Arab

Politics and
behind the

Arab Storm

Politics and Diplomacy behind the Gulf War

Alan Munro

I.B. TAURIS

LONDON · NEW YORK

For Grania,
and for all those friends and colleagues in the Kingdom
with whom we shared eventful times

Published in paperback in 2006 by
I.B.Tauris & Co Ltd
6 Salem Road, London W2 4BU
175 Fifth Avenue, New York NY 10010
www.ibtauris.com

First published by Brassey's in association with
the Royal United Services Institute in 1996

In the United States of America and Canada distributed by
Palgrave Macmillan a division of St Martin's Press
175 Fifth Avenue, New York NY 10010

ISBN 1 84511 128 1
EAN 978 1 84511 128 1

A full CIP record for this book is available from the British Library
A full CIP record is available from the Library of Congress

Library of Congress Catalog Card Number: available

Printed and bound in Great Britain by
TJ International Ltd, Padstow, Cornwall

Contents

List of Plates

PREFACE

From Success to Disaster

Our military operations have as their objective the defeat of the
enemy, and the driving of him from these territories. In order
to complete this task, I am charged with absolute and supreme
control of all regions in which British troops operate; but our
armies do not come into your cities and land as conquerors or
enemies, but as liberators ... You people of Baghdad are not to
understand that it is the wish of the British Government to impose
upon you alien institutions...

> *Proclamation to the inhabitants of Baghdad on 19 March
> 1917, by Lieut. General Sir Stanley Maude, following the
> occupation of the city by British forces*

The major changes to the political landscape which have been brought
upon Iraq through military conquest and occupation in the decade since
this book was first published have produced a dismal and chaotic sequel
to the efficient international action of 1990 and 1991 which rolled back
Iraq's illegal seizure of Kuwait. No long-term solution is readily available
to the intercommunal insurgency which has predictably followed the
American-led overthrow of Saddam Hussein and subsequent attempt to
convert Iraq into a beacon of liberal democracy. It is fitting to compare
the political contexts in which the two operations took place, and to
ask whether lessons to be derived from the success achieved by the first
coalition, with its carefully prepared military campaign and diplomatic
aftermath, and which were so recklessly ignored in the subsequent
engagement, can yet help salvage a disastrous outcome.

Indeed the risk of unleashing endemic internal tensions figured
prominently among the factors which deterred the members of the
coalition that ousted Iraq from Kuwait in 1991 from carrying their
battle through to Baghdad, for all the urgent pleas for intervention
from a brutally suppressed Shi'a insurrection in the south and a Kurdish
rising in the north. As Margaret Thatcher had put it, they should avoid

getting their 'arm caught in the mangle'. That limb is today well and truly caught in the snare of Iraq's chronic political dysfunction, just as General Maude and those who followed him were to find during the turbulent British mandate period ninety years earlier, for all their vain assurances of non-interference. History has thus come full circle, while its warnings have gone unheeded.

A distinctive feature of the successful operation to expel Iraq from Kuwait in 1991 was the broad international support it received, whether in the form of contributions to the military coalition, or of diplomatic support, albeit in varying degree, through the United Nations. Moreover this included a majority of Arab and Islamic states, as well as a crumbling Soviet Union. Even more significant was the measure of consensus that was achieved over the objectives of the operation, focused upon the liberation of Kuwait and the subsequent restraining of Iraq's regime – through sanctions and arms control measures – from any further acts of military aggression. In other words, the agreed objective was limited to putting Jack back in his box, and keeping the lid on. It was accepted, even by the governments in the forefront of the campaign such as the USA, Britain and France, and Saudi Arabia too, that their mandate did not extend to invading Iraq, or forcing a regime change.

The wisdom of this restraint has been much debated subsequently, but it was clearly recognised at the time that not only would such action fracture a carefully crafted international coalition, but it would also create major risks for the cohesion of Iraq and the consequent stability of this crucial region. The force of these considerations is now being amply demonstrated on the streets of Baghdad and Basra. Inevitably there were points of dissent amongst the international community, which Saddam Hussein skilfully exploited. But for all his defiance, and a policy of double bluff over continuing possession of weapons of mass destruction, his capacity for trouble continued to be inhibited.

By contrast the exercise in military pre-emption (or establishing hegemony as many Arabs see it), conducted in 2003 by a militant USA, and with the committed support of Britain's political establishment, was undertaken with little more than token regard for international consensus. It was prompted by a fervid and impatient mood in which an oversimplified mission to replace traditional autocratic government across the region with western democratic practice was combined with a frustrated urge, reinforced by the shock of the terror attacks on New York and Washington in September 2001, to settle scores with Iraq's regime, both real and imaginary. In part at least the action stemmed from understandable concern over erosion of the comprehensive control arrangements which had been applied to a stubbornly recusant Ba'athist regime in the aftermath of the Gulf War. But the caution which had characterised the campaign of 1991, and the sensibility to Iraq's inherent political complexity, together with the lessons of her recent history, were brushed aside. Superficial evidence of new military capability and of engagement in Islamist terrorism was taken at face value. Meanwhile provision for ensuring subsequent security and an orderly transition to a redistribution of power among Iraq's assorted communities and tribes was woefully inadequate.

Equally discounted was the animosity which military intervention and occupation in an Arab state would arouse across the Arab and Islamic worlds, particularly when contrasted with what was perceived as acquiescence in a tightening of control by Israel over occupied Palestinian territory. Nor was heed paid to warnings from allies in the region that upheaval in Iraq would serve to embolden the network of religious extremists whose capacity for acts of terror was now a matter of international concern. In short the consequences of this exercise in arrogance were never thought through. The result has been to draw occupation forces, mainly American and British, into a faltering and demoralising security role from which there appears no early exit.

It may now be too late to draw lessons from the earlier Kuwait conflict and its aftermath. Despite brave attempts to forge a new order of governance out of the wreckage of Ba'athism, Iraq still looks close to chaos, fragmentation and a resurgence of latent tensions between her neighbours. The gravity of this prospect however should now bring the international community to put aside its divisions and join once again in a broader coalition which would adopt a more assertive role on the political and security fronts to support Iraq's vulnerable political establishment and revitalise the crucial process of reconstruction. It would help minimise regional fall-out if such a coalition could include an Arab and Moslem presence – though probably not Iraq's neighbours, who would be perceived as partisan. This would include Saudi Arabia, who played such a pivotal role in stabilising the last Gulf crisis.

The prospects for such a coalition may appear unpromising, but the endeavour is justified, indeed essential. Without strong central authority, which the Iraqi government cannot establish on its own, liberal democracy can never flourish in Iraq.

And what of the Saudis, whose country played such a stalwart part in the dramatic events covered by this book? The process of drawing the Kingdom's sheltered community into a broader participation in national affairs and a more confident engagement with the outside world, which gained significant stimulus from the shock of the Kuwait crisis, has since been carried forward, albeit in cautious fashion, by the Al Saud regime, now led by King Abdullah. These are positive developments, and have been bolstered by a new era of oil-funded prosperity. They have however been accompanied by the emergence of radical Islamist groups, prepared to pursue their agenda of antagonism towards western, notably American, influence and its associated secular culture by acts of terror directed against western targets and the Al Saud establishment itself. This uncompromising cadre is still mindful of the rejection in 1990 by the Saudi government of a proposal by Osama bin Laden to provide an Islamist irregular force, fresh from an inflated role in the defeat of communism and Soviet occupation in Afghanistan, to replace infidel western troops arriving in the Kingdom. The fervour of its militant recruits was reinforced by the suicide attacks from the air on New York and Washington in September 2001 under the aegis of the amorphous al-Qaeda network. Here again events in Iraq cast their long shadow, fuelling public resentment over American-led occupation of Arab land and unease at the prospect of a Shi'a-dominated neighbour, as well as affording a springboard for extremist acts of violence within the Kingdom – and elsewhere in the region.

So much for time's turbulent march since Kuwait was liberated by force of arms in April 1991. Much has been written about the military aspects of that crisis, and particularly on the part played by the USA and Great Britain. Yet the campaign could never have taken place, let alone met with success, had it not been accompanied by an intensive and vigilant exercise in diplomacy, conducted at one level through international bodies such as the Security Council in New York and the Arab League in Cairo, and in parallel through direct contact between the players in the political as well as the military drama. The Kingdom of Saudi Arabia, by virtue of political resolve as well as of geography, found itself at the hub of this network of responses and acted as its linchpin throughout the months of arduous diplomacy. It took courage as well as skill to put together and hold in place amid the shifting sands of policy a coalition which had to transcend deep divergences not just of political alignment but of religious and ethnic status too.

Saudi Arabia, more accustomed hitherto to conciliation than to confrontation, assumed this role of leadership and coordination on multiple fronts with decisiveness and distinction. There was also a call for political subtlety, as relationships, which would respond to inducement one moment, often required a firm stand the next. The

Kingdom's was always at the centre of the drama. Its determination not only to respond to but also to reverse Saddam Hussein's overt act of banditry emanated from King Fahd himself, and he communicated it effectively to his own nation as well as those countries – Arab, western, Moslem and more besides, which gave their support. No understanding of the crisis can be complete without an account of the hectic diplomacy which underpinned the action of the United Nations, and of the unprecedented coalition which came together to free Kuwait.

This book represents an attempt to fill the gap. Written from the vantage point of Riyadh it seeks to give an assessment of the underlying causes of the crisis and to put on record the indefatigable sense of purpose of the Saudi leadership in sustaining the cohesion of a precarious alliance in the face of continual challenges of a political and propagandist nature upon which Iraq was counting to shipwreck it. The opportunity is taken to record the sequence of the Kuwait crisis, known in the West as the Gulf War, and Great Britain's key role in it, with armies dispersed into the desert while embassies stitched away to keep its diplomatic fabric intact. Meanwhile the civilian population, including British communities of substantial size, prepared themselves for war and underwent the unpleasant experience of random missile attack and the real threat of chemical weaponry. All this took place in the full view of a media army equipped with unprecedented facilities for satellite communication to bring the conflict into homes around the world.

Many friends and colleagues have made their contribution towards this book, with recollections and anecdotes as well as comment. It is impossible to mention them all. But I should like to record my appreciation for the encouragement given to me from the outset by H.R.H. Prince Saud Al Faisal, Foreign Minister of Saudi Arabia, who played such a central and effective political role throughout the crisis and its outcome. I am grateful for the support received from Dr. Hisham Nazer, former Minister of Petroleum, and from H.H. Prince Fahd bin Abdullah, Assistant to the Minister of Defence. Among other contributors I should like to acknowledge the support of H.H. Prince Abdullah bin Faisal bin Turki, former President of the Royal Commission for Jubail and Yanbu'; Shaikh Teymour Ali Reza who quoted to me the Arab proverb at the head of Chapter 4; the late Dr. Mamoun al Kurdi of the Ministry of Foreign Affairs; Dr. Shihab Jamjoom of the Information Ministry; the late Dr. Abdullah Dabbagh of the Saudi Chambers of Commerce; and a Kuwaiti friend, certain of whose relatives were still unaccounted for in Iraq long after liberation.

Among British friends particular thanks are due to General Sir Peter de la Billiere, Air Chief Marshal Sir William Wratten, Air Marshal Ian McFadyen, Brigadier Nick Cocking, Brigadier Peter Sincock, Padre Adrian Pollard, Don McClen, Harriet Bushman, Sandy Gall; and to many helpful colleagues in the Foreign Office and the British diplomatic missions in Saudi Arabia and the Gulf, including Derek Plumbly, Patrick Fairweather, Mark Scrase-Dickens, Chris Wilton, Peter Gooderham and Charles Hollis. My special gratitude is due to Charles B. Gray of the King Faisal Hospital in Riyadh for having generously allowed me to draw on his fascinating log of developments throughout the crisis as they were reported on local and international broadcasts. I am also grateful to Tessa Blackburn for permission to quote the poem 'Medina', by her late husband, Raymond Blackburn MP, and to I.B.Tauris for their belief in the ongoing value of this book.

Above all my gratitude goes to my wife, Grania, for her encouragement and support, and the undertaking of a valuable editorial role.

Chiswick, 2005

INTRODUCTION

The Kingdom and the War

Medina

Now slowly moves the shadow of the rock,
And cools parched bodies in a weary land.
'No God but God,' they cry – I cannot mock
Their absolute assurance of his hand
Outstretched to bless. They clearer see
Than the ungainly camel, or the hills
Ringed round the Prophet's tomb – their certainty
Allah to praise, whether he saves or kills.

His love may lurk even in the scorpion's sting,
His mercy in the maddening of the sun.
Of Him and in Him the cicadas sing,
Unseen persistent choirs till day is done,
And stars begin to wink, and men to nod,
Who, having nothing, yet have all their God.

Raymond Blackburn

Iraq's invasion of Kuwait on 2 August 1990 was not only an attempt to hijack by force that independent sheikhdom. It also delivered a set of severe shocks to Iraq's much more substantial southern neighbour, the Kingdom of Saudi Arabia.

These serious jolts, the effects of which are still at work, precipitated a number of sensitive issues for Saudi Arabia's ruling family, for the nature of her political society, for her relations with the outside world, and for her finances, as well as calling into question her defence capability. Not least, the arrival of great numbers of foreign, and in particular non-Moslem, troops to help defend the Kingdom and drive Iraq out of Kuwait produced a major dilemma for the government and for public opinion in the face of the exclusive and conservative religious attitudes which remain deeply rooted in Saudi society. All these aspects were to have an important bearing on the Saudi handling of the Kuwait crisis.

From Britain's point of view they had a direct influence on the relationship between Saudi Arabia and the members of the remarkable military coalition to which she acted as host. They affected the work of

xiii

diplomats, and conditioned the daily existence of the large community of British citizens who shared those difficult times with the Saudis and Kuwaitis and made their willing contribution on the home front.

To understand better the sensitivity and complexity of the background to this unprecedented exercise in co-operation which Iraq's leader sprung so suddenly upon us all in Arabia in the high summer of 1990, it is important to have an idea of the spirit and the society of this unconventional Kingdom, which suddenly found itself propelled into the limelight it had always sought to avoid.

Saudi Arabia is not Sparta. For all their feuding bedouin background, her people have experienced no more than skirmishes since 1932, when King Abdul Aziz Al Saud, known in the West as Ibn Saud, established the Kingdom as we know it today through a process of conquest and tribal consolidation. This began with a bold and successful raid in 1902 on Riyadh, right in the heart of the country.

The town was then a small mud-walled oasis in Nejd, the province from which the Al Saud family had governed the central deserts of Arabia since the middle of the 18th century. They had exercised their authority through military domination over the tribal confederations and scattered settled oases, buttressed by a spiritual leadership derived from their association with a rigorous puritanism involving a strict interpretation of the teaching of the Koran and its associated Hadith, or traditions. This fierce reformist movement had taken hold among the peoples of central Arabia through the preaching of one Mohammed Ibn Abdul Wahhab, a revivalist teacher who was invited under the protection of the ruling Al Saud around the year 1740; hence the term Wahhabis by which the adherents of this movement have come to be known, both within Arabia and further afield.

Building on this potent religious partnership, the Al Saud extended their sway out of their homeland in Nejd throughout much of the Arabian peninsula, including parts of the Gulf coast as far south as Oman, and northwards into the Ottoman-ruled territory of Iraq. In 1803 they occupied the Red Sea province of Hejaz, containing the holy cities of Mecca and Medina, which were governed on behalf of the Ottoman Sultan in Constantinople by an appointee from the Al Sherif family, descended from the Prophet Mohammed.

Al Saud rule within Arabia during the course of the 19th century was an uneven affair. They were four times driven out of their Nejd heartland and into exile by military expeditions organised by the Sultan, to whom, as holder of the Caliphate, a title which was anathema to the purist followers of the teachings of Ibn Abdul Wahhab, the Al Saud rule represented a twofold threat, political as well as religious, to Turkish influence. Their first and most significant defeat was at the hands of the Egyptian general, Ibrahim Pasha, who, acting on behalf of his father, Mohammed Ali, the Sultan's viceroy in Egypt, and in response to an act of iconoclastic fanaticism carried out at the Prophet's tomb in Medina by followers of the Al Saud ruler in 1810 on the occasion of the Hajj, or pilgrimage, undertook a prolonged and bitter campaign against the Al Saud and their bedouin allies, which ended six years later with the destruction of the Al Saud capital, Dira'iyah, near Riyadh.

The family's final exile occurred in 1885: weakened by rivalries and following defeat in the field by the Al Rashid of Ha'il, the second most powerful family within central Arabia who had joined forces with the Turks against the Al Saud, the Amir Abdul Rahman took refuge among the bedouin in the Eastern Province of al Hasa. He subsequently lived in Kuwait in the mid-1890s, under the wing of its forceful ruler, Sheikh Mubarak Al Sabah, whose small territory had benefited from British protection against Turkish and Al Rashid incursions for some 15 years.

It was from Kuwait, and with the backing of Sheikh Mubarak, that the future King Abdul Aziz Al Saud set out in 1902 to recapture Riyadh from the Al Rashid, and so set in hand the restoration of his family's rule and the eventual creation of the Kingdom of Saudi Arabia. It was thus a twist of historical irony, not lost on the present generation of the Al Saud, that when forced into summary exile by Iraq's military strike in the early hours of 2 August 1990, nearly a century later, it should have been to the Al Saud that the Al Sabah of Kuwait turned for refuge, and were readily given shelter.

The 30 years between the recapture of Riyadh and the establishment of the Kingdom of Saudi Arabia in 1932 represented a remarkable achievement in statecraft on the part of King Abdul Aziz. Through an incessant series of military campaigns, tribal and dynastic alliances, religious persuasion, diplomatic confrontation and magnanimity, and above all sheer force of personality, he succeeded in forging a state over two million square kilometres in size. This involved the successive incorporation of the Eastern Province following the ousting of the Turkish garrisons; of the northern region of Ha'il following defeat of, and subsequent reconciliation with, the Al Rashid; the assumption of authority over the mountainous Asir on the southern Red Sea coast, largely through a campaign led by the future King Faisal and involving the puritanical Wahhabi fighting levies; and finally in 1925 the military takeover of the Hejaz and its holy places from a failing Sherif Husain of Mecca and his son, Ali. The consolidation of the Kingdom was rounded off in a frontier war with Yemen which culminated in the Treaty of Taif in 1934. The borders with Yemen were only partly delineated, however, a deficiency which was to fester in the animosity that infected Saudi–Yemeni relations during the Gulf War.

A further remarkable aspect of King Abdul Aziz's formation of his huge kingdom, when seen against the background of the extensive Western involvement in the politics of the Middle East during the first half of this century, is that it was achieved with a minimum of outside sponsorship or interference. The entry of Turkey into the First World War on the side of Germany and Austria prompted a relationship with Great Britain, through which Abdul Aziz was able to increase his control within Nejd as a result of the supply of weapons and a small British subsidy he was given to keep the Turks and their Al Rashid associates on the hop. The relationship was fostered in intermittent fashion by a handful of British officials.

Notable among these was Captain William Shakespear, the political agent in Kuwait, who lost his life when he accompanied Abdul Aziz's forces into an inconclusive battle against the Al Rashid at Jarrab, south of Ha'il, in 1915. Another influential figure was Sir Percy Cox, the political resident in the Persian Gulf based at Bushire, who negotiated agreements with Abdul Aziz at Qatif in 1917 and at Uqair in 1922. These accorded a measure of British military support, fixed an annual subsidy and settled disputed frontiers with the British-protected territories of Iraq and Kuwait. Most significant of all was Harry St John Philby, who was to remain a close adviser to King Abdul Aziz, though increasingly hostile to British interests, right up to the King's death in 1953. So bitter did Philby become at what he regarded as Britain's failure to back the Al Saud in the Arabian territorial stakes after the First World War that, according to the eye-witness account of one of King Abdul Aziz's most senior sons, he went so far on one occasion in the late 1930s as to urge the King to align himself with Nazi Germany. Abdul Aziz's sharp reproof was to order Philby from the council chamber. These views earned Philby a spell of detention when he returned to Britain at the outset of the Second World War.

This early relationship with Britain was solid enough, but never particularly close. Until the ending of Sharifian rule in the Hejaz in 1925, alliance with the Al Saud took second place in the scale of British interests in Arabia to support for the Hashemite rulers of Mecca. This partnership was notable during the First World War for the revolt against Turkish rule by the Arab forces of the sons of the Sharif who, with the support of British irregular units including Colonel T E Lawrence (Lawrence of Arabia), helped drive the Turks out of the Hejaz, Transjordan and Syria.

With the ending of British subsidies to both the Sharif Husain and

Abdul Aziz in 1923, the Al Saud saw themselves with a free hand so far as British interests in the Hejaz were concerned. Their subsequent occupation of the Hejaz was recognised by the British government in a treaty signed at Jedda in 1927, when King Abdul Aziz for his part accepted the British-installed Hashemite rule in the new post-war kingdoms of Transjordan and Iraq, as well as British protection of the Gulf sheikhdoms. He also received backing from Britain in confronting a growing challenge to his authority at home from the puritanical Wahhabi contingents, whom he had recruited as the shock troops of his campaigns throughout Arabia. Some of these had begun to chafe at what they saw as restraints on their zealotry as Abdul Aziz sought to absorb and accommodate the various elements of his new state. The subjugation of these fanatical warriors was the first major test of King Abdul Aziz's authority, and it took force to achieve. Their legacy of aggressive piety has remained a powerful strand within Saudi society to this day, and was to resurface and call for sensitive handling when Western 'infidel' forces made their reappearance in the Kingdom as part of the coalition assembled in 1990 to liberate Kuwait from Iraqi occupation.

This consolidation of the new Kingdom by King Abdul Aziz was undertaken in circumstances of financial impoverishment, and without the benefit of the vast oil income with which Saudi Arabia is associated today. Oil was only discovered in the Eastern Province of Saudi Arabia in 1938 and its revenues did not become significant until after the Second World War. But just as significant for the future was the role foreign competition for the original oil prospecting concession was to play in establishing close links with the USA, which have meant so much to the subsequent history of the Kingdom.

Ever since the discovery of a substantial oilfield on the island of Bahrain in 1932 by the American firm Standard Oil of California (SOCAL), following an ill-judged conclusion by the British-dominated Iraq Petroleum Company (IPC) that no oil existed there, eyes had been cast across the narrow Gulf shoals towards the area of Dhahran on the Saudi coast, where similar geological structures might be found. IPC remained sceptical but, as dog in the Persian Gulf manger, felt constrained to compete with the Americans when a drawn-out round of bidding took place in Jedda in the spring of 1933. Abdul Aziz was prepared for the sake of his old association with Britain to see the concession go her way. But IPC were easily outbid by SOCAL. It is said that it was the British minister in Jedda, Sir Andrew Ryan, who himself advised the King to take the Americans' offer, which started with over £50,000 in gold – it would be money for nothing...

Although it took six years of prospecting and near despair before the Dhahran field was located, the subsequent record of Saudi Arabian oil production, in partnership until the mid-1980s with the American oil industry, has been prodigious. 1938 saw a mere half a million barrels produced, rising to 21 million barrels in 1945 at the end of the Second World War. Amid the crisis of the Iranian revolution in 1979 Saudi production peaked at 11 million barrels a day, dropping to as little as one-third of this figure in the glut conditions of the mid-1980s. By the end of the Gulf War production had climbed again to over eight million barrels a day, and Saudi Arabia was estimated to have a quarter of the world's oil reserves at her disposal.

It was the safeguarding of the American oil concession, as much as concern over the implications for the Middle East of East–West rivalry following the Second World War, which introduced an important political and military ingredient into Saudi-American relations from the mid-1940s onwards. In 1945 the US government decided to press ahead with the construction of a military airbase at Dhahran, as an earnest of longer-term American interest in Saudi Arabia. This same base, long since under full Saudi control, was to play a key part in the air war to recover Kuwait in 1991.

Thus by the time of his death in 1953 at the age of 77, and 51 years after he had reasserted the authority of the Al Saud by capturing the Riyadh citadel, Abdul Aziz had succeeded in uniting and pacifying the greater part of Arabia, establishing a kingdom with the apparatus of modern administration, securing its economic prosperity, and setting a pattern for security and stability within a framework of foreign alliance. This was a phenomenal achievement by any standard. Moreover, it took account of the tribal traditions of Arabian society, and of the conservative and uncompromising religious strand that was such a predominant feature of popular attitudes and behaviour, particularly within the desert heartland of Nejd. This puritanical outlook, which to the outsider, whether Muslim or not, can amount to narrow bigotry, had seen some of its excesses curbed by force of arms when in the early 1930s King Abdul Aziz recognised that the fanaticism of his religious warriors was becoming a threat to the new state itself. But the King also realised that in this environment of piety the exercise of authority had to be shared with the religious establishment, acting through a council of clerical elders or *ulema*. Thus religious fervour should become a force for stability within the Kingdom and not a focus of disruption.

In the 40 years since King Abdul Aziz's remarkable reign, the four sons who have so far succeeded to the throne have carried forward their country's development without seeking to challenge the pattern of centralised government which he bequeathed. The two most substantial reigns, those of King Faisal from 1964 until his assassination by a fanatic member of the Al Saud in 1975, and of King Fahd from 1982 to the present day, have seen oil wealth deployed to develop a modern economic infrastructure and a system of social welfare, as well as to build up a military capability that can at least stand guard over the Kingdom's sprawling frontiers and serve as a first line of deterrence to potential hostility on the part of neighbours, who in the turmoil of Middle Eastern politics over these last four decades have cast covetous or subversive eyes upon Saudi Arabia's economic prosperity and political stability. The result for Saudi society has been an era of peace and a turning away from martial feuding. Perhaps uniquely among Arab states, military parades are not a feature on the Saudi public agenda.

This stability and security has had its price. Opposition among sectors of Saudi Arabia's conservative Islamic society to what they see as an unwelcome compromise between the ruling Al Saud and an infidel West has continued as a latent factor in the political life of the Kingdom, erupting periodically in outbursts of protest, as occurred over the obtrusive presence of Western forces during the Kuwait crisis, and even of violence, as happened in 1979 when a group of fervid fanatics, led by a member of a prominent bedouin family, Juhaiman al Otaibi, seized the Great Mosque in Mecca in the cause of millenarist reform and were only dislodged with considerable loss of life. It has generally been the custom of the Al Saud to meet these tides of puritan opinion, which have demonstrated renewed vigour since the shock of the Gulf War, with a blend of conciliation and concession, and only rarely to resort to force. The voice of the clerical establishment is not to be disregarded in the formulation of policy in Saudi Arabia, although at the end of the day the Al Saud hold to Erastian principles and insist on the final word.

Outside her borders Saudi Arabia has over the years made an art of financial diplomacy, whereby she has sought to avoid confrontation by buying off through judicious subvention those who might disturb her prosperous existence. As is the way of the world such responses have rarely earned gratitude. Envy at the wealth of Saudi Arabia and of her oil-producing Gulf partners has become endemic in the popular attitudes of less well-endowed Arab states. This reflex had much to do with the degree of popular support which Saddam Hussein sought to exploit within the Arab world when he moved to seize Kuwait in August 1990. Yet the record of Saudi aid to her Arab partners has been far from parsimonious. Goaded by derogatory Iraqi propaganda in the early stages of the confrontation over Kuwait, the Saudi government broke with its customary avoidance of publicity for its regional aid and revealed that help accorded in crude oil and financial credits to Iraq during the eight years of her ill-advised war with Iran alone, up to its armistice in 1988, had totalled over $25 billion.

Saudi diplomacy has, however, more to it than money. The past decade has seen the Kingdom coming out of its shell and taking a more assertive role in regional affairs, as King Fahd has set himself to work for the moderating of some of the more intractable and acute disputes which could threaten his country's stability and put its cohesion and prosperity at risk. Of major local significance as part of this activity was the association in 1982 of Saudi Arabia and her five Arab neighbours along the western Gulf coast in the Gulf Co-operation Council (GCC). This required the putting aside of long-standing rivalries over issues of tribe and territory, the better to face a common threat of Iranian hostility during the Iran-Iraq war. Saudi Arabia's hand has also been in evidence in problems on a wider Arab front, including a consistent and effective prompting of the Palestinian Liberation Organisation (PLO) to adopt a less uncompromising position towards Israel. She has also assumed a leading role in working for an end to the Lebanese civil war. These are cases where Saudi Arabia's style of private intercession has met with a measure of success.

But there are shadows which linger from the days of conquest, notably unresolved border problems with Yemen, and an edginess to relations with Jordan which has its root in King Abdul Aziz's takeover of the Hejaz from the Hashemite forebears of King Hussein. Relations with Iran too are intrinsically precarious as a consequence of historical rivalry between Sunnism and Shi'ism, the two main branches of Islam. The puritanical Wahhabi elements within Saudi Arabia tend to despise Iran's dominant Shi'ism, while the militant zealotry which has emerged as a prominent feature of Iranian policy since the revolution of 1979 has not hesitated to challenge Saudi Arabia's jealously-guarded role as protector of the holy cities of Mecca and Medina and host to the annual pilgrimage. On the other hand there is no tradition of ill-feeling between the Kingdom and Iraq. The tribes and traders of northern Arabia have long had close ties with Basra and Baghdad and, despite Saudi Arabia's reservations over the wisdom of the quarrel Iraq's leadership picked with Iran in the 1980s, her support was readily forthcoming. In Saudi eyes it was Shi'a Iran that posed the greater threat to the calm and prosperity of the peninsula.

Thus Iraq's brutal seizure of Kuwait came as all the more of a shock from this Arab quarter. It aroused a profound sense of betrayal and anger in the minds of King Fahd and the Al Saud. This sentiment was widely shared within the Kingdom at large, mixed with a bewilderment at the possibility of a physical threat to their placid and insular existence. The sword emblazoned upon the Kingdom's flag, and used so effectively by King Abdul Aziz in creating the nation, had been sheathed for nearly 60 years until Saddam Hussein obliged it to be drawn once again. Quite possibly the Iraqi leader estimated that he could get away with intimidating a nation and a regime whose martial edge appeared blunted by comfortable and complacent decades of oil-fed plenty. If so, this was to be a serious miscalculation.

For the Saudi Arabia which was pitchforked into the eye of international crisis was a complex amalgam of pride and prejudice. To the outside world, and particularly in the West, the Kingdom had acquired a stereotyped image of a wealthy and arrogant society, wary of foreigners and their ways and inscrutable both in the process of government and in the conduct of private life. The Western press, too often frustrated at denial of access to see the country at first hand, sought in response to paint an exaggerated and inconsistent picture of Arabian Nights ostentation coupled with vivid accounts of family feuding, puritanical zealotry and harsh Islamic punishment. These caricatures tended to be unfair and grossly overdrawn. They missed the point that Saudi Arabia had remained since King Abdul Aziz's day, and despite the materialistic effect of unforeseen riches, a society which took itself and its practice of religion seriously, to an extent not seen in the West for over 200 years. It was not a particularly hardworking society nor by any means a killjoy one, but it accepted a culture in which piety conditioned pleasure, rigorous laws received through religious tradition were strictly and systematically applied, and the influence of external cultures was widely regarded as pernicious.

This last aspect, the source of an intolerance involving irksome and bigoted prohibitions and curbs on the activities of the multitude of foreigners who have found good employment in the Kingdom, was in large part due to the fact that alone among the countries of the Middle East, Saudi Arabia had never been protected, administered or even challenged by European or Western powers. She was ruled by a talented dynasty which could claim to have the longest suit of authority in all of Arabia, and had managed its fief in paternalistic fashion as a beneficial family co-operative. It had created the physical attributes of a modern and independent state within the cocoon of a confident and stable society which to outside eyes had its anachronisms, but which enjoyed strong cohesion within itself. The insidious and discredited currents of Egyptian-led pan-Arab republicanism of the 1950s and 1960s had been kept at bay. A wary and precarious compromise had been struck between the benefits of technology and material comforts of Western culture on

the one hand, and on the other a devout interpretation of Islam's ethi-
cal code and the *Shari'a* law through which this was applied. The give
and take of this sensitive compact with the West and its ways, by which
the Al Saud governed their desert kingdom, was to be put to the test by
the Gulf War.

CHAPTER 1

The Saddam Hussein Factor

Iraq's invasion of Kuwait in the small hours of 2 August 1990 caught the world off balance. One of the most cherished assumptions underlying the turbulent and often rebarbative relationships between Arab states is that however savagely they criticise each other through their media, they do not attack each other with force. The lightning strike which Iraq's president, Saddam Hussein, unleashed upon his small southern neighbour showed this up for an illusion. Saddam Hussein may have calculated that he could get away with his catch by playing upon political divisions and rivalries within the Arab world, and through the intimidation of those he menaced. Indeed, by a spurious presentation of Iraq's action as an instance of 'haves' against 'have nots', and by working on the ever-sensitive Arab nerve of Western and Israeli conspiracy, he did succeed in invoking a measure of support at public level and even with a handful of governments. But the main effect was to rally a substantial Arab front against him, motivated by a sense of shock and betrayal and a conviction that Iraq should not be permitted to get away with her assault.

Throughout the whole eight months of the crisis, from the invasion in early August to the liberation of Kuwait and the consequent international measures against Iraq the following spring, this Arab front, combined with an unprecedented coalition from among the wider international community, took heart from a resolute and consistent lead on the part of Saudi Arabia. There was a tenacity here for which Iraq had not bargained. The indefatigable part played in this drama by King Fahd bin Abdul Aziz and his government has been to some extent overshadowed in Western eyes by the overwhelming strength of the American military contribution backed up by the UK and France, and by the emphasis which, in their published accounts of the campaign, American and British commanders have laid on the roles of their own governments and the national forces under their command. There has been a tendency to take Saudi Arabia and the other Gulf and Arab members of the coalition for granted. But their part in the diplomacy of the episode, in the joint military command and hosting of the international coalition,

1

and in the liberation exercise and its aftermath, was no less significant to the outcome than what went on in the UN Security Council in New York, or in capitals like Washington, London or Moscow. It will help to fill this important gap in the record of the Kuwait crisis to give an account of the interaction between the Arab and international dimensions as it unfolded on the ground, from the ringside seat of the British embassy and community in Saudi Arabia as they participated in successive stages of the drama.

Iraq's foolhardy decision to seize Kuwait by force was the decision of one man, Saddam Hussein himself. It was to prove a gross miscalculation. The reasoning, or rather the impulse, behind this decision has to be sought in the aggressive nationalism which has been a predominant feature of Iraq's restless political scene since the overthrow of the monarchy in 1958, and more specifically in the impulsive and rancorous personality of Saddam Hussein himself, whose hold over his country after 11 years of supreme authority brooked no opposition to his plans for aggrandisement.

Iraq is an artificial state, whose form and administration was decided in the process of the dismembering and redistribution of the components of the Ottoman empire among the victorious European powers following Turkey's defeat in the First World War. In this contest for influence Britain secured mandatory authority from the newly-created League of Nations over the three former Turkish provinces of Basra, at the head of the Gulf; Baghdad, in the heart of the Euphrates basin; and Mosul, in the Kurdish-inhabited mountain territory adjacent to Turkey. She merged these regions into a single state, to be known as Iraq, and secured a formula, endorsed in the Anglo-Iraqi Treaty of 1922, whereby the new state would be a kingdom under British mandate, and ruled by Prince Faisal, one of the sons of the Hashemite Sharif of Mecca. Faisal had successfully led the Arab force which had played a part in driving the Turks out of the Hejaz and Syria alongside Allied forces in 1917 and 1918, but British undertakings to establish him as ruler of Syria after the war had been blocked by France. Britain thus took the alternative course of creating a kingdom for him in mandated Iraq.

But as a political entity Iraq lacked homogeneity, a feature which was to become a continuing source of instability in the course of her subsequent history. Indeed, from the outset there were voices in the British administration which expressed doubt over the political wisdom of the venture. These included the civil commissioner in Baghdad, Colonel Arnold Wilson, who considered the grouping together of the Shi'a Arabs of the Basra region and the distinct Kurdish population of Mosul under the governance of the more dominant but less numerous Sunni Arabs of

Baghdad province to be an arbitrary recipe which ignored historical realities and would make for future divisions within the new state of Iraq. With unconscious prescience Wilson forecast 'the result would be the antithesis of a democratic government'. Other influential British administrators, however, such as Gertrude Bell, favoured Hashemite rule. The Cabinet, under a Prime Minister, Lloyd George, who was determined to secure British interests in the Middle East following the defeat and collapse of Ottoman Turkey, and with support from the pro-consular Lord Curzon as foreign secretary, chose to disregard warnings from those on the ground and ignore Turkish claims to retain the Mosul province. Instead it went ahead with the establishment of the composite kingdom of Iraq under British protection. The kingdom had rich oil reserves, the importance of which was starting to be appreciated.

The course of Iraqi politics has proved to be a chronicle of turbulence and, since the bloody overthrow of the Hashemite monarchy in 1958, of violence and tyranny. Saddam Hussein was reared on this cult of violence, which came to be the key to survival in the vicious political life of Iraq. Born in 1937 in the town of Takrit, north of Baghdad in the Sunni Arab centre of the country, he is said to have suffered a brutal stepfather from whom he ran away at the age of nine and went to live with an uncle in Baghdad. By the time he was 20 he had earned a reputation for petty violence and was recruited into the Ba'ath party. The Ba'ath, or Renaissance, was an expression of Arab political nationalism which derived its philosophy from a blend of Marxist socialism and the cult of the Arab nation as a state. Prior to the overthrow of the Iraqi monarchy it operated clandestinely through a cell structure. Saddam Hussein was initially engaged as a party thug. When a group of nationalist officers under the leadership of Brigadier Abdul Karim Qasim overthrew the monarchy in bloodthirsty fashion in July 1958, murdering the young King Faisal II and members of the royal family and subsequently dragging the corpses of Crown Prince Abd al Illah and Prime Minister Nuri al Said through the streets of Baghdad, the Ba'ath came out of concealment and gave its support to the ending of a regime which it regarded as subservient to British imperial interests.

The revolution of July 1958 set a pattern for political turbulence and bloodshed which has characterised the politics of Iraq ever since. Within 15 months the Ba'ath party made an unsuccessful attempt to assassinate Qasim. Saddam Hussein was a member of the hit team. He evaded capture in the subsequent round-up and made his way to Egypt, where he spent the next three years. This was to be his only experience of life outside Iraq, a factor which may have had a bearing on the aggressive, insular approach which he was subsequently to show in regional matters as ruler of Iraq, and in his repeated misjudgements of international responses to his threats and actions. He returned to Baghdad in 1963 following a bloody coup in which officers of the Ba'ath persuasion overthrew the Qasim regime. Again divisions soon emerged and scores were violently settled. A distant relative from Takrit, Ahmed Hassan al Bakr, briefly became vice-president of Iraq, and Saddam was promoted on his coat-tails to run the party's intelligence apparatus, a post of sinister influence, and subsequently to membership of the party's regional council. He was now on his political way, despite a spell in prison where he is said to have spent time studying the writings of Hitler and Stalin.

Saddam Hussein's authority was consolidated further when the Iraqi Ba'ath party staged a fresh coup in July 1968. Al Bakr became chairman of a new Revolutionary Command Council which effectively governed the country. Saddam Hussein was appointed its deputy chairman, responsible for internal security. This position permitted him to set up an all-pervading intelligence and security apparatus, which became, and has since remained, a ruthless and violent tool for his exercise of absolute power through terror. The Ba'ath immediately launched into an orgy of witchhunts, trials of alleged spies and conspirators, and assassinations. The aim was to eliminate or cow all possible sources of opposition. At the same time the Iraqi army stepped up the brutality of its campaign against dissident Kurds in the north. In 1972 a Friendship Treaty was signed with the Soviet Union, which opened the way to substantial military co-operation and supply. This was to be a major factor in the subsequent massive build-up of Iraq's armed forces, to the point where at the time of the invasion of Kuwait in August 1990, and despite losses sustained in the eight years of conflict with Iran, Iraq maintained the fourth largest army in the world.

The Ba'ath government succeeded in putting an end to Kurdish resistance in 1975, following the signature of an agreement in Algiers with the Shah of Iran, whereby Iran ceased to give support to the Kurds in return for Iraq conceding partial Iranian sovereignty over the Shatt al Arab waterway at the head of the Gulf. This agreement was smartly abrogated by Saddam Hussein on the eve of his attack on Iran in September 1980, but was resurrected ten years later in a vain bid for Iran's support in the face of international opposition to the invasion of Kuwait. Having subdued the Kurds, the Ba'ath turned its attention to the Shi'a community in the south, which had become restless at the oppression to which it was being subjected. The execution of several Shi'a religious figures, and the deportation over the Iranian border of what is said to have amounted to some 200,000 Iraqi Shi'as, including their chief spiritual guide, the Iranian Ayatollah Khomeini who had been living in exile in the Shi'a holy city of Karbala, was an act of political highhandedness which would inevitably rebound at some stage upon Iraq. This reaction soon came in the form of provocative hostility and propaganda on the part of the Ayatollah's Islamic republican regime in Iran, following the violent overthrow of the Shah in February 1979.

Within a few months of the Iranian revolution Saddam Hussein's rise to the pinnacle of absolute power was accomplished when he unseated his cousin, Ahmed Hassan al Bakr, in June 1979 and assumed the presidency. Saddam followed this move with a characteristic ruthless purge of the Ba'ath command, leading to the execution of as many as 500 officials. Moreover, the purge was initiated in full public view, with a specially stage-managed conference of the party in Baghdad at which Saddam made a speech alleging a conspiracy and went on to read out the names of a number of associates present, who were then taken out from the hall by their loyalist colleagues, subjected to summary trial and conviction and shot by these same colleagues. In this ruthless fashion Saddam sought to engineer the unquestioning support of his regime by ensuring that their hands were stained with the same blood as his own.

Saddam Hussein went further and had the proceedings of this sinister meeting recorded on videotape, to be distributed throughout the party as a dreadful warning. This tape, with its chilling picture of Saddam Hussein's cold detachment and the hysteria and fear generated among those present, was shown again on a BBC *Panorama* programme in 1991 during the Kuwait crisis, and left no doubt as to the ruthlessly single-minded quest for power which was his motivating force.

With his reign by fear now in place, the mass of the Iraqi people found themselves brainwashed into a blind subservience, particularly among the younger generation who were to provide the shock troops for Saddam Hussein's ambitions for Iraq's aggrandisement. The slightest hint of disloyalty was likely to be picked up by ubiquitous informers and brutal retribution would follow, involving families as well as individuals. Those who might have sought to challenge, or even to question, their leader's decisions in matters of policy had been silenced. From now on Saddam Hussein would take his own decisions in isolation and according to the dictates of his personal complex of prejudice, anger, suspicion and ambition. It was to prove an erratic and dangerous blend.

Saddam Hussein's sudden move in launching a series of attacks across the border into Iran in September 1980 was an act of supreme miscalculation, political as well as military. It was also the forerunner of other miscalculations to come, including the invasion of Kuwait ten years later and his mishandling of the diplomatic aspects of that adventure. The roots of this rash decision to take on singlehanded his stronger neighbour and adversary, vibrating with a febrile religious revolution, must be sought in the character of Saddam Hussein himself.

Saddam Hussein has been described by Arabs who have known him and studied his political behaviour as having three dominant and mutually sustaining strands in his personality: the pursuit of power, a self-conceit leading to rash overconfidence, and a brooding resentment of people or policies that he finds in his way. In his perceptive study of the Kuwait crisis, Dr Ghazi al Gosaibi, the present Saudi ambassador to the UK, who as minister of industry had dealings with the Iraqi leader, defined this last element as amounting to a persecution complex where any imagined threat was seen as a challenge to his authority and by extension to the security of Iraq itself, thus justifying a ruthless punitive response. The design might be laid in advance, and in the case of Kuwait it probably was, but when it came to action, anger and impulsiveness overrode cautious consideration of the consequences.

Over the case of Iran and again with Kuwait, Saddam Hussein's sudden recourse to military attack has been dismissed as the action of a madman. Rather they were instances of a hubristic arrogance and self-deceit, deriving from his sense of absolute authority. In discussions during the Gulf War, King Fahd was wont to reject the suggestion that Saddam was mad, describing his affliction instead as megalomania, perhaps more in the tradition of Joseph Stalin's rule than that of Adolf Hitler. The King frequently related in public how, shortly before initiating his attack on Iran in September 1980, Saddam Hussein had told him of his outrage at Iranian propaganda and border provocations, and of his decision to make a military strike against Iran's Islamic regime. King Fahd had counselled firmly against such a step, as likely to achieve nothing beyond an intensification of Iranian hostility, which could in turn be directed at the Gulf states as well. But Saddam Hussein had paid no heed, his mind already made up and filled with ideas of aggrandisement.

Once Iraq's ill-prepared attack petered out and she herself came under Iranian pressure, the extensive assistance which Saudi Arabia and her Gulf partners gave her in oil credits, transit facilities and equipment was motivated more by concern to protect themselves from the antagonism which Saddam Hussein's rash action had gratuitously provoked on the part of Iran, than out of sympathy for Iraq's plight. Indeed, once Iran had gained the upper hand in the conflict, and particularly following her capture of the Faw peninsula in 1986 and the launching of Iranian naval attacks on Saudi and Kuwaiti shipping, it became an objective of Saudi diplomacy to work for a ceasefire.

At the Arab summit held in Amman in November 1987 King Fahd succeeded in switching the main focus of Arab diplomatic attention on to events in the Gulf and away from the traditional preoccupation with Palestine. It was also the Saudis who pressed in both London and Washington during the first half of 1987 for a UN Security Council resolution calling for a ceasefire and backed by a threat of sanctions. This led to the passage in July of Resolution Number 598 setting out the basis for a ceasefire, though there was to be a further year of bitter fighting before Iran came round to accept it.

It was this material support from within the Arab world, backed by massive military supply on credit from further afield, notably the USSR and France, and access also to American military intelligence from aerial surveillance, that enabled Iraq to emerge from the bloody stalemate of the war having regained the military edge. The war was fought at a very high cost to both sides in men killed and taken prisoner. Iraq showed herself prepared to go to great lengths to counter the fanatical Iranian tactic of deploying human screens of volunteer 'martyrs' to clear infantry minefields. When I was looking after Britain's military business with Middle East countries in 1981, I was even asked by an Iraqi general whether we would be prepared to reopen a production line for the Churchill flame-thrower tank to enable Iraq to counter these human waves. The idea was of course a vain one, not only given our strict refusal to supply weapons to either side in the war, but because the Churchill tank had gone out of production nearly 40 years earlier! But such was Saddam Hussein's military budget that he might well have been prepared to foot the enormous bill to bring such a dodo back into production.

Of more sinister significance, however, was the effective way in which Saddam Hussein exercised his authority with ruthless brutality at home to sustain popular support for the war and its sacrifices. He did this by suppressing, and indeed eliminating, any attempt by his commanders to question the inept and static conduct of Iraq's military strategy, of which he had arrogated the direction to himself. He succeeded in inducing the Shi'a soldiery within his armed forces to give their lives for their leader and their state, albeit against an enemy of their own religious persuasion. He also ran up massive international debts to establish an overwhelming defence inventory, including a sophisticated development programme for both nuclear and chemical weapons. This latter instrument, outlawed by international agreements to which Iraq was herself a party, was turned without compunction against his own Kurdish population in the massacre of the inhabitants of the northern town of Halabja in early 1988, and shortly afterwards in the successful action by the Iraqi army to dislodge the Iranians from the Faw salient, from where they had been threatening the city of Basra.

So it was that, following Iran's exhausted call for a ceasefire in July 1988, Saddam Hussein lost no time in throwing Iraq's considerable weight about once again on the Arab scene, with his customary mixture of bullying and blackmail, and through well-targeted deployment of the sophisticated propaganda apparatus which Iraq had developed during the conflict with Iran. He made no secret of his army's use of poison gas against the Iranian army, though he went to considerable lengths to stifle reports of its employment against Kurdish civilians at Halabja, including the expulsion of an American and a British diplomat who had attempted to investigate the affair in the area.

When, as deputy undersecretary in the Foreign and Commonwealth Office (FCO) responsible for relations with the Arab world, I was obliged to call the Iraqi ambassador, Mohammed al Mashat, into the FCO on more than one occasion during that summer to hear our protest at these grave breaches of Iraq's international undertakings, I was met with defiant and impenitent arguments, and allegations that Britain had been ready to do the same had the Germans attempted to invade during the Second World War. We had several sharp altercations on this gruesome subject of gas, made all the more poignant by the pervasive fragrance of the cologne with which the ambassador was wont to adorn himself. My secretary identified it as freesia. She may have been right, but in the context of our exchanges it carried a more nauseating message.

Despite his near defeat in the war with Iran, Saddam Hussein had snatched from its outcome a measure of diplomatic advantage and some enhancement of his status, at least among Arab opinion. Yet he was in serious trouble too. Iraq had by 1988 amassed debts in respect of her vast armament programme in the region of $80 billion, owed mainly to the Soviet Union and France as well as to her Arab neighbours in the Gulf, Jordan and Egypt. This would take years to repay, even given the resumption of Iraqi oil exports at nearly three million barrels a day, after Saudi Arabia the second highest level in the Organisation of Petroleum Exporting Countries (OPEC) and on a par with Iran. This bleak outlook for the economy had implications for Saddam Hussein's second major problem: what to do with Iraq's huge army of nearly a million men, the justification for which had vanished with the ending of the war. Yet if they were demobilised they could not easily be absorbed into the depressed civilian economy, and so could become a focus for social discontent.

The characteristic response of Iraq's leader to this predicament was to perpetuate the myth of danger, both within Iraqi society and from outside. Those suspected of opposition were sought out and removed, and fresh purges among officers took place. Terror became re-established as an instrument of government. Once again the Kurds took the brunt. In a campaign of unprecedented ruthlessness during 1988, Saddam Hussein had his army raze over 1,000 Kurdish villages in the north in an infamous operation of ethnic cleansing with the codename Al Anfal. The inhabitants were taken into captivity, under the pretext of relocating them in new settlements in southern Iraq. Evidence which has subsequently come to light indicates that large numbers of them, perhaps over 100,000, were exterminated in mass graves into which earth was then bulldozed. From outside all we heard were reports of a Kurdish resettlement programme, presented as a benign scheme to provide new lands and mix Iraq's communities in the interests of national homogeneity. Of the abhorrent reality of the project there was not a whisper.

So far as relations with Britain were concerned, Saddam Hussein continued to play cat and mouse over the long detention in prison of a British businessman, Ian Richter, held by Iraq on trumped-up charges as a pawn to try to gain the release of a convicted Iraqi assassin serving a sentence in the UK. I went out to Baghdad in the autumn of 1988 on behalf of the Foreign Secretary, Sir Geoffrey Howe, to remonstrate with Iraq's foreign minister, Tariq Aziz, over certain unacceptable activities on the part of the Iraqi embassy in London, the premises of which in Queen's Gate, Kensington, had become the scene of protest and picketing by Iraqi exiles which had led to dangerous confrontations.

My meeting with Tariq Aziz in a drab room in the Foreign Ministry was a chilly affair. He sat apart in the severe olive green uniform which Saddam Hussein had decreed for all members of the Revolutionary Command Council. His accompanying officials were wooden and ill at ease. We talked past each other, and the encounter did nothing for our already strained relations. Baghdad itself had a ominous feel to it as our ambassador, Terry Clark, and I drove round the city, the old heart of which had been almost entirely remodelled on Saddam Hussein's instructions into a characterless concrete monolith with memorials commemorating himself and his achievements at every vantage point. This act of civic vandalism had been carried out despite the preoccupations and financial drain of the early years of the war with Iran, in preparation for what Saddam had planned to be Iraq's victorious hosting of the summit of non-aligned nations in 1982. In the event the dream evaporated as Iraq lost ground to Iran's fierce counterattack. With relief we slipped into the shade of the old Tijani mosque to catch a vestige of the Baghdad that was no longer. At a dinner that night with my counterpart in the Iraqi foreign ministry, there were moments when his guard dropped enough to allow touches of the good feelings which many Iraqis retain for their links with Britain. But these were quickly masked in the interests of political correctness. It was no hardship to leave Baghdad that night.

In this militant post-war mood Saddam Hussein sought to regain for Iraq a key position of influence in Arab diplomacy. To this end he persuaded three states which at that time were not yet members of any regional grouping, Egypt, Jordan and Yemen, to band themselves with Iraq in a new club for closer political and economic association, to be called the Arab Co-operation Council (ACC). It had been Iraq's intention to give this body a military ingredient, but this was resisted, notably by Egypt, who was just re-emerging into the mainstream of Arab politics after ten years of ostracism following her signature in 1979 of the Camp David Accord with Israel. Iraq had therefore to make do with what she could get, in effect a club of nations each deeply in debt and in no position to help each other with more than rhetoric.

The establishment of the ACC had the effect, however, of sending warning signals to Iraq's Gulf neighbours, and particularly to Saudi Arabia, who saw in this move an attempt to encircle her with potentially hostile states. Her relations with Yemen were already poor owing to border disputes, those with the Hashemite regime in Jordan were as ever uneasy, and those with Egypt were only beginning to come out of the deep freeze. Elsewhere in the circle Iran pursued her attempts to subvert Saudi Arabia's guardianship of Mecca and Medina, while Sudan had adopted an extremist Islamic tone of hostility towards the Al Saud, despite the Kingdom's strict practice of religious orthodoxy. Thus by early 1989 the Saudi government had good reason to feel uncomfortable over where Saddam Hussein's ambitions might lead next. They were not taken in by a fierce and well-orchestrated campaign unleashed during 1989 by Iraq to create the impression of an imminent Israeli aggression against Iraq and perhaps more widely. This was suspected to amount to an elaborate Iraqi exercise in camouflage, but for what alternative objective was not clear. King Fahd's policy in response was to seek to contain Iraq by humouring Saddam and avoiding cause for provocation.

Saudi unease was heightened by an unsolicited proposal on the part of Iraq in early 1989 for a non-aggression agreement with Saudi Arabia. There seemed no good reason to decline. The Saudi–Iraqi border, including the partition of a diamond-shaped neutral zone which had existed since the negotiations between Sir Percy Cox and King Abdul Aziz at Al Uqair in 1922, had been definitively settled between the two governments in 1985, during Iraq's war with Iran. A non-aggression agreement had attractions for Saudi Arabia in the context of her unease over Iraq's latest move in initiating a new regional grouping in the ACC. But there was also reason to conjecture why Iraq should suddenly wish to buttress her generally good relationship with the Kingdom through a device designed to insure against aggression from that quarter. Nevertheless Saudi Arabia consented to Iraq's sudden proposal, and the non-aggression agreement was duly signed in Baghdad by King Fahd and Saddam Hussein.

Another aspect of Iraq's behaviour following the ceasefire with Iran, which contributed to misgivings in Saudi Arabia and further afield too, was the continuing high level of Iraqi expenditure on armaments and military infrastructure. It had been expected, by ourselves as well as by Iraq's neighbours, that with an end to the fighting which had so bled both Iraq and Iran in terms of manpower and economic resources, both protagonists would turn their attention to civil reconstruction and take a break from military expenditure. But by the end of 1988 the evidence was starting to accumulate that Saddam Hussein had no intention, despite Iraq's massive indebtedness, of easing up on this front. Rather he was putting considerable effort into building up a domestic armament capability involving high-grade weapons of mass destruction, and was seeking to obtain critical components and plant from a variety of Western European suppliers, using surreptitious means to evade arms export restrictions. These controls remained tight in the case of the UK, leading Iraq to deploy tactics of brazen deception. Iraqi weapons activity included work on extending the range of her Soviet-supplied stock of ground-launched Scud missiles as well as developing the chemical weapons already used to devastating effect against the Kurdish community at Halabja and Iranian forces in the Faw peninsula.

These ominous indications led to the British government stepping up from 1989 onwards its scrutiny of exports to Iraq. The results were disturbing. They confirmed suspicions that Saddam Hussein was engaged in acquiring from European suppliers an extensive selection of designs and components for the production of sophisticated weaponry, some of it outlawed by international agreements to which Iraq herself was signatory. Moreover she had managed to cover her tracks with ingenuity, taking advantage of looser export regimes applying at the time in certain countries, such as West Germany and Switzerland, where suitable technology was to be found. In Britain the Iraqis had concentrated on machine tools and specialised metal parts which could be presented as having a legitimate non-military purpose. They had even gone so far as to buy control of one of the country's leading makers of digital machine tools, Churchill-Matrix. Iraqi orders during the late 1980s kept the firm in business.

But Iraq's ambitious programme did not stop with missile technology and chemical weaponry. Indications emerged that she was actively engaged in the development of a crude nuclear capability. This was confirmed in the spring of 1990 when a consignment of components essential to the manufacture of a triggering mechanism for nuclear explosions was discovered under false documentation and seized by British customs authorities. This Iraqi attempt at deception received wide publicity and added to the growing wariness of Iraq's Gulf neighbours.

The most sensational revelation, however, was the unearthing, again by British customs authorities in early 1990, of the 'supergun' project. This was a scheme, verging on make-believe, for the construction of a cannon of unprecedented range, sufficient to launch projectiles from Iraqi territory against Israel, or for that matter the eastern cities of Saudi Arabia. It was in effect a crude terror weapon, the brainchild of a Canadian ballistics designer, Dr Gerald Bull, who met his death in suspicious circumstances in Brussels in early 1990.

The project came to light through the impounding of a large consignment of very heavy steel pipe sections at the British port of Middlesbrough. Two British special steels companies, contracted to manufacture the pipes to high specifications, had been told that they were intended for a petrochemical plant. There had accordingly been no problem over export clearance, and two consignments had already been shipped. At the time of the discovery one shipment had reached Iraq and the second was en route by road in Greece, where it too was impounded. Investigation of the pipe sections showed their strength to be far in excess of any likely use in process plant.

The trail led to the conclusion that Iraq had for some considerable time been working on the development of the Bull long-range gun, an operation the fanciful scope of which strained the credulity of her Arab neighbours and Western governments too. It only obtained final confirmation when UN weapons inspectors discovered the prototype gun barrel fully assembled at a secret test site in Iraq following the Gulf War. Indeed, I had difficulty at the time in convincing the Saudi foreign minister that the project was for real, and that the publicity was not just a crude campaign against Iraq on the part of Britain and other Western powers, as the agile Iraqi propaganda machine was quick to allege. As I assured Prince Saud, the allegations might sound like something out of Hollywood, but they were in dead earnest. He made it clear that Saudi misgivings over Iraq's continuing militancy following the 1988 ceasefire were again on the increase, though Saddam's intentions were as ever difficult to read.

By the latter part of 1989 the Gulf states which had shown support for Iraq in the war with Iran were beginning to sense fresh danger. In particular there were signs that Saddam had the intention of putting the screws on Kuwait and Saudi Arabia. He had surprised both countries earlier in the year with a renewed request for money, said to have been in the region of $10 billion. The request was coolly received, given that the war with Iran, to which the two countries had contributed some $40 billion between them in one form or another, was now at an end and Iraq was once again exporting oil at her maximum rate of around three million barrels a day. Indeed, though perhaps imprudently as things turned out, Kuwait had begun to hint to a resentful Saddam Hussein that she was interested in seeing a start made on the repayment of the 'loans' already made to Iraq. Saudi Arabia chose a less provocative stance on this point; in all likelihood they had for the present written off in their minds the prospect of repayment, given Iraq's precarious financial position and Saddam's unpredictable moods. In a minor attempt to keep Iraq off their backs, both countries arranged in early 1990 to pass on to Iraq a large stock of second-hand plant for use in Iraq's reconstruction programme. But the Iraqi leader was not to be deflected from his more sinister purpose.

CHAPTER 2

The Gathering Storm

In the light of hindsight Saddam Hussein's intention to seize the resources of Kuwait for the benefit of Iraq's aggrandisement and economic recovery probably took shape a year or more before the actual invasion. With the sudden and inconclusive ending of the conflict with Iran, the Iraqi leadership found itself in a very tight corner. Prices for crude oil were weakening as the world economy began to move into recession, yet the country was crippled with debt and faced huge reconstruction costs. Moreover, in these circumstances demobilisation of even part of the million-strong army would be far from straightforward.

It was therefore predictable that among his options Saddam Hussein's restless attention should revert to Iraq's longstanding claim to sovereignty over Kuwait. From here it was a small step to the conviction that Iraq was being denied her due share in Kuwait's wealth, which would provide the answer to her economic plight. Further pretexts for grievance were not hard to fabricate out of instances of Kuwaiti insensitivity towards her powerful neighbour. These gradually built up in the Iraqi leader's mind into a paranoid image of a conspiracy to deny Iraq her rightful position of influence, with Kuwait acting as a front for Western interests, notably the USA and Britain. Plans to escalate pressure on Kuwait were carefully laid and executed, though the actual timing of the onslaught probably owed something to the strand of impulsiveness so predominant in Saddam Hussein's personality.

Despite this ominous crescendo it seemed inconceivable to Iraq's Arab neighbours, as to others involved with the region, that for all her threats and pressures Iraq would attempt an unprovoked attack on the state of Kuwait whose support she had taken such pains to cultivate during the previous eight years of war with Iran. Indeed, co-operation had developed to the point where Kuwait herself had become a target for Iranian attack through artillery bombardment, threats to her tanker fleet in the Gulf, and subversion of Kuwait's Shi'a minority which led to an attempt to assassinate the Amir, Sheikh Jabir al Sabah, in 1985 while he was driving through Kuwait City.

Yet as early as the spring of 1989, within nine months of the ceasefire

14

in the war with Iran, Saddam Hussein had begun to signal an intention to bring pressure on Kuwait and resurrect Iraq's longstanding claim to her territory. This notice took the form of an official communication to the Kuwaiti government that Iraq laid claim to a segment of land in the north of the country, involving about a third of Kuwaiti territory down to what came to be known as the 'Saddam line'. It contained no centres of population, but covered the major Rumaila oilfield which straddled the existing frontier, as well as affording coastal space for Iraq to extend her very limited access to the Gulf in the shallows of Umm Qasr. As a result of earlier encroachment on Kuwaiti territory, she had already established a naval base in this area. At this early stage the Kuwaiti government did not appear to have taken Iraq's demands seriously, though the Saudis, themselves under simultaneous Iraqi pressure to conclude a non-aggression agreement, raised an eyebrow. Kuwait had by now grown accustomed to border violations by Iraq, and probably counted as in the past on being able to buy off such needling.

Iraq's claim to Kuwait was a long-running sore. It was based upon the disputed issue of Ottoman Turkish claims to sovereignty over the sheikhdom prior to the establishment of Iraq and Kuwait as separate states under British protection after the First World War. Legally it did not hold water. Of more practical relevance was the fact that Iraqi public opinion had for three decades been conditioned both at school and through constant propaganda to consider Kuwait as rightfully part of Iraq. Saddam Hussein himself, as the personification of Iraq's statehood and ambitions, would have needed no convincing on the point. According to the Iraqi case Kuwait had formed part of the Ottoman vilayet of Basra right up to the creation of the state of Iraq under British mandate in 1921. Accordingly, as the successor regime to Ottoman rule, Iraq had assumed sovereignty over Kuwait at that time, particularly as the Ottoman Sultan had refused to accept the validity of the protection agreement which Britain had signed with the ruler of Kuwait, Sheikh Mubarak, in 1899. The subsequent Anglo-Ottoman agreement of 1913, which recognised Kuwait as a state, had never been ratified by Turkey. The First World War had intervened, and blocked the process.

This Iraqi argument contained significant historical omissions. It ignored the formal recognition of Kuwait's existence, although this had been extended by Iraq in 1932 when at British urging the frontier between the two countries, which had been set in 1923 by Sir Percy Cox, the British High Commissioner to the recently-mandated Kingdom of Iraq, was defined on paper as a prelude to Iraq joining the League of Nations as a sovereign state. It also took no account of Turkey's renunciation of former Ottoman claims to territory outside her modern borders, as settled in 1923 in the Treaty of Lausanne, whereby with British support Iraq had gained the oil-rich region of Mosul. Successive Iraqi governments had, however, continued to dispute details of the 1932 border. In 1961 things came to a head when the full claim to Kuwait was resurrected by Iraq's first republican government under Abdul Karim Qasim, on the occasion of Kuwait's formal independence from Britain in June of that year and her subsequent application to join the Arab League.

Qasim backed up this bid for Kuwait by the despatch of troops to the border. Kuwait's ruler, Sheikh Abdullah al Salem al Sabah, recognised the danger that, despite the Arab League's prompt condemnation of Iraq's threat, the claim might be backed up with force. With British encouragement he activated his newly-signed defence agreement with Britain, resulting in the despatch of British land, sea and air forces to secure Kuwait's independence against any Iraqi attempt at seizure. At this time, prior to her military withdrawal from Aden and the Gulf, Britain still kept a considerable military garrison in the area. The force despatched to Kuwait consisted of a combined infantry and armoured brigade, normally based in Kenya and Aden, a small naval task force with a Royal Marines battalion operating from the aircraft carrier HMS *Hermes*, and an RAF squadron of Hunter aircraft, normally based at Muharraq airfield on Bahrain.

During this crisis I was myself assigned temporarily to the British embassy in Kuwait as information officer, responsible for liaison with the press. I flew over from Beirut in late June, a week or so after the arrival of the British forces, and took up my duties in the elegant embassy on the shore of Kuwait City, with its cool verandas redolent of the days when official representatives in Kuwait were appointed from New Delhi by the British government in India. It was this same solid building which 30 years later would serve as both refuge and prison for our ambassador and consul during the months when they stuck out Iraq's occupation of Kuwait prior to Operation DESERT STORM. In the hot June of 1962 I found the compound humming with unwonted activity, as military personnel came and went and urgent telegraphic communications were laboriously coded and decoded with the aid of the time-consuming manual cipher system then in use.

The arrival of British forces sufficed to block any Iraqi idea of an attack on a fledgeling Kuwait. But it was a cumbersome exercise when compared with the well-integrated yet far larger British mobilisation in the Gulf 30 years later. This first Kuwait operation marked the dying days of the old and jealously-preserved single service command arrangements, particularly where the Royal Navy was concerned. The commanding admiral, Fitzroy Talbot, declined to locate his head-quarters alongside the army and air force, and insisted on running the naval side of the affair from HMS *Hermes*, anchored some kilometres off-shore on account of the shallows.

The joint force commander was Major-General John Walker, a former Gurkha officer of somewhat choleric disposition, who had no patience with the hesitations which the Amir of Kuwait was showing over some aspects of the British deployment. For his part the Amir was coming under criticism from the Egypt of Gamal Abd al Nasser and other Arab nationalist circles, reacting in those post-Suez years to an instinctive sense of outrage at the spectacle of British military activity on Arab soil. Sheikh Abdullah accordingly saw a need for circumspection despite the evident threat to his state; a preoccupation which was, despite the ebbing of the high tide of Arab nationalism, to re-emerge for King Fahd of Saudi Arabia in his decision to invite Western arms in to help meet a threat from Iraq 30 years on.

In the event there were no hostilities, although Iraqi forces remained in strength on Kuwait's northern frontier for the next two years and Iraq continued to maintain her claim to the former sheikhdom. British infantry troops spent an uncomfortably hot July and August dug in along the Mutla Ridge to the north of Kuwait City or cooped up on board ship, while an armoured car squadron reconnoitred the desert frontier ahead and a regiment of Centurion tanks was held in reserve. The intense summer heat made for a harsh environment. I recall a visit to the Manchester Regiment, in trenches on the ridge looking north-wards across a bleak desert landscape. The sun temperature was over 130°F and they had only the thinnest of camouflage netting to shield them. Life inside their old-style tin helmets must have been infernal.

There were, however, Iraqi attempts at sabotage. On one occasion shortly after the British brigade commander had taken off from Kuwait airport in a Beverly transport, there was an explosion which blew out the cargo cabin loading door. The passengers found themselves looking down into the blue waters of the Gulf. The hatchway into the flight cabin above their heads opened and the RAF loadmaster sergeant's head emerged. Seeing the damage, he remarked 'Sorry, Brigadier. We've got mice', and they carried on their way.

It came as a considerable relief, not only to the Kuwait government but to ourselves as well, when in August the Arab League came up with a pro-posal to replace the British force with a composite Arab one. This was to be the first occasion for a joint Arab force to undertake a peacekeeping role in place of Western troops, and was only made possible by the fact that Iraq had in pique absented herself from Arab League meetings.

This was not to be so in the Kuwait crisis of 1990, when Iraq made a point of attending all Arab League meetings, thus thwarting initial Saudi and Egyptian efforts to unite an Arab front to oppose her action. In this earlier instance, however, the Arab force, wearing green berets and under the command of a Jordanian general, took over the defensive role at the end of August with a screen of troops behind the frontier with Iraq. There were units from Jordan, Egypt, Saudi Arabia, Syria and Sudan. They had never worked together before, yet settled down well under their unified command and for the next two years sat out the sentry role.

I went with a correspondent from the Egyptian daily, *Al Ahram*, to see the last British units fly out to Aden in their Beverley transports. 'Another British withdrawal', he remarked, having the Suez encounter, only five years before, still fresh in his mind. But this amicable hand-over, organised under mutual agreement, marked a new era and he knew it. By way of a backup arrangement under our defence agreement with Kuwait we left behind the tanks as a stockpile in case of future threat, together with a military mission to see to their maintenance. This mission was still operating as a training team for the Kuwait army's British-supplied armour when the Iraqis invaded in August 1990. Its luckless members were rounded up and held hostage in Iraq, along with British and other western civilians.

The overthrow of Abdul Karim Qasim's regime in a bloody *coup d'état* in February 1963 organised by the Ba'ath party brought an end to Iraq's military threat. The new government, headed by Abd al Salaam Aref, a former army officer, accorded recognition of Kuwait's independence and accepted the existing frontier in October of that year, receiving in return a cash payment from Kuwait of £31 million, still a substantial sum in those days. The exchange of letters confirming Iraq's recognition was officially lodged by Kuwait with the UN. It subsequently became a key piece of evidence to controvert Saddam Hussein's renewal of the Iraqi claim in 1990, on the grounds that Iraq had not formally ratified the 1963 agreement.

Meanwhile Iraq had continued to prevaricate over the establishment of a joint commission to demarcate the frontier on the ground, and in the intervening years had advanced her border posts at a number of points, particularly in the area of the new naval base at Umm Qasr. A harder Iraqi line, with frequent armed skirmishes along the frontier, became a feature from the time that the Ba'ath returned to government in Iraq following the overthrow of the Aref regime in July 1968. This marked a significant step in Saddam Hussein's own political advance, as the president of the new Revolutionary Command Council (RCC), set up by the Ba'ath party, was his relative and patron, Ahmad Hassan al Bakr, who put Saddam Hussein in charge of internal security, a position of influence from which he made his own successful bid for power through a further bloodletting purge in mid-1979. Shortly thereafter Saddam Hussein launched his ill-considered campaign against Iran, for which Kuwait's material support became essential. Nothing more was accordingly heard of the border dispute until, following the 1988 ceasefire, the Iraqi leader chose to resurrect it in the early months of 1990.

In some measure Kuwait herself contributed to Saddam Hussein's search for a pretext for his designs upon his neighbour. During their three decades of independence since 1961, the Kuwaitis acquired something of a reputation for the pursuit of self-interest which was at odds with their generosity towards their partners within the Arab community. The narrow basis on which Kuwaiti citizenship was defined produced a sense of resentment among Palestinian Arabs, who had taken up residence in large numbers since independence and provided the country with a core of professional skills. Some bedouin groups who had traditionally migrated across the sheikhdom found themselves ineligible for citizenship, although many were serving in the Kuwaiti forces. The regime also courted unpopularity among certain sections of Kuwait's own citizens by its action in closing down the elected national assembly in response to criticism of government policy within that institution. By early 1990 there were demonstrations and petitions calling for the restoration of the assembly, prompting the regime to come up with proposals to reintroduce it but on a more restricted basis. These stirrings of domestic discontent provided issues which Saddam Hussein would seek to exploit in August 1990, with a fraudulent claim that the invasion had been in response to public clamour.

In regional matters, too, the Kuwaitis had sometimes chosen to go their own way, opening their diplomatic and military lines to the communist regimes of the eastern bloc at a time when their Gulf partners abstained from such contacts. At the same time they showed themselves lukewarm over the process of closer integration with their neighbours in the Gulf Co-operation Council. At the time of Iraq's invasion Kuwait was not yet a signatory to the GCC's defence pact. Moreover, in the eyes of other Gulf states there was an overconfidence to Kuwaiti foreign policy. King Faisal of Saudi Arabia was reputed to have complained with some exasperation in the 1970s that there were not two but three superpowers in the world: the USA, the USSR and Kuwait.

In economic affairs Kuwait's record of support for development projects and to governments and private institutions throughout the Arab and developing worlds was a notable one. In particular she had been in the front rank of those Arab states giving support both in funds and services to Iraq during the war with Iran, and had come under physical attack from Iran for doing so. Moreover, the management of her oil wealth was marked by a thrifty housekeeping, and by the investment of surpluses in productive ventures abroad, designed to guarantee the state's future prosperity against the day when oil revenues would diminish. Yet these virtues tended to be offset, even among those who benefited from them, by a cruder image of a self-indulgent society.

The impression of a shortsighted pursuit of self-interest was enhanced in 1990 by Kuwait's production of crude oil at a level in excess of the quota which she had agreed with her partners in OPEC. This disregard for OPEC's sensitive quota system became a source of irritation to other members, not least Saudi Arabia, who had continued to do her bit to sustain oil prices by keeping her production down to some 5.4 million barrels a day during the first part of 1990 and was now finding it galling to see her neighbour flouting her quota. The Kuwaiti plea that she qualified for an exemption, on the grounds that her extensive overseas refining ventures had to be kept supplied, cut little ice. Above all the Kuwaiti action afforded a source of particular grievance to Iraq, already in the mood to find cause for affront, and faced with a calamitous economic situation and a need to maximise oil revenue to cushion her transition from an all-out war effort to a civilian economy. It thus contributed to stoking up Saddam Hussein's sense of injury, and may even have encouraged him in a misapprehension that he could get away with seizure of Kuwait and her tempting assets.

Iraq's ready sense of resentment was carried a step further by the opportunity taken by Kuwait to remind her unpredictable northern neighbour of the loans, mainly in oil credits and amounting to some $12 billion, which had been advanced to her during the war with Iran. The Kuwaiti finance ministry made a point of publicly recording these debts in their International Monetary Fund statistics for 1990, and even pressed Iraq to start repayment. By contrast the Saudis more prudently chose not to make an issue at this stage of their somewhat larger war credits to Iraq. In Saddam Hussein this parading by Kuwait of Iraq's debts, incurred in a cause which he considered had involved the defence of the Gulf states as much as of Iraq herself against Iranian expansionism, provoked a sharp irritation.

This renewed hardening in Iraq's attitude towards Kuwait, which started to show itself in the early months of 1990, ran parallel to Iraqi activity on a wider diplomatic front to rally opinion within the Arab world against an alleged Israeli and Western conspiracy to injure Iraq. This campaign may have been intended in part for internal consumption, to shore up the support of the long-suffering Iraqi public for a regime which had nothing but human loss and economic hardship to show for the eight years of war, and no early prospect of alleviation. It also served Saddam Hussein's compulsive quest for a leadership role within the Arab community at large. In some degree he had probably convinced himself that Iraq was at risk. Memories were not so distant of the devastating Israeli air attack in June 1981 on the Osiraq nuclear reactor, which Iraq had under construction with French technology, and which was widely suspected of being intended for the development of a nuclear military capability rather than its designated energy research programme. Subsequent efforts by Iraq to persuade France to rebuild the reactor had as a result of international concern come to nothing, and a long-shot attempt in 1989 to prompt the Saudis into meeting the costs had produced no response.

This paranoid sense on the part of Saddam Husein of a plot to frustrate his leadership was intensified by the restrictions on the part of most Western countries on supply of the high technology ingredients for Iraq's continuing armaments programme. An element in this obsession on the part of the Iraqi leader was contributed by the tragic case of Farzad Bazoft, a journalist working for the London *Observer* newspaper, who was arrested while on a visit to Iraq in September 1989 as a result of having taken himself off to investigate the site of an explosion known to have occurred at one of Iraq's major armaments factories at Al Hilla, near Baghdad. Bazoft, who was of Iranian origin, persuaded a British nurse employed at a Baghdad hospital to drive him on this risky investigation. Both were subsequently arrested by the Iraqi security services and were interrogated with brutality. Bazoft was made to sign a confession, the sincerity of which was rendered doubtful by its artificial language, that he had worked on behalf of British and Israeli intelligence. He was given a summary trial in March 1990, when he sought unsuccessfully to disavow his 'confession', and was sentenced to death. British consular help in the trial was denied him.

Bazoft's conviction unleashed a storm of public obloquy in Britain in which Mrs Thatcher herself gave full vent to her outrage. Intercession with Iraq was requested from a number of Arab governments, despite their hesitations over the increasingly aggressive tone of Saddam Hussein's behaviour in the region. The sentence of death was however carried out with a minimum of delay, perhaps with a view to pre-empting any intercessions which our friends in the region might be disposed to make in Baghdad.

The affair coincided with Tom King's first visit to Saudi Arabia as Defence Secretary, when he called on Crown Prince Abdullah, the commander of the National Guard with which the British army had for many years had a training mission, and on Prince Sultan, the Defence Minister. Discussions were concerned with our well-established co-operation in the security field, and particularly the important Al Yamamah programme, under which British Aerospace (BAe) and other firms were providing Tornado and Hawk aircraft together with flying and technical training to the Royal Saudi Air Force (RSAF) and minehunting ships to the Royal Saudi Navy. At this stage there still seemed no reason to suspect Iraq of military adventurism, nor how soon this defence co-operation between us was to be put to the test of hostilities. Bazoft's summary fate, however, afforded yet another reminder of the ruthlessness which characterised Iraq's leader.

Throughout the early months of 1990 Iraq's influential propaganda machine raised the temperature of its rhetoric against its traditional bogeys of the USA, Britain and Israel. Saddam Hussein's design in this was to work the campaign up to its highpoint in time for an Arab summit meeting which he had engineered to host in Baghdad, as a gauge of Iraq's claim to a leading role in Arab affairs now that the conflict with Iran was over. It can be argued that this bid for a summit to rally the Arab world afresh against Israel was intended all along as a smokescreen for Iraq's own designs on Kuwait. Certainly the political preludes were orchestrated in elaborate fashion.

A summit, held in Amman in February to mark the first anniversary of the new Iraq-led grouping, the ACC, comprising Egypt, Jordan and Yemen and aimed particularly at bringing Egypt out of her years of ostracism and into alliance with Iraq, was used by Saddam Hussein as a platform to work up anti-Western rhetoric and beat the Palestinian drum with a warning, calculated to appeal to Arab public opinion, about the threat posed by the new wave of Jewish immigration into Israel from the Soviet Union. In a bid for Islamic respectability, Iraq also played host to a conference of Arab religious personalities whose influence on public opinion, not least in Saudi Arabia, was recognised to be significant. Shortly after this conference I found myself on a flight from Jedda to Riyadh in conversation with a Saudi journalist, who told me how attendance at this well-staged conference had persuaded him that the Ba'athist creed possessed stronger Islamic credentials than he had previously believed to be the case. Here was an example of Iraq's insidious tactics.

Meanwhile the anti-Western rhetoric went down well in Palestinian circles, and with much of public opinion in Egypt, Jordan and Syria too, as well as further afield in North Africa. More blatant tactics to win friends were also adopted. Influential personalities among Iraq's new partners in the ACC were said to be susceptible to the offer of Mercedes limousines. Yemen, occupying the key Arab seat on the UN Security Council, was wooed with military aid. Even in remote Mauritania on the Atlantic shore, Iraq's arm reached out with the tempting offer of military aid in return for facilities for flight testing Iraq's ambitious missile programme.

It was very much a part of Saddam Hussein's policy to keep Saudi Arabia onside and to make the most of areas of common interest, such as a shared concern to see Kuwaiti overproduction curbed. But the way he went about this only served to heighten Saudi mistrust. Saddam Hussein followed up his springing of the idea of a non-aggression pact on King Fahd in the spring of 1989 with a return visit to Saudi Arabia in February 1990. King Fahd accepted the proposal with little show of enthusiasm and arranged for it to take place out of the public eye at the military base of Hafr al Batin, not far south of the Kingdom's borders with Iraq and Kuwait. The venue was chosen as a subtly-coded message to remind the Iraqi leader of the extent of Saudi territory and her readiness to defend it.

From accounts I subsequently heard from members of the Saudi ruling family who turned out at Hafr al Batin for the occasion, the visit was a distasteful affair with ominous overtones. The Iraqi leader's obsessive sensitivity over his personal security meant that Saddam Hussein and his entourage arrived from Baghdad in a fleet of aircraft without telling his hosts which of them contained the President himself. The Saudis were offended by this, seeing in it a mistrust of their tradition of hospitality by which they set store. They were further put off by the overbearing tone which Saddam Hussein adopted. He pressed the King to attend the Arab summit which Iraq was to host in May. A pitch was also made for additional financial help, accompanied by an attempt to exploit Saudi Arabia's known irritation at Kuwaiti overproduction of crude and to make common cause on this issue.

The upshot was to raise Saudi wariness of Iraq, though with no clear indication of where Saddam Hussein's predicament and ambition would lead him next. His mounting sense of grievance against Kuwait was evident, but there was nothing to indicate that this would be expressed in any form beyond an economic and diplomatic squeeze. Nothing more had been heard of Iraq's claim a year earlier to the slice of territory in northern Kuwait together with free port facilities and transit rights. Meanwhile, the Iraqi leader had diverted Arab attention towards his campaign against Israel and the West for seeking to inhibit Iraq's recovery from the burdens of the war with Iran.

Nevertheless, ever since Saddam Hussein had disregarded his advice in 1980 and gone ahead with his attack on Iran, King Fahd had recognised a potential threat to the Kingdom and its Gulf partners from Iraq's forceful leader. As the King told me when I presented my credentials to him in Jedda in October 1989, it was with the need in mind to ensure the protection of his country's extended frontiers, including the Iraqi flank, that he had entered with Britain into the huge Al Yamamah project for developing the RSAF, to improve Saudi Arabia's capability to deter outright attack. Iraq's move to establish a formal association with Jordan, Egypt and Yemen so soon after the end of hostilities with Iran had reinforced a Saudi premonition of danger which Saddam Hussein's unsolicited visit to Hafr al Batin had done nothing to allay.

The Arab League summit, held in Baghdad in the last week of May 1990, was intended to serve as the high point of Saddam Hussein's design to put himself at the head of a revived Arab mood of hostility towards the West and Israel, under cover of which he would find himself with a free hand to bring whatever pressure he might choose upon Kuwait and other Gulf oil producers to help extricate Iraq's collapsing economy. The meeting was preceded by a stream of invective through the medium of Iraq's propaganda machine, alleging Western conspiracy and calling for Arab vigilance. American radio broadcasts critical of Iraq's human rights record, and British action to block the export of military components, as well as allegations of espionage, all went into the Iraqi dossier. A reassurance of good relations conveyed to the Iraqi leader by a US Senate delegation in April, led by Senator Robert Dole, brought no change of tone. Concern over the implications of a new wave of immigration of Soviet Jews to Israel as part of a recent improvement in relations between the USSR and Israel was also exploited by Iraq to fuel Arab sentiment.

Worried at the implications of this febrile anti-Western prelude, King Fahd tried to cool things by seeking to have the summit postponed. He also took the precaution of sharing his concern with President Mubarak, in itself a significant diplomatic step towards an Egypt which Saudi Arabia had hitherto kept at arm's length since the Camp David agreement and as a result of Egypt's link with Iraq in the suspect ACC. Circumstances, however, now called for renewed contact with this important Arab player. The King had growing reason to suspect that behind the Iraqi polemic on traditional themes lay an intention to use her control of the summit to mobilise opinion against Kuwait and other Gulf states.

Iraq's growing sense of grievance in this quarter had been further exposed to the Saudis a few weeks before the summit, when the Iraqi leader had alleged to Hisham Nazer, the Saudi oil minister, that Kuwaiti overproduction was aimed at damaging Iraq. The Iraqi deputy Prime Minister, Saadoun Hammadi, had taken this further, claiming that Kuwait was ganging up with Saudi Arabia and the UAE to prejudice Iraq's oil revenues. Hisham Nazer subsequently told me he was left with the clear impression at the time that Saddam Hussein was already working up this grievance in his mind as a pretext for some kind of action against Kuwait.

In the event Saddam Hussein was not prepared to be deterred from holding his summit. It went ahead at the end of May with King Fahd a reluctant participant. With support from King Hussein of Jordan and Yasir Arafat, the Iraqi president sought to point the conference towards a condemnation of Western activity. Behind this screen, however, he vented his resentment against the Gulf states, and particularly Kuwait, for a failure to show Iraq the support which was her due. In an ominous warning to the Amir of Kuwait, which the latter appears to have chosen to ignore at the time, Saddam Hussein is said to have offered to 'surprise' him with a visit and a definitive solution to their border dispute.

Together with President Mubarak, King Fahd worked hard at the summit to head off the more outrageous Iraqi accusations over Palestine and allegations of Western hostility in the wake of the foiling of the 'supergun' episode, while seeking to avert a new and damaging split within the Arab world. It was apparent, when the King received Douglas Hurd a week later at his house on a small island just off the Red Sea coast some 80 kilometres north of Jedda where he was taking a break after the strains of the conference, that it had not been an easy meeting. The Saudis seemed as puzzled as were we at what lay behind the heightened invective which the Iraqi leader had unleashed on the Americans and ourselves. The anger shown by Saddam Hussein at seeing himself denied critical components for his armament programme was predictable, yet it did not appear to account entirely for the bitterness of his attacks, nor for his efforts to work up wider Arab opinion to a pitch of antipathy not seen for many years, indeed since the Suez war between Israel and Egypt in 1973. The effect was to arouse mistrust rather than solidarity. But so forceful was Iraq's diversionary campaign on this front that there seemed no reason to suspect it might all be a smokescreen for a brutal grab at Kuwait's resources.

We therefore pondered what Iraq might be up to and how we could help to restrain Iraq's polemic now that the summit was past. Saddam Hussein might be resentful at not getting his own way in the Baghdad meeting, but he did not appear to be looking to pick a further quarrel. We concluded from Douglas Hurd's talks in Jedda with the King and the Foreign Minister, Prince Saud, that one useful contribution which the

British government could make in this unsettled state of Middle East affairs was to pursue actively with the USA and Israel the idea of a fresh attempt to get a dialogue going over the Arab–Israel peace process. A move to restart talks, which the Americans had launched the previous year following Yasir Arafat's significant renunciation of the use of violence and acknowledgement of Israel's right to exist, had bogged down yet again through a combination of stiff Israeli reaction to the *intifada* uprising by Palestinians within the West Bank and Gaza, and Arab concern at the way in which migration to Israel by Soviet Jews was turning into a flood. For their part the Saudis undertook to use their considerable financial clout with the PLO to point them towards talks. In this way we could try to pre-empt the destabilising tension, which Iraq was seeking to escalate within the Arab world in a bid to enhance Iraqi influence.

Iraq's first direct warning shot against Kuwait occurred on 16 July, with the publication of a letter sent the previous day by the Foreign Minister, Tariq Aziz, to the Secretary General of the Arab League in Tunis, in which Iraq accused Kuwait of responsibility for the low oil price which was damaging Iraq's economy. Tariq Aziz then went on to allege that Kuwait had compounded this hostile act by taking and selling Iraq's share of production from the Rumaila oilfield. He demanded reparations amounting to $2.4 billion, as well as the cancellation of Iraq's war debt to Kuwait of $12 billion and a further payment of $10 billion to help tide Iraq over her financial problems. This barefaced exercise in extortion had menace added to it the following day when, in a speech on the occasion of Iraq's national day, the Iraqi president raised the stakes by accusing Kuwait – and for good measure the UAE too – of stabbing Iraq in the back. He went on to accuse both Kuwait and the UAE of conspiring against Iraq in conjunction with Western imperialism and Zionism, and gave a veiled warning that Iraq might be obliged to take action to secure her rights if dialogue did not work.

Iraq's sudden and intemperate move to raise the stakes in her dispute with Kuwait came as a surprise to the Saudi government, just as it did to Kuwait. The Saudis hoped that they had managed to defuse Iraq's sense of grievance over Kuwait's overproduction and the consequential downward pressure on oil prices – a grievance which, as the Iraqis knew, Saudi Arabia herself shared – through calling a meeting of Gulf oil producers in Jedda on 11 July at which Saudi Arabia had prevailed upon the Kuwaitis to observe their OPEC quota. This was seen as an important prelude to a regular OPEC meeting due to take place on 25 July in Geneva at which it was assumed Iraq would be making an issue of the problem. The Saudi petroleum minister told me, when I went to Jedda to discuss Iraq's demands with him on 17 July, that he believed Kuwait was now doing enough to satisfy Iraq. To the Saudis the Iraqi outburst to the Arab League and in the president's national day speech thus looked like a move to engineer a pretext for further pressure on Kuwait, presumably to extort more money. The idea of a physical attack may already have featured in Saddam Hussein's calculations at this stage, but it did not occur to his neighbours.

The Iraqi action nevertheless had the effect of moving Arab diplomacy into high gear, with a flurry of contacts in which King Fahd, President Mubarak and Ahmed Klibi, the Tunisian Secretary General of the Arab League, all sought to lower the temperature and press for dialogue in place of threats. The Kuwaitis had gone so far as to request that Iraq repay $2 billion by 31 July despite the latter's acute financial quandary. The Iraqi demand for the $2.4 billion compensation for oil allegedly stolen from the Rumaila field might have been designed as a specific retort to this bid. A recalcitrant statement made directly after the Jedda agreement by the Kuwaiti petroleum minister, to the effect that Kuwait did not regard this as applying beyond the autumn, was seen by many, including our Saudi contacts, as needlessly provocative to an already aggrieved Iraq.

All the same the Saudis were prepared to respond to Kuwait's appeal for help in mediation, and to give their backing to Kuwait's reply put to the Iraqis on 19 July. In this Kuwait rejected Iraq's allegations of ill intent, and recalled Kuwait's solidarity with Iraq during the conflict with Iran in the face of Iranian attacks. The Iraqis were reminded of their failure to fulfil their undertaking in the border agreement of 1963 to join in demarcation of the frontier. The Kuwaitis denied having pumped more than their share of the Rumaila field; their extraction rate had been a mere 10,000 barrels per day, while the Iraqi offtake from their section of the field came to 200,000 barrels. Moving on to a more conciliatory note, the Kuwaitis agreed to consider foregoing repayment of the Iraqi credits. On the matter of a further financial contribution, they explained that they were not in a position to offer more than $500,000 over five years.

The Iraqis were not, however, prepared to let their prey off the hook so easily, as Tariq Aziz made plain in a further communication to the Arab League on 21 July in which he restated Iraq's accusations and demands. On the same day the Iraqi posture assumed a more threatening aspect with the move of troops, estimated at some 20,000 in strength, to the vicinity of the border with Kuwait. In response Kuwait's small army, or rather such of it as was not abroad on summer vacation, was placed on alert, though in contacts with their partners the Kuwaitis sought to dismiss the Iraqi troop movements as an exercise in sabre-rattling.

Such was Saudi concern at the course of events by this stage that King Fahd sent the Foreign Minister, Prince Saud al Faisal, to Baghdad on 21 July with a personal message to Saddam Hussein urging restraint. President Mubarak himself visited Baghdad and Kuwait on the same errand three days later, coming on to Jedda that evening to talk with King Fahd. When I had earlier that day seen the assistant minister in the Foreign Ministry in Riyadh to obtain a readout on Saudi efforts in Baghdad, I was told that the main thrust of Saudi and Egyptian activity at this time was to dissuade Iraq from indulging in further strong-arm tactics until the OPEC meeting on oil pricing and quotas took place on 27 July, when the Kuwaitis were expected to confirm their readiness to fall into line over production limits. It was hoped this would lead to a moderation in Iraq's aggressive conduct. I told the Saudis that in response to our own intercession with the Iraqis the British chargé d'affaires in Baghdad, Robin Kealy, had been left in no doubt of Iraq's resentment at the Kuwaiti position over both oil pricing and debt repayment. It had been explained that Iraq was facing a shortfall of one third in her budgeted oil revenues, for which she held both Kuwait and the UAE responsible. We had, however, been assured that Iraq was seeking to settle things by diplomatic means.

In this discussion we agreed that, while this might all be elaborate bluff, the way in which the Iraqis had steadily worked up their grievance against Kuwait into a crisis, and were backing it with intensive military activity in the border area, albeit described as manoeuvres, gave the situation ominous aspects. Even an act of belligerence could not be ruled out, inconceivable as this appeared in terms of the conventions governing inter-Arab relations. The Kuwaitis might be indulging in overconfidence. I was told that if Kuwait now sought to pay danegeld in order to see off Iraq's browbeating, Saudi Arabia would have no cause to object. Such a demand now looked inevitable, whatever emerged from the forthcoming OPEC meeting. I was told there were limits to the pressure which the Arab world could bring to bear on Iraq. The Arab League was divided, for Saddam Hussein had made sure of his friends in that council. Nor would the GCC states put on at this stage a show of deterrent force through joint mobilisation, as this could risk escalating a dispute which all would prefer to contain. In any case, Kuwait was not a party to the GCC defence arrangements. Instead Saudi Arabia was concentrating on prompting other major Arab states to join with her in interceding in Baghdad. Egypt could play a key part here by virtue of her membership of the Iraqi-inspired ACC.

Also on 24 July King Fahd sent his nephew, Prince Bandar bin Sultan, the Saudi ambassador in Washington, to see the British Prime Minister in London to compare thoughts on the outlook. Prince Bandar explained to Mrs Thatcher that the Saudi government was finding it difficult to judge Saddam Hussein's real intentions. The extent of Iraq's diplomatic and military pressures suggested there was more to the issue in the Iraqi leader's mind than just an exercise in browbeating the Kuwaitis to write off Iraq's war debts. There might be a wider stratagem afoot. Saddam Hussein's recent actions were believed to have included an attempt to bribe the Yemenis to close the Bab al Mandab straits at the southern end of the Red Sea, thus provoking a quarrel over navigation with both Israel and Western powers. It was also said that Iraq had offered money to Egypt to stay out of the crisis (an offer subsequently confirmed by President Mubarak, who had given the proposal an emphatic rejection). Jordan's show of support for Iraq's accusations posed a further worry.

On the other hand, and despite his despatch of troops to the vicinity of the Kuwait frontier, Saddam Hussein had given King Fahd an assurance, on the occasion of Prince Saud's recent visit to Baghdad, that he had no military intentions. The King set store by this as coming from one Arab leader to another. (In an exercise in glib self-justification after the war, the Iraqis claimed that this assurance had been given on the condition that negotiations made progress, conveniently ignoring the fact that it takes two to have a negotiation.)

In reply the Prime Minister put Iraq's latest actions down to Saddam Hussein's arrogant ambition. We needed to watch developments carefully. Prince Bandar confirmed the King's intention to stand by Kuwait whatever happened, not only for the sake of solidarity among GCC members, but in the direct interest of Saudi Arabia's own security too.

At this point indications began to gather that Iraq might be heeding outside pleas for restraint. President Mubarak reported to King Fahd that Saddam Hussein had given him an assurance, in similar terms to that vouchsafed to Prince Saud, that he did not intend to move his forces closer to Kuwait. Furthermore, he had accepted the idea of a meeting on 28 July with the Kuwaitis in Jedda under Saudi and Egyptian auspices. The absence of urgency was given further credence the following day when Saddam Hussein summoned the American ambassador, April Glaspie. The substance of this crucial encounter has subsequently been the object of much speculation, not least because of a doctored version of it which was subsequently released by the Iraqis during the autumn and sought to imply a measure of American acquiescence in Iraq's action in Kuwait. The Iraqi leader evidently made it plain that he remained much vexed by what he claimed to be Kuwait's part in Iraq's acute financial predicament. He also reacted in hostile fashion to an American move, taken in response to Iraqi troop movements, to bring forward the timing of an amphibious military exercise in the UAE involving US marines and Emirate forces.

At the same time, however, Saddam Hussein gave the ambassador to understand that no act of aggression was imminent. In the course of the meeting Saddam Hussein received a telephone call from President Mubarak confirming that the Kuwaitis had agreed to attend the proposed discussions in Jedda the following week – a further pointer against hostilities. According to April Glaspie's subsequent testimony before the US Congress in March 1991, she told Saddam Hussein that the United States did not consider border disputes to be her business, but 'it was emphatically our business that they make the settlement in a non-violent way'. The ambassador left Baghdad five days later on summer leave, and, as I subsequently learnt from an acquaintance to whom April Glaspie spoke on her way through London, apparently did so with a clear conscience, having before her departure handed the Iraqi Foreign Minister a message of reply from President Bush.

The Foreign Minister took a similarly moderated line with the British chargé d'affaires when he sought to check out the American assessment. In the light of these exchanges, and with Kuwait now prepared to stick to her OPEC quota, the risk of an Iraqi attack appeared to be subsiding. The force which the Iraqis were continuing to deploy near the border was not at this point being strengthened further, and was looking more like a crude instrument of pressure to persuade the Kuwaitis to come up with more money at the next round of talks. The immediate crisis seemed to have passed and the Saudis started to relax, as did we. Even the Kuwaitis were not ringing alarm bells and their military forces were only on semi-alert, though it was evident to their partners that their government remained in a state of considerable nervousness.

These hopes that Iraq's pressure might be easing were quickly proved false. At the OPEC pricing meeting in Geneva on 27 July the Iraqis resumed their aggrieved tone. They gave no credit to Kuwait for her cut in production and were not even mollified by a Kuwaiti assurance, extracted after Saudi intervention, to extend observation of the quota right through to the end of the year. Indeed, the Iraqis tried to take on the whole of OPEC by insisting that production be cut all round to the point where prices could be forced up to a new ceiling target level of $25. The majority in OPEC, and in particular the Saudis, saw this as unrealistic as well as detrimental to the future of the industry. The Iraqi proposal was therefore rejected and Iraq was obliged to settle for an increase in the target price to $21. She took it with bad grace, and the episode only served to fuel further her resentment and belief in a conspiracy.

The following days saw the Iraqis moving more troops into the frontier area. Meanwhile, the idea of a meeting in Jedda had slipped as Iraq resumed her blackmail tactics against Kuwait by reaffirming the full suit of claims which she had paraded in Tariq Aziz' letter to the Arab League. King Fahd accordingly sent Prince Saud urgently to Baghdad on 28 July to try to reinstate this crucial meeting, which the Kuwaitis had declared themselves ready to attend. With difficulty the Saudi Foreign Minister secured Iraqi agreement to the meeting going ahead on 30 July.

Finding themselves unable to obtain Kuwaiti acceptance of their demands in advance, the Iraqis next sought to have the meeting qualified as a procedural affair to be followed by a substantive meeting in Baghdad, where they could bring greater pressure to bear on Kuwait. Prince Saud succeeded in getting them to drop this precondition. He indicated that Kuwait was prepared to come up with some financial offer. Saudi Arabia herself was prepared to help by resurrecting an existing offer, made originally to Iraq by the King's predecessor, King Khaled, for the reconstruction of Basra after Iranian attacks had damaged the city in 1981. This substantial offer of some $1 billion had been renewed once already on the occasion of the signature of the Saudi–Iraqi non-aggression agreement in 1989, but the Iraqis had never taken it up.

It was made clear to me by the Foreign Ministry in Riyadh that in deciding to relaunch their offer at this point the Saudis were well aware of the risks they ran by so doing in the context of Iraq's extortionate pressure on Kuwait. But the urgent priority was to ease Iraq's aggressive mood. Moreover, these Saudi funds were already pledged. To ensure that they would be used for the intended purpose, the Saudis now proposed to donate them to Iraq through the medium of the Jedda-based Islamic Development Bank, a condition which does not appear to have mollified the Iraqis. At this stage Saudi opinion was swinging back once again to the view that Iraq's show of military strength might after all be a feint, and that Saudi mediation stood a fair chance of working. In our assessment the situation was still dangerous, but hostilities looked on balance unlikely. To the Saudis, and probably the Kuwaitis too, they were still an unthinkable eventuality, breaching all the canons of Arab relations. There could be no question of mobilisation so long as talks were under way, though the Defence Minister, Prince Sultan, took the sensible precaution at this point of dispersing some of the front-line war planes of the RSAF in case of some surprise attack.

In an effort to gauge opinion on the crisis more generally among the

Gulf states, I also took soundings from Dr Saif al Maskeri, the Omani deputy Secretary General of the GCC, who was based in Riyadh. Saif al Maskeri was clear that while the Council's other members were concerned at the implications for themselves of Iraq's bullying of Kuwait, they were not prepared to risk provocation by bringing direct pressure to bear. Accordingly they were pinning their hopes on Saudi and Egyptian mediation. I had the impression that among the GCC states, Oman's position was perhaps the least firm towards Iraq, reflecting not only her distance from the scene of the crisis, but also a certain longstanding mistrust of the political objectives of her partners – Saudi Arabia in particular. All this made of course for just the mix of uncertainty and hesitation which Iraq's leader was playing for.

In cat-and-mouse fashion the Iraqis postponed the Jedda meeting by a further day. There was considerable relief when the vice-chairman of the Revolutionary Command Council, Izzat Ibrahim, accompanied by the Iraqi deputy Prime Minister, Sa'doun Hammadi, and the local government minister, Ali Hassan al Majid, turned up in Jedda on 1 August. The trio were all close to Saddam Hussein. Izzat Ibrahim, an unlikely-looking Iraqi with his ginger hair, fair skin and tall stature, was related to the president by marriage, and Ali Hassan al Majid was a kinsman of the same Tikrit origin as Saddam Hussein. Al Majid was subsequently to become notorious for the ruthlessness of his rule when he was appointed shortly afterwards to govern Kuwait as Iraq's 19th province. The Kuwaiti side was led by the Crown Prince, Sheikh Saad, who held the post of Prime Minister and was considered in effect to be the leading figure in the ruling Al Sabah family.

We passed a busy and anxious week in the embassy in Riyadh, keeping in close touch with the Saudis over their efforts at mediation, and in local assessments of the Iraqi threat to Kuwait as it ebbed and surged. From our vantage point events were taking on an increasingly ominous aspect. But it was a relief to find that our large British community were showing no particular signs of concern. For one thing it was Kuwait against whom Iraq's diatribes were being directed, and there was a lot of desert between Kuwait and the main urban centres of Saudi Arabia such as Jubail and Dammam on the Gulf coast and Riyadh in the Kingdom's centre. Moreover, the Saudi press were being discouraged from playing up the crisis, lest this affect public morale and prejudice the all-important talks due to be held in Jedda.

Fortunately we had earlier in the year updated and computerised our records of the British community in the Kingdom, now nearly 30,000 strong. This made it one of the largest British expatriate communities anywhere outside the Commonwealth countries, the USA and South

Africa. We had also taken the opportunity to review our warning system throughout the Kingdom, which operated by means of wardens in each locality – responsible British residents who volunteered to serve as links between the embassy and consulates and the members of our large community in case of emergency. Little did we know how indispensable these good citizens were to prove within a short space of time.

With the Jedda talks now firmly in prospect, I took the opportunity of the lull in tension to visit Abha, the capital of Asir province in the south-west of the Kingdom bordering on Yemen. This is a mountainous region of startling beauty, cool in summer, well watered by the fringe of the monsoon, and a great contrast to the arid heat of the plains and dunes of the centre. As St John Philby wrote, during his mapping expeditions in this area on behalf of King Abdul Aziz in the 1930s, 'the Garden of Eden must be very like this'. From the Red Sea coast a spectacular escarpment rises some 9,000 feet to the uplands where Abha lies, reached by two highways through tunnels and viaducts which are vertiginous marvels of engineering. Near to Abha, at Khamis al Mushait, is one of the main bases of the Saudi Air Force designed to secure the southern region of the Kingdom in the face of longstanding claims by Yemen to sovereignty over parts of the southern provinces of Asir and Najran. In 1963 civil war in Yemen, in which the republican forces had Egyptian backing, had led to the bombing of Asir towns by Egyptian aircraft, with considerable loss of life.

By 1990 relations between the Kingdom and Yemen were still uneasy, despite the presence of nearly one million Yemenis in Saudi Arabia, where they had the privilege of being able to enter and work without requiring a visa. With Iraq raising the temperature over Kuwait, the Saudis were uncomfortably aware that the Yemen government of President Ali Abdullah Saleh had particularly close relations with Ba'athist Iraq, and was indeed a member of the ACC, which Saddam Hussein had recently taken the lead in setting up. I wanted to visit Asir at this time to see something of the local reaction to the crisis, and to discuss the Yemen dimension with the province's experienced governor, Prince Khaled al Faisal, a son of the late King Faisal and elder brother to the Saudi Foreign Minister.

The visit also gave an opportunity to meet members of our community in this region, over 100 strong and consisting mainly of hospital personnel, and BAe and Royal Air Force personnel with their families who were working in support of the Tornado aircraft stationed at Khamis al Mushait under the Al Yamamah project. I was joined at Abha by Nick Pile, vice-consul from our consulate-general in Jedda, in whose area of consular responsibility the Asir lay. Nick, together with Abdullah, a

Yemeni driver with many years in British service, made the long drive up
to Abha from Jedda, some 800 kilometres north, while I flew down from
Riyadh on a Saudia internal flight. It was strange after Riyadh's relentless
summer heat to emerge from the aircraft into a rain shower and to have
no need of air-conditioning in the bedroom of the old-fashioned hotel
where we stayed. The more gentle pace of Abha also came as a relief
after the anxieties of Riyadh.

The governorate offices, where I called on Prince Khaled, were
thronged in the usual way with people from the town and local villages
and tribes, some of whom had come with petitions to give the governor
at his customary public audience or *majlis*, the traditional point of contact in Arabian society between governor and governed. The scene in
the town was more colourful than would be found elsewhere in the
Kingdom, as the uniform long, white *thobe* and headcloth of the Saudi
men and the black robe, or *abaya*, of the women were mixed with the
brighter headdresses, a few even adorned with flowers, of the tribesmen
from the rugged mountain areas along the Yemen frontier and the Red
Sea escarpment. It seemed a world away from the ominous atmosphere
of the capital.

I found our community wardens in good heart and we passed a convivial evening together over a Lebanese-style dinner in the hotel – that is,
as convivial as the imbibing of apple juice and soda water, a concoction
known deceptively as Saudi champagne, would permit. They seemed
confident of their responsibility for co-ordinating contact with the community in the area should trouble reach this corner of the Kingdom, an
eventuality which we all saw as unlikely despite uncertainty over the position Yemen might adopt in the event of hostilities with Iraq.

When I saw Prince Khaled, however, he took a sombre view of where
Saddam Hussein's ambitions might now be leading. He might be bought
off by Kuwait on this occasion, but we could not be sure of this. The talks
being held in Jedda that very day would tell. Even if the present crisis of
Iraq's making was defused, she was bound to resume an aggressive pos-
ture at some subsequent point. Prince Khaled appeared to regard
Saddam Hussein as a compulsive troublemaker with ambitions to dom-
inate his region. An underlying intention was to destabilise Saudi Arabia.
Prince Khaled gave a prescient warning that, while local relations with
Yemen were in reasonable shape, trouble could not be ruled out in the
event of hostilities to the north, in view of Iraq's strong influence with the
Yemeni regime in Sana'a. But given the effectiveness of Saudi defences in
the region, these were unlikely to go beyond political obstruction.

Prince Khaled may at this point have already had in mind the suspicion, shortly to take firm hold among the Al Saud and more widely

within Saudi opinion, that the Iraqi leader had been working on both King Hussein of Jordan and President Saleh of Yemen to conspire to partition the territory of the Kingdom between them following an Iraqi attack beyond Kuwait, with the objective of toppling the Al Saud. Under such a plan the ruling Hashemite family in Jordan might recover the Hejaz province on the west, which King Abdul Aziz had occupied and incorporated into the expanding Saudi lands in 1925. At the same time the Asir uplands and Tihama coastal plain would be given to Yemen, despite her renunciation of these areas in the treaty signed in Taif in 1934. Thus did territorial disputes and grievances linger on in Arabia to be exploited in times of crisis. Whether true or not, the idea of a plot touched Saudi Arabia on a raw nerve and was lent credence by the support which both Jordan and Yemen were subsequently to show towards Iraq through their efforts to avoid penalising her in the process of dislodging her from Kuwait.

It was significant to find Prince Khaled taking this hard-headed view of Iraq's ominous posture, with the probability that, even if the Jedda talks produced some agreement, it was unlikely to involve more than a breathing space before Saddam Hussein turned the heat on again. As tends to be the case on the eve of a crisis, there was a good deal of wishful thinking about, on the part of the British and other Western partners as much as among Arab governments. Despite Iraq having in the past few days increased her military force in the border area to some 100,000 men, the idea of outright attack still seemed remote. Diplomatic reporting out of Baghdad, including from our own embassy, subscribed to this opinion. Moreover, there were the assurances so recently given to both King Fahd and to President Mubarak by Saddam Hussein.

The possible imminence of hostilities looked all the more distant as Nick Pile and I took a break during our last afternoon in Abha to see a falcon breeding centre in the mountains, which Prince Khaled had arranged for us to visit. Our route took us along the rim of the spectacular escarpment, scattering troupes of baboons as we climbed up to the Intercontinental Hotel, built in lavish fashion to accommodate the inaugural GCC summit in 1982 in a mountain eyrie with magnificent views dropping 9,000 feet to the Tihama plain.

As I flew back to Riyadh on the morning of 1 August the news came through that the Jedda talks, which apart from Crown Prince Abdullah's attendance at their inaugural session were a strictly bilateral affair between the Iraqi and Kuwaiti delegations, had finally got under way that day. There were no other details, but at least this seemed a hopeful sign. I went straight to the embassy where Peter Gooderham and Charles Hollis, who were looking after the political section in the absence on

summer leave of my deputy, Derek Plumbly, were keeping an eye on
Saudi news bulletins. The general impression among our Saudi friends
was that Saddam Hussein had to be bluffing; a way around the crisis
would be found, even if it had to be an expensive one. An act of physical
aggression was for them inconceivable in terms of relations between
Arab states.

In the FCO in London a special emergency unit, with extensive
communications around Whitehall and facilities for round-the-clock consular and evacuation arrangements, had been put on alert as a sensible
precaution. It being August most senior ministers, including the Foreign
Secretary, were away on holiday. The FCO was in the charge of Douglas
Hogg, minister of state responsible for the Middle East. The Ministry of
Defence was being caretaken by the minister of state responsible for
equipment procurement, the effervescent Alan Clark, who was very
much the Prime Minister's man. Mrs Thatcher herself had just gone to
the USA, where she was due to join President Bush at the opening on 2
August of the Aspen Institute Conference and to make a speech three
days later on East–West relationships and democratic rights. The fortuitous presence together at Aspen and subsequently in Washington of
these two leaders in the immediate aftermath of Iraq's invasion of Kuwait
was to have a significant bearing on the prompt and resolute response
displayed by the USA and the UK, as well as by Saudi Arabia and Egypt.

By late afternoon the continuing absence of news on the Jedda talks
was beginning to look ominous. From several telephone conversations
with Rob Young, head of the Middle East department, it looked as though
the FCO were in two minds as to what the next hours would bring. The
latest information on the massing of troops near the Kuwaiti border
made it difficult to believe Saddam Hussein could still be bluffing. Yet the
Whitehall assessment was properly giving weight to the assurances from
Baghdad. Moreover, rather to our surprise there was nothing to suggest
particular alarm on the part of the Kuwaiti government. All attention was
focused on the talks still taking place in Jedda. Nevertheless the three of
us in Riyadh parted that evening with a sense of foreboding.

Our fears that the talks were not going smoothly were reinforced by
the first item on Saudi television's Arabic language news bulletin in mid-
evening: a statement in which the Saudi government took the unusual
step of issuing a disclaimer concerning its role in the meetings between
Iraq and Kuwait. In somewhat cryptic terms the statement stressed that
the Custodian of the Two Holy Mosques, King Fahd, having bidden
farewell that day to the participants, wished to make it clear that the
Kingdom's role had been confined to providing a cordial atmosphere
for the discussions without any participation in the bilateral meetings. It

was hoped that the negotiations would continue until the interests of both sides were met. To those of us accustomed to Arab circumlocution this read like a warning signal that the talks had got nowhere, and that the Saudis were taking the prudent course of dissociation to avoid any accusation of partisanship in whatever recrimination was to follow. I telephoned Rob Young in London to give him this negative assessment, though the hope of further talks expressed in the Saudi statement gave some grounds to believe the process might not yet be dead. From his own considerable experience of service in the Arab world, Rob Young shared the view that things had reached a dangerous point; the next hours would be critical.

This tension was eased by a report later that night on Saudi television which showed the chief Iraqi negotiator, Izzet Ibrahim, breaking his journey back to Baghdad at Medina, where he and his party went, in the company of the governor of Medina, to pray at the tomb of the Prophet Mohammed. This unexpected act of demonstrative piety might, I felt, yet constitute a sign of peace. I made a late-night call to the department in London and got through to Stephen Lamport, the assistant head, to whom I noted it as a possibly helpful development. Stephen, another Gulf specialist from earlier service in Iran in the eventful period of the Islamic revolution which had overthrown the Shah, undertook to pass the glimmer of hope on to Douglas Hogg that night. I went uneasily to bed, concluding that on balance Saddam Hussein looked like continuing to play his cat-and-mouse game a bit longer before springing a trap.

According to the account of these eleventh hour talks given by the Saudis, and subsequently recounted on several occasions by King Fahd himself, the Iraqis came to Jedda with no intention to negotiate in serious fashion. In the initial meeting, in the presence of Crown Prince Abdullah, Izzet Ibrahim tried to stall by resurrecting the claim that this was no more than a protocol discussion. Having got over this obstacle the Saudis left the two sides to hold private discussions. But Izzet Ibrahim had then feigned a headache, and had proposed that the talks be suspended and resumed in Baghdad on 6 August. He and the Kuwaiti Prime Minister, Sheikh Saad, went for a final gathering with King Fahd at the Al Salaam palace. By his own account the King was encouraged to find that the two leaders had come in the same car to see him, and to hear from them that a further meeting had been arranged. But as events in the course of that very night were to show, all this, and the pious stopover in Medina, amounted to no more than another elaborate and deceitful piece of theatre on the part of Iraq, a charade which aroused a personal sense of anger and betrayal on the part of King Fahd, running far deeper than Saddam Hussein had bargained for.

CHAPTER 3

The Reason Why

'Take but degree away, untune that string,
And, hark! what discord follows; each thing meets
In mere oppugnancy.'

William Shakespeare: *Troilus and Cressida*

Iraq's invasion of Kuwait, in the small hours of 2 August, caught everyone off balance; Kuwaitis, Saudis and their Gulf partners, Iranians, Egyptians, to say nothing of the USA, Britain, France and the rest of the Western world. Even Iraq's closest outside associate in terms of military support, the USSR, appears to have had no insight into Iraq's plans to attack. It has been suggested that the decision to launch an all-out attack and seize the whole of Kuwait was taken by Saddam Hussein in a fit of anger at Kuwait's refusal in Jedda to meet Iraq's demands in full. But from the Saudi account of Iraq's tactics during these talks, and the proposal that a further round be held in Baghdad five days later, it seems more likely that Saddam Hussein used the Jedda meeting as a smoke-screen with which to put the Kuwaitis, and the rest of the world too, off guard over the imminence of his plundering attack, of the justification for which he had convinced himself some while beforehand.

If this was indeed the case, his stratagem worked impeccably. The Kuwaitis took his threats as bluff. They had declared no state of emergency and their forces were only on semi-alert. The Saudis too had hesitated to mobilise. So far as the Americans and ourselves were concerned, the fact that the Jedda talks did not appear to have broken up in acrimony suggested that, despite the ominous indications from satellite surveillance that Iraqi armoured forces were positioned in strength along the Kuwaiti frontier in what could presage an attack, we still had a breathing space for further diplomacy.

Yet, as we were to ask ourselves in the days and weeks following the Iraqi strike, how had we all failed to read the signs right, at least to the point where firm warnings against any act of aggression might have been issued from Western capitals in those final days when intelligence indicated an intensification of the Iraqi buildup along the frontier? Or for that matter, how had nobody picked up clues as to the ultimate intentions of the Iraqi leader and his close associates? As Margaret Thatcher defined the position in a conversation we had some three years later, it was not so much a failure of intelligence gathering as of intelligence assessment. But perhaps in our appreciation of the situation we also to some extent allowed the wish to become father to the thought.

One factor here was that Western intelligence activity in the region had, since the Iranian revolution and during the eight subsequent years of conflict between Iran and Iraq, been directed primarily against Iran, whence the main threat to stability in the Gulf was considered to come, rather than against Saddam Hussein's Iraq despite her vicious domestic record of terror. With an end to the fighting in mid-1988 some of us who felt uncertain about Saddam Hussein's future agenda had urged that we should step up our focus on Iraq. But this would take time, and resources were scarce. Moreover, it was difficult to conceive that Iraq, emerging with her economy and society in serious disarray from eight years of costly and inconclusive war with Iran, would go to the lengths of an attack in her own Arab backyard against those who had helped to sustain her through the conflict. Nevertheless the Bazoft affair, plus the alarming evidence which came to light from early 1989 of deliberate Iraqi attempts to circumvent Western controls on the supply of material related to her ambitious armaments programme, did have the effect of putting the British government on its guard.

By contrast the American State Department seemed prepared to take a more relaxed view, perhaps as a result of a greater preoccupation with Iran. Charles Freeman, recently arrived as US ambassador to Saudi Arabia, and I exchanged in early spring our growing worries over Iraq's resumption of a more forceful tone with her neighbours. He subsequently made a case to Washington for greater vigilance on this front, though his shrewd advice did not appear to receive much heed.

The Arab states of the area, too, tended to give priority to a preoccupation with the threat of subversion and hostility from the fundamentalist regime in Tehran. In this confrontation Baghdad was seen as a part of their own front line. Foolhardy as Saddam Hussein's original attack on Iran in 1980 had been, once launched his Arab neighbours felt obliged to ally themselves in Iraq's support. The war over, and with Saddam Hussein showing fresh signs of throwing his weight about in Arab company, their first wary instinct was to placate him. An outright attack on an Arab partner, whatever the pretext, was in Arab eyes off the screen of possibility, and an eventuality they were disinclined to entertain. This Saddam Hussein realised and exploited.

So it was that both Western and Arab governments continued to take Iraq's assurances of no hostile intent and her pretence of negotiation at their political face value. The American administration may have missed an opportunity to put down a categoric warning at the highest level in Baghdad when their ambassador had her crucial meeting with Saddam Hussein on 25 July. But it is still questionable whether the Iraqi leader, keyed up as he had become by his sense of grievance and inflated by a mood of invincibility, would have paid any heed. Certainly there was no foundation to the fantasy, still current in some Arab circles, that his aggression formed part of an American design to foster an instability which would serve to secure economic dominance.

Yet it was not until the eve of the invasion that Western military intelligence evidence appears to have pointed conclusively to preparations for an attack on Kuwait. Meanwhile, the political assessments in both Washington and Whitehall tended towards the conclusion that, despite the more menacing tone which Iraq's bullying tactics were assuming, her sabre would for the present remain sheathed. At the most the Iraqis might go for a limited objective consistent with their demands, such as the Rumaila oilfield along the frontier or a repetition of previous border incursions. Perhaps we clutched at straws; but if so, then Saddam Hussein had made sure there were plenty to clutch at. The concealment of both intention and timing for his attack on Kuwait was Saddam Hussein's one and only success in the whole affair. From this point on he never managed to put a foot right.

Moreover, even had we concluded in those final days that hostilities seemed inevitable and a firm Western reaction was called for, we would have run up against opposition on the part of the Saudis and other Arab governments much closer to the action than we were. There was a report that when the Americans, as a precaution in the face of the evidence of major Iraqi troop mobilisation near to the Kuwaiti frontier, offered to make a show of air strength over Kuwait, the Kuwaiti government declined. This response may well have resulted from concern that such intervention would not deter but rather afford a pretext for further aggression by Iraq, and reinforce the jaded but still emotive rallying-call to Arab opinion to resist imperialist interference.

Iraq's Arab neighbours were instead inclined to try to divert Saddam Hussein's agitation into less bellicose channels. In discussions with Prince Saud and with others in the Saudi Foreign Ministry during late spring, I found myself reproached over the possible provocative effect of the warning bells which the British government had started to sound over Iraqi intentions, in the wake of the execution of Farzad Bazoft and the revelations of the 'supergun' plot. There was even suspicion of a vendetta against Iraq on our part, leading to initial Saudi hesitations over the implications for her precarious relations with Iraq of the visit which Douglas Hurd proposed to make to the Kingdom in early June. Hence the intensive efforts on the part of the Saudis and Egyptians, as Saddam Hussein turned up the heat on Kuwait, to bell the Iraqi cat through Arab diplomacy alone. So long as these contacts were alive the Arabs could not afford to contemplate the possibility of hostilities. Once bitten twice shy, however: Iraq's perfidy over Kuwait meant that Saudi Arabia took no second chances once Saddam Hussein went on to concentrate his forces along Kuwait's frontier with the Kingdom herself.

But just as the Kuwaitis and Saudis, and we too, misjudged Saddam Hussein, he in his turn made far more serious errors of judgement in going for Kuwait. At the time, and certainly in the light of hindsight, it was puzzling why he should have taken this gamble which was to unite opposition within the international community to a degree unprecedented in recent history. The succession of miscalculations made both at the outset and thereafter by the Iraqi leader was prodigious, on both regional and wider international fronts. It had the effect of stacking the odds against him to the point where he was eventually obliged by force of arms to retreat from Kuwait with a defeated army and nothing to show for his adventurism.

Many were the occasions in the months which followed when we pondered among ourselves and with the Saudis this perverse succession of miscalculations. Indeed, as the crisis developed we came to count on responses from the Iraqi leader which ran contrary to the diktats of common sense. A supreme instance was his dogged refusal to save his army and his face by withdrawing intact from Kuwait under the umbrella of the diplomatic mediation in which the Russians took a lead on the eve of the coalition's ground attack in February. At an earlier stage he might even have got away with limited territorial gains, including the Rumaila oilfield and some border adjustments. But he spurned such half measures. For Saddam Hussein it was to be all or nothing.

His personality played a major part here. In power and before Saddam Hussein had never brooked opposition, and through a combination of ruthlessness and political guile had always succeeded in having his way. As he saw it he had even come out on top from the war with Iran. This despotic temperament was, after more than a decade of absolute authority, liable to vent itself in acts of impulsive rancour. No doubt these dominant features played their part in his decision to break out of Iraq's economic impasse, into which his grandiose schemes of military supremacy had led her, by a take-over of Kuwait and her assets. His action was, however, compounded by two other factors in his personality:

a paranoid suspicion of conspiracy on the part of those who sought to challenge him, coupled with a self-conceit which showed itself in a disregard, bordering on contempt, for the reactions of other players. These tendencies were accentuated by his own political isolation, in which his capacity for self-delusion was fed by the distorted accounts of the external scene filtered through to him by his sycophantic circle. His own contact with the outside world was minimal, even with Arab states around him, which, as in the case of Jordan, he tended to treat as dependent clients of Iraq.

The paranoia showed itself in his delusion that Kuwait was deliberately seeking to obstruct Iraq's return to prosperity after the sacrifices of the eight years of war with Iran. This may have been coupled with a belief that the USA, whose attitude towards Iraq had in early 1989 begun to shift from a measure of collaboration to criticism over the issue of human rights, had a hand in Kuwait's defiance. In an interview after the war Tariq Aziz, the Iraqi Foreign Minister, claimed that the Iraqi leadership had become convinced that the USA was preparing to strike at Iraq through Kuwait, and that Saddam Hussein's decision on the timing and extent of the invasion of Kuwait had the object of forestalling this strategy. The account, while irrational, yet seems plausible. As for the conceit factor, this showed itself in Saddam Hussein's misplaced conviction throughout the course of the Kuwait crisis that, through raising the stakes of battle with missile attacks on Israel and by parading the shibboleths of anti-imperial rhetoric, he could yet split the assorted alliance which had come together to challenge him.

Moreover, in the misconceived and impulsive timing of his decision to seize Kuwait, Saddam Hussein denied himself the full effectiveness of the arsenal of mass-destruction weaponry on which his regime had lavished so much skill and resources. As UN inspections after the war were to reveal, he had been too impatient to await completion of Iraq's programme of developing long-range missiles with chemical and biological warheads, or to bring his sinister nuclear programme to the point where it might have afforded a credible threat. I heard from a Palestinian source on the eve of the expiry of the UN deadline for Iraq's withdrawal in mid-January that Saddam Hussein had spoken to Yasir Arafat of a secret weapon which would turn the tide of battle. It has since been revealed that he had prepared a deadly arsenal of biological and chemical weapons, as well as launching a crash nuclear programme following his seizure of Kuwait. In the event whatever he may have had in mind was, in the face of grave warnings by coalition governments, mercifully never deployed in hostilities. The fact that his major terror weapons were still under development was indeed a blessing to the coalition, though at the time we did not know precisely how close some of them were to production.

At the strategic level the Iraqi leader's most serious miscalculation was to ignore the ending of the Cold War and attack Kuwait just at the moment when Soviet policy under Mikhail Gorbachev, and particularly Eduard Shevardnadze, had shifted decisively away from confrontation with the West in the Arab world, towards co-operation with the USA in return for desperately needed economic aid and support for political change. The consequence for Iraq was that for the first time since the Second World War the USSR saw her interest as identical to that of the West, and joined promptly in the international embargo of supplies to Iraq. This action on the part of Iraq's main military supplier constituted a serious setback for Saddam Hussein.

Soviet action went further, to the point where, having seen their instinctive attempts to broker a political solution rebuffed by Iraq, the USSR acquiesced in the eventual use of force by the American-led coalition. A generous financial subvention from the Saudis also helped here. But the implications of this turnabout in Soviet foreign policy were lost on Iraq's leadership until it was too late. Subsequent attempts by Saddam Hussein to bully the Russians with threats over the security of the numerous Soviet military advisers in Iraq got him nowhere. At root he failed to see that the Kuwait crisis was providing the world with the first test of a new post-Cold War order.

There was a string of other false assumptions behind Iraq's decision to invade. Saddam Hussein appeared to bank on no more than diplomatic outrage on the part of the USA and Britain. He may have doubted whether France would go even this far, given that Iraq was her largest customer for military equipment and the extent of Iraqi indebtedness on this score. Moreover, the French Defence Minister, Jean Chévènement, even held a senior position in a Franco-Iraqi friendship society. On all these counts Iraq got things very wrong.

More significant yet was Saddam Hussein's misreading of King Fahd's reaction. The Iraqis had probably calculated that by playing on earlier Saudi exasperation over Kuwait's overproduction of crude oil, and by following up the invasion with blatant military intimidation along the Kingdom's border with Kuwait, they could secure sufficient Saudi acquiescence to ensure that no military challenge was mounted, and certainly not one which would bring the Americans and other Western powers into the act. King Fahd's resolute reaction to the Iraqi strike, involving the prompt formation of an Arab and Islamic front with refuge for the Kuwaiti government, and acceptance of Western and other outside help in defending his country, amounted therefore to a crucial setback to Saddam Hussein's aggressive designs.

King Fahd, along with other Gulf rulers, saw Iraq's action as a direct threat to their own security, if not today then tomorrow. The killing of a senior member of the Al Sabah family, Sheikh Fahd al Sabah, during the Iraq assault on the Dasman palace in Kuwait City, and the savage treatment accorded to Kuwaitis who continued to put up resistance, were further factors. Saudi Arabia was also allied with Kuwait through the GCC. But beyond these considerations King Fahd felt a deep personal sense of injury at what he saw as Saddam Hussein's betrayal of his assurances that Iraq had no aggressive intention. The Iraqi leader could never be trusted by Saudi Arabia again. From this point the King's animosity towards the Iraqi leader turned into an unremitting determination to see the seizure of Kuwait reversed and Saddam Hussein's manifest threat to the Kingdom and her neighbours removed once and for all.

The same went for the Egyptian leadership, where the Iraqis had probably expected compliance in view of their treaty association through the recently formed ACC. Instead, President Mubarak showed himself quick to share Saudi Arabia's sense of outrage, spurning a blatant offer by Saddam Hussein to match the financial assistance which Saudi Arabia was offering to Egypt in return for her provision of troops to help in the Kingdom's defence. Within Kuwait herself the stubborn resistance of many inhabitants to the Iraqi occupation must also have come as a surprise. Indeed, the patriotism shown in adversity by Kuwaitis, both under occupation and abroad, played an important part in sustaining the momentum of public support throughout the crisis.

As the crisis wore on, time and again the Iraqi leader showed himself prone to misjudgement. His holding of Western hostages in Iraq, and his subsequent gesture in releasing them, earned him no advantage but only served to intensify international hostility. His Scud missile raids on Saudi Arabia did not intimidate, but aroused an unwonted martial spirit. His supreme gamble of launching missiles against Israel, in a bid to provoke Israeli retaliation and so split the coalition, failed to come off. Saddam Hussein's basic assumption that the coalition represented an unnatural political association whose cohesion was bound to erode proved groundless. As his misjudgements multiplied we came to see them as a sensational instance of hubris, perhaps best summed up as the arrogance of ignorance.

CHAPTER 4

Invasion and Response

'On 2 August 1990 Iraq invaded Kuwait. Following the passing
of United Nations resolutions, the United Kingdom contributed to the build-up of a military presence in the Gulf to
defend neighbouring States from Iraqi aggression and to
secure an Iraqi withdrawal from Kuwait. The United Kingdom's
military involvement was called Operation GRANBY.
Diplomatic attempts to secure an Iraqi withdrawal failed and
hostilities began in mid-January 1991. The Allies' objectives
were achieved and fighting ceased at the end of February 1991.
The withdrawal of most United Kingdom forces took place
between March and May 1991.'

British Ministry of Defence:
Report on Costs and Receipts arising from the Gulf Conflict

The morning of Thursday 2 August dawned with a rude shock, with the
news on the 7am BBC bulletin that Iraqi forces had invaded Kuwait at
2am, and had swiftly taken control of Kuwait City with a combined
armoured thrust and airborne landing. So Saddam Hussein had not
been bluffing. Izzat Ibrahim's participation in the Jedda meetings had
been yet another piece of elaborate theatre on the part of the Iraqi
leadership, calculated to serve as a platform from which to administer
the *coup de grâce* to Kuwait and deploy Iraq's artifice of grievance to the
wider Arab community. Meanwhile the day of sterile discussion had
afforded cover for Iraq to put the finishing touches to the mobilisation
of her troops along the Kuwaiti border in preparation for the strike into
Kuwait in the small hours.

I recalled Prince Khalid al Faisal's perceptive warning when we had
met in Abha two days previously. All that last-minute activity which both
Saudi Arabia and Egypt had put into the search for a compromise, to
head off the threat of military action and at least buy a margin of time,
had been an exercise in wishful thinking. Saddam's mind had been
made up to seize Kuwait as soon as he saw a pretext to do so, counting
on his illusion of dominance on the Arab scene and his overwhelming
military arsenal to muzzle any serious reaction from within the region.
Now the test would come as we saw how far the Arab world would go in

45

standing up to this act of raw aggression, which had driven a coach and horses through cherished principles of inter-Arab solidarity and the resolution of disputes by compromise.

Right up to the last hours of the talks in Jedda with the Kuwaiti Crown Prince, there had seemed some hope that a way could be found to defuse the crisis. Not only had Saddam Hussein given assurances to both King Fahd and President Mubarak that he did not intend military action, but the Jedda talks had concluded with an evening meeting with King Fahd and Crown Prince Abdullah to which Izzat Ibrahim and Sheikh Saad had travelled in the same car in an illusion of amity. They had announced that there would be a further meeting the following week in Baghdad, thus pointing to a breathing space in the crisis. Indeed, on his return to Kuwait Sheikh Saad appears to have been of the firm opinion that there was no imminent danger. The state of alert of the Kuwaiti forces was not raised to a higher level that night, and the Kuwaiti secretary-general of the GCC, Abdullah Bishara, accepted an invitation to accompany him back to Kuwait. He was bundled out of Kuwait and back into Saudi Arabia by the Iraqis the next day.

It thus came as all the more of a shock when, having lulled his prey with this play-acting, Saddam Hussein responded to Kuwait's refusal to be browbeaten in the Jedda meeting by moving his forces across the border before dawn in a lightning attack. The capital fell quickly to an airborne assault which linked up with the armoured and infantry units, some 100,000 men strong, that the Iraqis had concentrated on the Kuwait border in the month preceding the invasion. Without clear orders from above the Kuwaiti forces were unable to put up more than isolated and token resistance. One tank regiment, equipped with British Chieftains supplied some 12 years previously, engaged in a firefight with the advancing Iraqi armour, but were soon forced to withdraw southwards over the Saudi border to the military base at Hafr al Batin. A good portion of the Kuwaiti air force managed to escape to Saudi Arabia; the rest of their warplanes were seized by the Iraqis.

The Iraqi invaders met with some spirited opposition on the part of the civilian population. Pockets of active resistance were to endure throughout the long months of occupation, despite savage Iraqi attempts at suppression. The Amir of Kuwait, with senior members of the Al Sabah family and other government figures, were roused in the early hours of 2 August, only a brief interval before Iraqi troops reached the city, and made their way overland to Dammam on the Saudi Gulf coast, whence they were taken by the Saudi government into a secure and comfortable exile in the Sheraton Hotel at Al Hada, requisitioned for the purpose and close to the mountain resort of Taif on the Hejaz escarpment behind Jedda. A younger brother of the Amir, Sheikh Fahd, stayed behind to join with loyal guards in resisting the attack on the Dasman Palace, where he lost his life. By the evening of 2 August Kuwait City was effectively under Iraqi control, and military units were advancing into the oilfields of southern Kuwait. Over the next two days Iraqi troops built up positions along the Kuwaiti border with Saudi Arabia, while additional forces were moved into Kuwait.

Nothing more was being heard of Saddam Hussein's initial fiction that he had moved into Kuwait in support of a popular uprising by opposition political figures. But on 4 August he sought to confuse the picture by claiming Iraq was prepared to start withdrawal, leaving behind a government friendly to Iraq. This ploy was accompanied by television pictures of Iraqi units purported to be on the way out. The general view, however, was that they were going south, as the road signposts belied the Iraqi claim. By 6 August there were 11 Iraqi divisions in the country. At least 30,000 troops were by now estimated to be along its frontier with Saudi Arabia, in a strength which was difficult to reconcile with defence against any sudden counterattack from the south.

The first effect of the Iraqi blitzkrieg among her neighbours was one of deep shock and uncertainty. Given the ingrained Arab attachment to the goal of solidarity in the face of potential external confrontation, in the shape of Israel or Iran or even the old, but not yet expired, bogey of Western imperialism, the possibility of one Arab state launching such an attack upon a neighbour strained credulity. It also, as Saddam Hussein had probably calculated, produced an initial reluctance to adopt a confrontational response for fear of where it might lead. This aspect was particularly acute for Saudi Arabia, threatened as she quickly perceived herself to be by evidence of Iraqi troops moving south to concentrate along her border. The Kingdom's first reflex was therefore to abstain from any public comment while efforts might yet be made in private to find a political way out of the nightmare and avoid provocation of Iraq.

Accordingly, no confirmation of the invasion was carried in the Saudi press or media for nearly three days. This silence had the effect of contributing to a mood of unease among a population which was left to gather its information from the BBC, Voice of America, and other sources, not least the agitated local rumour mill, and led to a corresponding loss of credibility for the Saudi information system which was to hamper its subsequent influence on public opinion. During this tense interval there was no move to mobilise Saudi army or National Guard units, which remained in camp. The air force did, however, come to a state of readiness and redeployed its fighting aircraft. Meanwhile the whole emphasis was on urgent, if stillborn, contacts to try to set in motion an 'Arab solution'.

This initial caution on the part of leading Arab governments meant that the first public countermoves against Iraq came from outside the Arab world. On the day of the invasion, and helped by the eight-hour time difference between Kuwait and the eastern USA, the British and American governments took the lead in condemning the attack and acting swiftly to freeze all Kuwaiti assets to prevent these falling into the hands of the Iraqis. They also moved to block trade with Iraq. Others quickly followed suit, notably France, Germany and Japan. The UN Security Council was also prompted that same day in New York to pass a resolution of condemnation which was supported by 14 of the Council's 15 members, though Yemen, the Arab representative, recorded an ominous abstention. This vote signalled a new unity of approach between the permanent members, and in particular between the Americans and the USSR in the immediate aftermath of the Cold War, a feature which was to lead to an unprecedented degree of co-operation between the Russians and the West throughout the crisis. Saddam Hussein thus found himself thwarted from the start in his aim of setting East against West in his incessant diplomatic manoeuvring to divide the Arab and international alliance which quickly coalesced against him.

The contrast between vehement Western reaction and initial caution on the part of the Saudis and other Arab governments showed itself in a telephone conversation between President Bush and King Fahd on 2 August. By mischance so far as Iraq was concerned, the President was that day due to join Mrs Thatcher on a visit to the Aspen Institute in Colorado, where he was to make a speech. It seems clear that the Prime Minister, finding herself alongside the President at this critical time, brought her own outrage at Iraq's action and her resolve to see it reversed to bear on President Bush in stiffening his response. Subsequent accounts of their discussions on a ranch near Aspen, and again four days later in Washington, have given rise to the 'Don't wobble, George' attribution. Whether true or not, it was clear from an account which we heard later from King Fahd of his telephone conversation with the President in Aspen on the day of the invasion, that he was heartened to meet such a robust response from President and Prime Minister. The King gave much credit for this to Mrs Thatcher.

Nevertheless, the King was not in this early stage looking primarily to his Western friends for military help to defend Saudi Arabia. Initially attention was focused on events in Kuwait, and the King's priority in those first days was an attempt at personal intercession with the Iraqi leader. By the account which King Fahd himself subsequently gave to his people of events during the immediate aftermath of the invasion, his efforts to reach Saddam Hussein directly by telephone early on 2 August were fobbed off in Baghdad with excuses that the President was out of reach. Later in the morning Saddam Hussein came on the line to tell the King that he was sending his Vice-President, Izzet Ibrahim, back to Jedda to explain Iraq's position. Izzet Ibrahim did not arrive until two days later, when he said no more than that Kuwait was a part of Iraq and had returned to its proper status. King Fahd's rejoinder that Iraq had as recently as 1963 formally recognised the independence of Kuwait was of no avail and the meeting was terminated. It was now plain to the Saudis that withdrawal was not on the cards. Saddam Hussein had crossed the Rubicon.

The King was also sensitive to the need to pay heed to calls from certain Arab quarters, notably King Hussein of Jordan and the PLO, for an 'Arab solution', faint though the prospects appeared. At the same time he was working to bring together as large a front as possible within the Arab world to call a halt to Iraq's aggression, and bring pressure on her to reverse it. Also in the King's mind was a concern lest immediate recourse to Western, and in particular American, military help should provoke a negative reflex among Arab states upon whose support Saudi Arabia, and Kuwait too, needed to count in the period ahead. This reaction was also likely to have echoes within some sections of Saudi public opinion itself, notably the more conservative religious elements, despite the Kingdom's evident vulnerability to an Iraqi attack.

These sensitivities over Western involvement in Arab affairs had lain dormant for several years, as the legacy of imperialism and the fever of Arab nationalism faded and other preoccupations diverted attention from American links with Israel. Yet they were never far below the surface of Arab consciousness, and in Saudi Arabia's devout Moslem society were mingled with a strong religious ingredient. Indeed, the agile Iraqi propaganda machine quickly saw this as a nerve to play upon, and to some effect too. Crown Prince Abdullah and Prince Sultan, the Defence Minister, were thought to be among those in the Saudi leadership who urged the King to proceed cautiously on the issue of Western military help in these early stages of the crisis.

Accordingly the King and Prince Saud devoted all their effort in the aftermath of the invasion to trying to secure a swift and categoric Arab rejection of the Iraqi action. Mobilisation of the Arab League was facilitated by the fact that Saddam had ineptly chosen to move on a day when a substantial number of Arab and other Moslem foreign ministers were gathered in Cairo for a ministerial meeting of the Organisation of the Islamic Conference. Had he waited a couple more days it could have been a less straightforward matter for the Saudis and Kuwaitis to mobilise such a prompt Arab gathering in response to his aggression. As it was, an emergency Arab League meeting was convened that same day, at which the Saudis and Kuwaitis took the lead in calling for a resolution demanding immediate Iraqi withdrawal. In this they received firm support from their Gulf partners as well as welcome backing from Egypt; King Fahd's policy over previous months in renewing Saudi ties with President Mubarak despite Egypt's membership of the Iraqi-inspired ACC had started to bear fruit.

The Arab League discussions revealed serious divisions among Arab governments, however. These were to persist right through to the time of Kuwait's liberation seven months later. It was to take constant encouragement, both diplomatic and in kind, on the part of Saudi Arabia to sustain Arab pressure on Iraq in the face of Saddam's persistent attempts to capture popular sympathy. In the event the Arab League's resolution of 2 August only just secured the support of the majority of League members. In addition to condemnation of Iraq's invasion, it called for immediate withdrawal and took cover in a proposal for an emergency Arab summit.

Significant among those withholding support were Jordan, Yemen and the PLO. All three had benefited from assiduous and generous cultivation by Saddam Hussein in the recent past. In Jordan's case her economic prosperity had become closely linked to Iraq through serving as one of the major supply lines to the outside world during the eight years of Iraq's war with Iran. Perhaps as a consequence of this degree of dependence, or even for reasons of a deeper dynastic nature, King Hussein showed himself from the outset inclined to accept at face value allegations on the part of Iraq's leadership that, in her highhanded responses towards Iraq's economic grievances, Kuwait was acting in collusion with the USA and Britain in a conspiracy to cut Iraq down to size.

Immediately following the invasion King Hussein took the lead in a round of contacts with Saudi Arabia, Egypt, Yemen and Saddam Hussein himself, with the aim of setting up a summit meeting beween them to try to resolve the issue and so avoid the prospect of wider international intervention in an Arab crisis. Participation by the Kuwaiti leadership does not, however, appear to have featured on the Jordanian menu. When they met in Baghdad on 3 August, Saddam Hussein is said to have given King Hussein a glib undertaking that Iraq would withdraw, but on the condition that Arab states should refrain from criticism of Iraq's action. The passage of the Arab League resolution by its narrow majority soon afforded the Iraqi leader a convenient pretext to decline to attend a summit.

But despite this rebuff King Hussein refused to take sides against Iraq during the crisis, partly perhaps in deference to a mood of sympathy with Iraq within Jordanian opinion, and particularly its large Palestinian component, but also as a matter of deliberate political alignment. This aroused intense and enduring irritation not only on the part of the Kuwaiti leadership in exile in Saudi Arabia, but from King Fahd and President Mubarak also. At the Arab League meeting in Cairo the Jordanian delegation, under instructions to support Iraq, argued for the further round of talks in Jedda. Finding this was a non-starter, they are said to have contacted Amman to try to get their instructions changed. They failed however, and so voted against the resolution. The shock of Jordan's evident sympathy for Saddam Hussein was felt beyond the confines of the Arab world, and particularly by the British government, given Britain's long and close association with King Hussein and the respect in which he was held.

Yemen, too, had developed a close relationship with Iraq's Ba'ath party and had received considerable military aid and training from the Iraqis. Her attitude was no doubt also affected by her long-running disputes with Saudi Arabia over border issues, which dated back to the 1930s. As for the PLO, Saddam had drawn Yasir Arafat into his net over a number of years, not only with financial assistance but also through the provision of training bases in Iraq for PLO military units on a scale greater than any other country. Added to these various bonds was an irrational but persistent sentiment on the part of popular opinion among Palestinians and Jordanians, as well as in several other less prosperous Arab societies, that the Gulf states had been insufficiently generous in redistributing their resources more widely.

These attitudes ignored the very substantial ways in which less well-endowed countries had benefited from Gulf largesse, a point which Saudi Arabia would be stung into spelling out at a later point in the crisis. In the case of Jordan, Yemen and the PLO, all three had been recipients of substantial economic help from Saudi Arabia as well as from Kuwait. Jordan was at the time receiving a major part of her oil requirements through the Tapline pipeline from Dhahran, for which she had fallen into arrears over payment. She had also recently received Saudi assistance in cash form to help offset the effect on her economy of a sharp drop in revenue from Palestinians in the occupied West Bank. The PLO too was receiving a grant of $6 million each month from Saudi Arabia, as well as enjoying the proceeds of an eight per cent levy on the incomes of the large Palestinian community working in Saudi Arabia, collected by the Saudi government in support of the *intifada* uprising. This financial help exceeded that which the PLO was getting from Iraq.

But despite these considerations the trio, as well as Libya and Sudan, chose to stand back from support for their Gulf neighbours and the international alliance formed to secure Iraq's withdrawal from Kuwait. At the popular level this sentiment intensified once the forces of the USA and other Western powers took up position within Arabia; indeed, it had an effect on public attitudes in several other Arab states too, whose governments had come out in support of the Kuwaiti and Saudi calls for Arab solidarity. The shadow of Palestine and Israel thus over-hung the crisis from the outset and distorted the Arab response, an aspect which Saddam constantly sought to exploit in the months ahead. In the case of the Sudan, another recipient of Saudi aid, the negative vote reflected a mixture of envy and religious animosity on the part of Sudan's extremist political establishment towards both Kuwait and the Al Saud.

Prior to the taking of the vote on the Arab League's withdrawal reso-lution, the Iraqi delegation tried the tactic of having it declared invalid on the grounds that resolutions invoking the Arab Defence Pact were required to be unanimous. This stratagem was countered by the Egyptian Foreign Minister who, with Saudi support, claimed that the vote was procedural in nature as it was a prelude to the extraordinary Arab summit to be convened in Cairo within a few days. Accordingly, under Arab League rules, if the resolution was not carried, those in the minority supporting it would not be obliged to observe the result. In the event the vote went through at the cost of a serious split in the League.

For Saudi Arabia, however, the main benefit was to have given the idea of an Arab solution a fair chance, while securing a resolution which afforded Arab cover for a wider international coalition to oppose Iraq and, most important, for the sensitive issue of the deployment of Western, non-Moslem forces on Saudi territory. 'How,' asked Prince Saud, 'can they call for an Arab solution when they then take a negative position on efforts to find one?' To have secured the clear support of both Egypt, despite her partnership with Iraq in the ACC, and Syria, as one of the more radical elements in the Arab world, was a considerable asset for the Saudis and the Kuwaiti government.

Saudi diplomatic activity continued at full pitch during these first days following the invasion. From Jedda King Fahd kept up an intensive round of contacts with other Arab leaders, to enlist their support for pressure to persuade Saddam to withdraw, despite a growing conviction that once inside Kuwait nothing was further from his mind. King Fahd talked by telephone with his Gulf partners, President Mubarak and King Hussein, against the background of the Arab League discussions taking place in Cairo and attended by Prince Saud. President Ali Abdullah

Saleh of Yemen came briefly to Jedda to see the King. The position which Yemen would adopt over the Iraqi attack held particular significance as she was currently occupying the Arab seat on the UN Security Council. Her ambivalent and occasionally negative voting record during the crisis was subsequently to be construed as showing sympathy for Iraq. It aroused an animosity on the part of the Saudi government, which led to the expulsion of around half a million Yemeni workers from the Kingdom. At this early stage there was talk of a special summit of Iraq and Kuwait to be held in Jedda, but the idea was not a starter. Things had gone too far for any reversal to be possible.

The focus of Saudi diplomatic attention moved on without respite to securing similar condemnation from the Moslem world at large. The Organisation of the Islamic Conference, which had been meeting at foreign minister level in Cairo when the invasion took place, was prompted to issue a statement that same day calling for withdrawal. This helped produce offers from a number of non-Arab Moslem countries of token forces to help defend Saudi Arabia. The GCC too, whose six members gave a useful lead to the Arab League pressure on Iraq, held a special session of its foreign ministers in Riyadh on 7 August. A statement issued following the meeting condemned the Iraqi invasion as a violation of the sovereignty and independence of a member state.

For King Fahd and Prince Saud their intensive and indefatigable diplomatic campaign had now begun to produce a dependable political line-up within the Arab and Islamic communities with which to confront Iraq if this had to be done. At the same time it was essential to keep in step with rapidly moving developments on the UN and international stages. A prompt UN Security Council resolution (No 660) of 2 August, calling upon Iraq to withdraw, was followed by a second one on 5 August (No 661) which imposed tight economic sanctions against Iraq and covered Kuwait too while under occupation. This step was followed by rapid action on the part of the EC, the USA and other Western governments to impose sanctions and freeze assets. The better to co-ordinate British actions with Saudi diplomacy, I flew down from Riyadh to Jedda early on 4 August to catch Prince Saud on his return there from the Cairo meeting. I took with me a copy of the draft UN Security Council sanctions resolution then in course of preparation among the three Western permanent members of the Council.

I came early to Prince Saud's elegant house on Jedda's northern shore. It was a morning of brilliant light, too soon as yet for the day's heat to raise the stifling humidity off the Red Sea which can make August such an enervating month along this coast. While waiting in Prince Saud's study I saw he had on the table a copy of *Republic of Fear*, a chilling record of the blood-letting violence perpetrated upon the people of Iraq since the middle of 1968 by Saddam Hussein and his clan within the Iraqi Ba'ath party in a long orgy of terror. The book had been written pseudonymously under the name of Samir al Khalil by an Iraqi, Kanaan Makiya, who had taken refuge in America from Saddam Hussein's regime. Published several months before Saddam Hussein picked his quarrel with Kuwait, the invasion quickly gave the book a wide influence on Western opinion by bringing home the monstrous nature of the regime which was about to be confronted.

Prince Saud was courteous as ever, but looked exhausted. He described the marathon of his discussions with Arab partners in Cairo over the past two days, which had revealed the extent of the divisions over the Iraqi aggression. The Arab League looked unlikely to take a firm stand. He was, however, encouraged at the way all Kuwait's partners in the GCC had given their full and prompt support, and for the response from Egypt, Syria and Morocco. We discussed action taking place in the UN Security Council. Prince Saud welcomed the proposal on which we and the Americans were taking the lead, to impose an immediate and rigorous trade sanctions regime on Iraq, and accepted that this must cover Kuwait too. Iraqi oil exports across Saudi Arabia via the recently-completed pipeline to Yanbu on the Red Sea coast would be stopped. He was concerned, however, that some provision be made so as not to shut off the resources of the large numbers of Kuwaitis who had either been caught abroad on summer travels or who were already starting to flock over the border in their thousands to seek refuge in Saudi Arabia before the Iraqi forces could shut the crossings. I gave Prince Saud the draft text of the sanctions resolution, as this might help him to stiffen Arab reactions. He showed sharp concern at the attitudes which Jordan and Yemen were adopting, and criticised Yemen's attitude in the UN Security Council. These two countries were leading the call for an Arab solution to the crisis, but this looked like no more than a delaying tactic to forestall outside intervention. Prince Saud made it clear there could be no question of compromise over the Iraqi action.

There was no doubting Prince Saud's sense of outrage at what had happened. Initial shock and disbelief at such a stab in the back of a fellow Arab state was now past. Any hopes the Saudis might have harboured that Saddam Hussein would stay his hand after the inconclusive Jedda talks had been abruptly shattered, and maximum diplomatic pressure had now to be mobilised. Our talk on this occasion did not yet cover possible military involvement. There still seemed no immediate threat to Saudi Arabia's own security that she could not handle herself. For it was

only that day that Iraqi forces, having consolidated their control over
Kuwait City, began to take up positions along Saudi Arabia's 220 kilo-
metre long frontier with Kuwait, and so to signal a direct threat to the
Kingdom itself.

President Bush had, with the encouragement of Mrs Thatcher, raised
with King Fahd the idea of military reinforcement when he first spoke to
the King by telephone on 2 August. He had also taken the precautionary
action of ordering the aircraft carriers *Eisenhower* and *Independence* to the
area from the Mediterranean and the Indian Ocean. The President had
also discussed possible deployment plans with Defence Secretary
Cheney, General Colin Powell, chief of staff, and the recently-appointed
commander of Central Command, General Norman Schwarzkopf, who
from his headquarters at Tampa in Florida had an area of responsibility
covering the Middle East and Asia.

By the time the President spoke again with the King on 4 August, the
prospect of an Iraqi attack on the Kingdom could no longer be discounted. It was at this point that American and British attention became
focused on the provision of military assistance to deter Iraq from rolling
her attack on into Saudi Arabia and the other Gulf states with whom our
interests, economic as well as political, were so closely engaged. We were
encouraged in this approach by a significant and impromptu meeting
which the American Secretary of State, James Baker, had held with
Foreign Minister Shevardnadze at Moscow airport on 3 August, at which
the Soviets had agreed on the need for Iraq to withdraw and to halt
Soviet military supplies to Iraq. This was seen as a preliminary signal on
the part of the USSR that her policy was to be one of co-operation with
the West in opposing Iraq's action. If Saddam Hussein had been banking
on automatic Soviet support in a Cold War mode it was evident he had
made a mistake.

King Fahd now agreed that Defence Secretary Cheney and General
Schwarzkopf should fly out to Riyadh to discuss the deteriorating military situation. Contingency arrangements were also made for two
squadrons of US Air Force (USAF) F-15 fighter aircraft to stand by to go
to the Gulf, and long-range B-52 bombers were deployed to the
American base on Diego Garcia in the British Indian Ocean Territory.
US Navy supply ships, carrying armour and equipment for a Marine
brigade, were ordered to sail for the Gulf from Diego Garcia and from
Guam in the Pacific.

Cheney's discussions with the King, attended by Crown Prince
Abdullah and other leading members of the Al Saud, took place on
6 August. By the end of that day, and after prolonged talks with his
brothers and advisers, some of whom professed reservations about the

shock to Saudi and other Arab public attitudes if Western, non-Moslem troops were invited to deploy in Arabia, the King took the bold decision to accept the American offer of help in defending Saudi Arabia. Given the way in which Iraqi forces were by then massing in considerable strength along the Saudi border, the Kingdom's need for such assistance was plain, risks and all. Nevertheless this unprecedented decision required political courage, both in terms of Saudi domestic opinion and in the wider Arab world. By now, however, it was plain that the idea of an Arab solution was a non-starter. Military help had also been pledged from friendly Arab quarters. King Fahd was not prepared to heed those who urged appeasement of the aggressor.

Once the King had accepted the reality of this threat to the Kingdom, the news blackout on the crisis which had produced a confused hiatus in all domestic media reporting on the Iraqi action during the first three days was converted into martial announcements, intended to make public opinion aware of the danger and so prepare it for the shocks to come. Even then the Saudis could not bring themselves to talk of invasion, preferring the euphemistic word 'raid' – *ghazzu* in Arabic – to describe Saddam's suffocation of Kuwait. This sudden switching-on of the media megaphone had the effect on many Saudis, irritated at having been kept in the dark hitherto, of raising questions about the government's preparedness.

To get the message across better in public, the Amir of Kuwait appeared on television with a pledge to repel the aggression and restore Kuwait's independence. Fine words but a low-key performance in which Sheikh Jabir still seemed dazed by the sudden calamity. King Fahd himself issued a public call for assistance from Arab, Islamic and other friendly countries. The sequence was significant, with the aim once again of playing down the significance of American and Western military help in the public eye, and particularly among the conservative religious element in Saudi society.

With Iraqi forces now concentrating in strength on the border, and little to impede a swoop on the oilfields of Saudi Arabia's Eastern Province and beyond, action was now taken to mobilise Saudi Arabia's own armed forces. The RSAF, equipped with British Tornado fighters and ground-attack aircraft recently supplied under the Al Yamamah programme, as well as up-to-date American F-15s, had sensibly taken precautions to arm and deploy its aircraft from the outset of the crisis, against the event of a surprise Iraqi attack. Its early warning radar AWACS aircraft had also stepped up surveillance patrols to ensure a measure of warning in the event of a surprise attack. As one of the best trained air forces in the Middle East, the RSAF would at least have given a bloody nose to any

Iraqi advance into the Kingdom. But it could not alone have withstood the overwhelming strength of Iraq's military machine.

The Saudi land forces were less prepared, being unused to deployment in the field and lacking equipment which could match the armour of Iraq. Troops were, however, moved into the frontier area on 6 August, earlier hesitation over provoking Saddam by such action having been overtaken by the gravity of the situation. First into the field was an infantry brigade of the National Guard, a land force kept distinct from the army and under the command of Crown Prince Abdullah. Saudi television began to show unaccustomed scenes of defensive positions in the desert. Slowly, and with a reluctant incredulity, the Kingdom began to put itself on to a war footing, a situation without precedent in its nearly 60 years of existence.

Whether Saddam Hussein was consolidating his forces on Kuwait's southern border as a prelude to moving on to seize the major Saudi oilfields, the nearest of which, the Japanese-managed Al Khafji offshore field, lay well within artillery range, may never be known. In my own view it seemed most likely he had assumed he could intimidate Saudi Arabia by a show of force into acquiescing in his seizure of Kuwait. But given the overwhelming strength of his attack, such a limited objective certainly could not be taken for granted.

King Fahd thus found himself confronted by a clear menace of military attack accompanied by hostile broadcasts. The time for hesitation was past. All that stood in the way of the Iraqi forces was a screen of Saudi troops backed up by the air force and the Peninsula Shield contingent, a mix of token units from her GCC partners grouped in a joint brigade under Saudi command and still in its trial phase. Beyond this Saudi Arabia had only her non-aggression agreement with Iraq for comfort, and Saddam Hussein had just demonstrated by the flouting of his assurances to both the King and to the Egyptian President how cynically he regarded such political undertakings.

Once the King had made up his mind to invite foreign, including Western, forces in to help defend Saudi Arabia, his resolve in the face of Iraqi bullying and manoeuvring remained unflinching. He demonstrated that the characteristic of political caution which he had inherited from King Abdul Aziz, the Kingdom's founder, could become transformed, as in the case of his father, into resolute decisiveness. It evidently came as a surprise to the Iraqi leadership to find themselves faced with this degree of firmness on the part of the Al Saud in defence of the Kingdom and in support of Kuwait's independent existence. In the event this was to prove one of the most crucial of Saddam Hussein's series of miscalculations.

King Fahd's response to Defence Secretary Cheney was nevertheless accompanied by important provisos over the prior need for Saudi political authority for any military engagement, and a prompt withdrawal of American forces once the crisis was past. These points, which would be applied with equal insistence to British and other foreign forces, were seen as essential against the background of anticipated public disquiet at the arrival of such forces. The decision to invite Western military help had, however, been made easier for the King by the welcome agreement of President Mubarak to send Egyptian troops to Saudi Arabia. Their presence would help presentationally to dilute the American element in Arab eyes.

The King's go-ahead was passed by Cheney in Jedda to the President on 6 August during a further round of talks with Mrs Thatcher in Washington. President Bush promptly ordered the departure for Saudi Arabia of attack and support aircraft, together with marines from Diego Garcia and the 82nd Airborne Division from Fort Bragg. General Schwarzkopf left behind him in Riyadh the nucleus of an American military headquarters under his USAF commander, General Chuck Horner, with instructions to set up all the logistic arrangements for the arrival of American forces. Schwarzkopf himself returned to Tampa to oversee the troop deployment movement.

The first air force elements reached Dhahran in the early morning of Wednesday 8 August, six days after Saddam had unleashed his attack on Kuwait. A massive and incessant military supply airlift from the USA followed as the American strength was built up, under the operational codename DESERT SHIELD. King Fahd, as ever with an eye to Saudi public reaction, went on television himself on 9 August to castigate Iraq's invasion as the most shocking act of aggression that the Arab nation had known in its modern history, and to demand the restoration of the status quo ante in Kuwait. He went on to explain that, faced with this reality, Saudi Arabia had agreed to have friendly forces of other nations protect the country's territory and economy. The American forces now arriving were there at his request for the purpose of helping protect the homeland. They would leave as soon as the Kingdom asked them to do so. Meanwhile the Amir of Kuwait, in an interview from Taif, was expressing doubt over the effectiveness of economic sanctions imposed by the UN as an instrument to get Iraq out of Kuwait. He hinted that military intervention might yet be needed.

The American move was quickly followed by a British offer of assistance with air defence, plans for which had been set in hand while the Prime Minister was in the USA. On her return to London on 7 August, Mrs Thatcher spoke to King Fahd from Downing Street, when the King made it clear he welcomed this additional support. Arrangements were immediately made for a squadron of RAF Tornado air defence fighters and another of Jaguar ground-attack aircraft to go to the Gulf. Having, unlike the Americans, a preference for random codenames for British military operations, the Ministry of Defence (MoD) chose to call this one GRANBY, a title more usually associated with public houses and far removed from Saudi Arabia's strict temperance society.

The decision to deploy resulted in a flurry of somewhat unco-ordinated instructions reaching us from the MoD in London during the morning of 8 August seeking urgent clearance for the Tornadoes to be based in Saudi Arabia, preferably alongside the Americans at the vast Dhahran airbase. It was also decided to reinforce the Royal Navy's Armilla patrol in the Gulf, currently three frigates strong. Thus the die was cast and we went into action.

Ever since the crisis broke on 2 August the embassy in Riyadh had been going flat out to handle an avalanche of telegram traffic, as well as liaison with the Saudis on the fast-moving political front and advice to the FCO. Together with our consulate-general in Jedda we were working hard to reassure and steady the large British community, particularly in the Riyadh area in the centre of the country and in the cities of Dhahran and Al Khobar, the port of Dammam and the industrial city of Jubail, strung along the Gulf coast. Despite the summer holiday season, their numbers were still some 25,000 strong, including families. Their morale was not being helped by the effect on their relatives at home of unduly alarmist reporting in the British press. The work of many of these British technical and managerial personnel was of major importance to Saudi economic and military activity, and would remain so throughout the months of the crisis. British staff were to be found in responsible positions in many areas of Saudi Arabia's national infrastructure. Particularly important to us at this critical stage was the key part being played by BAe technicians engaged in training and engineering work under the Al Yamamah programme for the RSAF, now constituting the country's front line of defence.

We were very much aware of finding ourselves at the centre of a drama where, in the first test of the post-Cold War era, the world had its chance to show that aggression would not be tolerated. As the threat to Saudi Arabia herself became evident, it seemed natural as a close friend and partner to offer help with defence. This principle was every bit as important in our minds as the parallel consideration of the security of important Gulf oil resources; moral arguments carried just as much weight as those derived from expediency. The pressure on us was not helped by the fact that we were in the middle of the summer leave

period, when we took it in turns to take a leave break from Saudi
Arabia's searing summer heat with shade temperatures in the region of
110°F. I was myself due to fly to England on 5 August to join my wife who
had returned a week earlier, but it was soon all too clear that leave was to
be a non-starter.

The deputy head of mission, Derek Plumbly, cut short his home leave
and flew back to Riyadh a couple of days after the invasion. This was an
enormous help as he and I were then able to divide the burden of political work, now running at a hectic pace. I made a point throughout the
long months of the crisis of having each section in the embassy – political, press, military, consular, commercial and management – responsible
for initiating its own responses to relevant aspects of the crisis. Every day,
seven days a week for much of its duration, all section heads met
together in mid-morning and again in the evening to compare notes,
update each other on developments and set our tasks for the next stage.
This took time but was necessary to enable us to keep in step. The whole
embassy responded with good spirit to all this activity. We lost the sense
of days and sometimes found ourselves working round the clock. In the
rush I forgot my own 55th birthday, and only caught up with it late in the
evening when Nick and Anna Cocking of our mission to the National
Guard managed to cajole me out of the office for a bite of supper, to find
their home full of British and Saudi friends determined to celebrate the
occasion. It was a kind touch.

To help keep the embassy's political section going, two of our secretaries, Karen Williams, who had been posted to New York, and Heather
Wilson, who was returning to England to have a baby, nobly stayed on in
Riyadh until replacements could arrive from London. I was particularly
fortunate as, finding myself suddenly without a personal assistant when
the invasion took place, a volunteer of exceptional standard, Lisa Jacobs,
came out to take over this work. Lisa stayed on through the Gulf War and
beyond. She was an organiser of rare efficiency and sorted out the pressures of events whatever the time of day or night, while managing always
to look as though she had just stepped out of a bandbox. Military headquarters officers, drawn into her office, were firmly kept away with the
point that while they might not have a war on their hands, she did.

The crisis soon became a way of life for us all. John Mitchell, the
embassy's indefatigable wireless operator, was at his machines for nights
on end during August, to cope with the receipt and transmission of our
mountain of additional telegraph traffic, which made up our incessant
dialogue with London and other embassies in the region, as well as with
the UN in New York and other capitals. At the London end Roger
Tomkys as deputy under secretary and Rob Young as head of the Middle

East department found themselves carrying the brunt of the onset of the crisis, which had inevitably exploded while Whitehall was in full leave season. We could not have asked for better support and contact round the clock. Mercifully the FCO waved a magic wand, or at least came up with some extra funds, and converted us within a few weeks to a computerised secure telegraph system. This made a huge difference to our effectiveness in the months ahead by giving us almost instant communications. Most important, it also enabled the operators to have some sleep.

The whole embassy, families included, responded to the challenge and strains brought by the sudden crisis as a close team. The pressures of the hour were leavened by the essential ingredient of laughter. Yet despite the occasional irreverence to ensure no one took themselves too seriously, we shared a conviction of the rightness of what we were doing, and of the importance of seeing it through. There was little time to brood on how things might turn out. For the benefit of the surge of visitors which the crisis brought from London, I kept a copy of Tom Lehrer's off-beat songs on the residence piano, open at that old favourite, the 'Mushroom-Coloured Cloud'.

These first days and nights were nevertheless nervous ones, particularly between 4 and 8 August once it had become clear that Saddam Hussein was not prepared to withdraw in response to international condemnation, but instead was building up his forces and posing an onward threat to the Kingdom. We were also getting stark descriptions of Iraqi brutality towards the inhabitants of Kuwait from British expatriates who managed to escape across the frontier into Saudi Arabia, disregarding the British government's controversial instruction to stay put for their own safety. Our own colleagues in Kuwait were holed up in the embassy or in their homes; two of them, the ambassador, Michael Weston, and the consul, Larry Banks, courageously agreed to stay on in an important gesture of diplomatic defiance of Iraq's illegal occupation, and had a grim four months of confinement ahead of them.

Each morning during that first week we awoke uncertain whether the Iraqi juggernaut would have rolled forward yet again during the dark hours, to be followed by relief on realising there had been no such move. In reality, given the strength of the support for Kuwait and Saudi Arabia which had been so quickly mobilised on the part of the international community, it seemed plain beyond doubt that any further Iraqi thrust south would bring severe retribution. There was also, as our Saudi friends reminded us, a long stretch of inhospitable desert between Kuwait and Riyadh's oasis. But the Gulf coastal cities were a more accessible target. Having already seen Saddam Hussein's blind impulsiveness in action, one could not be sure he would not seize the moment of vulnerability before outside help could arrive to press on and secure the main Gulf oilfields.

It was a great relief therefore to feel the threat begin to recede with the arrival in the Kingdom on 8 August of the first USAF units, followed the next day by RAF Tornadoes and a headquarters under the command of Air Vice Marshal Sandy Wilson. Western support was further reinforced by a statement by President Mitterrand that France would increase her military presence in the Gulf. The Canadian and Australian governments also announced the despatch of warships to join in patrolling and control of Iraqi shipping in implementation of Security Council Resolution No 661, which had been passed on 5 August, again with a Yemeni abstention, to impose a rigorous ban on trade with Iraq and occupied Kuwait in all but strictly humanitarian goods.

The Arab League duly convened in summit session in Cairo on Thursday 9 August although few heads of state chose to go. The Amir of Kuwait, Sheikh Jabir, came from his refuge in Taif, still evidently suffering from the shock of his flight by night, a move which was important for sustaining the legitimacy of the Kuwait government, yet had aroused somewhat unjust criticism on the part of Kuwaitis caught in Saddam Hussein's net. King Fahd attended and gave a robust performance. The conference was skilfully managed by the Egyptian President, who left no doubt where Egypt stood in opposing Iraq's use of force. He also succeeded in outmanoeuvring an attempt by the Iraqi representative, the deputy Prime Minister, Taha Yasin Ramadan, to exclude the Amir of Kuwait from the proceedings.

The summit passed a resolution reiterating the League's condemnation of the Iraqi invasion, and agreeing to send Arab forces to Saudi Arabia and the Gulf states to protect them against possible attack by Iraq. But again the deep split within the Arab world was apparent; Iraq's claque of Yemen, Jordan and the PLO were joined by other radical Arab states, Algeria, Sudan, Mauritania and Libya in resisting the resolution in one form or another. The meeting saw an ill-tempered confrontation between the Iraqis and Kuwaitis, which went beyond verbal abuse when a member of the Kuwaiti delegation threw a dinner plate at the Iraqis. President Mubarak rounded off the proceedings by putting Egypt's rejection of the invasion firmly on the record with the media and press.

From this point on, the divided Arab League itself was unable to play any further useful part in a resolution of the Kuwait crisis. But it had at least provided the Saudis, Kuwaitis and others opposed to Iraq's action with a majority statement of Arab condemnation, including the support of Syria from among the radicals, and a useful endorsement of external military help. Perhaps, given the divisions within the Arab world on which Saddam Hussein had been counting, this was as good as could be expected. It was certainly a considerable achievement on the part of the Egyptian and Saudi leaderships.

But there could be no let up for Saudi diplomacy, now closely co-ordinated with Egypt and the Gulf partners. Attention was turned to making a reality as quickly as possible of the collection of Moslem countries prepared to contribute military units to the coalition forming in Saudi Arabia. While these might not amount to a major contribution in military terms, they nevertheless constituted an essential element in countering Iraqi-fed criticism of Saudi Arabia's break with Arab princi-ples by inviting in a Western presence.

Morocco and Syria were the first to follow the GCC states and Egypt in offering to send troops. King Hassan of Morocco had long been one of the Al Saud's closest associates in the Arab world, and could be counted upon to come to their help. Indeed his links with the Kingdom went back more than a century, as his branch of the ruling dynasty in Morocco originated from the Hejaz, and was connected with the Sherifian families from whom the Hashemite family of King Hussein of Jordan was also descended.

A contingent of Moroccan troops arrived in short order on 11 August, the same day as an Egyptian armoured brigade started to move in. The Moroccans took up defensive positions alongside Saudi forces in the vicinity of the military base at Hafr al Batin in north-eastern Saudi Arabia, some 100 kilometres south of the Kuwait frontier. There they would remain for the duration of the crisis, for, having made this impor-tant gesture, King Hassan found himself running up against volatile public opinion which quickly showed its antipathy to the idea of Moroccan troops being associated with the presence of American and Western forces in Arabia. To his credit King Hassan kept his contingent in the Kingdom, even though their role had to be circumscribed. Like other Arab and Moslem contingents in Saudi Arabia, they came under the overall command of General Prince Khalid bin Sultan, the Sandhurst-trained commander of the Saudi Air Defence Command, who was appointed in mid-August to act as joint commander responsible for the Saudi and non-Western wing of the coalition, in parallel with the American commander of CENTCOM, General Schwarzkopf.

Syria was a less straightforward ally, though President Assad's prompt offer of troops was gratifying. The Syrian decision was to some degree opportunist. Since the recent ending of the Cold War and its stimulus of Western–Soviet rivalry and client relationships in the Middle East, Syria had found herself out on a political limb, forsaken by her main sponsor, the USSR. Accordingly she had good reason to reinsure with wealthier Arab partners such as Saudi Arabia and the Gulf states, and had already begun to do so. In offering military help in line with the decision of the Arab summit she sought to drive a hard financial bargain in return, and succeeded in doing so to the tune of obtaining Saudi promises of immediate aid of the order of $1.5 billion.

But this was not the only factor. A deep and bitter rift had divided the Syrian Ba'ath party of President Assad from its counterpart in Iraq since the 1960s. It followed that anything which put Iraq offside in the Arab power game should be to Syria's benefit. For example, lining up against Iraq afforded a pretext for Syria to postpone her military withdrawal from the Lebanon where Saddam Hussein had been giving support to last-ditch Maronite resistance to the Taif settlement of the civil war. Syria may also have spotted the prospect of mending fences with Western governments, including the UK, with whom relations had been severed since the El Al airliner sabotage attempt in 1986.

Together with the Americans, the Saudis also sought to enlist Turkey's support. This would tighten the noose around Iraq significantly. Turkish interests hitherto had pointed towards keeping on terms with Iraq, given the Turkish perception of a common problem over separatism on the part of their respective Kurdish minorities. Turkey also received half of her oil needs by pipeline from Iraq, as well as earning royalties of some £300 million a day from the transit of Iraqi oil to the export terminal at Ceyhan on the Mediterranean. To cut off this export route in accordance with UN Security Council Resolution 661 would involve a considerable loss of revenue.

But Saudi Arabia too was a major trading partner of Turkey, particularly for Turkish construction workers, who were employed on projects in the Kingdom such as the extension of the sacred mosques of pilgrimage at Mecca and Medina. Saudi Arabia had for her part agreed to close the two Iraqi export pipelines crossing the kingdom. In the event the Turks gave their support to the international effort by closing their pipeline, agreeing to American and other NATO aircraft being based in eastern Turkey, and stepping up their own army strength on the Iraqi frontier, thus tying down Iraqi troops. In return Turkey was compensated by Kuwait for her losses. She also subsequently received a credit of £2 billion from Saudi Arabia for oil purchases and the acquisition of fighter aircraft from America.

King Fahd's appeal for military help from other Moslem countries brought a prompt offer from Pakistan of 5,000 men, in return for which Pakistan received a supply of Saudi crude oil. Pakistan's readiness to play a part may also have been in reaction to Saddam Hussein's misjudgement in rounding up and detaining large numbers of Pakistanis working in Kuwait. His callous action in holding and then expelling thousands of Asian as well as Western expatriates contributed to the high degree of solidarity which Asian countries generally showed with Kuwait during the crisis. Other minor troop contributors from among Islamic states were Bangladesh and Senegal. None of these forces, however, performed a role going beyond the defence of Saudi Arabia.

But it was Egypt who by the middle of August was by far the most significant non-Western troop contributor, with 5,000 men in northern Saudi Arabia and more to come. In return Egypt received a pledge of $2.5 billion from King Fahd, of which $1.5 billion was budgetary aid in cash and the balance for capital investment. In addition Egypt was forgiven her outstanding debts by Saudi Arabia and other states, including Britain, as well as some $6.7 billion of military debt by the USA. It was already evident that the crisis was going to prove an onerous financial burden for Saudi Arabia and Kuwait, with benefits for those who came to their support. Yet Egypt's ready backing on all fronts meant a great deal to Saudi Arabia, and the price attaching to this was willingly accepted by the King.

Meanwhile Saddam Hussein quickly ran into trouble in his attempt to consolidate his claim to Kuwait. Having failed to prevent the Amir and other senior members of the Al Sabah from eluding his grasp and taking refuge in Saudi Arabia, he had declared the formation of a puppet republican government in Kuwait, in response to an alleged public uprising against the ruling family which Iraq's intervention had been designed to assist. Those named as its leaders looked to us like a handful of renegades or else Iraqis with flimsy Kuwaiti connections; in other words, men of straw. This charade was dropped by 8 August, when it was clear that no such uprising existed and that the Kuwaiti people were demonstrating a courageous resistance to the occupation.

Iraq then opted for a harsher approach, with the declaration that Kuwait no longer existed but had been incorporated into Iraq as the 19th province. This turnabout raised the question of whether Iraq had fully thought through her intentions for Kuwait at the time of attack. Certainly from the outset the Iraqis pillaged Kuwait, as well as treating her population with brutal coercion. To those suspected of resistance no quarter was given, and accounts of atrocities began to circulate in Riyadh, serving to stiffen public resolve to stand up to Saddam, who was increasingly seen as having designs on the Kingdom's livelihood as well as that of Kuwait.

The two UN Security Council resolutions imposing economic sanctions (661) and declaring void Iraq's annexation of Kuwait (662) had the

immediate effect of goading the Iraqi leader into a vehement campaign
of abuse directed against the West and designed to discredit the Al Saud
in Arab opinion. Iraqi propaganda now began to play on the sensitive
nerve of Islamic sentiment, which it hoped to arouse in protest at
Western intervention at the popular level both within the Kingdom and
more widely. In a broadcast on 10 August, Saddam Hussein made a traditional rallying call for a holy war, or *jihad*, with the unfounded and
provocative allegation that infidel troops were threatening the holy city
of Mecca. He claimed to have entered Kuwait to clean up Western cor-
ruption, and went on to call for an end to Al Saud rule.

In another surprise move he sought to engage the support of his
recent enemy, Iran, with an offer to revoke his abrogation, 12 years earlier on the eve of his invasion of Iran, of the 1975 Algiers agreement by
which Iran had secured shared sovereignty over the Shatt al Arab waterway to the Gulf. Saddam Hussein also offered to return to Iran the
various pockets of territory which Iraq had held on to at the end of the
war, and to ease his country's hitherto uncompromising position over
compensation and the return of prisoners of war. This move puzzled us.
It seemed a desperate expedient, for it surrendered in one go Iraq's few
gains from eight years of conflict which had produced only economic
hardship, heavy indebtedness and the loss of tens of thousands of Iraqi
lives. How was the Iraqi leader going to explain this to his people, and in
particular to his army? It turned out to be yet another misjudgement on
Saddam Hussein's part as the Iranians pocketed the offer, yet kept their
distance from Iraq throughout the crisis.

For Saudi Arabia the gloves now came off. Steps were taken to counter
Iraqi allegations and try to gain the propaganda initiative. This proved
difficult, as the Kingdom's information system, traditionally geared to
the restraint of debate rather than the stimulation of comment, was no
match for the agility of Iraq's information machine, long tried in the art
of misrepresenting the iniquities of its regime to the outside world. As a
result Saudi Arabia's performance in this key area was by comparison to
appear wooden and reactive. But the King lost no time in putting it on
the record that Saudi Arabia was under threat and would fight any
aggression.

This martial note was, as I began to find in contacts with the Saudi
business community, starting to make a positive impact as initial
incredulity at the rush of unaccustomed events wore off. It was particularly significant to find a solid support for the King's stand on the part of
senior Saudis in the Hejaz, where opinion sometimes tended to be sceptical, even disdainful, of rule from the centre of the Kingdom. On visits
I paid to Jedda and the Gulf cities during the first weeks of the crisis, I

was struck by a new spirit of national solidarity which the attack on Kuwait and the threat to the Kingdom appeared to have induced.

It was also significant to find influential Hejazi families, some of which had links with the Hashemites going back to the Sharifian period, vehement in their condemnation of Jordan for her partisanship towards Iraq. The theory was afoot of a conspiracy to which King Hussein had been a party, together with Saddam Hussein and the Yemen, to divide Saudi Arabia between them with Iraq taking the eastern oilfields, Yemen exerting its old claims to the Asir province in the south, and the Hashemites restoring their authority over the Hejaz and the holy cities. Far-fetched as this idea appeared, it had wide currency in the nervous mood of the time.

In a further response to Iraq's behaviour the Saudi government threw its doors open in generous and wholehearted fashion to the stream of Kuwaitis who fled by land into the Kingdom during the first two weeks of the crisis, before the Iraqi forces, now some 150,000 strong in Kuwait, took steps to seal off the frontier. Even thereafter some bold individuals, including British and other foreigners, took the risk of making their way to refuge across the flat desert. By this time the Iraqis had begun to round up foreigners, decanting around one million Asians in summary fashion across the frontier into Jordan, where they were accommodated in temporary camps run by the Jordanian Red Crescent. Meanwhile, Westerners and Japanese were detained as 'guests', in effect hostages, in Baghdad or at key security sites within Iraq, to serve as political bargaining counters in the months ahead.

The inrush of Kuwaitis was accommodated with open arms in hotels and school buildings throughout Saudi Arabia, and without charge. Others were given the use of apartment blocks in Dammam, Riyadh and other major cities, which had been constructed in a misconceived housing project some ten years before, but never occupied as the bedouin families for whom they were intended rejected the idea of moving to the confines of an apartment block, so alien to their tradition. Thus spare infrastructure was ready to hand when the crisis came. Further benefits accorded to the Kuwaitis included food on credit, a living allowance for each family, education in Saudi schools, and free petrol for their cars. Kuwaiti dinars, now much discounted on the financial markets, could be exchanged at their pre-invasion parity. In addition Kuwaiti merchants were allowed to carry on business in Saudi Arabia, and to sell their import shipments on the Saudi market.

All this amounted to an act of hospitality towards a refugee population which must be without parallel. Saudi citizens took it in their stride, seeing it as consistent with their tradition of hospitality inherited from tribal custom. In a neat historical touch it also represented the repayment of the earlier debt to the Al Sabah for the hospitality the present Amir's forebear, Sheikh Mubarak, had extended to King Fahd's grandfather, Abdul Rahman, and to his father, later to become King Abdul Aziz, when they were driven out of Riyadh by the Al Rashid of Ha'il in the 1890s. Significantly, it was from Kuwait that Abdul Aziz had set out across the desert with a few companions in 1902 when in a daring raid he successfully captured the Mismak fort in Riyadh and set in hand the process of consolidation of territory which was to lead to the formation of Saudi Arabia.

Yet the absorption of such a flood of refugees was not without problems. The luxurious hotels in which they were initially accommodated quickly showed signs of wear from rampaging Kuwaiti children, whose parents, bereft of the servants who had looked after their households, let them run out of control. There were stories of Kuwaiti families being shown the kitchen in their new apartments and asking where was the cook. A group of Saudi ladies in Jedda offered to purchase any necessities for those suddenly uprooted to the region, and were aggrieved to find the shopping lists returned to them contained expensive French perfumes and cosmetics. Particularly controversial in the eyes of many Saudis, with their strict interpretation of Islamic practice, was the sight of unveiled Kuwaiti women driving the cars in which they had made their escape. A stop was put to this activity before it aroused wider public outrage, although resentment reoccurred when vehicles were seen being driven in Riyadh and the eastern cities by American servicewomen.

Many of the Kuwaitis who sought refuge in Saudi Arabia took their exile in despondent fashion. The menfolk were to be seen in sad and taciturn groups in hotel lobbies, waiting for the tide to turn. Some exasperation became apparent on the part of the Saudi authorities, as the weeks wore on, at the failure of the Kuwait government in exile to shoulder some of the growing financial burden. The energetic governor of the Eastern Province, Prince Mohammed bin Fahd, whose administration had handled with great efficiency the first influx of refugees along the Gulf coast, told me in Dammam in mid-August that there were already some 100,000 Kuwaitis in the Kingdom, mostly in his parish. The Finance Minister claimed in October that the unstinted hospitality had already cost his exchequer the equivalent of a billion pounds; he was looking for a Kuwaiti government contribution now that they had re-established a cash flow, partly through Saudi help in releasing crude oil on credit to the Kuwait Oil Company so it could fulfil its main supply contracts.

This mood of apathy among Kuwaitis was in part a reflection of the absence of a rallying lead from the Amir and his ministers on their hill-top at Taif. Once it was clear that a government in exile was in existence there, I suggested to the FCO that we second a diplomat, preferably someone who knew the Kuwait scene, to undertake liaison with the Amir and his government. This official could be based in the consulate-general in Jedda, 128 kilometres from Taif at the base of the mountain escarpment. The FCO agreed and appointed Ian Blackley, currently serving as deputy head of mission in Kuwait, who had been on home leave when the Iraqi attack occurred. Ian Blackley's familiarity with the leading Kuwaiti personalities enabled us to keep close alongside them in their exile and give them encouragement and advice in presenting their case to the world at large as well as in preparing for their eventual return and the reconstruction of their country. With sardonic humour Ian had himself described as British Representative to the Government of Kuwait in Exile – BREPGOOKIE for short. The appointment was welcomed by the Kuwaiti leadership, and by Prince Saud too, as a way to give international recognition to the continuation in authority of the Kuwait government. Our move was shortly followed by the Americans and French.

As soon as Ian Blackley arrived I flew down to Taif to meet him there to call on the Kuwait government personalities based in the Sheraton Hotel, which had been commandeered for their use. It was a surreal and depressing experience. The Amir and other senior members of the Al Sabah, many of whom held government portfolios, occupied separate floors of the high-rise hotel. They sat about in dejected fashion, still shocked by their experience. All were listening incessantly to Arabic and English radio bulletins, and to the new CNN satellite television news broadcasts, which had just made their debut when the crisis broke. We found a combative spirit in Sheikh Saad, Kuwait's Crown Prince and Prime Minister, who was clearly pleased at Ian Blackley's appointment, and welcomed our suggestion that Douglas Hurd, with accompanying journalists, should come to Taif to see the Amir when he paid a visit to Saudi Arabia at the beginning of September. We also had a lively lunch with the deputy Foreign Minister, Sheikh Nasser al Sabah and the Minister of Public Works, Sulaiman al Mutawa, who recognised the need for the Kuwaiti leadership to come out of its corner and stand up to Iraq. They could not expect others to make all the running.

By mid-August the Saudi government was also having to turn its attention to domestic opinion. Abroad they now felt well buttressed by Arab and international support, and with five UN resolutions in force, including an enforcement of the naval blockade. Even Iran had declared her support for the embargo. But with American, British and other foreign contingents building up rapidly – there were by now around 30,000 American troops in the Kingdom, as well as units in the Gulf and in other GCC states – the problem of public sensitivity over the Western presence, exploited by Iraqi broadcasts, was requiring attention. There was also a lingering incredulity at the idea of a threat to the Kingdom from another Arab quarter, so conditioned had opinion become to the concept of Arab solidarity.

Crown Prince Abdullah took a leading part in countering these hesitations with a series of well-publicised speeches to Saudi military contingents in the field. In vehement terms he emphasised the threat from Iraq, and with due invocation of the Almighty justified the need to defend the Kingdom. The Interior Minister, Prince Naif, also took the floor, presenting to the Saudi media the case for mobilisation and defence. A sense of patriotism was further fostered by a call for young men, and women too, to enlist as reservists for civil defence. Ponderous though these moves appeared, they had a galvanising effect on the Saudi people. Volunteers came forward in their thousands, while loyal messages of support poured in and were read out to the point of tedium on television and radio. Complacency was rudely shaken, to the point where there was a danger it might be replaced by alarm. Indeed this was a balance we all had to watch with care in handling public reaction to the crisis.

At the same time the King and his ministers took pains to meet the reservations expressed in conservative religious quarters with arguments of Islamic precedent, rather than by tackling dissident voices head-on. A firmer hand became necessary at a later stage, but for now the much-respected head of the Higher Council of Ulema, or elders, Sheikh Abdul Aziz bin Baz, was prevailed upon to issue an edict, known as a *fatwa* in Islam, in which he condemned Iraq's aggression in terms of *Sharia* law and endorsed the King's decision to invite non-Moslem as well as Moslem forces to help defend the Kingdom. There was, however, a grudging tinge to the statement, reflecting the real reservations felt by substantial elements among the Saudi religious establishment, and in the population at large, over the King's recourse to infidel military help. Iraq, for all the iniquity of her action, was yet a Moslem state.

This pronouncement by the leader of the Kingdom's religious establishment was reinforced by the convocation in Mecca in early September of a conference of senior figures from around the Islamic world. This meeting, organised by the Jedda-based Moslem World League, heard speeches from King Fahd and the Amir of Kuwait, justifying their call to arms and appeal for help from the Moslem world and beyond as consistent with the Koran. The conference was given the widest publicity within the Kingdom.

We encouraged Barnaby Mason, an experienced BBC World Service Middle East correspondent based in Cairo, who up to that time had been unable to secure a visa to enter Saudi Arabia, to take the opportunity afforded by the conference to give a first-hand account of the resolute mood of the Saudi government in the face of Iraq's aggression. He took full advantage of the chance, and his reporting helped to counter some of the misconceptions of the Saudi position being put about with Iraq's encouragement. For the moment the incipient ferment of religious reaction to the presence of Western forces was contained. But it remained an issue for Saudi public opinion, and had to be constantly addressed by all of us throughout the crisis to an extent redolent of mediaeval scholasticism in impatient European eyes, yet very much a feature of contemporary life in 20th century Saudi Arabia.

In the last days of August we had our first opportunities for direct exchanges between British and Saudi ministers on the state of the crisis and the way ahead, with a visit by Prince Saud to London and the first of several visits to the Kingdom by the Defence Secretary, Tom King. Prince Saud's tour also included Paris, where he obtained President Mitterrand's agreement to send a contingent of helicopter-borne troops to Saudi Arabia. The Saudis suspected the French of being half-hearted in their commitment to the military aspects of countering Iraq; and with some justification, for opinion in the French government was divided on the question, not least because France was said to be owed some $12 billion by Iraq, while her Defence Minister, Jean Chévènement, had close personal links, holding a senior position in the Franco-Iraqi friendship association, and having overseen substantial French military equipment sales. For the French aircraft industry Iraq was a customer of an importance comparable to what Saudi Arabia represented for Britain and BAe through the Al Yamamah programme, now being put to the test against the threat from Iraq's air force. France's initial pledge of military help to King Fahd had been confined to the despatch of the aircraft carrier *Clemenceau* to the Red Sea, with helicopter troops embarked, and four warships on patrol in the vicinity of the Gulf, operating out of the French naval base at Djibouti. The *Clemenceau* was subsequently withdrawn, as it was claimed she could not make enough speed to windward to permit her modern aircraft to take off safely.

In London Prince Saud called on the Prime Minister at Downing Street, when he made plain King Fahd's determination that Saudi Arabia would stand up to Iraq and that Saddam must be obliged to withdraw from Kuwait. The Saudis appeared content with the degree of solidarity which their prompt diplomacy had achieved within the Arab world, in which Egyptian and Syrian support had been prime objectives. They were far from happy, however, with Jordan's response, and with the extent to which King Hussein appeared to be under Saddam Hussein's influence. This was helping divide Arab opinion. Prince Saud held that the Iraqi invasion had been planned in advance, and that the Iraqis had been prepared to continue down the Gulf if they had not been quickly blocked. It was reassuring for the Saudis to hear Mrs Thatcher insist that there should be no negotiation with Saddam over the basic question of Iraq's illegal occupation of Kuwait. The Prime Minister shared the disillusionment with King Hussein's position. She pointed to the need for action to counter Iraq's sophisticated propaganda message more effectively. Even at this stage, with sanctions starting to take effect, the Prime Minister did not conceal her conviction that it would take a fight to get Iraq out of Kuwait.

Prince Saud also pointed to the implications for the Palestine question of Iraq's action in Kuwait; Saddam Hussein must not get away with posing as the champion of the Palestinians through confrontation with the international community. The need to see momentum restored to the Arab–Israel peace process, but without linkage to the Kuwait issue, was to become a significant refrain in Saudi diplomacy in the months ahead, as Saddam Hussein sought to gain sympathy with Arab public opinion by deploying this drumbeat. In the back of all our minds was the eventuality of Saddam Hussein, once he found himself in a corner, putting the cohesion of the international coalition under ultimate strain with a missile attack on Israel.

Saudi outrage at Iraq's seizure of Kuwait was reaffirmed in clear terms when Tom King came out on 28 August. His meeting with Prince Sultan in Jedda was concerned with the handling of the British forces now arriving in the Kingdom, and with issues of wider strategy. Although Prince Sultan was his customary genial self there was no call this time for the ceremony which had accompanied a visit Tom King had paid to the Kingdom only a few months previously. We were now into serious business together. The Prince showed concern that things should not drag on too long, and made it clear we all had to keep the option of offensive action in mind.

We went on to see King Fahd in the elegant Al Salaam palace on its island in Jedda bay. Tom King was received with great friendliness by the King, who made clear his appreciation of the prompt military as well as diplomatic support shown by Britain from the outset of the crisis. This was in the tradition of our long and close association. The King made no secret of his bitterness over the act of perfidy on the part of Saddam Hussein, to whom Saudi Arabia had given generous backing during his long war with Iran. King Hussein's support for Iraq's action was also a matter for deep regret, and might even have been part of a wider plot. We categorised Saddam Hussein's rash invasion not so much as the action of a madman as of a megalomaniac, which was just as dangerous. Saudi Arabia had found herself in real peril.

There were already signs of scepticism on the part of the Saudi leadership over whether sanctions against Iraq would achieve their objective, though it was accepted these needed to be given a chance. At the same time delay was seen to pose certain risks for the solidarity of the alliance. A factor in their minds here may have been the emerging shadow of Islamic resentment at the presence of Western troops. They were also alert to the uncomfortable implications of Saddam Hussein raising the stakes by threatening an attack on Israel in a bid to split Arabs and others ranged against him – the 'Armageddon scenario', as we came to term it.

The Defence Secretary was urged to keep open the option of military action to enforce UN Security Council Resolution 660 through a multinational force, but with the clear proviso that this would have to be under UN aegis. Tom King made it plain we were committed to seeing the Iraqis out of Kuwait; but for the present we believed political and economic pressures had to be given time to work. There were substantial obstacles to a more martial posture at this early juncture, both in the international arena and with public opinion too.

During our discussions in Jedda Sandy Wilson's attention was drawn to a suspected threat to the Kingdom from Iraqi aircraft and missiles believed to have been based on Yemeni territory. Launch pads were said to have been set up on the island of Perim, off Aden. There was a real sense of vulnerability. Tom King flew on to Bahrain that evening considerably delayed, but in no doubt of the grave view King Fahd and his government took of the outlook for war, and of the unprecedented extent of the co-operation he was looking to have with us in the months to come.

CHAPTER 5

Light Blue

Just as the Saudi people had instinctive difficulty in coming to terms with the possibility of an attack by their Arab neighbour, Iraq, so we for our part found it hard to contemplate the deployment of British military forces in the Kingdom. Apart from occasional joint exercises with local troops, mainly in Oman, where our active military links were strongest, there had been no deployment by any British forces in Arab territory or airspace since our withdrawal from Aden in 1967, and subsequently from Bahrain and the Emirates in the Gulf in 1971. With Saudi Arabia in particular, Britain's relations had been strained during much of King Saud's reign in the late 1950s and early 1960s as a result of British action in 1955 in blocking Saudi Arabia's claim to the southern oasis of Buraimi, as well as reaction to Britain's involvement with France in the military invasion of Suez the following year.

For British diplomats involved with the Middle East the tortuous road of British military withdrawal, beginning at Suez in 1956 and continuing through Iraq, Libya, Jordan and finally the Arabian peninsula, had closed a chapter. Throughout the 1970s we had chosen to turn our backs on the idea of security links with Arabia and the Gulf. Labour government ministers during this period were intellectually and emotionally sceptical about the durability of the traditional Gulf rulers. It was only with the upheaval following the fall of the Shah in Iran in early 1979, and the return of a Conservative government to office in the general election of that April, which brought Lord Carrington into the Foreign Secretaryship, that those dealing with Middle East policy in the FCO were able to embark on renewed involvement in the security of this key region.

An important difference, however, was that henceforward this was to be based on co-operation in the development of local defence forces, through advice, training and the provision of equipment. This approach had proved itself to be a healthier basis on which to build a firm relationship. It was also more consistent with our diminished resources, and with the complementary, if sometimes competitive, involvement of the USA in a custodial role in the Gulf with its growing significance for Western energy supplies.

Moreover, we were ever conscious, perhaps to the point of oversensitivity, of latent Arab resistance to foreign military involvement. The bogey of Western imperialism still sent its echoes down the years from the Arab nationalism of Nasser's Egypt and the bitter experience of Algeria's war to secure independence from France. In the case of Saudi Arabia, no foreign troops had ever had a presence in the Kingdom except as advisers, a point in which the Al Saud regime took pride. It was true that the Royal Navy had resumed direct operations in Gulf waters through its Armilla patrol once the Iraq–Iran war began to present a threat to British and other international navigation in the early 1980s, and enjoyed the benefit of shore facilities in Dubai and Bahrain. But this activity had not compromised our policy of abstinence from direct involvement in security matters in the Arab world, and particularly in Arabia and the Gulf.

To those of us on the ground it therefore came initially as a jolt to find that the British government, alongside the Americans, was considering supplementing the rigorous regime of international sanctions so promptly imposed upon Iraq with a physical military presence. Yet from the third day after the invasion aerial surveillance left no doubt of a real threat to Saudi Arabia by the Iraqi forces concentrated along the frontier with Kuwait. With Saudi ground forces only starting to deploy into the field, there was clearly a need for outside help to deter any Iraqi designs on Saudi Arabia, and perhaps on other Gulf oil producers beyond. The information, given to us by the American embassy on 5 August, that Defence Secretary Cheney was on his way to see King Fahd about the despatch of ground and air forces, and the knowledge that US Marine elements were already embarked for the Gulf from their advance base on the British island of Diego Garcia in the Indian Ocean, was followed by a telegram from the FCO saying that RAF units had been put on standby to go to the Gulf, perhaps to the Kingdom. Our preconceptions from the past had swiftly to be jettisoned.

Yet once faced with what had seemed unthinkable, the switch came easily enough. It was helped in no small measure by the ready cooperation shown from the start by the Saudis and other host nations along the Gulf. Once King Fahd's crucial decision was taken on 6 August to accept the American offer of military support, things moved fast. A massive American airlift from the USA to Saudi Arabia was launched the following day, involving F-15 fighters and transport aircraft to ferry the troops of the 82nd Airborne Division, together with tankers and additional airborne surveillance aircraft. The first elements arrived at Dhahran airbase on the Gulf early on 8 August and immediately began air patrols, while the ground troops joined with Saudi forces in protection of oilfields and other key installations between Dhahran and the Kuwait frontier, 320 kilometres north. Other support elements were deployed to Riyadh's military and international airports.

The extravagant scale of Saudi Arabia's civil and military infrastructure was to prove a real bonus when it came to absorbing the huge armada of a foreign presence – British, French, Egyptian and others as well as American – which now began to pour into the Kingdom and was to continue without interruption for the next four months. Even so, in those early days there were signs of strain as the Saudi military establishment struggled to avoid being overwhelmed by the sheer volume of the American airlift, and to allocate space for aircraft arriving by the hundred and personnel by the thousand. For days on end the sound of heavy jet aircraft landing and taking off every few minutes from Dhahran, and with almost the same frequency at Riyadh too, became a part of the background to our existence. It also did a lot for morale, faced as we were with the threat of Iraqi attack on the Kingdom's eastern cities.

As soon as the American airlift had been launched, Mrs Thatcher, on her return to London from Washington on 7 August, followed through with her own telephone call to King Fahd in Jedda. In this conversation, which we set up through the staff of the Royal Diwan, the Prime Minister made an offer of British assistance with air defence, and if necessary with ground forces. The King welcomed the air support; not only would this be valuable in itself, but a British ingredient in the Western defensive shield would also help to leaven potential antipathy to the American presence. King Fahd made his sense of outrage at Saddam Hussein's behaviour plain to the Prime Minister, and found it fully reciprocated. There was some pained discussion of King Hussein's unhelpful action in seeking to make excuses for Iraq's deeds. Both leaders found this difficult to explain.

The RAF quickly moved ahead with preparations for the despatch of a Tornado air defence squadron to Saudi Arabia, as well as a squadron of Jaguar ground attack aircraft which it was proposed to base in Oman at Thumrait, whence they could operate in reserve or be moved further forward in the event of an Iraqi attack. At the Riyadh end we had the essential administrative task of ensuring that deployments did not take place without full Saudi clearance. On this first occasion a somewhat peremptory instruction, received in the embassy on the morning of 9 August, came in the form of a telephone call to the defence attaché, Peter Sincock, from the assistant chief of air staff, requiring us to let the Saudis know the Tornadoes and their support staff would arrive the next day, to be based at Dhahran.

Knowing well that even in a crisis Arabs are not to be rushed, I expected that the arrangements for the RAF's arrival and basing would involve negotiation. For one thing the King's authorisation would have to be passed down the line from Jedda through Prince Sultan to the RSAF command in Riyadh. For their part the Americans had sent a specialist team to go over such details with their Saudi counterparts. Without having more detail on what we wanted by way of facilities our approach, for all the urgency of the situation, was going to look improvised. Whitehall's reaction was to tell us there was no time for this. We were to to open Saudi doors without more ado, and quickly, as the Prime Minister intended to announce the deployment that same afternoon. There would be no further briefing.

With no room to consider more thoroughly the options for our deployment, the situation called for a bit of diplomatic theatre. I made an immediate appointment to see General Beheiry, the commander of the RSAF, and a good friend to us through the Al Yamamah programme. Peter Sincock and the air attaché, John Ambler, went quickly home to change into their service uniforms, complete with gold braid, so we could muster our most imposing front for our mission as a trio. On our arrival at the palatial air force headquarters building, soon to be turned into the nerve centre of air operations, we were shown straight into the general, to whom I explained the prompt despatch of the Tornado squadron following the King's talk with the Prime Minister. We planned for them to arrive tomorrow, and asked to base them at Dhahran.

General Beheiry had as yet had no word of the King's agreement to our deployment. This would first have to be confirmed through Prince Sultan. I stressed the urgency of this clearance; the die was already cast at the London end, where an announcement was imminent. The press would naturally want to record the departure of the Tornado squadron, and postponement would look poorly. General Beheiry was also doubtful there would be space for the RAF at Dhahran. He was evidently feeling somewhat sore at the extent to which his airspace was being monopolised by the density of the US airlift, with aircraft going in all directions. The shield they would help provide was welcome, but, as he put it with a nice wry touch, the main danger to Saudi Arabia at that moment was not so much the Iraqis as a mid-air collision! He asked that the RAF go to Khamis al Mushait instead.

We pointed out that this was not acceptable. The whole point of our prompt deployment, agreed between the Prime Minister and the King, was to show a British presence alongside the RSAF and the Americans, in the defence of the Eastern Province. The message in this for the Iraqis was political as much as military. It would not be achieved by our isolating ourselves from the theatre of operations by positioning ourselves in the far south near the Yemen frontier. The general took the point and proposed as an alternative Tabuk, an airbase in the north-west of the Kingdom near the Jordanian frontier but still some flying distance from Kuwait. I explained that this still did not fit with our air defence role. For our contribution to be effective it had to be Dhahran. Surely space could be found in that vast expanse of airbase? Finally General Beheiry agreed to make our points to Prince Sultan, when he passed on our request for clearance. Seeing the pressure upon him from the myriad administrative problems being thrown up by the American airlift we took our leave, after stressing once again the urgency of our request. We had made the best case we could and must rely on General Beheiry's considerable goodwill to clear our path.

A nervous couple of hours followed, during which we came under tedious MoD pressure for the answer we did not yet have. The French ambassador, Jacques Bernière, joined me to discuss the latest developments. He had as yet had no indication from Paris as to what contribution, if any, his government might make towards Saudi requests for help against the threat of an Iraqi attack. General Beheiry was, however, as good as his word and rang back in the early afternoon, having spoken with Prince Sultan in Jedda. It was with considerable relief that I heard him say our arguments had been accepted, and that all was clear for the Tornado squadron to fly out right away and be based alongside the Americans at Dhahran. We would, of course, have to sort out our own administrative arrangements there. We got this news back to the MoD in Whitehall just in time for the Prime Minister to make her statement, but it had been a close-run thing.

For the present all was under control. We looked forward to the arrival of the RAF for the contribution their presence would help to make in lifting the morale of our British community. They had been going through a difficult patch with the nightly threat of an Iraqi move into Saudi Arabia, combined with the effect of over-sensationalised reporting in the British media of the accounts given by British escapees from Kuwait and of the Kingdom's vulnerability to attack. The problem was not so much the effect these reports were having on the British community directly – they were indeed for the most part showing laudable resilience – as the secondary effect on their morale of calls from close relatives at home, who had been understandably worked up by this scaremongering and were pressing them to come out of danger. The Prime Minister's announcement of the despatch of the Tornadoes to Saudi Arabia and the Jaguars to Oman, as well as the reinforcement of the naval Armilla patrol in the Gulf and the sending of three minesweepers to back up this naval capability, thus provided a useful shot in the arm at this juncture.

Moreover, it was well received at both official and public levels in Saudi Arabia, not just as a political offset to the American presence, but in its own right as a contribution from a longtime friend to the Kingdom's defence. Cynical comment in some circles at home, as in the USA, that it was only our concern for Arabia's oil which had brought us this far, was overridden in our minds by the conviction that this military display represented a rightful response to an act of international brigandage, which might not yet have run its course and had to be stopped.

But we had little time for reflection as we plunged into arrangements to receive British forces in Dhahran and Riyadh. An RAF advance party was immediately flown out to prepare the way for the Tornado squadron, and to liaise with our defence section over clearances and logistic arrangements. A headquarters for the British forces in the area, together with a communications network by satellite, was to be established in Riyadh to liaise on the ground with the American and Saudi commands, as well as with ourselves on the political side. We decided the best place for this was the embassy itself. With some doubling up we could find space for the purpose in our chancery building, constructed only five years previously when the Saudis had required all foreign embassies to move the 960 kilometres inland to the austere environment of Riyadh from cosmopolitan Jedda.

Early on 11 August the Tornado squadron took up its position in Dhahran, and straightaway commenced combat air patrols alongside those being mounted by the air defence Tornadoes and F-15s of the RSAF and the newly-arrived USAF units. The same day the Jaguar squadron flew to Thumrait in Oman, together with refuelling tankers and a Nimrod maritime surveillance aircraft to assist in the watch for Iraqi cargo ships seeking to evade sanctions.

The RAF operation finally clicked into place with the arrival in Riyadh on 12 August of the officer appointed to command the British force in Arabia, Air Vice Marshal 'Sandy' Wilson. This marked for me the start of a close and stimulating partnership which was to last for the next two months until the arrival of major army formations obliged the RAF to relinquish command in theatre. Sandy Wilson was an excellent choice to establish the British force in the area. From the outset he was determined to see that the RAF were effectively linked to the dominant American flight activity, and had the right facilities to do so. At the same time he was ever alert to the political dimension of our military presence and the sensitivity this could present for our Saudi hosts.

He readily took the advice that British servicemen must be scrupulous in observing Saudi Arabia's prohibition on alcohol, irksome though this might be when off duty. As for servicewomen, having seen something of the shock already given to strict Saudi conventions on the seclusion of women by the presence in the streets of Riyadh and the eastern cities of American servicewomen on patrol duty, we agreed that for the present it would simplify matters to have a male-only force, a restriction which we subsequently lifted as our force expanded and the Saudi public became more accustomed, though never fully reconciled, to women in combat uniform.

Sandy Wilson quickly got on to close terms with General Beheiry, a step which was very important to the basing arrangements for the RAF in the Kingdom. In this he was helped by having previously done a stint in charge of the development of the RAF's Tornado programme at the time when the RSAF had first ordered the aircraft. This had involved visits to Riyadh when he had made the General's acquaintance. So it was that when Sandy Wilson called on General Beheiry on arrival he was greeted with a 'hello, Sandy, nice to see you back.' This set the scene for a close working co-operation between the RAF and the Saudi airforce both on the ground and in the air throughout the eight months of the Kuwait crisis, and beyond too when air patrols over Iraq from Saudi Arabia resumed a year later.

Sandy Wilson's good relationship with his Saudi counterparts was a great help in enabling the RAF to set up an operational headquarters right beside the airforce headquarters building in the city centre. This was initially in a tent until a neat temporary building was constructed for their use. It was to serve the RAF well throughout the crisis. We also provided Sandy Wilson with offices in the embassy for his intelligence and communications sections. He had his own office next door to mine, which helped our liaison over the matters of policy which soon began to inundate us, both locally and from the UK end. Sandy Wilson held the appointment of Commander, British Forces Middle East, or CBFME, a grandiose title which had not been seen since our withdrawal from Aden nearly 20 years before. In his turn he came under a joint forces headquarters located at High Wycombe in Buckinghamshire, under the command of another senior RAF officer, Air Marshal Paddy Hine.

This somewhat cumbersome chain of command had been used during the Falklands War of 1982. The existence of the joint headquarters back in England facilitated operational and support aspects of the management of British forces in theatre from the British end, and Paddy Hine rightly made it his business throughout the crisis to visit the Kingdom regularly and keep in close personal touch with the American and Saudi commanders of coalition forces on the ground. But there were occasions when the interposition of the High Wycombe element appeared to us in theatre to constitute a supernumerary filter between ourselves and those who were responsible for the direction of affairs at both military and ministerial level in Whitehall.

In my own case I enjoyed the advantage of having direct access to the FCO for prompt political direction. But there were occasions when CBFME was to feel himself hindered by the need to go through a superior headquarters in Britain to obtain decisions on major issues. Certainly Sandy Wilson found himself spending long periods each day – and night too, as a result of the three-hour time difference – in consultation by secure telephone with the staff at High Wycombe, a performance which did not always do much for his normally cheerful composure.

But the pace of events in those first hectic days of deployment gave CBFME little time for his office. We met together when we could snatch moments to do so, often late at night on his return from a sortie in his HS125 executive jet, which was kept at Riyadh's downtown military airport, to visit his far-flung units around the Gulf. One of our first concerns following the precipitate arrival of the Tornado squadron and its supporting personnel at Dhahran was to secure suitable accommodation for them. It was clearly out of the question to use Dhahran's smart and expensive hotels, but with the rate at which American forces were by now pouring into the Eastern Province, accommodation of a suitable standard was in short supply. Indeed, some of the American ground troops were having to endure living in tents in an August shade temperature of around 110°F.

Fortunately BAe were able to come to our aid with the offer of housing on a compound close to the airport, used by their personnel working for the RSAF on the Al Yamamah project. A good Saudi friend, Teymour Ali Reza, whose firm operated compound and catering facilities in the vicinity, also came up with a very fair offer to take in the remainder, and thus the problem was solved. In Riyadh, however, the headquarters staff remained in hotels for several weeks. Eventually their growing numbers and concern for their personal security led to the renting of a vacant compound, while we found CBFME himself a villa belonging to the Saudi-British Bank, conveniently located in central Riyadh.

On the operational front, the relationship with the USAF command was of foremost importance from the very outset. The initial wave of American forces airlifted to help in the defence of Saudi Arabia comprised, in addition to USAF units, an army airborne brigade and two Marines brigades. These forces were under the command of a three-star USAF general, 'Chuck' Horner, whose normal role was in command of the air forces attached to Central Command (AFCENT), based at MacDill Airbase in Florida. The air patrols which the RAF Tornadoes based at Dhahran were mounting, in conjunction with American and Saudi squadrons, were placed under American tactical control. It was also essential if operations were to be effectively co-ordinated that all three air forces should operate on the basis of identical rules governing the engagement of any hostile Iraqi incursion. There was no intention in the nervous atmosphere of the time to provoke the opposition. It was thus important to be sure of the identity and purpose of any aircraft which attempted an incursion from the direction of Iraq or Kuwait into Saudi airspace.

This need for common rules of engagement, known as ROE, became a source of some early friction between ourselves and the USAF. Sandy Wilson was from the start rightly concerned that RAF pilots should have a clear double-check on any intruding aircraft's identity before an engagement took place. Otherwise there was a risk of confusion between friendly forces on separate patrols. The Iraqis might also attempt deception by flying captured Kuwaiti Air Force aircraft of French, American or British types in service with coalition forces. A substantial part of the Kuwaiti Air Force had managed to escape to Saudi Arabia, only to find themselves grounded for this reason. This same risk was also subsequently to make it impossible for the French Air Force to deploy its Mirage aircraft in the Gulf theatre, as both the Iraqi and Kuwaiti Air Forces were equipped with similar types and there could have been confusion over their 'friend or foe' identification systems in combat.

In the view of the RAF, both in theatre and at Paddy Hine's headquarters in High Wycombe, the ROE as originally set by the Americans were insufficiently rigorous to offset the risk of a mishap, or of a loose response to the kind of lure which Iraqi pilots were starting to deploy by darting briefly into Saudi airspace and back again in the hope of attracting the fire of coalition aircraft. This could then be presented to Arab opinion by Iraq's sophisticated propaganda machine as an aggressive move on the part of American, British or Saudi forces.

At this initial stage USAF and Marines pilots were required to obtain a single positive confirmation of the identity of a hostile aircraft in Saudi airspace. In the more cautious British view it was desirable to have a cross-check of two confirmations before an attack was authorised. This should not present difficulty given that the area was under thorough radar surveillance by American and Saudi early warning (AWACS) aircraft around the clock. In plain words the RAF saw the Americans as adopting a cowboy approach, while General Horner and his staff regarded the RAF's attitude as wimpish. Discussion developed into argument without any resolution of the difference.

We became increasingly concerned that, given the nervous situation in the air with Iraqi pilots becoming bolder in attempts to dare coalition pilots to come for them, we could find ourselves provoked into a wider engagement affecting Saudi Arabia's security, and for which the coalition forces were not as yet prepared. At the same time the RAF's approach risked imposing too tight a rein on pilots who might find themselves in combat before they had time to verify a contact. We remained uncomfortably aware that it was still a very thin shield defending the Kingdom against the massive Iraqi threat along the Kuwaiti frontier. A precipitate air battle might yet provide Saddam Hussein with a pretext to carry his aggression forward.

Somehow this unsatisfactory situation needed to be sorted out urgently, and clearly this would have to be done between military staffs in Washington and London. At this point, however, an opportunity arose for us to raise the issue with the MoD at the political level. Sandy Wilson learnt from his joint headquarters at High Wycombe that Mrs Thatcher was sending Alan Clark, a minister of state in the ministry with whom she was particularly close, on a rapid visit to the Gulf to show our support to certain of the rulers and prepare the way for further RAF deployments. As is clear from Alan Clark's subsequently published memoirs, the idea of the visit did not find favour with Tom King, the Defence Secretary, who was at the time away from London on summer holiday in Scotland. After some sharp exchanges he gave his assent to Alan Clark's foray, but on the condition that he did not visit Saudi Arabia, with whom he regarded our close defence relationship as very much his own preserve. Accordingly, and with ill-concealed chagrin, Alan Clark confined his itinerary to Bahrain and Abu Dhabi in the UAE, where he was given a warm welcome.

As a consequence of the unorthodox way in which the tour had been set up, we in the embassy received no advance warning from London of Alan Clark's movements in the area. It was therefore a surprise when on 17 August Sandy Wilson came into my office with the news that Alan Clark's RAF VC10, an air tanker pressed into ferry service and carrying a number of defence correspondents as well as the minister's party, would make a technical stop at the Riyadh military airport the next night to refuel before flying back to Brize Norton. Here was our chance to put over our concern at the loose ends in the ROE and the need for these to be sorted out at the highest military level. But there was a snag. CBFME had a hint from High Wycombe of the fuss over the Clark tour and had been discouraged from making contact during the Riyadh stopover.

While no strangers to the controversy which tended to accompany Alan Clark in Whitehall, this seemed to both Sandy Wilson and myself to be an unnecessary gag at a time where we were facing a real problem with our American partners in the handling of joint operations. In any case I had no instructions to keep my distance; indeed it would be discourteous of me not to greet a British minister in transit through Riyadh, even though he had no business with the Saudi government. We therefore agreed to go to the airport when the VC10 staged through and put our concerns to Alan Clark. For good order's sake I telegraphed the FCO to let them know of this intention.

Around midnight on 18 August Sandy Wilson and I found Alan Clark aboard the VC10. He was glad of the chance to stretch his legs, so he and I wandered off on the darkened airfield among parked Saudi and American transport aircraft, to be out of earshot of the journalists in the party while we discussed the ROE problem and our worry lest a mishap provoke a wider conflict such as our forces were there to help avoid. Alan Clark took the point readily and agreed to pursue it with the MoD and the Prime Minister herself on his return the next day. He was also proposing to recommend in favour of RAF reinforcement in theatre, and had had a positive response on this from the Amir of Bahrain, Sheikh Issa Al Khalifah, one of Britain's closest friends in the Gulf region. Having said my piece I left Alan Clark with Sandy Wilson in the shadow of the VC10, while members of the minister's staff had begun to hunt for him across the apron preparatory to departure. Their calls were drowned in the din of the AWACS and heavy transport aircraft, as they landed and took off in frequent succession, a backdrop which was becoming a feature of life in the Saudi capital.

It had been a useful night's work, for within days the MoD agreed to slightly tightened American ROE. The air patrols continued, sometimes with British and Saudi Tornadoes flying in tandem. Iraqi attempts at provocation persisted, but no one took the bait. The shield seemed to be working. I therefore took the opportunity to go down to Dhahran on the Gulf coast, and join Sandy Wilson in a visit to the recently-arrived British squadron. This also afforded an opportunity to brief a number of British defence journalists who had been flown out by the public relations people in the MoD on a special Hercules flight from Brize Norton to see how the RAF were settling in. It was important to have British journalists reporting how the operation was getting into its stride in professional fashion and with the ready co-operation of the Saudi airforce and the Americans. This might also help to correct the overexcited and even alarmist tone of some reports in the British media.

I also had the chance during the visit to meet with our citizens in the eastern cities and to give them steadying news of how they were now at far less risk from Iraqi attack. I called with CBFME on the governor of the Eastern Province, Prince Mohammed bin Fahd, the King's eldest son, who went out of his way throughout the crisis to make things smooth for our troops, as well as giving every help to Britons who managed to escape from Kuwait.

The Tornado aircrews and ground support units were in good spirits, and making the best of their makeshift facilities on the crowded airbase. General Beheiry had not been exaggerating in describing the scale of the USAF armada that was descending on Dhahran. Combat aircraft and military helicopters stretched in endless rows, an inviting target in the unlikely event that an Iraqi pilot succeeded in penetrating the assorted American, Saudi and RAF patrols. Huge transport aircraft from the USA, some military and others chartered from airline services, took off and landed every three minutes or so, perhaps the largest military airlift in history. We visited the Tornado flight line and the pilots' briefing centre. There was a communications centre set up by the Royal Signals and, as an additional but necessary precaution given what we knew of the capability Saddam Hussein had in chemical and biological weapons, a special Royal Engineers unit specialising in toxic detection. This grim and outlawed aspect of warfare was to preoccupy us increasingly throughout the crisis.

Sandy Wilson and I went on to hold a press conference with the visiting journalists, some 30 in number including television crews from BBC, ITV and Sky, who been round the operation and seen something of the RSAF too. The scale of the airlift had undoubtedly made an impression. We got the point across that an adequate defensive shield was now in place, and that Iraq would be wise to think twice before taking on Saudi Arabia and the friends who had come to her support. We then responded to requests for photographs by going outside into the midday heat, and with a palm tree to serve as a suitable backdrop, raised our eyes to the aircraft overhead; a somewhat theatrical pose but, from what we heard, it gave the right message back home. Only the strains of the 'Dambusters March' were missing.

At this early stage in the crisis the Saudi authorities had not yet faced up to the fact that they would have to overcome their characteristic aversion to the idea of foreign journalists visiting the Kingdom and prying into its conservative and sheltered society. This shock was yet to come. Saudi press visas were thus like gold dust, and only an ingenious handful of pressmen had managed to gain entry, for the most part across the causeway road from nearby Bahrain island. On this visit the press party was restricted to the Dhahran military airbase. The RAF

officer accompanying the group flown in from England was worried
that some might refuse to re-embark despite their lack of Saudi visas.

This could have presented real difficulty with the Saudi military, still
recovering from the speed and scale of the response to the King's
request for foreign military help. To have American troops on vehicle
patrol both on and off the airbase was proving a shock to the system, and
all the more so when these included gun-toting Annie Oakleys in the driving seat. Some were piloting transport aircraft too. A female pilot of one
of the huge Galaxy transport aircraft had told us how a startled con-
troller at the Riyadh airbase had refused to clear her to land until he
heard a man's voice on the aircraft radio. This presented a problem as all
her flight crew were female. In the end there was nothing for it but to get
the male loadmaster to talk the aircraft down. To have such contrasts
played up in the Western press before the Saudis had more time to
come to terms with the experience could do damage to our partnership.
It was with relief therefore that we saw the party on to the Hercules, leaving behind only a handful of colleagues in the fortunate possession of
visas.

Meanwhile the decision was taken in London to reinforce further
with a squadron of Tornado GR1 ground-attack aircraft, to improve the
defensive capability and counter any attack into Saudi Arabia by the
massed Iraqi armoured force. At this early stage the aim of coalition
strategy remained a defensive one of forestalling any inclination on the
part of the Iraqi leader to move against other Gulf states and their oil
resources. Rigorous international sanctions were seen as the most
appropriate instrument for obliging Iraq to give up Kuwait, long though
the haul might be.

Given the tight fit in Saudi Arabia, it was proposed to base this fresh
Tornado squadron at Muharraq international airport on Bahrain. This
airfield had housed an RAF station up to Britain's withdrawal from the
Gulf in 1971 when Bahrain's protected status, along with that of the
other smaller Gulf states, had come to an end. It nevertheless took some
negotiation by Sandy Wilson and our ambassador in Bahrain, John
Shepherd, to secure Bahraini clearance for the deployment, not for reason of hesitation on Bahrain's part, but because space throughout the
whole Gulf for the location of the fast-growing numbers of American aircraft was now at a premium. The Bahraini government was also keen to
see provision made by us for the defence of Muharraq from possible
Iraqi air attack, and was preoccupied by the risk of terrorist action. To
help assuage these concerns it was agreed to bolster the squadron with
a detachment of the RAF Regiment. All was now clear for the squadron
to arrive from Britain on 22 August.

Although the aircraft were to go to Bahrain it was still important that we should clear the deployment with the Saudis, not least because the squadron would need to overfly the Kingdom en route. Through the FCO and High Wycombe, CBFME and I managed to get this prerequisite across to a reluctant RAF staff, who were no doubt feeling the force of Mrs Thatcher's characteristic impatience for action. Instructions reached me late on the evening of 21 August, the night the aircraft were due to depart from England, to seek urgent Saudi clearance. It was not to be the last time when I would be grateful for the habit of King Fahd and his brothers of working through the night until the dawn prayers. At three that morning Prince Sultan confirmed his welcome for our reinforcement, a message which we lost no time in passing on. In the event it was just as well we had put the Saudis on notice, as one of the aircraft was obliged to make a diversion to land at the small Saudi town of Baha in the west. The RSAF flew in an RAF repair team from Dhahran to get the aircraft on its way.

With the arrival in the region of British forces to take their place within the coalition came questions of a wider operational kind. These ranged from practical issues concerning the legal status of our troops in the Kingdom to matters of policy over the role of foreign forces and what part, if any, they might play towards the longer-term objective of getting Iraq to withdraw from Kuwait. We also needed to work out arrangements for the operational command of our RAF units, as well as their relationship with the predominant American presence on the one hand and on the other with the Saudi military establishment as our hosts.

The Saudis had by now appointed as joint theatre commander General Prince Khalid bin Sultan Al Saud, a son of the Defence Minister, Prince Sultan. The general, who was in his 40s, had done his officer training at Sandhurst and had subsequently had staff training in the USA. He had built up a position of influence within the Saudi military hierarchy as a specialist in air defence, and for some years previously had had command of the air defence force, which held the status of an independent command within the Saudi armed forces. Prince Khalid had succeeded in moulding this into a very well-equipped force, with French and American advice and equipment. What he lacked in experience of active service and joint command, Prince Khalid amply made up for by his ability, helped by his royal status, to cut through Saudi bureaucracy and get things done, an attribute for which we and other coalition forces in the Kingdom had frequent cause to be grateful in the months ahead.

Prince Khalid was to play a key role in providing Saudi logistic and administrative back-up to all the forces from no less than 37 nations which eventually made up the military coalition, as well as having operational command over all non-Western units, plus the French contingent up to the eve of the offensive to recover Kuwait. Since his Sandhurst days, however, he had not had much contact with the British military; our links were traditionally closest with the RSAF and the National Guard.

On the American side General Norman Schwarzkopf, the head of Central Command (CENTCOM), was still in the process of moving his headquarters from Tampa in Florida to Saudi Arabia. He arrived in Riyadh on 26 August to become the counterpart to Prince Khalid as joint commander, taking over command of US forces in theatre from General Horner, who remained in tactical charge of all air force activity including RAF participation.

It was to discuss these broader issues, as well as to see something of RAF and Royal Navy forces in theatre, that the Defence Secretary, Tom King, decided to visit Saudi Arabia, Bahrain and Oman at the end of August. Sandy Wilson and I planned for him to start with an early morning visit to the Tornado squadron at Dhahran, where he could also meet the RSAF commander, Prince Turki bin Nasser, and see over the modern air defence operations centre on the airfield. We would then fly back across Arabia in the VC10 to have talks with Prince Sultan in Jedda, the summer seat of the King and his senior ministers.

I was hopeful that Tom King would also call on the King, though in the customary Saudi way this would not be disclosed to us until the last moment. It might not take place until well into the night, given King Fahd's predilection for meetings in the small hours, no mean test of the endurance of visiting ministers and foreign ambassadors. This could present us with a timing problem as the Defence Secretary was due to go on to call on the Amir of Bahrain that night, before going to sea briefly on HMS *York* on patrol in the Gulf. We had planned for him to stage back through Riyadh a couple of days later for a talk with the newly-arrived General Schwarzkopf.

To help get a feel for Saudi thinking on the steps ahead in preparation for Tom King's meetings, I flew down to Jedda a few days before his visit to have a talk with Prince Fahd bin Abdullah, a former senior officer in the RSAF, who had been a pilot on Lightnings and subsequently director of operations, and was now serving as an assistant Defence Minister. In this capacity Prince Fahd had the ear of Prince Sultan and was thus an important figure in the formulation of military policy. We had worked together ten years previously when I had been in Riyadh looking after our co-operation with the RSAF prior to the Al Yamamah Tornado programme.

It was encouraging to find Prince Fahd firm as a rock in his determination that Saddam Hussein had to be confronted and obliged to give up Kuwait. Saudi Arabia would not let herself be browbeaten by his military threat or propaganda campaign. At the same time it was a surprise to hear the Prince talking of joint military action by coalition forces against the Iraqi army in Kuwait, on the grounds that economic sanctions were most unlikely to achieve Iraqi withdrawal despite their rigorous enforcement through naval blockade.

In an analysis of the Iraqi leader's intentions, which proved in the light of subsequent events to be perceptively accurate, Prince Fahd argued that, having rashly undertaken the invasion of Kuwait and in the process misjudged Saudi Arabia's strong reaction, Saddam Hussein now found himself obliged to forgo his plans for extending his empire over Gulf oil resources. Instead he had to devote his attention to survival. This meant he was likely to aim to sit tight while banking on seeing international resolve to force him out of Kuwait through sanctions erode by the end of the year. Alternatively he might play canny and undertake a partial withdrawal, thus saving face and rallying a measure of popular Arab sympathy while holding on to a part of the spoils, notably the Rumailah oilfield which he had made into a source of grievance against his neighbour.

It was evident, however, that in the Saudi view there was some risk that the groundswell of international outrage, together with the prompt and unprecedented show of military support for Saudi Arabia, could indeed begin to unravel as the weeks wore on and other political considerations came to bear on governments. Accordingly we could not afford to hang about, but should start to consider a military response. Prince Fahd had two options in mind to discuss with us. From the political aspect there was much to be said for taking a leaf from the Korean War and working towards securing UN Security Council authority for the establishment of a UN operation, under joint American and Saudi command, to evict Iraq from Kuwait.

Surprised at the boldness of this proposal, I rehearsed a number of reasons for not rushing into military action on these lines. We needed to give time to judge whether sanctions were having their intended effect or needed to be followed up by other means. There were significant difficulties in the way of securing a UN Security Council decision in favour of UN military action on the lines of the Korean precedent. Prominent here was the position of the USSR. It had been gratifying to find Moscow prepared to join with the Americans in unprecedented fashion to condemn Iraq's action when James Baker had met Eduard Shevardnadze a fortnight previously. But this was well short of endorsement of Western-led military action under the UN colours. Moreover, in the Korean case the UN Security Council's decision had only been possible because the USSR had absented herself from participation in the Council's activities. There were other states, too, for whom such a move at this stage could impose a strain on their support.

We then considered whether an alternative course might be for the Saudis, Americans and ourselves to plan together to move over to an offensive stance. This could still have some form of UN endorsement. It would have to involve land as well as air action, though the latter would be important against supply lines. The Saudis held a low opinion of Iraqi morale and believed that their military opposition was likely to crumble, a forecast which subsequently turned out to be close to the mark. The shock of events could even provoke the overthrow of Saddam Hussein.

The case for action on these lines before our solidarity had a chance to wane was evidently a major preoccupation in Prince Fahd's mind. It would be expressed by Prince Sultan and other leading Saudi military figures at subsequent intervals in the crisis, while the Western commanders remained hesitant of rushing into conflict. There was for the Saudis a justified concern over how long their public opinion at large could live with the political and cultural shock of the presence of Western forces, coupled with less well-founded doubts over the political will of their coalition partners to go through with things as time wore on. Moreover they still had cause to feel threatened by Iraq's military build-up in Kuwait, now estimated at some 150,000 men. Saudi scepticism over the ability of sanctions to achieve Iraq's withdrawal was deeply instilled.

One point on which Prince Fahd and I firmly agreed in our talk was the importance of Arab forces, notably the Kuwaitis as well as Saudi units, being seen to take part in the vanguard of any clash with the Iraqis, or of an eventual liberation of Kuwait. For this reason the Saudi army, National Guard and frontier force were already providing the advance screen along the border with Kuwait, with the US Marines and airborne divisions in reserve further down the Gulf coast. Kuwaiti forces who had managed to make their escape were meanwhile regrouping and undergoing training in Saudi Arabia. They included elements of an armoured regiment which had fought an engagement with the advancing Iraqis before being forced to withdraw into the Kingdom with their ammunition exhausted. Their vehicles were now being readied for fresh service with British Army help.

In several respects this revealing discussion with Prince Fahd set the tone for the subsequent development of our close and effective cooperation during the months of crisis. More immediately it prepared the way for Tom King to stress emphatically to both Prince Sultan and King Fahd when he saw them a few days later the British government's commitment to see Kuwait's sovereignty restored, and that our will in this respect would not erode. At the same time we should not rush into an offensive option, as sanctions needed time to show an effect.

So far as the UN Security Council was concerned, we were clear in our minds that Article 51 of the UN Charter, providing for the right of individual or collective self-defence in the event of armed attack against a member state, afforded sufficient legal cover for military action by the international coalition in support of the Kuwait government, now in exile. This was a point to which Mrs Thatcher in particular attached significance, as a means of avoiding the UN Security Council restricting freedom of action over Kuwait. It had, however, already become a point of difference between ourselves and the Americans, who for reasons of domestic politics and with an eye to the precarious relationship with the Soviets, preferred to see any military action receive UN Security Council authority under Article 42 of the Charter. It was made clear in Prince Sultan's conversation with Tom King in Jedda that the Saudis were of similar mind, in the interest of holding firm the Arab front they had successfully put together.

Numerous other dimensions affecting our military units present in the Kingdom and elsewhere in the Gulf were now cropping up daily for the embassy and Sandy Wilson's headquarters staff to sort out with the Saudis. Tom King usefully secured Prince Sultan's agreement to the RAF Tornadoes undertaking low flying training in the east and to the use of Saudi bombing and weapons ranges. The Defence Secretary also obtained permission for Royal Navy ships enforcing the blockade in the Gulf and Red Sea to enter Saudi waters in pursuit, and if necessary to bring suspect vessels into Saudi ports for inspection. This clearance was important for the US Navy and ourselves, as well as for warships of other navies now being added to the sanctions patrols, including the French, Dutch and Australians.

The three frigates in the Royal Navy's Armilla patrol at the outbreak of the crisis had recently been authorised to take a more forceful part in the stop-and-search activity in the Gulf, following signs of ruffled feelings on the part of the American naval commander, Admiral Maurs, that they were spending too much time at their shore base in Dubai. Sandy Wilson had been hampered in sorting this out by a lack of direct communications with his naval element, which reported direct back to High Wycombe and to the fleet commander at Northwood. This show of individualism on the Navy's part was soon put straight, and a better co-ordinated activity foilowed.

The need for access to Saudi and other Gulf ports became clear after one of the first interceptions involving Armilla ships during August, when a cargo vessel boarded in the Sea of Oman by Royal Marines was found to be carrying flour for Iraq. The Oman authorities, however, jibbed at allowing the cargo to be unloaded in Muscat, with the result that the operation had to be awkwardly undertaken at sea. A repetition needed to be avoided if the sanctions regime was to be credible.

Another issue broached by Tom King concerned arrangements to govern the legal status of British forces in the Kingdom. It was obviously desirable to get this agreed as soon as possible against the chance of some mishap or incident involving our troops. British military personnel already working in Saudi Arabia as advisers were covered by long-standing special agreements. But the influx we were now seeing was of quite a different order. Having secured the Saudi go-ahead, Derek Plumbly, who was a fluent Arabic speaker, started on the process of working up a diplomatic agreement with the Saudis. The pressures of the crisis greatly speeded the process and I was able to sign with Prince Sultan in mid-October a formal memorandum which ensured the legal protection of our forces, the strength of which in the Kingdom, by the time our deployment reached its peak in January, was not far short of 40,000. It was a relief to have this loose end under control, given the ever-sensitive attitude of extremist religious elements within Saudi society towards the presence of Western and non-Moslem troops in their midst.

Sandy Wilson and I slipped up on one point of protocol in making our plans for Tom King's visit. It was important that the Defence Secretary should have the chance to meet General Norman Schwarzkopf at his headquarters in Riyadh to discuss aspects of our operational co-operation, and in particular to open the way to British participation in the detailed military planning, including air strategy, which the Americans had already put in hand. Sandy Wilson rightly did not want to have RAF units involved in actions over the preparation of which we had not been consulted. We had omitted, however, to suggest that when Tom King returned through Riyadh for this meeting he should also pay a call on the Saudi joint commander.

General Khalid bin Sultan was put out at this lapse of courtesy and expressed sore feelings to me in a telephone call on the night before Tom King's return. We certainly wanted to avoid seeing our working relationship with the newly-appointed Saudi commander get off to a bad start. It was by then too late to arrange a call, however, and there was nothing for it but to regret the oversight, and take note for the future that we could not afford to bypass the Saudi chain of command. In due course this led to an involved exercise involving Paddy Hine, as British joint commander, in the devising of a command pattern whereby due account could be taken of General Khalid's central administrative responsibilities alongside the American commander under whose aegis our forces were to operate.

Sandy Wilson and I followed up with an early call on Prince Khalid bin Sultan in the imposing new Ministry of Defence building in the centre of Riyadh. The general, who had the tall stature and large frame of his father, Prince Sultan, as well as his jovial manner, gave us a warm welcome. We were plied with the cappuccino coffee which was for all his Allied visitors to become the hallmark of visits to the Saudi commander, and Sandy Wilson quickly established a friendly relationship. There were reminiscences of Prince Khalid's time at Sandhurst and an invitation to him to pay a visit to the RAF at Dhahran. Sandy Wilson undertook to keep in frequent touch and was glad to have the general's offer of assistance with any problems we might encounter of the logistic side. Here, we realised, was someone who had the personality to cut through obstacles and red tape.

At this stage, in addition to the Saudi forces and contingents from partners in the GCC, Prince Khalid was engaged in allocating tasks to the army units under his direct command which were starting to arrive from several Arab and Moslem countries, including Egypt, Syria, Pakistan, Bangladesh and Senegal – a mixed bunch, yet providing a tangible signal to Saddam Hussein that he was not facing just a Western conspiracy, as his propaganda sought to portray. I suggested to Prince Khalid that our co-operation could be usefully reinforced by an exchange of intelligence on Iraqi activity and intentions, an idea which he quickly endorsed, leading to the establishment of an Intelligence Corps liaison with his headquarters throughout the crisis.

In London the political mood, spurred on by the Prime Minister's conviction that in the end things would have to come to blows, was taking on an increasingly hawkish tone. The Americans were steadily reinforcing their military presence in the region and were keen to see us do likewise, including ground troops. Following a debate of good quality in the House of Commons on 6 September, in which the opposition joined with the government in giving full support to international action through the UN to achieve Iraq's withdrawal from Kuwait, and to the British military deployment, the decision was taken on 13 September to reinforce our forces in the Kingdom with additional Tornado ground-attack and air-defence aircraft, and also by the deployment from Germany of a full-strength armoured brigade, the 7th Armoured, known since the North African campaign of the Second World War as the Desert Rats after the jerboa, which also inhabited the Arabian desert. As it happened I had served with this brigade back in the 1950s.

The despatch of an army formation was particularly significant as it marked a considerably greater commitment in manpower. It also gave the first signal of a readiness to contemplate an eventual land offensive to dislodge Iraq, if diplomatic and economic pressures proved ineffective. Additional forces would meanwhile help strengthen Saudi defences against a possible Iraqi attack by land as well as in the air.

This danger could not yet be discounted, although it was some relief to know that the 150,000 Iraqi troops now inside Kuwait had gone into defensive positions in their concentrations along the Saudi frontier, and that their formidable Revolutionary Guard units had been pulled back in reserve. Still the Iraqis could muster some 1,200 tanks in Kuwait by American estimates, with only light Saudi and American armour to face them. Hence the case for the deployment of the 7th Armoured Division with their Challenger heavy tanks. The Americans too were in the process of stiffening their armoured presence with a division, equipped with the new Abrams heavy tank, though it was evident from my regular exchanges with Chas Freeman that the US administration were still committed to giving sanctions every chance, for reasons of sustaining Soviet and other international support as well as for domestic and congressional considerations. As the White House adviser, Brent Scowcroft, put it early in September, it was all right for the USA to be seen as the world's number one policeman, but not as its number one gunslinger. Chas Freeman showed surprise when I told him of the way both the King and Prince Sultan had talked to us of an eventual military option under UN auspices.

At the London end the Prime Minister was already looking to the likelihood of an offensive, if necessary without further UN Security Council endorsement. For Douglas Hurd and the FCO, however, such talk sounded premature; we should take a further look at how sanctions were going in mid-autumn. It might have to be a longish haul.

Thus in announcing on 14 September the decision to send the armoured brigade Tom King was careful to emphasise its primary role of strengthening the defensive shield, while adding the warning that if Iraq did not implement the UN Security Council resolutions, then other options remained available to the international coalition. The hasty timing of the announcement left us in no doubt that the MoD were again coming under impetuous pressure to get reinforcement under way from the Prime Minister, who sometimes seemed to be on a military high. It was an uphill task to get it registered in Whitehall that care should be taken to consult Prince Sultan over our major decision and its rationale, and to get his agreement. We could not risk a repetition of our earlier exercise in bouncing him into agreement in the middle of the night. In any case Sandy Wilson wanted the new Tornado deployment to be divided between Dhahran and the well-equipped RSAF base at Tabuk in the north-east, near the Jordanian border. In the event we had to enlist General Schwarzkopf's support to secure Saudi agreement to share Tabuk with us.

I finally took this point of protocol up directly with Tom King, who promptly put Prince Sultan in the picture by telephone, albeit only the day before the announcement of deployment. Prince Sultan's ready clearance only reached me at 1.00am – another close-run thing, and even then I was out of bed again at four to take a call from Chas Freeman in Washington to say the Americans were agitated lest we jump their gun by telling the Saudis of the planned US reinforcement before they had a chance to do so. Largely as a result of the Prime Minister's impatience, we had managed to do just that. The Americans would have to pick up the pieces, I told myself on returning to what was left of my night's sleep.

This reinforcement brought to a head, however, the need to sort out the complexities of how British forces were to fit into the coalition's chain of command, now starting to take shape with the arrival in Riyadh of General Norman Schwarzkopf with his CENTCOM headquarters. The RAF units in their air defence role were tied in with the Americans under the operational command of General Horner. The ground attack Tornadoes now to be deployed to Tabuk would come under the same arrangement.

Problems arose, however, over accommodation there for the pilots. Sandy Wilson was insistent that all his pilots must be billeted in good-quality hotels. I found this surprising, as many of their American counterparts were in hutted or tented accommodation around the Kingdom's airfields. Moreover, the RAF pilots were apparently only required to do a two-month tour in theatre as compared with the six-month stints or longer of the Americans. Hotel comforts were proving difficult to find in Tabuk. I therefore flew up there at the end of September with Sandy Wilson to seek the help of the governor, Prince Fahd bin Sultan, in allocating hotel accommodation for the Tornado pilots. Prince Fahd, the owner of some fine bloodstock on the English turf, agreed to sort things out for us.

As we flew back across the desolate dunes of the Nefud desert north of Ha'il, and on over the irrigated circular wheatfields of Qassim province, with Sandy piloting the HS125, we were tracing a route taken by the first European explorers to come into central Arabia over a century before; Doughty, Palgrave and the Blunts. Over to the west it was

possible to make out the line of the derelict Hejaz railway, the scene of
T E Lawrence's sabotage activity in the First World War, on the last occasion when British troops had fought alongside Arabian forces. Now we
found ourselves in partnership again.

This time, however, it had been decided that 7th Armoured Brigade
needed to operate with the American forces in the east and come under
American tactical command in the field. Accordingly the British ground
forces were to be grouped with the US Marines division, commanded by
General Walt Boomer and located, since their arrival at the outset of the
crisis, as a defensive screen alongside Saudi and other GCC units south
of the Kuwait border and near the Gulf coast, where the main highway
ran north to Kuwait from the port of Dammam and the new industrial
city of Jubail. With its refinery, water desalination plant and petrochemical installations, Jubail was a prime area for protection. It also afforded
a superb supply base for American and British troops with its newly-
built port facilities and extensive compounds.

But account had also to be taken of the fact that Saudi Arabia was the
host country for all foreign forces, was providing support and logistics
free of charge, and moreover had appointed her own overall commander, General Prince Khalid, who had already had cause to remind us of
his role. The Americans were, we knew, already having difficulty in iron-
ing out a system of parallel command which acknowledged Saudi
participation at the top tier, yet afforded General Schwarzkopf effective
control over planning and operations throughout the coalition, which by
early September had collected land, sea and air forces from no less than
22 countries. The ground forces sent so promptly by Egypt and Morocco,
and in slightly slower time by Syria, Pakistan and Bangladesh, were firmly
part of the Saudi-commanded wing under General Khalid, as were GCC
forces. A tentative Saudi approach to Moscow to provide a battalion as a
sign of solidarity had got nowhere; not surprisingly the USSR was not yet
prepared to back its about-turn in foreign policy with a military involvement. The French, who by this time had a helicopter-borne light brigade
on the way, had opted to go under Saudi command, though after considerable tergiversation they switched some weeks later to the
US-commanded wing.

Air force units were by now stretched around the Gulf region wher-
ever airfield space could be found. The French Air Force had a Jaguar
unit based at Al Kharj, south of Riyadh. A Canadian squadron put down
in Qatar alongside Americans, with Italian Tornadoes in Abu Dhabi and
RAF Jaguars and tankers still down in Muscat from where Sandy Wilson
was trying to relocate them northwards to be nearer the action. He
eventually succeeded against fierce competition in squeezing the Jaguars

into Bahrain. Room was found for the tankers at Riyadh's busy King Khalid civil airport, which also became the hub for the RAF's ferry service from home. Sandy Wilson secured this valuable concession through his close working relationship with General Beheiry, though the general suffered a number of what Sandy Wilson used blithely to call 'sense of humour failures' along the way.

As for the navies, it was initially a case of each for himself in the seas around Arabia. The American, French and British vessels were being joined by Australian, Canadian, Belgian, Dutch, Danish and even Argentinian warships, with a Soviet presence in the background to keep an eye on things. The European element ran into command complications at the outset, with the French making a somewhat petulant bid for control by virtue of their current presidency of the Western European Union (WEU). We and others were less keen on the idea. It was finally agreed, following an inter-naval conference in Bahrain, that we would each be responsible for patrolling our own boxes inside the Gulf while keeping in close touch. The Saudi navy was covering its own territorial waters, and the Royal Navy was working more harmoniously by now with the Americans in stop-and-search activity to keep the essential tanker and supply ship lanes free from harassment and mines. For this last purpose British and Belgian minehunters had been deployed, as the US Navy had turned out to be less well equipped to deal with this hazard, having minesweepers close to Second World War vintage.

It was to try to codify this confused and *ad hoc* pattern of responsibility that Paddy Hine came out to Riyadh in the middle of September. He brought with him General Michael Wilkes, his deputy as joint commander, who from his headquarters at Wilton near Salisbury was overseeing the deployment of British Army units to the Kingdom, and also Brigadier Patrick Cordingley, the commander of 7th Armoured Brigade, whom I had last seen when we had found ourselves stationed together in Benghazi in Libya in 1965.

Paddy Hine recognised that not only deference to Saudi susceptibilities, but also the reality of logistic support and the protection of our forces' status in the Kingdom, required that we match our proposal to have British forces in Saudi Arabia under American tactical control with some formal link to the overall local authority of Prince Khalid. He came up with an ingenious 'wiring diagram' for command arrangements which he, Sandy Wilson and I spent several hours adjusting and adapting. It took three days of intensive talks to finalise its complexities with General Schwarzkopf on the one hand and General Khalid on the other. In its final form the diagram resembled a cat's cradle, with solid lines here and dotted lines there. Predictably the MoD found cause to jib, but Paddy succeeded in overcoming their reservations. There were occasional moments when we wondered with whom we were tangling: Saddam Hussein or our own MoD. The formula did the trick, however, and ensured both honour and operational needs were satisfied. Paddy Hine's persistence and skills in military diplomacy were rewarded when I was informed a week later that on General Khalid's recommendation Prince Sultan had accepted our command diagram. I was relieved not to have had to explain it to him, let alone in Arabic.

The tasks of diplomatic liaison with the Saudis and Kuwaitis and with our coalition partners in Riyadh, plus handling our community and the British press and smoothing the path for our military, were by now placing a heavy burden on the embassy. People rose to the occasion splendidly, invigorated by the challenge and their sense of outrage. Saddam Hussein's savage record against his own people was once again being given full rein in a vicious maltreatment of the Kuwaiti 'subjects' he had come to 'liberate', and in the illegal detention of British and other foreigners taken hostage or mouldering in transit camps on Iraq's frontier with Jordan. Such actions left us in no doubt that he had to be confronted. Personally I had come to feel he had forfeited his right to membership of the human race. On rising each morning I was confronted from the bedroom window with the brooding bulk of the Iraqi embassy building, recently completed in a mausoleum style some 200 metres away across the diplomatic quarter, and now housing a skeleton staff who rarely ventured out.

In throwing ourselves into these challenges we were greatly helped by the friendly operating style of Sandy Wilson and the RAF, working in our midst. The embassy's three attachés, Peter Sincock, the senior of them, Nick Kerr on the navy side and John Ambler for the air force, gave all their attention to keeping the wheels turning as smoothly as possible for our personnel in the novel and sensitive environment of Saudi Arabia. There were a number of ground rules which we had to agree from the outset. These included no alcohol for consumption, in deference to Saudi Arabia's tenacious attachment to its prohibition on religious grounds. This was a tough pill for the military to swallow, but they took it well, and while in Saudi Arabia to all intents and purposes stuck to it throughout the crisis and the campaign. Perhaps in consequence their disciplinary record was exemplary; it would have rendered the Duke of Wellington incredulous.

Another sensitive area for Saudi opinion was religious services, as the strict Islamic conventions of the Kingdom did not allow public non-Moslem worship, though in practice it was condoned in private. I explained to Paddy Hine and Sandy Wilson that we needed to respect this way of handling the issue. Of course the Saudi authorities recognised our troops must have access to spiritual contact; they were the last people to deny the importance of this benefit to those who were facing the possibility of death or injury in battle. But for the sake of their easily-aroused public opinion, the Saudis were asking us to be discreet. Iraq's ever-astute radio propaganda was already putting it about that American soldiers were defiling the holy cities of Mecca and Medina, and there was even a story in the rumour-mill that Jewish rabbis were active on Saudi soil. All this could easily generate active antipathy. The Americans had agreed to term their chaplains 'morale officers'. This sounded to us excessively euphemistic, but some caution was in order. We agreed to speak of 'welfare', and I asked that chaplains should avoid wearing any clothing or insignia bearing a cross or identifying their calling, summed up as no dog-collars and no collar-dogs. Paddy Hine rightly objected that this would not do if troops were engaged in combat, and we settled for this distinction. In the event our forces handled this area with good sense and at no inconvenience, a restraint in the interests of amity within the coalition.

Another area where the sensitivities of Saudi society had to be taken into account was in the provision of entertainment for our forces. This was going to be an important feature in their existence, for while most would be out in the desert and on training or flying operations for much of the time, they were to have a recreation facility in a camp we had taken over in Jubail. We were discouraging them from visiting the souks of Riyadh or Dammam for fear of some uncovenanted incident. The aggressive Saudi religious police had, we knew, had their fervour curbed to some extent by the Saudi government to minimise the possibility of confrontation with infidel troops, particularly females, but their indignation rumbled not far below the surface. Cassette tapes of sermons by firebrand Saudi preachers, particularly from the puritanical Qassim oases north of Riyadh, were starting to circulate among the public, with inflammatory texts which, while careful not to condone Iraq's action, were nevertheless hostile to the presence of infidel forces with allegations of pork-eating and other profanities. As our best Arabist, Derek Plumbly monitored several of these. They were heady stuff, though it was believed that US forces did have pork in their rations; so the mischievous story went, the carcasses had been accounted for on arrival as sheep with gas masks.

Things had already threatened to go sour shortly after General Schwarzkopf's arrival when King Fahd, along with many of his subjects, had been shocked to see on one of the flamboyant newscasts run by the new satellite-based CNN television channel out of Atlanta, a spectacle of American troops dancing with members of the opposite sex at a location said to be Dhahran, Saudi Arabia. The telephones between the US head-quarters, the American ambassador and the Saudi commander went red-hot as explanations of this serious breach of the Kingdom's moral code were sought. It turned out to have been part of an entertainment laid on in good faith by American families employed at the Saudi-American oil company, Aramco, under the provocative title of 'The Best Little Whorehouse in Texas'. Red faces all round, but thenceforward all live music and dancing were out for the troops. Oliver Cromwell would have approved.

In the light of this episode I put it to Sandy Wilson that visiting enter-tainers for British forces in the Kingdom must be confined to comedians and conjurors. He looked at me as if I was out of my mind. Who was this spoilsport? No drink, no sex, no bacon, no religion, and now no fun! How could such fare possibly satisfy soldiery? We left it at that for the moment. Christmas still seemed a long way off. But in the event the high points of the forces' entertainment calendar turned out to be none other than Harry Secombe and Paul Daniels (minus his nubile assis-tant), and very good entertainment they gave.

Meanwhile the stream of military and other visitors from home was turning into a flood. Sandy Wilson took the brunt of it, but there were political aspects to be discussed with many of them, matters involving Saudi and Kuwaiti policy, the position of other coalition members, intel-ligence activity and liaison, and so forth. There was also entertainment to be offered, an area which my wife handled in style until the train of visitors was cut off on the eve of hostilities. Grania had returned to Riyadh from England in mid-September. It was great to have her back, and a help to community morale too. Our visitors were on the whole good company, and showed much consideration for the pressures upon the embassy. We got off lightly compared with the Americans, whose vast military presence generated a horde of callers – commanders, con-gressmen, and experts of every kind. Chas Freeman dubbed Saudi Arabia the world's first military theme park, and so it felt.

The steady growth in the numbers of British servicemen was having implications for the local costs of our military deployment. Sandy Wilson and I were by September becoming uneasily aware that so far very little control was being imposed in this field from the MoD in Whitehall. Newly-arrived unit commanders were having to forage on the local mar-ket for many requirements; mainly rations, accommodation and transport. We had done our best through embassy contacts with the Saudi business community to open lines of supply at reasonable prices. But basically this was a matter for those on the ground.

For their part the Saudis, as host nation, were being generous in meeting the local operational costs of our forces, notably aviation fuel. This was one of the benefits which had prompted Sandy Wilson to move the RAF tankers up from Oman, where we had been obliged to pay for their refuelling loads. The Saudis had also indicated a readiness to cover our other costs, along with the Americans, either by arranging direct supply or reimbursing our expenditure. But this could only be done on the basis of properly organised accounts. This accounting task, normally the responsibility of a civil secretariat attached to headquarters, had by early October still not been set up for British forces, while both the Americans and the more recently arrived French had kept their accounts from the outset.

I had drawn this omission to Tom King's attention when he came out at the end of August, to be told that there was a problem as provision was no longer made for civilian manpower to undertake civil secretariat work. Volunteer candidates were being sought, but this would take time. On his side Sandy Wilson was regularly pressing his joint headquarters at High Wycombe to remedy the situation. The absence of supervision meant that we were inevitably spending more than was necessary. For example, aircrews were being billeted in hotels at standard rates. The situation did indeed lead to awkward questions later on. We risked forfeiting eventual Saudi repayment for lack of proper accounts, and this led to the writing-off of some millions of pounds when, on the eve of hostilities in January, we finally concluded our agreement with the Saudis over what they would reimburse us as host nation.

We took up this issue again with the Minister of State for Defence, Archie Hamilton, when he came to the Kingdom at the beginning of October. The matter lay within his field of responsibility. Tom King had let it be known shortly before that the deployment was already costing us in the region of £2 million a day, while capital expenditure to date was put at around £100 million. Like the Americans we had started to hand the hat round to our friends in the Gulf and the West.

The Saudi Deputy Defence Minister, Prince Abdul Rahman, a full brother to the King and Prince Sultan, made it clear when he saw Archie Hamilton in Jedda on 6 October that the Kingdom was prepared to deal generously with us over the costs of coming to her defence. But he plainly found it difficult to understand why we were being so slow off the mark in producing accounts. Archie Hamilton had brought out with him Norman Abbott, who had just been nominated for the civil secretary post. This was welcome, but it was frustrating to discover that he was not to take it up for another three weeks. Once established Norman Abbott did a good job in getting expenditure under better control. But he and his small staff in Riyadh had no time to catch up with much of the backlog.

The bureaucratic delay over the civil secretary appointment was also compounded by argument within Whitehall over the provision of political advice to CBFME. The MoD held that the British commander required a civilian specialist in defence policy to serve as the interface between the military command and the ambassadors in theatre, as well as the political establishment at home. In my view, and more importantly in that of Sandy Wilson, this function was in most respects being carried out in practice by myself. Moreover, we had operated like this from the start. Sandy and I had adjacent offices in the embassy chancery, we understood each other, and we got on well. There was no need to interpose someone, especially as he was unlikely to have experience of the local political and social considerations which were proving so relevant to the operation of the coalition. As for the other Gulf states, our ambassadors in those capitals were providing Sandy Wilson and his staff with the right advice and contacts on the local scene. The Royal Navy, with their support base established at Jebel Ali port in the UAE, had attached a liaison officer to the embassy office in Dubai.

Sandy and I therefore put it to our respective contacts at the home end that we saw no need for a change. The FCO were content to have myself and other Gulf ambassadors in direct liaison with the military. Tom King had seen for himself how things were working well on the ground. As joint commander Paddy Hine was using the embassy to good effect as his source of political advice during his periodic visits to discuss command and other strategic issues with Norman Schwarzkopf and Prince Khalid. Paddy Hine and I spent an evening at my house in mid-September talking over the issue of political advice for whatever lay ahead. I suggested it might suit his purposes better if he had access to this at High Wycombe, where the shifts in the diplomatic and political picture could be plotted and analysed on the basis of the reports which we and other embassies around the world were constantly sending back as the crisis developed.

I also put this suggestion to Roger Tomkys and David Gore-Booth, the two under-secretaries in the FCO who were steering the diplomacy of the crisis at the London end. They had evidently been thinking on similar lines. Paddy Hine followed it up on his return, with the result that the FCO seconded two senior officials, Peter Wallis and Andrew Palmer, to High Wycombe for the duration of the crisis. Intelligence specialists were also attached, while Sandy Wilson at our end received similar support in this important field, in co-operation with the Americans and Saudis and drawing on sources inside Kuwait as well as on the extensive aerial surveillance facilities which the Americans had diverted to the region. As for the idea of a political adviser in Riyadh, this was quietly dropped. When he eventually took up the post of civil secretary in late October, Norman Abbott's remit was to concentrate on financial control and matters of forces' status. In the area of policy advice his role was limited to MoD questions such as rules of engagement. This made sense and suited fine.

Thus by late September we had a smooth working system in place, and were ready for the arrival of the additional RAF units and the 6,000 men of 7th Armoured Brigade. We still saw their role as primarily defensive, and as a deterrent against further rash action on Saddam Hussein's part while sanctions were allowed time to achieve an Iraqi climbdown and even, we dared hope, provoke a collapse of his reign of terror. We were, however, coming to share the Al Saud view that more than sanctions might be needed to shift him from Kuwait, and that the window for a military standoff was finite.

From an early stage in the crisis, work had begun on contingency plans for an eventual air campaign to dislodge the Iraqis. The American chief of the air force, General Michael Dugan, had been summarily dismissed by Defence Secretary Cheney in mid-September for opening his mouth too wide about these preparations to journalists during a flight back to the USA. General Dugan was of the school that believed in the ability of bombing and air superiority to clinch a a battle. Sandy Wilson, together with General Schwarzkopf, took the alternative view that wars were not won in the air; ground still had to be captured and held. Hence the need to build up army strength within the coalition.

Sandy Wilson was by now well established as the British forces commander with Saudi leaders and other Gulf figures. He had succeeded in building up a close working relationship with General Norman Schwarzkopf, not always easy to achieve given Stormin' Norman's reputation for irascible impatience. Liaison between our air forces was going well. Relations were also sweet on General Khalid's front. But Sandy Wilson was shortly to be uprooted, to his disappointment and against the background of a strong rearguard action in Whitehall from the RAF. With the arrival of 7 Brigade, however, British military strength in theatre would increase eight-fold, with the Army predominant. The political view in Whitehall, led by the Prime Minister, was that this called for a soldier with full general rank as commander. The RAF would retain an air marshal in the joint commander's post at High Wycombe. Moreover, the current Chief of the Defence Staff, Air Chief Marshal Sir David Craig, was also from the RAF. So the change was made, with the appointment as Commander, British Forces of General Sir Peter de la Billière, Mrs Thatcher's personal choice for the post. He was fortunate to have had the way well prepared by Sandy Wilson.

CHAPTER 6

Business as Usual

Iraq's sudden strike at Kuwait on the night of 2 August came as a rude shock to the large British community in Saudi Arabia as well as to British expatriates elsewhere through the lower Gulf. For those in Kuwait, and in Iraq itself, the invasion was the start of an agonising ordeal of captivity, separation and danger, as Saddam Hussein played cat and mouse with their safety and sought to use them as pawns in his efforts to divide the coalition raised against him.

In Saudi Arabia an initial sense of alarm within the whole foreign community was heightened further when it became apparent that Iraqi forces were gathering in strength along the frontier, with little to block their rolling forward to seize the oilfields and cities of the Kingdom's Eastern Province. This would also put Riyadh at risk, as the capital was largely dependent for its water supply on a pipeline running some 350 kilometres inland from desalination plants at Jubail on the eastern coast. The sense of unease was made more acute by the Saudi government's policy of discouraging the reporting in the local press of Iraq's military build-up against Kuwait during the final days of July, followed by the prohibition on local reporting of the Iraqi invasion for 48 hours following the event.

The British expatriate community of some 30,000 resident in Saudi Arabia was at the outset of the crisis the largest Western community in the Kingdom, slightly ahead of the American total, and over twice that of the French. Other substantial Western communities included Canadians, Germans, Australians, Italians and Irish. Foreign communities from Asian countries, notably the Indian subcontinent, the Philippines, Thailand, and, in the Arab world, from Yemen, Jordan and Egypt, were of a different order of magnitude altogether. The largest, from the Philippines, exceeded half a million. It is no exaggeration to say that Saudi Arabia's economic infrastructure, in social services, maintenance of utilities, agricultural and construction labour, commercial activity, and even baseline military support, depended on the presence of this army of foreign workers. Indeed, it was through their activity that Saudi Arabia had applied her oil wealth so successfully to the country's prosperous development over the previous three decades.

It was thus of crucial importance for Saudi Arabia to retain this foreign workforce in the face of the threat presented by Iraq's invasion of Kuwait. A mass exodus provoked by an epidemic of alarm would have had a grave effect on the functioning of the Kingdom. In this sensitive situation it was clear to us, as it was to the Saudi authorities, that the reaction and comportment of the British and American communities, which constituted the most extensive foreign presence at a managerial level, would be a major factor in setting the example for other communities, large and small. This meant that in our duty of making provision for the security of the British citizens under our charge, we in the embassy, together with those at the FCO in London who were responsible for the consular aspects of the crisis, had to bear in mind the impact which advice to our community might have on other national groups who might look to us for a lead. We also needed to consider how our responses might affect morale within the Saudi population among whom we lived.

All these aspects called for a balancing act which was not easy to maintain. As the crisis worked through to its climax there were occasions when it proved difficult to reconcile concern for the safety of our own people with the essential part which many of them were called to play on Saudi Arabia's home front. This required careful judgment and a network of communication on which our citizens could depend. Above all we had to retain the confidence of the British community in the advice we were giving them, and avoid arousing undue alarm. The contribution of the media at the UK end was not always helpful to this endeavour. It was very much to its credit that the British community as a whole carried on working with steadiness and good spirits throughout the long months of the crisis, and set an example from which other expatriate groups took heart, and which was much appreciated among Saudis.

Fortunately the advent of the summer holiday period, when many expatriates sought to take a break from the great summer heat of Arabia, meant that our community was already considerably reduced when the crisis arose at the beginning of August. Its numbers were for the most part divided equally across the Kingdom between Jedda, Riyadh and the Gulf cities of Jubail, Dammam, Al Khobar and Dhahran.

Of the 12,000 or so living in Jedda, most were engaged in commercial and manufacturing activity on behalf of British and Saudi firms with a number also employed by the national airline, Saudia, and in local hospitals. Riyadh's slightly smaller community had a more mixed composition of business people, medical staff, engineers and technicians with Saudi government departments, and BAe employees involved

in the Al Yamamah project and at the RSAF flying academy. In addition
there was the staff of our embassy and of the British Council's main cultural office in Saudi Arabia, comprising some 80 British expatriates
including families. Riyadh was also the centre for two British military
missions with the RSAF and the National Guard.

As for the Gulf cities, the two largest employers of British personnel
were BAe and Aramco, the state oil company. There was also an element
with local Saudi firms and in the newly-established petrochemical centre
at Jubail. All these larger centres of our community were served by
British-run schools, and each region also ran a businessmen's association. There were a few hundred more British citizens scattered through
smaller centres around the Kingdom, from the airbase at Tabuk near the
Jordanian border in the north-west down to Abha in the mountainous
south. In the main people tended to spend two or three years working in
the Kingdom, though some had lived there for considerably longer and
had developed strong feelings of attachment to the country and a familiarity with its desert environment and secluded society. British
expatriates had recently produced illustrated studies of Saudi plant and
bird life, as well as of the handsome traditional architecture of the towns
of central Nejd. A number of British women were married to Saudis.

The network of contact throughout the British community which we
put into effect from the beginning of the crisis had its centres in the
embassy in Riyadh, the consulate-general in Jedda and the small trade
office which we maintained in Al Khobar. By fortunate chance we had
undertaken an operation a few months previously to transfer the
standard register of all British citizens known to be in Saudi Arabia,
such as is maintained by all British diplomatic posts abroad against a
civil emergency, on to a computerised record to facilitate reference.
This exercise had afforded the opportunity to publicise the register and
ask all British citizens in the Kingdom to update their details. This had
brought a surprising number of new names out of the woodwork.

We had also taken steps to review the system whereby volunteers from
among the community acted as wardens in each residential centre and
compound and in major work locations, with the role of acting as the
main channel of communication between the consulates and British
families and individuals. This well-tried system had never had to be activated in the peaceful conditions of Saudi Arabia. But it was there to
hand and was quickly brought into effect when the balloon went up.
That it served us well throughout the most difficult moments of the
next seven months was due to the public spirit and commitment of the
wardens, numbering some 200, who gave their time to this key activity.

A second important channel for passing advice and instructions to the community during the crisis was by means of announcements from the FCO in London over the short-wave English-language broadcasts of the BBC World Service. These could be issued at short notice, and could be counted on to reach a wide cross-section of the community who were staying closely tuned to BBC bulletins. A complication here, however, was that the same broadcasts were also listened to by many English-speaking Saudis and other Gulf Arabs, as well as serving as an information point for expatriates of other nationalities. This meant that any messages for our community that sounded too stark or alarmist in tone could set off a wider reaction. We had therefore to be careful in the preparation of the text of any advice we put out over the BBC, and depend on them to relay it accurately over the air and without embell-ishment. In the event we found this was not always carried out scrupulously, resulting in some instances of confusion on the part of our community and of suspicion on the part of the Saudi authorities that our solidarity might be less solid than we professed.

Immediately following the invasion the FCO manned its emergency consular unit, housed in a specially-equipped suite of rooms in the base-ment of the old India Office in Whitehall. The political element of this emergency team had already been activated under the supervision of Rob Young, the head of the Middle East department, who had long experience of Middle Eastern affairs. The consular unit was from the start preoccupied with the plight of the several thousand British citizens caught in Kuwait, as well as the smaller number of British technicians who were working on projects in Iraq. We lost no time in working out with the consular unit a line for use with the community on the ground as well as for enquiries from the public and press at home.

In this initial advice we encouraged people to carry on with their work and daily lives. If they were out of the country on leave, as we knew many to be, they were recommended to extend their absence until the situation became clearer. We did not suggest that those pre-sent in the Kingdom had any cause to leave, unless they were living in the Eastern Province. In this case we suggested that dependents might consider taking a short break outside. But we deliberately avoided any encouragement of a large-scale departure.

On 7 August we sought to give this guidance a wider circulation, partly in response to a fresh wave of concern among the community. This was a result of sensationalist claims of danger to those in Saudi Arabia which had begun to feature in the domestic media in Britain and was having the effect of alarming relatives of many expatriates and lead-ing to family pressure for them to come home. We needed to counter this unhelpful process before it got out of hand. Accordingly we agreed with London that the BBC should be asked to carry in a news bulletin the line we were taking to reassure people. It should be presented as guidance rather than in the form of a FCO statement. In the nervous mood prevailing at that vulnerable time we feared the latter course might imply a greater risk than the situation warranted, and might also have a knock-on effect on other communities.

This tactic backfired, however. Not finding themselves constrained by a formal text, the BBC news staff succumbed to the temptation to ginger up the guidance, giving the impression that our advice amounted to urging people to take a break from the Gulf area, a line not far short of a call to evacuate. The FCO promptly issued a statement correcting the picture, which an impenitent BBC still managed to misreport. The damage was done, and for us a lesson had been learnt. The broadcasters' irresponsible gloss upset the community and led to a stream of anxious telephone calls to our consulates, as well as raising the level of alarm at home. A few people even showed up with their luggage at the embassy gate, asking to be repatriated. We sought to talk through their worries before passing them across to British Airways. The airline was fortunately continuing to fly scheduled services into Riyadh and Dhahran despite the shock to crew morale which had resulted from the misadventure of a British Airways 747 having landed at Kuwait just before the Iraqi airborne assault on the airport, with the result that its British passengers and crew were being held captive.

This edgy period also saw sharp exchanges between radio interviewers in London and those of us in the embassy in Riyadh who were caught to take part in telephone broadcasts. Requests for interviews were thick on the ground in the early days, particularly as few British or other foreign correspondents had managed to secure visas to enter the Kingdom. We were thus the only eye-witnesses to hand. These contacts were shared in Riyadh between myself, Derek Plumbly, Clive Woodland, the consul-general, and Nick Abbott, our information officer who carried the main burden of our busy relationship with the press throughout the crisis.

I recall some two days after the invasion being rung by one of the early morning radio news programmes and finding myself plunged into a live, and somewhat hostile, interview at the hands of Angela Rippon, who accused me of adopting a cavalier attitude towards the safety of British expatriates in the east. She implied that by urging them to stay calm and carry on rather than advising them to leave, I was putting them at risk. They were already within range of Iraq's artillery, so what was I going to do about it? I pointed out this was not the case; the nearest British community to the frontier was at Jubail, which was still some 320 kilometres south. 'We have experts in the studio,' I was told tartly, 'who can vouch they are much closer.' 'Then I suggest they get a better map,' I could only reply.

This temptation on the part of the media at home in the early stages to overstate the predicament of British people in Saudi Arabia and elsewhere in the Gulf began to have an erosive effect on morale, and to complicate our task of keeping people steady. Worried families, worked up by nightly television film of Iraq's military forces in Kuwait and speculative reports of Iraq's capability in chemical weapons, as well as by the martial predictions of armchair pundits who joined Peter Snow in moving model divisions around the desert on the BBC's *Newsnight* sand-table, began pressing their relatives working in the Gulf to come out of danger. Stories of Iraqi brutality, brought by Kuwaitis who were still being let out of their country and a small number of British expatriates who had managed to get out through the Iraqi net, also fed the disquiet. We did our best to counter it, though it must be said that in those first critical days before help got under way the danger was a real one.

Fortunately we had a strong consular staff in Riyadh, which had been reinforced in recent years in step with the rapid growth of the British community. Clive Woodland and the consul, Alan Sutton, were both well cast for the task of conveying confidence, being caring of manner and large of frame. Together with the two vice-consuls, Patrick Owens and Simon Wilson, they gave much time to going the rounds of the various establishments in Riyadh and other centres where there were substantial numbers of British employees, to reassure people that there was no cause for fear and that their security was very much a priority, with arrangements in hand to look after them should things deteriorate. We all took turns to give regular briefings on the situation to the community wardens, who were diligent in passing advice down the line. In this crucial contact work we were helped by the service attachés, who brought a useful military perspective to bear on the briefings. The attachés were also much in demand by other Western embassies to reassure their communities, though some fainter hearts may not have found the descriptions of the growing firepower of the coalition's air defences around their homes all that comforting.

The highest level of anxiety within the British community was to be found in the Gulf coast cities, where people were closest to the shadow of Iraqi military activity. Our consular staff had from the outset been receiving a stream of worried telephone calls from residents in this area, by night as well as by day. I asked Peter Ford, the counsellor in the embassy in Riyadh responsible for trade work, to move across to the east to reinforce our two hard-pressed officials who had been dealing with the crisis there.

Not surprisingly the flow of business visitors from Britain had tailed off to virtually zero, and the stout few who did come out were being asked to pay ludicrous premiums at home for insurance cover.

A particular point of concern to us was the large BAe workforce engaged in training and technical support for the RSAF Tornado and Hawk aircraft based at Dhahran. It was essential to Saudi Arabia's air defence, and by extension to our whole relationship with the Saudis at this critical time, that this group should carry on with their activity, target though the Dhahran airbase was likely to be should the Iraqi's unleash an attack. The BAe personnel in the east were responding well to the strains of the crisis, with a cool and firm leadership from their manager at Dhahran, Phil Champness, who had the experience behind him of some ten year' working in the Kingdom. The BAe staff had earned credit in Saudi eyes from the outset for staying at their work when expatriate employees of certain other key foreign firms working in the Kingdom, including Japanese and Americans, had been pulled out without warning.

It was therefore worrying when the chief executive for the Al Yamamah project, Don McClen, came to see me in Riyadh within a few days of the invasion to ask whether I was considering strengthening the advice we were giving to those living in the east that dependents should consider taking a break outside. The BBC's irresponsible misrepresentation of the FCO advice had had the effect of unsettling the BAe personnel and their families in the Dhahran region, and some in Riyadh too. The BAe board in Britain believed that the danger of an attack on the Eastern Province was real. Families at home were worried, and had been pressing the firm to do something. The company were therefore on the point of chartering aircraft to bring out all dependents from the Dhahran area, though employees would remain. It would help with the presentation of this step if it were to coincide with our official advice.

I knew both Don McClen, and his director back home, Mike Rouse, to be steady operators, in no way given to bouts of alarm. He was carrying a heavy responsibility for his 4,000 or so personnel and their families in the Kingdom, many engaged in work essential to Saudi Arabia's defence. I told him that, much as I would have liked to ease the difficult decision which BAe were proposing to make, the mixture of factors which we had to take into account did not justify the withdrawal of British families from the Eastern Province for the present. Military help from abroad to reinforce Saudi Arabia's defence was on its way. Saddam Hussein had stayed his hand so far over an attack on the Kingdom; indeed the time for such a move might now be passing. In this situation we had to think very carefully before taking an initiative to pull out people on the ground, and before any other foreign government had decided to do so.

BAe were not the only large employer of British staff in the area to be affected. There was also Aramco, with around 1,000 British personnel and families spread through the oilfields and facilities along the Gulf coast. Many were now outside the country on leave, which helped. But for the present I saw no need to insist that dependents should go. A decision on withdrawal at this stage would thus have to be for BAe to make. I could see that in their case it might help the morale of those who worked on the airbase to know that their families were at home.

Don McClen accepted the position and saw that the company would have to take its own course. Several hundred dependents were flown out over the next few days. The company's decision did not, however, have support from the senior MoD official responsible for overseeing the Al Yamamah project, Air Marshal Ron Stewart Paul, who came out quickly from London to check that the morale of BAe employees was holding up and that the large RAF team, based in Saudi Arabia to ensure good working liaison between the RSAF and BAe, was not affected. He found both operations in good shape, and his own brisk approach to the dangers of the moment had a steadying effect. Once this issue was out of the way Don McClen and his BAe staff gave a resilient performance throughout the crisis, sometimes in dangerous conditions, which earned them the warm appreciation of the Saudis and did a great deal for the excellent climate of our military co-operation.

The return of the BAe families from Dhahran was of course headline news at home. It also provided another opportunity for provocative interviews suggesting scant official concern for the safety of those left behind. I took one of these radio calls on the morning the first BAe charter reached home. Fortunately I could hear on the monitor a preceding interview with a resilient lady, who identified herself as Mrs Jones from Peterborough, and who was protesting indignantly at the speed with which she had been uprooted from her husband and home in Saudi Arabia to be brought to England. As far as she was concerned they had all been getting on with their daily lives, so why all the fuss? Bless you, Mrs Jones, I thought, as I went on to commend her gameness. Her spirit was a tonic. I suspected the interviewer might be regretting having picked on this unflappable lady for a comment.

During these first nervous days we were also working hard to ensure that the various western missions in Riyadh, both those within the EC and others outside, kept in close step over the advice given to our communities. A premature move by one could start a chain reaction among others. This liaison took up a good deal of time but was well worth it. So far as the 11 EC embassies were concerned, we were fortunate to have in the revolving six months' presidency at the time the crisis blew up a wise and energetic Italian ambassador, Mario Maiolini, who was strongly committed to the belief that the EC should demonstrate in this affair its ability to work in unison on the ground, no matter how member governments might find themselves differing over the politics of confrontation with Iraq.

Mario Maiolini telephoned me on the morning of the invasion to suggest that he convene an immediate meeting of the 11 of us, and to ask for British support in establishing a common approach. I warmly endorsed this, and we all met together an hour later, for convenience sake in my house in the diplomatic quarter, to discuss where the night's dramatic events might be taking us and hear Mario Maiolini enjoin us all to work in close harmony over our communities. For the next month we met almost daily in the Italian residence, dropping thereafter to once or twice a week as the security situation entered a more stable phase with the buildup of forces. Under Mario Maiolini's watchful eye, and from January onwards under the lead of the Dutch ambassador, Heinrick Philipse, we achieved a real measure of practical co-operation, and set a solid example for other countries to follow.

This European co-operation was also valuable in our dealings with the Saudi authorities over the foreign communities. Much of Saudi Arabia's national infrastructure, particularly outside the military area, was inextricably tied up with the presence and performance of foreign civilian technicians. At the same time we could not have our citizens in a situation where they might find themselves detained by Saudi employers in circumstances of real danger. This awkward situation was not helped by Saudi Arabia's restrictive rules over the employment of foreign staff. These had been designed for the purpose of keeping a tight control over foreigners entering and leaving the Kingdom, partly to maximise employment openings for Saudis, but also for reasons of security and as a means of guarding Saudi Arabia's conservative way of life, ever a point of particular sensitivity for the Saudi regime and a source of inconvenience to expatriates.

The upshot was a cumbersome and bureaucratic system whereby almost all foreigners received visas providing for single entry only. To leave the country a fresh visa was required which might take several days to obtain, particularly from outside the main cities. If the person was returning to the Kingdom, the period of absence had to be stipulated for the purpose of re-entry. There were also controls on the movement of expatriates within the country, though these tended to be less rigorously enforced. Foreigners were meant to obtain a pass from the regional governorate if they were travelling outside its bounds. In addition wives and children of expatriate employees were not issued with their own identity cards – or *iqamas* – but carried copies of that of the employee. This could complicate separate travel.

In practice these restrictions were not as inhibiting as they sound. The Saudi immigration and security authorities generally applied them efficiently and in good faith. But they were time-consuming and had not been designed for an emergency situation where large numbers of expatriates might seek to depart or move around the country at short notice. The headache which this produced for our consular services was compounded by a practice, not governed by regulation but to which many Saudi employers were strongly attached, of keeping the passports of foreign employees in their custody. In theory this was done to facilitate the administration of visa procedures, but in practice it afforded a means of tying workers to their employer. It was particularly applied to labourers from Third World countries, whose total numbers in the Kingdom ran into millions, but many Western employees found themselves in the same predicament.

One of our first tasks therefore was to work out with the Saudi authorities some way to ease these restrictions on the movement of our expatriates, to cover an eventuality in which evacuation became necessary in the face of a successful Iraqi attack or even air raids involving the use of chemical weapons. The sense of having their exit in an emergency blocked was already giving rise to problems of morale among some British and other expatriate groups, particularly those employed in the medical services and with the national oil company, where managers sought to hold on to their expatriate staff for operational reasons.

Within a few days of the invasion the Saudi Foreign Ministry sensibly took the initiative by calling all ambassadors with communities in the Kingdom to a meeting, at which we were assured that the security situation was under control and that there was no cause for foreigners to feel alarm. At this early and uncertain stage of the crisis we could see, as could the Saudis, that there was a certain element of piety in such an assurance. But we also realised how important it was for us all to demonstrate our solidarity. The Saudi official who presided over this meeting, Jaafar Alaqani, went on to complain about the unfortunate BBC report calling on people to leave the Eastern Province, and claimed this had a widely unsettling effect. He saw no need for us to put out such advice. I assured him it did not represent our official guidance, and that we had insisted on the broadcasting of a correction. But, speaking for many of the others present, I said we must see an easing of the exit regulations to facilitate free movement in an emergency. This should not lead to an early flight of expatriates, but rather would give them the heart to stay at their jobs once they felt their exit was not blocked. We would meanwhile make a point of keeping in close touch with the Saudis over the advice we gave to our community on their security.

Regulations are not, however, easily changed in Saudi Arabia's cautious bureaucracy. The Foreign Ministry took our points readily enough, and the next month saw a succession of meetings in which the Europeans and Americans took a leading part. It took strong intervention on the part of the Foreign Ministry with their colleagues in the Interior Ministry to secure a concession whereby foreigners would be issued more rapidly with exit visas, including a more generous interval for return. It was also tacitly accepted that in an emergency situation individuals could leave on the authority of a document issued by their consulate.

These limited measures were sufficient for our needs, and helped give confidence to our expatriates. Pressure to depart began to ease, and people settled in to the new and unaccustomed routine of keeping an ear on the wireless and an eye on their warden, with a suitcase packed just in case. We failed, however, to get action obliging Saudi employers to give up the custody of passports. To their credit a number of private employers did so, recognising the psychological importance of this step for sustaining the morale and loyalty of their expatriate employees. We encouraged the practice as far as we could. But there remained pockets of employment where this did not apply. The morale of British employees in these areas was to call for particular attention in our consular work during the crisis.

Clive Woodland and others on the consular side in Riyadh and Al Khobar, as well as in Jedda despite its greater distance from the Iraqi threat, all spent much of these early weeks visiting places of work in the cities and towns around the Kingdom, where British communities existed, to give assurance on the security situation and explain how to keep in touch. Their travels took them to Abha and Najran in the south, and to Tabuk and Ha'il in the north. We devoted particular attention to the most exposed section of the community in the east, where Britons in employment included a number of women working as hospital nurses and as secretaries with Aramco.

When I went down to Dhahran in August to see the RAF operation, David Lloyd, who was in charge in Al Khobar, gathered many of our community in a hall on one of the compounds so we could talk things through. They were tense and going through a nervous time, despite the presence of military vehicles patrolling the area and the din of jet fighters overhead. I commended them on the way they had stuck things out, pointing to the real contribution this was making to Saudi Arabia's performance at this time of unprecedented crisis, and to the example they were setting for others who looked to them as one of the largest Western communities for a lead.

To their worried enquiries about security I responded with a description, in considerably more confident tones than would have been justified ten days previously, of the extent of the defensive shield now being put in place to protect the Eastern Province. They could start to relax under this umbrella, noisy as it might be. It was by now very unlikely that any Iraqi aircraft, or even missiles should Saddam Hussein decide to use them, would get through. Moreover, Saddam could now have no doubt that any attack would lead to a massive retaliation. We considered the chances of the Iraqis using chemical weapons to be remote. The defensive shield was being strengthened with the new anti-missile Patriot launcher system, the bulky shapes of which they could already see in position around Dhahran airfield.

As for evacuation, there was no call for this at the present. We had our plans in hand should it become necessary to advise them to go. Such information would be given to them through wardens or over the BBC, who I expected to get it right next time. In such an event we would ensure employers did not get in the way of their going. But for the present they should carry on.

This explanation seemed to produce a measure of relief, though there were still a few doubtful faces. I was particularly asked about the position of the large group who worked for Aramco, where the management was making departure difficult and talking of applying financial penalties to expatriate employees who insisted on leaving. This pressure was having a particularly demoralising effect on female employees, many of whom were being pressed to leave by alarmed relatives at home.

Morale among Aramco expatriates, and others in the eastern cities, had not been helped by a circular purporting to emanate from the company, but more likely the result of a misplaced attempt at graveyard humour, in which employees were recommended as a security precaution to take a careful look out of the window before going out in the morning. Should they notice anything untoward, such as birds falling out of trees or cars crashing into each other, this indicated a gas attack, in which case they should stay indoors. In the prevailing mood of jitters this broadsheet had aroused some alarm, though there was still sufficient humour in the community for someone to comment that, if people driving into each other was sufficient cause to stay indoors, then he would never go to work anyway as it was nothing unusual.

David Lloyd had arranged for us to call on the president of Aramco at its Dhahran headquarters the next morning, when I took this problem up with him. Dr Ali Naimi responded seriously. It was of course critical to the defence of the Kingdom, as well as to the broader objective of maintaining a steady flow of oil to international markets, that Aramco carried on functioning. He agreed, however, that expatriate staff were showing loyalty and sticking at their work. It might therefore be better to release the few who were fearful and wanted to go, as this should help the morale of those who stayed.

Some easing of Aramco's practice did follow, but relations with their expatriate staff never fully recovered during the crisis. At a meeting which Clive Woodland held with the company's British employees some weeks later, the problem of liberty to leave surfaced again, when it was claimed the embassy should have done more to get this settled. Discussion started to become heated, but turned into good-natured resignation when one speaker reminded his colleagues that they were after all there for the money and should get on with the job. No one quarrelled with that. In the event the large British staff in Aramco more than did their bit to keep the oil flowing through the crisis, and during the fight when it came.

In a small gesture to help convey the impression back home that the community was carrying on in good spirits, and to counter some of the more alarmist reporting of those early days, I made the road trip from Riyadh to Al Khobar for this August visit in the official Rolls Royce. Being ten years old it was asking quite a bit of the elegant vehicle to cover the 800-kilometre return journey in an August shade temperature of some 110 °F. But she made it without mishap, and provided some upbeat television shots for British networks looking for a bit of colour and a change from warplanes.

Ali, the Yemeni driver, and I had an eerie drive across the featureless landscape of dunes and baked scrub through which the Riyadh–Dammam motorway snakes a monotonous route. The road, usually bustling with convoys of heavy trucks hauling food, fuel and other supplies from the Gulf ports to Riyadh and the interior of Nejd, was almost deserted, an indication of the extent to which the shock of Iraq's invasion had brought Saudi Arabia's economic life to a near standstill even two weeks on. The journey afforded a sharp contrast to the palmy days when I had last visited the Eastern Province, a few weeks prior to the invasion, and had returned to Riyadh in elegant style in the Saudi Railways royal coach, which had been attached to the Dammam–Riyadh express.

As Ali and I now made our solitary way we reflected how everyone must be lying low, with their ears close to the radio. Nearing the coastal cities the highway began to fill with the unaccustomed sight of long convoys of American and Saudi military vehicles – trucks, artillery, personnel carriers and tanks on transporters – heading north towards the frontier. In the reverse direction came groups of dusty cars with Kuwaiti licence plates, crammed with baggage and carrying families who had managed to make their escape through the Iraqi military lines and into Saudi Arabia, often by cross-desert routes. The polished Rolls made a conspicuous contrast in all this company.

The visit to our community on the Gulf coast left me in no doubt that this was the quarter where we needed to have the closest liaison. As the press corps built up over the months, with its largest contingent alongside British and American troops in the east, so it became all the more important to keep in touch with British civilians in the area. David Lloyd and the two vice-consuls, Rick Girdlestone and Geoff Plant, were indefatigable here with great support from their wives and the dedicated local wardens. Among the most vulnerable were the hundred or so Britons working in the petrochemical plants and other industrial facilities at Jubail, 80 kilometres up the coast towards Kuwait.

John Wakeham, who in addition to being Secretary of State for Energy was also a member of Mrs Thatcher's crisis committee within the Cabinet, came on a brief visit to Riyadh at the beginning of October to discuss issues of oil production policy with the Saudis, including whether the British government had the powers to divert North Sea crude to help Saudi Arabia meet the coalition's needs should her fields be put out of action. I took him across to Jubail to meet the British and Dutch staff of the refinery there, jointly owned by Shell and Aramco. For this trip we were lent the executive jet owned by the Royal Commission for Jubail, the authority responsible for the planning and administration of this new industrial city. Its director was Prince Abdullah bin Faisal bin Turki, a nephew of King Fahd and a graduate of Nottingham University. Prince Abdullah, or AFT as we knew him, was an unfailing source of support to us and the British forces based in Jubail in numerous ways throughout the course of the Kuwait crisis.

John Wakeham had a positive meeting with the Shell expatriates. He made it clear that were they to come under threat we had plans to evacuate them out of danger. Meanwhile they were, through their work at the refinery, making an important contribution to the ability of Saudi Arabia and her partners to stand up to Iraq's threat. From what Tom Higgins, Shell's energetic representative in the Kingdom, told me after the visit, these words from a Cabinet minister had given heart to both expatriates and Saudis at the plant.

But while things were to continue to look tense for those in the east, the growing evidence that the Iraqis were no longer poised to attack Saudi Arabia, but were instead taking up defensive positions along the frontier, meant that by the last week of August we felt able to relax our advice somewhat over travel to the Kingdom. Our consular colleagues in the FCO were still finding themselves under constant pressure from families, the press and members of Parliament to play safe to the maximum degree. They agreed, however, that it was no longer necessary to discourage travel to the centre and west of the Kingdom. This helped encourage those living in Riyadh and Jedda to resume a more normal pattern of life, and to bring their children back to start the new term at the British schools. It also reopened the way for businessmen to visit, although such activity was, with the exception of military business, to remain at a low ebb for the next eight months. We still discouraged a return of dependents to the east, with the result that the two British community schools there began their autumn term at about one-third strength.

When Douglas Hurd came out to see King Fahd and Prince Saud, the Foreign Minister, in Jedda early in September, we arranged for him to meet with wardens and other leading figures in the British community there. He joined them in the hall of the consulate-general compound, and emphasised the importance of justifying our reputation for steadiness in the period that lay ahead. His words of encouragement were subsequently circulated among members of the community elsewhere in the Kingdom through the newsletters of the three regional British business groups.

In fact, Jedda was never within range of Iraqi attack from the north, though people there were disquieted in the early stages by unfounded rumours of Iraqi missiles in Sudan and Yemen. Such risk as did exist came from the possibility of Iraqi-inspired terrorism or sabotage, of which there was an isolated instance later when shots were fired in Jedda at a bus carrying USAF personnel. In the event, when it came to war many British expatriates in Jedda gave helpful shelter to their compatriots from nearer the action.

As we moved into autumn the community's mood entered a more stable phase. The risks had for the moment subsided into a state of phoney war which we felt could last some while. Two British employees of Aramco chose to ignore the crisis altogether, and were indignant to find themselves apprehended by the Saudi police while on an ill-considered birdwatching expedition in the vicinity of the oil pipeline to Jordan, north of Jubail. David Lloyd had his work cut out convincing the Saudis that, despite their presence in a military zone complete with cameras and binoculars, the interests of the pair did not extend beyond ornithology.

Conversation was, of course, constantly focused on the crisis and the fast-growing presence of American, British and other troop contingents, with their desert-brown overalls providing a startling contrast to the immaculate white dress of the Saudi population. It was a time for humour, too. The enterprising British business group in Al Khobar entered the competition to come up with the catchiest T-shirt with a vest bearing crossed Union Jack and Stars and Stripes with the caption 'These Colours Don't Run'. There was a rash of sardonic humour: 'What do Saddam Hussein and his father have in common?'; answer, 'Neither knew when to withdraw.' It all helped with morale.

Meanwhile our attention was becoming diverted towards the predicament of those being held within Kuwait, and with the growing number of British expatriates who were taking their chance in making a dash for the safety of the Saudi frontier. As early as 17 August, Iraq announced that all Westerners in Iraq and Kuwait were to be detained and held at key military and civil installations, in effect as hostages, though the Iraqi media sought to describe them as 'guests'.

International revulsion at this step was compounded, in Saudi Arabia as well as in the West, by television news pictures of Saddam Hussein patting the head of a young English boy, one of a group of women and children being detained in Iraq who had been marshalled to meet the President in a display intended to demonstrate they were being well treated. The boy, Stewart, did not conceal his aversion to finding himself in Saddam Hussein's embrace and the object of solicitous enquiries about his cornflakes ration. That this clumsy attempt at propaganda misfired so conclusively was due to the fortunate presence of a BBC television team led by John Simpson, one of a small and respectable band of Western journalists operating out of Baghdad who were not taken in by Iraq's information machine. They had just arrived, and were on hand to relay the charade to the outside world.

The taking of Western expatriates into custody, and the deployment of the men among them as a human deterrent shield at military locations while Iraq tried to bargain for their release, epitomised the tactics of ruthless terror which Saddam Hussein was prepared to employ to try to break the resolve of the international community standing up to him. Many Kuwaitis, and some Saudis too, were placed in detention within Iraq. Several hundred Britons were caught in this net, though a small group of employees of the Bechtel construction company managed to take refuge in the grounds of the spacious British embassy compound on the banks of the Tigris. Here they camped for several weeks in the eye of the media, with supplies from the embassy and encouragement from the ambassador, 'Hookey' Walker, to keep a stiff upper lip until their freedom could be secured without ransom.

Western women and children were soon allowed to leave, along with a multitude of Asian and Egyptian workers, by the rough expedient of decanting them into Jordan or Saudi Arabia. The Saudi government for its part took on the transportation of several thousand labourers across the Kingdom to Egypt. The Iraqi move was swiftly countered by a unanimous UN Security Council resolution demanding that all foreigners be permitted to leave. In advice which was to prove a source of controversy, the British government urged Britons in Kuwait first to lie low, and then to follow instructions for assembly issued by the occupying Iraqi authorities. They were discouraged from attempting to make a bolt for Saudi Arabia. This cautious advice made sense in the violent circumstances prevailing in Kuwait City at the time, and when Iraqi troops were known to be patrolling the frontier.

We were therefore surprised in the last days of August, when the Iraqis had started to round up foreigners and take them into custody, to find a trickle of British expatriates joining the southwards exodus from Kuwait and daring a dash over the desert frontier. The news reached us first in a telephone message from a remote border post at Al Ruq'i, at the western extremity of the Saudi–Kuwaiti frontier, where the regional governor, a local sheikh, asked for the embassy's help in handling these British exfiltrators, as they came to be known in the jargon.

Simon Wilson, one of our vice-consuls in Riyadh, readily agreed to drive forthwith to Al Ruq'i, a distance of some 480 kilometres, to set up a reception point for Britons reaching Saudi Arabia by this route and help them on their way to Dhahran, where they could catch flights out of the Kingdom. We also made this a contact point for other Western escapees from Kuwait. It was less necessary to have a consular checkpoint at the main road crossing into Saudi Arabia at Al Khafji on the coast, as the Saudi Frontier Force were accustomed to refugees there and the road ran on south to Dhahran. Moreover, Al Ruq'i appeared to offer a safer route for evading Iraqi patrols.

Simon Wilson set himself up at the border with a table and flag. So that there should be no doubt as to his identity, he also brought a solar topee from his collection of headgear, a sensible precaution in the noonday sun. This led to a report in the next issue of the embassy's 'underground' newsletter on the crisis that a member of the élite consular guerilla force had been sent to the front line to interrogate Iraqi applicants for entry to Britain, with a visa stamp for a weapon. He was replaced in this vigil a week later by Warrant Officer Dave Muir of the defence section, and in mid-September the watch was taken over by consul Alan Sutton. We then stood down, but resumed the checkpoint for a spell at the end of the month when a second brief wave of British exfiltrators appeared.

Thereafter the flow stopped, as the remaining Britons were either rounded up as hostages or saw out the next five months until liberation in hiding under the protection of the movement established by groups of resourceful Kuwaitis to resist the Iraqi occupation. Sandy Wilson gave considerable thought to the possibility of an airdrop of food to help the small group who remained shut up in the British embassy compound in Kuwait City, but the idea had to be dropped as impracticable. We managed, however, to maintain an erratic radio voice-link with our colleagues there, whose plight was becoming increasingly grim.

By early October some 160 British citizens had managed to make their escape through Al Ruq'i. They were quickly sent on their way home with the help of British Airways. Several were able to give us useful, if sombre, accounts of Iraqi strength in Kuwait and of the brutal retribution which was being meted out to Kuwaitis who defied the invaders.

Not all escapees made it, however. Particularly tragic was the case of Douglas Croskery, who set off in early October across the desert towards Al Ruq'i in a four-wheel drive vehicle. With not far to go to the frontier he stopped to help a Kuwaiti family push their car out of a patch of soft sand in which it had become bogged. As he went back to his own vehicle an Iraqi army truck appeared. One of the soldiers from it stopped him and shot him in cold blood. The Kuwaiti group he had helped to save managed to cross the frontier and gave an account of his heroic action to the Saudi border guards. The Saudis later went into Kuwait to recover the vehicle, but all traces of Douglas Croskery's body had been removed and despite extensive searches it was never found.

The governor of the Eastern Province, Prince Mohammed bin Fahd, rang me that night from Dammam as soon as he received the report from Al Ruq'i of this brutal murder. He took a direct hand in efforts to discover what had happened. The tragedy was widely reported and probably served to discourage others from attempting what had by now become a very hazardous journey.

Kuwaitis themselves were by this time being encouraged by the Iraqis to leave their country in what looked like a deliberate policy of depopulation, with several thousand crossing the Al Khafji border point each day to add to those who had already taken advantage of Saudi Arabia's refuge. By late October when the flow dried up it was estimated by our Kuwaiti contacts that nearly a half of Kuwait's national population of some 800,000 was now abroad, with the largest number in Saudi Arabia, and others taking refuge elsewhere in the Gulf and in Egypt, Britain, France and the USA. The Saudis told me some 65,000 Kuwaiti-registered cars had crossed into the Kingdom. It came as a shock to Kuwaiti women to find they could not drive during their Saudi refuge.

For the Saudis this second sudden influx of refugees brought with it the risk that the Iraqis would try to infiltrate agents and saboteurs into the Kingdom under cover of the Kuwaiti exodus. Fortunately an official of the Kuwaiti Interior Ministry had the considerable presence of mind at the time of the invasion to bring out with him a disk with the computerised citizenship records. It passed through the Iraqi frontier guards concealed in a baby's nappies. The details were incorporated in Dammam into a fresh data bank using facilities provided by a local businessman of Kuwaiti origin, and proved a invaluable record for checking the identity of those coming across and so trapping any Iraqi infiltrators.

Many Kuwaitis who stayed behind carried on a clandestine resistance to the occupation despite the risks of brutal retribution if they were caught. For several weeks they were able to get messages out to contacts in Saudi Arabia through the Kuwaiti mobile telephone network, which the Iraqis initially overlooked in their takeover of Kuwait's communications system.

For Western expatriates in Kuwait and Iraq, however, release had now become the object of a disgraceful game of political ransom. In his misconceived conviction that such traffic in human safety could serve to divide the solidarity of the international front ranged against Iraq, Saddam sought to negotiate the release of detained citizens of major Western states in return for political gestures and visits to Baghdad by prominent Western figures. In the event this trafficking earned Iraq nothing but opprobrium, and was terminated in early December by Iraq with the release of all remaining Western hostages, a major reversal of policy by Saddam Hussein under the pretext that by this time the detentions had secured for Iraq an interval in which to improve her defences against attack. In practice the solid wall of international condemnation, mobilised by the British and other Western governments whose citizens were being held hostage, played a part in leading him to reconsider the wisdom of the detentions, which even those Arab leaders most sympathetic to him made no attempt to justify.

There were two sources of international influence where our efforts to urge protest met with muted response. The International Committee of the Red Cross took the position that, to preserve their neutral status and responsibility under the Geneva Conventions to secure access to prisoners in conflict situations, they could not afford to be drawn into criticism of this kind. In the event this profession of impartiality got them nowhere with the Iraqis, who consistently denied them access to detainees and military prisoners. The local Iraqi Red Crescent, however, managed to its credit to visit some of those held and report on their condition. My Italian colleague, Mario Maiolini, and I also suggested the Vatican might raise its voice in support of the hostages' cause. Approaches were made by the Italians and by John Broadley, our ambassador to the Holy See. But again we found a reluctance to become involved. A determining factor here may have been concern for the consequences which Vatican criticism might have held for the small Chaldaean Christian church in Iraq, which was in communion with Rome. Nevertheless the silence was a disappointment.

Moreover, our own front was not entirely united. During the weeks prior to the decision to release the hostages we were treated to the galling spectacle of a trail of Western personalities, starting with Edward Heath in mid-October, visiting Saddam Hussein, to the benefit of Iraq's propaganda machine, to solicit the release of their nationals. Unofficial delegations came from Germany (led by ex-Chancellor Brandt), France, Italy, Ireland, the USA (in the shape of visits by Jesse Jackson and Mohammed Ali), Japan and others, including a conciliatory call by Tony Benn.

In response to these supplicants to Saddam Hussein's court, token packages of detainees, both men and families, were allowed to leave. In some cases medical and food supplies were sent in return. Attempts were made to keep up the fiction that the hostages were living in comfort by such devices as televising a grotesque Thanksgiving dinner given for a group of American detainees at a Baghdad country club and hosted by the Iraqi Foreign Ministry. The Iraqis also made a concerted but fruitless effort to use the French detainees to sap France's political commitment to the coalition. A Soviet special envoy, Yevgeni Primakov, negotiated at the end of October the departure of some 3,000 Soviet citizens working in Iraq, including military advisers, in return for an assurance of Soviet efforts to work for a negotiated outcome to the crisis.

All this contact with Baghdad over the hostages inevitably had the effect Iraq intended of raising in Saudi minds doubts over our commitment to our stated policy of no compromise with Iraq. To counter this we made the most of statements by British ministers dissociating the government from any moves to kowtow to Saddam Hussein over the hostages, while stressing the illegality of Iraq's action in holding them in captivity around the country. Our refusal to respond to Iraq's efforts to cut deals over the detainees received a boost in terms of publicity when on 4 October three British technicians working on a gas platform on the Iraqi shore of the Shatt al Arab waterway succeeded in reaching Saudi Arabia in a daring escape in a small open boat.

By fortunate coincidence Grania and I had driven down to the

Eastern Province that morning to join the British community in a reception on board HMS *York*, the flagship of the Royal Navy flotilla in the Gulf which was on a brief visit to Dammam. The huge port presented an astonishing sight with acres of compounds already filled with American military equipment, which was now reaching the Gulf in a special sealift operation from the USA. The tonnage of cargo thus carried eventually exceeded by four times the amount shipped across the English Channel in support of the D-Day landings in 1944.

We nearly came to grief on the journey down, as the armoured Range Rover with which I had recently been provided as a security measure had a tyre blow-out and, being heavy with armour plate, went out of control in the middle of the desert highway full of speeding long-distance trucks. Only skilled driving by Ali saved the situation. It was no consolation to be subsequently told by the manufacturer that an armoured Range Rover should not be driven at speeds over 80 kilometres an hour owing to its instability; Saudi Arabia was far too large a country to cruise around at that speed. So we had the car exchanged for a more nimble armoured Jaguar, having put the Rolls temporarily into retirement.

During the afternoon, while seeing some Saudi contacts, I heard of the presence in the International Hotel at Dhahran airport of the gas engineers, Ivan Manning and his two colleagues. The party, which included two Frenchmen, had come ashore the previous day at Mina al Saud, an oilfield terminal just south of the Kuwaiti frontier, and had spent the night recovering with the Saudi coastguard at Al Khafji before being driven down to Dhahran. Together with David Lloyd and Rick Girdlestone, I went round to the hotel to meet the group and arrange for their prompt departure for London. Clearly there was going to be much press interest in their escape, not least because the hotel where they had been taken was also serving as the centre for all foreign press activity in the Eastern Province. Many journalists would be around, keen to make the most of this gallant episode. Yet presentation would need to be carefully handled, to minimise the risk of an Iraqi reaction which would make the lot of Western hostages even harder, or lead to reprisals.

On getting to the hotel I found the trio with the governor, Prince Mohammed, and in the course of being interviewed by the Saudi press and television. They were tired but elated at their escape. It had been a close-run thing. Unlike most Western males held in Iraq and Kuwait, they had not been sent to camps at strategic military sites but had been obliged to carry on with their contracted work on the gas platform. Under cover of darkness the five had slipped downstream in the workboat with limited food and fuel, and with the general idea of making their way east across the Gulf to an Iranian port.

Having set this course, however, they had second thoughts about the reception they might receive in Iran, with which at that time Britain had no relations. They therefore turned about and set off south-east, hoping to skirt the Kuwaiti coast and make landfall in Saudi Arabia. It then occurred to them there might be mines about, so they spent the night and the next day on anxious watch. When they came close to the coast they saw offshore oil installations, but had no means of telling whether these lay in Saudi Arabia or Kuwait. They headed for the nearest point but then decided to go on a bit further. Finally they hailed a boat full of very surprised Japanese, who took them back to their base.

By good fortune they had reached the most northerly oil terminal in Saudi territory. Had the party gone ashore at the first point, they would have fallen back into Iraqi hands. The Saudi coastguard commander at Al Khafji debriefed them and gave them a chance to rest. He also to their surprise gave each of them 5,000 riyals, equivalent to about £800, which was the bounty generously offered by the Saudi government to each person taking refuge from Kuwait, to help meet their immediate expenses. The five went into the souk to replace their tattered wardrobe. It was a bit like passing 'go' in a game of Monopoly.

It seemed to me that with this story to tell there was much to be said for letting Ivan Manning and his colleagues give the foreign press an account of their escape, provided they revealed no details of locations and gave no encouragement to others to risk similar hazards. It could give a morale-boosting lift to public opinion in those countries engaged in the confrontation with Iraq. In any case over 100 British and foreign journalists were now gathered in the press hall, clamouring to meet the party. The French pair had been refused clearance to give an interview, apparently on instructions from Paris. This had not improved the journalists' humour. Having ascertained from the trio that, for all their exhaustion, they were game to go through with a press conference along the lines we had worked out together, I secured by telephone the agreement of the FCO. This was given with some hesitation in view of the predicament of our several hundred hostages still in Iraq or in hiding in Kuwait, but we were rightly allowed to go ahead.

In the event the trio gave a great performance. It must have been an alarming sensation to find themselves suddenly the cynosure of the world's media interest, facing rows of cameras and journalists firing questions, while they were still in a state of some bewilderment at their adventure. One of them told me this experience was more harrowing than the escape itself. But the story of their cockleshell flight gave everyone a timely lift. Predictably some British journalists sought to trip me up with questions about how we regarded the adventure in view of our advice to detainees not to take risks. 'Well done them,' I said. It was no time to grudge anyone their freedom. We somehow extricated our heroes from the crush and took them on board HMS *York*, where the Navy looked after them royally until it was time for their overnight British Airways flight home.

The plight of the hostages, and the cat-and-mouse game Saddam Hussein was playing with them, continued to be features of our lives right up to the time of their final release in December. As the probability of hostilities grew, much thought was given in military planning by the Americans and ourselves to ways in which they might be protected, or even rescued, in the event of air attacks on the military locations where many were being held in defiance of the Geneva Conventions of 1949 to which Iraq was a party. The International Red Cross, as the body responsible for upholding the Conventions, had by now with some intercession from ourselves succeeded in overcoming Saudi hesitations, stemming in part from the offence which their emblem of the cross might give to oversensitive elements among Saudi society, over the establishment of a special mission in Riyadh. A determined and dedicated Swiss, Arnold Leuthold, was appointed to head it.

Our awareness of the awful predicament of the British and other Western hostages was sustained daily by the Gulf Link programme broadcast each morning following the early news bulletin on the BBC World Service, with half an hour of messages from families and friends to those held in captivity. The contents of these programmes were brave and touching, a mixture of news, matters of resettlement where families had been released leaving husbands behind, and sometimes snatches of poetry or other words of encouragement. They were moving to hear and the programme set us off each morning with a lump in the throat. It was as well the messages were not rebroadcast on the British radio, for while they did a great deal for the morale of the hostages, they could have had a sapping effect on national opinion.

Just occasionally a less tender communication slipped through the screen. One morning a harsh voice came on the air, upbraiding a husband over a report that he had been 'comforting yourself in captivity'. It went on to warn that what was sauce for the gander was sauce for the goose. Not a message calculated to raise morale if one is staked out on an Iraqi airbase. Apparently there were also instances where messages of affectionate encouragement to a hostage arrived at the BBC from more than one woman, presenting the programme with a ticklish question over which to broadcast. Nevertheless the BBC did a great job with the programme, which was subsequently copied by Voice of America.

We also found ourselves involved with the Gulf Crisis Line, a telephone counselling service run by volunteers, which was set up in London in close co-operation with the consular emergency service of the FCO to help with advice and comfort for the families of those being detained or in hiding. Our daughter, Joanna, had been with us in Riyadh during July, working for the local office of UNICEF which was run by Sabah Allawi, an Iraqi exile in Saudi Arabia. The Iraqi threat put a stop to this employment, so Joanna joined the Crisis Line telephone team in London. When in early December Prince Abdullah bin Faisal, the direc- tor of the Royal Commission for Jubail, was sent by King Fahd with a group of senior Saudis to Britain to put across Saudi Arabia's determi- nation to see Iraq out of Kuwait, we suggested he and his party should visit the Gulf Crisis Line centre. The operation made such a favourable impression that Prince Abdullah offered to meet their telephone bills, a generous Saudi gesture to this dedicated group.

As the autumn advanced with still no indications of imminent hostil- ities, the British community got on with its job and kept in good spirits. This positive mood helped us to head off pressure from London, and from some of our European partners, for advice to leave to be strength- ened. By contrast, however, the advice being given to the large American community seemed at times almost too laid back, to the point where it unsettled many Americans. Right up to the eleventh hour before the January UN deadline for Iraq's withdrawal from Kuwait the American embassy was in the awkward position of having no authorisation to thin out its numbers in the Riyadh area. This appeared to be the result of a policy decision taken by the White House, largely as a result of lobbying by major American corporations operating in Saudi Arabia and the Gulf, fearful that advice of such a precautionary nature might have the effect of prompting an exodus of staff.

As a result of this policy, however, the American community found itself increasingly out of step with other expatriate groups as the crisis developed, resulting in unnecessary alarm. Having the largest Western community alongside the USA, we did our best to keep in step over advice. But this became progressively more difficult as the deadline approached and the risk of air attack rose.

To their credit the British schools stayed open, even in Al Khobar, though numbers both there and in Riyadh were down considerably as many families stayed away. Grania and others in the embassy made a point during this waiting period of visiting the schools and other organ- isations with which we had regular contact, to reinforce the image of business as usual. Mercifully the usual hectic autumn social round had subsided under the threat of hostilities, and anyway there was no time for a social circuit. But we kept up our contacts with Saudi friends. Indeed, these friendships took on a deeper quality under the stress of events, and helped our sense of common purpose in whatever lay beyond the present stage of phoney war.

Many of us in the embassy seized the occasional chance of a break into the desert. One November afternoon Grania and I took off with Nick Cocking in two Range Rovers for some sand-driving in the golden dunes which run like a sea below the sheer Tuwaiq escarpment to the west of Riyadh. It was a liberating sensation to traverse this spectacular terrain, a perfect way to relieve the strain under which we had been operating, even though we emerged minus one vehicle.

We also regained occasional touches of normality through the visits of undaunted businessmen and academics from Britain. Professor Rex Smith, who had been our daughter's Arabic professor at Durham University, turned up to lecture at the King Saud University on early Arabian inscriptions, and we passed an enjoyable evening at the home of Clive Smith, the British Council representative, in discussion of antiquities and other such interests with Saudi academics, thus putting the crisis firmly behind us for a few hours.

The arrival from late October of large numbers of army personnel in the east and at headquarters in Riyadh helped to ease further the sense of insecurity felt by the British and other expatriate communities following the shock of the summer. But it also put them on notice that hostilities to liberate Kuwait, with the attendant risks of Iraqi retaliation, were very much on the cards. Thus the 'promenade concerts' given each November in Riyadh by the expatriate concert band held a particular poignancy for us all that autumn, and 'Land of Hope and Glory' was sung with added emotion by the large audiences.

This growing sense of anticipation also marked the annual festive season gatherings, held in December by the British business groups in the east, in Riyadh and in Jedda, at which it was customary for the ambassador to speak about the state of Britain's affairs in Saudi Arabia. Numbers were somewhat depleted, but spirits were not. I took the opportunity at all three gatherings to stress the vital part which those who had stayed were playing, and might yet be called upon to play in our common task of seeing an end to Iraq's seizure of Kuwait and the threat this posed for the whole area with which our interests were so closely bound up. The way in which the community had faced the crisis had helped to steady others. There might well be a need for cool nerves in the weeks ahead if things came to war. But their security would be our first priority, and I had no doubt they would meet the challenge if it came.

Meanwhile, for the sake of morale, and with the UN Security Council deadline for Iraq to withdraw not due to expire until mid-January, we raised no objection to families reuniting in Saudi Arabia over the Christmas holiday, except in the Eastern Province. Our twin sons came out for the university vacation and found themselves impressed into the unloading into the embassy compound of a large consignment of gas masks intended for issue to the British community in the centre and east in the event of war.

But the moment for scaling up our precautions to this level had not yet come. We were still some way from having an agreed line with London over the advice and evacuation measures to be adopted in the event that hostilities put the community at risk. Indeed, we were still far from certain what dangers the community might have to face from Iraqi air attacks, and saw no point in arousing alarm through excessive precautions now that the mood had steadied. We were not at this point convinced that Riyadh could be reached from missile launchers in Iraq or Kuwait. The American embassy shared these doubts. So far we had managed to keep more or less in step with our Western partners and the Saudi authorities over provision for the security of our civilian communities. In terms of overall civilian morale it was important to do so.

With the approach of the deadline for withdrawal, further assessment of the range and warhead capability of the programme we knew the Iraqis had been working on to enhance the performance of their Soviet-supplied Scud missiles now became an urgent requirement. With our community still some 13,000 strong between Riyadh and the Eastern Province it was not something over which we could afford to take chances. We therefore asked the military intelligence people in Whitehall in early December to give us an updated assessment.

Our liaison with the FCO over imminent and crucial decisions on advice and evacuation plans in the event of hostilities was greatly helped by a visit which the head of the consular department, Christopher Denne, and his assistant, Martin Warre, paid to Saudi Arabia and other Gulf states at this point to see the state of community morale and the practicability of evacuation at first hand. They were carrying a heavy responsibility for the safety of the 40,000 or so British citizens throughout the whole Gulf, with its grave implications for public attitudes in Britain were things to go wrong on this front. At the same time Christopher Denne saw the harmful effect which an overreaction would have on Saudi society and on the coalition's ability to perform.

The need to strike the right balance between these factors was to remain one of our major preoccupations as we felt our way towards a safe yet sensible approach, and would produce some acute differences with London and among our embassies in the area before all was in place for our communities to face the test of war.

CHAPTER 7

The Long Haul ...

ana wa akhi 'ala ibn 'ammi,
ana wa ibn 'ammi 'ala al-gharib.

My brother and I against my cousin,
But my cousin and I against the stranger.

Arab proverb

British community morale was a comparatively straightforward matter by comparison with the task faced by King Fahd and his government in sustaining the commitment of Saudi public opinion to Iraq's withdrawal from Kuwait at the risk of a war with participation by Western forces. This challenge on the home front was matched by a need for constant vigilance to hold together the unprecedented and precarious international partnership which had come together in August in response to Iraq's invasion. As the weeks passed this impromptu solidarity found itself constantly subjected to erosive pressures, which Iraq's agile propaganda campaign set itself to exploit.

The resolute determination which King Fahd and his ministers showed from the outset to see an end to Iraq's occupation of Kuwait and the threat she presented to the security of the Kingdom was shared by Saudis in all walks of life. For some, however, it was mixed with a mood which ranged from incredulity at the idea of Saudi involvement in hostilities between brother Arab states to shock at the arrival of Western forces, bringing with them infidel and emancipated customs into Islam's Arabian homeland. These were not superficial prejudices. They presented a real obstacle to the close working relationship which was a prerequisite for effective political and military co-operation between Saudi Arabia and the Western countries which had joined with her to resist Iraq's expansionism.

At the same time the King, supported by Prince Saud, the Foreign Minister, exhibited a high degree of diplomatic persistence and skill in holding at bay recurrent pressures from within the Arab and international communities which were urging compromise in the search for a negotiated settlement to Iraq's invasion. To its credit the Saudi leadership never lost sight of the single-minded course which King Fahd set for his country from the outset of the crisis. This firm position served as an example and a point of reference for others within the coalition. It also led to an impatience to see things brought to an early conclusion, if necessary by a military offensive, and to a growing scepticism over the efficacy of the UN sanctions regime as the weeks of diplomatic and economic pressure on Iraq turned into months with little visible effect.

The Saudi people, along with other members of the Arab community, had long been conditioned to a climate of political culture in which inter-Arab disputes were traditionally resolved through mediation and negotiation without coming to blows. In the rare case of regional hostilities it was almost axiomatic that these would be confined to confrontation with non-Arab states, such as Israel or Iran in recent memory, or in an earlier stage with Western 'imperialism'. Consequently many Saudis, accustomed to their prosperous and protected existence, found the idea of conflict with their Iraqi brothers almost inconceivable. Indeed, despite the shock of the invasion of Kuwait, many found the possibility of an onward attack on Saudi Arabia herself hard to accept.

This background, coupled with a historical tradition in which the major Western powers were associated in the popular mind with an era of political domination and support for an expansionist Israel, produced a far from negligible measure of public disquiet at the sudden and obtrusive appearance of large Western military contingents in Saudi Arabia. There were even those, including some among our friends, who were susceptible to the fanciful theory of an American-led conspiracy to entice Saddam Hussein into attacking Kuwait in order to have the pretext to deal Iraq a blow.

It was to counter this unease that King Fahd devoted so much effort in the opening weeks of the crisis to the securing of military help from as wide a range of Arab and other Moslem countries as possible. Egypt, Syria and Morocco were first in the field, but others were subsequently persuaded to join the party, if only with token forces and in return for useful financial inducements. By the end of the year Prince Khalid bin Sultan, the Saudi joint commander, had forces from 24 Moslem states under his authority in the non-Western wing of the coalition, although of these only the GCC states, the Egyptians and Syrians showed themselves ready to join in the Allied offensive to liberate Kuwait when the moment came. Nevertheless, the visible participation in the defence of the Kingdom of these co-religionaries, drawn from West Africa and the Indian subcontinent as well as a cross-section of the Arab world, helped the Saudi government to parry sensitive accusations from at home or overseas that it had put itself in hock to the old imperialists.

At the same time the Saudi government worked hard throughout the autumn to counter public incredulity at the idea of confrontation with Iraq. Maximum publicity was given to the young men and women who had responded in large numbers to the call for civil defence volunteers launched in August. Recruitment centres around the country were swamped with volunteers in what was the first exercise of its kind since the founding of the Kingdom nearly 60 years before. The men were given uniforms and basic part-time military training, while the women underwent courses in nursing care.

Newspapers and television were also mobilised to beat the patriotic drum. This had some effect, though the techniques were all too often pedestrian and cumbersome in style, the result of a media scene in which originality and controversy had hitherto been discouraged. By contrast the Iraqi information system, although far more strictly controlled, was of a different order of agility and sophistication, and at least in the early months of the crisis had a considerable edge over its Saudi counterpart, particularly through well-targeted special broadcasts to the Kingdom such as Radio Medina, which sought to arouse popular hostility to the presence of foreign forces with provocative reports of infidel troops defiling Islam's holy cities. Towards the end of the year the Saudi Ministry of Information realised it must respond with a more populist approach. It took a leaf out of the book of the Western press by authorising the publication of a number of tabloid dailies which did not hesitate to publish in sensational detail accounts of Iraqi atrocities in Kuwait. This unaccustomed fare turned out to have an appeal for the Saudi public. It did not, however, survive the ending of hostilities.

Yet despite these rallying measures Saudi public attitudes towards the crisis required constant care. In a break with custom the King, with Crown Prince Abdullah and Prince Sultan, undertook a series of public speeches to refocus popular attention on the fate of Kuwait and the threat this presented for Saudi Arabia. It seemed clear that the great majority of people were not being taken in by spurious Iraqi claims to the moral high ground. But there were a few febrile pockets of religious dissent.

The crisis was also provoking stirrings of a more profound kind within Saudi public opinion. The jolt which it delivered unleashed a degree of political debate uncharacteristic of the Kingdom's prosperous and acquiescent society. There was a measure of polarisation here, with on the one hand a conservative and Islamic segment deeply perturbed by the Western military presence, and on the other a more pragmatic and liberal element of opinion to be found mainly within public administration and the business community. Many of the latter were asking why the

Kingdom found herself in this sudden predicament, confronted by an Arab neighbour whom she had sought to appease, and with her defences, on which so much had been spent, unable to see off the threat without outside help.

This thinking gave in turn fresh impetus to debate about the need for broader consultation in the process of government, a development to which it was known that the King had been giving thought for some years past, but had hesitated so far to take the plunge. Under the pressure of the crisis certain groups of merchants in both Riyadh and Jedda took the step of preparing petitions to the ruling family proposing the establishment of machinery for wider consultation. These sought to resurrect the idea of a national consultative council, or *majlis al shura*, which would have a part in the formulation of national policy alongside the senior members of the Al Saud and the Council of Ministers. Some of those pressing for these changes also saw the Council as an institution which could help to stem moves by the conservative religious establishment to strengthen its hold over Saudi society.

At the same time approaches were made to outsiders deemed to have influence with the Saudi regime, such as the Americans and ourselves, to use the issue of the present crisis to press for a wider democratic process. In the latter part of September petitions on these lines were put to two of the King's full brothers, Prince Salman, the governor of Riyadh, and Prince Naif, the Minister of the Interior, by two groups made up of merchants and liberal academics in Riyadh and Jedda. The proponents may to some extent have been emboldened by the recent holding under the chairmanship of the Kuwaiti Crown Prince, Sheikh Sa'ad, of a 'solidarity conference' in Jedda at which leading Kuwaiti citizens, including former opposition members of the National Assembly which had been dissolved some years before by the Amir, were given an undertaking that on the restoration of the Al Sabah to government they would be afforded a fresh participation in affairs.

Before the regime could give its response to these approaches a predictable reaction emerged from the traditionalist wing of Saudi society, with the argument that if there were to be changes these should be in the direction of reordering society on even stricter Islamic lines. The counterblast against the presence of non-Moslem forces began to work up into a fresh crescendo, with the circulation of cassette tapes of inflammatory sermons by well-known preachers, such as Salman al Auda from Buraida, a traditional centre of Wahhabist zealotry, and Safar al Hawali, an influential teacher at the Um al Qura Islamic college in Mecca, which sought to stir up public sentiment by putting infidel troops on a par with Iraq's Ba'ath party. Meanwhile the religious police, or *mutawa'in*, joined by self-appointed religious vigilantes, stepped up their harassment of foreign civilians, and of Saudis too, for breaches of the Islamic dress code and other customs. There were even episodes where *mutawa'in* broke into private homes, on casual tip-offs that riotous parties were taking place.

This angry reaction from the zealot quarter came to a peak in early November following a sensation in Riyadh when a group of some 40 well-connected Saudi women, who had learnt to drive during spells outside the Kingdom, decided to take advantage of the new climate of public debate and the presence of large numbers of Western journalists to mount a demonstration against the Islamic prohibition on women drivers. Having tipped off the foreign press, they assembled on 6 November at the Fal shopping centre on one of Riyadh's main streets and, dismissing their drivers, took the wheel in a procession of elegant cars towards the city centre. The police quickly stopped the parade and gently took the drivers into custody, as much as anything for their protection against any violent reaction from conservative quarters. To their credit they refused demands from the religious police that the drivers be handed over to them for punishment, for having broken Islamic rather than civil law.

The episode backfired badly on its participants. This was not the time, in the face of a national emergency, for the government to have to cope with a bitter rift within Saudi society itself. The women involved in the demonstration misjudged the timing of their protest. Their action shocked a wide range of Saudi public opinion beyond the most conservative elements, to the point where the government, some of whose members were known personally to favour greater social freedom for women, felt obliged to try to calm the ferment with concessions to the religious camp. The women concerned were released on the order of the governor, Prince Salman. But a furious reaction ensued in which conservative elements in Saudi Arabia's influential religious establishment gave vent to their wider frustration over the libertine influences which they considered Western forces to be introducing into the Kingdom.

An unprecedented public demonstration in Riyadh by male Islamic students, which converged on the governorate offices in the old quarter of the city, had to be dispersed by the police. Deputations called on Prince Na'if, the Minister of the Interior, and Prince Salman to demand punishment. Sermons in mosques disparaged the women concerned in furious terms and castigated secularist tendencies in society as the road to perdition. Even the official Higher Council of Ulema, the ultimate authority on social and religious discipline, was pressed into issuing a decree asserting that driving by women contradicted Islamic tradition. For their part the women concerned found themselves widely ostracised. Some who were teachers by profession found their classes boycotted by female students.

In the face of this fierce public reaction the government responded by making driving by women a legal offence; hitherto its interdiction had been backed up by custom alone. To their credit the authorities resisted calls for judicial action to be taken against the drivers, but as a penalty their passports were withdrawn for a spell. During a dinner at the house of a Saudi friend on the evening before the demonstration one of the women involved told my wife and myself of their plans. Asked whether this was really a suitable moment, the query was brushed aside with the argument that Western women had secured their emancipation in the early part of this century largely through the pressures of a war economy. Saudi women now faced a similar opportunity and should act.

In the event, far from helping to break down deeply-ingrained attitudes on the position of women within Saudi society, this theatrical gesture at a time of national crisis had the effect of setting back their cause. The publicity which the showdown received in the international press only served to fuel popular disapproval. However much liberal elements within the Al Saud leadership privately sympathised with the women's aspirations, there was no way they could afford to take on conservative religious opinion at this time of national crisis.

Moreover, the episode delivered a setback to the broader campaign to liberalise the Kingdom's political processes, which had up to this point been gaining momentum. Among the measures which the King had set in train in response to these pressures was the preparation of a new judicial code. This was intended to clarify and in some respects ease Saudi Arabia's strict rules of detention and legal process, based hitherto on a rigorous interpretation of the Islamic *Shari'a* law. In the face of the wave of conservative outrage with which he found himself confronted, this measure was shelved.

The King did, however, hold out some encouragement to the liberal camp when, only three days after the women's demonstration, he gave a briefing to Saudi newspaper editors in which he announced that finishing touches were being given to studies for government reform, to include the establishment of a national advisory council and wider participation in regional administration. King Fahd was careful to cite religious precedents for such developments, and stress that any changes to the Kingdom's system of government would be guided by Islamic principles. The King also took the opportunity to rehearse for public benefit Saudi Arabia's clear conditions for a settlement with Iraq,

including the restoration of Kuwait's legitimate government and guarantees that Iraq would commit no future aggression. He reminded the
public of the approval originally given by the leaders of the Kingdom's
religious establishment to the presence of foreign troops to help defend
the Kingdom.

But any hope there might have been of retaining the support of hard-
line religious opinion for such constitutional ideas foundered in the
backlash of outrage engendered by the driving episode. In the event the
King chose to wait a further 18 months to allow the controversy aroused
by the affair time to settle before promulgating his proposals for changes
to the system of government. There would be a further interval until the
end of 1993 before the new councils were finally established.

The King's statement of early November was followed by outbursts of
religious agitation. At the end of the month the King gave a further
speech to the nation to help steady opinion. Despite the religious furore
he repeated his support for wider consultation, while stressing that
change and greater individual liberty needed to be exercised within an
Islamic framework. He sought to refocus public attention on the paramount need to secure Iraq's withdrawal from Kuwait, and gave his word
that foreign troops would leave as soon as the danger was over.

To give support to this important assertion, I urged Whitehall that in
public statements and speeches by ministers we should make a point of
repeating our intention to go once the job was done. I also emphasised
to the British commanders the need to ensure their troops were made
aware of Saudi religious susceptibilities and gave no cause for offence. As
it happened, most of the troops were located well away from centres of
population. Those in Riyadh and the eastern towns observed the rules
scrupulously, to our great relief.

By December the religious ferment had to a considerable extent subsided. To avoid a recurrence, however, the government found itself
obliged to resort to direct measures to maintain control over the more
fanatical elements. Warnings were given to the most hot-headed preachers, while the aggressiveness of the *mutawa'in* was curbed by dispersing
the more fervent among them out of the main cities to provincial centres where they could remain out of the way until the crisis was over. The
sense of relief at these measures on the part of expatriates, and many
Saudi families too, was palpable. Nevertheless, fed by Iraqi radio propaganda, a conditioned disbelief in the acceptability of hostilities between
Moslem Arabs and the myth of a Western conspiracy against Iraq persisted in the minds of many Saudis right up to the eve of war.

This ability of the conservative religious camp within Saudi society to
arouse public feeling reinforced the wish of the Saudi government to see

the Iraqis out of Kuwait as quickly as possible. This conviction lay behind the questions which we and the Americans increasingly faced in our contacts with the Saudi leadership, and particularly with Prince Sultan, the Defence Minister, over how long sanctions should be given to take effect before a military option needed to be considered.

This sense of the dangers of delay also reflected a parallel concern on the part of the Al Saud over the risks of seeing international resolve erode as governments began to count the cost of sanctions for their own economies, while Iraq worked away to restore her image with public opinion in Arab and other Moslem countries. To their credit the Saudi leadership never once wavered in their conviction that Saddam Hussein had to be got out of Kuwait for the sake of the security of the Kingdom and of the other states of Arabia, and that it was for Saudi Arabia to give a lead to this end. Such was the sense of bitterness on the part of the King and his brothers at the way Saddam Hussein had repaid Saudi Arabia's substantial investment in support for Iraq during the eight years of war with Iran, that this objective was accompanied in their minds by a certain hope that the outcome would also involve an end to the menace posed by Saddam Hussein's rule. Until then Saudi Arabia, let alone Kuwait, could never regard herself as safe.

It was clear from the outset of the crisis that the solidarity in support of Kuwait and Saudi Arabia which had been so quickly rallied within the UN, as well as among Arab and Moslem states, could easily start to falter. Indeed, it was a prime objective of Iraqi policy to encourage this process by stringing things along and exploiting divergences as they arose. To keep these weaker links in good repair called for a prodigious exercise in diplomacy, accompanied by no small generosity on Saudi Arabia's part. Over the nervous weeks of stalemate prior to the launching of the coalition's offensive to liberate Kuwait, the Saudi leadership undertook this role indefatigably and with a skill which was impressive. It was made all the more arduous by the fact that the Kuwaiti leadership in its refuge at Ta'if remained in a shocked and demoralised state for many weeks after its flight, and had to be pushed by the Saudis, as well as by ourselves and the Americans, to go out and drum up support for its own restoration.

This vigilance on Saudi Arabia's part had to be exerted simultaneously on a variety of fronts. Prince Saud constantly found himself needing to be in several capitals at once, while foreign political figures streamed into Jedda and Riyadh to see the King and Prince Sultan, often late into the night. We obtained a feel for the strain this was imposing when Douglas Hurd came to Jedda at the beginning of September for talks with Prince Saud, who took him on that night to see the King.

These encounters provided a valuable opportunity to establish how close we stood in our mutual determination to hold together the international pressure on Iraq to get out of Kuwait. Prince Saud made plain Saudi concern at Iraq's efforts at wedge-driving. Only the day before a contact had appeared with a request from Saddam Hussein to meet the Crown Prince. This was seen as a clumsy attempt to probe for divisions within the Saudi leadership. The Iraqis had also been putting it about that the Kingdom was lukewarm in its support for Kuwait.

More insidious in the Saudi view were Iraq's moves to curry popular favour within the Arab world by posing as the champion of the Palestinian cause, and seeking to link a withdrawal from Kuwait with a call for a reciprocal Israeli withdrawal from the occupied West Bank and Gaza. This could have some appeal for public opinion, and needed to be countered. Douglas Hurd agreed we could accept no linkage here: Iraq's withdrawal had to be unconditional. At the same time we should be looking for a fresh approach over Palestine. Present circumstances might, for example, permit reconsideration of an international conference under the sponsorship of the five permanent members of the UN Security Council, a proposal which had hitherto proved unacceptable to Israel and the Americans, mainly as it would involve the USSR.

Both the King and Prince Saud were, however, vehement in their insistence that there could be no compromise with Iraq. They had no time for the kind of brokered Arab solutions which were being peddled by King Hussein, and lately by King Hassan of Morocco despite his staunch despatch of a contingent of Moroccan troops to help in the defence of Saudi Arabia when the crisis had broken. The Saudis realised that the Moroccan government was, along with other Arab states of North Africa, having to face a groundswell of public sympathy for Iraq, with its origins in an instinctive sense of respect for an Arab regime seen to be standing up against Western strength and in the name of Palestine. This was the case in Tunisia, and particularly in Algeria, where popular demonstrations had occurred in support of Iraq and the government was keeping its head well down. As the Algerian ambassador reminded me, 'for Algeria it only takes one French soldier on Arab soil to produce this reaction, whatever the cause'. Perhaps, too, Kuwait had neglected to cultivate the Arab states of North Africa as effectively as Iraq had been doing for some years past.

No such excuses could be accepted, however, on behalf of King Hussein, nor of Yasir Arafat. Saddam Hussein's propaganda had succeeded in arousing wide popular support for Iraq among Palestinians, both in the occupied territories and in Jordan and elsewhere. But this did not explain the way in which King Hussein persisted in excusing

'Our Men on the Spot' ran the caption in *The Times*: Air Vice Marshal Sandy Wilson and the author at Dhahran air base, August 1990. (*Press Association*)

A prime target for Iraq's Scuds: Jubail Industrial City. (*Royal Commission for Jubail and Yanbu*)

Prince Sultan bin Abdul Aziz with the author at the embassy residence in Riyadh. (*Crown Copyright*)

King Fahd attends the Cairo emergency Arab Summit called on 10 August to discuss the Iraqi invasion. He is flanked by his Foreign Minister, Prince Saud al Faisal (left) and by Prince Abdul Aziz bin Fahd. (*Saudi Press Agency*)

Many young Saudis answered the call for volunteers to help defend the country from the threat of Iraqi attack in August 1990. (*Saudi Press Agency*)

King Fahd with Sheikh Jaber al Ahmed al Sabah, the Ruler of Kuwait, to whom the Kingdom gave sanctuary following the invasion. (*Saudi Press Agency*)

Patriot air defence missiles in position at Riyadh military airport. (*Raytheon Company*)

President Hosni Mubarak of Egypt, a staunch ally, visits King Fahd in Jedda to discuss the crisis. (*Saudi Press Agency*)

Tom King, British Secretary of State for Defence had a good meeting with King Fahd in November to discuss troop reinforcement: to his left are seated Derek Plumbly, General Peter de la Billière and the author. (*Saudi Press Agency*)

President George Bush came to the Kingdom over the Thanksgiving weekend in November 1990. (*Saudi Press Agency*)

Comparing notes in mid-crisis: Chas Freeman and the author. (*Crown Copyright*)

John Major visits 4 Brigade in training south of Kuwait, January 1991. (*Author/Crown Copyright*)

Postcards sent by Kuwaiti children in Saudi Arabia to British troops: this one carried the message 'Love is my Life – Zahra'. (*Author*)

TO THE HEROES OF
DESERT STORM:

Dear Courageous Soldier:

On August 2ⁿᵈ as everyone Knows,
Our former brothers became our foes.
They invaded our land at night as we slept,
Over our borders by the thousands they crept.
In helicopters and trucks and in tanks they came,
The evil warriors of Saddam Hussein.
But then YOU came and brought hope to us all,
That Kuwait would be free and Saddam would fall.
We'd like to thank you for your courageous stand,
To expel the Iraqis and free our land.
You're in our hearts
this Valentine's Day,
And you're in our prayers
EVERY day.
Sincerely,
The Kuwaiti People

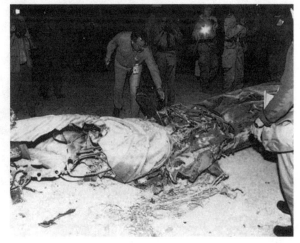

The wreckage of a Scud missile which fell in a Riyadh street without exploding after being intercepted by a Patriot. (*Saudi Press Agency*)

Scud missile damage in central Riyadh. (*Saudi Press Agency*)

Saudi infantry in action to recapture the town of Al Khafji, occupied by the Iraqis at the end of January 1991. (*Saudi Press Agency*)

Iraq's violation of her Arab neighbour, while looking for a compromise way out which would leave Iraq with something to show for her aggression. Rumours persisted that Saddam Hussein had some months previously suggested to his Jordanian and Yemeni associates within the ACC that the day of the Gulf sheikhs was over and their lands should be divided. The King revealed to Douglas Hurd that, on learning of Iraq's invasion early on the morning of 2 August, one of his first actions had been to telephone King Hussein to discuss urgent Arab action to stop Iraq. But from the outset Jordan's efforts in the Arab League and beyond had been unhelpful.

We pondered why King Hussein should be showing this degree of support for Saddam Hussein. Iraq's regime held no affection for the Hashemite dynasty; an Iraqi mob had murdered King Hussein's cousin, King Faisal, in 1958. Perhaps the Jordanian King had fallen under the influence of Saddam Hussein's forceful personality in some way over the years of close Jordanian association with Iraq during the war with Iran. Douglas Hurd explained how deeply we too felt let down by our long-time friend, and found it difficult to account for the position he was adopting. Mrs Thatcher had taken King Hussein to task a few days earlier in London. Douglas Hurd was himself going on from Jedda to Amman, and would press the Jordanians to share our stand over Iraq. We shared the view that King Hussein would continue to have an important part to play in the cause of Arab stability, not least in the search for a solution over Palestine. But Saudi chagrin at Jordan's behaviour over Kuwait, despite earlier openhandedness, was plain.

Yemen for her part came in for vigorous condemnation, in which all Saudi Arabia's accumulated suspicion of the past 70 years came into play. The Yemeni action in using her position as the Arab representative on the UN Security Council to abstain on several of the resolutions condemning Iraqi actions over Kuwait was seen as sympathy for Iraq. Like Jordan and the PLO, the Yemenis had been the recipients of generous Saudi help. This was how they repaid it. The idea of retaliation was in the wind, and two weeks later Saudi resentment came to the boil. By long custom, which suited the economies of both countries well, Yemeni citizens had enjoyed the unique concession of being allowed to come to Saudi Arabia to work without the need for a visa or work permit. As a result Yemenis provided much of Saudi Arabia's labour force in key areas such as construction, transportation, agriculture and clerical work. Many, particularly those from the Hadhramaut in the south, owned trading businesses and ran shops throughout the Kingdom. Most of the bakers were Yemenis.

At a stroke this privileged status was cancelled, and the Yemenis were given 90 days to settle their affairs and return home. This drastic penalty meant severe inconvenience to the Kingdom. Yet we found few Saudis who did not share in the mood of resentment at Yemen's refusal to back UN Security Council action against Iraq or give their full support to this reprisal. There were some scuffles in Riyadh's Al Batha souk, the heart of the Yemeni community. Around a million Yemenis were estimated to be living in Saudi Arabia at the time. At least a half of these sold up and trekked back southwards through the mountains to a life of considerable hardship at home. Many had lived for years in Saudi Arabia, or were even born there. It was a sorry trail to see the convoys of laden vehicles moving south out of Jedda through October and November. Others succeeded through their Saudi employers in securing precious work permits, particularly when after a few weeks the Saudi authorities eased up on this front. To our relief we managed to obtain them for the Yemenis who had given long service to our offices in Riyadh and Jedda. For my own part I could have ill-afforded to lose the cheerful resourcefulness of Ali as my driver during these busy times.

At the same time Saudi Arabia moved to penalise Jordan. The supply of crude oil by pipeline from the Gulf coast was cut off. The reason given was that over 18,000 barrels had been supplied since Iraq's invasion of Kuwait without any payment being received. But it was clear to all that Saudi feelings ran much deeper, in the face of what was seen as King Hussein's subservience to Saddam Hussein and his tolerance of a campaign in Jordan's Palestinian-dominated press which sought to attack Saudi Arabia and Kuwait and to disparage the Al Saud.

The sense of offence among the Saudi leadership was compounded by an announcement by King Hussein that he wished to resume the title of Sharif, which had been the prerogative of his family in the period up to 1924 when they had ruled the Hejaz and the holy cities of Mecca and Medina. To the Al Saud, ever-sensitive to Hashemite pretensions, this looked like a veiled attempt to reclaim this role, and led to suspicions that King Hussein might even in the present crisis be resurrecting dynastic ambitions in the direction of Iraq.

On a visit to Jedda in October I was struck to find influential Hejazis fierce in their condemnation of what they regarded as quisling behaviour on King Hussein's part. Some believed him to be privy to an Iraqi plan to partition Saudi Arabia, and even to look towards the Hejaz as his refuge from problems in Jordan as the Palestinians consolidated their influence over his country. Fanciful as such ideas appeared, they were prevalent nonetheless. Indeed, the Saudi government may have taken precautionary steps to reinsure its position through reopening old links with the Howeitat and other bedouin tribes in southern Jordan, in areas which had formerly been attached to the Hejaz.

The suspension of oil supply was accompanied by other measures, including the closure of the Saudi border to Jordan's important truck trade in fresh foods with the Kingdom and other GCC states, and the denial of re-entry visas to Jordanians and Palestinians who decided to leave. The embassies of Yemen, Jordan and Iraq were reduced to a small core of staff. Contacts with the PLO were also interrupted, and the valuable monthly subvention of $6 million paid to them by Saudi Arabia, as well as the levy on Palestinians in the Kingdom which was intended to help finance the *intifada* uprising in the occupied territories, were suspended.

When Hani al Hassan, a leading figure within the Fatah movement and Yasir Arafat's main link to King Fahd, came to Riyadh in November on a fruitless mission to try to keep PLO lines open to Saudi Arabia, I asked him why Arafat persisted in showing such open support for Saddam Hussein. Hani al Hassan explained that, as much as Palestinian public sentiment, it was Iraq's provision of training facilities for the Palestinian army which persuaded Yasir Arafat to keep on terms with Saddam Hussein. If a choice had to be made, these counted for even more than Saudi Arabia's generous financing.

Although the basis for Saudi Arabia's outrage over the behaviour of her two neighbours was well understood by the British government, the policy of ostracism was seen as carrying risks for the Kingdom's security as well as for the solidarity of the Arab front over Kuwait. I was consequently instructed during the latter part of September to explore whether some mitigation of its full rigour could be achieved. In particular we were concerned that the cut-off in oil supply would have the effect of driving Jordan yet more closely into Iraq's embrace, by forcing her to make up the energy shortfall from supplies delivered by road from Iraq despite the UN-authorised boycott. Jordan simply had nowhere else to go, and it was no part of our policy, nor in practice that of Saudi Arabia, to see Jordan's monarchy under threat, with all that would imply for the frail state of Israeli–Arab relations at this critical juncture.

Having warned the FCO that, given the extent of Saudi feelings towards both countries, I expected little change from such representations, I took the matter up at senior level in the Foreign Ministry. To have approached Prince Saud directly over the issue at this heated time could have produced doubts about our commitment in support of the Kingdom.

The response was a courteous but firm negative. Ismail Shura, the political director in the Foreign Ministry, with whom I had many close and productive dialogues during the crisis, made it plain that we were wasting our breath. The decision on the oil blockade had only been taken after careful consideration. In the Saudi estimation things would not reach the point where Jordan's stability was threatened. Oil could still be supplied from other sources. But Jordan's attitude since the start of the crisis compelled a firm Saudi sign of disapproval. The same went for Yemen and Yasir Arafat. When I took John Wakeham to see Hisham Nazer, the Minister of Petroleum, in Riyadh in early October he took a similarly firm line over Jordan's oil supply. It was clear the Saudis were not going to shift.

In the talks which Douglas Hurd held on his September visit to Jedda with both Prince Saud and over a supper with his brother, Prince Turki al Faisal, the head of Saudi foreign intelligence, it emerged that the Saudis fully shared our concern to keep all five members of the UN Security Council working within the bounds of their new-found unison. There were continuing signs of equivocation in the French position, despite their decision to respond to Saudi Arabia's request for military help. The attitude of the coalition government's Defence Minister was recognised as playing a part here. We agreed the French needed more time to sort out their position. The real test, however, of the 'New International Order' recently proclaimed by President Bush would be whether the USSR, having put aside the Cold War, would forswear her ties with Iraq and stand beside the West over Kuwait. So far the new orientation in Soviet foreign policy had held. Prince Saud himself intended to visit Moscow shortly, feeling the circumstances of the present crisis justified a change in the Kingdom's longstanding policy of having no relationship with the USSR. We concurred that it made sense for Saudi Arabia to open her lines in this direction.

In the event Prince Saud's doubts about the extent of Soviet solidarity proved well founded. The months leading up to hostilities saw growing Soviet efforts to mediate a compromise settlement, and to insist that all enforcement activity be conducted through the UN and its long-moribund Military Staff Committee. President Gorbachev also showed himself susceptible, during his summit meeting with President Bush in early September, to the Iraqi leader's calculated proposal that withdrawal from Kuwait be linked to the Arab–Israel question through an international conference. Prince Saud's journey to Moscow provided the occasion for the announcement on 17 September of the restoration of Saudi Arabia's diplomatic relations with the USSR, and a Soviet chargé d'affaires appeared in Riyadh shortly before hostilities began in January.

October, however, saw a determined bout of mediation by President

Gorbachev's emissary, Yevgeny Primakov, but the exercise proved still-born in the face of Saddam Hussein's intransigence. Prince Saud made it clear to me in a discussion at the beginning of November that the Saudis shared our view that this compulsive Soviet meddling only mud-died the waters and gave Saddam Hussein the illusion of international support. When Primakov had come from Baghdad to Jedda on 29 October to see King Fahd with a Soviet formula for a peaceful settlement which might head off the prospect of an American-led military offensive, the King had initiated Saudi Arabia's newly-established dialogue with the USSR by giving him short shrift.

After these efforts the USSR in the end went along with American proposals for a UN Security Council ultimatum to Iraq which carried the threat of force. In reaching this difficult decision they were no doubt helped by the inducement of a judicious Saudi offer of $5 billion in soft aid loans, made in late November when Prince Saud again visited Moscow together with the Saudi Finance Minister, Mohammed Aba al Khail. Ironically this visit coincided with the presence in Moscow of Tariq Aziz, the Iraqi Foreign Minister, on a vain mission to solicit Soviet opposition to the proposed UN Security Council resolution authorising the use of force if Iraq did not withdraw. President Gorbachev's response was uncompromising, though this was not to be the end of attempts by the indefatigable Primakov to find a way out of the embarrassment of condoning Western-led military action.

In the work of trying to retain Soviet support, the Americans and Saudis paid the greatest attention to the need to take Soviet sensitivities into account. In their negotiations over a UN Security Council deadline for Iraq's withdrawal, the USA deferred to the Soviet wish that the effec-tive date be delayed until 15 January. Further concessions of a diplomatic kind were made by the Americans at the time of the last-ditch Soviet attempt to broker a compromise once the air offensive against Iraq had begun.

The importance of carrying the USSR with the coalition proved on the other hand to be something of a blind spot in Britain's approach to the diplomacy of the crisis. Mistrustful by instinct both of the UN and of Soviet ambitions in the Middle East, despite the evidence that they could no longer afford the expense of Cold War rivalries, the Prime Minister from the outset of the crisis set a policy aimed at keeping to a minimum opportunities for the Soviets to meddle in any military action against Saddam Hussein. In the event the American approach carried the day and we fell into line. Had Mrs Thatcher not been obliged by the Conservative Party to resign the office of Prime Minister in late November, she might have sought to carry her resistance further.

But it was the task of holding together the Arab and Moslem portion of the front against Iraq which constituted the greatest challenge for Saudi Arabia during the final months of 1990, and accounted in large measure for her growing sense of impatience at the long-haul approach advocated by her main partners. The fragile package of Arab and Asian opposition to Iraq, which the Saudis had taken such a skilful lead in putting together in the first weeks following the invasion, showed increasing tendencies to unravel as events in the region put strain on its cohesion. For King Fahd and Prince Saud all fronts had to be watched at once. As soon as one loose end was pinned together another would threaten to unpick.

In this connection it came as a blow to Saudi Arabia to observe how various leading Islamic figures abroad, whose friendship Saudi Arabia had for some years past sought to cultivate, lost no time in declaring their support for Baghdad and the questionable religious credentials of the Ba'ath leadership once the chips were down. Saudi support for Islamic personalities, known to have a radical political agenda, had already become a point of controversy in the Kingdom's relations with certain Arab and Moslem governments in whose countries these individuals were based. Saudi policy towards them had been dictated not so much by a sense of identity with their brand of zealotry with its political overtones, but rather by the hope that such contact could serve to temper their extremism and discourage their adherence to the alternative militant and revolutionary Islamic message which Iran was actively addressing to the Moslem nation at large.

Prominent among the targets of this Saudi attention were Abbas al Madani in Algeria, Rashid al Ghannouchi in Tunisia, Hassan al Turabi in Sudan, and the most hard-line of the leaders among the Afghan *mujaheddin* guerrillas, Gulbuddin Hekmatyar. Yet none of these made an effort to disguise an opportunistic support for Saddam Hussein in his confrontation over Kuwait. It was a chastening experience for Saudi Arabia.

Even in Britain Iraq's propaganda reached out to sow doubt in the minds of sections of the Moslem community over the Koranic justification for the decision of Saudi Arabia and Kuwait to invite unbelievers to help in defence against a fellow Moslem, and in such close proximity to Islam's holy places. One influential British Moslem, the singer Cat Stevens who had converted and taken the name Yusef Islam, was courted by Iraq. In consequence he was invited on a couple of occasions to Saudi Arabia during the long prelude to hostilities in an attempt to convince him of the rectitude of Saudi Arabia's stand.

Abdullah Nasif, the director of the Moslem World League, Saudi

Arabia's instrument for influencing opinion within the Moslem world, and himself an unusual blend of religious scholarship and a Western scientific education, having a doctorate in geology from Leeds University, told me in Jedda in October that he had been having considerable difficulty in his contacts with British Moslems in countering Iraq's ill-founded accusations of religious heresy on the part of the Saudi regime. It was one of the features of the crisis that we had throughout to keep in mind theological as well as political and strategic considerations in determining our policy. From London such factors often seemed arcane, but to those of us operating in the Kingdom, the very crucible of Islam, they formed an ineluctable part of the picture.

One major Arab source of uncertainty throughout these five months of waiting time was Syria. President Assad's initial and welcome response to King Fahd's request for Arab military help to withstand the threat of Iraqi attack had been motivated by complex political factors. There was Syria's long-standing and deep hostility towards her Ba'athist rivals in Iraq, reflected in personal animosity between President Assad and Saddam Hussein. A more recent, but just as compelling, element was Syria's predicament with the ending of the Cold War, which had left her bereft of her traditional prop in the form of Soviet support and subsidy, both financial and military, in the confrontation with Israel.

The Kuwait crisis with the opportunity it gave for close association with Kuwait and Saudi Arabia offered an expedient way to break out of this awkward isolation within the Arab world, and to gain an alternative source of subvention. Syria might also acquire a freer hand in Lebanon, where the Saudi-sponsored Ta'if agreement between the warring parties was being resisted by the right-wing Maronite leader, General Aoun, with considerable support from Iraq. But Syria soon made it clear she had her price. She began by prevaricating over the despatch of the armoured brigade she had offered to send, obliging the Saudis to meet the cost of transport and provide shipping for the purpose. Saudi Arabia's offer of a grant of $1.5 billion to Egypt in return for her prompt commitment of military forces was also quickly matched by a grant of £1 billion to the considerably smaller Syrian economy.

In a further move to tie the Syrians into the coalition against Iraq, the Saudis sought to mediate an end to the diplomatic estrangement between Britain and Syria which had prevailed since we had broken off diplomatic relations with Damascus following Syrian complicity in an attempt to place a bomb on an Israeli airliner at Heathrow airport in 1986. This summary move by the British government had in large part been taken on the insistence of Mrs Thatcher. Five years on tempers had cooled, but it was not easy to see a way back. For our part we required

assurances from the Syrians of abstention from future terrorist involvement. At the same time it complicated our liaison with the Syrian
government, now that we found ourselves on the same side in confronting Iraq, to have no channel for official communication. The crisis
presented an opportunity to put our relations in order.

Prince Saud was one of the first to recognise this. In a talk with Mrs
Thatcher at the UN in New York at the beginning of October he asked
if we would restore our relations with Syria, given the latter's welcome
support for Saudi Arabia and the help she was also giving to keeping the
Iranians onside. Prince Saud offered to help in preparing the way for us
in Damascus to secure the assurances we sought. Although it went
against her grain, the Prime Minister agreed to explore the ground.

From there things moved ahead swiftly. The Saudis took soundings
during October which produced an encouraging response. I had a number of sessions with Prince Saud to discuss the terms of the assurances on
terrorist acts and punishment of officials implicated in the El Al affair,
on which we were insisting. He was invariably helpful and constructive.
There was no doubting Saudi keenness to see this irritant in Syria's attitude towards the coalition removed.

When Tom King came to Jedda in mid-November one of his party was
Rob Young, the head of the FCO Middle East department, who had
been counsellor in our embassy in Damascus at the time of the breach in
1985. He and I met Prince Saud to tell him we were now ready to go
ahead with resumption of relations. These were formally restored a fortnight later following a visit to Damascus by David Gore-Booth, the
under-secretary in charge of the Middle East and a leading FCO trou-
bleshooter during the Gulf crisis. Saudi diplomacy had helped us resolve
a tricky impasse. As for the Syrians, following a meeting with the Saudis
and Egyptians in Damascus in early November when the idea of military
action was discussed, they announced that they were ready to increase
their forces in Saudi Arabia to 20,000, including an armoured division.
But this did not prevent their turning the heat on their Saudi benefac-
tors once again as the January deadline drew near.

The commitment of Syria, together with that of other Arab partners, came under fresh strain from an unwelcome quarter when on 9
October the Israeli police killed 21 Palestinians, and wounded many
more, when they opened fire to disperse a demonstration outside the Al
Aqsa mosque in Jerusalem, always a flashpoint for confrontation
between Arabs and Israelis. This lamentable event played right into the
hands of Iraq's propaganda, and caused reverberations throughout Arab
public opinion. Not only Palestinians but even some Saudis found themselves susceptible to Iraq's well-aimed question whether the Arab nation

could afford to be divided over Kuwait when its common adversary in the shape of Israel sought to take advantage of Arab disarray in this brutal fashion.

Iran too, who had so far shown a surprising degree of resistance to Iraqi inducements to bury the hatchet of their eight years of war, including the unilateral return of pockets of occupied Iranian territory, the release of prisoners of war, and calls to join in resisting American-led military involvement in the region, showed her outrage at the Israeli action. The situation required an urgent demonstration of Western-led international condemnation before Arab reaction risked getting out of hand. For Saudi Arabia it was crucial that the front against Iraq, on which she had expended so much political capital, should hold. The Egyptian government found itself similarly placed. The Speaker of the Egyptian National Assembly was gunned down in Cairo two days after the Jerusalem episode, an act which some saw as an Iraqi-inspired attempt to shake Egyptian commitment to Kuwait.

There was thus considerable relief when the UN Security Council was able to agree on 12 October on a unanimous resolution condemning the killing of the Palestinians and instructing the Secretary-General to send a fact-finding mission to Israel. This last provision was a device to permit American support for condemnation. Little matter that Israel predictably refused to receive the Secretary-General's representative; at least the resolution put a stop to Iraq's exploitation of the shootings and cleared the way for attention to be turned back to Kuwait. The affair illustrated, however, how the precarious unity of the coalition against Iraq depended crucially upon Israel keeping out of the limelight. This message was not to be lost on Saddam Hussein when things came to a fight.

Other quarters also demanded attention from the Saudis and ourselves. The decision was taken in London shortly after the onset of the crisis to try to use our common purpose in opposing Iraq's seizure of Kuwait to resume the long search for a formula which would permit a resumption of diplomatic relations with Iran. These had been interrupted more than once since the overthrow of the Shah in the Islamic revolution of February 1979, as a result of the anti-Western fever which that event had unleashed. The most recent breach had occurred early in 1989 following the publication in Britain of *The Satanic Verses*, a novel by the lapsed Moslem author Salman Rushdie, which many Moslems understandably saw as a work of blasphemy against the Prophet Muhammad. Iran's extreme reaction had been a call by the religious authorities for the author's death. Such official incitement was clearly quite unacceptable to the British government and had put a sharp stop to the process of reconciliation.

Now, as in the case of Syria, a common hostility to Iraq's attack on Kuwait afforded a basis for a resumption of relations, together with a measure of official Iranian dissociation from the pronouncement over Salman Rushdie. It was in our interests to have lines open to Iran at this critical time, when her contacts with the Americans and Saudis remained frozen and Iraq was doing her utmost to engage Iran's support.

The satisfactory upshot was the return to Tehran in late September of one of our most experienced Iranian specialists, David Reddaway, to reopen the capacious British embassy there. The Saudis wished to follow suit. Their diplomatic relations with Iran had been broken off in April 1988, after a serious bout of rioting by Iranian pilgrims during the Haj in Mecca the previous July had had to be stopped with loss of life. This had been followed by Iranian attacks on Saudi shipping in the Gulf. Subsequently there had been incidents of attempted sabotage against petrochemical installations in Saudi Arabia's Eastern Province, where the large Shi'a population had shown itself susceptible to Iranian propaganda against the Al Saud.

Iranian aggravation continued during the Haj of 1989, with bombing incidents in Mecca carried out by a group of Shi'as who turned out to have been recruited by Iran in Kuwait. Nineteen were caught and convicted of terrorism. Sixteen of these received capital sentences and were executed in late August. The severity of the sentences demonstrated the strength of Saudi concern over Iran's activities at this juncture. They also put strain on the Kingdom's relations with Kuwait.

Matters were thus at a low ebb when Iraq's invasion of Kuwait occurred. Iran's prompt condemnation of the occupation afforded some grounds for encouragement, though this was offset by a hostile reaction to the arrival of American and other Western forces in the Gulf, a development which was bound to touch a raw nerve in revolutionary Iran, and particularly among the radical religious elements within her society which President Rafsanjani had been seeking to curb. It was clearly of major importance for Saudi Arabia's leadership of the Arab and Moslem front facing Iraq, just as it was for Britain and other Western participants, that Iran should at least remain neutral in the crisis and be discouraged from affording Iraq physical or diplomatic support. Saddam Hussein could be counted on to play upon Iran's sensitivities over Western military involvement. Moreover, Saudi Arabia's own serious dispute with Iran over the Haj pilgrim quota, with its impact on religious opinion, remained an obstacle which would have to be resolved before relations could be improved.

Nevertheless feelers put out by the Saudi government during the autumn, partly through the good offices of Oman as the GCC member having the most comfortable relationship with Iran, evoked positive if cautious responses from Tehran. President Assad of Syria was also persuaded to use his regime's long-standing alliance with Iran to seek undertakings of moderation. Yet, perhaps for internal consumption, Iran continued to make ambivalent noises about the crisis, leading to suspicion that some measure of sanctions-breaking might be taking place across the long land frontier.

It was not until the end of December that President Rafsanjani announced that Iran would remain neutral in any conflict, and followed this up by making it plain to a senior Iraqi delegation, which Saddam Hussein promptly despatched to Tehran, that Iraq should withdraw from Kuwait and could not expect Iranian support were Iraq to carry out her veiled threat to extend the crisis by attacking Israel. Iran continued, in the context of a subsequent non-aligned movement initiative at mediation, to talk of conditional withdrawal, and predictably refused co-operation with coalition forces in the Gulf. But President Rafsanjani's assurances represented an important conciliatory step and opened the way to discreet direct contact with Saudi Arabia, starting with a meeting between Prince Saud and the Iranian Foreign Minister, Ali Akbar Velayati, in Bonn in February as a prelude to the renewal of relations a month later.

But the long weeks of waiting for sanctions to take effect meant that Saudi Arabia's diplomatic marathon had to cover yet more fronts, both in the wider Islamic world and her own GCC backyard. To hold these countries to their initial pledges of political or military support, in the face of Iraq's agile propaganda tactics and repeated hints at compromise which would avert hostilities, required diligent attention and a measure of largesse too.

Turkey, ever careful of her relationship with both Iraq and Iran, with whom she shared common frontiers and an irredentist Kurdish population, had declined to send troops to the Kingdom. She had, however, at considerable economic cost to herself applied sanctions by closing one of Iraq's main oil export pipelines to the Mediterranean, and had reinforced her border with Iraq, thus usefully tying down Iraqi troops on this northern flank. Turkey had also agreed to the stationing of American and other Nato airforce contingents in proximity to the Iraqi frontier.

Pakistan also constituted a key Moslem ally who had sent troops to Saudi Arabia, but where public opinion was showing some sympathy for Iraq, not least through Saddam Hussein's attempts to turn his seizure of Kuwait into a bargaining counter over Palestine. Here again a substantial financial grant for the purchase of oil helped to induce Pakistan to stand by her commitments within the Moslem wing of the front, although it was made clear that Pakistani forces would not participate in any eventual offensive against the Iraqis.

Bangladesh was rewarded for her despatch of ground forces with assistance in their equipment, and the small Senegalese detachment represented in some respects a response to Saudi Arabia's undertaking to fund the construction of an international conference centre to be inaugurated with the summit meeting of the Islamic Conference Organisation, due to be held in Dakar under Senegalese presidency in 1992. A small army contingent from Niger was sent, partly in recognition of the fact that the Secretary-General of the Jedda-based Organisation of the Islamic Conference was a former Prime Minister of that country. Specialised military units had also come from Poland, Hungary and Czechoslovakia, who provided a useful chemical warfare detection team. These three countries were losing no time in trying to establish a relationship with the world's wealthiest oil-producing state.

The insidious effect of Iraq's propaganda continued to have its effect on Moroccan opinion. This prompted King Hassan to call on 11 November for the holding of a 'last chance' Arab summit to try to avoid a war over Kuwait. The proposal was seized upon by Iraq in a flurry of diplomatic contacts with Arab states regarded as susceptible to proposals for dialogue. It also brought the Chinese Foreign Minister to Baghdad, where he saw both Saddam Hussein and Yasir Arafat with talk of Chinese support for a peaceful solution. In a hasty tour of North African states the Iraqi deputy Prime Minister, Taha Ramadan, made it clear that Iraq still intended to dictate terms for such a summit, however, including the rescinding of the Arab League's August resolution requiring Iraq's unconditional withdrawal from Kuwait and the inclusion of Palestine on the summit agenda.

In response to the Moroccan King's unwelcome proposal for a summit, Saudi Arabia and Egypt moved once again to stop the rot and shore up the Arab front. President Mubarak went to Libya, and also saw President Assad in Damascus. On 14 November Prince Saud made a firm statement that before any summit could take place Iraq would have to observe the Arab League and UN resolutions on withdrawal. Otherwise it would be a waste of time. In the face of Iraq's obduracy over unconditional withdrawal, Egypt and Syria applied the *coup de grâce* to the summit idea two days later with a joint statement that Iraqi conditions had made such a meeting impossible, and putting responsibility for this failure to find a political solution squarely on Iraq. Here in effect was another instance where Saddam Hussein's personal inflexibility blocked what might have been an opportunity for Iraq to salvage some political advantage from her aggression. Saddam Hussein's response to the collapse of the Moroccan initiative was a defiant announcement that Iraq was sending a further 250,000 troops to Kuwait.

Meanwhile, to sustain the solidarity of the core of Arab opposition to Iraq within the GCC itself, the Saudis arranged for a special meeting of the foreign ministers of its six members to be convened in Riyadh at the end of October. With a strong lead from the GCC's Kuwaiti Secretary-General, Abdullah Bishara, they reaffirmed their determination to see Iraq out of Kuwait and the legitimate government restored. There were, however, some shades of divergence over means, with Oman, traditionally the most conciliatory of the Gulf states where relations with the big brothers to the north and east were concerned, countering Kuwaiti and Saudi impatience to see things brought to a conclusion with a plea for more time for diplomacy to work. Nor was Oman prepared to share with her Gulf partners in making a financial contribution towards the cost of foreign troops, although she had given base facilities to RAF Jaguars and tanker aircraft and continued to allow Nimrod surveillance aircraft to be based at Thumrait.

In late November the Omani government went so far as to accept a visit from the Iraqi Foreign Minister with a message to Sultan Qaboos from Saddam Hussein on the eve of the UN Security Council's ultimatum on withdrawal. This Iraqi attempt to drive a wedge into GCC solidarity caused the Saudis some concern, though in the event Oman stood by her commitments to her GCC partners. Oman also made a point of keeping open her lines to King Hussein of Jordan. In practice this may have helped serve as a brake on Jordanian support for Iraq.

All these regional alarums constituted an incessant preoccupation for Saudi Arabia's tireless diplomacy. We gave what support we could, but no sooner had one point of discord been patched together than another emerged in a different quarter, affording fresh scope for Iraqi efforts to fragment the motley coalition. But while these side-plots called for constant attention, they were nevertheless subsidiary to the prime objective of sustaining the closest co-operation and trust between the Kingdom, at the head of the Arab and Moslem front committed to Iraq's withdrawal from Kuwait, and the USA, Britain and France as the main contributors to Western diplomatic and military pressure on Iraq.

It was to this essential task that we gave the highest priority in our diplomatic work throughout the autumn and winter, both in London and in our Riyadh embassy. There was the occasional insinuation from some Western quarters that in taking such an active role we were boxing above our weight. But the part we were playing on the diplomatic front, and the lead given to European partners, made an important contribution to the course of events.

With the Saudis we worked together in remarkably close harmony. Ministers and emissaries went to and fro from both sides. In the embassy we were able to take advantage of an unprecedented degree of access to senior Saudi ministers and their advisers, and in particular to Prince Saud, who rightly set store by regular contact with the Kingdom's main partners to minimise the kind of misunderstandings to which our differing perspectives and priorities in foreign affairs were likely to subject our incongruous alliance. King Fahd's personal staff, and indeed the King himself when occasion required, made themselves available at any hour. This open association made a great difference to the success of our venture.

It was also very necessary. For, almost as soon as UN sanctions and measures for their enforcement were voted into place by the UN Security Council in August, differences began to appear between the Saudi government and the Kuwaitis in their exile in Ta'if on the one hand, and the main Western partners on the other, over the nature and the pace of the pressures to be put on Iraq to get out of Kuwait. Nor were such issues only to arise between the two wings of the coalition. They also were a source of division from time to time among the three main Western partners themselves, with Britain showing the greatest measure of impatience, at least while Mrs Thatcher remained Prime Minister until late November, and the American administration inclined to allow longer for diplomacy to work and for public and congressional opinion to come to terms with the prospect of hostilities.

France for her part found herself with a coalition government divided over support for Saudi Arabia and Kuwait and confrontation with Iraq, as against the securing of the major political and financial investment which France had made in Saddam Hussein's regime in recent years. This dilemma was evident in acute form to France's partners, and not least to the Saudis. It did not resolve itself in a firm French commitment to military action until almost the eve of the expiry of the UN Security Council deadline in mid-January.

CHAPTER 8

. . . And Longer

The questionable durability of Moslem opinion was thus not the only factor inclining the Saudis and Kuwaitis towards a minimum of delay. They were uncertain of the resolve of their Western partners and the international community to sustain confrontation with Iraq while paying the economic penalty which a rigorous application of the sanctions regime involved. Congressional opinion in the USA was known to be still not wholly behind President Bush's firm stand, with its risk of war. Diplomatic initiatives directed towards a settlement involving compromise, emanating not only from the USSR and non-aligned quarters but from Europe too, also fed Saudi scepticism.

There was the fear, too, that Saddam Hussein would be bold enough to raise the stakes with an air attack on Israel, to invite a retaliation calculated to strain the coalition to breaking point. As time passed so the unwelcome prospect grew that Saddam Hussein might take advantage of the delay to make a partial withdrawal, with some gain to show for his aggression. In the event it was one of the Iraqi leader's major miscalculations that he failed to exploit this opening. There were also problems ahead associated with the calendars of climate and religion. The fasting month of Ramadan, when the military effectiveness of Moslem troops might well become problematic, would begin in the third week of March, followed in May by the onset of the hot weather which would make conditions of existence in the desert very difficult, particularly for European troops.

On top of these factors there was also pressure for action from the Kuwaiti Amir and his ministers and family, increasingly anxious to see their country freed of the invader, particularly as reports accumulated of the coercion which the Iraqi administration and troops were inflicting on Kuwaitis under occupation. Many were understood to have been transported off to captivity in Iraq.

This restlessness on the part of the Kuwaiti government was made plain when Douglas Hurd flew briefly up to Ta'if to meet the Amir and Crown Prince Saad during his visit to Jedda at the beginning of September. Our stay was slightly extended as a result of the VC10 puncturing a tyre on landing at Ta'if's high altitude airport, but the RAF crew quickly effected running repairs and we put the extra time to useful purpose. Sheikh Jabir gave a limp and dejected performance, and needed encouraging to go out and speak up for Kuwait's plight on the international circuit, advice which he eventually adopted with a round of visits to the UN in New York and a number of Western capitals. The Crown Prince. on the other hand. welcomed the solidness of our political and military response and did not hide his conviction that force would be needed to dislodge the Iraqis. He evinced no patience with sanctions.

Later that night in Jedda King Fahd also pondered a military option, though, as he had told Tom King the previous week, any such action needed to be backed by UN Security Council approval. Prince Saud indicated a similar preference for facing the consequences of military action to liberate Kuwait, rather than sitting out what might become a tedious and inconclusive stalemate while sanctions were applied. For him too a UN umbrella was essential. Kuwait's Crown Prince Saad, on the other hand, took the view that we and our partners in the coalition already had sufficient authority to mount military action, on the basis of Kuwait's inherent right to engage collectively in self-defence, accorded under Article 51 of the UN Charter.

This divergence of approach had its reflection in a disagreement which had emerged since the first days of the crisis between Mrs Thatcher and the Americans, notably Secretary of State Baker, over the question of military action and the authority on which this would need to be based. Instinctively impatient to see Iraq's aggression terminated, the Prime Minister was firmly of the view that Article 51 of the Charter, combined with the UN Security Council resolutions requiring Iraq's withdrawal from Kuwait, permitted the adoption of military measures on the basis of a formal request for such assistance from the Kuwait government. This would avoid the need for a more specific UN Security Council resolution, when two permanent members, the USSR and China, might choose to jib or impose limitations. It would also get round the emphasis which the USSR had begun to lay on having any military action supervised by the moribund UN Military Staff Committee.

The Americans, as the major players in the military coalition, were however most uneasy about an attempt to take international opinion for granted in this fashion. In particular they did not want to invite the strain which unilateral action was likely to impose upon their new and fragile co-operation with the Soviets following the ending of the Cold War. They were also aware of Saudi hesitations over action outside the UN framework.

In his discussions in Jedda and Ta'if, Douglas Hurd had argued for giving sanctions a reasonable time to work. But the Prime Minister subsequently badgered him and the FCO to get ahead with setting up a formal Kuwaiti request for intervention under Article 51. This led to my receiving instructions towards the end of September to put to the Kuwaitis the draft of a letter from the Amir to the Prime Minister requesting our military intervention in accordance with Kuwait's right of self-defence.

I went across to the imposing Kuwaiti embassy on the diplomatic quarter to see Sulaiman Shahine, the Secretary-General of the Kuwaiti Foreign Ministry, who had based himself in Riyadh to handle liaison with the Saudi government and other foreign missions on diplomatic issues. Sulaiman Shahine had impressed me as an effective operator with a sensible and realistic approach to the crisis. When I showed him the draft letter he welcomed this statement of our forthright support for the recovery of Kuwait, and saw no difficulty in having the request confirmed by the Amir. He was concerned, however, that we should keep in step with the Americans. We agreed that Saudi reservations about unilateral action without some form of UN Security Council cover also needed to be taken into account.

I therefore suggested to the FCO that we proceed with less haste by a two-stage approach. The Kuwaitis now had our draft of the letter. We should not press them for their formal request until options became clearer on the other fronts, lest we run the risk of raising Kuwaiti expectations of early military action to an extent which we were not in a position to fulfil. Meanwhile we should talk things through further in Washington to try to align our positions more closely. Chas Freeman had made it clear to me that so far as the State Department was concerned some further UN Security Council authority under Article 42 of the Charter, which provided for military operations to restore the peace in the event that other measures proved ineffective, was going to form an important tactical element in American policy. We were unlikely to shift them from this intention, despite the Prime Minister's close personal relationship with the President.

Moreover, at this stage the US administration was, largely for reasons of internal politics, considerably less prepared than the British government to give an impression of readiness to contemplate military action to evict Iraq from Kuwait, despite the planning which General Schwarzkopf's headquarters was already undertaking for such a contingency. The shadow of military losses in Vietnam still overhung public attitudes at home. Mrs Thatcher's impetuosity was thus risking taking us well ahead of the game, to the point of causing irritation to our main partners, except for the Kuwaitis, who were not in the driving seat.

In the event it was the American and Saudi preference for UN Security Council cover for a possible military offensive which carried the day, and we found ourselves obliged to follow suit. This course had from the start made more sense to the FCO, just as it looked more realistic to us in Riyadh, engaged as we were in ensuring a close working relationship with the Saudis. The Prime Minister, however, remained attached to the option of using Article 51, and accordingly pressed the Kuwaiti Amir, Sheikh Jabir al Sabah, for Kuwait's formal request for armed support when he saw her in London on 23 October in the course of his round of Allied capitals.

It was a further month before the Americans were ready to make a similar approach to the Kuwaitis over a request for military assistance. By this time they had, after detailed discussion with the Saudis and ourselves, and negotiating crucial Soviet acquiescence, put together an ingenious formula whereby the UN Security Council would be asked to set a deadline for Iraq's withdrawal, failing which those members of the UN who were co-operating with the government of Kuwait would be entitled to use 'all necessary means' to implement the UN Security Council resolutions requiring Iraq to leave Kuwait.

Any military action would be undertaken with full UN authority, but without the inhibitions of UN command. Instead, control of a military offensive would be handled on an independent basis under dual arrangements. After some touchy discussion the American and Saudi military commands had succeeded in working these out on a pragmatic basis, which assured for the Americans a prime responsibility for the planning and conduct of any offensive operations to secure Iraqi withdrawal from Kuwait, while the Saudis had a lead in any military activity in defence of the Kingdom. This unprecedented arrangement afforded the best of both worlds; an international force with objectives established with full UN authority, yet under the joint command of the participating nations.

On 29 November the UN Security Council duly issued its ultimatum to Iraq as Resolution 678, setting a deadline of 15 January for her voluntary withdrawal from Kuwait. In the voting Yemen put herself definitively offside in the Saudi view by joining Cuba in the only negative votes. The Chinese abstained.

From Saudi Arabia's point of view the resolution represented a satisfactory outcome after a period of growing impatience with the Americans, and to a lesser extent with ourselves and the French, over a timetable for achieving a solution to the crisis. The concern over the possible effects of delay in securing Iraq's withdrawal, which Prince Sultan had expressed to Tom King at the end of August and which both King Fahd and Prince Saud had reiterated to Douglas Hurd in early September, had become more evident during the weeks that followed, as the main Western partners let it be known that they were prepared to allow a period for the effectiveness of sanctions to be judged. Saudi scepticism over the efficacy of sanctions continued to grow. They were diligent in investigating occasional allegations of breaches on the part of their business community, and in bringing similar reports from other quarters to our attention. In particular they were concerned by evidence on their air traffic radars of possible supply flights to Iraq from Yemen and Sudan, flying up the Red Sea and across Jordanian airspace.

We did our best in public statements and in our contacts with the Saudi and Kuwaiti leadership to leave no room for doubt that we were every bit as committed as they were to see Iraq out of Kuwait. This went for all sides of the political spectrum in Britain, as Gerald Kaufman, foreign affairs spokesman for the Labour Party, confirmed emphatically when I took him to call on Prince Saud in Jedda on 9 September. He repeated this message of solidarity when Ian Blackley took him up to Ta'if to see Kuwaiti ministers the next day. Taking a point from the recent House of Commons debate on the Kuwait crisis, Gerald Kaufman made it plain that Britain's prompt association in Saudi Arabia's defence, and the lead we were taking in bringing international pressure to bear on Iraq, were not just an opportunistic response for the sake of the region's oil resources, as Iraq would have had the Moslem world believe. There was a wider principle of acceptable international behaviour at stake. Had Kuwait simply grown carrots, this same principle would apply. But then, had it been a question of carrots, Saddam Hussein would not have coveted Kuwait or other Gulf resources in the first place.

Such assurances on our part, and in particular Mrs Thatcher's vehement public definition of Iraq's retributive actions in Kuwait as war crimes, were welcome in Saudi Arabia. But the regime's impatience to see the message of a possible military option spelt out to Iraq ran just below the surface. It came through clearly when I took General Peter de la Billière to pay his introductory call on Prince Sultan on 14 October. Sandy Wilson was with us, and we had the opportunity for a useful talk on timescales and strategy.

Prince Sultan did not hide his concern at the erosive effect he believed a lengthy delay for sanctions to take hold would have on the coalition's political cohesion. He saw problems on two fronts here. With the passage of time, and the advent of major festivals in the Christian and Moslem calendars, the resolve of both wings of the coalition to keep their troops in the field was likely to fray. Moreover, he was acutely conscious of the undercurrent of hostility to the presence in the Kingdom of Western forces, which was being constantly nourished by extremist elements within the Islamic hierarchy, both at home and abroad. This could not be held in check indefinitely. Prince Sultan recognised that in both political and military terms the coalition was not yet prepared for the idea of an offensive. But he saw risks in leaving such an option beyond December. To this end he welcomed Peter de la Billière's appointment and also the imminent arrival from Germany of 7th Armoured Brigade.

The conviction that things would have to be taken to a military conclusion before Saddam Hussein could be dislodged from Kuwait was also being put to me by other senior members of the Al Saud. Among these were Crown Prince Abdullah and Prince Salman, the governor of Riyadh and full brother to King Fahd and Prince Sultan, who had raised the likelihood of a military option when John Wakeham and I saw him earlier in October. The Energy Secretary had conveyed this impression back to London. Prince Sultan's full brother, Prince Abdul Rahman, the deputy Minister of Defence, had shown his impatience with a military standoff in speaking to Archie Hamilton in Jedda, when he had taken the view that the Iraqi forces would be incapable of resisting a military strike and that Saddam Hussein's huge arsenal had to be dismantled, a point which the Saudis were glad to find that Mrs Thatcher was also stressing in public.

When Peter de la Billière and I saw Prince Salman again later in the month he gave us his stark assessment that Saddam Hussein's conceit and self-delusion would prevent his releasing his grip on Kuwait unless he were forced to do so. It was doubted whether, in view of what the Saudis understood to be the poor state of training and morale of the Iraqi army in Kuwait, it would be necessary for the coalition to build up significant further reinforcement. One sharp blow should suffice to break its resistance.

I found myself increasingly concerned by this evidence of a growing sense of haste on the part of the Saudi leadership, lest the coalition should start to fall apart and public support fade. For his part Peter de la Billière had well-founded doubts over whether it was right to assume that a military offensive from a position of considerable numerical inferiority would be a walkover. Above all it was essential to see the basis of political trust between the Saudis and the Americans and ourselves as their principal Western partners preserved in the face of these divisive factors, which Iraq would be quick to exploit.

A recent statement by Prince Sultan to press correspondents, which had been reported as indicating a softening in the Saudi position over possible territorial compromise, had raised a measure of alarm in London, not least on the part of the Prime Minister. We had sought urgent clarification, and had been relieved to hear Prince Sultan put the record straight with an assertion that Iraq's unconditional withdrawal must precede any longer-term settlement. It may have been that in making his statement Prince Sultan was flying a kite to test indications put out by the Iraqi leader that he was considering withdrawal. But if so these amounted to no more than another Iraqi feint. Nevertheless the international reaction to press reports of the affair demonstrated the ever-sensitive nature of the relationships which underpinned our remarkable enterprise, and how these called for constant vigilance to sustain.

To help in preparing an assessment for Whitehall on this important issue I took the occasion of a visit by Alan Thomas, the industrialist in charge of British sales of defence equipment abroad and responsible for the smooth operation of the Al Yamamah deal, to compare ideas once again with Prince Fahd bin Abdullah, the assistant Defence Minister, over dinner in my house on our consulate-general compound in Jedda. Prince Fahd was as ever forthcoming and clear in his analysis of Saudi thinking. He confirmed that for the Saudi leadership the time fuse for waiting for Iraq to get out of Kuwait was shortening. There were real worries about the endurance of Allied resolve as well as over domestic public reaction. None of our troops could be kept out in the field in inhospitable conditions indefinitely.

Moreover, there was a growing suspicion that Saddam Hussein would seek to turn the tables by settling for a partial withdrawal under international pressure. This would leave him still presenting a threat to Kuwait and her neighbours and with his dangerous arsenal unimpaired, while the international front would start to fragment. A military blow seemed essential to avoid this situation. We could expect any conflict to be brief in view of the reports of low Iraqi morale. But action must be covered by some form of UN Security Council approval, at least involving all five permanent members. Sanctions were proving too slow to take effect, and Arab resolve was giving cause for concern, particularly following the events in Jerusalem.

I put the case for holding back for a while yet, not least to ensure wide international support for any offensive and permit coalition forces to be assembled in sufficient strength. We could not count on an Iraqi rout; there were nearly half a million Iraqi troops in and around Kuwait. Moreover, there were risks in an ultimatum which could lead Saddam Hussein to pre-empt the deadline with just the kind of partial withdrawal of which the Saudis were wary. But the dangers in stretching things out too far, which Prince Fahd had described, needed to be taken seriously.

I was particularly alive to his point about domestic public attitudes, which as the crisis proceeded through the prolonged interval of 'phoney war' were starting to question the need for all this mobilisation.

Discussing all this subsequently with Chas Freeman, it emerged that he shared the concern that our joint approach towards seeing Iraq out of Kuwait might be falling out of step with that of our Saudi hosts. Critical decisions were about to be taken in Washington on whether the USA should increase her military commitment, and visits to the Kingdom by Secretary of State Baker and Defence Secretary Cheney to discuss these options were in the offing. Chas Freeman suggested we first ask to see King Fahd together to get an authoritative feel for Al Saud thinking on a military option and its timing.

Having received the go-ahead from the Royal Diwan, we flew down to Jedda on 23 October expecting to have an audience that night. Chas Freeman gave me a lift in one of the USAF Lear jets, based in Riyadh for communications work. It was like squeezing into a cigar container, and I found myself wishing I had instead offered him the hospitality of the more commodious HS125. We disembarked on the air force base side of Jedda's mammoth airport, on a tarmac filled with the bulky silhouettes of American K105 tanker aircraft. I noticed that each had the name of a different state of the Union painted on its tail, and was told that the tankers belonged to the American National Guard, whose part-time crews had been called up for the emergency. Apparently the unit was infused by a spirit of lively competition between the different states represented, in the fashion characteristic of the regimental system in the British Army. As we passed through the crew hall it was noticeable how many of the aircrew were women.

In the event we did not see the King; other visitors supervened. But we were given to understand he shared Prince Sultan's preoccupations over the erosive effects of undue delay. Fortunately Paddy Hine was out from High Wycombe on one of his liaison visits at this juncture, and he, Peter de la Billière and I agreed on the need to straighten out with the Saudis the main lines of our policy. I therefore sent the FCO a detailed account of how our options for action and the timetable looked from the vantage point of Riyadh, taking into account such diverse factors as public sentiment, religious festivals and weather, as well as the possible context for a fight if there was to be one. All in all the Saudis were right that we did not have that much time in hand, though perhaps a few weeks longer than they were suggesting.

It was a comfort to find David Gore-Booth in London in agreement that to avoid confusion and crossing of wires we needed to talk objectives through with the Saudi leadership, even though American policy still appeared in search of Congressional endorsement. Peter de la Billière and Sandy Wilson made similar recommendations up their military chain, taking advantage of a visit to the theatre by the Chief of the Defence Staff, Sir David Craig.

The upshot was a telephone call from Tom King offering to come out in the next few days to see Prince Sultan and perhaps King Fahd too. I welcomed this as a way to re-establish a common policy approach. It would also usefully reaffirm our public message to Iraq to get out of Kuwait. At the same time Peter de la Billière was keen to have the Defence Secretary see something of the recently arrived 7th Armoured Brigade undergoing desert training. I always found visits by Tom King positive events. We had known each other since our time at Cambridge, where we had bibbed together for the university in the annual winetasting match against Oxford – not an activity to be easily repeated in the teetotal circumstances of Saudi Arabia. Tom King always spoke to good purpose with the Saudis and was on close terms of trust with Prince Sultan.

Tom King's talks in Jedda turned out to be a help in getting things back on a more even keel. The Saudis made plain their welcome for the visit by laying on an exceptionally full programme of meetings with the King, Prince Saud and Prince Turki, the head of Foreign Intelligence. Prince Sultan also offered a banquet in his elegant palace. Tom King was able to assure Prince Sultan that while our public emphasis would continue to be laid upon sanctions for the present, the military option was by no means ruled out, as the arrival of 7th Armoured Brigade demonstrated. We now saw merit in demonstrating a capacity to resort to force as a way of getting the message through to Saddam Hussein that, if he continued to flout international condemnation backed by economic sanctions, then other measures would be needed.

Planning should go ahead between us all on the form of a possible military offensive. It would take time to prepare ourselves, but the clock had now started with an announcement by President Bush on 8 November that he was sending more troops to the Gulf to ensure the coalition had an adequate offensive military option, should this prove necessary. This marked a significant shift towards a more offensive stance on the part of the US administration. We recognised that the window of the cooler winter conditions, and before the onset of Ramadan, was a narrow one. We were also aware of Saudi Arabia's wish to see any eventual use of force covered by UN Security Council approval in some form; work on this had already begun in New York. Tom King mentioned the proposal, which Peter de la Billière had been discussing with him, to double the size of the British Army contribution by the addition of another armoured brigade to bring us up to division strength.

Prince Sultan appeared well satisfied at these developments in our thinking, and at our readiness to contemplate military action. But there was still pressure for decisions over the timing of an offensive and for an ultimatum to Iraq, as well as concern about the problems of a prolonged military stand-off. Saddam Hussein was evidently playing for time in the belief that in this lay his best chance of driving a wedge through the coalition's solidarity. It was put to us that the UN Security Council should set an early deadline; no purpose would be served by a further Arab summit. The discussion went on to cover various outstanding points affecting our deployment, notably the generous contribution which Saudi Arabia was making to our billowing costs and the possibility of further financial help.

When we saw the King that evening he was in a confident and expansive mood, and clearly pleased to have the visit. As we sipped the refreshing carrot juice which was always offered to his guests along with cardamom-flavoured Arab coffee, he spoke of his anger at Iraq's deceitful action against Kuwait, and his determination to see the menace which Saddam Hussein continued to present to Saudi Arabia and her neighbours removed once and for all. Our co-operation was of the first importance, and would remain so in view of the growing likelihood of force. We would have to judge when the time was ripe for this, and might want to wait until the New Year.

We already knew of Saudi concern over the possibility of secondary attacks against the Kingdom on the part of Yemen and Jordan. Saddam Hussein had recently been putting out feelers via Yemen, but this was no more than another attempt to play for time. The King gave his ready agreement to our reinforcement. His appreciation of the firm stand taken by Mrs Thatcher and the uncompromising tone of her public statements was very evident. Tom King sensibly made no mention of what he had earlier told Peter de la Billière and myself about the storm clouds which were beginning at that point to threaten the Prime Minister's survival in office from within the Conservative Party. But the King's words of appreciation brought it acutely home to me that, if Mrs Thatcher were to go at this critical juncture, the transition to a new leader would need to be very carefully handled indeed if Saudi confidence in us as allies was not to suffer serious damage. Personal relations counted for a great deal in the politics of Arab society, and King Fahd's regard for Mrs Thatcher was of long standing.

After a brief stop in Riyadh for talks with General Khalid bin Sultan, who also counselled against too long a delay before deciding on military action, and with General Schwarzkopf, Tom King went on to see British armoured units in eastern Saudi Arabia and finished with a late stopover at Tabuk in the north to visit the RAF ground attack Tornado squadron there. Sandy Wilson and I flew back from Tabuk to Riyadh in the early hours, where I faced a night of drafting a reporting telegram on the visit for the FCO's insatiable appetite. It had been well worth while in terms of our relations with the Saudi leadership.

For my part I was off back to London with Grania, taking advantage of what I hoped would be a lull in our diplomatic activity to make an over-due attendance at an investiture at Buckingham Palace and discuss with colleagues in the FCO how we should tackle the next stages of the crisis. Derek Plumbly's safe hands would see that all went well in Riyadh and could handle our relentless flood of visitors, among the next of whom would be members of the House of Commons Defence Committee, led by Michael Mates. We had asked for them to have a chance to hear the Saudi view of the crisis from King Fahd himself.

We got back on 19 November to find London in political convulsion over whether the Prime Minister would survive in office. For the next week the country held its breath and the business of government was vir-tually suspended as knives came out within her party amidst Michael Heseltine's challenge for the leadership and the rallying calls of alter-native candidates. From my own point of view the interval afforded an opportunity to have a series of valuable sessions in the FCO and else-where on steps towards the increasingly likely eventuality of offensive action to get the Iraqis out of Kuwait, as well as on the handling of our community in the case of war. I was encouraged to find a general mood of public support for military action, a spirit which Mrs Thatcher's con-sistent and determined backing for Kuwait and for Saudi Arabia had done much to inculcate. Now the irony was that having brought things so far she was about to be jettisoned. To King Fahd and his brothers, steeped in the tradition of personal leadership, this was bound to appear perverse, if not inexplicable. Indeed her sudden resignation came as a shock to our own forces in the theatre, and to the Americans too. General Chuck Horner, the US air force commander responsible for planning the air campaign, told his morning staff meeting in Riyadh he would begin with the bad news that Margaret Thatcher had resigned. But the good news, he went on, was that he heard she had applied to join 7th Armoured Brigade! The only one to take comfort from her dis-appearance was Saddam Hussein whose propaganda machine went into overdrive in claiming the affair as a victory for Iraqi policy.

At the same time it struck me that a change of Prime Minister, drastic as it would be, could bring the incidental benefit of helping to close a gap which had been emerging between 10 Downing Street and the FCO over the political conduct of the crisis and the need for any further international authority for military action. It was clear from my talks with the two under-secretaries who were sharing the direction of the political aspects of the crisis, Patrick Fairweather and David Gore-Booth, that we were now working closely with the Americans through our Permanent Representative at the United Nations in New York, David Hannay, to go for Security Council confirmation of a formula for a with-drawal deadline and the concomitant prospect thereafter of the use of force by the coalition, albeit outside the formal United Nations military framework. This was an important development in our policy, which from my point of view took account of Saudi concern to secure the widest possible degree of international cover. It also marked a step away from Mrs Thatcher's aversion to a further reference to the Security Council to clear the decks for possible military action.

I also spent time with Rob Young, now translated to a windowless cubby-hole of an office in the emergency unit in the depths of the FCO. The unit was humming with activity, and fully manned with staff drafted in to enable it to provide a round the clock service on political, military and consular, as well as press, aspects of the crisis, in contact with Riyadh and other embassies in the region and with all parts of the Whitehall machine. The staff were working under pressures very similar to our own in the field, albeit on a shift system which did permit occasional breaks. The daily round of briefing meetings started by seven each morning and went on until late into the night. It was impressive to have this glimpse of Whitehall at war, and to know that if the balloon went up we would be getting such capable and ready support. I also had talks on the military side, and rounded off with an eye to the aftermath of the crisis by speaking to a gathering of businessmen and industrialists about the opportunities which they should now be preparing themselves to seize, both in a liberated Kuwait in the process of reconstruction and in the Saudi market too, once the crisis was over. I was sure they would find a very positive climate on which to build fresh business.

On 29 November the Security Council duly approved Resolution No. 678 with its ultimatum to Iraq. The same day John Major emerged as the new leader of the Conservative Party and took up office as Prime Minister. Grania and I had taken a refreshing couple of days break on the South Downs. On return to London I discussed with Rob Young how we should handle the abrupt transfer of leadership with the Saudis. The paramount need was to convey an immediate assurance to the King of a firm continuity of purpose over Kuwait on the part of the new Prime Minister.

Although John Major had had a brief stint as Foreign Secretary prior to becoming Chancellor of the Exchequer the previous year, he had not had time to establish contact with Arab governments and was in consequence an unknown quantity so far as the Saudis were concerned. Mrs Thatcher on the other hand had acquired considerable stature in the eyes of the Saudis and other Gulf rulers. We agreed that the most effective way to present the change was for the new Prime Minister to send an immediate message to King Fahd, pledging his support for the task in hand and his intention to carry forward the close co-operation which his predecessor had enjoyed. I would ask for an audience to hand over this letter on my return to the Kingdom two days later. I telegraphed Derek Plumbly asking him to set this in hand. Number 10 readily agreed to this course of action, and a personal message from John Major was quickly on its way to Riyadh.

Grania and I flew back on 1 December from a heavily guarded Heathrow airport, accompanied by some feeling of unreality that we were returning to a situation which seemed increasingly likely to result in war. Yet we knew that if this was the only way to put a stop to Saddam Hussein's record of tyranny and aggrandisement, then it had to be so. The pieces were at last falling into place to achieve his removal from Kuwait. At root one found oneself hoping he would not play the card of a partial withdrawal, and counted on his self-conceit and intransigence to divert him from this tactic. There was a mountain of work to catch up with on return. But for once the political action had been concentrated in New York. Peter de la Billière and his staff were deeply engaged in the deployment to Saudi Arabia of the additional army formation, 4th Armoured Brigade, the decision to send which had been taken by Mrs Thatcher in her final days in office. The British headquarters in Riyadh was now swelling in size by the day and was moving into a more spacious building downtown, built originally as the BAe offices in the days of the Lightning aircraft project. With the passage of Security Council Resolution No. 678 there was a new sense of purpose to their planning and co-ordination with the American and Saudi military. In the embassy too we set about clearing the way for possible hostilities as the countdown to the 15 January ultimatum got under way.

My summons to see King Fahd to deliver John Major's message came through quickly, and on 4 December I flew down to Jedda for an audience at the Al Salaam palace. The King was most friendly, and had arranged the nice gesture of inviting his son, Prince Mohammed, the governor of the Eastern Province who had been so helpful to us over British escapees from Kuwait, to join the meeting. In a mood of fond reminiscence the King stressed the importance he had always attached to Saudi Arabia's close relationship with Britain, never so close as at the present time. Prince Mohammed subsequently told me when I took

Peter de la Billière to meet him in Dammam a few days later, how struck he had been at the warmth with which his father had spoken of our relationship. King Fahd paid a sincere tribute to all that Mrs Thatcher had done to create these ties. He did not dwell on the causes of her leaving office, though no doubt he found these difficult to comprehend. Certainly Crown Prince Abdullah did when I saw him later that month and found myself shrewdly questioned over how our democratic political system permitted a leader to be ousted from office without any reference to the electorate. It was not an easy question to answer.

King Fahd gave careful attention to John Major's letter. He was clearly reassured to receive it and to hear that we remained committed to our common purpose to see Iraq out of Kuwait and no longer a threat to the region. Looking ahead he indicated that hostilities seemed likely. The coalition had to make sure it was well prepared. But it was also important to keep to the deadline which the United Nations had now set. In this connection I sensed some concern at an offer, made by President Bush in a broadcast to the American people on 30 November following the Security Council resolution, to 'go the extra mile for peace' by inviting the Iraqi Foreign Minister to come and see him in Washington and sending Secretary Baker to Baghdad to see Saddam Hussein in a last effort to find a political solution. The President had made it clear this would not involve any compromise over the requirement for Iraq's total withdrawal and the restoration of the Kuwaiti government, as well as for the freeing of all hostages the Iraqis were holding. He had however proposed that the Baker visit could take place on a date right up to the 15 January deadline.

The Saudi leadership were evidently taken aback by this last minute offer of talks, which might signal to Baghdad a loss of resolve and open the way to further Iraqi prevarication. It looked to me as though the Americans had omitted to brief them on this move. For all I knew they had not discussed it with us either. Pressed to offer an explanation for it off the cuff, I suggested it reflected a tactical need on the President's part to secure the widest possible support for the prospect of hostilities from a Congress where opinion was still divided about committing American troops to fight. This assessment turned out to be close to the mark, though it subsequently emerged that the need to secure Soviet backing for Resolution No. 678 had also played a part in the offer. In the event the Saudi prediction that the Iraqis would use the proposal to try to drag things out proved correct. Before traversing the Kingdom from Jedda to Al Khobar the next day, to give my annual address to the British business community in the east (or what by then remained of it), I passed a warning to Chas Freeman about this concern and the need to reassure the Saudis that no compromise was in the wind.

It was however a relief to find the King reacting in so steady a fashion to the shock of Mrs Thatcher's disappearance from office. The next step would be for John Major to pay a visit to the Kingdom and meet King Fahd in person, as President Bush had just done on the occasion of Thanksgiving Day in late November. Once again I had been struck by the King's lively engagement in all aspects of the crisis, and his resolute and uncompromising approach to an unconditional outcome, if necessary through hostilities. His working schedule, night and day, during the past four months would have been punishing for anyone, let alone a man in his seventieth year. Yet he continued to give a firm lead to his allies and to his own people on the multitude of issues and challenges thrown up by the crisis. Under the Saudi system one could be sure that whatever the buck it would eventually stop with the King. Nor was there to be any let-up in the pressure. On the contrary, as the deadline neared, so from all corners attempts at mediation gathered to try to find a way out of war while saving something of Iraq's face. Some emerged from within the coalition itself. The containment of these manoeuvres and of Iraq's efforts to exploit them was to impose yet further burdens upon King Fahd and his government as we moved into the new year.

CHAPTER 9

Khaki

'For, lo, I will raise and cause to come up against Babylon an
assembly of great nations from the north country: and they
shall set themselves in array against her; from thence shall she
be taken: their arrows shall be as of a mighty expert man; none
shall return in vain.'

Jeremiah ch. V, vs. 9.

The British government's decision, announced by Tom King on 14
September, to reinforce the British forces already deployed to the Gulf
by the despatch of 7th Armoured Brigade from Germany had the effect
of moving our activity at all levels of the embassy into a much higher
gear. The brigade commander, Brigadier Patrick Cordingley, paid an
early reconnaissance visit to make contact in Riyadh and with the US
Marines division in the east, under whose command his brigade was to
operate, as well as to see something of the desert conditions his troops
and tanks would face on the ground. We had last met 25 years earlier in
another desert, the Sahara, during my time in the embassy in Benghazi,
where Patrick had been a subaltern with the 5th Inniskilling Dragoon
Guards, garrisoned in Cyrenaica in the mid-1960s during the last years of
the Senussi monarchy in Libya.

It was good to have an old acquaintance commanding our armoured
force in the field, although in the event we were to see little of Patrick in
Riyadh. From the moment his brigade began to form up north of Jubail
in the middle of October, he dedicated himself to leading them in an
intensive programme of training in desert tactics, which continued with
hardly a break up to the final deployment for the land battle during the
latter part of January. It was interesting to hear his comparison between
conditions for armoured vehicles in the Libyan and Arabian deserts;
the grittier sand of North Africa made for easier running and maintenance than the finer sand of Arabia, in which 7 Brigade would now have
to operate.

The most significant feature of the decision to commit British land
forces was the transfer of their overall command from Air Vice Marshal
Sandy Wilson to Sir Peter de la Billière, a lieutenant-general in the

British Army. The choice of Peter de la Billière to take over command in the Gulf had not been without controversy in Whitehall and within the British military establishment. The RAF had been understandably reluctant to lose the command appointment in the field, so ably filled by Sandy Wilson, who was in any case on the point of gaining his promotion to full air marshal rank.

At Paddy Hine's request I agreed to put in a word in support of Sandy Wilson's claims to remain in the post. No sooner was it clear that a full armoured brigade in the field called for an Army commander, however, than it became evident to us in Riyadh that voices were being raised at a senior level within the Army itself questioning the candidature, put forward on the personal recommendation of Mrs Thatcher, of Peter de la Billière. From what we heard it was being argued that General de la Billière was about to retire from the Army, that he lacked experience of armoured warfare, and that he had never commanded a major formation in the field, as other army candidates for the appointment had done.

But Mrs Thatcher's mind was already made up. She admired Peter de la Billière's record as a fighting commander, having seen at first hand his successful direction of the Army's special forces during the Falklands War. His previous service in Arabia, in both Aden and Oman, was also relevant to the task in hand with its need for close co-operation with Arab allies. The Prime Minister therefore overcame resistance from within the military in characteristically summary fashion with the threat that, if she did not get her man into the job, she would outflank them by making General de la Billière her personal adviser on the campaign. His appointment to Riyadh went ahead.

It turned out to be an inspired choice. Peter de la Billière brought a combination of qualities which were ideally suited to the mixture of leadership and diplomacy for which the appointment called. His gentle manner overlay a determination to see British forces used to the best effect in whatever conflict might come, yet without putting them at needless risk. His relish for soldiering communicated itself to his commanders and their troops, whether Army, Navy or RAF, while his calm professionalism earned him a real respect on the part of the American and Saudi military commands and secured for Britain an influence in the planning and conduct of operations which was greater than our substantial contribution in manpower might have warranted.

He lost no time in establishing a basis of close trust and co-operation with his overall commander, Norman Schwarzkopf, whose fuse could be notoriously short, and in different vein with the Saudi joint commander, Prince Khalid bin Sultan, where the fuse tended to look longer but was not necessarily so. In both cases the co-operation developed during the months ahead into real friendship. Indeed, some of Peter de la Billière's sharpest passages at arms were in the event to be with Whitehall rather than with his partners in Riyadh.

From the start it was a pleasure to work with Peter de la Billière. Finding myself in effect his chief political adviser in theatre, it was clear to me how important it would be for us to begin on the right note. I had no need to worry on this score. From our first meeting in the embassy on the morning of Peter de la Billière's arrival in Riyadh on 7 October after an overnight journey by RAF supply flight from Brize Norton, a solid bond of comradeship, indeed at times of complicity, existed between us. This was to be a major asset over the months ahead in our countless discussions together, often way into the night, on issues ranging from broad questions of strategy and coalition policy to the minutiae of public relations, troops' welfare and the snares of our infidel military presence amid the devout Islamic society of our Saudi hosts. Behind Peter de la Billière's gaunt features lay an alert sensitivity and sharp appreciation, coupled with a rich sense of humour, all invaluable attributes for the unprecedented exercise in collaboration which we were about to face.

Unfortunately this key transfer of command was handled in awkward and insensitive manner by the MoD authorities. It was bound to be difficult for Sandy Wilson, as a commander who had successfully set up an active service operation, to find himself obliged to hand over its command to a fellow officer from another service. The fact that the level of command had been raised did not help soothe these feelings. The predicament was compounded by a question of personality, for Sandy Wilson found it difficult to let go the reins of decision to his new commander. Yet he and Peter de la Billière were made by their masters in London to spend six long weeks in uneasy tandem in Riyadh before Sandy Wilson was released from his position as deputy commander to take over command of the RAF in Germany on promotion. The result was a growing irritation and tension in the relationship between the two commanders.

In operational terms it was very helpful to have on hand the benefit of Sandy Wilson's experience of the early stages during October and early November when we were much engaged in dialogue with Whitehall and with Paddy Hine at High Wycombe over options for possible offensive military action, while the American, British and French troop strength steadily built up in theatre. By the time of his final departure on 16 November, critical decisions had been taken by the Americans, Saudis and ourselves on the eventuality of an offensive to get the Iraqis out of

Kuwait and its possible timing. But the RAF were asking a lot of Sandy Wilson by keeping him on for so long in a deputy role after he had successfully set up the British military presence in the Kingdom. Once his place as RAF deputy commander had been taken by Air Vice Marshal Bill Wratten, Peter de la Billière was at last able to get fully into his stride as commander.

Sandy Wilson and I had agreed that, despite the intention to place our ground forces under American tactical command in the event of hostilities, it was important for protocol reasons that the general should pay his first formal call on Prince Khalid bin Sultan as Saudi joint commander. Accordingly we all went round that same evening to see Prince Khalid in his office in the Defence Ministry building in central Riyadh. It was good to see the two commanders quickly hit it off together. Prince Khalid plied us with his special brew of cappuccino and came out with warm recollections of his time as an officer cadet at Sandhurst. He invited Peter de la Billière to meet regularly with him to sort out any problems of co-operation which might arise. He sensibly made it plain that the Saudis had no intention to cut across the recreational activities of our troops, but at the same time he asked that we keep publicity for entertainments to the minimum, in deference to the sensitivities of many Saudis on this score. The same went for our religious services.

Prince Khalid expressed satisfaction with the arrangements for reconciling authority over the British forces in the Kingdom with the joint command structure, which Paddy Hine had worked out so painstakingly with him a few weeks previously. This news came as a considerable relief to us, and was confirmed by Prince Sultan three days later. Peter de la Billière decided to make full use of the access for discussion which Prince Khalid offered, and made a point of going to see him at least weekly throughout the crisis. For his part it was clear that the Prince also set store by the opportunity to have the occasional benefit of Peter de la Billière's advice, particularly given his own lack of experience of multiple command. There were to be moments, indeed, when Peter de la Billière's steadying presence helped to soothe ruffled feelings between the American and Saudi commanders.

A week later, after Peter de la Billière had spent a few days going with Sandy Wilson around his Gulf theatre of command with RAF units in Bahrain and Oman and some of his own special forces undergoing desert training in Abu Dhabi, I took him to call on Prince Sultan in Jedda. It was on the flight down in the HS125 that a growing edginess in relations between general and air vice marshal became evident.

Early autumn is an unpleasantly humid season in Jedda, but we met Prince Sultan in the cool of his elegant house. He gave Peter de la

Billière a warm welcome to his new command and left us in no doubt of his satisfaction at the Prime Minister's decision to add an armoured brigade to the British contribution to Saudi Arabia's defence. Prince Sultan took the opportunity to raise with us for the first time his impatience at the absence of results from the UN sanctions regime. It looked increasingly as though military action would have to be considered if Iraq was to be dislodged from Kuwait. This militant tone took us somewhat by surprise. But while Prince Sultan did not appear to have a specific time-scale in mind, he nevertheless spoke with emphasis and left us in no doubt that for the Saudi leadership the military option had now to be considered. His words set the scene for the dialogue which Peter de la Billière and I were to have with London and with our American counterparts in Riyadh over the next month.

Our call also provided the occasion for Prince Sultan and I to sign our agreement on the conditions which would govern the legal and operational status of British forces in the Kingdom for the duration of the crisis. This was an important document for both countries. On our side it ensured that British forces would remain under British military jurisdiction. The document also defined the role of British forces in helping to counter the threat of aggression, subject to any other purposes that might be agreed. It provided for their prompt withdrawal once the crisis was over, and the requirement for a joint decision before any offensive action could take place. As Prince Sultan explained in a meeting with the international press, this last point was essential to meet Saudi Arabia's need to be able to show her Arab partners that she had not abdicated authority over combat issues to Western powers.

We were unable to meet a proposal that British forces should technically come under overall Saudi command while in the Kingdom. For Whitehall this was a sticking point; British troops had to remain under a British chain of command, although they would be under American tactical control in the field. We found a way around the difficulty with a formula which the Saudis, being accustomed to the idea of monarchy, could readily understand. British forces would operate along lines consistent with the 'overall strategic guidance' of the supreme Saudi Arabian military authority – in other words, King Fahd. In return we retained ultimate British authority over our troops by invoking the constitutional role of the Queen in this respect. For all that it had been two-and-a-half centuries since a British monarch last commanded a British army in the field, it was nevertheless a great help on this occasion to be able to claim the inalienable royal right to ultimate command. The arrangement worked out happily in our case.

Our republican allies, however, found it less easy to come up with a formula to fit their circumstances. Indeed, in the French case the matter of national command became an issue of contention, despite France's political gesture in brigading her land forces with the Saudi wing of the coalition when they arrived in the Kingdom during September.

It had been a considerable achievement to complete the negotiation of this sensitive and unprecedented status arrangement in such a short time. We were helped in some respects by the lead from the Americans with their far more substantial military presence in the Kingdom. But much of the credit was due on our side to the imaginative diplomacy of Derek Plumbly, who led our small embassy and MoD team in the lengthy rounds of discussion. His fluency in Arabic, extending to technical and legal language, was a particular asset.

The process was also greatly helped as a result of Prince Saud's appointment of a highly experienced senior diplomat, Dr Mohammed Omar al Madani, to lead the Saudi side in negotiating status agreements for the various foreign military contingents. We had good cause on this occasion, and at numerous subsequent stages during the crisis, to appreciate his calm good sense in reconciling the essential principles of Saudi Arabia's position as host country with the administrative and operational demands of coalition forces.

One example which illustrated the singular nature of issues which tended to complicate co-operation within the unique coalition was provision for burial of Christian troops killed in action. Saudi Arabia's puritanical society made no provision for non-Moslem burial. Yet with Dr al Madani's help this and many similar problems were resolved. Once things came to war his experience in international law was a great help in ensuring observance of the Geneva Conventions in relation to prisoners of war, and in establishing a monitoring role for the International Committee of the Red Cross.

Our status agreement with the Saudis took the form of a memorandum of understanding and served its purpose ideally throughout the campaign. In the event there were almost no instances of breaches of Saudi law by British forces, an admirable record which some attributed to the absence of alcohol as much as to their busy training regime. I passed a copy of our final agreement to the French ambassador to serve as a guide for his negotiations. The text was also used as a model for Saudi agreements with other coalition partners who subsequently sent military contingents to the Kingdom, such as New Zealand, which provided an air transport unit to help out the RAF, the Canadians, and European countries which later supplemented British medical resources with military hospital units. Our agreement was also drawn upon for local arrangements by British embassies elsewhere in the Gulf.

Shortly after Peter de la Billière's arrival I had my first opportunity to meet General Norman Schwarzkopf, when he came to a dinner I gave in Riyadh in late October on the occasion of a visit by the Chief of the Defence Staff, Sir David Craig. Peter de la Billière had lost no time in getting on close terms with Norman Schwarzkopf, and had succeeded in building up a relationship of trust which was to stand us in very good stead as the coalition's position developed from a defensive into an offensive mode.

One of the earliest products of this liaison was the appointment of a British colonel, Tim Sulivan, to participate in CENTCOM's restricted planning cell in Riyadh. To get around tight American restrictions on access to information, and avoid giving offence to the other coalition partners who did not enjoy this privileged access to the planning scene, Tim Sulivan had to masquerade in the tiger-spotted US battle fatigues in place of regulation British Army desert camouflage. Norman Schwarzkopf made it plain to us during dinner how much store he set by having the RAF and 7th Armoured Brigade under his tactical command.

Norman Schwarzkopf had by this time already acquired a reputation in Saudi Arabia as a commander of determination and thoroughness but with a short temper. It was known that he had lost patience on occasions with the sensitivities and circumspection which were characteristic of the Saudi command hierarchy, and that the diagram which had been worked out for the division of command arangements between the Saudis and the Americans had only been agreed with difficulty. His own staff officers were said to hold him in considerable awe. On the other hand, to the rank and file in the field his commanding personality and physical size lent him an heroic quality. Peter de la Billière had developed a strong respect for his professionalism as a soldier, as well as for the valuable influence he carried with General Colin Powell, the US chief of staff, and through him into the intricate military policy machine in Washington.

For all his sometimes intemperate approach to his own officers, Norman Schwarzkopf took care with his relations with the Saudis and other coalition commanders, and to his credit sustained harmony within the unprecedentedly disparate military alliance. In this endeavour he was probably helped by a personal familiarity with the culture and style of the region, as a result of his own upbringing in Iran, where his father had for a spell in the 1940s been in charge of the imperial gendarmerie. It was a fortunate turn of fate that at this critical time the American general responsible for central command should early in life have had first-hand experience of the Gulf area.

For his part Norman Schwarzkopf left me in no doubt of the value he placed on Peter de la Billière's advice and experience. This became particularly relevant in the field of special operations, an area of activity to which Norman Schwarzkopf brought an in-built scepticism. Peter de la Billière was able progressively to overcome this, to the point where both British and American special operations units were deployed to good effect within Iraq during the DESERT STORM campaign. But at the time of the dinner for David Craig all this lay in the future. The idea of an offensive to re-establish the Kuwaiti government, on which the Saudi leadership was beginning to focus its attention, was still far from being a declared option in Western policy, particularly for the Americans and French, despite careful plans which Norman Schwarzkopf had begun to lay for such an eventuality.

General Schwarzkopf's attendance at the dinner was preceded by a certain amount of turmoil as his personal bodyguards gave my house their security once-over. His level of protection seemed considerably in excess of the discreet yet effective cover given to Peter de la Billière by his Royal Military Police guards.

For all the reputation as a demanding and irascible personality which Norman Schwarzkopf had built up for himself during his first two months in theatre, he turned out to have his humorous side and to be excellent company. His presence, and wearing a suit, was a considerable gesture to us, as he told me it was the first evening he had spent outside a headquarters and battle fatigues in the two months he had been in theatre. Both he, and the French commander who was present, took full part in the evening's discussion. Norman Schwarzkopf had the American gift of vivid idiom – in Hollywood cowboy language the coalition forces were for him 'the guys in the white hats', while the Iraqis wore the black.

Growing Saudi anxiety at the prospect of a prolonged stalemate while economic sanctions were allowed more time to bite, and with the Iraqi leadership showing no sign of easing its military grip on Kuwait, brought the option of a military offensive more clearly into focus in the exchanges which Peter de la Billière and I had with our counterparts at home during October. Prince Sultan's words to us in Jedda on the need for an early decision were backed up by other leading figures who shared a conviction that, given his manic conceit, Saddam Hussein's threat to the whole region would not be removed unless he was dislodged from Kuwait by force. This would have the support of Saudi public opinion, despite querulous voices in some quarters.

From our vantage point in Riyadh these arguments had a certain force, and prompted us to put together in a paper for Whitehall various factors of a diplomatic and operational kind, including timing and environmental aspects, which were now pointing towards a military offensive.

There were of course obstacles involved in raising the coalition's military profile in this way, notably on the American political scene and within the UN Security Council in New York, as well as the likely need for further troop reinforcement to tackle the strong defences which the Iraqi army had by now built up in Kuwait. A feature which gave Peter de la Billière much preoccupation was the problem of how to avoid putting at risk the several hundred Western hostages, mostly British, known to be held as a human shield in military target areas within Iraq, or still in hiding in Kuwait. Consideration was being given to using British special forces in a role here. But the chances of their succeeding in any attempt at rescue looked remote.

It turned out that thinking in Whitehall, spurred on by the Prime Minister, had also been moving in the direction of a military option. Talks were also under way in Washington, and the further major US reinforcement for which Norman Schwarzkopf had been calling in order to take on an estimated Iraqi military strength of nearly half a million men in the Kuwait theatre was at last receiving serious consideration, following a spell when the senior military staff in Whitehall had found thinking among their American counterparts to be at sixes and sevens over the implications of an offensive strategy. For his part Peter de la Billière had come up with the ambitious idea of increasing the British Army contribution to the size of a complete armoured division. This would have the advantage of ensuring that the British force operated in any land attack to best effect as an integrated element within the framework of overall American command.

The reinforcement was also seen as affording a means of remedying a predicament which was causing Peter de la Billière considerable unease. On current plans the 7th Armoured Brigade, now assembling with its armour in the desert to the south of the Kuwait frontier as part of the land shield against any sudden Iraqi thrust, would in the event of an offensive find itself as part of the US Marines division attacking along the coastal axis at what was calculated to be the Iraqis' most heavily defended sector. They would no doubt give a good account of themselves in this role and were already into an intensive programme of field training. General Walt Boomer, their US Marines divisional commander, had developed considerable respect for Patrick Cordingley and would be loath to lose them.

But, as Peter de la Billière saw it, there was little to be said for a situation in which the comparatively small British Army contribution might find itself fighting over coastal terrain strewn with obstacles for which its long-range armour was not best suited and taking a disproportionate share of battle casualties. There was no doubting that, given the scale of

Iraq's military strength now in theatre and her known capability in battlefield chemical weapons, a land campaign could bring a heavy toll in casualties.

We had considerable discussion on how the bid for a second brigade and a divisional headquarters could most effectively be presented within Whitehall. Peter de la Billière was already showing irritation over what he saw as financial niggardliness on the part of the civilian establishment in the MoD, as every request by his headquarters for additional resources to cope with the growing complexity of the operation seemed to meet with negative response and calls for further justification. In practice it was probably pressure from the Treasury, as custodians of the national purse, which was at work here. But Peter de la Billière suspected a lack of backing on the part of the armed forces ministers, which he found at odds with what he knew of the Prime Minister's commitment to provide all necessary military support.

From the point of view of the embassy there was an inconsistency in all this. If tight financial controls were being applied at home, they were not in evidence in theatre. Three months into the crisis the MoD had still to appoint a civil secretariat staff to oversee local expenditure by British forces. Meanwhile individual unit commanders had more or less a free hand in providing for their essential logistic needs at base and in the field. Some local contractors were starting to raise prices as demand for their services reacted to the growth of foreign forces. I was also increasingly aware that our Saudi hosts, no amateurs when it came to financial negotiations, might find reason to jib at reimbursing costs for which the British forces could not account in proper fashion. I had already made my concern on this aspect clear to Archie Hamilton during his visit on 6 October, but financial controllers had yet to materialise.

The bid by Peter de la Billière for a substantial further reinforcement, launched while the first British armoured units were still arriving in the Kingdom and accompanied by proposals for additional RAF and naval resources, was asking a great deal of Britain's stretched military establishment. To put together a second armoured brigade at full wartime strength out of units in Germany and at home would impose much strain on manpower and equipment. In giving the idea my backing through the FCO channel, I stressed the case being made to us by Prince Sultan and other senior Saudi ministers for an acceleration of action to get Iraq out of Kuwait. There was no doubt the additional contingents would now be welcomed by our hosts.

At the same time, however, the resentment which lay not far below the surface of public opinion over the presence of Western forces had in no way diminished. For many conservative Saudis there was a feeling that their closely-regulated world was becoming untuned. Blame for this was more easily attributed to the libertine influence of the growing Western military presence than to the threat posed for the Kingdom's prosperity and way of life by Iraq's sacking of Kuwait. It remained a constant pre-occupation of King Fahd and his government to prevent this atavistic and powerful reflex from getting out of hand, in the face of stimulus by deft Iraqi radio propaganda and from the pulpits of certain mosques.

In this situation it was more than ever necessary that we clear our lines on any further reinforcement well in advance, to give the Saudi author-ities time to prepare their public. These considerations, so peculiar to the Gulf campaign, may have been a source of some exasperation to those responsible in Whitehall and in Washington for decisions on troop deployment. But for the sake of smooth co-operation with our Saudi hosts they were in the first rank of importance. It was a great help throughout the crisis to be able to count on the understanding of David Gore-Booth, Rob Young and others in the FCO, whose familiarity with the cultural environment of the Middle East led them to ensure that these eccentric considerations were given due weight in the MoD and elsewhere. In the present case we had a useful opportunity to talk through these aspects of the proposed reinforcement with Tom King when he came to Saudi Arabia in mid-November to see 7th Armoured Brigade on training.

Meanwhile, the influx from the middle of October of the 11,000 troops of 7th Armoured Brigade and its support elements gave the whole embassy plenty to do. There was a flurry when a Tornado bound for Bahrain from England had to divert to Medina – the kind of incident which would feed Saddam Hussein's insidious propaganda allegations about the presence of Western forces in the holy cities. Fortunately the RAF got the aircraft on its way in quick time.

By now we were receiving an incessant stream of military visitors from home, whose briefing and guiding placed an additional load on both headquarters and embassy. The defence section were particularly stretched to deal with calls for advice on local contacts and conditions. Peter Sincock, together with John Ambler, the air attaché, and our newly-arrived naval attaché, Trevor Waddington, managed to take it all in their stride. While Warrant Officer Dave Muir went off to do a stint receiving British escapees up on the Kuwait frontier, the RAF sergeant, Gordon Carstairs, was kept busy obtaining clearances for the stream of supply flights to the Kingdom. The good relations he had developed with the Saudi aviation authorities were invaluable in keeping the air-bridge going, and somehow his counterparts were never fazed by his rich Scots voice over the telephone.

As BFME's headquarters grew it had to move out of our chancery and nearer to the main joint command centre in the Saudi Defence Ministry and the USAF headquarters. General Chuck Horner's air defence nerve centre had been set up here, partly below ground and partly in a vast tent where radar screens blinked out their vigilant message night and day in a cavernous gloom. There were problems over finding a suitable building downtown, with the result that until January Peter de la Billière and his staff were squeezed into a couple of floors of an office block which they shared with the US Marines command. It became a very tight fit as servicemen arrived by every trooping flight to join different parts of the command structure.

The MoD sprung another of its backhanders on Peter de la Billière towards the end of the year with a proposal that his brother, a captain in the Royal Navy, should take over naval liaison at BFME headquarters. It was decided that one de la Billière was probably enough. It was already confusing for some of our coalition partners to have an American commander with a German name and a British commander with a French one.

Some elements of the RAF's communications network back to the UK continued to operate from the embassy compound, and Sandy Wilson also left his RAF intelligence cell in the chancery, where it remained throughout the campaign. To permit close liaison between the embassy and the downtown headquarters, a secure telephone link was installed by a team of cheerful Gurkha signalmen. This proved its worth on a number of occasions, though it had a maddening habit of going on the blink at critical points in urgent conversations between Peter de la Billière and myself, necessitating a switch to clumsily-coded exchanges on the open telephone which often left us thoroughly bemused.

We established a system whereby Peter de la Billière's personal staff officer, Lieutenant-Commander Colin Ferbrache, a bright and effective Guernseyman, or his ADC, Captain Mark Chapman, who kept a thorough watch over his general's programme, would attend the briefing meeting in the embassy each morning, and often at the end of the day too. Peter de la Billière's own headquarters meeting first thing each morning, when his new chief of staff, the ebullient Air Commodore Ian MacFadyen, provided a briefing on military developments during the previous 24 hours, was attended by Peter Sincock or one of the other attachés.

All this helped us to work in close harmony during the hectic months of military preparation and build-up, and to ensure that local political factors were kept in view. Physical arrangements for the arrival by air of 7th Armoured Brigade's troops, mostly at the half-constructed airfield at

Jubail which had rapidly been brought into service by the Saudis at the outset of the crisis to accommodate American helicopter units, and for their interim accommodation in tented and hutted camps while awaiting the arrival by sea at Jubail port of their vehicles and equipment, was greatly facilitated by the assistance we received from the administration of the Jubail industrial city.

Prince Abdulla bin Faisal bin Turki, the head of the Jubail Royal Commission, did all he could to put facilities at the disposal of the British army logistics teams for their landing and reception facilities. Jubail's huge and under-utilised commercial port was already filling up with acres of recently arrived American vehicles. Now the British sea-train of equipment was about to add to the congestion. An unoccupied construction workers' compound was taken over as a base for the first of the British Army's field hospitals to be set up in the Kingdom. It also served as a recreation facility where troops under training in the desert could take periodic breaks, not least for a shower and some laundry. With typical military humour the camp was christened by the soldiers Baldric Lines, after the moronic batman in the BBC's *Blackadder* television comedy, and the Army logistics base set up in Jubail adopted a black adder for its shoulder insignia to distinguish it from the desert rat of 7 Brigade.

The business of handling the clearance and berthing of the long sea-lift of the brigade's equipment from Europe to Jubail was entrusted at our suggestion to the Saudi firm of Kanoo. This was an exercise which, with the subsequent despatch of a second British brigade, was to go on right up to the start of hostilities in January, using a motley assortment of British and other merchant ships as well as Royal Fleet Auxiliary vessels like the *Sir Tristram, Bedivere* and *Percival,* veterans of the Falklands campaign.

Kanoo's shipping agency had been long established throughout the Gulf, and acted as agents for numerous British commercial interests. In the early part of the century the firm's founder had been appointed by the British authorities in India to handle the official subsidies then paid in gold to the various rulers in the Gulf area as part of the Pax Britannica. Once again the firm found itself acting in the service of the Crown, and made a very good job of it. The flow of merchant shipping into the capacious ports of Dammam and Jubail, where military vehicles soon stretched for kilometres along the shore, was able to take place free from risk of Iraqi interception thanks to the coalition's control of the air and sea lanes. There were, however, shipping delays with some of the less seaworthy vessels which had been pressed into service at short notice.

There was also a risk of drifting mines in the northern Gulf, where the

Iraqis had scattered them on a considerable scale. A flotilla of Royal Navy minehunters, eventually five strong, joined the British destroyer force engaged in enforcement of the trade sanctions on Iraq. The naval force was under the command of Commodore Paul Haddacks, the Senior Naval Officer Middle East, or SNOME, a title not used in the Royal Navy since its withdrawal from the Gulf in 1971. Paul Haddacks was succeeded in early December by Commodore Christopher Craig, who saw the Royal Navy contingent through the fighting stage of the crisis.

I fully supported through the FCO Peter de la Billière's insistence that British command arrangements should be integrated throughout the region on the lines of the Americans. Even so the MoD still managed an own goal during the last stages of our supply sea-train to the Gulf in January, by issuing an advice to British shipping to avoid all Saudi and other northern Gulf ports for risk of mines. This instruction was quickly brought to the embassy's notice by the Saudi Petroleum Ministry, who pointed out the drastic consequences for their shipment of essential oil exports to the international market. BFME headquarters and the local P&O representative added their voices, alarmed lest the instruction should stop the military sea-train en route for Jubail. The Royal Navy minehunters had succeeded so far in keeping these sea lanes open. Pressed by us all to think again, the MoD was persuaded to adapt the advice to an agreement to navigation during daylight hours. It may all have been a case of one part of the MoD coming under pressure from the marine insurance industry, which had already imposed heavy premium supplements on shipping in the Gulf, and failing to consult the other half.

By the time of Tom King's visit in mid-November there were some 17,000 British personnel in the Kingdom, mostly tucked well away from public view in their desert training area north of Jubail, but with substantial numbers in the Riyadh headquarters and with the RAF Tornado squadrons at Dhahran and Tabuk in the north. There was a Tornado squadron at Muharraq in Bahrain, where Sandy Wilson had succeeded in also squeezing in the RAF Jaguar squadron sent out to Oman back in August.

Following his talks in Jedda with King Fahd and Prince Sultan, I flew with Tom King in his VC10 across Arabia to the Gulf coast. Peter de la Billière had arranged a busy round of visits to all three services, starting with the logistics base in Jubail port and a helicopter flight out to see 7 Brigade in the desert. We nearly lost the Defence Secretary at Jubail, when some of us became stuck with him in the lift at the top of the port authority's control tower. We were about to try to climb out through the cabin roof when someone below found a button to get it in motion. An Iraqi gremlin at work, we assumed.

We wanted to use this stage of his visit to put out a message through the press that we were serious in our purpose to see Iraq out of Kuwait by one means or another. Tom King made this plain in a well-attended press conference which the Army laid on in a tent at the end of his run in a Challenger tank amid a brigade exercise to practise an advance through minefields. The Defence Secretary left room for no doubt that, so far as the British government was concerned, we meant what we said about resort to the military option if there was no withdrawal from Kuwait. Saddam Hussein would gain nothing by a policy of playing for time. This was just the message for which the Saudi government were looking from us, and the press conference, helped by its dramatic location, received wide coverage in the Kingdom and at home.

7 Brigade made an impressive sight as the two armoured regiments, the Royal Scots Dragoon Guards and the Queen's Royal Irish Hussars in their Challenger tanks, together with its infantry battalion from the Staffordshire Regiment in Warrior armoured carriers, and the scout cars of the Queen's Dragoon Guards, rehearsed an advance on a wide front across desert terrain. Obstacles had been set to simulate the physical barriers it was known the Iraqis were erecting on the Kuwaiti side of the frontier to obstruct a possible offensive. These involved pipelines, deep trenches to be filled with crude oil which could be ignited, and earthwork berms. The brigade was laboriously engaged in clearing obstacles in its path with the help of the armoured earth-moving vehicles of its engineers, while infantry soldiers swarmed to the attack out of their carriers and the radio network chattered with commands. Enemy opposition was simulated by units of the US Marines with whom 7 Brigade were grouped. As I chased after the Defence Secretary's tank in the commander's seat of a Warrior, little but the surroundings seemed to have changed in the 40 years since I had taken part in similar exercises on Germany's Luneburg Heath during my National Service.

It was all pleasantly informal and the soldiers seemed in cheerful heart, despite the desert heat and absence of alcohol. The army cooks produced a good lunch, which I was relieved to see included no pork, though I gathered that bacon occasionally found its way to breakfast. The British rations were reputed to be far superior to the MRE rations issued to the US Marines, popularly known as 'meals rejected by Ethiopians'. There was a lively business in the exchange of British ration packs for marine cot beds. Tom King took on board the main complaint about the absence of an active service allowance. He also found himself having to explain the inconsistency between such a large military deployment and the government's 'Options for Change' programme which had just been launched to achieve major reductions in Britain's fighting strength following the end of the Cold War. To many servicemen now in the field this just did not add up.

Striking while the iron was hot, Peter de la Billière used the contact with Tom King to press his bid for a second brigade to make up a single British division. Indeed, we had gone so far in the meeting with King Fahd in Jedda as to obtain his approval in principle to this reinforcement. Our proposal coincided with a crucial decision by the American administration to prepare for a military option and authorise a massive troop reinforcement for this purpose. General Schwarzkopf had been pressing Washington on this for several weeks; indeed, his initial bid had been considerably higher, based on what some considered to be an over-cautious estimate of the capacity of Iraqi forces to resist a ground offensive.

An announcement was accordingly made by President Bush on 8 November, having first seen the Congressional mid-term elections out of the way, that he had decided to double American combat strength in the Gulf to some 450,000 men and women, including four additional armoured divisions as well as 300 combat aircraft and two more carrier groups. James Baker had also succeeded in negotiating with the Saudis a joint command structure wherein the Saudis would take the lead in the event of an Iraqi attack on the Kingdom and the Americans would do so should the coalition go on to the offensive. This cleared the way for the massive American reinforcement.

We did not get all we were asking for. General Khalid jibbed when Tom King put it to him in Riyadh that it would make sense for the Kuwaiti armoured regiment, equipped with British Chieftain tanks and trained by British advisers, which had escaped south into Saudi Arabia in August, to be grouped with British armoured forces. Their tanks were currently being restored to battleworthy condition by a team of British REME engineers at the northern Saudi base of Hafr al Batin. The Prince insisted, however, that he must have all Arab forces under his wing of the joint command structure. It was already understood that Arab, and particularly Kuwaiti, troops deserved to take part in the vanguard of any eventual move to recapture Kuwait. In Prince Khalid's view this meant that all Kuwaiti fighting units must come under his command.

We did, however, secure a helpful addition to the RAF's hard-stretched air transport network: the loan of some Kuwait air force Hercules aircraft and a Boeing 747 airliner of Kuwait Airways for use in ferrying troops from the UK to Jubail, in greater comfort moreover than Transport Command could offer. Prince Khalid also cleared the way for the RAF to have full use of Saudi practice bombing ranges and to undertake low-flying training. All in all it was a helpful session.

We flew on that evening to Tabuk. The governor, Prince Fahd bin Sultan, who greeted us there, showed concern at what he saw as the threat of Iraqi-instigated subversion or sabotage across the province's long desert frontier with Jordan. The way in which his friends in the Jordanian leadership had effectively taken sides with Saddam Hussein was plainly a source of sadness to him.

We went to visit the operations and briefing centre of the RAF Tornado squadron, and found it ingeniously improvised in a heavily sandbagged pair of cargo containers, set end to end and all blacked out in the dark. With its dim interior lighting and a certain tension in the air, the setting had more than an echo of a scene from a production of *Journey's End*. The Tornados were lined up on the tarmac while their technicians armed them with coffin-like cratering bombs, almost as long as the aircraft that carried them. One of these aircraft was a few days later destroyed in a landing mishap after a training sortie, but the pilot and observer were fortunately able to eject at ground level and survived.

Tom King gave an upbeat talk to the British service personnel on the base. They seemed in good spirits despite the hard routine of their existence and the uncertainty of what the future held. Around midnight he headed on back to London, where Michael Heseltine had just fired the first salvo in his bid to unseat Mrs Thatcher. It was the early hours of the morning when Sandy Wilson and I got back to Riyadh.

The visit proved well worth while. On 22 November, at Mrs Thatcher's last Cabinet as Prime Minister, the decision was taken to double the strength of the British combat forces in the Gulf with the despatch to Saudi Arabia of 4th Armoured Brigade from Germany plus substantial artillery support. This brought the British land forces up to divisional strength. Additional aircraft and naval minehunters were also to be sent. These substantial increases had the effect of bringing the total strength of British forces in the theatre to some 46,000 by the time hostilities began in mid-January, the largest contingent after the Americans and Saudis, and a significant help in enabling the coalition to match the half-million troops to which Iraq's military strength in the Kuwait area was built up during November and December.

Nor was our military contribution confined to front-line resources. Our discussions with Paddy Hine and other visitors had pointed up a lack of reliable first-hand human intelligence on Iraqi intentions, troop dispositions and morale, as well as the need to develop a capability in the event of hostilities to undertake sabotage and other activity behind Iraqi lines. With the agreement of the Saudis and Kuwaitis a centre was set up near Taif with British Army instructors, headed by an experienced British intelligence officer, to train selected Kuwaiti personnel in the techniques of sabotage and other clandestine operations. They proved keen students and subsequently played a useful part in inhibiting Iraqi military activity within Kuwait.

At the same time a villa in Al Khobar was equipped as a communications link through Saudi and other intermediaries to sources of information among Kuwaitis who had gone into hiding within their country and were putting up a fierce and risky resistance to the Iraqi occupation. I dropped in there one foggy evening in December to find a charmingly old-fashioned cloak-and-dagger atmosphere. The Arabic-speaking official who ran the operation was also participating in debriefing defectors from the Iraqi forces, who were prepared to risk a bullet from their own side to cross the Saudi border and give themselves up. Once the air bombardment began in mid-January this source of information turned into a flood, though its accuracy proved difficult to verify.

The rapid expansion in our military forces did not only produce a busy liaison burden for the embassy. We also did what we could to help with their amenities. Grania put together a committee for troops' welfare, which operated in both Riyadh and Al Khobar with willing help from wives in the embassy and in the wider British community who had opted to stay on. Right up until hostilities began in January, and particularly over the Christmas period, British soldiers and airmen were entertained in people's homes during breaks from duty, cakes were baked and delivered up the line to Jubail and beyond through a chain organised by families in the British Military Mission, and a regular soft drinks canteen run was organised by a public-spirited expatriate in Jubail, Laurence Oates, for troops in the armour training area to the north.

A large quantity of books and videos was collected, mainly by BAe families in Riyadh and Dhahran. The taste in literature was sometimes a bit lurid, and would have upset the Saudi censorship department, but it all went down well with the customers. In Jedda too the community organised a library, which they delivered up to the RAF at Tabuk. Grania also arranged with good friends at home to collect books locally and send them out on the RAF flights from Brize Norton. In anticipation, mercifully unrealised, of sight casualties from chemical weapons, the Talking Books organisation in Britain generously provided special headphone tapes, which were distributed around the military hospitals.

Other comforts were purchased locally with funds contributed by British business groups in Riyadh and the east. These included cosmetics and even Tampax for the female personnel, who were now becoming

numerous in theatre but whose special needs apparently had yet to figure in the quartermaster's stores. The regimental sergeant-major of the
3rd Royal Fusiliers asked for a collection of volleyballs, while the battalion doctor countered with a request for Tinaderm powder for athlete's
foot. Both were promptly despatched up the line. One gift we particularly appreciated was of a supply of UNICEF greetings cards for the use
of British troops, donated by an Iraqi friend living in Saudi Arabia in
exile from Saddam Hussein's regime.

The matter of recreation and amenities for British forces involved
much other activity. Saudi agreement was readily given for a forces post
office to be set up to handle the huge amount of personal and fan mail
which our troops were receiving from home. Towards the end of the year
the Army postal service became overloaded with gift parcels from well-
wishers, particularly consignments of the 'battlecake', a heavy honey
cake for which the *Daily Star* newspaper had published a recipe with
encouragement to Women's Institutes all over Britain to bake it and
send it to the front. The response was enthusiastic and things reached
the point where it looked as if essential military supplies to the forward
units might be restricted in order to get the cake parcels through. The
headquarters in Riyadh was deluged to the point where battlecakes
might have to be used for sandbags. With their nigh-indestructible consistency they would probably have served the artillery well as
ammunition. It was a touching venture, but the volume proved to be
beyond even the Army's substantial appetites.

Just as important as mail was the provision of a radio station by the
Forces Broadcasting Service. We wondered how the Saudis would take to
an invasion of their strait-laced airwaves by a diet of Western pop culture.
The Americans obtained Saudi agreement during September to the establishment of a local forces broadcast in Riyadh and Dhahran, and Tom
King secured Prince Khalid's approval to our following suit in November,
though once again financial objections at home had to be overcome. It
did us all good to be able to tune in during the day to a familiar programme of popular music and news relays. The headquarters also
published a lively weekly newspaper, *The Sandy Times*, printed by a local
Saudi firm and affording a valuable and at times outspoken vehicle of
communication for commanders and servicemen. Its weekly column of
readers' poetry was a poignant feature as we all prepared for possible war.

As a result of his visit, Tom King also agreed to meet the cost of
nudging the BBC's European TV satellite into an orbit which would permit reception by forces in the Gulf. This was a real breakthrough for us,
as it not only brought us via a small dish aerial access to regular BBC
programmes, but also gave us, and a number of key Saudis to whom the

FCO agreed we should present receiving equipment, the opportunity to vary the unremitting diet of CNN's repetitive, and sometimes tendentious, news menu with the BBC's more reputable bulletins. For the troops in the field TV receivers were donated by the British Legion and the *Daily Mirror*. Together with the forces radio this gave a welcome change from the naive radio diet of propaganda and music which the Iraqis had started to beam at the Western forces from Baghdad in a derisory attempt to subvert morale.

BFME headquarters also introduced a regular video series, recording the activities of different units as they underwent training in theatre. Apart from the interesting record this afforded of preparation for possible combat, it was an inspired way to keep the three services in touch and so build up a corporate spirit between them.

The Saudis did, however, hold to their line over live musical entertainment. This was in part the unfortunate result of the musical evening organised for American forces in Dhahran at the outset of the crisis, the transmission of which on CNN had so upset the Saudi establishment. General Khalid had asked Peter de la Billière and me to take particular care on this front. It was as well we did so, as the French found their relations with Prince Sultan prejudiced by an episode in December where their Defence Ministry went ahead, against the French ambassador's advice, with a concert tour by a popular singer to which the French press gave wide publicity. This aroused a forthright Saudi reaction, in the face of which the singer concerned, Eddy Mitchell, returned to France without giving a performance, apparently on the instructions of the French President himself. The affair coincided with a visit to French forces in Saudi Arabia by M Chévènement just before Christmas, and led to the cancellation of a meeting between him and Prince Sultan.

For our part we faced considerable pressure from home to allow tours by well-known singers and other entertainers. My own image in the eyes of the headquarters as Gradgrind – or rather, with the approach of Christmas, as Scrooge – reached a low point when I opposed the concert schemes and continued to insist that only comedians and conjurors should come out. How, I was asked, could servicemen be expected to accept such childish fare?

In the event the two main British entertainment tours were undertaken by just this combination, first by the magician Paul Daniels, though his glamorous assistant stayed behind, and soon afterwards by that indomitable trouper, Lance-Bombardier Sir Harry Secombe. American forces were treated to Bob Hope. They were a great success all round, and the Saudis had no cause for worry.

Harry Secombe stayed with us in Riyadh and kept us in stitches. He arrived back in Riyadh one evening with a nasty cut on his head. Apparently the naval helicopter bringing him to shore from a visit to a frigate off Jubail had dived sharply to sea level when for some reason its warning system indicated a hostile radar had locked on to it. Harry had been jolted off his bench and had literally hit the roof. The operation had to be repeated before the helicopter flew clear, by which time a shaken Harry had reached what he described as the tuneless whistling stage. Asked what might have been the cause of the emergency, he presumed it must have been the action of someone who didn't care for his BBC *Songs of Praise* programme. The visit finished with his leading rousing carols at an embassy party.

Another irony arose from the presence among the British forces of no less than 19 military bands, in a country where all live music was officially regarded as profane. This odd situation was the consequence of the sensible practice in the British forces of training bandsmen to double up, and earn their place in war, as medical orderlies and stretcher-bearers. Owing to the ample deployment of military field hospitals which Norman Schwarzkopf and Peter de la Billière regarded as essential, given the real threat of Iraqi chemical attack, bands were drafted in large numbers to the Gulf from all three services. Practice had to be undertaken well away from population centres.

For us the bonus was that when Grania and I came to plan our annual end-of-year party at the embassy, we were generously given the pick of the country's most famous military bands for the occasion, all of whom would welcome a break from medical standby. We opted for the Scots Guards, whose director of music produced not only his dance band but the concert band too. In their desert fatigues and with Red Cross armbands they looked a far cry from their resplendent costumes of London parades and balls. But the music was superb and the evening in the mild winter's night air of the embassy garden was memorable, all the more so for being tinged with the unease we all felt over what the next few weeks would bring. For some of the headquarters staff there were shades of the Brussels ball held on the eve of Waterloo. The dancing went on into the early morning, by which time it was Christmas Eve. 'We normally play at the Savoy tonight,' said the director of music to me with a touch of wistfulness.

There were other breaks too, so important to us all amidst the pressures of our daily round. The conviction was growing in us that at the end of the day Saddam Hussein would choose a fight and take the beating he merited, rather than opt for the more rational course of exploiting the UN Security Council's deadline to leave the field unbeaten, and perhaps with a portion of his ill-gotten gains intact.

Shortly before Christmas we persuaded Peter de la Billière to take a short break in the villa on our Jedda compound. He and Colin Ferbrache were well looked after by the consul-general, Hugh Tunnell, and his wife Margaret, who took them out into the Red Sea for a day's snorkelling amid the spectacular coral growths and tropical fish along the offshore reef. It refreshed them both. Hugh Tunnell had staying with him his father, then in his early 90s, who had served as a pilot in the very earliest days of aviation in the First World War. Oliver Tunnell enjoyed a rather special moment that autumn during a visit to Jedda port of an American aircraft carrier, the *Franklin D Roosevelt*. In a tour of the ship's modern fighting aircraft the young pilot escorting them round was surprised by the knowledge and technical interest which his elderly visitor was showing, until he discovered he had one of the pioneers of air warfare on his hands. Things had come a very long way since.

Back in Riyadh, Grania and I had Patrick Cordingley with us for a break from his intense two months' stint of bringing 7 Brigade up to its high pitch of readiness. He had also survived an unpleasant traffic accident. We had an enjoyable if somewhat unreal English day of croquet on the lawn, when Nick and Anna Cocking brought round the colonels of the three 7 Brigade regiments. As Arthur Denaro, who commanded the Royal Irish Hussars, wrote to Grania afterwards, he was not quite sure whether it had been a break from reality or a return to it, but 'please God, whatever happens over the next month or so, we will all be able to come back and say our farewells'.

The small club on our embassy compound also provided a friendly port to those based in Riyadh with the BFME headquarters. Harold Formstone ran it in lively style along with Phil Haggar, who put his droll turn of humour to good purpose by making an irreverent video film of embassy activity throughout the crisis, under the title 'Embassy at War'. Our relationship with the military had its occasional ups and downs, but at base it was a happy one.

As Christmas approached everyone did their best to offer a hospitable break to the personnel of the headquarters. There were of course calls in the press at home for the troops in the Gulf to be given a traditional Christmas. This was fair enough, until some bright spark in the MoD suggested that each man should get two cans of beer with his turkey and trimmings. When Peter de la Billière came to me about this, I had no option but to put on my Scrooge-like mien and say no. There was no doubting that one of the reasons for the extent to which Saudi popular opinion had so far acquiesced in the presence of non-Moslem forces in such large numbers had been the willing observance of the Kingdom's prohibition on alcohol on the part of Western forces. It would have been folly to put this confidence at risk on the eve of possible hostilities by breaching our undertaking, even for Christmas. Peter de la Billière agreed and the idea was dropped, but not before it had been given an airing in the British press, and had come to the attention of General Prince Khalid. He was manifestly relieved to learn of our decision.

Over Christmas worship, too, our arrangements to proceed with all discretion were not helped by attempts in certain newspapers to dramatise and distort the position. The Saudi authorities sensibly recognised that our troops had a right to their worship, especially at this time. But as always it was publicity which complicated things for them. Fortunately many of the journalists in the Kingdom opted to go home for Christmas, taking a chance that Saddam Hussein would not choose that moment to make a move. We finessed a well-intentioned proposal by the BBC to broadcast a carol service uniting troops in the Gulf with their families at home by arranging for representatives from each unit in the Kingdom to go across to Bahrain, where there was no problem over Christian worship, and participate from there. The programme was a great success. Thus the fuss evaporated and we all got on with our festival. One of the most touching features, told to me by several in the headquarters, was the number of Saudis who, on passing our soldiers in the streets of Riyadh on 25 December, gently bade them a Merry Christmas.

As our military strength built up, and the UN Security Council's countdown for Iraq's withdrawal drew on, so the pressure of senior visitors from London became yet more intense. Most stayed either with us or with Peter de la Billière. Grania kept the hospitality going at a remarkable pace. We introduced Paddy Hine to the pleasures of the hubble-bubble pipe, while Peter de la Billière's vice turned out to be chocolates. Grania kept him plied throughout the crisis, to sustain his remarkable energy. The welfare side of things was very active, and our community came up with all kinds of hospitality and comforts.

Things did not always go according to plan, however. There was an occasion in early December when Grania travelled to Jubail with a colleague to deliver books and videos to the British field hospital. Her companion was in a fairly advanced state of pregnancy, and by the time they reached the hospital was showing signs of imminent miscarriage. As the Range Rover entered the camp gate, the sentry was startled to be asked urgently for a gynaecologist. It was stiffly pointed out that this was a war hospital and not equipped for childbirth. To their credit, however, the Medical Corps produced a nursing sister with midwifery experience, and crisis was narrowly averted.

With the turning of the year, however, Peter de la Billière decided he must call a halt to visitors, in order to focus effort on final arrangements for the likelihood of hostilities. 4th Armoured Brigade from Germany with its slow sea-train in tow was forming up during December and early January, and needed time to acclimatise and get its desert training to the pitch achieved by the Desert Rats of 7 Brigade. 4 Brigade was commanded by Christopher Hammerbeck, a tank officer, and its major fighting units were the 14th/20th King's Hussars with Challengers, and two Warrior-equipped infantry battalions, the Royal Scots and the 3rd Royal Regiment of Fusiliers. The new division was also to have a strong Royal Artillery and Royal Engineers element, and the 16th/5th Lancers for observation work. The whole show was now to operate as an independent British division, commanded in the field by a paratroop officer, Major-General Rupert Smith, as part of the American VII Corps under General Fred Franks.

All this represented a very substantial increment to the British strength on the ground, yet gave little time to prepare men and equipment before the end of January, the date set for the division to become operational. In January Paddy Hine raised with me again the status of the growing numbers of female military personnel being sent to the Gulf as our strength built up. He was particularly keen that they should drive military vehicles as their American counterparts were doing. Among the American forces the proportion of servicewomen was considerably higher; indeed by then the number of American women personnel in theatre was said to exceed the total of all British troops.

With hostilities looking imminent, there seemed no further cause to be as restrictive as hitherto over the tasks which British servicewomen personnel could perform in Saudi public view. The initial widespread sense of outrage visible in response to the American female presence had by now abated, particularly with the steps which had been taken to cool down the more vehement Friday sermon against the presence of infidel troops in the Kingdom. For their part our forces' commanders had shown real forbearance over this problem, and had earned credit from the Saudi authorities.

Indeed, the behaviour of British forces since their first arrival in the Kingdom had been exemplary. As an American military policeman put it, 'the Saudis have eliminated the main causes of most problems, namely wine, women and song. Without them there ain't much left to get in trouble over.' We agreed therefore to let driving go ahead, though I asked that this should not take place in the cities. It also made sense for military chaplains to wear their insignia while with their units. As Paddy Hine rightly put it, they had to be identifiable in action.

The Americans still had major reinforcements *en route* from Germany and the USA, which needed to be fitted into the battle plan now starting to take shape. In addition Egyptian and Syrian armoured units were still arriving in the Kingdom, and the French had yet to decide on where their forces were to come under command. We had had a moment of slight awkwardness on this last point during one of our regular meetings of EC ambassadors in Riyadh, when the Frenchman had somewhat rashly vaunted the numbers of French forces now in theatre until gently asked by the Italian which way they were pointing. French indecision, while their coalition government tried to make up their minds just how committed they were to seeing Saddam Hussein driven out of Kuwait by force, was provoking irritation within the military alliance, and not least to the Saudis.

Nor was it only the headquarters that still had considerable clearing of decks to do as the New Year approached. In the embassy we found ourselves interceding with the Saudis to open the way for representatives of the International Committee of the Red Cross, with its Swiss secretariat based in Geneva, to operate in the Kingdom and carry out its international responsibility of supervising, at least on the coalition side, proper observance of the various Geneva Conventions governing the conduct of war and the treatment of prisoners.

Initially the role of the Red Cross in this important area was not fully understood by the Saudi authorities. There were questions about what kind of status should be accorded to the ICRC's staff, and even some hesitations over whether their insignia of a cross would arouse public antipathy among puritanical elements of Saudi society. We were able to help reassure the Foreign Ministry on a number of these points, with the result that by January the ICRC had a representative, Arnold Leuthold, in place who devoted himself indefatigably over the coming months to such matters as the release of prisoners of war and civilians detained in Iraq, and subsequently to the plight of Iraqi refugees who sought safety in Saudi Arabia from Saddam Hussein's post-war pogroms.

We also managed to help the British forces finalise their lengthy negotiations with the Saudi military on the terms of host nation financial support, covering issues ranging from repayment by Saudi Arabia of costs incurred by our troops in the Kingdom to arrangements for the temporary burial of British personnel. Derek Plumbly and the other members of our chancery who were involved in these negotiations had worked patiently to help bring things to a conclusion. I made a point of pressing Peter de la Billière to sign the agreement before the date when hostilities might begin, as thereafter both the Saudis and ourselves would have our attention focused elsewhere. It was a relief when he told me on 15 January, the last day before the UN deadline, that he had signed with Prince Khalid bin Sultan, just in time for war.

Even then a few of the Saudi contractors our forces had engaged showed reluctance to transfer their contracts to the Saudi military command, though whether because of the possibility of seeing their margins trimmed or through other financial considerations was never entirely clear. So far as the British forces were concerned, they all gave us good service.

To demonstrate to his own people, as well as to Iraq and her few clients within the Arab world, that the military coalition was indeed a reality King Fahd arranged in early January for a major parade of coalition forces to be held in the northern desert near Hafr al Batin. There was initial American hesitation as to whether to take the time off to participate, but good sense and solidarity prevailed. For our part we emphasised to Whitehall the importance of participating in this display, and permission was given.

Peter de la Billière collected together an assortment of British troops from all three services, plus one of the military bands to add a bit of martial colour, which went down well. The King used the opportunity to make a strong speech justifying the cause of liberating Kuwait and calling for Iraq's withdrawal before it was too late. After he had inspected the assembled forces everyone joined in a traditional Arab feast, with rulers, commanders and troops all sitting together on carpets spread on the desert floor. It was a picturesque and typically Saudi event which received useful media publicity in the Kingdom and throughout the region.

In these last weeks before the deadline expired we received two visitors of exceptional significance from home: the Prince of Wales and, two weeks later, the new Prime Minister, John Major. The Prince came on 22 December, just before Christmas, and spent two days in Saudi Arabia seeing the whole range of British military activity, and spending a night afloat in the Gulf on HMS *Brazen*. His visit had been set up at short notice from London. It appeared in part to have stemmed from suggestions in the more restless quarters of the British press that both the Prince and Princess of Wales should pay a Christmas visit to the forces. When the FCO told me of the proposal only ten days beforehand, I welcomed the idea of the Prince coming out, not only for the good this would do for our forces, but also on the diplomatic side for the message of solidarity it would give to the Saudi leadership and people, while sending an important contrary signal to Baghdad.

I was, however, less enthusiastic about the presence of the Princess on such a mission. Given the sensitivities of Saudi protocol where women were concerned, and particularly at a time when crisis circumstances and tight timing made it difficult for the Saudis to arrange their customary programme of hospitality, I was convinced that her coming would cause them embarrassment. Also in my mind was the certainty that the large British press contingent now in the Kingdom could not be restrained from playing up the Princess' visits to units in the desert with images of tank rides in military gear. This was bound to afford conservative elements within local opinion yet another pretext for criticism of the presence of infidel forces with their female component, and so apply further strain to popular misgivings which the Saudi government was already stretched to control. Moreover, Iraq's agile propaganda machine was bound to exploit this aspect.

I discussed these reservations with Peter de la Billière and Paddy Hine, who happened to be in Riyadh, and was relieved to find that they had their own misgivings about a visit by the Princess, based on security considerations in a theatre of war. The Prince could more easily fit into the operational military environment, including the night aboard HMS *Brazen*. Accordingly we recommended through our respective channels that the Prince of Wales should come unaccompanied. The MoD suggested that the Princess should instead visit Germany to meet some of the families of those serving in the Gulf. Apparently our discouragement of her visit came as a disappointment, and it was indicated to me that it had led to some uncomfortable exchanges in Whitehall. But Peter de la Billière and I had no doubt that it was the right decision in the circumstances.

For their part, and despite the short notice and their other preoccupations, the Saudis pulled out the stops to welcome the Prince. King Fahd was away at the GCC summit meeting, taking place in Doha, Qatar's capital. His brother, Crown Prince Abdullah, did the honours, giving a congenial banquet in his palace in Riyadh which was attended by a large contingent of the Al Saud family, Saudi ministers and some members of the British community who were staying to see things through. Prince Sultan broke off an engagement with the French Defence Minister to be present. The Saudi joint commander, Prince Khalid, was also there. One of the Prince of Wales' closer acquaintances among the Al Saud, Prince Sultan bin Salman, who had participated as an astronaut in an American space flight, was absent, however, flying patrols with the RSAF. The Crown Prince took a characteristically robust line over the need to put a stop to Saddam Hussein's expansionist ambitions, and made the point that there could be no security until he was ousted. He clearly welcomed the presence of the Prince of Wales as an important demonstration of our common purpose.

The main purpose of the Prince's visit was to meet British troops. These were now building up fast, as 4 Brigade was ferried in from

Germany. Having seen off Archie Hamilton, the Minister of State, at the end of a flying pre-Christmas visit to the troops and to talk with his Saudi counterpart, I flew across to Jubail with Peter de la Billière the night before the Prince's arrival. A Kuwait Airlines 707, on loan to us for trooping, had landed from Germany just ahead of our HS125. The airfield showed no lights, and it was a dramatic sight to see the long, dark line of soldiers descending from the aircraft and forming up on the tarmac, silhouetted in a clear desert moon.

We were back at the airfield early next morning to meet the Prince of Wales on his arrival from Britain. The tarmac was cluttered with American military helicopters, being reassembled for operations. The governor of the Eastern Province, Prince Mohammed bin Fahd, had also come out to give a greeting. The Royal Flight BAe 146 soon arrived and, despite the tight schedule of military visits which the headquarters had arranged, we took a cup of Arabian coffee with Prince Mohammed before the party was whisked off by helicopter to be briefed in the desert by General Rupert Smith, who had taken up command of 1st Division.

The Prince packed in visits to 7 Brigade and the logistics base at Jubail, as well as spending the night on patrol with HMS *Brazen* and an early morning with the Tornado squadrons at Dhahran. In Riyadh he made a tour of Peter de la Billière's cramped headquarters and had a talk with Norman Schwarzkopf at the Defence Ministry operations centre. We visited the air defence control centre in a marquee behind the USAF headquarters, entering into a gloom broken by the dim lights of countless dials and monitoring screens, over which crouched American, Saudi, British, French and Canadian personnel, ready to throw aircraft into action should any signal of hostile action come from the airborne radars. The busy atmosphere brought it home that here was possible war in earnest, and with an impressive high-tech co-operation arrayed to meet it.

There were welcoming smiles all round for the Prince of Wales. His visit to the theatre had been thoroughly worth while both for morale and for our partnership with the Saudis at this time of danger. Not least welcome was the supply of videos which he brought out for the troops. As one of the American marines with 7 Brigade put it, 'Last month we had a visit from President Bush, but now we've got a real VIP.'

John Major's visit to Saudi Arabia on 7 and 8 January had a particular importance, not only for its opportunity for contact between the new Prime Minister and our commanders and servicemen in the field, but also to reaffirm the confidence of our political relationship with King Fahd and his government, which had taken a knock with the abrupt disappearance from office of Margaret Thatcher. The Prime Minister began with a call on the Amir of Kuwait in his exile in Taif, and came on to Riyadh for a dinner with Crown Prince Abdullah, who once again turned out the great and good of the Kingdom to meet him. This was followed by a late session with King Fahd. The conviction was growing on all sides that Saddam Hussein's intransigence would lead to war, though he might yet have a trick up his sleeve. Much was to depend on a crucial eleventh hour encounter between the American and Iraqi foreign ministers, expected to take place in Geneva on 9 January.

With all of us, British and Saudis, the new Prime Minister came across very well. I noted at the time how approachable he was, and the clear-headed view he took of the issues confronting us and of sensitivities within the coalition. He was particularly concerned with his message to the British troops. As Peter de la Billière and I flew with him in the VC10 from Riyadh to Jubail early on 8 January, he told us of his sense of humbleness before these men and women who might shortly be going into action. We agreed he should set out the principles and issues at stake and assure them that all at home were 100 per cent behind them in whatever lay ahead.

From the moment we came down by helicopter into the swirling sand of 4 Brigade's training area south of the Kuwait frontier, John Major launched himself into a succession of informal gatherings with infantry and armour, transport drivers and tank workshops, as well as seeing an impressive review of Navy strength in mid-Gulf, and meeting RAF and BAe personnel gathered round the Tornadoes at Dhahran.

With all he hit just the right note, with his plain man's approach showing a blend of encouragement and of modesty in the face of their duty to come. As he put it to one gathering, 'Unless Saddam Hussein gets out of Kuwait, we will invite you to remove him. Whatever needs to be done could not be in better hands.' There were no histrionics, rather a lump in many throats. I found myself relieved that it was John Major's calm tones which were sending these troops to battle; had it been Mrs Thatcher I suspected she would have been carried away by her martial spirit and aroused embarrassment. Even the REME mechanics in their grimy overalls gave the Prime Minister a rousing cheer and clustered to be photographed with him in front of a Challenger.

He had the same steadying effect on members of our civilian community when he saw them in Riyadh. There was cheerful backchat in the desert with the Fusiliers and the Hussars. A Fusilier, unrecognisable in full battle kit, greeted me. It turned out to be the padre, Adrian Pollard, who had been our embassy chaplain in Algiers six years before and was now in the thick of soldiering. We arranged to meet up in Riyadh when it was all over.

With the Hussars Peter Sincock and I took photographs of several troopers with their regiment's Roman Catholic padre, to send back to their families and girlfriends. We became so caught up with the friendly enthusiasm of the soldiers that we missed most of the Prime Minister's desert press conference to the scores of international journalists who had been ferried out to hear him repeat our commitment to see Saddam Hussein out of Kuwait. It was a dramatic setting in which to put the message across. At Dhahran airfield that evening the aircraftsmen hung out a banner proclaiming 'We want Kate Adie', the BBC's troubleshooting correspondent who had become something of a mascot figure. John Major enjoyed the jibe, and wished us all luck as he flew off to London.

As Charles Powell, the private secretary John Major had inherited from Margaret Thatcher, put it to me, a lot had been learnt in these two days. For us, as for the Saudis, they had been well worth while and we returned to Riyadh buoyed up by the visit. By now hostilities looked all but inevitable. Our last senior military visitors, the chief of the general staff, General Sir John Chapple, and the Chief of Air Staff, Air Marshal Sir Peter Harding, came out for a final look before the shutters came down on all visits. We all still had much preparation and liaison to do before the decks would be clear.

CHAPTER 10

Oil and Money

The crisis over Kuwait, and the heavy burden of expenditure which it imposed, hit Saudi Arabia at an awkward moment. Despite harbouring over a quarter of the world's proven oil reserves, twice those of Iraq, Saudi Arabia's economy had been going through a bad patch. By 1990 it was just starting to show signs of recovery from the collapse of the country's legendary oil boom, brought about by the low crude oil prices which had been a feature of the international economic scene throughout the 1980s. This sharp decline in Saudi government oil revenues, from $37 billion in 1983 when prices were still around the $30 a barrel mark, to a low point of under $14 billion in 1986 with prices down to $12 a barrel and Saudi production cut to just over four million barrels a day, a level below that of the UK, had led to a series of deficit budgets and cutbacks in the Kingdom's ambitious civil development.

At the same time expenditure was being swollen by a surge in military projects, such as the Al Yamamah programme with the UK for the supply of Tornado and Hawk warplanes and naval minehunters, and similar programmes with the Americans and French for the supply of combat and early-warning aircraft, air defence systems and frigates. This military re-equipment programme was far from a superfluous exercise. It was seen as necessary to counter a genuine threat to the security of the Kingdom and her smaller Gulf partners, principally from Iran, locked into a stalemate conflict with Iraq and hostile in her post-revolutionary fervour to Saudi Arabia's custodianship of Islam's holiest shrines.

The Kingdom was also developing, with due foresight as it turned out, a mistrust of the expansionist ambitions of Saddam Hussein's Iraq. But in this case she sought to neutralise potential aggression through costly subvention of Iraq's military chest in the war against Iran, and perhaps of her armaments manufacturing programme too. In January 1991, goaded by Iraqi propaganda accusations of Saudi niggardliness towards her less wealthy Arab neighbours, King Fahd disclosed that assistance to Iraq during the long-running conflict with Iran had amounted to $25.7 billion, a munificent contribution against the background of the weak oil prices of the 1980s and one which the Kingdom was to regret, though it may have seemed an act of prudent reinsurance at the time.

Until 1988 it was possible for the Saudi Finance Ministry to fund the consequent budget deficits without recourse to borrowing, by drawing down on the massive reserves which had been built up during the boom years of the 1970s. From 1988, however, these had diminished to the point where it was necessary to find additional resources to meet the budgetary deficit by raising funds from local private and parastatal sources through the issue of government development bonds and treasury bills. In effect this meant the creation of a national debt, a step which called for very careful presentation in view of the deep-seated resistance on the part of the conservative Islamic element in Saudi society to the practice of borrowing at interest. Economic activity within the Kingdom had also slowed down from the frenzied pace of the late 1970s, as the country's gross domestic product exhibited low growth during the mid-1980s and even showed a fall in 1987.

Nevertheless, by the outset of 1990 the clouds were starting to clear. In its budget for that year the Saudi Finance Ministry felt able to project a more encouraging picture for the recovery of the economy. During the previous year oil prices had returned to around $17 per barrel on the back of an incipient recovery in international economic activity, as well as a stricter observance of production quotas by OPEC members. In this exercise in self-discipline Saudi Arabia had demonstrated her readiness to play tough with her fellow oil producers. There were grumbles from some quarters in OPEC, led ominously by Iraq, at Saudi Arabia's refusal to join in forcing the price yet higher through additional production restraint, and some sour accusations that in going for moderation in oil prices the Kingdom was dancing to an American tune.

In practice, however, Saudi Arabia had her own sound reasons for resisting pressure to bring the price of crude back up to the elevated levels of a decade earlier, which she recognised as having contributed to the subsequent market contraction and its associated price collapse. With a price per barrel at around $17 the Kingdom was by the beginning of 1990 producing at a volume of five-and-a-half million barrels a day, still only half the record levels she had achieved in the boom of ten years earlier, but on the mark of her quota target of one-quarter of OPEC's total production. Her revenues from oil in 1989 had recovered to $24 billion and were expected to reach $30 billion by the end of the year. It was being suggested that within three years the budget deficits might be a thing of the past, and depleted financial reserves could start to be restored.

The initial effect of the Iraqi invasion of Kuwait in August 1990 was to give a sharp boost to oil prices, when supplies amounting to some five-and-a-half million barrels a day from Iraq and occupied Kuwait were suddenly lost to the market as a result of the prompt imposition of sanctions by the UN, followed by the blocking by Saudi Arabia and Turkey of Iraq's main oil export pipelines across their territory to the Red Sea and the Mediterranean. Two Iraqi tankers which arrived at the Iraqi pipeline terminal near Yanbu on Saudi Arabia's Red Sea coast a few days after the invasion, in what was evidently a move to test Saudi resolve, were denied permission to berth and sailed away unladen on 19 August. When I raised the arrival of these vessels with the Foreign Ministry in Riyadh shortly after the passage on 6 August of UN Security Council Resolution 661, prohibiting trade with Iraq, I was assured that no loading of oil would be permitted.

The price of some crudes rose to touch $40 for a brief moment during August. But it dropped by some ten dollars later in the month, following a statement on 18 August by the Saudi Petroleum Minister, Hisham Nazer, that the Kingdom intended to raise production to as much as ten million barrels a day to help stabilise the market and ease the shortage.

This was a bold and important decision on the part of the Saudi government. It was taken with the prime aim of avoiding the kind of disruption to world economies which had occurred during the oil price panic of the late 1970s. It also had the purpose of forestalling resentment on the part of consuming countries at the sight of oil producers profiting on a major scale from oil sanctions on Iraq, with a consequent loss of sympathy for Saudi Arabia and other Gulf states whose security was under serious threat.

In practice the Kingdom still enjoyed a windfall benefit in oil revenues, as the producer with the greatest capacity to sustain a sudden rise in output. By the end of the year Saudi Arabia had raised her output from five-and-a-half million barrels a day to over eight million. Abu Dhabi also pushed up her production, but elsewhere within OPEC increases were small or negligible. Largely as a result of the Saudi increase, which had the effect of raising her share of OPEC's total to 35 per cent, the organisation had by December more than made up for the shortfall in world production, and prices had dropped to around $25 per barrel, a level which was still sufficiently high to satisfy pressure among less well-endowed members of the organisation for some revenue benefit from the crisis.

The increase in oil prices from August onwards, plus the 50 per cent rise in the volume of Saudi output, produced a leap in the value of the Kingdom's oil export revenues from $24 billion in 1989 to $40 billion by

the end of 1990. But even this spectacular increase was to be overwhelmed by demands on the Saudi exchequer imposed by the crisis.
These claims came from all sides, building up massively as the crisis
drew on. By the time Iraq was finally evicted from Kuwait and the foreign
contingents were packing up to go home in the spring of 1991, the
Saudis put their costs of the crisis, both military and diplomatic, at $55
billion, nearly a half of the value of the Kingdom's gross domestic product for 1991. It is to their credit that the Saudi government did not cavil
at this onerous burden, but met it in generous fashion.

The costs fell broadly into three categories. The largest was the direct
cost of military forces, both Saudi and other contingents, which came to
the Kingdom's defence from the West and from Moslem states. By the
time of the offensive to liberate Kuwait these involved, according to the
Saudi joint commander, Prince Khalid bin Sultan, 37 national contingents, of which 24 were in the Moslem wing of the coalition under his
direct command. The American contribution had grown to over half a
million service personnel in the Gulf theatre, followed by the British,
which at the outset of hostilities totalled some 46,000. The next largest
was Egypt, with 40,000 armoured troops, followed by the Syrians with
some 20,000. French land, sea and air forces in theatre totalled not far
short of this number, and there was also a small Canadian air force contingent in the Kingdom and in Qatar, and an Italian Tornado squadron
based in Abu Dhabi. In addition there were the costs of Saudi Arabia's
own expanded armed forces, some 118,000 strong, and units from all
her GCC partners, including Kuwaiti forces reformed and trained at
Saudi expense.

All these elements in the coalition took part in some form in the
eventual action to recover Kuwait. Contingents of varying sizes from
other states also answered the call to the defence of Saudi Arabia and the
enforcement of the naval blockade of Iraq, but stopped short of joining
the military action against Iraq in Kuwait. These ranged from land forces
from Morocco, Pakistan, Bangladesh and Senegal among leading
Moslem states, to naval units from Denmark, Holland and Belgium,
Canada, Australia and Argentina (the friendly co-operation established
in the Gulf between the Royal Navy and their Argentinian counterpart
less than ten years after the Falklands War was noteworthy). In addition
there were support units in transport, medical and anti-chemical warfare
roles from a wide variety of Western and former Soviet bloc countries,
including Canada, Spain, Portugal, the Scandinavians, Hungary,
Czechoslovakia, Romania, Singapore and New Zealand.

In all these cases Saudi Arabia readily carried the substantial costs of
accommodation and replenishment where troops were deployed within

the Kingdom. But the costs did not stop there. Led by the Americans under pressure from Congress, the three main Western contributors to the coalition sought from an early stage to have the wider costs of their deployments reimbursed by their Saudi hosts. Contributions were also sought from other governments with funds to spare but which were unwilling or unable to contribute directly to the military effort. Notable among the latter category were Germany and Japan, still operating since the Second World War under a self-imposed prohibition on the partici-pation of their forces in international military activity.

So far as the Saudis were concerned, when I first raised the idea of a financial contribution to the broader costs of the British deployment with the Saudi Finance Minister in October 1990, Sheikh Mohammed Aba al Khail suggested that the windfall oil revenues which Saudi Arabia was receiving should make this possible. By the end of the crisis six months later, however, the scale of the payments made by the Kingdom to the USA, and on a lesser scale to ourselves and the French, towards the costs of our military deployment far exceeded the estimates which both of us had in mind in this first discussion.

In an open-handed show of appreciation for the prompt military response to the crisis by the three main Western participants in the coalition, King Fahd authorised payments in the early months of 1991 of $13.5 billion to the Americans, as well as $1 billion to ourselves and $500 million to the French, to help meet the costs of deployment and re-equipment. This was in addition to the costs in the Kingdom which his government was already picking up. It was a munificent contribution which amounted to about one-third of the total cost of British military deployment. Inadequate accounting by the MoD, however, meant that a substantial portion of our administrative costs in Saudi Arabia in the early stages of the deployment was not recovered.

The Saudi treasury also faced major expense in respect of military and political support from other key quarters. The Egyptians received an outright grant of $1.5 billion for their ready military response and in recognition of Egypt's crucial role in standing up to Saddam Hussein within the Arab League. This grant comprised a portion for immediate support for Egypt's balance of payments, with the remainder dedicated to the funding of capital development projects.

Syria too was rewarded for her support and despatch of troops with a grant of $1 billion. Keen as always to drive a hard bargain, the Syrians began to play up in the period before the launching of the coalition's offensive in January with indications that they might jib at committing their forces to the liberation of Kuwait. By this calculated threat to the carefully co-ordinated battle plan of General Schwarzkopf and Prince

Khalid bin Sultan, the Syrians managed to extract from the Saudis an advance deposit of $500 million, a characteristic Syrian price for the token part she was to play in the military offensive.

Other payments by the Kingdom went towards securing political support on a wider international front. Turkey had a key role to play here. With some urging from the Americans and ourselves the Saudis came up with a generous offer of $2 billion of help for Turkey, of which $1.5 billion was to meet the cost of oil purchase and the balance for the acquisition of American military equipment. This financial assistance played a significant part in ensuring Turkey's support for the international effort to achieve Iraq's withdrawal from Kuwait. But given the sensitivity of her bilateral relationship with Iraq, stemming from a mutual concern over Kurdish irredentism in their frontier region, the Turks were not prepared to take part in direct military action against Saddam Hussein, nor to respond to a Saudi invitation shortly after the invasion of Kuwait to contribute to the international deployment within the Kingdom.

Another major beneficiary of Saudi financial largesse was the USSR. Soviet support, or at least acquiescence, in the incremental stages of Western-led action within the UN Security Council to force Iraq out of Kuwait, was from the start essential to the success of the operation. With the recent burying of the hatchet of the Cold War, Soviet support for Iraq in the face of Western resistance to her occupation of Kuwait was no longer an automatic reflex. Saddam Hussein had made a serious miscalculation in this respect. Nevertheless there were still those within the USSR's military and political hierarchy who were uneasy at the unprecedented degree of adherence to the Western line in the UN Security Council adopted by President Gorbachev and Foreign Minister Shevardnadze. This was particularly the case within the officer corps of the Soviet Army, which had long enjoyed a close co-operation with the Iraqi armed forces. Indeed Iraq, with the fourth largest army in the world, was one of the USSR's leading customers for military equipment.

With the resignation of Eduard Shevardnadze in December 1990, Soviet concern to play a more prominent role in averting hostilities by seeking a negotiated solution to the crisis became more evident, and led to greater efforts to harmonise policy on the part of the Americans. As part of the effort to retain Soviet support, the Saudi finance and foreign ministers visited Moscow in January 1991, shortly before the expiry of the UN deadline for Iraq's withdrawal, with a substantial offer of a soft loan of $4 billion. Although Soviet attempts to mediate continued right up to the launching of the land offensive into Kuwait in late February this Saudi gesture, representing a breach with some 55 years of diplomatic ostracism of the communist and godless USSR, no doubt played its part in securing Soviet readiness to leave Saddam Hussein to his fate when the chips went down.

In the event the breakup of the USSR occurred before the disbursement of this aid had taken place. It was subsequently divided by the Saudis, with half allocated to the newly independent Moslem states in Central Asia which had seceded from the Union.

There was recompense too, if on a lesser scale, to other states who had come with a price tag to Saudi Arabia's defence. Pakistan received three months' oil supply, and Bangladesh and Senegal also benefited. Bilateral contacts were established with Zimbabwe, as a new member of the UN Security Council who had been cultivated in the past by Iraq. On the other hand, Saudi assistance to Jordan was terminated, despite tentative intercessions by the Americans and ourselves to suggest its resumption, and also to Yemen, evidence of whose partiality towards Iraq was giving deep offence.

The Saudis were also irritated by exhortations from certain Western quarters, notably within the US Congress and from the German foreign minister, that they and their Gulf partners should in future contribute more generously to the welfare of their less well-endowed Arab neighbours. This provoked from King Fahd an uncharacteristic exercise in trumpet blowing to remind the world that the Kingdom produced one of the highest per capita rates of international aid donation. A seed was nevertheless planted which resulted in the establishment of a new Gulf Fund by the GCC states some months after the crisis.

These heavy military and political costs to the Kingdom, which were to carry forward as a burden on the Saudi budget for at least four years after the liberation of Kuwait, were compounded by other expenses resulting from the upheaval of the crisis. In the immediate aftermath of Iraq's invasion, while Saudi Arabia herself seemed under the threat of attack, there was a rush by holders of Saudi riyals, both Saudi nationals and expatriate workers, to exchange these deposits into dollars and other currencies. This produced a heavy run on the riyal in the first days of August, which threatened to upset the international value of Saudi Arabia's currency.

Already a similar wave of selling the Kuwaiti dinar had led to its substantial discounting on the international exchanges and even to refusal by some banks to accept the dinar. After hasty consultation between the governor of the Saudi Arabian Monetary Agency, Mohammed al Sayyari, and the heads of the leading banks in the Kingdom, a bold decision was taken to confront and turn the tide of selling by making foreign currency fully available from reserves, rather than introducing restrictions to restrain the outflow.

It was a gamble but it came off, to the credit of the Kingdom's financial reputation. By late September, with the coalition's military shield in place and the international community applying economic sanctions to Iraq, confidence in Saudi Arabia had returned to the point where the outflow had been entirely reversed. Indeed, under the stimulus of the military deployment a new boom became visible by the year's end, and 1990 ended with a net inflow of funds to the Kingdom of some $22 billion, in the circumstances a remarkable statement of confidence.

A greater financial burden for Saudi Arabia was the influx of refugees in their thousands from Kuwait. The first wave occurred in the wake of the August invasion, followed by a second flood in October when, having demonstrated their readiness to sack the country they had occupied, the Iraqis reopened the frontier with Saudi Arabia and encouraged Kuwaiti citizens, Iraq's new 'subjects', to take refuge abroad.

At both official and private levels the Saudis welcomed these refugees with generous hospitality. From the outset they were accommodated in hotels, schools and other emergency centres all over the country. They were given a daily allowance for food and free petrol in their cars. Their Kuwaiti dinars, now heavily discounted on the open market, continued to be exchanged at the pre-invasion rate, and, as in Britain, Kuwaitis were able to draw limited amounts from their blocked bank accounts. Influential social charities run by Saudi women with a lead from prominent female members of the Al Saud devoted their fund-raising activities that winter to assistance for Kuwaiti families who had taken refuge. As the crisis wore on and the number of refugees grew, blocks of empty government housing were made available. By the time of Kuwait's liberation at the end of February 1991 there were estimated to be around 350,000 Kuwaitis in the Kingdom, nearly a half of the native population of Kuwait.

This refuge involved a considerable cost, however, and by October we were receiving clear signals of exasperation on the part of Saudi friends at the failure of the Kuwait government, from their safe exile in Taif, to offer a contribution, particularly now their substantial overseas assets in London and elsewhere had been unblocked. I was told by the Finance Ministry that the refugees were costing the Saudis some $2 million dollars a day to house and feed.

In a further act of support to Kuwait, Saudi Arabia was making 600,000 barrels a day of crude oil available to her on credit, to enable the Kuwait Oil Company to fulfil contracts with its overseas refining and distribution subsidiaries. All this was starting to stretch the limits of traditional Arabian hospitality. Shortly afterwards the Kuwaiti government organised themselves to bear the living costs of the refugees and make a

contribution towards accommodation. But to their credit the Saudis
continued to provide the Kuwaitis with generous refuge right up until it
was safe for them to return home as Kuwait recovered from the occupation. By this time, however, a new refugee burden was starting to
materialise in the form of those forced to flee from Saddam Hussein's
acts of repression in southern Iraq.

This explosion in Saudi Arabia's national expenditure resulting from
the crisis was bound to drive her economy way off its course of recovery.
The Saudis own cost estimate of $55 billion was probably not far off the
mark. There was a gain in economic activity. The economy grew by a
quarter in 1990 and by a further ten per cent the following year, as private business boomed in the wake of military expenditure. But all this
had to be paid for. On top of it came a burst of spending on military
equipment, mainly for land forces, in which Saudi Arabia indulged as
soon as she came under Iraq's direct military threat. The lion's share of
these orders went to the USA, though the UK secured a portion.

An early consequence of this uncovenanted financial burden was an
approach by the Kingdom to the international banking system in March
1991, immediately following the end of hostilities, for a sovereign loan of
$4.5 billion. This was Saudi Arabia's first direct borrowing in the inter-
national market since the profligate days of King Saud's reign 40 years
earlier, and as such represented a certain humiliation for the country's
economic standing. In our own case the unfortunate refusal of the
British clearing banks to participate in this loan to tide Saudi Arabia over
the consequences of her open-handedness to us and to others was for
the Saudis a matter for pained surprise, only partially alleviated by the
participation of the Saudi-British Bank in a subsequent foreign currency
borrowing on the local market of $2.5 billion.

There were also Saudi hesitations lest this official initiative to borrow
money at interest from the West might unleash a reaction on the part of
conservative religious opinion within the Kingdom, already resentful
over having been unable to give full vent to its antipathy to the presence
of infidel forces and the scale of Saudi contributions to the American
and other Western war chests. In the event the international loan, presented as a consequence of Iraq's aggression, went ahead without
arousing comment, and the taboo was thus broken. It was to be the
forerunner of further borrowing before the Kingdom's onerous war
debts could be covered, against a background of a renewed slide in post-
war oil prices and a painful retrenchment in government expenditure.

For ourselves, however, as for the Americans, the generosity of financial contributions from Saudi Arabia, and other states to whom the hat
was passed round, came near to offsetting the considerable costs of our

military contribution. The British Government Audit Office reported in December 1992 that receipts from overseas amounted to just over £2 billion of overall costs of £2.4 billion. Of these contributions the Saudi share was the largest, closely followed by a contribution from the Kuwaitis, promised to Douglas Hurd by the Amir when they met in Taif in February in the middle of hostilities. Sheikh Zaid, President of the UAE, made a sizeable subscription of £330 million.

Japan, constitutionally disbarred from military participation in a theatre of war, made a contribution of $12 billion towards the coalition cause, but complicated things by making its allocation the responsibility of the Riyadh-based secretariat of the GCC. This funding proved a cash lifesaver to the American military build-up in the Kingdom in the early stages of the crisis. For our own part we eventually succeeded in securing some £120 million of it, though it required persistence on the part of our ambassador in Tokyo, John Whitehead, and considerable help from my Japanese colleague in Riyadh and the GCC secretariat, to hold off an American attempt to hijack Japan's generosity.

Closer to home the German government, also impeded from seeing her forces play more than a peripheral role in the military endeavour, made a helpful contribution to British costs, while smaller offers came from a variety of sources, including Oman and Hong Kong. It must have been one of the few campaigns in British history where the taxpayer was so little out of pocket.

CHAPTER 11

Cold Feet

'Diplomats are just as essential to starting a war as Soldiers are
for finishing it. You take Diplomacy out of war and the thing
would fall flat in a week.'

Will Rogers
(as recorded in *The Diplomat's Dictionary* by Chas. W. Freeman)

The passage of the UN Security Council's Resolution 678 on 28
November setting a deadline of 15 January for Iraq's withdrawal, after
which 'all necessary measures' would be permitted to remedy the situation, finally brought a real possibility of war. The response, as the
countdown proceeded through December and into early January, was a
crescendo of diplomatic initiatives aimed at averting hostilities and
exploring ways to open a dialogue which would secure Iraq's voluntary
withdrawal. Inevitably most of these moves involved compromise, sometimes presentational in nature but occasionally including points of
substance of a kind which would be bound to give comfort to Saddam
Hussein and feed his conviction that the solidarity of the coalition
arrayed against him could be sapped by Iraqi intransigence.

These initiatives came from all quarters: within Western Europe, the
Arab and Islamic world, the Soviet Union, and from a variety of multi-
lateral organisations and figures of international standing, including
the UN Secretary-General and the Pope. Hesitations over the justification for hostilities became apparent within the military coalition itself.
There were pressures for negotiation among public opinion in Egypt
and Syria; on the part of a significant section of the US Congress and the
American public, still to some extent inhibited by the experience of
Vietnam; and within the French government, where an element sought
to keep lines of contact open to Iraq, as a former major customer.

There were recurrent hesitations, too, from sections of the Saudi public, arising out of still lingering offence at the presence of Western forces
or, more prevalently, from a general disbelief at the prospect of a war on
their doorstep. Apart from Kuwait herself, as the impatient victim of
the aggression, support for military action was perhaps most solid in

Britain, and on both sides of Parliament. But here too there was opposition from pockets of pacifist opinion, as well as from elements among the country's Moslem population, susceptible to Iraq's persuasive allegations of foreign imperialist intervention in an Islamic issue.

It says a great deal for the consistent resolve of the Saudi leadership that they withstood these multiple pressures and manoeuvres week after week without ever losing sight of the objective of Iraq's unconditional withdrawal from Kuwait on terms consistent with successive UN Security Council resolutions since the beginning of the crisis. King Fahd and his Foreign Minister, Prince Saud, found themselves throughout December and the first half of January beset by initiatives designed to afford Iraq a means of extricating herself from Kuwait. Almost without exception these were regarded with scepticism and misgiving, as opening the way for Saddam Hussein to secure some return for his aggression.

In the eyes of the Saudi government there must be no question of a dividend for Iraq, or she would contrive to salvage some credit from her aggression and remain a menace to the region. In particular Saddam Hussein should not be permitted to get away with his blatant yet seductive attempt to link withdrawal with the question of Palestine. Certainly the Kuwait crisis reinforced the paramount need for a fresh attempt to deal with the cancer of Palestine within the politics of the region, but not as a product of Iraq's aggression. There was concern moreover that, irrespective of these exercises in mediation, Saddam Hussein would extract a last-minute gain through partial withdrawal from Kuwait while retaining the northern oilfield and some coastal territory. In this situation there was seen to be a real risk of the gesture vitiating the determination of certain members of the coalition to secure Iraq's total withdrawal.

This firm and consistent Saudi position accorded exactly with that of ourselves and of the American administration. With all these hares running loose it was of the first importance for us to keep in close contact with the Saudis for the sake of mutual reassurance and to harmonise our responses. Derek Plumbly and I accordingly found our time increasingly taken up at this stage with liaison with Prince Saud and his senior advisers in the Foreign Ministry over the diplomatic state of play, as reported to us from the FCO in London and our missions at the UN and elsewhere. Our Saudi counterparts were by now working under great pressure as unwelcome essays in mediation multiplied about them. Yet they made themselves unfailingly available to us day and night, with helpful counsel and a courtesy that meant a great deal.

Prince Saud had over his long watch as Foreign Minister built up a strong and experienced team of senior officials operating from the

ministry's elegant headquarters in Riyadh. Its fortress-like exterior concealed an oasis of cool courtyards and fountains linked by a labyrinth of
passages, where the visitor needed to equip himself with Theseus' ball of
thread to be sure of finding the way out. These officials were constantly
on the move around the region, and never more so than at the present
time when incessant liaison was called for to keep the coalition in shape.

Our main contacts were with the deputy minister, Abdul Rahman al
Mansouri, an international lawyer of wide experience; the director
responsible for political affairs, Ismail Shura, a diplomatic strategist of
considerable ability; and Nizar al Madani, the director for Western relations and a right-hand man to Prince Saud. Others who shared the
burden of holding their partners steady and sustaining the pressure on
Iraq were Mamoun al Kurdi, who had particular responsibility for the
economic aspects of the crisis, and Prince Turki bin Mohammed, the
deputy head of the Western department, who had studied international
relations at Cambridge.

On the consular side we kept in close touch with Vice-Minister Abdul
Aziz al Thunayan and with Ibrahim al Mashat, the director of consular
affairs. He had the challenging responsibility of meeting the insistent
concerns of foreign embassies for the security of their nervous expatriate communities in the Kingdom while discouraging the kind of exodus
which would have left sections of Saudi Arabia's infrastructure and economic activity inoperative.

Scarcely a day passed during this tense period of waiting when we did
not need to make contact over some development that might generate
misunderstanding between us or obscure the objectives of our alliance.
The co-operation between us had developed to a point of unprecedented interplay, not only with the Foreign Ministry but with other
sections of the Saudi government too, including the Royal Secretariat
and the Defence and Petroleum Ministries. It was essential to keep it on
this close footing in the face of errant initiatives and Iraq's ceaseless
and often skilful attempts to drive wedges into the front lined up against
her.

Yet if precarious international support was to be sustained, members
of the coalition needed to be careful about appearing to dismiss mediation out of hand. At base we all subscribed to the wish to see an
unconditional Iraqi withdrawal from Kuwait without the need for force.
But as the deadline approached with no sign of anything but intransigence from the Iraqi leadership, both the Saudis and ourselves came to
see force as the most decisive, and perhaps the only, remedy.

Saddam Hussein had demonstrated his defiance in the face of the
threat of military action from the first passage of Resolution 678, to

which he responded with a burst of invective confirming Iraq's claim to Kuwait and castigating Saudi Arabia as an American stooge. Douglas Hurd countered from London by making it plain that peace was up to Saddam Hussein and that the military option was not bluff. In a public reaffirmation of the firm Saudi position, King Fahd added his voice in early December to those urging Iraqi withdrawal to avoid the disgrace of defeat and spare the region from war. This had the effect of spelling out the Kingdom's readiness to face hostilities if the deadline were not observed. The Saudis also acted promptly to meet in Cairo with their two main Arab coalition partners, Egypt and Syria, in a fresh sign of their joint backing for the UN Security Council's action.

At the same time the three partners welcomed the proposal, made by President Bush immediately following Resolution 678, for a meeting with the Iraqi leader to discuss withdrawal. This was a deliberate move by the Americans, partly in response to domestic pressures and also with Soviet hesitations in mind, to be seen to go the last mile for peace. Saddam Hussein's initial reaction, however, was to accept the invitation but prevaricate over dates and, with an eye to Arab public opinion, reiterate Iraq's insistence that discussion of the Palestine issue must be a prerequisite for any talks. He followed this in mid-December with a truculent rejection of the range of dates offered by the Americans, and a proposal that James Baker and Tariq Aziz, the Iraqi Foreign Minister, should meet on 12 January, hard up against the UN deadline and so allowing virtually no time for adequate withdrawal.

Towards the end of the month Saddam Hussein stepped up his shrill bluster with the threat to attack Israel in the event of war. He still showed no flexibility over a date to meet the Americans, and reaffirmed that Kuwait was now Iraq's 19th province and that Palestine must be settled first. For her part, Saudi Arabia was accused of betraying Islam by inviting in foreign troops. Increasingly the Iraqi leader seemed intent on painting himself into a corner.

At the same time, however, feelers for contact and dialogue continued to reach Baghdad, no doubt helping to confirm the Iraqi leader in his conviction that he should play for time. Two of his closest Arab associates over the crisis, King Hussein and President Ali Abdullah Saleh of Yemen, went to Baghdad on 4 December, together with Yasir Arafat, the PLO chairman. Their meeting with Saddam Hussein led to reports of a proposal for summit meetings between King Hussein, King Fahd and the Amir of Kuwait, and a subsequent meeting between King Fahd and Saddam Hussein. None of this could hold any appeal for the Saudis or Kuwaitis, whose position on the need for prior Iraqi withdrawal was categoric.

One useful result of this get-together may, however, have been to persuade Saddam Hussein that he had only to lose by his policy of holding on to the foreign hostages and releasing them in dribs and drabs as a device to gain time and stall an attack. Two days after the meeting, Iraq announced that a decision by the President to release all hostages would be put to the national assembly for approval. Saddam Hussein told the assembly the decision had been taken on humanitarian grounds, and that the hostages' detention was no longer necessary as it had afforded time for Iraq to improve her defences. It seems more likely that the point was made to him by his visitors that the reprehensible hostage operation only served to consolidate international hostility towards Iraq, and that the dispersal of the foreigners to military target sites was unlikely to deter Western and Arab members of the coalition from attacking these locations from the air. Certainly Yasir Arafat subsequently sought to take some credit for having persuaded the Iraqi leader to set the remaining hostages free.

Saddam Hussein may also have deluded himself that release would earn him credit on the diplomatic front. If so then he will have been quickly disabused of this illusion. Foreigners who had spent time in concealment in Kuwait brought accounts of Iraqi brutality and gross mistreatment, and of the spirit shown by the Kuwaiti resistance movement in the capital. Speaking to Parliament once the several hundred British citizens who had been held in Iraq had been airlifted home, Douglas Hurd put Saddam Hussein firmly on notice that Iraq must still implement the UN resolutions by withdrawing unconditionally and permitting Kuwait's legitimate government to return. The Saudis welcomed this firm statement of our position, and President Bush's comment that Iraq would not be rewarded for the release of those she had kidnapped, and that the return of the hostages made it if anything easier to go to war if that should prove necessary.

Certainly their providential evacuation removed one major headache which had been exercising Peter de la Billière and others responsible for putting the final touches to the coalition's military plans for an offensive.

Having seen a number of British citizens who had gone to ground in Kuwait since the invasion safely on their way back to London, our ambassador, Michael Weston, and the consul, Larry Banks, finally departed from the beleaguered embassy building in the city, where they had been surviving on tinned tuna fish and vegetables grown in a patch on the compound. Our direct contact with them via a radio link operated by Gordon Horne and Derek Smith, our two indefatigable registry officers in Riyadh, had proved intermittent in recent weeks and it was increasingly difficult to relay messages. But their presence throughout Kuwait's occupation had done much for morale and symbolised Britain's rejection of Iraq's aggression and pillage. They were the last foreign embassy to close down; the rump of the American embassy, including the ambassador, Nat Howell, an old colleague of ours from Algiers, had departed a couple of days earlier leaving the Stars and Stripes flying.

On the positive side there was a useful sign of Iranian support in early December when the Foreign Minister, Velayati, made a statement on 7 December giving backing to Resolution 678, while qualifying this with a warning that Iran would not join in hostilities and a call for all foreign forces to leave the area once the crisis was settled. This was as encouraging a line as could be expected from an Iran still nursing her wounds from the bloody conflict with Iraq, yet fiercely opposed to any sign of a resumption of Western and non-Moslem military influence. Our Kuwaiti contacts in Taif told us that they had been given a similar private assurance by the Iranians when the Kuwaiti Foreign Minister had recently visited Tehran to press for Iran's support.

The Iranian statement gave a timely boost to Saudi Arabia and her GCC partners, who were about to hold their annual summit meeting at which future relations with Iran would be discussed. It held little comfort for Saddam Hussein, however, with its indication that his recent territorial concessions along their common frontier and the Shatt al Arab waterway, through the reversal of his 1979 abrogation of the bilateral Algiers agreement of 1975, had gained him no more than Iran's wary neutrality.

The six Gulf states held their summit in Doha from 23 to 25 December, hosted by the Amir of Qatar, Sheikh Khalifa bin Hamad Al Thani. Coming at this critical moment for Gulf security it was probably the most significant meeting yet in the GCC's short life, and as such called for a firm show of unity and support for Kuwait's recovery. This was forthcoming in the shape of the Doha Declaration, in which the members made an unqualified call for Iraq's unconditional withdrawal and the restoration of the Al Sabah's government.

In a lengthy communiqué the GCC leaders turned their attention to the future of their region, with a pledge to develop their joint capacity for self-defence and strengthen their ties within the wider Arab world through the establishment of a new fund for Arab economic development and enhanced political co-operation with the Arab states who had come to their support. These features, which derived from a Saudi initiative, were to evolve over the coming weeks into a more specific association between the GCC states, Egypt and Syria. An olive branch was also held out to Iran. Nevertheless, the territorial squabbles which beset intra-Gulf relations still managed to obtrude when sharp differences between Bahrain and Qatar over ownership of the small island of Hawar lying between them held up the opening of the conference and called for strenuous mediation on the part of King Fahd.

This key summit by no means marked the end of hesitations within the Arab world and further afield at the prospect of hostilities. Right up to the deadline on 15 January, the Saudis found themselves having to work without a break to sustain the commitment of some of their partners. This activity called for a good deal of mutual reassurance and parallel intercession on our part, not least on the European scene, but also among the members of the UN Security Council.

So far as the Moslem world was concerned, Iraq's agile propaganda continued to play on Islamic and anti-imperialist sentiment to the point where public opinion in both Syria, and to a lesser extent Egypt, began to demonstrate discomfort at the prospect of going to war alongside Western forces against a fellow Arab state. Hints that Syria might after all decline to have her armoured division in Saudi Arabia join in an offensive into Kuwait was causing concern to coalition military commanders by early January. Algeria too sent a signal of support to Baghdad with the chartering of a cargo ship, the *Ibn Khaldun*, to a group of Arab and European peace campaigners, both male and female, who were intent on challenging the naval blockade in the Gulf with food for Iraq. After refusing to change course the vessel was boarded on Christmas Day off the Omani coast in an operation by the British, American and Australian navies. Fortunately there was no need for force, and the ship was brought into the port of Mina Qaboos.

This rot needed to be stopped, not least on account of the importance for the campaign's credibility in Arab eyes that Kuwaiti and other Arab forces should be seen to be in the vanguard of land operations to recover Kuwait, a point on which the Saudis rightly laid considerable store. The Syrian hesitations necessitated a bout of diplomatic shuttling to Damascus by the Saudis. An advance deposit of half of the $1 billion which Saudi Arabia had pledged to Syria in aid helped to bring them back into line.

The Syrian Foreign Minister, Farouk al Shara', came to Riyadh with the Egyptian Foreign Minister on 5 January. When I met him at a dinner at the Saudi Foreign Ministry that night, he seemed relaxed about what lay ahead and confirmed there should be no specific linkage between Kuwait and Palestine. He also showed satisfaction that our bilateral relations were now back in place. Prince Saud assured me the next day that the Syrians were now prepared to join an offensive into Kuwait. After the failure of James Baker's last-chance meeting with the Iraqi Foreign Minister in Geneva on 9 January seemed to foreclose all options but war, the Syrian Vice-President, Abdul Halim Khaddam, came promptly to Riyadh with a final reassurance for the Saudis on this crucial issue.

The Moroccans too, who had been among the first to rally to Saudi Arabia's defence back in August, opted in the face of domestic pressures and public manifestations to confine their force's role to the territory of the Kingdom. Fortunately no such major hesitations emerged on the part of the Egyptians, though they joined in calls in early January for further dialogue. Egyptian public opinion, particularly among its Islamic political movement, was by no means solid on the use of force in association with the West to dislodge Iraq, and the government took the precaution of having the Grand Mufti of Egypt visit Egyptian units in the field to reaffirm to them the propriety of a fight to relieve Iraqi oppression of their Kuwaiti co-religionaries. Such moral and spiritual reinforcement remained a feature of major importance for the whole Moslem wing of the coalition, and needed to be given due weight by Western participants if our hybrid military alliance was not to get out of step.

Efforts to urge a negotiated settlement were sustained right up to the deadline by those Arab interests who had shown some common bond with Iraq. The leaders of Jordan, Yemen and the PLO appeared to get little change from Saddam Hussein on the issue of withdrawal when they met him in Baghdad in early January, but each followed up with calls for negotiation. King Hussein, who was having to cope with a wave of conditioned emotional support for Saddam Hussein from among his Palestinian subjects, but was also seeking for his own reasons which were far from clear to us to ease things for the Iraqi leader, set off on a fruitless round of calls in Western capitals to argue for more time.

Yemen came up with a plan for conditional withdrawal, and her Foreign Minister waylaid James Baker in Cairo and subsequently claimed American support for this. Eventually finding herself getting nowhere with either side, Yemen took the course of declaring herself non-combatant a few days before the deadline, thus relieving Saudi Arabia of a potential threat from her southern flank.

As for the PLO, Yasir Arafat, keyed up by the strong groundswell of Palestinian elation at Saddam Hussein's calculated bid to have withdrawal linked to Israeli relinquishment of Palestinian territory, played this card for all it was worth. Indeed, Arafat seemed carried away to the point where he was putting at risk the significant support which his recent political restraint over the Palestine question had gained for his movement in moderate Arab circles, and in the West too. His rash conviction that Iraq's occupation of Kuwait could be turned to the advantage of the Palestinians was even becoming a point of concern to more rational heads within the PLO leadership.

One of his leading advisers on foreign relations, Hani al Hassan, made this clear to me when he came to Riyadh in early January in a forlorn attempt to salvage something of the PLO's strained relationship with the Saudis, whose crucial monthly subsidy to the organisation had been suspended. The excuse that, if forced to choose between the subsidies from Saudi Arabia and Iraq, the PLO had to opt for Iraq in view of the training facilities she provided to the Palestine National Army, did not fully account for the enthusiasm Yasir Arafat displayed for Saddam Hussein.

The PLO command did at least appear to be restraining the movement's more militant elements from indulging in acts of terrorism and sabotage at Iraq's behest, actions which would have brought universal condemnation. Yasir Arafat's blind support for Iraq, however, earned him profound Saudi animosity and was to have the effect of sidelining him for a lengthy period once serious negotiations over the Arab–Israel question resumed in the wake of the Kuwait crisis.

The Saudis met these multiple instances of cold feet with a single-minded consistency of approach – there could be no going back on unconditional Iraqi withdrawal and the full application of the various UN Security Council resolutions. The hesitations also served to reinforce Saudi conviction that, if there was to be no withdrawal before the deadline, then there must be no question of any grace period beyond it. Otherwise they saw a clear risk of further backsliding.

Their impatience for a military move as soon as the deadline was past, coupled with a conviction that Iraqi forces would crumble and a land offensive might not even be required, was put to Defence Secretary Cheney when he came to Riyadh in mid-December to set the seal on the complex negotiations which General Schwarzkopf had been having with Prince Khalid over arrangements for command of an offensive into Kuwait. For their part the Americans were not prepared to bank on an Iraqi collapse, but must be ready for a prolonged and fierce campaign, for which the forces still arriving in theatre needed time to prepare themselves.

This realistic concern was, however, given an ill-judged airing by the deputy American commander, General Calvin Waller, in remarks to the press on the eve of Richard Cheney's arrival, when he disclosed that American forces would not be ready until the middle of February and that 15 January was not therefore a formal deadline. This bloomer was not only a gift to Iraqi propaganda; it also resurrected doubts in Saudi minds over the solidarity of the US military commitment. The Defence Secretary was obliged to devote time to allaying these suspicions. A corrective statement was issued: the USAF would indeed be ready by the deadline. Confidence was thus restored, but the episode only served to reinforce the Saudi view that the coalition could not afford delay.

Pressure for dialogue did not only come from within the Arab community. A wider movement for a negotiated solution emerged at the end of December from the Non-Aligned Movement, a body held in some suspicion by Saudi Arabia on account of its socialist credentials. Shrewdly prompted by Iraq with a bid for a non-aligned conference to be convened in Baghdad to discuss the crisis, and with support from leading members such as India, Malaysia and Pakistan, the Yugoslav Foreign Minister, Aloncar, visited Baghdad at the end of December for talks with Iraq's leadership, to be met with a defiant insistence on Kuwait's status as Iraq's 19th province and on priority being given to Palestine.

Aloncar then came on to Saudi Arabia early in the New Year to urge delay and possible compromise to avert hostilities. The Saudis neatly managed to confront him with the Egyptian and Syrian Foreign Ministers alongside Prince Saud, and jointly made plain their refusal to dilute their insistence on full withdrawal or to go along with the Iraqi-inspired call for a non-aligned summit meeting. The exercise faltered and Pakistan's Prime Minister subsequently visited his troops stationed at Tabuk and Arar in the north of the Kingdom to show support for their presence. Saudi steadiness had seen off another initiative likely to play into Saddam Hussein's hands.

But the coast was still not clear. Shortly before the deadline the Organisation of the Islamic Conference, a body which, with its head-quarters in Jedda, usually gave ready support to the Saudi position in issues dividing the Moslem world, came out with its own call for dialogue, perhaps with Pakistani and Iranian encouragement.

The USSR also kept up rearguard attempts to acquire a mediatory role, particularly after the resignation of Eduard Shevardnadze in early December led to renewed questioning in Moscow of the benefits of a policy of following an American lead at the expense of the Soviet Union's independent global role. Belonsov, the Soviet deputy Foreign Minister, came to the Kingdom in late December, but was no more successful than Primakov had been some weeks before in persuading the Saudis to open a dialogue on the crisis. Despite the substantial Saudi carrot of $4 billion as a soft loan, Soviet attempts to promote a negotiated solution and spare their former ally the humiliation of defeat continued beyond the UN deadline with an appeal for delay, which President Gorbachev unsuccessfully attempted to press on the Americans through his newly-established communications with Saudi Arabia.

But of as much concern to the Saudis as any of these intercessions were the signs from late September onwards of second thoughts and pressures for a negotiated settlement on the part of certain European countries. Conscious of the general persistence in the West of misconceptions about Saudi Arabia and her policies, King Fahd had in early December taken the elaborate step of despatching special missions to Britain and other major European states, as well as to North America and Japan, to improve public awareness of the Kingdom's firm position towards Saddam Hussein's seizure of Kuwait and its appreciation of international support and military help.

The group to visit Britain was led by Prince Abdullah bin Faisal bin Turki, the British-educated head of the Jubail Royal Commission, already well-known in London media circles. Others included Professor Assad Abdo of King Saud University, who held a doctorate from Durham, and Abdul Aziz Kanoo of the Gulf merchant family with long connections with Britain. It was a well-chosen party and succeeded in putting across a positive public message, though their programme of contacts suffered initially from the surprisingly limp performance being played on the British domestic scene by the Saudi embassy in London. Fortunately the Saudi Information Ministry through their London representative, Dermot Graham, and with support from the FCO and British friends of the Kingdom, managed to put together a useful clutch of public and media encounters.

Elsewhere, notably in the USA and France, the Kingdom's embassies were acting more effectively to counter the impact of Iraq's ever-subtle propaganda. There were contacts in the reverse direction, too, with visits to the Kingdom by congressional and parliamentary groups. One interesting party from Britain at this time, put together by St John Armitage through his long-standing connection with the Saudi Information Minister, Ali Shair, consisted of specialists from the three main centres of defence and diplomatic studies, the Royal United Services Institute, the International Institute for Strategic Studies, and the Royal Institute for International Affairs. They saw Saudi and British troops at the front, had a session with General Khalid bin Sultan, and also met an articulate selection of Saudi opinion at my house in Riyadh.

The Kuwaitis, too, began at last to come out of their state of shock and do more to work up international support for the recovery of their country. Ministers, and the Amir himself, left their refuge in Taif to visit Western capitals and New York to put across their impatience to see Iraq ejected. They drew on an increasingly well-documented background of atrocities being committed against Kuwaitis under occupation. Kuwaiti communities abroad were also active in raising funds for refugees without resources. A particularly strong publicity campaign was mounted in Britain. At our end we encouraged the Kuwaitis to set up an information desk in the news clearing centre which had taken over the huge lobby of the International Hotel at Dhahran.

Despite all these efforts by Saudis and Kuwaitis to put across their call for action, the final weeks of the Italian presidency of the EC, which ended with the turn of the year, saw proposals backed by Prime Minister Andreotti and Foreign Minister de Michaelis for negotiation through the resurrection of a long-standing Italian project of a Mediterranean security conference, in which the problems of the Gulf would also be considered. The Saudi reaction was distinctly cool, as was our own. Such a conference would dilute the focus on Kuwait and establish the linkage we sought to avoid with the Palestine question. But the assumption of the EC presidency in January by Luxembourg, a country with no direct diplomatic representation in the region and in consequence susceptible to pressures from its larger European partners, allowed other initiatives from within the community, stimulated in particular by France and Germany, to open a European line of contact with Iraq on the back of the talks which President Bush had offered to Saddam Hussein.

Following Iraq's reluctant assent to meet James Baker in Geneva, a proposal was issued by Luxembourg on behalf of the European foreign ministers for a second meeting there. This was rejected by Iraq. As part of our efforts to shore up the resolve of certain of our European partners who seemed prepared to contemplate compromise, Douglas Hurd came out with a warning that any European contacts with Iraq must not be allowed to blur the essential issues. This was helpful in Riyadh, where the moves were starting to arouse Saudi misgivings about European solidarity.

Prince Saud saw me on 2 January to express to us, as the Kingdom's most solid European partner in the venture to see Iraq out of Kuwait, the gravity of his concern over what might emerge from the Luxembourg meeting and the encouragement this could give to Iraqi wedge-driving tactics, doubts which we entirely shared. Saudi concern was being fed further at this stage by statements by the German Foreign Minister emphasising the need for a peaceful solution. Herr Genscher had further upset the Saudis by questioning the restoration of Al Sabah rule in Kuwait and unequal distribution of wealth in the Gulf region.

French equivocation was causing even greater concern. Not only was there continuing uncertainty over the role which the French contingent would be authorised to play in an offensive, but also the poor relationship between Prince Sultan and the French Defence Minister, Chévènement, which came to a head with his failure to have a meeting with the Prince when he came to Riyadh in late December. Relations with France deteriorated further when the President of the Foreign Affairs Committee of the National Assembly, Vaizelle, visited Baghdad in early January and had a talk on the situation with Saddam Hussein. It was widely assumed that he must have gone with the blessing of President Mitterrand, and Saudi eyebrows were not the only ones which his journey caused to raise.

Doubts persisted with the subsequent announcement of a Franco-Algerian initiative to mediate, though we saw this as no more than a tactic to try to meet France's traditional concern for her southern Mediterranean flank. A suggestion by Luxembourg that she and the two other European states which formed the community's troika, Italy and the Netherlands, should try to meet Tariq Aziz in Algiers, was also suspected to have a French inspiration.

It was not until after the failure of the Iraqi–American meeting in Geneva on 9 January that French forces in the Gulf were finally committed to the coalition's offensive, to the relief of the Americans and ourselves, with whom they were to be deployed. There were still limitations on the air side, as French aircraft were not allowed to attack inside Iraq, the Jaguar aircraft could not fly at night, and Mirages could not be used for fear of confusion with the similar aircraft supplied in large quantities to Iraq during the war with Iran.

Even then there was a forlorn last-ditch attempt by the French government to draw back from hostilities when the deadline expired on 15 January. That same day the French put a draft resolution before the UN Security Council to authorise delay provided Iraq declared an intention to withdraw, in return for the calling of a peace conference under UN auspices and linkage to other problems in the region. This made a nonsense of the Council's stand over unconditional withdrawal, and the draft was summarily rejected by the Americans and ourselves as offering too little and too late. Having staged this piece of diplomatic theatre the French thenceforward played a full part in the coalition. But their ambivalence led to a degree of mistrust on the part of Saudi Arabia which was to linger beyond the crisis.

Concern over signs of division within Europe had become a major preoccupation for the Saudi leadership as the UN deadline approached. The failure to achieve sufficient identity of interest to forge a unified European policy left the Saudis with no option but to deal individually with the members of the community most directly involved in the diplomacy of the crisis. It was made clear to John Major when he visited the Kingdom in early January that the Kingdom looked to us for a lead. The Prime Minister left King Fahd in no doubt that he would have no truck with compromise. His firm statement before leaving Britain, that you did not negotiate with someone who had broken into your house, went down well.

We also made sure the Saudis knew of the affirmation after the Camp David meeting on 22 December between the Prime Minister and President Bush that there would be no compromises. As the deadline for withdrawal approached, policy among the members of the EC looked increasingly at sixes and sevens. In the Saudi view only Britain and the USA were standing unequivocally alongside them at this critical juncture.

As the firmest among the Europeans, it was of the first importance for us to demonstrate to the Saudi leadership the consistency and the resolve behind our position, not least in the wake of the abrupt change of Prime Minister in mid-crisis. John Major's visit to the Kingdom on 7 and 8 January, his first trip abroad since moving into Downing Street apart from his session at Camp David with President Bush before Christmas, thus held particular importance for the opportunity it gave him to confirm our solidarity of purpose and establish a basis for carrying forward the very close relationship with King Fahd and the Saudis built up during the 12 years that Mrs Thatcher had been in office. We also needed to convey a similar profession of our commitment to the Kuwaiti leadership in their impatient exile, and put across our interest in having a share in the work of repairing the ravages of Iraq's occupation once Kuwait was liberated.

The Prime Minister carried through this mission to good effect. He flew first to Taif, where the Amir of Kuwait put on a more robust show than on the occasion of Douglas Hurd's visit four months earlier. Sheikh Jaber al Ahmad showed concern that Saddam Hussein would try to turn the tables by engaging in a partial withdrawal in the context of the forthcoming meeting with the Americans in Geneva. This could leave the coalition high and dry. He was reassured to have John Major's assurance that for us there could be no halfway house solution. Our wish to participate in the business of reconstruction was also clearly registered. At the Riyadh end we had begun to pick up indications that the Americans might seek to monopolise this area of activity. We had accordingly been working with Whitehall to lay plans for a British role in Kuwait's recovery through appropriate sectors of our industry.

With King Fahd the Prime Minister quickly got on to terms. Their meeting in Riyadh, preceded by a hospitable banquet hosted by Crown Prince Abdullah, began late in the evening and went on beyond midnight. It took place in the monumental Al Yamamah palace, built in the 1980s on the rim of a spectacular and fertile cleft cut through the barren plateau by the Wadi Hanifah. There were several senior Saudis present, including the Crown Prince, Prince Sultan and Prince Saud. Peter de la Billière joined our small group.

King Fahd expressed to John Major the warmth he felt for our good relationship. This was followed by a detailed and bitter account, on the lines of the King's recent public addresses to his people, of Saddam Hussein's betrayal of his fellow Arabs and the danger which his ruthless ambition for power presented for the region unless he were stopped. The King had sought unsuccessfully to discourage Saddam Hussein from launching the disastrous attack on Iran ten years previously. King Fahd ridiculed Saddam Hussein's bid for Islamic credentials and in particular his fabricated claim to descent from the Prophet.

There was an echo of the suspicion voiced by the Amir of Kuwait that Saddam might yet have a trick up his sleeve to try to divide the front ranged against him. Egypt and Syria now seemed firm, but King Hussein's activity on Iraq's behalf was incomprehensible and a deep disappointment. A snap partial withdrawal would be intensely frustrating, and would leave Iraq's threat intact. Saddam had to be driven out of Kuwait; he was unlikely to survive the consequent disgrace of defeat. We should not hang about after the deadline. In Saudi minds there was a doubt about the will of the Iraqi army to fight, and a hope that Allied air strikes might suffice to bring capitulation, a point on which we were less sanguine. I recalled Sandy Wilson's comment at the time it had been decided to send out 7 Brigade, that air forces did not win wars alone; at the end of the day land had to be taken and held.

The Prime Minister's fervent assurance of his intention to carry forward Mrs Thatcher's commitment to see unconditional withdrawal and maintain our close relationship with the Kingdom was well received by the King. The meeting between James Baker and Tariq Aziz in Geneva two days later should show what the Iraqi leader had in mind. Turning to the future, John Major stressed the need for the GCC states to integrate their defence more closely and offered our co-operation in this process, while confirming to King Fahd that British troops would leave the Kingdom promptly once Iraq's withdrawal had been achieved.

This theme of tighter security arrangements among the Gulf states, which the GCC had itself set in hand at its summit, had already been broached by us in mid-December in a meeting in Riyadh between Archie Hamilton, the Minister of State for Defence, and his Saudi counterpart, Prince Abdul Rahman. Peter de la Billière and I had been giving thought to how we could draw on the new working relationship between British and Saudi forces which the crisis had produced to develop a wider basis for co-operation in advice and equipment once our forces had withdrawn after the crisis.

The Gulf states would need to strengthen their own line of defence against possible future threats to their security. Our co-operation with the RSAF was well established, and BAe had given excellent technical support since the start of the crisis under the keen supervision of the Al Yamamah project director, Air Marshal Ron Stuart-Paul. Brigadier Nick Cocking and his team were also giving sound advisory support to the National Guard, as part of the Kingdom's ground defences. Our interest was now focusing on developing links with the land forces. The Saudi response had been encouraging, though their priority at this stage remained to get rid of the threat from Saddam Hussein and his menacing armoury of weapons of mass destruction. Indeed, it was the Saudis who were increasingly urging the inclusion of this last point among the coalition's war aims. Perhaps they knew better than we what Iraq had been up to in this sinister area.

The meeting with King Fahd had a moment of drama when Prince Sultan was suddenly summoned from the room around midnight, returning promptly to whisper into his brother's ear. The King then told us that a report had just come in of the defection across the Kuwaiti frontier of six Iraqi helicopters. Was this, we asked each other, the first crack in the dam of Saddam Hussein's military façade? A trickle of Iraqi defectors had already begun to risk the hazards of slipping across the frontier. Their interrogation under Saudi auspices was proving useful in building up the coalition's inadequate picture of Iraqi military strength in Kuwait. Our hopes were premature, however. Whether the helicopters were phantom or not, the alert was attributed to a radar malfunction. But we parted from the King that night on an optimistic note.

The Prime Minister spent the next day with the British forces in the east and in the Gulf, and flew off that evening to Muscat where he was to meet Sultan Qaboos of Oman. It was a great relief to see his relationship with King Fahd start off in such positive fashion. But there was yet to be a hiccup. In the course of the flight from Dhahran down to Muscat Gus O'Donnell, the Prime Minister's press secretary, gave a briefing to the accompanying press party which led to a report that we were proposing to keep some forces in the Gulf area once the crisis was over. This was carried on the BBC Arabic Service in an evening bulletin and picked up by the ever vigilant King, for whom it touched a very sensitive nerve. The readiness of Western forces to pack up and go post-crisis was one of the cardinal elements in the King's constant efforts to allay hostility both at home and in the wider Arab world to his request for Western military intervention.

I consequently spent a hectic few hours that night on the telephone between Muscat and the King's private secretary in Riyadh, straightening out what had been said in order to set King Fahd's mind at rest. The point was not carried further in the British press and no harm was done. But the incident served to remind us of the precarious nature of the bond of trust which underpinned the unprecedented alliance we had fashioned.

The convening by Luxembourg on 14 January of a second meeting of European foreign ministers to discuss Kuwait in the wake of the abortive Geneva meeting brought these Saudi doubts into the open again. Prince Saud asked me to see him two days beforehand to discuss his concern over fresh moves by the 'Eurowimps' to have the troika foreign ministers make contact with Iraq. In his view it was now the Europeans and not the Arabs who were having cold feet. I made it clear there had been no dilution whatsoever in our line and put him in touch by telephone with Douglas Hurd, who was in Abu Dhabi on a last-hour tour of the smaller Gulf states, Jordan and Turkey to press for solidarity against Iraq.

Prince Saud repeated his concern at EC feelers towards Iraq. The situation called for steady nerves. Douglas Hurd told Prince Saud he too was working to stiffen the less resolute European partners, and confirmed our immutable commitment to an unconditional Iraqi withdrawal. Nevertheless the indefatigable Prince Saud felt sufficiently worried to despatch a senior emissary at short notice to the three troika capitals, to see the Dutch, Luxembourg and Italian foreign ministers with a message discouraging compromise and reminding them that any initiatives for talks with the Iraqis must be consistent with the strict terms of the UN Security Council resolutions. Proposals for a fresh start in negotiations over Palestine needed to be squared with the principle of no rewards for Iraq's aggression. Prince Saud also called in the Dutch and Italian ambassadors representing the European troika in Riyadh to give them a similar warning.

The statement issued from the Luxembourg presidency following the meeting on 14 January still suggested to the Saudis a possible link between withdrawal from Kuwait and Israel's occupation of Palestinian territory. This implied further European backsliding, which in turn could prejudice the sensitive discussions in which the Saudis were themselves involved to overcome Syrian reservations. Once again I spoke to Prince Saud to emphasise there had been no going back on European solidarity and that the fresh start over Palestine which we all had in mind was distinct from the problem of Kuwait.

Our resolute position as anchor within the European camp had become a major factor in sustaining Saudi Arabia's own sense of confidence during this stage of turbulent diplomacy. Indeed, our co-operation in these crucial weeks had never been closer. There were a few points of strain, notably over Saudi reluctance to open doors to the armada of representatives from the British media. Sensitivity over a BBC *Panorama* programme on the Saudi mood towards the crisis, which the

Saudis felt reflected negatively on their conservative political and religious culture, added an unwelcome complication. But these hindrances we managed to overcome.

The failure of the Geneva meeting between James Baker and Tariq Aziz on 9 January constituted a watershed in the hectic run-up to the UN deadline. In the eyes of the Americans, the Saudis and ourselves, Tariq Aziz's intransigent refusal in some seven hours of talks to discuss withdrawal, or even to accept the letter which President Bush had written to Saddam Hussein, in effect removed the last chance for peace. The Iraqis had clearly left themselves no room to change their position.

Late that night Grania and I watched the two ministers separately make their momentous statements to the world's press, on the CNN television satellite at the house of a friend, Ahmed Malik, a deputy governor of the Saudi central bank. Also with us were Teymour Ali Reza and his wife, and Andrew Buxton, chairman of Barclay's Bank, who had chosen to pay a bold business visit to Riyadh on the eve of hostilities. The sombre and fateful mood of the occasion affected us all. It was difficult to believe that Saddam Hussein had made his decision to face a war he could not win. Perhaps he still hoped to split the alliance, possibly through launching an attack on Israel in a desperate bid to neutralise the Arab element of the coalition.

It subsequently emerged that Tariq Aziz had indeed threatened James Baker with this eventuality – Iraq's Armageddon option – counting on it to split the Arab front against him. For his part James Baker had given Tariq Aziz a categoric warning that, if Iraq were to use chemical or biological weapons, the USA would 'exact vengeance' – perhaps implying possible nuclear retaliation – a message Saddam Hussein sensibly chose to heed. We saw it as indicative of Iraq's obduracy that Tariq Aziz did not deign to mention Kuwait by name in the course of his impenitent statement, and sought to divert attention towards Palestine. As we all digested the import of what we had heard, it became clear that the die was now cast and that within days we would be involved in a conflict. We parted solemnly for the night.

The bleak outcome of the Geneva meeting had the effect of concentrating the attention of all in Saudi Arabia on the prospect of imminent war. Yet there might still be a faint hope of averting hostilities. There were six days to go before the deadline expired. Before leaving London for the Gulf, Douglas Hurd called it a very great shame that Saddam Hussein had chosen not to reverse his aggression and leave Kuwait. He warned that, although war was not yet inevitable, the military option remained to be used after 15 January. He still hoped Saddam Hussein would realise he could not win a conflict and so would withdraw.

Nevertheless the British government followed the Geneva rebuff by expelling most of the staff of the Iraqi embassy from London, although the ambassador was permitted to remain.

An ultimate attempt at mediation was launched at the eleventh hour on 13 January by the UN Secretary General, who flew to Baghdad and saw Saddam Hussein. Perez de Cuellar claimed he had a moral duty to try to avert a war, and had the support of the great majority of member states. For the Saudis, as for ourselves, this looked a profitless and poorly-timed venture, affording Iraq yet another opportunity to spin things out. When I saw Prince Saud on 13 January, he expressed an earnest hope that Perez de Cuellar could be kept on a tight rein.

By the end of that day, however, it was evident that the Iraqi President was refusing even this last chance to salvage something from the wreckage. Baghdad radio was quoting him as reaffirming Kuwait's status as Iraq's 19th province and his intention to fight to hold it. The radio carried defiant claims that Iraq was ready for war, and bloodcurdling threats against Western troops in battle. On 14 January Perez de Cuellar returned to New York. He admitted he had made no progress and that he had found Saddam Hussein almost fatalistic about the approaching conflict.

Even at this final stage, with only hours to go before the expiry of the UN deadline at midnight, New York time, on 15 January, the French, whose collusion in the Secretary General's initiative became evident when he passed through Paris to see President Mitterrand on his way to Baghdad, came up with a final move to salvage something of their previous relationship with Iraq through a last-minute initiative in the UN Security Council. So far as Britain was concerned this action added insult to injury, as the Prime Minister had visited Paris that very day and discussed the state of play without receiving any indication from the President of what he had up his sleeve. I quickly reassured Prince Saud that we regarded this draft resolution as unacceptable. At this moment above all we needed to hold firm. The successive French manoeuvres, reflecting as they did discordance within the governing coalition, had certainly been trying Saudi patience as well as our own.

For the Americans, Saudis and ourselves, Iraq's rejection in Geneva of a peaceful withdrawal was the signal to set the final preparations for the hostilities which now seemed inevitable. With the possibility in mind that even at this late stage Saddam Hussein would signal some last-minute gesture over withdrawal, we had discussed with the Americans the kind of timetable we could accept for evacuation of the half-million Iraqi troops now believed to be in the vicinity of Kuwait together with their heavy equipment. A fortnight seemed adequate, after which there would still need to be an effective monitoring arrangement. This could be handled under UN auspices.

But such was the contumacy of the Iraqi leader's tone that it had by now become almost impossible to see a peaceful way out. Indeed, for many of us on the ground, keyed up by the activity of the past months and by what we knew of Iraqi outrages in Kuwait, it would have been a bitter experience to see Saddam Hussein's regime of vicious tyranny over his own people and his subjugated neighbour escape the retribution it merited, and with its menacing armoury intact. The confrontation had assumed a moral dimension. The opportunity was plain for Iraq's leader to wriggle off his hook through a partial withdrawal, which could erode the solidarity of the coalition and transform his climb-down into a propaganda victory for having stood up to America and the West. He might even salvage some territorial gain. As one candid Saudi officer put it to me, 'we Arabs have a way of turning defeat into a virtue'. Fervently we hoped Saddam Hussein would not take this option, and somehow felt he was too intransigent, even obtuse, to do so.

Among the Saudis, too, there was an evident impatience to get on with the business and well-founded concern to have no delay once the deadline expired. The resolve shown by King Fahd and his senior brothers had never faltered. Now our other contacts in the military and government seemed convinced a fight was coming. Prince Fahd bin Abdullah, the assistant Defence Minister, made it plain to me that Saudi policy continued to envisage Kuwaiti, Saudi and other Arab troops in the vanguard of the eventual liberation of Kuwait City.

James Baker came on to Riyadh from Geneva on 11 January and saw the King to tie up final details for the jointly-led offensive, including the all-important Saudi approval for the initiation of hostilities. The campaign would open with a programme of intensive air attacks on military and strategic targets in Iraq and Kuwait. The posture of the US administration had been much strengthened by the crucial approval of the use of force by Congress on 12 January.

On 12 January the American military command signed an agreement with the Saudis which provided for Saudi custody of the Iraqi prisoners of war captured by Western forces. This was a considerable relief to us and also to the International Red Cross mission, now established in Riyadh in preparation for carrying out their responsibility to ensure the observance of the Geneva Conventions. It meant that the Americans, French and ourselves would not be encumbered with the custody of the large numbers of Iraqi troops whom we expected to take prisoner once a land offensive was under way. We would still have to guard and transport them in the initial stage of capture, and subsequently fulfil the obligation under the Geneva Convention to ensure those we had taken prisoner were properly handled. The MoD had, at the insistence of the British forces headquarters, provided two infantry battalions for this task, the King's Own Scottish Borderers and the Royal Highland Fusiliers.

Our own preparations were also moving ahead swiftly. Our ambassador in Baghdad, 'Hooky' Walker, was instructed in early January to prepare to pull his staff out by road to Jordan on 10 January if the Geneva meeting should fail. For tactical reasons the FCO did not go for a formal breach in relations, and left the onus to do this on the Iraqis, a step they took once the offensive began. In a move timed no doubt to complicate our withdrawal, the Iraqis chose this moment to put on trial an Englishman, Patrick Trigg, whom they had picked up some weeks before trying to escape from Iraq across the desert. They already had a handful of British subjects in prison whom they were holding as bargaining counters. To afford such encouragement and consular protection as was possible at this critical stage, the counsellor in the embassy, Chris Segar, stayed behind to see Patrick Trigg through his trial, which much to our relief resulted in his release.

We also had to clear our own lines with the Saudis over authority for British forces to go on the offensive from Saudi territory, as provided for in the status of forces memorandum which I had signed with Prince Sultan in October. We nearly had a slip-up here. It had been expected in London that James Baker's discussion with the King on this point would also cover British and French forces. When I checked this with Chas Freeman on 14 January after James Baker had left Riyadh, I gained the impression that the clearance they had obtained only extended to their own troops. A quick telephone call to Nigel Broomfield, the deputy secretary in the FCO responsible for defence matters, suggested that all should be in order and that the Prime Minister would be seeing James Baker that afternoon at Alconbury, a military airfield in Huntingdonshire, on the latter's way back to Washington. Later that evening, however, Nigel Broomfield came on the telephone again to say that the assurance had been premature. We did after all need our own clearance and, what was more, that very night.

I had a quick word with Prince Saud at his home, and then met Derek Plumbly around midnight in the chancery to prepare in handwritten Arabic our formal request to King Fahd for his authority for British forces to join in the launching of an offensive from the Kingdom. The composition of this important document presented no problem, but setting it up on an Arabic typewriter was beyond us and at that hour no help was available. Shortly after one we drove to the house of Mohammed Sulaiman, King Fahd's ever-helpful private secretary, who gave us a cup of Arab coffee and undertook to obtain the King's reply immediately. He was as good as his word. Shortly after we got back to the embassy he rang to say the way was clear. I put a call through to Patrick Nixon, who had succeeded Rob Young as head of the Middle East department in the FCO and was in charge of the emergency unit that night, to give him the news, and went to bed with considerable relief. It was the day the deadline was to expire.

The prodigious work which the Saudis put into sustaining the commitment of countries associated with the international endeavour to get Iraq out of Kuwait without reward was duplicated for them on the domestic front. In dealing with public opinion all through the months of waiting, King Fahd found himself having to strike a difficult balance between preparing his people to face the unthinkable eventuality of hostilities with an Arab neighbour, and avoiding spreading excessive alarm which could erode national resistance. The threat from Iraq to the Kingdom, together with the shock of reports from Kuwaiti refugees of Iraqi pillage and ruthless brutality, had the effect of rallying the major part of the Saudi public behind its leadership in the unwonted preparations for war. Indeed, the crisis was helping to consolidate the sense of nationhood which the Al Saud had set themselves to create ever since the Kingdom's unification just on 30 years before.

Nevertheless, questions over Western motives behind the crisis over Kuwait were evident in some degree within Saudi public opinion. There was even a lingering suspicion that America and the West had somehow set up the whole crisis over Kuwait to humiliate Iraq. Such fantasy, born of the vestiges of anti-imperialist sentiment deep within the Arab mind, offered a foundation of prejudice which Iraqi propaganda exploited to the utmost. It also prompted sermons from a number of hard-line clerics, harshly critical of the presence of infidel troops and of their implications for devout Moslem society. These were being clandestinely distributed on tape to a widening audience.

Even among some of our more objective Saudi friends we occasionally found ourselves obliged during these months to counter an insidious assumption that Iraq's seizure of Kuwait formed part of a subtle American-inspired game of cat and mouse with Saddam Hussein, to create a pretext to destroy Iraq's strength for the benefit of Israel and achieve a freer Western hand in the Gulf.

It was not characteristic of King Fahd's style of rule to confront such issues in public fashion. But from the beginning of January, as the prospect for avoiding hostilities diminished, the King and his ministers went on an unaccustomed offensive to spell out to the Saudi people the reality of their predicament and the facts of Iraqi oppression in Kuwait in highly-coloured terms. Iraq's strident charges were at last being met by countercharges in similar vein.

Chas Freeman and I took the chance to give interviews in the Saudi press, both Arabic and English language, spelling out the commitment our countries shared with the Kingdom to see an end to Iraq's illegal occupation and her threat to Gulf security. Our message was that if things came to war, Saddam Hussein had only himself to blame. The quarrel was with him rather than with the Iraqi people.

The principal message was, however, spelt out by the King himself, accompanied by a certain amount of theatre. He opened with a rousing speech, delivered at a parade of all the 30 or so national forces gathered in Saudi Arabia held in early January in the desert south of the Kuwait frontier. King Fahd rehearsed in detail the stages in Iraq's actions prior to her invasion of Kuwait. These amounted to a sequence of duplicity and broken assurances. He had done his best to mediate right up to the moment of invasion. Having relied on assurances given to him by Saddam Hussein that Iraq did not intend to attack, he had then been presented with an unacceptable assertion of Iraq's sovereignty over Kuwait when the Iraqi Vice-President had been sent to see him in Jedda just after the invasion.

The King stressed that it was open to Iraq to withdraw without loss of face and try to find a peaceful settlement through the Arab League or other mediation. But withdrawal must be without conditions and lead to the restoration of the Kuwaiti government. King Fahd warned that if Iraq did not comply with the demand of the whole international community to withdraw peacefully, other means would have to be employed. Saddam Hussein alone would carry the responsibility for any war; he held the key to a solution. Iraq had meanwhile indulged in cheap insults and press campaigns against the Kingdom. He did not propose to respond in kind, but Saudi Arabia had a right to defend herself.

This robust and plain speaking was followed by the convening in Mecca four days later of a conference of the executive council of the Islamic Popular Conference, one of Islam's most influential theological bodies. The purpose of this gathering was to repudiate on behalf of the Moslem community the status of a conference, under the banner of the same body, which Iraq had organised in Baghdad earlier in the month in a brazen bid for the support of Moslem opinion by claiming Islamic legitimacy for her actions over Kuwait.

The Mecca conference, attended by Saudi Arabia's religious leaders and scholars from Egypt and a number of other Moslem countries, came out with a statement dismissing Iraq's claims with contumely, while bluntly accusing the Iraqi regime of standing for paganism and secular materialism, masquerading as Islam. It recalled Saddam Hussein's massacres of his Kurdish subjects and his detention of large numbers of Iraqis as political prisoners. The statement called on behalf of the Moslem *umma*, or community, for Iraq's withdrawal, and justified the presence of non-Moslem forces to help in the exercise of self-defence against aggression. Contrary to Iraq's propaganda, the holy places of Islam were well protected and undefiled. The statement enjoined Iraqi soldiers to disobey their orders, and warned those who took life in combat of the fires of hell.

Abstruse as such arguments may have appeared in Western eyes, they and the authority behind them were calculated to carry significance for all but the most hidebound conservative elements in Saudi Arabia's devout society. At the end of the conference King Fahd gave another opportune and well-publicised speech, in which he rehearsed at yet greater length the sequence of Iraq's deception and aggression and his deep personal sense of betrayal by Saddam Hussein, whom Saudi Arabia had supported in generous fashion during the years of costly war with Iran. It was now clear that, when Saddam Hussein had sprung the proposal for a non-aggression agreement in 1989, this had been part of his plan to neutralise the Kingdom and give him a free hand to pursue his expansionist aims in Kuwait and perhaps further along the Gulf.

With an eye to conservative religious opinion within the Kingdom, King Fahd took pains to refute the argument that foreign forces had no right to be in Saudi Arabia.They had come at his invitation to protect Saudi Arabia against the threat of invasion. If they were now to play a part in reversing the aggression against Kuwait, this was in response to Kuwait's request for international help. If it came to a fight then the coalition had a legitimate right to do so. By contrast Saddam Hussein, who exercised an absolute authority over his country, as he had demonstrated by his unilateral action in returning to Iran all the territory she had acquired from Iraq under the Algiers agreement of 1975, could surely have no problem over restoring the *status quo* in Kuwait to avoid a war.

King Fahd completed this heavy cycle of public exhortation with an open letter addressed to the Iraqi President on 14 January, following the Geneva meeting. It was cast as a reply to a message addressed to him by Saddam Hussein and broadcast by Baghdad radio, in which the Iraqi leader had produced a polemic of accusations of Saudi Arabian hostility towards Iraq, of infidelity to Islam and betrayal of the Arab cause,

without the least mention of the issue of Kuwait. The King opened his
reply with a quotation from the Koran:

> There is a type of man whose speech about this world may dazzle thee,
> and he calls God to witness about what is in his heart. Yet he is the most
> contentious of enemies. When he turns his back, his aim everywhere is to
> spread mischief through the earth and destroy crops and cattle, but God
> loveth not mischief.

He went on to say that he did not propose to trade insults with the
Iraqi leader, but to correct his lies. In unwontedly harsh tones he set out
once again Saddam Hussein's record of broken assurances and pretence
of peace, his threats and accusations against the Kingdom, and his false
claim to Kuwait. The King was particularly incensed by the gross misrepresentation of Saudi Arabia's generosity to Iraq and made a point of
putting the record straight. If Saddam Hussein was sincere in calling for
the restoration of good relations with the Kingdom and the departure of
foreign troops, it was up to him to prove it by first getting out of Kuwait
and removing his forces from the frontier with the Kingdom. Only thus
could bloodshed be avoided.

This elaborate barrage of public statements by the King, designed
not so much with the hope of securing a change of heart on the part of
the Iraqi leader as to spell out the case for war to his own people,
achieved a steadying effect on Saudi opinion. Some who had doubts
about the legitimacy of a campaign on religious grounds, and yet more
who simply found it difficult to contemplate the intrusion of hostilities
and danger into their accustomed routine and had been nursing an
illusion that compromise would be reached, were brought face to face
with the reality of the situation and took heart from the King's expression of a firm resolve. Wishful thinking faded into the background,
though there was still a general conviction that Iraq's will to fight would
crumble within days of air attacks. A distinction, encouraged by the
Saudi government, was established between the Ba'ath regime and the
people of Iraq, whose suffering deserved to be spared to the greatest
extent possible.

To be sure of sustaining this national resolve, however, it was also
seen as desirable to take out of circulation those elements which had
been playing a part in fostering public concern over the idea of war and
the presence of Western forces. Accordingly from early January the government began quietly to transfer some of the zealots among the
religious police in the main cities to smaller provincial towns, where
their prejudices and harassment would have less impact. This exercise in

rustication certainly removed one source of aggravation for Saudi families and expatriates during the tense weeks of air attacks on Riyadh and
the eastern cities, though it contributed subsequently to a backlash of
fanaticism once these custodians of public behaviour returned to their
beats after the crisis.

The Saudi government's decision to wait so long before winding public opinion up for war did, however, have negative consequences in the
field of civil defence. Saudi arrangements in this area, which were the
responsibility of the Interior Ministry, were fairly rudimentary. Prior to
the end of 1990 little had been set in hand to prepare for protection of
the civilian population against the air raids which could be expected in
the Eastern Province and perhaps in the Riyadh region too. The result
was a scramble in the last few days before the expiry of the deadline on
15 January to set up a system for the issue of gas-masks and launch an
information campaign on air-raid precautions. Sirens had been hastily
erected in a few locations, but warnings were mainly to depend on radio
and television and on mobile sirens carried on police patrol vehicles.
The first air raid practice only took place in Riyadh on 13 January.

Instruction in gas-mask drill and safety precautions in homes against
chemical attack was carried on television. This was in some measure
based on our own drill, and involved the issue of adhesive tape to stick
across glass windows against blast, and the preparation in each house of
a sealed area into which the inhabitants could withdraw until any poiso-
nous gas had dispersed. Citizens were also to be issued with a supply of
fullers' earth as an antidote to chemical burns. This unaccustomed substance was described reassuringly in public instruction as the material
used in England against chemical attack, as though we underwent this
experience frequently.

The position over the issue of gas-masks was even less satisfactory,
and caused us to be thankful that we had laid the preparations for our
own community in good time. It was only in the final weeks before mid-
January that the authorities began to look for supplies. By this time
newly-manufactured stocks around the world were already almost
exhausted. We were unable to meet a substantial Saudi order for the
much sought after model made by the Avon company in South Wales, as
even by working round the clock the factory was only just able to keep
pace with orders placed earlier in the crisis for British use and by countries and companies in the Gulf. In the event the Saudis ended up with
consignments of obsolete masks, mostly from Eastern European sources
and not designed to give great confidence to the wearer.

There were problems, too, over distribution. Masks had to be bought
through a system of first paying the cost at a bank and then taking the

receipt round to the distribution centre. People found themselves completing this routine only to be told that there were insufficient masks and to come back another day. Many did not obtain masks until some days after the start of air attacks, and some never received them at all. There was considerable criticism and morale suffered, particularly as the importance of gas-masks was by now being emphasised through regular programmes on television.

An entertaining episode occurred on Bahrain's English-language channel where, as the instructor was just reaching the critical point of what to do having donned the mask, the programme faded to one of the regular daily prayer schedules with an announcement that it was now time to pray. We also heard of problems faced by religious conservatives with long beards, who found it impossible to fit these badges of piety inside the chin of the mask.

The rush by the Saudis to prepare their civil defences against attack produced one episode which for a short period in January threatened to cast a cloud over our very positive co-operation on the diplomatic front. Early in January Abdul Aziz al Thunayan, the Vice-Minister for Foreign Affairs, asked me to see him to hear a complaint about the failure of a private British firm to deliver a stock of vaccines against the biological warfare threat of botulism and anthrax, which they had contracted to supply to the Saudi government. The firm were now pleading that the British government's chemical and biological research laboratory at Porton Down was unable to fulfil the Saudi order. The Saudis felt badly let down over the affair and, as the minister made clear to me, were looking to us to help sort it out. The vaccines were needed for the Saudi armed forces and no other sources of supply appeared to be available for these very specialised products. Saudi concern over the matter was repeated to me a few days later by a senior member of Prince Sultan's military staff.

Urgent investigation by the MoD in Whitehall produced an unsatisfactory picture. It appeared that an opportunist firm, trading in pharmaceuticals, had given undertakings to the Saudis which it was in no position to fulfil, perhaps banking on the British authorities authorising Porton Down to release a quantity of the limited supply of the vaccines once the Saudi order was revealed to them. As a result we now had a problem of good faith on our hands. There was apparently no way in which the laboratory could produce sufficient of the new and specialised vaccines to meet the Saudi order in the time provided by the contract. Priority had to go to production for British combat troops in the theatre, and there were also some earlier American orders to fulfil.

The matter was fortunately resolved through a decision by Tom King to divert a portion of the British forces' order to the Saudis as a first step, with the rest of the supply to follow. At the same time we arranged for General Crawford, the deputy head of the Royal Army Medical Corps, to come out and brief the Saudi military medical service and Health Ministry on the biological warfare threat and countermeasures. This was as much as we could do, but Prince Sultan accepted these offers with good grace and the awkward storm blew over.

Despite such mishaps things duly fell into place. There was some hoarding of water and foods, but to the credit of Saudi Arabia's well-developed distribution system the markets never ran short. Many families left for the comparative safety of Jedda and the south-western hill towns. Those who stayed battened down their hatches. The Saudi authorities had prudently delayed the end of the school and university winter holiday, partly to free families to move away from areas of possible danger, but also, we suspected, to forestall any risk of youthful demon-strations being incited by religious zealots among the teaching community. Hotels set up their air-raid shelters. A curious phenomenon was the virtual closure of Riyadh's normally active songbird market in the old town; it transpired that there had been a rush to buy all available birds to serve as a rudimentary early warning system for gas attack – shades of the canaries in Britain's 19th century coal mines.

CHAPTER 12

Clearing the Decks

The embassy's intensive preoccupation with diplomatic liaison during the six weeks of countdown to the 15 January deadline was fully matched on the consular side by the task of devising arrangements for the security and possible evacuation of our expatriate community. By the year's end, and despite a progressive thinning out among dependants and families, the number of British citizens still living and working in Saudi Arabia was estimated to have dropped by only just over a third, to a figure of some 19,000. This still made us the largest Western community in the Kingdom, with the Americans close behind. The French and Canadians had a few thousand citizens, while other European nationals, Australians and Japanese could be counted in hundreds. By contrast the workforce from Asian countries remained over a million throughout the Kingdom.

Despite this huge disparity in numbers we were very conscious that, as one of the largest Western communities, many of whose members were employed in technical and managerial roles in key areas of the Kingdom's economic and medical infrastructure as well as in military support, our response to the crisis would be bound to set a model for the morale of other groups. The Saudis continued to emphasise to us the importance for them of our doing our bit to keep civilian morale steady and avoid any precipitate reaction or advice which might have the effect of ratcheting up a more general alarm among their expatriate population, already nervous as the prospect of hostilities increased.

Yet our first obligation had to be to the safety of our citizens. As we saw it this did not have to involve their wholesale evacuation. On the basis of the assessments of Iraqi capabilities of attack available to us, the threat to security did not warrant such a measure. In any case about half our numbers were located in Jedda and the west, where they were well out of range of air attack. A considerable proportion of the British total in the Kingdom was of Asian origin, holding British citizenship but without right of abode in the UK. Moreover, of the 9,000 or so Britons who still remained by late December in the areas at risk in the east and centre of the Kingdom, many had made it clear they intended to stay to help see the affair through.

The need to achieve this difficult balance between protection and solidarity with Saudi Arabia dictated the adoption of an essentially pragmatic approach in providing for the security of the expatriates for whose safety we were responsible, and in the rationale behind our responses to a constantly changing scene. It was not only the effect of our actions on the Saudi front and the wider expatriate scene that we had to take into account. They also had to be acceptable to the FCO, which was answerable for the general safety of British citizens throughout the war zone. It was also important to standardise our approach with that of the four other British embassies in the Gulf states, two of which, in Bahrain and Qatar, had communities within range of Iraqi air attack. Finally there was the importance of keeping in step with other Western embassies in Saudi Arabia, particularly the Americans as our peers in size, and other EC members for the sake both of practical co-operation and in the interests of wider political harmony.

These often conflicting factors made for numerous headaches and inconsistencies. The general thrust of the approach we adopted in Riyadh was not to rush any fences over the issue of evacuation, leaving this decision so far as possible to individual judgment, while spelling out the dangers in realistic fashion and providing facilities and guidance on protection in the event of attack. This was seen by some as tending towards the riskier end of the spectrum, but given the extent to which our reactions were likely to be a focus for a wider public response within the Kingdom this seemed justified.

Indeed, by taking our warnings and precautions by successive stages we made a contribution towards steadying the foreign community at large when the attacks came. Several embassies in Riyadh sought to take their cues from us, including a number of Europeans and Commonwealth members, with whom we kept in regular touch on the consular side. Ironically, we were to find ourselves least in step with our two closest partners in the military effort, the Americans and French.

The former found themselves obliged, largely it appeared through indecision and inconsistency in Washington, to adopt a position over advice in the Riyadh region which many in their large community considered over-relaxed. This approach had been conditioned by lobbying in the early stages of the crisis on the part of certain major American corporations with workforces in the Kingdom, particularly in the hydrocarbons and military fields, aimed at discouraging any precipitate advice on evacuation which they feared could provoke a nervous exodus and leave their operations at a standstill. This attitude had, however, by the end of the year engendered a feeling of insecurity among significant parts of the large American community.

The unease was compounded when, shortly before the outbreak of hostilities, the Americans suddenly came out with cautionary advice about departure from the whole area of the Kingdom and began a belated issue of gas-masks. For practical reasons of harmonisation I sought for as long as possible to keep our precautions in step with the American approach. For his part Chas Freeman, who was rightly one of those most alert to the risks of chemical or biological attack on centres of population, did what he could to graduate the advice to his community as we were doing. But he had difficulties with Washington, and by early January the gap between us had become too wide to span.

The French position tended towards the opposite extreme. Through our regular consultations among EC embassies, both at ambassador level and involving consular staffs, we all managed until well into December to keep in step to a remarkable extent, thus avoiding any spiral of concern among our communities who lived and worked so closely together. Things became more complicated, however, after the French embassy were instructed from Paris in mid-December to advise all those in the Kingdom whose presence was not essential to leave by Christmas. This produced quite an exodus and led to unease among our own and other communities, whose advice had not been as categoric. Subsequently, a week before the expiry of the UN deadline, all French citizens were advised to leave the Kingdom, irrespective of where they were located. This was advice which went considerably further than we and our other Western partners saw as necessary. Fortunately French numbers were not great, and there was no serious knock-on effect from their decision to recommend evacuation.

On our own front the harmonisation of our local approach with that being advocated from London was much facilitated through a visit paid to Saudi Arabia and other Gulf posts in the first days of December by the head of the FCO consular department, Christopher Denne. Having come out with impressions understandably coloured by the pressures and concerns for the safety of those in the area to which he and his special crisis unit were being subjected by relatives and alarmist media at home, he was able to judge for himself the various political and security factors with which we were faced, and to have contact with the community and BFME headquarters.

In Riyadh and the east of the Kingdom he found people calm enough on the surface, though understandably apprehensive below. Our advisory system through the wardens was functioning effectively. In a final conference in Jedda on 9 December before Christopher Denne's return to London, we agreed the time looked close when we should need to replace our deliberately low-key warnings to the community in the centre and east, to take the Christmas break out of the Kingdom if they could, with a more specific message linked to the approaching UN deadline.

We also discussed options for the possibility of an assisted evacuation from the east and centre, slight though we believed the prospect of things coming to such a point to be. An air evacuation would be preferable but its feasibility would depend on the availability of airports, a factor which it was hard to assess at this stage. As a last resort we therefore planned on a long road evacuation southwards down the Gulf to the UAE or Oman, or across from Riyadh to Jedda. Christopher Denne agreed that our emphasis should remain on thinning out dependants and the protection of those who stayed. But he made the point that, in the nightmarish event of a chemical attack, it would only take one warhead to set off a scramble to get out, with major problems of control. Moreover, there could be irreversible public pressure at home to see an immediate evacuation.

On protection I took the line that, although the RAF were now delivering stocks of gas-masks from Britain sufficient for present numbers of the community in both the east and the areas of Riyadh and Tabuk, we were not proposing to issue these yet. There were several reasons for this. We did not want to get too far ahead of our foreign partners or the Saudis in the provision of equipment which would suggest, contrary to our belief at the time, that we had reason to expect chemical attack. Moreover, hostilities were at this stage not a foregone conclusion, so long as the proposed meeting between the Americans and Iraqis had still to take place.

We also had yet to be convinced that Iraq possessed the capability to 'weaponise' her stock of chemical and biological material. Her programme did not appear so far to have reached this stage of development (though subsequent revelations suggested our assumptions were wrong). So far as the Riyadh region was concerned, it was not clear whether the additional range which we knew the Iraqis had developed in their Soviet Scud missiles could match the city's distance of 560 kilometres from Kuwait, and yet further from Iraqi territory. The Americans seemed confident this was not the case, and we had therefore asked the intelligence people in Whitehall to give us their latest assessment. Indeed, the defence attaché had recently gone on record in briefing the Riyadh wardens with the opinion that no Scuds would reach the capital – words which we were obliged to eat two months later.

Behind all these considerations lay an uneasiness in my mind that the

issue of gas-masks, in a situation where we were discounting the probability of chemical attack, would be all too likely to provoke alarm within
the community, whose nerve had so far proved very steady. In its turn
this could lead to the exodus we aimed to avoid. In this forecast, however, I turned out to be quite wrong. Once we went ahead with the issue
of masks in early January, we found them to prove a source of reassurance rather than disquiet.

The upshot was agreement between the FCO and ourselves on the
text of a letter, initiating the second phase of our warning advice, to be
addressed by embassies to all members of their communities within possible range of air attack. This conveyed the message that 'in view of the
possibility of hostilities in the Gulf and the ensuing danger, British
dependants are advised to leave the area well before the deadline of 15
January which has been set by the Security Council for the withdrawal of
Iraq from Kuwait'. We emphasised that the advice only applied to dependants, and was thus a further step in our precautionary policy of
thinning out our numbers. It was not intended to affect the presence of
those working in the area. In the case of our own embassy, where several
of our wives were doing essential support jobs, particularly on the hard-
pressed consular side and with troops welfare, the FCO agreed that the
advice need not apply to them if they chose to remain. In the event
most of them did. It was only in the case of families with small children
that we firmly urged departure.

Otherwise we held to the principle that a decision on whether to go
or stay should be for each family to take. This applied throughout our
community. I was sure it was the right line in the circumstances, though
there were those who would have preferred to have the decision taken
out of their hands by the embassy, and told us so. Some firms with a large
British workforce, such as Cable and Wireless and BAe, took the decision
at this point to fly remaining dependants home from the east and centre
of the Kingdom, not only for safety's sake but also on the sensible
grounds that this would free the husbands of a preoccupation with the
security of their families if hostilities were to come.

People's worries about leaving were considerably eased by the helpful
action of the consular department in the Saudi Foreign Ministry in cutting through the bureaucratic complexities of residence procedures by
providing for exit visas to permit re-entry up to six months. We also
secured a tacit agreement that, in cases where expatriates' passports
were being held by employers, temporary documents issued by the
embassy would be accepted on departure.

To avoid our move to stronger advice on departure coming as a shock
to the Saudis, I saw Prince Saud on 16 December, 24 hours before it was

due to be issued over the BBC and through our wardens in Riyadh and the eastern region. I stressed that the advice amounted to a justified precautionary measure and did not constitute a British evacuation. In particular it was designed not to prompt those engaged in essential work within the Kingdom to pull out. To issue the warning at this stage would allow reasonable time for those who intended to go to leave in orderly fashion on the regular flights being operated to Britain by British Airways and Saudia. Indeed, the British Airways manager had told us that additional capacity would be laid on to London over the month ahead, which was a considerable help.

Prince Saud raised no objection to what we proposed to say. He showed some concern, however, over the possible local effect of the message being carried on the BBC, which was widely listened to in the Kingdom. I explained that we had already learnt the hard way at the outset of the crisis that it was safest to broadcast clear advice, rather than to go for a lower-key message which risked becoming garbled by the media. We had been careful to take Saudi preoccupations into account and must now go ahead.

The advice was duly issued on 17 December, a few days after the French and Italians had acted in similar fashion. It persuaded several hundred dependants to leave, but without denuding the British workforce or arousing serious anxiety on a wider scale, though we took some flak from a few Saudi employers whose mainly Asian expatriate workers were becoming increasingly nervous. It did, however, mark an end to our common front with the American embassy over advice to leave, and provoked some anxiety within the American community in Riyadh, which had received no official advice to reduce its numbers. Our assessments had begun to diverge.

By the turn of the year, with Iraq showing no sign of withdrawing and still prevaricating over the proposed meeting with the Americans, there was renewed pressure from London to get our numbers, which we reckoned still to be above 10,000 in the centre and east, reduced further. It was also proposed that we give preliminary advice to our communities on the contingency of a full-scale evacuation. This last point was supported by our embassy in Doha, where the British community was comparatively small and a land evacuation was geographically more feasible to organise.

The proposal that we should move automatically to a full-scale evacuation from the northern Gulf region in the event of a chemical air attack, or even heavy bombardment by conventional means, presented real difficulty for us in Saudi Arabia. We had by this time been persuaded, on the basis of an updated assessment of Iraq's missile capability provided by intelligence sources in London, that there was a chance, if only an outside one, that Iraq might attempt to arm her Scud missiles with chemical or biological warheads. The techniques were untested, but there was disturbing evidence that Iraq held stocks of three highly-toxic chemical agents, Sarin, Tabun and phosgene (mustard gas). There was also a suspicion, over which Chas Freeman told me the Americans were concerned, that Saddam Hussein might try to sow anthrax or botulism plague as a lethal biological weapon.

It had also become clear that the modifications undertaken by the Iraqis to extend the range of the Scud, renamed the Hussein, would put Riyadh within their range, albeit at the expense of a lighter warhead payload. Saddam Hussein obligingly put this beyond doubt, as well as giving us a seasonable preview of what he might have in store, when a long-range test flight by a Scud within Iraq was detected on 25 December, bringing BFME headquarters on to a premature alert and somewhat thinning out their attendance at our Christmas lunch.

Saudi centres of population would therefore have to depend for protection on the American Patriot missiles, which had already been set up at key points around Riyadh, Dhahran and Jubail. Their box-like silhouettes, pointing into the northern sky, had become a comforting sight, though the weapon had been designed for anti-aircraft rather than anti-missile defence and was being hurriedly adapted for its new role. Beyond this line of protection it would be up to individuals to wear gas-masks and take thorough precautions to proof their homes and workplaces against air raids.

Accordingly, and despite the American intention to continue to hold back, we took the decision at the end of December to go ahead with the issue of gas-masks to the 10,000 or so members of the British community who remained in the regions of Riyadh and the east, as well as to the couple of hundred Britons working in the northern airbase town of Tabuk. I presented this to the Saudis as a sensible precaution. Our decision may have had the side effect of prompting them to take the possibility of gas attack more seriously in their own belated civil defence precautions. Certainly those Western and European partners who had not already taken this step now went ahead with it, though the Americans, to the frustration of their community and embassy, continued to hold back.

We were, however, under no illusions as to the logistical nightmare which the organisation of a full-scale evacuation of this number of British citizens would involve, particularly if it was to take place in a rush and against the background of limited evacuation flights and a simultaneous road exodus to safer ground by Saudis and other expatriates. Indeed, in the event of a chemical attack it seemed to us that the safest course for at least the initial day or so would be to stay within a sealed area within the home or workplace, while the dust literally cleared. In any case, even in the event of a single attempt to use chemical weapons, a repetition seemed very unlikely in view of the sombre warnings of retaliation already broadcast to Iraq's leadership.

We therefore took issue with the FCO in late December over the proposal that we should plan on an immediate and complete withdrawal of the British community from areas of danger in the Gulf region in the event of chemical attack. After considerable debate by telegram between the FCO, ourselves and our embassies in Bahrain and Doha, our case for an initial stay-put policy was to our considerable relief accepted, despite FCO reservations derived in part from public criticism of similar advice which had been given to the British community caught in Kuwait following Iraq's invasion in August. In the present instance we understood that Douglas Hurd himself was opposed to a rushed evacuation.

This modified advice was to be included in a detailed letter from each of the three ambassadors to their communities, in which existing warnings to dependants whose presence was not essential to consider leaving before 15 January would be reinforced, and advice on measures to protect themselves in their homes offered to those remaining. A helpful draft, which reconciled the various points at issue between ourselves on the one hand and the FCO on the other, was put together by the ambassador in Bahrain, John Shepherd. It served as the basis for a key meeting of representatives from the consular department in London and the embassies concerned, plus the British headquarters in Riyadh, which took place in Doha at the beginning of January to thrash out a common approach on advice and evacuation. Clive Woodland attended on our behalf.

The upshot of this important meeting was a letter which I sent out through our warden system to all remaining members of our community in the centre and east of the Kingdom on 6 January. With our usual eye to avoiding wider alarm we decided not to use the local English-language press for dissemination. In preparing our letter we sought to convey a message which would be realistic yet not alarmist. In particular we wanted to avoid giving the impression that we were upgrading our previous advice on departure to include those in employment. For these the best course in the eventuality of a limited Iraqi air threat was to take precautions and sit tight.

The message therefore began with a repetition of our advice to dependants who were not in employment to leave as soon as possible, while explaining that this counsel was not directed at jobholders despite confusion on this point in some British media reports. The letter went on to give guidance on the preparation of safe areas in homes, with door and window joints to be sealed with tape against the event of gas attack. We considered this to be unlikely, but people were urged to collect their gas-masks. We discouraged the idea of movement in the event of hostilities, doubting this would prove necessary, and it could prove more of a risk. As matters stood we were likely to advise staying put. We warned of the awkwardness of a mass land evacuation, but explained that we had laid plans for this contingency. In case it should happen, people were asked to keep a store of petrol for their vehicle, plus food and a suitcase packed and ready.

This comprehensive message, designed to spell out the risks and how to meet them, was received calmly and sensibly by the community. We were relieved that it was not sensationalised by the large British press contingent by now arriving in the Kingdom. But things were complicated by the irresponsible action of a commentator on the BBC World Service choosing to embroider a FCO message on 11 January, with advice to dependants to leave following the breakdown of the Geneva talks, by announcing that all British nationals in the areas at risk should pull out. We promptly brought this lapse to the attention of the news department in the FCO, and a correction was secured. But once again confusion resulted and we had to devote considerable time to allaying a wave of concern among the community, who rightly were keeping their ears close to the radio.

The renewed advice on departure was heeded to a useful degree, and British Airways flew three additional flights from Dhahran and Riyadh back to London during the week before the UN deadline expired. By the time hostilities opened in the early hours of 17 January, we reckoned British community numbers in the areas at risk from air attack were down to around 5,000 in the centre and 3,500 in the east, plus a hundred or so in Tabuk – in all under a half of the normal complement. Of these perhaps ten per cent were dependants who chose to stay; several of these joined our wives in giving valuable help over the issue of gas-masks and the welfare of British troops.

Our initial advice on the preparation of a safe area in houses recommended sealing a ground floor room, but we subsequently changed this on military advice to an upper storey to be out of reach of gas with its tendency to concentrate at ground level. Most chose a bedroom for a safe haven, with adhesive tape stuck across the windows to help against blast and with plenty of water and other supplies.

Several other Western and Commonwealth countries took our warning letter as a model for a communication to their own communities. The fulminations of the Spanish ambassador at our weekly EC liaison meetings over the alleged faintheartedness of his Spanish colony, whom he was rightly determined should see out the crisis despite pressures emanating from the Madrid press to bring them home, afforded us some welcome theatre. The French went further, with advice in early January to all French nationals to leave the Gulf and Middle East region unless their presence was indispensable.

For its part the FCO extended the advice on dependants to the neighbouring countries of Jordan, Yemen and Sudan, where local sympathy with Iraq might erupt into hostile demonstrations in the event of a coalition offensive. It did not, however, apply to Israel and the occupied territories under Israeli control, where, although Saddam Hussein's defiant threats of missile attack were not to be dismissed, the wider alarm engendered by such an instruction would have greatly outweighed the prospective danger, as well as indicating a loss of political nerve.

Despite our emphasis on a stay-put policy we now gave urgent attention to laying plans for a possible full evacuation in the event of sustained chemical attacks. It was clear that the prospects for an airlift on a large scale from Dhahran were remote, though some might be got out of Riyadh by this means. The best exit would be by land convoys southwards from the Gulf cities to ports such as Fujairah and Muscat on the Indian Ocean coasts of the UAE and Oman, whence departure could be arranged by air or sea using RAF and charter aircraft and by naval ships or cargo vessels.

In Riyadh we had to plan for a migration to the safety of Jedda. Once there we would have to accommodate the refugees in a camp until they could get away. In both cases there were good highways to hand. But the road journeys would still be long and arduous – in the case of Jedda some 1,120 kilometres – and in conditions likely to be made chaotic by the simultaneous flight of other groups. Fuel and water supplies would be problematic, though we had been assured that border formalities out of the Kingdom on the route into the UAE would present no difficulty. Clive Woodland and other consular staff were kept very busy finding ways round all these obstacles. In Riyadh they reconnoitred the Jedda route and hired fuel bowsers to be stationed at intervals along the barren highway to replenish convoy vehicles, together with stocks of water. Twenty buses were stood by to ferry single female members of the community, mainly hospital nurses.

Down in Jedda, where living space was already at a premium, the consulate-general planned to set up a tented transit camp on empty land adjacent to its compound, which was usefully equipped with an amenity hall. Conditions would inevitably be basic, but the stay should be a short one and the large British community in the city could be counted upon to help make things tolerable. Fortunately it was the coolest time of the year, with coastal temperatures resembling an English May. Up on Riyadh's desert plateau it was colder, with even a touch of frost at night. The main problem might be torrential rain.

We all took pains to keep in close touch with our community, both directly and through the wardens, during this time of increasing tension. On the surface they were remarkably calm and steady as they went about their daily business. But, as was only to be expected, this overlaid a growing sense of jitteriness and uncertainty. The embassy's consular telephone line was always open to those seeking advice.

The consul, Patrick Owens, went up to Tabuk at the beginning of January to brief the small community there and arrange for the issue of their gas-masks. Clive Woodland and others had regular sessions with those in and around Riyadh, while Peter Sincock, the defence attaché, went to reassure the community in Jedda on the limited threat to the Hejaz province. David Lloyd was doing a very good job with the morale of those staying on in the east, helped by the two vice-consuls, Rick Girdlestone and Geoff Plant, recently arrived from London straight into the crisis.

When I went with Grania across to Al Khobar early in December I took the opportunity to speak to the wardens about precautions and explain that, while we saw evacuation as a last resort, we would implement it if danger got too close. 'How close is too close?' I was asked, reasonably enough. 'That we'll have to judge at the time,' was the best reply I could give, well aware that in the final analysis this was the crucial responsibility which each ambassador in the area would have to carry.

Much of the credit for the steadiness shown by our communities throughout the Kingdom during this time should go to the dedicated way in which the volunteer wardens carried out their duties of liaison between the consulates and the community groups for which they were responsible, either in the workplace or in residential areas. The unaccustomed treat of having a cheery local station of the British Forces Broadcasting Service open up in January, with popular music interspersed with relays of BBC World Service news, also provided a tonic. Some were even able to take advantage of the technological breakthrough of CNN and BBC television now being within receiving range by satellite.

The four regional business groups had a positive and buoyant lead from their chairmen, Alistair Allen, the BP representative in Riyadh, Patrick Arnold in Jedda, Syd Watson of P&O in Al Khobar, and Laurence Oates in Jubail. When I addressed a meeting of the Riyadh business group on 15 January, to brace them for what might follow the expiry that night of the UN deadline, the large turnout seemed in staunch heart and in the mood for some black humour – yes, it was bound to come to war; someone at home had overheard Dame Vera Lynn gargling.

The BAe workforce at Dhahran, whose support role was so crucial to the RSAF, were being kept hard at it by the dynamism of their chief, Phil Champness, and the British expatriates with Aramco did their bit to ensure that the voracious demand for fuel of the coalition forces never went short. In Riyadh Clive Smith commendably kept a programme of English language classes for Saudi students going at British Council centres throughout the crisis. The two British schools in Al Khobar showed creditable resolve in reopening after the end-of-year break, one of them on a skeleton basis as numbers were much reduced. The larger British school in Riyadh suffered a temporary loss of nerve when hostilities began. Several of its pupils were diverted to the British preparatory school in Jedda, where they were given a warm welcome for the next few weeks.

John Major did his bit to sustain the good spirits of the embassy and community when he met a cross-section of those in the Riyadh area at a lunch in our garden during his visit in early January. He spoke to them with informality and in terms of encouragement similar to those he used to such good effect with the British military units, emphasising the importance to Saudi Arabia and to Britain's part in the crisis of the role they were playing. The contact meant a lot to everyone present. Indeed, to their credit after all the months of a phoney war, the British community now looked in stalwart heart and as keen as anyone to get on with seeing Iraq out of Kuwait.

The issue of gas-masks to British subjects in the central and eastern areas, and to some Commonwealth citizens too, was a considerable task and took a good week to complete. It was not just a question of distributing the masks sent out from Britain. They had to be individually fitted, and detailed instruction given on the technique of donning them in a way that would ensure all possibly contaminated air was expelled and an effective seal created. At the beginning of January, following our decision to diverge from the Americans and go ahead with the issue of masks, members of the community were invited by wardens to collect them. In Riyadh we began issue simultaneously with the Canadians on 5 January, on the eve of the Prime Minister's visit. We were careful to avoid drawing the operation to the attention of the accompanying press, lest their reporting should alarm relatives at home. In Al Khobar, however, BBC television filmed the first day of issue with suitably relaxed comment from Geoff Plant.

The summons had the useful effect of bringing to our notice a considerable number of British subjects who had not previously registered with the consulates. Some were the wives of Saudis, living behind the veil. The work of checking identities in the long lines that collected in front of the embassy, and of handing out the masks, was undertaken by the consular staff with a number of wives in the embassy and the community. The Avon masks were much in demand for their quality. Many people suddenly remembered having British antecedents, including a number of Americans, frustrated at what they saw as their government's complacency. It was not until a couple of days before the deadline expired that the American embassy received clearance to start the issue of gas-masks.

Our operation was, however, a good-natured affair, and the relief to be getting the cumbersome masks was evident. Special plastic bags with a filtered air vent were provided to envelop very small children. At least one was issued to an expectant mother. The Treasury tried to insist that we make people pay for their masks. This was rejected as impracticable, though we did send a bill to large companies whose employees were fitted out. In a last-minute fit of dottiness the MoD instructed that all civilian masks should carry a blue paint mark to identify the wearer in conditions of war. This idea we quietly kicked into touch, while we got on with the work of issue.

To help with the task of giving advice on the fitting of the masks we turned to the military, who readily arranged for the RAF and Royal Navy to give assistance in Al Khobar and Jubail. In Riyadh some NCOs were sent to us from the Devonshire and Dorset Regiment. They were ideal for the task as with a comforting West Country burr to their voices they initiated nervous civilians into the unaccustomed techniques of gas-mask drills. Problems arose, however, in a few instances where British women who had married into Saudi families were in accordance with Saudi custom forbidden to raise their veils to have the soldiers fit their masks. Grania and the other ladies involved in the distribution had to step in on these occasions and undertake the task. There was a tender episode at Al Khobar where an elderly British lady, drawing on her mask, asked what she should do to protect her parrot. The mischievous reply that she should scrag it caused considerable distress, which had to be soothed with a dose of consular sympathy and an apology from a contrite airman.

As for the embassy itself, everybody gave all they had to get the show ready for what lay ahead. Intrepid volunteers from the FCO and Jedda joined us to reinforce our hard-pressed consular and secretarial staff in Riyadh and Al Khobar. Everyone, British and local, was ready to put all they had into a cause in which they had come to believe strongly. It was interesting to see how some, whom one might have expected to be among the more nervous at the prospect of hostilities, seemed in the event to take it in their stride, and vice versa too. We took to carrying our handsets and gas-masks all the time. Safe rooms, proofed against gas, were set up in our homes and tape stuck across all windows. It brought back for some of us childhood memories of the 1940s.

We had some awkward dilemmas to resolve over the degree of protection to give ourselves as compared with the community at large, notably over whether we should accept the military's offer of the full chemical protection suits issued to the forces, and also over access to the limited supply of antidotes to chemical and biological toxins. In the end we rationalised our need for the special clothing on the grounds that we might have to go across to the embassy building during an attack. As for the vaccinations, it was left to individual discretion on whether to be jabbed or take a chance. Some of the vaccines were understood not to be long out of the experimental phase.

But it was not only the morale and solidarity of our local British community to which we found ourselves having to give attention. We were affected too by echoes of the debate taking place at home over the propriety of going to war over Kuwait, particularly on the part of Britain's Moslem community. This controversy involved me in one of the more bizarre encounters of the crisis. On one of my frequent visits during early January to see Prince Saud at the Foreign Ministry, I was sitting in his waiting room when a Saudi official brought in a slim figure with a wispy beard, dressed in a white robe and turban and walking with a stick. He was introduced to me as Yusef Islam. Charles Hollis, who was with me, was quicker off the mark, saying in a stage whisper 'Cat Stevens'. Memories crowded back of pleasant hours in the company of his music, at an epoch which now seemed worlds away.

Here he was, a convert to Islam and a leading figure in the British Moslem community, on the eve of a war and with a theological difficulty on his mind: the religious morality of an attack on Iraq by a joint Moslem and Christian force. He explained how the irregularity of this had, predictably, been emphasised to him on a recent visit to Baghdad. He was now in Riyadh at Saudi invitation to seek the other side of the story, before making a judgment with his fellow Moslems in north London. He had found his meeting with Prince Saud very helpful, and would later be seeing the Kingdom's chief religious authority, Sheikh Abdul Aziz Bin Baz.

We had a talk together, as I suspected the Saudis had intended us to do. It seemed unreal to be having this fascinating if scholastic discussion

with Cat Stevens: angels dancing on the head of a pin while armies prepared for war. Yet it all mattered to the solidarity of our singular
coalition. I sought to ease his dilemma by challenging the assumption
that an offensive would constitute an act of aggression by the coalition.
Rather it was action in defence of the Kuwaitis, to enable them to recover
their state. They had requested help in this from both Moslem and non-
Moslem quarters. I understood such a step to have respectable Koranic
precedent, recalling the Prophet's recourse to assistance from a local
Jewish tribe when he had needed help in defending his base in Medina
from attack by his Arab enemies in the battle of Badr. This line of argument, sound if somewhat hastily assembled, seemed to open a fresh
perspective for Yusef Islam, and we went our separate ways. It had been
a strange encounter.

Hard as we all worked there was plenty of good humour to relieve the
tension. Occasionally this verged on hilarity as we were put through
instruction in the race to insert ourselves into our charcoal-filled chemical suits, with their complicated arrangement of boots and gloves, all to
be donned in less than a minute and with cries of 'gas – gas – gas' as we
thrust on our masks. Charles Hollis always seemed to be first out of the
trap. Paul Baines, an inveterate beard-wearer, had his growth shaved off
for charity, as beards were said to be unreliable as a chemical filter.

We were all issued with personal hand radios, a novel experience.
Communications drills were never our strong point, despite patient
instruction from our military colleagues. Some treated the network as a
glorified telephone party-line. The Royal Military Police sent us out a
specialist in counter-terrorist techniques, Sergeant Gorman, to give our
drivers a course in evasive tactics which Ali passed with flying colours. He
also gave instruction in anti-terrorist precautions in the home, a proce-
dure which involved somehow drawing all curtains before turning on the
lights when entering a room after dark, and produced more alarm than
reassurance.

The embassy's annual pantomime, a popular source of entertainment for the community, had to be cancelled. This was no time to be
frolicking with Ali Baba and his accomplices when the Thief of Baghdad
was already on the doorstep. We were into serious theatre instead. We
did, however, hold our seasonal ball where the carols were rendered
with gusto, and Grania went ahead with her regular party for the
younger embassy children, complete with a conjuring show. Harry Gray,
who kept the embassy's installations going without a hitch through the
long weeks of pressure, made a jovial and suitably bulky Father
Christmas. Many of the children were soon to leave with their mothers
for safer refuge in Britain or Jedda, whither they drove in early January

in a convoy led by Chris and Dianne Wilton, with Arab headdress helping to obscure the gender of some of the drivers in deference to Saudi regulations.

For New Year's Eve our New Zealand colleagues, the Cochranes, held a celebration where we put outside preoccupations behind us for a brief instant. We also enjoyed a memorable *meshwi* with a sheep cooked on the spit out at the desert camp of the ever-hospitable Prince Abdullah bin Faisal. It was a cold, star-filled night. We looked northwards to a horizon which would shortly be the setting for flame and smoke. Peter de la Billière was there with some of his staff, looking chilled in their thin khaki pullovers until warm *farwas*, the sheepskin-lined cloaks of the Saudi bedouin, were thrust over their shoulders.

As the deadline neared a final wave of dependants from Riyadh and the east caught the last commercial flights back to London, joined by some families who had come out for the holidays, among them our two boys. There had been little time for family activity, though we had occasionally managed to put the crisis behind us with visits to favourite spots, such as the tranquillity of Riyadh's cavernous carpet souk.The press corps remained in town in force, along with a few determined grandstanders whose personal links with the Kingdom led them to stay and see things through. Among these was David Sulzberger, a specialist in Islamic art, concerned for the fate of Kuwait's fine national collection which was known to have been hijacked to Baghdad.

Michael Weston also stayed with us at this time, recovered from the rigours of his spell under siege in our embassy in Kuwait. This gave us a chance to discuss plans for the return of his embassy following Iraq's enforced withdrawal, and for a British role in the work of reconstruction in Kuwait for which we had already begun to lay plans. He also had a useful opportunity to see Sulaiman Shahine, who from the Kuwaiti embassy up the road continued his effective co-ordination of Kuwait's foreign policy in exile. Together we pressed for an early return to Kuwait by members of the government on the heels of the liberating forces, to reassert authority and avoid indiscriminate settling of scores by those who were stoutly sustaining a national resistance under occupation.

I somehow found time in the first days of the New Year to compose my regulation annual review of 1990 for the Foreign Secretary. It was not easy to encapsulate all the frenzy of activity which had brought our unique coalition so far, and to reflect on where we might now be going. But of one thing I was sure: our resolute response had brought us closer to the Saudis than ever before, and would mean a great deal to our future relationship once the crisis was past.

CHAPTER 13

The Fog of War

On the evening of 16 January Peter de la Billière came over to the embassy to tell me that the first wave of the coalition air attack would be launched at 3am that night local time. The information was to go no further. It had been an uneasy day. The UN ceasefire expired at eight o'clock that morning, by our local time. There was no doubt in the minds of the Saudis, the Americans and ourselves that delay in following through with the launching of the air attack carried political risks, and presentational ones too, beset as we were by Soviet and other last-minute initiatives for negotiation and compromise.

On the Saudi side both Prince Saud and the joint commander, Prince Khalid, had made clear their concern to get on with the job of dislodging the Iraqis once the deadline passed. We were of similar mind, bolstered by the knowledge that the British and other coalition forces which would be participating in an offensive had brought themselves to a high state of readiness in the air and on the ground, and by a suspicion that the will to fight of Iraq's forces in the field was already starting to be sapped.

By chance Grania and I had picked this day some while before to give a farewell lunch for John Mitchell, our communications officer, who had worked tirelessly during the preceding six months to keep an avalanche of telegrams rolling through all the pressures of the crisis. He and his wife, Rosa, who had sustained us all in the first weeks of the crisis with her lunchtime canteen of Belgian cooking, were on their way to Rawalpindi. So Millen, our Indian cook, produced one of his memorable curry lunches. We were a large embassy party and our good spirits belied the tension we all felt as the clock ticked forward.

Shortly after one in the morning of 17 January the cat came out of the bag in spectacular fashion, as the sky over Riyadh's diplomatic quarter was blasted by the din of laden KC135 tanker aircraft heading north from the military airbase across the city, and dispelling any doubt that we were now involved in war. They were on their way to rendezvous with scores of American, Saudi, British and Italian night bombers and fighter escorts from airfields all over Saudi Arabia and the Gulf states, and from the American carrier force in the northern Gulf, which would refuel over the Kuwait border before pressing on to strike at strategic targets within Iraq and Kuwait. This air armada was supplemented by long-range B52 bombers, operating from as far away as Diego Garcia in the southern Indian Ocean, England, and even from the USA, as well as by American aircraft based in Turkey.

The BFME chief of staff, Ian MacFadyen, quoted the celebrated lines from Shakespeare's *King Henry V* to the meeting of his headquarters officers in Riyadh that morning, when all aircraft involved in the first wave of attacks had returned without loss.

> And gentlemen in England now abed
> Shall think themselves accurs'd they were not here . . .

Several of us were in the embassy through the small hours, standing watch against possible retaliation and responding to telephone calls for reassurance from the community. In fact there were few that first night. Our main problem was a Saudia flight bound for London which had been caught ready for take-off on the runway of Riyadh's King Abdul Aziz airport just as Saudi airspace was closed soon after midnight. Sixty luckless Britons were on board, understandably upset to find their evacuation route thus denied by minutes. They would now have to sit things out for some days until we could get them away on military flights.

The air war was to prove the most intensive, yet selective, bombing campaign in history, carried forward with some 2,000 coalition aircraft against military installations and key elements in Iraq's administrative infrastructure for the next six weeks without a break. It also had the advantage of unprecedented precision afforded by the computerised and laser beam accuracy of the 'smart' munitions, in the form of bombs and ship-launched Tomahawk cruise missiles, which were the result of American and other Western research during the preceding 20 years and were now making their debut in full-scale war.

Night air attacks on key command and infrastructure targets in and around Baghdad were carried out with accuracy by the American force of F-117 Stealth aircraft, the bat-like shape of which made them undetectable by Iraqi radar. Other night raids over Iraq and Kuwait were carried out by American, British, Saudi and Italian aircraft, and were carried on into daylight attacks and air patrols with French, Canadian and Kuwaiti warplanes joining in. In the first 24 hours alone over 1,000 sorties were flown, and this rate was subsequently stepped up to twice that intensity, despite unusually poor weather conditions which hindered target location and also complicated mid-air refuelling, especially by night.

The computerised planning of timing, routes and targets, which brought hundreds of aircraft on their conveyor belt of missions day in and day out through Iraq's air defences, was a task of incredible complexity, put together over many weeks by a combined air force team working in the depths of the RSAF headquarters in Riyadh and headed by a USAF officer, Brigadier General 'Buster' Glosson, the chief planner in General Chuck Horner's AFCENT.

There is a supposition that the launching of warfare marks the point where diplomats step down from the stage to the stalls, handing the direction of affairs over to their military counterparts. Nothing could have been further from the reality for all of us in embassies and consulates throughout the Gulf, as well as for our colleagues involved in the crisis in the FCO and elsewhere around the world. If we had been going hard before, we were to find ourselves for the next seven weeks going nigh round the clock, with snatches of sleep by night and occasional cat-naps by day. All our strands of activity in dealing with the Kuwait crisis and Iraq's threat came together in this period in a welter of instructions, decisions, plans and contacts.

Our need to keep in constant touch with developments on the military front was met through daily meetings in the embassy and at the headquarters of BFME, which had just moved into more ample premises downtown. Peter de la Billière and I kept in close contact by secure telephone. It was fascinating to view the detailed course of the coalition's military activity through his calm appraisal.

Though the British forces in theatre, totalling some 46,000 men and women by early February, had now been placed under American operational command, Peter de la Billière had his place close to General Schwarzkopf at all stages of the campaign. There was a real sense of trust between them, particularly over operations behind Iraqi lines. These were to play an important part in inhibiting Iraq's Scud missile onslaught on Israel and Saudi Arabia, as well as in cutting some of Iraq's main underground military communications links, results achieved in conditions of danger and with considerable courage and sacrifice.

Our close association during these eventful days brought me close to the ebb and flow of the military action. There were times when Peter de la Billière showed himself disconcerted at what he saw as interference, sometimes petty in nature, from the MoD. The launching of the air war found him frustrated anew at a lack of decision in London over the perennial issue of rules of engagement for combat aircraft. Tom King, the Defence Secretary, came in for his share of such complaint, particularly when he sought to put in his oar over the handling of press briefing, a key preoccupation for all of us in theatre and one to which Norman

Schwarzkopf and Peter de la Billière gave close attention. Both commanders adopted a forceful upbeat style in their press briefings. I reminded Peter that in fairness Tom King had given him good support, backing him on several points over terms of service, and above all securing him the additional armoured brigade.

In our close collaboration we covered not only the conflict day by day, but also looked forward to the post-hostilities phase and the securing of Kuwait and the other Gulf states against renewed threat. We were conscious that once the present crisis was past there were sound political reasons for Western forces not to hang about in Saudi Arabia for longer than necessary. Yet we also had an obligation and an interest in assisting Kuwait to mount guard until, perhaps with UN help, she could take this on herself.

The outbreak of hostilities saw no abatement of unwelcome diplomatic initiatives, from within the Arab world and further afield, aimed at a ceasefire, if necessary involving a price. These spawning developments necessitated close contact through January and March with Prince Saud and his colleagues in the Saudi Foreign Ministry, and with Chas Freeman too, as our governments worked to keep the coalition and members of the UN Security Council on course for the objective of Iraq's unconditional withdrawal, now that the going had begun to get rough.

Nor was our liaison only concerned with such initiatives. Interesting Saudi ideas were beginning to take shape over future Gulf security, based on a regional defensive shield which would in the first instance build on the newly-formed relationship with Egypt and Syria, and perhaps reach out to Turkey and Pakistan. There were other consequences of the crisis to be considered, such as the reconstruction of Kuwait. Above all there was an opportunity for a fresh start in the search for a settlement of the Arab–Israel dispute, particularly as the more uncompromising elements on the Palestinian political scene had put themselves offside through a misjudged support for Saddam Hussein.

But our activities did not stop there. The protection and encouragement of our community, now facing a random threat from Iraqi Scud missile attack every two or three nights in the vicinities of Riyadh and Dhahran, became a constant preoccupation. There was a call for close and constant liaison with the large numbers of British press representatives now in the Kingdom to report the war. We were also kept busy with activity, shared with the Saudis, to counter Iraq's act of unprecedented vandalism to the environment by the release in late January of several million tons of crude oil into the waters of the northern Gulf, followed by setting the torch to Kuwait's oilwells. At the back of our minds was the question of our own security, amid Scud raids and a risk of sabotage or terrorist attempts. But there was little time to give thought to these aspects. We never had a dull or idle moment, as everyone went about their work with good humour and a sense of dedication to the cause in hand.

Our liaison with the British headquarters fell mainly to the three service attachés, who attended the early morning meeting at BFME headquarters and brought news of developments over the previous 24 hours to our mid-morning gathering in the embassy. A member of the British forces staff came to our daily meeting to keep Peter de la Billière and his staff posted on political developments. The headquarters also had the benefit of briefing on the wider political scene through the two political advisers whom the FCO had seconded to Paddy Hine's headquarters at High Wycombe.

Our exchanges in Riyadh gave us a grandstand view of the course of the air war and the accompanying land and sea deployment as the ground forces slowly moved themselves into position for an assault into Kuwait and Iraq. The timing of this was in mid-January still a matter for conjecture within a window limited by the fasting month of Ramadan, due to commence in the middle of March by our Gregorian calendar. Gradually we became familiar with the mysteries of military jargon; terms like 'deconfliction' and 'resubordination' began to trip off the tongue, as Rupert Smith's 1st British Armoured Division, now forming north of Jubail, was switched from a diversionary role alongside the US Marines on the coastal eastern flank of the coalition line to a more substantial participation in the main tank thrust along Kuwait's western frontier with Iraq.

As the air war progressed and Iraq's air force stayed on the ground or began to seek an improbable refuge in Iran, the RAF moved away from the dangerous task of low-level attacks on Iraq's well-defended military airfields. The Tornado crews, with their Saudi counterparts playing a full part, had given a courageous and effective account of themselves, but at the high cost of the loss of several aircraft and personnel. They now switched, not without some resistance on the part of RAF diehards in Whitehall, to join the Americans in high-level precision bombing of strategic targets within Iraq, with the aid of Buccaneer laser targeting aircraft and the recently developed TIALD laser guidance system, operated by the observer in the Tornado itself.

Film of the bombs' controlled path and their impact on target was brought to our meetings by John Ambler. It provided dramatic footage and cockpit voice recordings, complete with expletives, which demonstrated the remarkable accuracy of these new weapons, as major bridges over the Tigris and Euphrates were taken out with minimal collateral damage to the civilian population of the neighbourhood. The hardened aircraft hangars on Iraq's airbases, built to withstand a nuclear attack, proved no match for the deep penetration bombs, dropped with surgical accuracy by the F117 Stealth bombers.

Trevor Waddington kept us well posted on Royal Navy activity, replete with nautical parlance about chopping command and boats in the bath. Christopher Craig's sizeable flotilla in the Gulf was having a busy time, with helicopter attacks on Iraqi patrol craft and escort duties with the American Second World War battleships as they fired their old-fashioned broadsides into shore targets in Kuwait. Destroyers armed with the uncanny Tomahawk missiles were surgically taking the heart out of Iraq's infrastructure and command network hundreds of kilometres distant. There was a spectacular incident one night in late January when HMS *Gloucester* succeeded in destroying with her air defence missiles a long-range Iraqi Silkworm aimed from the Kuwait shore at the battleship USS *Missouri*.

Equally arduous was the work undertaken in the northern Gulf off Kuwait by Royal Navy minehunters, which were leading the coalition's mine-clearing activity from their base in Dubai's Jebel Ali port. They managed to clear offshore areas close to Kuwait sufficiently to permit naval bombardment and attacks against Iraqi patrol vessels. The extent of the mine-clearing problem was, however, brought home when on 15 February the USS *Tripoli* and *Princeton* struck drifting mines and had to withdraw for repairs. The injured were treated on board the hospital ship HMS *Argus*.

Our close association with BFME headquarters during the five weeks of the air war phase gave us ample evidence of the reality of the cliché – fog of war. Information on progress in the air campaign and the results it was achieving came through in filtered form from a variety of sources: from the joint headquarters where General Schwarzkopf and General Prince Khalid had their respective command centres deep below the grandiose Defence Ministry building; from RAF squadron reports; from photographic reconnaissance of targets after attack, though this means of damage assessment was hampered by poor visibility and proved a subject of disagreement between CENTCOM and analysts back in the USA; from intelligence sources on the ground, both electronic and human; and even from the eye-witness accounts of Western correspondents still in Baghdad, whenever they managed to circumvent the vigilant Iraqi censorship.

It was nevertheless clear within the first week that the bombing campaign was taking a heavy toll of Iraq's key military and civil infrastructure, yet with minimal civilian casualties. This was an important aspect, as we and the Saudis were well aware of the propaganda advantage Iraq could take with public opinion in the Arab world, and in the West too, of any strike which caused substantial loss of civilian life. The aiming precision of the new generation of 'smart' weapons was proving invaluable in keeping down collateral damage. Moreover, certain targets where the Iraqis were known to have co-located military command centres with civilian occupation were off limits to attack. A prime example here was Baghdad's Al Rashid hotel, where the Iraqis had made a point of accommodating the Western press contingent they had admitted to Iraq. Meanwhile, communications and transport links, utilities, oil installations, military bases and factories were steadily being taken out.

By the beginning of February the coalition air forces had flown some 30,000 sorties with the loss of only 19 aircraft, while Iraq had lost 29 aircraft in the air, including two Mirages in a single encounter with a sharpshooting Saudi F15 pilot, and many more than that number on the ground through the precision targeting of hardened hangars. A good proportion of these sorties by day and night were being flown by the RSAF, and there was also participation by Kuwaiti, Bahraini, Qatari and UAE warplanes.

A disorderly escape of Iraqi aircraft over the eastern border into Iran now ensued. The background to this dash for refuge was hard to assess. While it may have started as defection by individual pilots, its scale, which reached a total of some 140 military and civil aircraft by mid-February, took on the appearance of a deliberate, if desperate, move by Saddam Hussein to salvage Iraq's modern air force. If so it proved to be another serious miscalculation, for the Iranians sent the pilots back but held on to the aircraft, thus making their unsolicited contribution to the coalition's acquisition of air supremacy. When in the middle of February Saddam Hussein sent his deputy Prime Minister, Saadoun Hammadi, to Tehran to request the return of some of the aircraft with the argument that they were needed to attack Israel, his mission was rebuffed by the Iranians.

The strategic bombing campaign was slowed down after the first couple of weeks to switch effort to the task of softening up Iraq's army units in defensive formation along the Saudi frontier with Kuwait and Iraq. At the outset of the campaign Iraqi army strength in the Kuwait theatre of operations was estimated to total somewhat over 400,000 men, with a massive armoured force of some 4,000 tanks as well as about 2,500 guns. With the exception of Iraq's elite Republican Guard armoured divisions, which counted for some third of the total, much of this force was already reckoned to be suffering low morale and a high desertion rate, despite savage reprisals on those who were caught slipping away.

A source of these reports was the growing number of Iraqis, including officers, prepared to risk death by crossing the heavily-mined no man's land into Saudi territory. Indeed, it was starting to be said that Saddam Hussein's vaunted secret weapon must be a white handkerchief. At Saudi Army request we had provided a team from the Intelligence Corps to advise on prisoner interrogation.

The direct air bombardment of Iraqi units in their defensive positions grew in intensity, with the use of devastating air-burst munitions and accompanied by a fierce artillery barrage, to the point where on the eve of the launching of the coalition land offensive on 23 February Iraq's active strength in theatre was already reduced by about a half. This gave the coalition forces the advantage of some two to one, a factor for offensive tactics which had at the outset seemed unachievable to the coalition's military planners.

Yet in those first uncertain weeks of the air campaign there was no reason to anticipate a walkover. We found ourselves sharing at close quarters the preoccupations of Peter de la Billière and his headquarters staff. I sometimes joined the morning briefing which he and Air Marshal Bill Wratten held in their new headquarters building. At last there was room for the staff to spread themselves. The building was guarded by a detachment from the Queen's Own Highlanders in full battle kit, who kept a tight eye on anyone approaching along the busy Riyadh street. One of them went so far as to immobilise our Rolls Royce, in which Derek Plumbly was visiting the headquarters while I was out of town. The canny Jock evidently considered this imposing vehicle to be hostile and so threw a chain of 'dragon's teeth' across its path, puncturing the tyres. We put it down to fog of war.

Several of Peter de la Billière's main concerns as the campaign got into its stride had a direct bearing on our embassy responsibilities on the diplomatic and community fronts. Foremost among these was the threat, which we no longer doubted was a real one, of the use of chemical weapons by Iraq, not only on the battlefield but perhaps also in long-range missile attack. The conventional version of the Scud missile, which the Iraqis had ingeniously adapted to give additional range, was now being deployed with an impressive degree of accuracy against Riyadh and the east coast, as well as against urban centres in Israel. It was to try to neutralise the mobile Scud launchers, which were proving far more elusive than the coalition had reckoned, that Peter de la Billière had persuaded Norman Schwarzkopf to deploy the Special Air Services, and subsequently US Special Forces, on dangerous and exposed missions deep into Iraq. This Scud hunt was also diverting precious air resources away from the bombing campaign into a frustrating game of hide and seek.

The land offensive was meanwhile being planned on the assumption that battlefield casualties, especially if chemical weapons were employed, would be high. To maximise the degree of protection for coalition troops against this threat, the coalition commanders insisted on a high level of military hospital back-up for the land campaign. On the British side this involved the activation by the NHS, in conjunction with the Red Cross, of a network of medical reception arrangements across Britain to cope with the possible repatriation of several thousand servicemen suffering from the effects of chemical attack.

The threat also required the calling up of medical reservists, in the shape of a territorial hospital unit of the RAMC based on the Scottish Lowlands and with its personnel mainly drawn from civilian medical services in the Glasgow and Birmingham areas. 205 Field Hospital duly arrived with all their equipment at Riyadh's King Khalid airport on the night of 20 January, just before a fierce Scud barrage from Iraq. Some of the Patriot batteries found their targets, and missile debris began to shower the runway. It was a baptism of fire for the territorials, straight from their hospitals and other civilian occupations.

To their credit the unit, commanded by one of Scotland's leading gastric specialists, went straight to work that night to set up their 500-bed hospital, complete with gas-proof operating theatres, in the vast concourse of one of the airport's four splendid terminal buildings, which the Saudis had made available for British military use. When Grania and I went out the next morning with the attachés to give them a welcome with books and other comforts, we found the whole show up and running. I asked one of the orderlies what he had been doing until the day before. 'Driving a London Underground train,' was the reply. So swift had been their departure that I wondered whether his train was still at Earl's Court.

The extensive medical deployment was, however, to give us a headache on the diplomatic side when, without any warning, the MoD had the bright idea of inviting a number of friendly countries to contribute medical facilities to the British forces in theatre. They cast their net wide, starting with NATO partners such as Canada, Holland, Denmark and Norway, but moving out into less customary territory such as the Swedes and Austrians with their tradition of neutrality, Singapore from the Commonwealth, and even putting the seal on the ending of the Cold War with invitations to Poland, Hungary and Romania. The response was gratifying. Offers of medical detachments and field hospitals came from almost all those approached. Even Sweden decided to qualify her long-established policy of abstention from military deployment in a combat situation, which, as the ambassador, Lennart Alvin, explained, had been scrupulously adhered to since her association with Napoleon's defeat at Leipzig in 1813. In a generous gesture the Swedes put a full-scale tented hospital under British command.

But from our point of view what the MoD had overlooked was that each of these states would need its own agreement on the status of forces to be negotiated with the Saudis, and with a war going on. Moreover, the East Europeans among them did not even have diplomatic relations with the Kingdom. It looked a diplomatic nightmare. With scant thanks to those in the MoD who had landed this on us, we managed to sort out the Saudi end in co-operation with the embassies concerned. The East Europeans proved too problematic, however, and never made it to the starting tape. Allan Lever, Canada's effective ambassador in the Kingdom, already had an agreement in place to cover Canadian air force personnel, while Lennart Alvin lost no time in concluding a Swedish agreement along the lines of our own, and in finding a desert site north of the city where his hospital could locate. He held a historic dinner to mark Sweden's return to active service.

In the merciful event very limited use had to be made of all these facilities, as Saddam Hussein prudently took heed of the firm warnings from the coalition leaders over the consequences of any attempt to employ his weapons of mass destruction. President Bush had left Iraq in no doubt on this score on the eve of the campaign. In London, Douglas Hogg summoned the Iraqi ambassador on 21 January to warn him against the use of chemical weapons. He coupled this with a forceful protest about Iraq's outrageous and illegal action in parading captured British and other coalition pilots on television, plainly under duress and in poor physical shape, in defiance of the Geneva Conventions on conduct in war. This display had aroused anger in Britain and with all of us in Saudi Arabia. It became yet another Iraqi own-goal with international opinion.

The International Committee of the Red Cross, exercising its supervisory role for the conduct of warfare, added its voice from Geneva with a reminder to both sides, but clearly intended primarily for Iraq, to refrain from the use of chemical and biological weapons, in accordance with the respective weapons conventions of 1925 and 1972. The International Committee's local mission had begun to check out the careful arrangements which the Saudis, Americans, French and ourselves were making for the handling of prisoners of war. It was a touch galling to be complying fully with international standards while the Iraqis were denying the Red Cross all access and were flouting their obligations towards British and other captured servicemen. For good order's sake we kept an eye on television footage of Iraqi prisoners taken by British naval and land forces, and found no breach of the rules of international humanitarian law obliging them to be treated with consideration and respect.

The first serious jolt to the coalition's military progress occurred late on 29 January, when an Iraqi tank force advanced into Saudi Arabia along the line of the coast road and, passing through an infantry screen lightly defended by the Saudi National Guard, seized the oil town of Al Khafji, the operations centre for the offshore fields of the Japanese-Saudi Arabian oil company. A further assault across the shore, with troops landed from Iraqi Navy craft, was halted by coalition naval patrols. The town of around 10,000 inhabitants had been evacuated some weeks before, as it lay within range of Iraqi artillery.

Once again Iraq's intentions behind this bold but futile action were hard to identify. It seemed to us most likely to have been intended as a show of bravado to rally Iraqi and wider Arab opinion. Alternatively it could have been a misconceived bid to deliver a challenge to Saudi morale by occupying a pocket of territory and taking prisoners who might serve as bargaining counters later. Perhaps Iraqi intelligence was suffering from its lack of aerial observation. Some even thought it a deliberate deception on the part of the coalition to tempt Iraqi forces to attack the territory of the Kingdom, as no attempt was made by the joint command to forestall it. The Iraqi attack came as a surprise; indeed the press first came to hear of it when a correspondent tried to telephone the town's hotel and found an Iraqi soldier answering the call.

Whatever its purpose, the foray had the effect of rallying Saudi opinion, already goaded by Scud attacks on civilian targets, to yet greater support for the cause of getting Iraq out of Kuwait. It also involved Saudi land forces in two days of tough fighting to recover Al Khafji. Their initial withdrawal was turned around when General Prince Khalid took personal command on 30 January of the National Guard and Saudi Army forces in the area, and prepared plans for an attack to recapture the town and rescue an American army observation unit which had been caught within it.

During that night the counterattack was launched led by mechanised infantry units of the National Guard, consisting mainly of bedouin soldiers, with tank support from the Saudi Army and a Qatari armoured force, plus artillery and air support from the US Marines. There was fierce fighting, but within 24 hours the Saudis had retaken the town. Two advisers from the British Military Mission to the National Guard accompanied the engagement. The fighting was vividly recorded on Saudi television. General Khalid was able on 1 February to claim a significant victory for Saudi forces, with over 400 Iraqi troops and much equipment taken with a loss of ten Saudi troops killed and about 30 wounded.

The outcome was a boost for Saudi morale; it was also good to see Saudi forces in the thick of action. The swift recapture of Al Khafji permitted the important Aramco offshore field to the south at Safania to resume production. For its part, Baghdad radio claimed the brief occupation of Al Khafji as a victory.

There were losses, however, among the American Marines, when soldiers in an armoured vehicle were killed in error by their own forces. This was to be the first of a series of incidents during the conflict to recover Kuwait in which American forces fired on their own, or in one case on British, troops in the field through misidentification in so-called 'blue on blue' engagements. It brought home to us how the remarkable improvements in Western weapon accuracy of the previous ten years had now produced a situation, in target-finding and gunfire as well as in aerial bombing, in which there was no longer any room for human misjudgment. For the first time in war, munitions had become as smart as the men who operated them, and occasionally smarter.

Yet this very precision, which was enabling Stealth bombers even to send bombs from high altitude down a laser beam and into the target buildings through their air-conditioning ventilation shafts, also carried risks in use against the enemy. The new ability they afforded to minimise collateral damage, for example to adjacent civilian areas, had the consequence in the public mind of highlighting those few but inevitable occasions when through misfunction or lack of accurate target intelligence a strike caused loss of civilian life.

Such was the effect of the precision bombing by American aircraft on 13 February of a camouflaged bunker in Baghdad, which had been identified as a military command centre. What was not known was that a few days previously the Iraqis had for some reason opened the upper level of the bunker to serve as a civilian air-raid shelter; some 300 civilians were killed. This tragic loss of life was vividly reported in the international media. Public concern was compounded the following day when one of a series of laser-guided bombs dropped in a raid by RAF Tornados on a key bridge over the Euphrates at the town of Falluja went astray and struck a nearby suburb. The Iraqis claimed 130 dead.

These two mishaps in quick succession helped produce a resurgence of doubt among some Saudis over the real war aims of the Western coalition partners. Even certain of our closest Saudi friends and contacts, who had earlier made plain their outrage at Iraq's attack on Al Khafji, began to ask whether we might be pursuing a private agenda which involved spinning out the air war, now in progress for a month, and holding back on the land attack into Kuwait to give more time for the destruction of Iraq's economy. Seeing a risk of harm to the all-important basis of mutual confidence between the Western and Arab components, which had held our precarious alliance together so far, we urged Whitehall to do more to talk up in public statements the effectiveness of the coalition bombing campaign to date and the remarkable absence of civilian damage.

This growing impatience to see the conflict brought to an early close was also countered by a useful press conference given by the Saudi joint commander, General Prince Khalid, on 9 February, when he made a robust statement emphasising the limited nature of coalition war aims in respect of the liberation of Kuwait and the restoration of her government. He pointed to discussions to be held in Riyadh that day with the American Defence Secretary and the chief of staff, General Colin Powell, when the next stages of battle would be considered. If hostilities had to stretch on into the fasting month of Ramadan, this need present no problem for Moslem forces in the coalition.

Nevertheless, as the weeks passed the arguments for an early move to the land offensive, which would administer the *coup de grâce* to Iraq's presence in Kuwait, gained in force both on the wider diplomatic front and in terms of Saudi opinion. It was, however, evident from our close links with the headquarters that there was still some way to go with assembling the full Western military strength in the Kingdom and moving the coalition's attack force into position. The latter step involved a bold and complex ruse whereby the main thrust of the American, British and French armoured strength was to be switched across to the western flank of the advance, with the Saudis and other Arab forces in the centre and the US Marines operating in diversionary fashion in an advance up the well-defended Gulf coast. This called for a massive transfer of troops, equipment and supplies, all to be carried out without alerting the Iraqis.

The deception plan was conducted successfully over some three weeks, and with a remarkable degree of secrecy in which press co-operation was an important ingredient. The British 1st Division took up its new position south of the Kuwait frontier, near its western junction with Iraq where the Wadi Batin valley made a deep cut northwards through the desert to mark the divide between the two countries. This was to be the division's line of advance within the US VII Corps, lately arrived from Germany under the command of General Fred Franks.

To retain the element of surprise in such a huge repositioning exercise, even with the Iraqis unable to get into the air, called for a prodigious feat of transportation and logistics along the single Tapline road running parallel to the now closed oil pipeline from Dhahran into Jordan. Conditions were not helped by uncommonly wet weather, which turned the desert clay into sludge. Yet by the middle of February the operation was complete. There was a nervous moment early in the month when a journalist accompanying forward American forces for the CNN satellite television network let slip their position on the west flank. This could have been a major giveaway and breath was held, but the Iraqis appeared not to have picked it up and continued to be taken in by the barrage of deception signals designed to give the impression of a major thrust along the coast.

The deception was buttressed with some successful strikes by special forces, as well as infiltration by some of the Kuwaiti volunteers we had been training in behind-the-lines operations. Their targets were key Iraqi lines of communication. There was even talk of a long-shot operation which might have caught Saddam Hussein during the only visit he paid to his forces in Kuwait during this period. The Iraqi leader was, however, proving elusive as a fox in the face of ingenious coalition attempts to get at him in one of his numerous lairs.

The Iraqi army's resolve was meanwhile being steadily eroded by the pounding which her forces in theatre continued to receive from the daily aerial and artillery bombardment. But there was confusion on the part of the coalition over the crucial assessment of damage being inflicted. Each morning Peter Sincock would relay to us the latest estimate of the reduced battle effectiveness of the main Iraqi troop concentrations. These suggested that the damage level might be high enough to permit a land attack as soon as the middle of the month. But it transpired that serious difference of opinion had arisen between the analysts on the staff of CENTCOM in Riyadh and those working on the same reports and photographic material in Washington, who were downgrading damage claims made in theatre and calling for further air strikes.

This disagreement was starting to have an impact on planning for the date of an offensive, and leading to pressure from Washington to allow more time for battle preparation. By the time of Secretary Cheney's visit to Riyadh on 9 February, CENTCOM were confident of having all ground troops in place and ready to go by the middle of February; 21 February was tentatively set for the land offensive. But this timing started to slide around again when a combination of poor weather and changes to the Marines' attack plans prompted two or three days' slippage at the Riyadh end. Meanwhile developments on the political front, resulting from renewed eleventh hour Soviet efforts to mediate a withdrawal, prompted President Bush to resist any idea of further delay. It was not until 20 February that the final all-clear was given, endorsed by King Fahd, for the land attack to begin on 24 February.

But it was not only the campaign in hand which took up our contacts with Whitehall at this busy time. We were also giving attention to the aftermath of war, and to a timetable for withdrawal which would avoid the impression that we sought to hang on, yet saw us playing our part in ensuring that Kuwait was secured against a repetition of Iraq's threat until other local or international protection could be moved into place. I opened discussions with Sulaiman Shahine of the Kuwaiti Foreign Ministry on an agreement we would need to cover the legal status of British forces once they were present in Kuwait. We also considered how Britain could build on the new co-operation, now being forged in the crisis to participate in Kuwait's recovery and the future security of the region.

This exchange led to a visit to Riyadh in mid-February by Nigel Broomfield, the FCO deputy under-secretary responsible for defence policy, and Andrew Palmer, who had been attached to Paddy Hine's joint HQ at High Wycombe as a political adviser, to see something of the campaign at first hand and discuss with the military and ourselves ideas on the rundown and the next stages in our co-operation with the Saudis and elsewhere in the Gulf. They also had a valuable talk with Prince Fahd bin Abdullah, whose advice on how things were likely to develop following Kuwait's liberation was as always most perceptive.

It was clear that we needed to lay plans to move our forces out of Saudi Arabia as expeditiously as we could. Any continuing support we could give in Kuwait would be welcome, and indeed some ongoing presence there while the Kuwaitis and the UN decided on the next steps looked necessary. As for the longer term, a wider measure of co-operation with the Saudi armed forces looked on the cards. Peter de la Billière floated the idea that we might leave behind some of our armour. A useful study on how we could develop our co-operation with the Saudi armed forces in the field of supply was put together by Bob Regan, the embassy's defence equipment specialist. Our thoughts on securing a share in Kuwait's reconstruction were also meeting with a positive reception. The Department of Trade appointed a diplomat, Christian Adams, to put together a joint government–business approach towards this challenge in co-operation with Ian Blackley, who continued from Jedda to keep in touch with the Kuwait authorities in their exile.

Meanwhile the Scud bombardments on both Riyadh and the eastern cities were keeping us busy on the community front. From the outset of the coalition's air campaign, the Iraqis lost no time in putting a stop to any lingering doubts we might have had over their capacity to reach both regions with the longer-range missiles they had been quietly developing since the last years of their war with Iran on the basis of the

The night shift is interrupted by Scud, the cat. (*Grania Munro/Crown Copyright*)

The Foreign Secretary visits Riyadh in February 1991: (left to right) Douglas Hurd, Prince Saud al Faisal and the author. (*Saudi Press Agency*)

General Prince Khalid bin Sultan briefs the media at the regular evening press conference given by the coalition command during the hostilities. (*Saudi Press Agency*)

Volunteers clean crude oil off a green turtle at the Wildlife Rescue Centre set up in Jubail. (*Michael McKinnon*)

A Socotra cormorant coated with oil slick on the Gulf shore. (*Michael McKinnon*)

Grania sees off an RAF Tornado patrol from Dhahran at dawn. (*Author/Crown Copyright*)

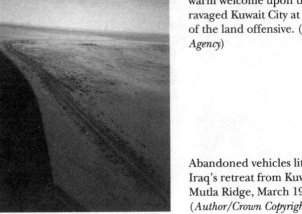

Saudi military personnel receiving a warm welcome upon their entry into a ravaged Kuwait City at the conclusion of the land offensive. (*Saudi Press Agency*)

Abandoned vehicles litter the road of Iraq's retreat from Kuwait City over the Mutla Ridge, March 1991. (*Author/Crown Copyright*)

Cratered runways and a hardened aircraft shelter penetrated by allied 'smart' bombing at a base in Kuwait used by the Iraqi airforce. (*Author/Crown Copyright*)

Oil wells near Kuwait City set ablaze by Iraqi forces. (*Author/Crown Copyright*)

Bombed tailplane of British
Airways jumbo jet stranded at
Kuwait airport since the night
of the Iraqi invasion.
(*Author/Crown Copyright*)

John Major welcomed by RAF
and Saudi airforce personnel at
Dhahran after visiting British
troops in Kuwait, March 1991.
His Private Secretary, Charles
Powell, is on the right of the
picture. (*Crown Copyright*)

The author and his wife, Grania, with the Royal Military Police close protection team. (*Crown Copyright*)

Congratulating General Prince Khalid bin Sultan at the Saudi Victory Parade – Eastern Province, May 1991: Chas Freeman, the author and Lennart Alvin. (*Saudi Press Agency*)

General Sir Peter de la
Billière in relaxed
mood after the war.
(*Author/Crown
Copyright*)

General Norman
Schwarzkopf with RAF
pilots shot down over
Iraq, Flight Lieutenants
John Peters (left) and
John Nichol. (*Press
Association*)

The author loses his bearings along the old Hejaz Railway. (*Author/Crown Copyright*)

Relic of another war: Patrick Fairweather inspects the wreckage of a Turkish troop train locomotive sabotaged along the former Hejaz Railway by Colonel T E Lawrence and the forces of Amir Faisal in the First World War. (*Author/Crown Copyright*)

Soviet-supplied Scud. They first struck at Israel, late on 17 January, in a high-risk stratagem to provoke an Israeli response and so rend the solidarity of the Western and Arab front ranged against them.

Each Scud missile launch had the effect of triggering the attack warning system, which the Americans had set up using a satellite in fixed orbit over Iraq. This satellite was programmed to pick up the flash of the launch, sending an instantaneous signal to a ground station in Colorado, which instantly repeated the message around the whole region including CENTCOM headquarters in Riyadh. The local alarms were then sounded by means of sirens installed by the Saudis throughout the cities, and by a newsflash on the local radio and TV channels. A direct radio message was also passed to each national military headquarters. HQBFME would then relay this to its outstations in the Kingdom, including the duty officer's post in our embassy, who in turn issued an immediate 'safe haven' warning to all embassy staff and families through our personal radios which we carried with us everywhere.

Remarkably this series of actions involving the transmission of warning messages over several thousand kilometres via outer space took only some five minutes to complete. This was just as well, as the Al Abbas improved Scud which the Iraqis used against long-range city targets in Saudi Arabia and Israel took only some seven minutes in flight. This meant that on the ground we generally still had a minute or two to spare between receipt of the local alarm and hearing the explosion which signalled the arrival of a missile or the roar from nearby as the Patriot air defence missiles were launched to try to destroy it.

Nevertheless, it was sometimes a close run thing. On a couple of occasions we had the bizarre experience of being woken up around 2am by a telephone call from our daughter, Emma, in London who, having seen a newsflash on British television that Scuds were approaching Riyadh, took on herself the role of remote air-raid warden and passed us the warning to take precautions before we had received it on our local net.

One drawback of this sensitive warning system was that the satellite could not distinguish the precise trajectory of the missile. This meant that we often received false alarms in Riyadh of missiles launched against Eastern Province targets and further afield such as Tel Aviv. A false alarm one afternoon was even suspected of being caused by a Scud launched by the Russian-supported government forces in Afghanistan against a guerrilla target. To take no risks the Patriot batteries set up in the vicinities of Riyadh and all the eastern cities, as well as the military bases in the north, were obliged to open up their radars on each warning to identify the line of fire.

Thus it was that we found ourselves caught out on the night of 17 January when the Iraqis opened their Scud campaign with the salvo on Israel. I was dealing with some late communications in the embassy when the sergeant in the RAF intelligence room upstairs came running down in full chemical suit, shouting to us to get into a safe haven. We did so, and for good order's sake donned our protective clothing too. The false alarm message came through some minutes later, bringing a sense of anticlimax as we clambered out of the heavy suits.

We did not have long to wait, however, for our baptism of fire. The next night saw a Scud attack on Dhahran, a move which neatly negated any propaganda effect intended by the Iraqis in Saudi Arabia by the attack on Israel. Fortunately the missiles used in this first assault on the Kingdom were taken out in the air by the Patriots, a success which did a great deal to convince the public of the effectiveness of this defence against Scud attack. The psychological gain at this early stage was enormous, and withstood the subsequent erratic record of the Patriot in hitting its elusive targets.

This said, it was still a remarkable achievement to adapt the Patriot system, designed originally as an anti-aircraft defence, to intercept supersonic missile targets. In a study prepared after the war it was estimated that of 48 Scuds aimed at Saudi Arabia, 11 were taken out by the Patriot system, and of 40 fired at Israel 34 were intercepted. In both cases several Scuds went off course and were allowed to fall wide. Saudi and expatriate confidence in the Patriot endured throughout the war; the joke went round the British community that there were two things which worked – Patriots and expatriates.

There was another Scud attack on Dhahran the following night, and late on the night of 20 January came the first attack on Riyadh in the form of six Scuds. They were successfully intercepted by a massive barrage of Patriots launched from the northern edge of the city, in which some 35 missiles were fired. It was a spectacular *feu de joie*, which we reckoned had, at some $800,000 a projectile, cost over $25 million; perhaps the most expensive fireworks display in history. Thereafter the Patriots were reprogrammed to give a more economical response.

Few witnessed the show, however, as we lay low and waited for the all clear. Some of us were caught in the embassy when the attack came. We made an incongruous party as we sat in one of the sealed offices in our chemical suits, making muffled jokes through our gas-masks. We kept an emergency telephone line open round the clock to respond to enquiries from members of the community and offer reassurance. The embassy's Indian telephonist, William, had to be entreated to join us in the refuge, so reluctant was he to leave his place of duty on the exchange. All was over in 15 minutes, but they seemed to pass very slowly.

This first raid marked another success for Patriot to the benefit of local morale. But at least one Scud had got through. It struck the local office of the Sun Alliance insurance company, an asset which ironically the company had decided not to insure – a matter for some subsequent ribbing at the expense of the expatriate manager. Mercifully there was no loss of life on this occasion, though subsequent raids caused a number of deaths in the city. The raid took place just as a five-man Royal Military Police protection team led by Staff Sergeant Steve Brumpton, which the FCO had sent out to ensure my protection and that of the embassy against possible terrorist attack, arrived in Riyadh via the nightly RAF shuttle. It made for a lively welcome as they got themselves to the embassy compound. The team quickly settled in to the house, and became firm friends as Grania and I spent a great deal of the next six weeks in their vigilant company.

Thereafter we found ourselves interrupted every four or five nights by Scud alarms, sometimes genuine and sometimes false, but always involving a measure of tension and often the loss of precious sleep as we donned gas masks before taking 'safe haven' refuge in our homes or offices. Results from the diversion by the coalition command of precious military resources to hunting down elusive Scud launchers deep in Iraq were slow to come, but the activity did at least help to deter unilateral Israeli action against Iraq's provocative attacks. It was mid-February before the frequency of Scud attacks on Riyadh and Dhahran began to diminish.

One unexpected problem faced by the Patriots in interception was that, in modifying the Scuds to achieve greater range, the Iraqis had used inferior welding techniques. This resulted in some of the warheads coming adrift from the motor section on re-entering the atmosphere above the target. The heat-seeking Patriots then went for the motor, leaving the warhead cone to fall unscathed. During the second raid on Riyadh on the night of 22 January a complete motor section of a Scud fell into one of Riyadh's main streets, where it lay smoking like an overlarge cigar. The spectacle made for good television pictures around the world, though these also led to renewed concern on the part of families in Britain about the security of relatives in the war zone.

During a raid one night I had a call from England from a worried husband whose wife was working as a nursing sister at one of the Riyadh hospitals. He was clearly upset at the dramatic images on his television set. I sought to reassure him and the next morning managed to contact his wife who was in commendably stout heart. He kindly wrote afterwards to say how our brief talk had cheered him amidst all the sensationalism on the media.

The initial Scud raids on Riyadh and Dhahran led nevertheless to nervousness among the large numbers of British and other expatriates who had elected to stay and see things through. It was for many a disconcerting experience to sit in an insulated room with a gas-mask on, listening to uncomfortable bangs in the night and wondering about chemicals. Clive Woodland, Peter Sincock and I had met all our wardens in the Riyadh area for a final briefing on 19 January, and had found them in good spirits and in touch with all those in their charge. They, and their counterparts in Jubail, Al Khobar, Dhahran and elsewhere in the Kingdom, did a great job of keeping people steady once the balloon went up.

But the shock of missile attack led a few people to have second thoughts about the wisdom of staying put. On the morning after the first raid on Riyadh I was asked by the BBC World Service for a message of advice to the community, who were sure to be listening attentively to the shortwave. In line with what we had agreed with the consular side in the FCO, I suggested people carry on as normally as possible, but should keep tuned to the radio and 'keep their heads down'.

This diversion into the vernacular proved a mistake. In the small hours of the following night, when Grania happened to be doing a stint on the community 'hot line' in the embassy, a telephone call came from a member of the community with an Indian accent, who explained in worried tones that he and his family had diligently followed to the letter my injunction that morning that they should keep their heads down. Some 15 hours later, however, they were in difficulty as the posture was causing them headaches. Could they now straighten up? Grania gently assured them that this was quite in order. A further call that night came from an English woman who had managed to get her gas-mask on but was having difficulty putting the cat in her handbag. Did we have any other suggestions? Such human episodes meant a lot.

Nervousness among the community reached its peak on about 24 January, following a dual missile raid on Dhahran and Riyadh. One of the chief causes of unhappiness was the feeling that no one could get out, as all air services had been suspended out of the Kingdom on the launching of the air war on 17 January. It would have been unsafe for civil air traffic to try to fly through the wall of warplanes and tankers constantly in the air over most of the Kingdom. The British headquarters helpfully came up with an offer to make seats available out of Dhahran on the Boeing 747 of Kuwait Airlines which the Kuwaitis had put at their disposal for trooping requirements from the UK. This proved a lifesaver.

Christopher Wilton moved down to Al Khobar with a consular team and one of the secretaries who had volunteered to come out from London to reinforce us. They joined David Lloyd and his two colleagues in sustaining community morale and organising the transport to Britain of those who wanted to go.

We found that once people knew that a line of escape existed, their anxiety diminished. Only 170 out of a residual community in the east of some 5,000 chose to take seats on the first backloading flight. We offered the balance to other nationalities. On the next flight there was only a handful of takers. The evacuation brought its crop of anecdotes. The lady with the parrot surfaced again to ask if she could take it with her on the flight. Another passenger insisted on choosing her seat and wanted to know what film would be shown. Patiently it was explained that this was a trooping flight without such comforts, but she appeared unconvinced. Predictably, when the evacuees were met by the press on arrival in Britain, the television news let her give full vent to her grumbles and ignored the other 169 satisfied customers.

In Riyadh, too, there was some jitteriness. The city itself had an eerie air of emptiness, with little traffic in its normally crowded streets and the resplendent shopping malls deserted. The National Guard ran armoured car patrols through the city, and there were gun emplacements at some key points. But their activity was discreet and road checkpoints were few, a feature which helped to give an air of normality and reduce alarm. Air-raid warnings were handled efficiently by the police and civil defence organisation. Some Saudi families had moved to safer areas in the west and south, while the menfolk stayed on. The decision by King Fahd that he and other senior members of the Al Saud and their families would remain in Riyadh, set a confident example and helped public morale.

The Saudi leadership also rejected the option of retaliating in kind to Iraqi terror tactics by activating their force of surface-to-surface missiles, recently acquired from China. It was wisely recognised that to reply in Iraq's own coin with random attacks on civilians would cancel out the moral advantage which the coalition had secured through confining its devastating air strikes to weapons capable of precision targeting.

Meanwhile, ministers and government officials were at their desks and carried on with business. It was a great help to have the Foreign Ministry operating at full pitch night and day under Prince Saud. The spirit of the mainly Asian expatriate workforces was helped by the constant and confident presence in the office or factory of many of their Saudi employers. Moreover, immense activity was generated within the Saudi economy by the requirements of armies at war.

In the Eastern Province, which underwent the most intensive Scud bombardment and where key RSAF and petroleum facilities were located, the governor, Prince Mohammed bin Fahd, and his deputy, Prince Fahd bin Salman, took a high profile by going out and about, and appearing on television, to encourage a public already infused with indignation at Iraq's random attacks on their cities. The powerful Al Zamil industrial group took the opportunity to show their confidence by laying the foundation stone, with the help of Prince Abdullah bin Faisal bin Turki, of a new chemical plant in Jubail.

Prudent action taken by the authorities during January to move religious figures opposed to the conflict away from contact with their associates in the main cities also helped to keep the political temperature down while hostilities were in progress. Support was further consolidated in this important quarter with a statement issued in late January by the head of the religious establishment, Sheikh Abdul Aziz bin Baz, who had hitherto shown himself distinctly lukewarm at the involvement of Western forces, in which he justified the offensive against Iraq's leader as a *jihad* or holy war, waged against an enemy of God. The authorities followed up this approbation with a conference on the subject of *jihad* held in mid-February at Riyadh's Islamic University and attended by religious figures from within the Kingdom and around the Arab world. In two addresses to the participants, the King rehearsed the events which had led to the present offensive and made a careful exposition of its justification in terms of Islamic exegesis. The wide publicity given to this conference helped to preoccupy the attention of conservative elements in Saudi public opinion as the air offensive ran on into a second month.

As a rule people tried to be home early in the evening or else stayed the night with friends to avoid being caught abroad during a raid. A friend of ours asked an American who had come for an evening's bridge what was in the suitcase with which she had arrived. 'It's mah jools,' was the reply. The Austrian ambassador went so far as to set up a camp for his small community along the Wadi Hanifa north of the city. Given the missile debris that tended to fall on the surrounding countryside, we were not sure they were any safer there.

Anxiety was, however, mounting as the sleepless nights took their toll on nerves and the occasional Scud missile got through the Patriot screen, causing injuries and some fatalities. The community was further worried by reports of a belated US government advisory notice urging American dependants to leave all parts of Saudi Arabia. On the night of 26 January one missile hit the downtown building of the Ministry of the Interior where Riyadh's traffic offence records were kept, bringing a ray of relief and gratitude on the part of some local motorists. A Scud hit a residential area on the east of the city during a raid in early February, while another fell close to the quarter where the Royal Palace was situated, demolishing the garages of the royal car pool. The missile warheads had been reduced in the interest of longer range, and tended to cause more noise than destruction. There was nervousness in Jedda, too, following an isolated shooting attack on a bus carrying American military personnel.

To help ease the stress on community members in Riyadh the headquarters agreed to make available spare seats on RAF transports returning to bases in Britain, a tedious trip in a Hercules but at least a way out. Our Riyadh wardens were doing a great job in keeping people steady, and in the event few sought to go. Places were also offered us on USAF transports to Frankfurt or Spain, as well as on the military flights of European and Western partners – Portuguese, Spanish, Dutch, Argentinian and Belgian – the last offering some amends for the outrage felt in our headquarters some weeks previously when the Belgian government had declined, on the plea of neutrality, to meet a British request for much-needed tank ammunition.

To help settle this bout of nerves Clive Woodland wrote a further letter of reassurance in late January to all community members in the central and eastern districts. In this we repeated the advice to carry on working but lie a bit low. We told them the Patriot defence system was doing its job, and there was unlikely to be a need for evacuation. Passages to the UK were available on the Kuwaiti 747 from Dhahran, whither the road was open and the railway was also running. Emergency cases might obtain places on RAF flights out of Riyadh. Saudia had resumed flights down to Jedda, and was now running limited services from there to Europe.

For their part British Airways had been running some flights round the south of Arabia to the UAE. Having heard they were ready to resume direct flights as far as Jedda via Cairo, I asked Prince Fahd bin Abdullah, who was responsible for civil aviation, if he would agree, as an exception to the military block on foreign civilian flights, to allow them an occasional frequency. This would help to calm anxieties and also give an important demonstration of 'business as usual'. Prince Fahd readily took the point and gave his assent, subject to air traffic conditions as Jedda airport was by this time serving as a base for B52 long-range bombers engaged in softening up Iraq's military positions. BA were back on the Jedda route in the first days of February, the only foreign airline to do so and providing a valuable route of access into the Kingdom, not only for those who wanted to leave but also for those coming out to join the BAe workforce in Dhahran.

On 29 January I flew over to Jubail, partly to learn about the effects on its important industrial and water desalination plants of the flood of crude oil which the Iraqis had begun to release into the northern Gulf waters from Kuwaiti terminals, and also to see how the community was coping in this vulnerable location. They all seemed in robust heart, and the British engineers were reassuring about the ability of the desalination plant, on which Riyadh depended for most of its water, to keep operating.

I went on to join Grania in Al Khobar, where we also found people's spirits beginning to recover as they became more accustomed to missile raids and had so far come to no harm. Iraq's failure to use chemicals and the knowledge there was an air route out in emergency had also helped restore morale. Contact with our reinforced consular office was close. The BAe technicians were doing a stout job in supporting the RSAF through all the alarums of Scud attacks on the Dhahran airbase, as were civilian specialists from other British equipment firms giving back-up to British forces in the field. Grania went to visit one of the British schools in Al Khobar, which was keeping classes going under its resilient Welsh headmaster, Leighton Brunt. She had a confident and happy morning with the pupils. Next day, while waiting in the dawn for the HS125 to collect us at Dhahran, we went over to the RAF apron to see Tornado ADVs off on morning combat patrol, with Grania on the cockpit access ladder for the final crew checks.

The mood in Riyadh, where our community numbers were still around 7,000, also became steadier by early February. The incidence of Scud raids diminished as coalition forces began at last to restrict Iraq's missile launchers in the south. We had a noisy raid during the visit of Nigel Broomfield and Andrew Palmer. I found Andrew complete with gas-mask in the bedroom corridor going down to join the close protection team's vigil; but nothing would awaken Nigel. Knowing he only had a couple of hours to go before catching the VC10 back to Brize Norton, I left him to sleep in peace.

The consular people in the FCO, prompted by overdramatised reporting of Scud raids and the possibility of chemical attack, renewed their pressure for more families to leave. By this time, however, we regarded the signs of returning confidence within our community as a positive factor which we did not want to upset. The carefully graduated approach, which with FCO support we had adopted over consular advice, appeared to have struck the right balance in bracing people for risks without prompting precipitate departure. Our postbag from members of the community now had a more confident tone, and calls for advice or comfort were few. Indeed, some people were becoming blasé and had taken to watching the Patriot fireworks from roofs and windows.

The hectic activity and interrupted nights inevitably brought strain for the embassy staff. Behind the good humour and stiff upper lip there were real worries over personal security. Half an ear was always cocked for the embassy duty officer's disembodied voice to emerge with the 'safe haven, safe haven' warning from the radio handsets we carried everywhere, to be followed by bangs and the occasional tremor if an impact was close, and then the silent wait for the all-clear once it had been established there was no gas about. The Iraqis generally seemed to pick a night when Charles Hollis was our anchor man on Scud raid duty, though the voice of Gordon Carstairs also lingers in the memory as we deciphered his 'wee sitreps' delivered in broad Glaswegian. One of the earliest raids drove Grania to her easel to spend the remainder of the night expurgating through paint her sense of protest at the indiscriminate nature of Iraq's attacks on the city and its people. It was a help to morale all round when the FCO agreed to our giving an extra month's salary to all the locally-engaged employees who were standing so stoutly by us. They also granted an additional home leave journey to British staff, which gave people something to look forward to once the crisis was over.

Marcelle Abbott, the Belgian wife of our press attaché, restarted with help from the residence staff a 'soup kitchen' where everyone could catch a hot meal during the middle of each hectic day. We had the occasional entertaining night, in the company of one of the embassy reinforcements from London who had moved in with us, having a grandstand view of the fireworks from the windows of our insulated room. A cat, presumably cast out when her owner evacuated, adopted us and immediately produced a litter. She was a character and we called her Scud.

Messages of good wishes from friends and family at home were a great encouragement; my aunt once rang from Ireland in the middle of an air-raid warning and could not understand why the line was so poor until I managed to convey I was speaking through a gas-mask filter. A touching letter of support came out of the blue from the sergeant of my tank troop in Germany nearly 40 years before.

We managed to have the occasional lunchtime gathering with Saudi and other friends. It was important to keep in touch while times were so out of joint. In the middle of all these events Grania and I succeeded in contracting pneumonia, as a result of leaving the air humidifier operating in the sealed atmosphere of our room. There was no question of going to bed, and we were kept on our feet by the medical skill of Kieran MacCormack, an Irish doctor who was seeing things through in Riyadh.

The January weather was proving unusually cold and wet, a feature which was making life unpleasant for troops up on the frontier as they completed their muddy deployment into position for an offensive. Some 500 kilometres to the south in Riyadh, the winter rain took on a dark tinge which left black streaks on the sandstone of the embassy walls and the city's immaculate white villas, and gave an oily smell to the air. This was our first taste of the campaign of vandalism which Saddam Hussein unleashed a week after the coalition launched its air attacks, in the form of the release of millions of barrels of Kuwaiti crude oil into Gulf waters, to be followed later by the torching of over 500 of Kuwait's oilwells to fill the sky with dense smoke. This vindictive attempt at a scorched earth policy only earned Iraq further international obloquy, despite her spurious appeal to the world's ecological lobby to press for an end to fighting. By 26 January the growing oil slick had spread south as far as the Saudi coast, while black rain was reported across the Gulf from Iran.

It became clear that unless the oil flow could be stopped it would soon present a major threat to fresh water supplies to the eastern cities and Riyadh, as well as Bahrain and Qatar, and to crucial industries and refineries along the Gulf coast. It also threatened a major disaster for fish and other wildlife. Peter de la Billière told me the USAF were urgently considering ways of destroying the oil outlet manifolds at the Mina al Ahmadi terminal to try to block the flow. On 27 January they succeeded in doing so through precision bombing. But by then some eight million barrels of oil were already spreading southwards in a thick slick, augmented by crude now being released from Iraq's own terminal at Mina al Bakr.

The Saudi authorities mounted a prompt response to this danger. Responsibility was shared between the government's environmental protection agency and Aramco. Surface booms were quickly brought in from Britain and other centres with oil disaster resources, to try to screen the intakes to the coastal refineries and water installations. An international appeal was launched for funds to help fight the threat, for which the British government led the way with a contribution of £1 million and the Japanese gave generous help. The RAF joined in flying protection equipment to Dhahran, and the US Coastguard, with the recent experience of the *Exxon Valdez* disaster to hand, produced valuable technical advice. Remarkably there was no significant effect on crude production in the coastal oilfields.

We also arranged for the RAF to fly out a film team, led by Michael McKinnon, an environmentalist who knew the Gulf well. His Kuwaiti wife, Fawzia, had been playing a leading part in drumming up support in Britain for her captive country. The television films on the disaster which resulted from his visit helped alert international opinion to the scale of the environmental damage inflicted on the region by Saddam Hussein's vindictive act.

Our first warning of water supply trouble for Riyadh came three days after the oil valves were opened. The domestic water suddenly acquired a brackish taste as the supply of sweet water along the pipeline from the huge desalination plant at Jubail was reduced and replaced by reserve supply from artesian wells below the Nejd plateau. When I went down to Jubail on 29 January to see what we might do to help, I was encouraged to hear that much of the slick drifting south was being trapped by easterly winds and the configuration of the Saudi coast in a bay to the north of Jubail formed providentially by the small Abu Ali peninsula. Pumps and skimmers were already at work to try to prevent the oil spreading further south. There seemed a chance these efforts would be successful.

I went on to see the head of Jubail's Royal Commission, Prince Abdullah bin Faisal, who had based himself in the city to accompany its inhabitants through the crisis. He was concerned at the risk of floating oil getting into the system of cooling canals on which Jubail's industries depended. These had originally been designed by the British consulting engineers, Sir Alexander Gibb and Partners. Prince Abdullah asked if they could give advice. From his office I telephoned an old friend at Gibb's headquarters in Reading, Bill Pirie, who knew Saudi Arabia well. He arranged for an engineer who had worked on the original project to fly out with the RAF shuttle that very night. It was prompt and effective service.

Prince Abdullah then mentioned his deep concern at the effect the oil slick was having on Gulf wildlife, notably the population of cormorants, and on sea creatures such as turtles and even dugongs. He was ready to provide facilities for a rescue centre where birds could be washed clean and recuperate, provided we could help with expertise. This seemed an obvious case for the RSPCA or RSPB, with whom we made prompt contact through the FCO.

Their response was impressive. Brigadier Jack Westlake came out within days via the RAF with an RSPCA team and washing equipment. Under Prince Abdullah's enthusiastic lead, and with help from the Saudi Wildlife Commission and local volunteers, both civilian and military, the bird-washing operation was in full swing by the first week in February. For some curious reason the washing had to be done in Fairy Liquid, but we managed to identify a similar local soap product from the Ben Zagr factory in Jedda. The venture came immediately to public attention in Britain as Sandy Gall of ITN happened to be in Jubail the morning of my visit, on the chance of an environment story. He interviewed us about our plans, while Prince Abdullah made for good television with a revolver strapped across his white *thobe*. The report received prominence on News at Ten that night, and no doubt contributed to the success of the two wildlife societies in raising a generous sum for the project through an appeal to the British public.

CHAPTER 14

Diplomatic Distractions

If war is said to be the continuation of diplomacy by other means, our experience in Riyadh during the coalition offensive of early 1991 was to be the exception to the rule. The beginning of the coalition's offensive on 17 January brought no let-up in the succession of diplomatic initiatives, tailored to secure a ceasefire and a political settlement. At a time when Iraq continued to parade her defiance, such mediation seemed bound to have the effect of letting Saddam Hussein off the hook, at the expense of the unconditional terms for withdrawal and the restoration of Kuwait's sovereignty and security which the UN Security Council had laid down in successive resolutions.

It was the Saudi government which bore the brunt of these pressures and intercessions. To their credit they gave a lead which held unflinchingly to the principle of withdrawal without conditions, while facing with a robust patience the appeals and propositions which came to them from within the Arab and Moslem worlds and beyond. The political risks which this solid stand carried within the Arab community were magnified by Saddam Hussein's decision at the outset of hostilities to lead with what he regarded as his trump card of direct missile attacks on Israel. This was an arrogant stratagem designed to provoke her into a military retaliation which would put the relationship between the Western and Arab wings of the coalition under impossible strain.

The Kingdom's success in withstanding these currents of compromise was in large measure inspired by the resolute, indeed pugnacious, spirit shown by King Fahd himself right up to the day Iraq's withdrawal was complete. This determination, which many contrasted with the King's reputation for preferring to exercise diplomacy through conciliation and inducement rather than confrontation, set a standard which was fully shared by his brothers at the head of government and did much to sustain the nation's resolve through its unprecedented predicament.

It was bolstered by the bond of support and co-operation which the King had forged with President Mubarak of Egypt from the very outset of the crisis, and to which Egypt's firm commitment on the political front and in the field remained constant. The price in terms of financial assistance, coupled with the waiving of earlier loans, seemed entirely reasonable when judged against the political benefit in terms of Arab backing which the partnership with Egypt, Iraq's former associate, brought to the Kingdom. Indeed, the benefits which Egypt garnered from around the world for her participation in the coalition against Iraq were a triumph of economic diplomacy, estimated in all at some $13 billion of new grants and debts forgiven.

The burden of pursuing this singleminded course amid the shoals and diversions of the diplomatic scene fell as ever upon Prince Saud and his staff, who were called upon to demonstrate yet greater capacity for endurance and sound judgment. It was not only mediation that took their attention during this hectic time. They were preoccupied too with the architecture of a post-war environment designed to ensure a better guarantee of security for the Gulf region. This tied in with the sensitive issue of the coalition's war aims and the future status of Iraq, points on which it was essential for Saudi Arabia and her GCC partners to achieve understanding with the Western members of the coalition. When the offensive began some aspects of this issue had yet to be thought through. Over the ensuing weeks our constant dialogue was much concerned with future plans.

Iraq's selection of Israel for the opening shot in her Scud missile campaign on the night of 17 January put the coalition's solidarity under its most extreme test to date, and had us all holding our breath for several uncomfortable days. In reality the Israelis, unaccustomed to turning the other cheek when subjected to Arab provocation, came very close to retaliation of a military nature, even though this might have amounted to little more than gesture. On the night of the first Scud raid Israeli warplanes were ordered into the air, but the command to go on the attack was not given.

The second missile raid against Israel two nights later, in which some 30 civilians were injured, brought proposals for a major retaliation from which the Israelis were only with difficulty dissuaded. Conscious of the immense strain which such a response would inevitably have placed on Arab solidarity in confronting Iraq, the Americans brought all their considerable influence, military as well as political, to bear in an effort to urge restraint on the Israeli government. Messages of the utmost urgency were sent to Israel's leadership to make the point that retaliation would be to play Saddam Hussein's game.

At the same time they took steps to reduce Israel's vulnerability to missile attack. Technicians and supplies of missiles were diverted urgently to hasten the process of bringing Israel's Patriot system into operation around Tel Aviv, which appeared to be Iraq's chosen target. On top of this assurances were given that, despite the impediment to the coalition's strategic bombing campaign, resources would be diverted to locate and destroy the Scud launchers in western Iraq which were delivering the attacks on Israel.

Nor did American efforts stop at persuasion. Deterrence of a firmer order was also employed to discourage Israel's military intervention. An idea for Israeli association with the coalition command structure in Riyadh was seen as a step too far, and there was talk of keeping Israel's air force off the pitch by withholding the identification codes used by the coalition air forces over Iraqi airspace. The lack of this information would have made it virtually impossible for the Israeli airf orce to oper- ate in Iraq's skies.

In parallel with these American intercessions the British ambassador to Israel, Mark Eliot, was sent into bat by the FCO to add Britain's voice to the pressure for restraint. Once he had done so in Jerusalem, I went to see Prince Saud on 19 January to let him know of our action and dis- cuss the implications of an Israeli reaction for the coalition. Prince Saud urged that we keep up the pressure on Israel to play things coolly. He considered that now the coalition was engaged in action to liberate Kuwait, its resolve would not necessarily be checked by an Israeli inter- vention. But he insisted there could be no question of Israel using Saudi airspace to gain access to Iraq. This was a point on which the King had also given the Americans a firm negative.

It turned out to be a prudent line, as within days Iraq's propaganda machine was alleging that Israeli warplanes were using Saudi airfields, a charge which the Saudis firmly rebutted. For their part the Saudis delib- erately avoided any mention in their own news bulletins of Iraq's salvos against Israel, lest this arouse instinctive approbation among less sophis- ticated elements of public opinion.

The session with Prince Saud at this critical moment was marked by another episode which contributed to the surreal impression of the experience through which we were passing. As a sequel to our exchange on possible action with the Israelis, Prince Saud sought to have a quick word with the American Secretary of State on how things stood. He went to his desk and, although it was by then after midnight in Washington, dialled the number of the State Department. Prince Saud asked to speak to Secretary Baker, giving his name as Saud Al Faisal, the Foreign Minister of Saudi Arabia. 'Who?' came the reply. 'Saud al Faisal.' 'How do you spell it?' 'S-A-U-D A-L F-A-I-S-A-L,' he spelt patiently. It was being taken down laboriously at the other end. Then, after a pause,

'Well, he's not here,' was the abrupt response and the line went dead. Prince Saud's wry look said a lot. I made a note to pass on a friendly tip to Chas Freeman.

Saudi anxiety at this point was eased by helpful public statements from both Cairo and Damascus, emphasising the solidarity of purpose of the coalition despite Iraq's blatant appeal to Arab antipathy towards Israel. The Syrians warned, however, that direct Israeli military intervention would put a different complexion on things. Partly to scotch Iraqi suggestions of rifts within the Arab front, President Mubarak paid a high-profile visit to King Fahd in Riyadh at the end of January, when they held a joint press conference to demonstrate their identity of purpose and repeat the call for Saddam Hussein to end hostilities by withdrawing from Kuwait without conditions.

The calls for a cessation to hostilities were given an early lead by King Hussein of Jordan, evidence of whose continued sympathy for Iraq's action remained a source of concern to the Americans and ourselves, and a matter for outrage on the part of Saudi Arabia. We also had reason to suspect the Jordanians were turning a blind eye to the transport of goods into Iraq in breach of UN sanctions. Two days after the launching of the air campaign, King Hussein issued an appeal for an end to attacks to allow a chance for dialogue. In Riyadh his call was regarded as a ritual one. It was repeated in early February, with the old refrain that the West was in reality waging a war against Arabs and Moslems in order to carve up the Arab world. The solid response from Washington was that nothing less than Iraq's complete withdrawal would stop the bombing campaign.

The call was also taken up by Yasir Arafat, who was making no attempt to conceal his personal support for Saddam Hussein. The surge of anti-Western emotion which had gripped the Palestinian community both in the occupied territories and throughout the world, in response to the Iraqi leader's spurious bid to be acting in the Palestinian cause, was being intensified by the thrill of unprecedented missile strikes on Israel. Yasir Arafat chose to associate himself with this mood, thereby effectively forfeiting for himself and the PLO the financial backing of Saudi Arabia and other Gulf states. There were still a few within the Palestinian leadership who saw this for the rash move it was, and endeavoured to keep doors open in Riyadh. But for the Saudi leadership the wound was too deep.

Hani al Hassan, briefly back in Saudi Arabia, came in for a talk the evening after the first round of Scuds on Tel Aviv. He deplored the PLO leader's sycophancy towards Saddam Hussein, which he perceptively recognised as an error of judgment with serious implications for the future of the Palestinian movement. Arafat had allowed his emotions to get the better of him. The final straw, however, came with a return visit to Baghdad by Yasir Arafat after the launch of hostilities, when his support was consummated with the award by Saddam Hussein of the Order of the 'Mother of all Battles', the title chosen by Iraq's leader to describe the rout he was about to undergo at the hands of the coalition's Operation DESERT STORM.

Hani al Hassan's call at the residence coincided with an air raid warning. This turned out to be one of the false alarms, but for half an hour he and I retired to our bedroom keep, where I furnished him with an Avon gas-mask and we continued our talk in muffled fashion. We must have made a rare sight, and the irony of one of the leaders of the Fatah movement being issued with a British gas-mask for his protection seemed a nice touch at the time. He was most appreciative.

When I saw Prince Saud again on 22 January he made it plain that the Saudi government had no time for renewed calls for a pause to permit talks. We agreed that in the absence of Iraqi readiness to withdraw without conditions there was no point in discussion. Baghdad continued to make defiant noises, and a break would only serve to gain time for Iraq.

There was concern too over Iran's position. She had, following the outbreak of hostilities, declared her neutrality in the conflict. This was a helpful step. But the Iranians then muddied the water with a call a few days later for an Islamic summit, combined with an attempt to enlist the Jedda-based Organisation of the Islamic Conference in this cause. They followed this with a proposal for a conditional withdrawal by Iraq, linked to the idea, which also had support from Pakistan, of a meeting of the Non-Aligned Movement to broker a solution. In an effort to hold the door open to Iran and offset the activity which Iraq was undertaking in Tehran to seek the return of her military aircraft and persuade Iran out of neutrality, the Saudis took their own initiative towards a restoration of diplomatic relations. Prince Saud visited Bonn in early February to meet the Iranian Foreign Minister, Velayati, for discussions along lines similar to those we had pursued with Iran two months earlier.

But as the air campaign got into its stride vigilance was called for on a wider diplomatic front. Iraq's summary abrogation, announced on 21 January, of the 1985 border agreement with Saudi Arabia was resented in Riyadh as unlawful and served to heighten antagonism. Two weeks later the Iraqi government finally broke off diplomatic relations with Saudi Arabia, at the same time as she did so in London, Washington and Paris. The gaunt Iraqi embassy building close to our own compound on Riyadh's diplomatic quarter had been empty of life for some weeks already. It was now given a thorough going-over by the Saudi security

forces, after which the water was turned off and the tall palm trees encircling the building began slowly to die.

Meanwhile diligent preparation went into a meeting of GCC foreign
ministers to be held in Riyadh on 26 January. Particular attention was to
be paid to securing the support of the two southernmost members, the
UAE and Oman, in issuing a strong statement of solidarity with the
coalition's offensive. Prince Saud, with his deputy minister, Abdul
Rahman al Mansouri, and the indefatigable team of senior officials in
the Foreign Ministry, seemed to be perpetually in orbit during this
period as they criss-crossed the Moslem world to sustain support and
head off possible defections. It was a formidable performance.

Among Moslem countries Pakistan, Malaysia and the states of North
Africa were seen as points of potential weakness where initial support for
moves to achieve unconditional withdrawal from Kuwait was in danger of
being eroded by public susceptibility to Iraq's meretricious anti-Western
message. Sudan was regarded as a lost cause. The wider Third World
front had also to be watched. Prince Saud discussed with me in early
February how we might combine our efforts at this critical stage of pressure on Iraq to hold in line Commonwealth countries on the UN
Security Council, notably India and Zimbabwe, and those among the
leaders of the Non-Aligned Movement.

Differences also resurfaced at this point in the uneasy relationship
with Syria, now expressing fresh doubts about going over to the attack.
These hesitations on Syria's part had put considerable strain on General
Schwarzkopf's working relationship with Prince Khalid bin Sultan a
month earlier, and had led to an agreement that Syria's awkward sensitivities would be accommodated by giving her the role of reserve force to
the Saudis and Egyptians in the Arab wing of the land offensive. The
Syrian government now seemed to be playing up again, though whether
this marked a response to incipient popular support for Iraq in the wake
of the defiant missile strikes on Israel, or was rather a tactic to extract further economic benefits from Saudi Arabia as a price for participation,
was not clear.

Saudi exasperation was evident as Prince Saud led yet another mission
to Damascus to straighten things out, through an offer to establish a
joint committee on economic co-operation and make an advance
deposit of half a billion dollars out of the Kingdom's original pledge of
financial aid for Syria's economy.

At the same time as they were putting so much effort into holding
together the Arab and Moslem front, the Saudis were also devoting
attention to the political lessons of the crisis in terms of future regional
security and relationships within the Arab world itself. Saudi Arabia's

political instincts made her less inclined than her smaller Gulf partners to rely, at least through formal agreements, on direct Western military support in the event of future threat. The regime's difficulty in containing antipathy and outrage on the part of religious conservatives during the present crisis tended to reinforce this conclusion.

Alternative ideas for some kind of international security provision under the umbrella of an extended Conference on Mediterranean Security, which the Italian Foreign Minister, Gianni de Michaelis, had begun to canvass, found no favour with King Fahd and Prince Saud. Yet the brutal shock of Iraq's attack on a fellow Arab state had brought Saudi Arabia and some of her partners to question the basic assumptions about Arab unity and consensus on which co-operation within the framework of the Arab League had been founded for the past four decades. The effect of Iraq's unprecedented action had been to divide the League's membership into two camps, and render the alliance powerless.

Prince Saud and his advisers were accordingly giving thought to new arrangements which would give a higher profile to mutual security and supplement rather than substitute for the provisions of the Arab League Charter. Ismail Shura, the political director at the Foreign Ministry who took a leading part in the preparation of this initiative, described these as intended to reshape inter-Arab relations by giving priority to a shared respect for the interests of individual states alongside their common bond over Palestine.

The existing combination of the six GCC states plus their two principal Arab allies in the present crisis, Egypt and Syria, was to be taken as the starting point for this new concept, which would initially involve co-ordination in defence and perhaps an Egyptian and Syrian military presence in the Gulf region. It would be buttressed by wider political co-operation and GCC financial assistance for the economic development of their less well-endowed partners. Although specifically aimed in the shorter term at strengthening the capacity of the Gulf states to deter aggression through the association of Egypt and Syria with their defence, it was not seen as a new alliance but as a project which could eventually embrace the whole Arab community. A second layer of security was envisaged, which might involve other regional powers such as Turkey and Pakistan. Western help was, at least in Saudi thinking, to be relegated to the status of ultimate recourse, though they recognised it would be a considerable time before this could be entirely written out of the script.

These initiatives were raised by King Fahd with President Mubarak during the latter's visit to Riyadh at the end of January, and were followed through by Prince Saud in Damascus and Cairo in early February.

They found favour with the Egyptians and Syrians, not least for the prospects they opened of further economic assistance from the Gulf and a wider strategic role. Plans for launching the exercise through a joint declaration by the eight countries concerned were carried forward at an important meeting between the Saudi, Egyptian and Syrian foreign ministers held in Cairo in the middle of February, though it was not until after hostilities had ceased and Kuwait had been liberated that the plan finally came into force with the signing in March of the Damascus Declaration.

Alongside all this active Arab diplomacy, attention had constantly to be given to the preservation of the essential bilateral relationship between Saudi Arabia and her three main Western partners, the USA, Britain and France. Despite our intensive co-operation at the military level in the air campaign now well under way, harmony could not be taken for granted. Given the unprecedented nature of our common venture, misunderstandings over performance and objectives were never far distant, and had to be minimised if the operation was to succeed.

Relations with France continued to pose the most awkward issue for the Saudis, due in large part to their sense of mistrust over what they saw as ambivalence in France's commitment to the joint objective of seeing Iraq out of Kuwait on an unconditional basis, if necessary by the use of force. France's eleventh hour activities in the UN Security Council to gain more time for negotiation had not helped here. Moreover, her defence minister's personal association with the Franco-Iraqi military relationship still gave ground for doubts, despite the presence of some 11,000 French ground troops in the Kingdom and the participation of her air force in raids on Iraqi targets in Kuwait.

The fact that at the outset of hostilities the French troops were finally committed to the offensive under American operational control had been a positive step, but earlier misunderstanding lingered. Already some Saudi orders for military equipment had been diverted to the Americans and ourselves at the expense of France. Jean-Pierre Chevenement came out to Riyadh two days after the air campaign was launched to try to clear up the differences with Prince Sultan. But his position as defence minister was fast becoming untenable, and on 29 January he resigned.

His successor, Pierre Joxe, lost no time in working to close this awkward chapter and establish a better relationship. For the French forces, and indeed for the whole coalition, the new sense of commitment which he brought to French policy came as a considerable relief. The French Prime Minister, Michel Rocard, followed him with a visit to King Fahd in mid-February, when the King took the opportunity to make it plain that his intention to see Saddam Hussein out of Kuwait and his capacity to threaten the region removed remained as staunch as ever.

With the Americans, too, there were occasions for misunderstanding. The Saudis were taken aback by an American statement on 28 January, made jointly with the USSR, which pointed to the possibility of a ceasefire if Iraq showed clear evidence of her intention to withdraw. From the questions which Prince Saud put to me on this move when we met the following day, it appeared that the Saudis had not been consulted or briefed on what lay behind the statement. I suggested it demonstrated how the American administration was leaning over backwards in its efforts to retain the support of an increasingly restive Soviet leadership for an offensive which was putting Soviet diplomatic activity in the shade. Chas Freeman subsequently confirmed that it was indeed a tactic to keep the USSR in play. But the Saudis evidently feared it would afford the USSR further scope for misplaced attempts at mediation, which would only gain time for Iraq.

The Americans also faced by early February signs of Saudi impatience over the duration of the air campaign, which some had expected to be over within a month. The longer it drew on without an Iraqi collapse, the greater the worry in Saudi minds that Saddam Hussein's stature in Arab popular opinion would recover for having stood up to the West. There was still the myth to be watched of a Western conspiracy behind the whole crisis. So far the Iraqi leader had enjoyed only limited success in rallying Arab opinion, and the old war cries about Western imperialism and Palestine were proving less compelling than in past times. But things needed to be brought to a conclusion. The significant financial burden of prolonged operations by American and other coalition forces was beginning to add to Saudi preoccupations.

A visit to Riyadh on 9 February by Defence Secretary Cheney and the chief of staff, General Powell, to finalise with Norman Schwarzkopf the plans and timing of the land offensive fuelled speculation that the final stage might be imminent. It was confirmed with King Fahd that no move should be made until all the coalition forces were ready in position. These preparations could still require another 12 days, after which the offensive could go ahead. But the crucial decision had now been taken. The visitors also squared things with Amir Jaber al Ahmad in Taif.

But it was our own crucial relationship with the Saudis, and with the Kuwaiti authorities too, to which we gave our main attention during these hectic first weeks of hostilities. There were many aspects to this work. It was great good fortune to have such able colleagues as Derek Plumbly, Peter Gooderham and Charles Hollis in the chancery at this time, well tried by now in the Kingdom's often enigmatic ways.

There were substantial bilateral issues to be dealt with. By early January the Americans had concluded arrangements for the Saudi government to reimburse them for a large portion of the overall costs of the US forces sent to the Gulf area, to the tune of $13 billion in addition to the local costs which the Saudis were already bearing for coalition forces in the Kingdom. Pressure from Congress and within the American administration for financial compensation on this scale had been intense, but even so King Fahd's response was generous, particularly as his country's economy was only starting to recover from the depressed oil revenues of the 1980s. Kuwait and the UAE had also pledged substantial sums.

In these circumstances it was understandable that the British government should seek similar recompense for the huge costs incurred in coming to help with the defence of the Kingdom and the liberation of Kuwait, on a pro rata basis to what the Americans might receive. The size of our military contribution at the outset of hostilities meant that this worked out at roughly eight per cent of the American total.

By late January we were coming under pressure from the MoD in London, themselves being pushed in turn by the Treasury, to obtain Saudi Arabia's response to the bid for a financial contribution which the Prime Minister had put to King Fahd when they met in Riyadh. I was concerned, however, not to present our request in a fashion which might appear importunate, particularly at this critical juncture. It was apparent to us that the pressure the Americans had been bringing to bear over the financial issue had produced a sour taste in Saudi mouths and was arousing critical public comment. It thus seemed sensible to press our bid discreetly through a letter to the King from John Major. The FCO promptly set this up, and I delivered the communication to Prince Saud a few days later. The message was followed up by a positive telephone conversation between King Fahd in Riyadh and John Major in London in early February, on the eve of a visit by Douglas Hurd.

More significant in our intensive bilateral relationship during this period was the harmonisation of coalition war aims and the associated question of how the security of the Gulf states was to be assured once Iraq had withdrawn. These issues featured prominently in discussions which Prince Saud held with myself and the American ambassador as the prospect of Kuwait's liberation approached. Some public debate had begun to emerge in Britain over how far coalition forces, and in particular the Americans and ourselves, should go in pursuit of Iraq's leadership and the establishment of a more benign and representative government in Baghdad. Mrs Thatcher, now on the back benches in Parliament, was fierce in urging that Saddam Hussein should be run to earth and brought to book for his crimes. We had much discussion in Riyadh on what was justifiable and, more important still, what was politically and militarily feasible.

It was evident to us on the ground that there were real practical limitations to a policy of following the liberation of Kuwait through to the gates of Baghdad. In the first place the coalition had no authority to do so. The operation had been deliberately put together under the auspices of the UN Security Council, whose endorsement extended only to the objective of restoring Kuwait's sovereignty. Indeed, some were saying that military operations within Iraq herself, so essential to the achievement of the Council's objective, were not covered by the remit. Egyptian and Syrian forces were, for example, confining their participation to the territory of Kuwait. In this unique instance of united international action to counter an act of clear aggression, we all saw it as particularly important to be scrupulous about the legitimacy of the steps we took, despite the likelihood that, once the Iraqi forces had been driven out of Kuwait in a much-weakened state and with their military infrastructure and command system all but destroyed by air attack, there would be little to obstruct a coalition advance on the capital.

Alongside these considerations was the political factor that if the coalition, and particularly its Western members, were to involve themselves directly in the replacement of Iraq's regime, they were all too likely to find themselves drawn into the morass of Iraq's deeply-divided ethnic and political scene, from which it would be difficult to extract themselves. Saddam Hussein might find asylum elsewhere, and so remain a destabilising presence on the stage. Moreover, as we knew from our contacts with the various Iraqi political figures in exile in the West and Saudi Arabia too, the outlook was unpromising for the succession of a democratic regime capable of achieving cohesion within Iraq's precarious ethnic balance of Sunni, Shi'a and Kurd with their traditional antagonisms. These differences might in turn be exploited by Iraq's neighbours.

Moreover, the whole Arab world continued to harbour a long and aggrieved memory of Western political domination. Britain and France had particular cause to recall the lessons of that interlude, and had abjured its repetition. Not only would our Arab partners in the coalition stop short of participation in any action intended to provoke the overthrow of a fellow Arab government, even one as iniquitous as that of Saddam Hussein, but we would inevitably find that if we were to go for such a course ourselves, we would alienate Arab opinion and place our relations with even our closest Arab partners under excessive strain. In short we would end up holding the very thick end of a stick.

As for future security in the region, there was no doubt in our minds that somehow the Arab and other states of the area had to be encouraged to establish a greater political and military equilibrium, which would enable them better to avert the danger of mutual threat or aggression. Some ultimate back-up on the part of the West and other elements in the new international order produced out of the ending of the Cold War might be required for some period ahead. But we could not afford to take a nostalgic approach to Gulf security, and neither was this in the interests of the countries of the region. The Arab states of the Gulf needed to work out their own means to deter or defend themselves against any attempt at aggression, at least until outside help could be mobilised.

Both we and the Americans were taking opportunities to urge this approach on the Saudis. We found it harmonised with the ideas which the Saudis themselves were starting to put together as the basis for a new inter-Arab defence arrangement, although certain of the smaller GCC states, including the Kuwaitis, continued to talk to us of renewed Western defence commitments.

To help in their consideration of future security arrangements on these lines, we prepared a paper in February for the GCC secretariat which emphasised the importance of closer regional defence co-ordination, starting with the Gulf states themselves and encompassing undertakings and confidence-building measures involving other countries in the region, including Iran. This produced a wry comment that the first requirement was for confidence-building measures within the GCC. We recognised there would probably be a need for a Western contribution to an international military shield in Kuwait, but this should be for a limited period. Peter de la Billière suggested we might leave some of our armour behind for the Kuwaitis to use.

All these ideas were the subject of detailed exchanges with colleagues in the FCO during the first hectic weeks of the offensive. It was a great help to be able to compare ideas with those involved in the crisis at home, whether in the FCO, the MoD, or at the joint headquarters in High Wycombe, at any time of day or night. Our thinking on future stages ran very close. They too were working under great pressure, but were always ready to toss ideas around with us and provide, sometimes at the shortest notice, the briefing so essential to our dialogue with Saudis and Kuwaitis. Indeed, the unity of approach on policy within Whitehall at this juncture was an impressive tribute to the efficiency of its crisis machinery, and compared favourably, as we saw it, with the manifold points of consultation to which our American and French colleagues had to address themselves in their capitals.

Saudi concern over how far their Western partners intended to press the coalition offensive was first expressed to me by Prince Saud in late January, as a result of media publicity over an outburst by Tom King in which he called for the destruction of Iraq's whole war machine. In the circumstances this seemed an understandable objective and one over which the Saudis fully shared our concern, not least from what they knew of Saddam Hussein's sinister programme to develop weapons of mass destruction. An assumption was, however, emerging on the part of the Saudi leadership that Saddam Hussein was likely to be toppled by his own people in the disgrace of defeat. We ourselves fervently shared in this hope.

These preoccupations were reiterated more intensively to us as the campaign moved towards its climax. Stress was also being laid on the need to differentiate between Iraq's vicious regime and the Iraqi people, who had suffered so much under it. In the event that sanctions needed to continue to be applied for a period following Iraq's withdrawal, this aspect must be borne in mind, with provision for prompt humanitarian aid to be directed towards the Iraqi population. There was thus a solid case for restraint on the part of the coalition in the interest of Iraq's future stability and her integrity as a nation. A defensive screen should be retained in Kuwait following the ending of hostilities, but it would be preferable for this to take the form of an Arab force, perhaps under UN auspices. It was still evident that for reasons of internal policy the Saudis wished to see Western forces vacate Saudi Arabia as rapidly as possible.

With a sense of history perhaps more acute than our own, the Saudis showed particular concern to avoid leaving Iraq in the position where she found her military capability reduced to the point that she could no longer offer a defence against predatory moves by certain neighbours in the aftermath of her defeat. The ghosts of the post-First World War division of the former Ottoman empire were again stalking the stage after an interval of 70 years. Dormant claims on the part of Turkey to the Kurdish Mosul province in northern Iraq could still be resuscitated. Iran for her part might lend military backing to the Shi'a community of southern Iraq to exploit their resentment of Baghdad and so provoke either secession or a Shi'a takeover of government, which could prove inimical to the security of the Kingdom and her Gulf partners. Even Syria might harbour territorial ambitions towards the east.

These preoccupations took us on a fascinating tour through the byways of history, but they held some substance too. They were also causing serious concern to our major partner in the crisis. In discussion of them I sought to give a contemporary perspective and so to discount their gravity. Was it really so probable that the Turks would move to consolidate the territorial claims denied to Kemal Ataturk in the early 1920s; or was Iran, beset by her own problems with her Kurdish population in the north, likely to seek to provoke the dismemberment of Iraq and absorb her Arab Shi'a population, which had in eight years of war demonstrated its readiness to fight for nation rather than religious confession? But these responses did little to mitigate Saudi concern to leave Iraq able to defend herself, however fervently they wanted Saddam Hussein out of the way.

Seeing some risk of incipient misunderstanding between us over the crucial issue of what our precise objectives were in the present conflict, I raised with David Gore-Booth in London the possibility of a visit by the Foreign Secretary to go over these matters with Prince Saud and the King. It was essential to have our war aims clearly defined between us, and with our other main partners. The contact would also provide an opportunity to follow up the matter of a contribution to our costs.

In addition there was much to be said for a meeting with the Kuwaiti leadership in Taif, to discuss defence in the immediate aftermath of liberation as well as the contribution Britain expected to make to the task of reconstruction, for which we were already laying plans. This would give an opportunity to follow through a request for a Kuwaiti contribution to our military costs, which had been put a few weeks earlier to the Kuwaiti foreign minister in London. The idea had then been floated that Mrs Thatcher, who was fretting on the sidelines of the action, should come out to Saudi Arabia to press this request herself with the Amir. I had, however, strongly discouraged this flight of fancy. It would have put King Fahd in an awkward predicament to have his close and trusted ally, Margaret Thatcher, visit the Kingdom for the primary purpose of seeing the Kuwaitis in exile and at a time when he would not be free to give her the attention and hospitality which he would have wished.

It was good to discover that the FCO already had the idea of a visit by the Foreign Secretary in mind, and that Douglas Hurd was keen to come out at this crucial stage. A visit was welcomed by the Saudis, not least for its public demonstration of our mutual solidarity at this active stage of the crisis, and we therefore set up plans for a visit to Riyadh on 9 and 10 February, stopping *en route* in Taif to see the Amir of Kuwait and Crown Prince Saad. It was also planned that in the sessions with the Kuwaitis Douglas Hurd should be backed up by a group of senior British business figures from appropriate sectors of construction and manufacturing, led by the chairman of GEC, Lord Prior.

But all was not to be entirely plain sailing. Six days before Douglas Hurd was due to come I was telephoned late in the evening by Prince Saud, asking that I come round urgently to his home. It transpired that the Saudis were concerned over a report carried on the BBC Arabic service. This had indicated that an address which Douglas Hurd was due to give that evening to a local Conservative Party meeting in the village of Blaby in Leicestershire would include a comment on the scope for further assistance by the oil producers to their Arab partners once the crisis was over.

Prince Saud rightly reminded me that, as the King had made clear in the face of derogatory Iraqi propaganda, Saudi Arabia's record in this regard was exceedingly generous. Moreover, we ourselves recognised that the Saudis were contributing handsomely towards the military costs of their partners in the coalition as well as opening discussion of new channels for Gulf aid. To avoid misunderstanding it seemed important to put the record straight. I therefore arranged during the night for the Foreign Secretary, who was by then in Brussels for a EC Foreign Affairs Committee meeting, to speak to Prince Saud with reassuring words of clarification. In the event the Blaby speech, with its affirmation in strong and positive terms of our commitment to see Iraq out of Kuwait and of our solidarity with Saudi Arabia and our other coalition partners, was well received in Riyadh.

Douglas Hurd duly had constructive talks with the Amir and members of the Kuwaiti government in Taif on 9 February. Kuwaiti impatience to see the final stage of liberation on its way was evident, reinforced perhaps by information about continuing acts of atrocity by occupying troops against Kuwaiti citizens in retaliation for resistance activities, and reports that large numbers of Kuwaitis, including members of the Al Sabah family, were being transported into Iraq and held captive there. An offer was made of £660 million towards the costs of the British forces and gratefully accepted.

The opportunity was taken to urge on Crown Prince Saad the earliest possible return of the Al Sabah and the Kuwaiti government to Kuwait to re-establish order and rally the national forces, including resistance groups. This was a point which we had also been making to Kuwaiti representatives based in Riyadh. A warning was also given against summary justice or the taking of reprisals against those suspected of collaboration. Such measures would do Kuwait's reputation great damage. The point was also put across to Kuwait's economic ministers that we looked to play a significant part in the task of physical recovery and reconstruction.

The party came on to Riyadh that evening, when discussions were opened over a dinner in the main guest palace. Prince Saud and his brother, Prince Turki al Faisal, led on the Saudi side. It felt strange to be in this sumptuous building amid signs pointing to the air-raid shelters. In fact Saddam Hussein missed his opportunity that night, as not only the

Foreign Secretary and his party but also the American Defence Secretary and chief of staff were sleeping there. He left them undisturbed.

Our discussions over dinner and again the following morning ranged widely, covering war aims, the prospect of an imminent land offensive, the need to preserve Iraq's integrity as a state, the future of Gulf security through strengthening of the GCC's own defences, the uncertain relationship with Iran, and Saudi ideas for a new basis for inter-Arab co-operation through links with Egypt and Syria. The Saudis were envisaging a series of circles for Gulf security, radiating outwards from an Arab core to a regional layer, beyond which might lie ultimate recourse to Western and international assistance. With his customary perspicacity Prince Saud also stressed the need to grasp the opportunity presented by the shock of Iraq's action and the discrediting of the PLO through their blind support for it, as well as by Iraq's missile attacks on Israel, for the West to launch a fresh initiative in the search for a solution to the Palestine issue. This would now have wide Arab support. The matter of who should speak for the Palestinians could be left on one side for the moment.

There were also discussions with Peter de la Billière and his staff on the next steps in the campaign, which we still saw as a possibly long-drawn-out affair with the threat of chemical weapons. Douglas Hurd just had time for a quick word with embassy staff at lunch in our garden before we were summoned to see King Fahd.

The King received us in his private villa next to the Al Yamamah palace. Both Crown Prince Abdullah and Prince Sultan were present, plus Prince Saud. The King's welcome to Douglas Hurd was very warm. He spoke at length about the outlook for the campaign and for Iraq's future. It was a relief to find the King in no rush to start the land offensive, despite pressures on him at home to get the crisis over with, and from various external quarters to agree a ceasefire. He had seen Dick Cheney the day before, and agreed to a timing in the last week of February. The King recognised the importance of making sure coalition forces were in the right shape for an offensive against what still looked a well-prepared enemy, and to allow time for attrition through air attack.

There was unease at the prospect of a ceasefire that left Saddam Hussein in charge of Iraq and with the capacity to retaliate. His objective was judged to have been the extension of Iraqi control over the whole Arab side of the Gulf, and he could still present a danger in defeat. There was no doubt in our minds that the Saudis hoped to see the end of Saddam Hussein, although they realised that his generals could not be counted upon to get rid of him.

Iraq's armoury therefore had to be destroyed, to inhibit her ability to relaunch an aggression. At the same time the limits set by the UN Security Council's remit had to be observed, and Iraq's integrity as a state sustained. There might even be fresh ambitions on the part of the Hashemite family to see their rule over Iraq restored. Looking to the future, we agreed that the Gulf states needed to assume primary responsibility for their own defence. This would require further building up of their armed forces, in which Britain could help. Douglas Hurd was given an assurance of Saudi financial assistance over our military costs. It was an excellent meeting which demonstrated our close identity of approach as the crisis entered its final stage.

On return from seeing the King we all took a welcome spot of exercise with a walk through the palm groves in the wadi which ran through Riyadh's diplomatic quarter, and then went on to a meeting with Abdullah Bishara, the Kuwaiti Secretary-General of the GCC, impatient as ever to see his country liberated and perhaps more sanguine than us about prospects for security co-operation throughout the Gulf after the war.

Douglas Hurd rounded off this very full day by meeting the world's press in the glaring lights of the Hyatt Hotel press centre, used each evening by the military commanders and their press officers for daily briefings on the progress of Operation DESERT STORM. In an interview with Sky TV the Foreign Secretary made it plain we did not intend to keep troops in the Gulf after the war. Nor had we widened our war aims to include a change of regime in Iraq, though he made it clear no tears would be shed if Saddam Hussein were to fall by the wayside; words which were welcome to our hosts and a broad hint for Iraq. As we left the building Norman Schwarzkopf swept theatrically past us, accompanied by his posse of personal guards, to deliver that night's briefing. The show was going on.

But not without a further eleventh hour hiatus. The same day marked the start of yet another climax in activity by the USSR, ever restive at finding herself sidelined in the crisis, to secure a ceasefire which would spare humiliation for her former ally, Iraq, and salvage something of Soviet prestige. On 10 February the tenacious Yevgeny Primakov found himself despatched once again on a round of visits, starting with Baghdad, for the purpose of reopening a dialogue on mediation. At the same time President Gorbachev issued a warning to the coalition not to exceed the mandate set by the UN Security Council. Saddam Hussein responded characteristically by stringing things out, while Primakov came on to Riyadh where he received fairly short shrift from the King for this latest meddling. By this time direct diplomatic relations had been re-established between the Kingdom and the USSR after an interval of 55 years, and a Soviet chargé d'affaires had arrived in Riyadh.

The next move came on 15 February with an Iraqi announcement that they were ready to withdraw, but still subject to conditions. These included the withdrawal of American and other Western forces and their equipment from the Gulf and elsewhere in the Middle East, as well as an Israeli pull-out from the occupied Palestinian territories, Lebanon and the Golan in Syria. Iraq should be allowed one month for her withdrawal from Kuwait. These terms were clearly unacceptable, and the British and American governments lost no time in rejecting them as a hoax.

President Bush was provoked to go further with an invitation to the Iraqi people and the military to force their leader to step down, an off-the-cuff invitation to insurrection which, taken with remarks in similar vein made by John Major a few days previously, was to raise false hopes and recoil on the Americans with Saddam Hussein's savage suppression of uprisings in both southern and northern Iraq in the immediate aftermath of the war.

The Saudis joined in a robust rejection of the Iraqi proposal as being inconsistent with UN and Arab League resolutions, and this was reaffirmed by all six GCC states, Egypt and Syria when they met in Cairo on 16 February to discuss plans for their future co-operation. Only the Soviets gave Baghdad's ideas a welcome.

In a surprise move the Iraqi Foreign Minister, Tariq Aziz, set off for Moscow on 16 February, travelling overland to Iran and arriving the following day. He was presented on 18 February by President Gorbachev with a Soviet proposal for a ceasefire which contained eight points, and left immediately for Baghdad to discuss these with Saddam Hussein.

Meanwhile the Soviets released details of their peace plan. Its main ingredients were full and unconditional withdrawal, to begin within two days of a ceasefire; withdrawal from Kuwait City within four days and from the country within three weeks; some sanctions to be lifted once two-thirds of Iraqi forces had withdrawn, and the rest following total evacuation; all prisoners to be released on the ceasefire; and the UN to supervise the withdrawal. There was no mention of Kuwait's future security. On 21 February Iraq announced her acceptance of these proposals, though Saddam Hussein still sought to set conditions by insisting that all other UN Security Council resolutions be annulled once withdrawal was complete.

The Soviet action provoked a flurry of diplomatic activity on all sides. The proposals were met with categoric rejection from the British and American governments. The Prime Minister described them as insufficient to meet the requirements of the UN Security Council resolutions. They were not unconditional. Saddam Hussein must accept the resolutions in full or face a land war. President Bush described the proposals as falling well short. There could be no concessions to Iraq. He expressed appreciation for Soviet efforts, though the Americans declined a Soviet suggestion that they jointly present the plan to the UN Security Council.

These responses came as a relief to the Saudi government, as I found when I saw Prince Saud on 22 February to pass on to him the Prime Minister's firm reaction. The Saudis had been seriously taken aback at the Soviet initiative, and where Iraq's fudged acceptance of it might lead. Saddam Hussein was rightly seen as again playing for time, and a prompt expression of support from King Hussein did not help. Nor did favourable signals on the part of the French, Italian and Spanish governments.

Emissaries had immediately been despatched from Riyadh to the Kingdom's main Arab partners in the coalition to establish their reactions. Finding all were prepared to hold firm to the principle of unconditional Iraqi withdrawal and were committed to a land offensive as the only sure means to achieve this, the Saudis made a statement on 21 February endorsing American rejection of the Soviet plan and insisting on full Iraqi compliance with UN Security Council resolutions.

There was no doubt in Saudi minds what elements needed to be covered for an Iraqi ceasefire offer to be acceptable at this late and active stage of military engagement. Iraq had to withdraw from Kuwait and along her border with the Kingdom; Kuwait's legitimate government had to be restored; Iraq must agree to pay reparations; provision had to be made for her arsenal of weapons of mass destruction to be destroyed; and she should give guarantees of no further aggressive intent. Moreover, Iraq's word alone was no longer seen to be good enough, and the Saudis were unhappy to have the Soviets in the role of go-between. It was now for the coalition to decide on any ceasefire, rather than the UN Security Council.

Meanwhile, as we held our breath, there came a typically ambiguous Iraqi response to the Soviet plan. Tariq Aziz had returned to Moscow on 21 February to tell President Gorbachev that Iraq accepted it but would not agree to a surrender. The response was further confused by a defiant broadcast by Saddam Hussein in which he abused President Bush and King Fahd, and claimed that Iraq would continue the struggle. This was accompanied by the firing of a further series of missiles into northern and eastern Saudi Arabia, and by the multiple igniting of oil wells across Kuwait, hardly to be interpreted as acts of conciliation. Most of the trajectiles were successfully intercepted by the Patriot system, but one, which fell near the military base of Hafr al Batin, wounded some soldiers from a Senegalese contingent.

At this point the American administration ran out of patience, and took the crucial decision that the time had come for the coalition to turn on the heat by spelling out its own ultimatum to Iraq. After some pressure from Washington, General Schwarzkopf's agreement was obtained that conditions would be acceptable for the land offensive to go ahead on 24 February. It was now accepted by the coalition commanders in the field that Iraq's stalling tactics did not offer a way around the option of a ground fight, with the heavy loss of lives this might involve. President Bush accordingly laid it down on behalf of the coalition governments in a statement from the White House on the morning of 22 February that Iraq had 24 hours to start pulling her forces out of Kuwait, with a further 48 hours to be clear of Kuwait City and one week to have all troops, as distinct from their equipment, out of the country. With this decisive move the Soviet peace initiative petered out.

Iraq's only response was to launch a further series of Scud missiles into Saudi Arabia and one against Israel. The deadline passed at 8pm Riyadh time with no indication that the Iraqis were preparing to withdraw. We went to bed in the sombre knowledge, not unmixed with a tinge of relief, that by dawn the next morning the final battle for Kuwait's liberation, for which we had all worked so long, would at last be joined, and that Iraq would soon taste the bitter fruits of her aggression.

CHAPTER 15

Climax

The land offensive to clear Kuwait of Iraq's occupation was carried through with a speed that took us all by surprise. The feeling among the military in Riyadh was that, while the outcome was beyond doubt, it could take at least a fortnight to clear Iraq's weakened but still massive occupation force out of Kuwait, though the Saudis continued to forecast its swift collapse.

On paper the Iraqis were reckoned to have up to half a million troops in the theatre of operations, of whom about half were in Kuwait. The élite Republican Guard was reckoned to compose over a quarter of these forces, though Saddam Hussein had taken the precaution of moving them into reserve in southern Iraq, covering the approaches to Basra at the mouth of the Euphrates, a critical escape route of which they could avail themselves in the event of retreat. Tank strength was put at over 4,000, with over 3,000 artillery pieces including missile launchers. There was reason to expect chemical weapons to be used on the battlefield, despite warnings of grave consequences from both the American administration and London.

As a result of insufficient intelligence, however, these totals may have involved a substantial overestimate. The picture of how things stood on the eve of the land offensive was obscured for the coalition's commanders by a lack of detail. There was still disagreement between analysts in Washington and at CENTCOM in Riyadh over the extent of the damage caused to Iraqi units in the field by the crescendo of activity to soften up the resistance of Iraq's front-line defences through incessant air and artillery attack, as well as by aggressive cross-border patrolling in the final days to open gaps in the minefields and other physical defences arrayed along the Kuwait frontier.

General Schwarzkopf had set a target of inflicting a 50 per cent degradation on Iraqi capability in the field before launching the offensive. In the event this proved very difficult to assess. Aerial surveillance was hampered by bad weather and, in the last stages, by the pall of smoke which overhung much of southern Kuwait as the Iraqis ignited the explosive charges they had set to over 600 oilwells in an orgy of spiteful vandalism while the Soviet peace plan was yet under discussion.

It was nevertheless clear, in particular from the accounts brought by the growing numbers of demoralised Iraqi soldiers who were giving themselves up, that rates of injury and desertion, despite harsh penalties for the latter, were proving high and damage to combat equipment extensive. A major operation to drop leaflets in Arabic over Iraqi troop positions inviting them to give themselves up, with assurances of good treatment, was beginning to show results. On the British side cassettes had been compiled which combined catchy Arab music with stirring exhortation to give up the fight. We had stacks of these in the embassy for dropping by the RAF; they may by now be collectors' items in Iraq. There were already some 2,500 Iraqi prisoners, mostly being held in camps in Saudi Arabia with a few hundred in Turkey in the north.

An American assessment after the war brought Iraq's effective troop numbers in theatre down to less than a quarter of a million by 23 February, with only some 2,000 tanks in fighting condition and around 1,300 artillery weapons. American military personnel alone had now peaked at twice this Iraqi figure.

It also looked as though Norman Schwarzkopf's bold plan of deception to camouflage the switch of the major part of coalition ground forces to the western portion of the front for their main thrust, rather than along the Gulf coast, had been brought off without Iraqi detection. This was a considerable achievement, involving a barrage of decoy radio communications to suggest heavy manoeuvring to the east, backed up by diversionary naval movements and amphibious operations conducted by the Marines against shoals and islands off the Kuwait mainland.

The CENTCOM plan for attack assigned roles to the three Western participants who had committed ground forces to the coalition, as well as to the Arab contingents from Saudi Arabia and her five GCC partners, plus the Egyptians and Syrians. It involved an advance on a front some 560 kilometres wide. On the western flank a highly-mobile American and French force was to race north-west across Iraq from the Saudi border to secure a military airfield to the north of the theatre in the rear of Iraq's forces. In parallel the American 101st Division was to make an airborne assault on a position near the Euphrates north-west of Basra, from where it could block the main highway to Baghdad, only some 240 kilometres distant.

The main armoured thrust, in which Rupert Smith's 1st British Division formed part of the US VII Corps under General Fred Franks, was to cross the border into Iraq just to the west of the Kuwait frontier and advance in an eastward arc through the front-line troops to tackle the well-armed Republican Guard divisions that constituted the main threat. Next in line of advance was the main Arab armoured force of Saudi and Egyptian units, with the Syrians in reserve. Their task was to advance direct towards Kuwait City through Iraqi defensive obstacles in order to be in a position to lead the recapture of the capital. Two other lines of advance were to be undertaken near the Gulf coast, one involving two US Marine divisions and the other a light armoured force of Saudi troops with detachments from the other five GCC states, including regrouped Kuwaiti armour. All Arab forces were under the command from Riyadh of General Prince Khalid bin Sultan, as coalition joint commander, while General Schwarzkopf had overall control of the offensive operation.

A news blackout was imposed until the close of the second day of the land attack, by which time it was clear that the coalition advance was going smoothly and its pace exceeding expectations. Back in Riyadh we were dependent on information filtered through to us from BFME headquarters, whence Peter de la Billière, having transferred operational command of his forces to the Americans, was closely accompanying developments on the battle front through Norman Schwarzkopf's war room below the Defence Ministry building.

There seemed no reason to expect a walkover, and we felt very conscious of the dangers now faced by the young soldiers whom we had met in training on our occasional visits up the line over the past five months. Our television screens showed dramatic pictures of Royal Artillery gunners conducting a massive long-range engagement over the border against Iraqi positions, in an operation described as their heaviest barrage since the battle of El Alamein in 1942. The saturation effect of their recently-acquired MRLS rocket launchers was said to have been particularly devastating.

The morning of 25 February brought signs of frustration in headquarters over time lost overnight in 1st Division's move through the border breach. The delay was attributed to a decision by General Franks to halt VII Corps' advance during the hours of darkness. This step had, perhaps unjustly, caused Norman Schwarzkopf, who had the previous day brought forward the timing of VII Corps' start in order to hasten the advance against the Republican Guard units, to blow one of his ever-volatile fuses. Uncharitable comparisons were drawn with General George McClellan, the Unionist commander during the American Civil War, notorious for his reluctance to advance and described by an exasperated President Lincoln as 'a stationary engine'. Once through the gap, however, VII Corps and its British armoured division set a good pace as they wheeled across Wadi al Batin into northern Kuwait. Despite numerous tank engagements they were never checked for long.

To remind us that Iraq had still to be reckoned with, a renewed flush of Scud missiles was directed against both Riyadh and the Eastern Province during the first three days of the offensive. On 26 February two neighbouring Gulf states, Bahrain and Qatar, received their first Scuds of the war, though no damage was done. Ironically this last throw in the missile campaign against the Kingdom was to cause some of the most significant damage and loss of life. On the night of 25 February a Scud which Patriot defences failed to intercept struck a warehouse in Al Khobar that was being used as a barracks for American support troops. Twenty-eight personnel were killed and nearly 100 wounded in what was Iraq's biggest single military cull of the war. Realising that the building which had been hit was only some 400 metres from the compound inhabited by the staff of our Al Khobar office, I rang David Lloyd to hear with relief that they were all fine, if a bit shocked by the missile's impact.

A genial anecdote subsequently emerged from this tragic episode. One of the female welfare officers supplied to our military hospitals by the British Red Cross and Order of St John Societies happened to be outside a shopping centre close to the barrack room when the missile struck. In a letter to Grania after the war she described how, with all the others around, she had thrown herself to the ground. As they picked themselves up from the dust, rather shaken by the experience, she was addressed by a Saudi beside her who, seeing her uniform, asked if she was English. On hearing this was so he went on, 'Oh, good. I do like Victorian architecture. Do you know Harrogate?' His unruffled, if incongruous, introduction meant a lot to her at that difficult moment.

In Riyadh a Scud got through the Patriot screen on 24 February and demolished one of the city's largest schools, the Nejd School in the northern suburbs. Fortunately the building was deserted, though the Sheraton Hotel nearby, mainly occupied by Kuwaiti refugee families and Western military personnel, had a number of windows blown in. The tremor from this strike was felt in our house a good four kilometres away, and must have contributed to a surprise the next morning when a section of the ceiling tiles in our dining room dropped on Grania as she was preparing lunch. To be safe we stripped the rest of the ceiling, with the result that the room looked a bit like an aircraft hangar for our entertainment of the stream of political and military visitors we received once hostilities were over. The Scuds and their Patriot intercepts over Riyadh that night and the following one, when the skies were for once clear, afforded a dramatic sight and permitted some spectacular photography.

A preoccupation for us, as for our colleagues in the American embassy, at the outset of the land campaign was to try to counter the re-emergence of doubt in some Saudi minds over the motives behind the coalition decision to press ahead with the ground offensive when the Iraqis had declared their acceptance of the Soviet peace proposals. We had no doubt that the King and his government were just as resolute as ourselves in the conviction that Saddam Hussein would seek to spin things out and secure advantage from a ceasefire, which at this stage would still leave him capable of a threat to his southern neighbours. For their part the Kuwaiti leadership felt strongly that the attack must be pressed through to the point where Saddam Hussein suffered a defeat.

Once the land battle was joined it did have a rallying effect on Saudi public sentiment, with the end of the affair at last coming into view. But some sections of opinion were ever susceptible to Iraqi propaganda, which was now switching to the line, guaranteed to find a sensitive Arab nerve, that the Western members of the coalition intended occupying southern Iraq, and had launched the land war to this end.

On 25 February General Khalid bin Sultan spoke in a press conference of the necessity for the land offensive. He went further with a suggestion that the liberation of Kuwait might in turn lead to the liberation of Iraq's army and people from their tyrant. His remarks were tempered with the assurance that the coalition bore the Iraqi people no ill will. Only Iraqi troops who showed resistance would be engaged in battle. Prince Khalid added that the first stages of the offensive were going well, and that no less than 20,000 Iraqi troops had surrendered in the first 24 hours. He sent a message of encouragement to those in Kuwait that relief would soon arrive.

For my part I gave an interview on Saudi television on the day the coalition's ultimatum to Iraq was due to expire, in which I emphasised there could be no room for compromise in our common objective to see Kuwait liberated and Iraq's threat to her Arab neighbours eliminated. We were all now entering the final stage of the crisis which Saddam Hussein had brought upon the region; our quarrel was not with the Iraqi people. The interview had a stale feeling to it; perhaps fatigue got in the way. It was nevertheless carried that evening as the deadline ran out, and again the following day.

I also briefed a number of British journalists, gathered at the embassy by Nick Abbott, on the political background to the land offensive and the outlook for future security, and had an interview with the two main Arabic and English-language dailies, in which I went in some detail over the reasons for rejecting the eleventh hour Soviet peace plan. Its proposals still fell short of what was demanded. They only covered Iraq's acceptance of the UN Security Council's Resolution 660, concerning withdrawal from Kuwait, and ignored implementation of the 11 subsequent resolutions on Iraq's aggression. Iraq's response was insufficient too, being confined to an offer to withdraw under certain conditions. Having invaded Kuwait in two days, Iraq did not need three weeks to complete withdrawal minus heavy equipment. I paid due tribute to Saudi resolve and the morale of our community who had stayed to make their contribution at work. As for the future, it was up to the states of the region to make their own security arrangements in the light of the present experience; British forces would stay no longer than they were wanted.

I had another talk with Sulaiman Shahine at the Kuwaiti embassy, to urge that the Kuwaiti government take steps to counter Iraq's latest propaganda barrage by publicising their insistence that there be no conditions attached to an Iraqi withdrawal, even if this involved force of arms. We also discussed the next steps in securing Kuwait after an Iraqi withdrawal. The Kuwaitis were keen to see British troops stay on a while, along with other Western and Arab forces, to provide a defensive screen against any renewed Iraqi threat. I responded that I expected we would pull out our units in stages, but Kuwait should be thinking in terms of a GCC and wider Arab contribution to help in the longer term, perhaps under UN aegis. Sulaiman Shahine was not prepared to consider an Arab League force, such as had helped stand guard in Kuwait during the Iraqi threat 30 years before.

As it happened, 25 February was Kuwait's national day, marked by a wave of optimism in which we all shared. In a moving celebration in the Kuwaiti embassy in Riyadh's diplomatic quarter, attended by Prince Saud and Prince Salman, the children of Kuwaitis who had taken refuge in the Kingdom sang of their appreciation and their hopes for a return home, which at last seemed imminent.

A difference was, however, starting to emerge between Saudi and Kuwaiti thinking. The former were making it plain to the Americans, French and ourselves that they wanted our forces either into Kuwait or backloaded from the Kingdom as quickly as possible, with Arab forces or UN contingents replacing them to form a tripwire on the Kuwait–Iraq border. The Kuwaitis, however, had little faith in the deterrent value of their Arab partners and were hanging out for a more concrete Western commitment to carry them through the next phase.

CENTCOM's response at this stage was to air the possibility of establishing an advance headquarters in one of the lower Gulf states, where reaction to the presence of US forces might be less sensitive, and of setting up equipment stockpiles around the area, including the Kingdom – an idea which quickly ran into problems with the Saudis over control. In our own case the initial BFME estimate was that it might take us up to a year to backload all our equipment out through the Kingdom's ports. It was clear to me, however, that we were going to have to speed up this exercise substantially if relations were not to go sour.

By the second day of the land attack there could be no doubt that the resistance of Iraq's forces was crumbling beyond recovery. A few Iraqi units in Kuwait tried to put up a fight, but the great majority had no stomach for it. They had been taken by surprise by the eastward flanking movement of the main coalition armour, and by its speed despite unusually wet conditions. Indeed, the advance was in some danger of being impeded by the thousands of Iraqi soldiers who sought to give themselves up. Even the three Republican Guard divisions to the north, armed with the latest Soviet armour, were putting up only patchy resistance and looking for an escape across the Euphrates over pontoon bridges in the vicinity of Basra, as all fixed bridges had been damaged by air attack.

One group of Iraqi soldiers surrendered to a surprised group of Western journalists who had set off on their own for the front and ran into more action than they had bargained for. We also heard of an American soldier in a jeep who became bogged in mud and thought his number was up when he saw an Iraqi tank approaching. It drew up beside him, whereupon the crew dismounted and towed the jeep out of the mud before giving themselves up to the driver. Baghdad radio during these first two days took on a shrill note, with messages from Iraq's leader urging his troops to fight and kill, while Arabs were incited to attack infidel Western targets anywhere.

Norman Schwarzkopf and the other coalition commanders took advantage of these early successes in the field with bullish press conferences to describe how well things were going. As Schwarzkopf put it in his own forceful style on 25 February, 'I'm going to go around, over, through, on top, underneath and any other way'.

Peter de la Billière spoke in similarly positive terms of the progress of 1st Division. His headquarters in Riyadh were showing much satisfaction at the verve of its two brigades, with their strong artillery support, in overrunning a series of Iraqi armoured positions as they motored north into Iraq on a front shared with two American armoured divisions and then wheeled east to cross into the Kuwaiti desert.

It was evident that the Challengers' gunners were having a field day, being able to outgun the opposition in range and through their crucial advantage of being able to pick out targets at night and in foul weather conditions with the help of the thermal imaging sights with which their tanks were equipped. The Iraqis' Russian armour had nothing to match this new technology. Both tanks and infantry were also greatly helped in the featureless desert conditions by the facility of the GPS satellite navigation system, known as Magellan, which enabled each commander to ascertain his position to within metres with the aid of a hand-held receiver. No longer was there any reason to lose direction in battle.

Above all there was relief that Iraqi units had not sought to introduce their supply of chemical weapons into the battle; the warnings on this appeared to have got through. But from what we heard in Riyadh, some of the infantry engagements were fierce. A soldier of the Staffordshires, Corporal Heaven, was badly wounded in a trench-clearing operation and transferred in an unrecognisable state back to No 33 Field Hospital at Jubail as one of a group of wounded Iraqis. Heavy sedation meant that he was initially unable to communicate with the medical staff, and it was some days before he managed to explain that he was not a prisoner of war but a British soldier. (Corporal Heaven was subsequently chosen as one of a military party invited back two years later by the Kuwaitis to attend the dedication of a memorial to the British personnel who lost their lives in the campaign. The event was marred by a fatal collision between two Kuwaiti helicopters during an air display off the shore. In a courageous sequel to his earlier experience, Corporal Heaven was one of several British servicemen to plunge straight into the oil-filled water to try to free the aircrew, for which he received a commendation for bravery.)

The satisfaction which BFME headquarters was conveying to us was, however, cut brutally short on 26 February by a report of an incident in which, following a successful attack by the 14th/20th Hussars, Royal Scots and 3rd Royal Fusiliers of 4 Brigade on a well-defended Iraqi position, two US aircraft, called up to fire on the brigade's next objective, had attacked in a tragic error one of the Fusiliers' Warrior armoured vehicles, despite coalition identification marks. Nine soldiers were killed and 11 wounded, the largest single loss of life suffered by British forces during the whole campaign.

Peter de la Billière's sense of shock was plain. But he rightly insisted there be no recriminations. Indeed, such incidents were afflicting American units in the offensive to an even greater degree, as tank formations crossed each others' path in the fast-moving battle on a narrow front. The accuracy of modern weapons ensured that friendly fire, or 'blue on blue' actions as they were known, did not miss. Norman Schwarzkopf supported the decision that no hasty judgment on the episode be made while the battle went forward and an inquiry took place. But General Chuck Horner, the USAF commander, showed a more defensive reaction to suggestions that his pilots might have been at fault. I could see that the affair, and the subsequent difference with General Horner, had deeply upset Peter de la Billière's customary calm, as well it might.

This was the day on which the first elements of the coalition forces reached the outskirts of Kuwait City. In last-minute anticipation of military defeat, Baghdad radio that morning sharply reversed its defiant line with an announcement that the Revolutionary Command Council had ordered all Iraqi troops to withdraw from Kuwait to the positions they had held prior to the invasion of 2 August. It was a forlorn attempt to present a rout as an act of policy.

From this point the scenery began to move very rapidly. Later that morning Saddam Hussein himself came on the radio to announce that Kuwait was no longer part of Iraq and that a complete withdrawal would take place within the day. Somewhat unconvincingly, given the rash of white flags appearing all over the theatre, he assured Iraqis that the victory was theirs. This statement gave the signal for a disorderly scramble of Iraqi troops heading north out of Kuwait City, taking all kinds of loot with them along the single highway across the frontier to Basra. On our television screens we saw pictures of Iraqis rejoicing in the streets of Baghdad at the news of withdrawal.

But the celebration was premature. President Bush dismissed Saddam Hussein's announcement with scorn. The only way for Iraq's troops to save themselves was by throwing down their arms. Meanwhile the advance would continue. The Prime Minister gave an equally firm rejection in London, saying there could be no ceasefire until Iraq accepted all the resolutions and her unrenounced threat to Kuwait was removed. It was for the UN to set the terms for a ceasefire, not Iraq. Similarly firm rejections came from the Saudis, French and Italians. The only favourable noises of which we heard came predictably from the USSR, Jordan and Sudan, while within Europe the Spanish government indicated a welcome. The Soviets convened an urgent meeting of the UN Security Council in New York to hear an Iraqi request for a ceasefire, but the session adjourned inconclusively.

On 27 February the coalition advance reached its climax with the entry into Kuwait City of the vanguard of General Khalid bin Sultan's Saudi, Egyptian and Kuwaiti forces to lead the act of liberation. For the past two days and nights they had been methodically ploughing their way through Iraqi obstacles towards the city, taking several thousand prisoners *en route*. Meanwhile the American Marines had encircled the city from the south-east and taken its badly-damaged airport.

After some further chivvying on the part of Norman Schwarzkopf, General Fred Franks' VII Corps had made contact with the main tank forces of two Republican Guard divisions in southern Iraq the preceding night, and was causing heavy damage to them, while the third division started to make its getaway towards Basra. The crucial aim was to cut off their retreat before the Euphrates river, thus catching virtually all Iraq's forces and their equipment in a vast bag. The day brought another inadequate Iraqi call for a ceasefire in return for Iraq's acceptance of three of the resolutions: those concerning withdrawal, an end to annexation, and payment of reparations. But victory was now close, with no less than 29 Iraqi army divisions *hors de combat.* The attack was now to be pressed on the forces pulling out of the capital and, in particular, on the Republican Guard divisions to the north to prevent their escape.

It had been carefully planned among the three Western commanders that as soon as Kuwait City was entered the deserted British, American and French embassies would be taken back into occupation. Peter de la Billière had arranged to give the British task to a boarding party from the Royal Navy's Special Boat Squadron, who formed part of the special forces under his command. There was some laughter up the sleeve in our Riyadh headquarters when, having been given the go-ahead – and the door key – by Colonel Ian Talbot, the BFME armour adviser who had gone ahead to set up an advance headquarters in the remains of Kuwait's airport terminal, the SBS team chose as a precaution to enter the hard way, blowing out the front door, which had stood there since the building was designed for the old Indian Government early in the century. The embassy turned out to be empty and devoid of booby traps, and it was left for the carpenters of the Royal Engineers to repair the damage.

But no one seriously begrudged the moment of drama. Our self-esteem also received a boost when a British diplomat who had joined the first wave to enter Kuwait City was approached in the makeshift airport office by a French special forces officer, who asked if he by any chance knew the location of the French mission. His unit had been tasked to reoccupy it but could not find the place. Their awkward problem was quickly solved by a message back to the FCO, who came up with location and map reference for the grateful French officer.

The forces, both Arab and American, who were first into the capital found themselves fêted by a display of emotion far removed from the undemonstrative reserve characteristic of Arabia. Kuwaitis, many of whom had suffered grievously under the harsh occupation of the past seven months, came out from the refuge of their homes in a release of joy. Our colleague who had helped the French to locate their embassy told me of finding himself mobbed and hugged as he and his party tried to drive their Land Rover with its Union Jack through the streets on arrival. 'It was like Brussels in 1944,' he said. We pointed out that in the case of Kuwait the embraces had presumably been bestowed by males and not the fairer sex.

We saw scenes on Saudi television of Arab troops entering the city to an ecstatic greeting. But the city itself had a grim appearance, accentuated by the dense black smoke from nearby oilwell fires which the Iraqi forces had set since the start of the land offensive, and which was now obscuring the sun and in the oilfields turning day into suffocating night. On the afternoon of 27 February the Saudi joint commander, General Khalid bin Sultan, announced the liberation of the capital, but cautioned the thousands of Kuwaitis in the Kingdom and elsewhere from rushing back to their homes before the city had been made safe for occupation. Following the prompt declaration by the Amir of Kuwait of a state of emergency, General Khalid took action to put all Kuwaiti forces under his command back under the authority of their own government to consolidate order in Kuwait City.

The unexpected speed of the ground advance and the absence of serious resistance on the part of the Iraqi army gave a real lift to all our spirits in Saudi Arabia, which not even the final Scud volleys could dampen. A fresh rash of T-shirt slogans appeared around the British community – mostly on the Scudbuster theme. The school in Riyadh was able to reopen on 23 February with 120 pupils, a strong sign that things were steadier.

Grania and I flew down to Jedda on the evening of 26 February; Lisa Jacobs came too as there was a great deal of FCO telegram traffic flying around at this hectic stage. I found a more relaxed and bullish mood among Saudi business figures than had been the case for many weeks. All were relieved the long period of waiting and uncertainty was almost at an end. In an interview with one of the Arabic-language newspapers I felt able for the first time in months to take a thoroughly positive view of the future.

Everywhere there was a real feeling of comradeship to our meetings. While Grania went with Margaret Tunnell to visit one of our community's schools in the city, I gave a talk to the Jedda British businessmen's association, with the message that now Kuwait was about to be liberated their firms should go out for a share in what we expected to be a huge task of rebuilding the country's ransacked infrastructure, much of it of British origin. A group representing a cross-section of British industry and services was poised to assemble on the east coast prior to establishing itself in Kuwait to co-ordinate opportunities for reconstruction work.

The speed with which the coalition advance had reached Kuwait City meant that plans for the British, American and French ambassadors to reopen their embassies in the capital as soon as conditions permitted suddenly looked like being put into effect on the last day of February. The newly-appointed American ambassador, Skip Gnehm, and the

Frenchman, Jean Bressot, who along with Michael Weston had stayed at his post during much of the Iraqi occupation, were already in Riyadh poised to return. They had spent the preceding weeks ensuring liaison with Kuwaiti ministers in Taif, as Ian Blackley had been doing on our behalf from Jedda.

Michael Weston, who had returned to London after a spell in Taif, was due to fly out to Riyadh via the RAF overnight shuttle on 27 February to be in time for the co-ordinated return. That evening, while I was still in Jedda, he rang through to say that his aircraft was stuck at Brize Norton with little prospect of taking off for several hours. There was a real possibility he might miss the synchronised reopening of missions in Kuwait. Here was 'Murphy' at work again. With all the build-up which had gone into this step, both with the media and as an encouragement to the Kuwaiti government itself to lose no time in re-establishing its authority, we could not afford to have Britain miss the boat.

At a pinch Ian Blackley, who had been accredited to our embassy in Kuwait until the previous summer and was with us in Jedda, could have stood in. But it would not have been the same thing and he had hesitations about doing it. I even thought of asking Peter de la Billière if he could lend us one of his officers now in Kuwait City to raise the flag over our compound. Then Michael Weston rang again with the welcome news that they were about to take off. It would be a close-run thing, but he could transfer directly to a Hercules at Riyadh to get him straight on to Kuwait. For once 'Murphy' had relented.

We flew back to Riyadh late that evening, but as we prepared to board the RAF HS125 at Jedda things nearly went off the rails again. When we were putting our cases through the scanner I noticed Sergeant Andy Worrall, the member of the Military Police close protection team who had accompanied us to Jedda, making feverish signs to me and pointing to his briefcase. 'Come along, Andy,' I said, 'put it through the machine.' 'I can't, sir,' he gasped. Only then did it dawn on me that his 'briefcase' was a very special one cloaking a sub-machine gun which was ready for action as soon as a button on the handle was pressed, causing the case to detach and fall away. The contents could have given the Saudi security official operating the scanner a heart attack. Fortunately he proved to be a broadminded man, and readily took as adequate my hasty explanation that the case belonged to my bodyguard and so need not be examined.

We had a bumpy two-hour flight back in the rain and cloud which had been dogging the land campaign to the north. Coming in to Riyadh's military airport, with rows of American and Saudi radar reconnaissance planes and tankers crammed onto the tarmac, it was almost unreal to think that their job was virtually done, and that the huge military armada which had accumulated all over the Kingdom for so long would soon be dispersed.

On getting back to the embassy around midnight I was greeted with the news of a decision from Washington to bring a suspension of operations into effect from as soon as 8am local time next day. My first reaction was one of surprise. Though Kuwait City had been retaken that day, virtually without a fight, and Iraqi forces were streaming north out of the country, there were still large concentrations of troops in the area between the Kuwaiti frontier and the Euphrates at Basra. These included the three armoured divisions of the Republican Guard, which I had understood it to be among the coalition's objectives to put out of action. But it was late and we were pretty exhausted, so the answers could wait for the morning. At least the war seemed over, which was a great blessing.

Michael Weston turned up early next morning for a quick tidy-up at the house before going on to Kuwait to reopen the embassy. It was a day of cloud and rain, made yet darker by the pall of oily smoke drifting south from the well fires across Kuwait, 500 kilometres to the north. The heavy smell of crude oil was in the air and the rain brought down streaks of soot. We sent Michael Weston on his way with plenty of rations, as there was no way of knowing what conditions would be like. I undertook to come up with more supplies and keep him and his colleagues replenished from Riyadh as soon as pressures permitted.

In the event the Kuwaiti government tarried two more days before the Prime Minister, Crown Prince Saad, re-entered the city from which he and other members of the Al Sabah family had departed in such abrupt fashion in the small hours of 2 August the preceding summer for sanctuary in Saudi Arabia. We were concerned that with each day that passed without visible re-establishment of the Al Sabah's authority, those elements in Kuwait which had so courageously resisted the occupation and its brutalities would take things into their own hands and indulge in acts of retribution against suspected collaborators, particularly among the large Palestinian community, which would tarnish Kuwait's reputation at large.

The Crown Prince first paid an important and ceremonious call on King Fahd at the Al Yamamah palace in Riyadh on 1 March, when he asserted that Kuwait would never forget the stand taken by the King and the Saudi people in resisting Iraq's aggression and seeing things through to the liberation of Kuwait and the final ejection of Iraq. He pledged closer co-operation with the Kingdom in the future. It was a well-deserved tribute, and suggested a lesson learnt too.

In his reply, which was given wide publicity, King Fahd commended

Kuwait's spirit of resistance and pointedly looked forward to a new spirit
of national unity under Al Sabah leadership. He rehearsed his conviction
that it had been Saddam Hussein's intention to extend his control over
the whole of the Gulf's Arab coastline, and went so far as to hope that a
new and responsible government would now emerge in Iraq. The Iraqi
people had nothing to gain from a tyrant as their leader. The King had
hard words for those Arab states which had sided with Iraq's aggression,
and with an eye to the future he held out an olive branch to Iran across
the Gulf.

The decision to call an early halt to the land campaign has been
much debated since the Gulf War, with the suggestion that it was fum-
bled by the American leadership. Certainly I found my own surprise at its
sudden application shared by Saudi contacts on the morning of 28
February, when it came into effect. We knew it had never been the Saudi
intention to see the coalition forces carry the advance deep into Iraq,
nor to leave her without the ability to defend her territory against possible encroachment or dismemberment from other neighbouring
quarters in the aftermath of war. In our own minds we were clear that an
occupation of Iraq would not only overstep the bounds of the UN
Security Council's authorisation and alienate Arab opinion, but would
also draw the Western partners in the coalition directly into Iraq's political morass. It had been assumed therefore that those elements of the
Republican Guard which had been held in reserve north of the
Euphrates and around Baghdad would survive without damage.

The Guard's armoured and infantry divisions in southern Iraq were
another matter. If they were allowed to get away without the loss of their
modern equipment, they would reinforce a continuing threat to Kuwait
and the Kingdom. It looked as though some portion of these forces was
now slipping north across the river near Basra, where the Americans had
not yet had time to close the top of their encircling bag. Moreover, there
was no sign of the forecast uprising against the Iraqi leadership from
within the army or other quarters. Although President Bush's announcement early that morning local time, to the effect that Kuwait's liberation
was complete and the military objectives of the international coalition
had been met with the defeat of Iraq's army, had been cleared with all
partners, there was still a certain ruefulness and unease detectable in the
Saudi reaction that day.

From the background which Peter de la Billière gave me that morning on the decision as it had developed at CENTCOM in Riyadh, it also
looked as though General Schwarzkopf had himself been taken aback by
the sudden anxiety in Washington to halt the offensive before the net
had been finally drawn tight in front of Basra and the river. It was

suggested that those taking the decisions in the White House had been made nervous by initial reports in the press of the decimation met by fleeing Iraqi troops as they scrambled out of Kuwait City along the single highway over the Mutla Ridge to the north, and became sitting ducks for coalition pilots. There was concern, shared at senior military levels in London, over the possibility of a deeply negative public reaction emerging were the rout to turn into a 'turkey shoot'.

Yet the line of retreat for Republican Guard units and other Iraqi forces south of Basra had not been fully cut off. It was clear that VII Corps still had some way to go. The British 1st Division had successfully completed a gallop in the last hours before the early morning ceasefire which brought it astride the road north out of Kuwait, amid the shambles of the Iraqi retreat. By this time they had with their Challengers destroyed some 200 Iraqi tanks, as well as artillery and other armoured vehicles, while several thousand prisoners had been passed to the rear in a demoralised state, helped along by their captors with some decent rations.

The American armoured divisions leading the corps' attack were still engaged in fierce fighting to the north with two of the Republican Guard's three armoured divisions, and had yet to make contact with the third. The thirsty gas turbines of the Abrams tanks, for which the latest Soviet T72s of the Guard were proving no match in firepower, appeared to be near the limit of their fuel replenishment chain. Nevertheless it seemed clear that another 24 hours of offensive could have meant putting these powerful units beyond further operations. This, we had understood, was what Norman Schwarzkopf had in mind, a position which in a press interview some months later he suggested had been the case. But he loyally came into line, rounding off with an ebullient press briefing on the evening of 27 February in which he described the various phases of his victorious campaign and its successful deception strategy in fascinating detail.

Still, for reasons not fully clear at the time, President Bush, with the support of his military and political staff, decided to blow the whistle. In practice, although another day for mopping up would have been useful, the escape of one mauled Republican Guard division across the Euphrates was not going to make a significant difference to Saddam Hussein's ability to salvage his greatly-reduced fighting capability or military prestige. He had already taken the precaution of keeping a proportion of his strength out of the battle for Kuwait. Meanwhile, soldiers' lives would be saved. Yet some Iraqi armour did get away, to reappear within weeks in the repression of internal uprising.

Subsequent debate has focused on such issues as whether it was understood in Washington that there was still some way to go before the encirclement was complete and Norman Schwarzkopf's 'gate was closed'; whether coalition pilots and tank crews had the will to go on hammering a beaten enemy; and whether public opinion, including that in Britain, would stomach scenes of savage destruction on its television screens. All these factors may have played a part in some degree, though we had no reason to believe that our own government was pressing for a premature truce.

At the time, however, the case for a halt, as justified by the coalition commanders, seemed convincing enough, even if it left a feeling more of relief than elation that the war was so quickly over, and with a lingering sense of unfinished business. Anyhow there was little time for reflection. We had plenty to get on with as we watched to see if Iraq would respect the suspension of hostilities, and turned our attention urgently with our headquarters to the meeting between senior military commanders of the coalition and Iraq to establish a formal military ceasefire, which President Bush had stipulated should be convened within 48 hours.

CHAPTER 16

Anticlimax

'Better they do it imperfectly than you do it perfectly, for it is
their country, their war and your time is limited.'

T. E. Lawrence (of Arabia): *The Seven Pillars of Wisdom*

The impression has been current, ever since President Bush made his
historic statement on 27 February in which he called for a suspension of
hostilities with effect from midnight New York time that night, that having decisively won the war the coalition went on to bungle the peace.
Certainly there were false assumptions made about the consequences for
Iraq's discredited leadership of the fact that the 'mother of all battles'
had ended in humiliating rout.

   The ability of Saddam Hussein to reassert his despotic rule over both
his defeated army and a significant core of the Ba'ath political machine,
and to use them to reassert his authority over his countrymen through
ruthless suppression of insurgency among the Shi'a of the south and the
Kurds in the north, confounded predictions which we had all been
making, Saudis and Kuwaitis just as much as their Arab and Western
partners, over the likelihood of the tyrant's imminent overthrow at the
hands of his people. There were catches dropped, too, in the preparation and outcome of the military ceasefire talks, which the two joint
commanders hurriedly arranged with Iraq's military representatives at
an airstrip under American occupation at Safwan in the desert area of
southern Iraq.

   Yet in practice, although the outcome had its inconclusive and untidy
aspects, it nevertheless succeeded in assembling a skein of controls and
deterrent measures which have so far sufficed to contain the Iraqi
regime's potential for a resumption of aggressive behaviour and adventurism towards its neighbours during the five years following its defeat in
Kuwait. In this time, moreover, certain key requirements set by the UN
have been secured, notably the recognition by Iraq of Kuwait and her
newly-delineated frontier, and the dismantling, despite constant obstruction, of much of Iraq's immediate capability in chemical and biological

315

weapons and long-range missiles, together with her well-advanced nuclear programme.

Above all, these pressures have been sustained with a remarkable degree of solidarity by the international community under the authority of the UN Security Council. The dividend of conflict has thus been by no means negative in terms of the restoration of security in this important yet volatile region, despite its high price in terms of hardship and repression for the Iraqi people, whom Saddam Hussein has continued to hold to ransom by his failure as yet to fulfil all the conditions laid upon him as a result of his ill-judged aggression.

The decisive stand taken by the international coalition, and not least by its Arab members, also produced significant bonuses in other quarters. Notable among these was the opportunity it created for a fresh and more pragmatic approach from all sides towards negotiations over a settlement of the intractable Arab–Israel dispute – a road which was to lead to the watershed conference in Madrid only eight months later. Other problems besetting the Middle East region also drew indirect benefit from the confrontation with Iraq: the Saudis were able to put their relations with Iran back on a working basis, as indeed was Britain, a step which helped secure the release of British hostages held in Lebanon by groups sympathetic to Iran; the right-wing Maronite faction in Lebanon, under General Michel Aoun, which had resisted by force of arms the settlement brokered by Saudi Arabia at Taif in 1989, lost its main prop in the shape of Iraqi support; and Syria also finally came in from the cold.

The crisis over Kuwait had other repercussions upon political conventions and relationships among Arab states themselves. For Saudi Arabia and her Gulf partners, the shock of Iraq's aggression and their inability on their own to forestall, let alone withstand, the threat to their security discredited some cherished assumptions about the inviolability of the principle of Arab unity. It also gave birth to debate on the business of government on an unprecedented scale, and emboldened sections of the community to press for a role in discussion of policy.

In Saudi Arabia political ideas began to be voiced which even questioned the social contract that had served the Kingdom well enough hitherto. They ranged on one side from calls for wider public participation in government and the dismantling of some of the more restrictive regulations which, in deference to the Kingdom's puritanical religious traditions, governed many aspects of social behaviour for both men and women, to a countervailing movement rooted in some mosques which argued for a yet more rigorous application of religious orthodoxy and the judging of all government actions according to strict 'Islamic' criteria, to be set by the religious establishment. Saudi Arabia would never be quite the same again, and for King Fahd and the Al Saud family the path to be steered between advocates of theocracy and of modernist reform called for a new degree of deftness and sensitivity.

All these developments lay imperceptibly ahead of us as the embassy got down in the first days of March to the work of liaison with the Saudis and our own military over steps to ensure a ceasefire, to be followed by a secure peace and our orderly withdrawal. In his call for hostilities to be suspended on the morning of 28 February after only 100 hours of land battle, President Bush proposed action in parallel in the UN Security Council and on the military front in theatre to consolidate this into a more formal arrangement.

It quickly became apparent that, so far as the political track was concerned, the range of requirements which Iraq should be called upon to fulfil in consequence of her aggression against Kuwait and her wider threat to the security of the area needed to be discussed in rather slower time. Accordingly the Americans proposed a two-stage approach through the UN Security Council, beginning with a short resolution to hold the ceasefire in place. A draft was quickly prepared by the Americans and our own mission in New York, calling on Iraq to accept the Council's 12 previous resolutions on the crisis, including renunciation of her annexation of Kuwait and agreement to pay reparations, plus the release of all prisoners, co-operation over removal of mines, and return of stolen property. Hostile acts including missile attacks and flights by combat aircraft had to cease. This initial Resolution 686 was approved unanimously by the Council on 3 March, and accepted by Iraq the following day.

The preparation of this draft resolution produced an incongruous exchange at our end. I happened to be going over its ingredients by telephone with Prince Saud on the preceding evening when a call came through from a friend in London on another line asking my urgent advice on the sale of a painting through Sotheby's. I told my caller that I had more pressing matters of policy in hand, but he was insistent. Overhearing this exchange, which had interrupted our conversation, Prince Saud asked if there was a problem. On learning what was up he gently suggested that I deal with Sotheby's first and come back to him. It was this nice sense of humour which made our frequent transactions a pleasure throughout all the pressures of the crisis.

Plans were being laid at the Riyadh end for General Norman Schwarzkopf and General Khalid bin Sultan, accompanied by the commanders of the other coalition forces involved in the action to liberate Kuwait, to meet two senior representatives of the Iraqi military at the

Safwan airfield for the purpose of spelling out the coalition's conditions for the military aspects of the ceasefire. This meeting was not an occasion for a formal surrender, but was nevertheless to be a conspicuous affair in the full glare of the world's media. A press briefing would follow, giving an opportunity to confirm publicly Iraq's failure to get away with her seizure of Kuwait.

From the outset, however, we had an uncomfortable feeling that the Safwan event was being rushed by the American military. There was an embarrassing hiccup at the start when, having settled on Safwan as the venue, it emerged that VII Corps were still short of this objective at the time of the halt to hostilities on 28 February. A show of force by General Rhame's 1st Infantry Division was hastily ordered by Norman Schwarzkopf to remove the detachment of the Revolutionary Guard still occupying the airfield. They fortunately withdrew without a shot having to be fired, thus averting an embarrassing incident. Elsewhere in southern Iraq, however, an armoured column of the Republican Guard tried to break through the American screen two days after the fighting ended. It was destroyed in a fierce engagement. Our reaction was a grim one of good riddance; a few less Iraqi tanks left to fight another day.

The Safwan meeting finally took place on 3 March. I was surprised to hear from Peter de la Billière that he and other national commanders were not to be seated in the front rank in the conference tent, but were rather attending in the capacity of observers. Indeed, at one point it looked as though we would need to press for their participation at all. Nor was CENTCOM giving its partners much of a sight of the agenda, or the conditions which with Washington's approval it was proposed to put to the Iraqi side. The meeting looked like turning into a somewhat unscripted event and, so far as we could see, without much input on the political side. I knew from talks with our Foreign Ministry colleagues that the Saudis also had reservations on this count.

We were all starting to come to terms with the discouraging possibility that Saddam Hussein might yet survive the ignominy of defeat, and that sanctions and other pressures would have to be sustained on his regime for a while to come. The face-to-face encounter at Safwan thus afforded an important opportunity to transmit the coalition's common resolve. It also emerged that General Prince Khalid was unhappy to find the Americans had settled for the Iraqis to be represented at a step below the most senior military level, by two lieutenants-general, one the deputy chief of staff and the other the commander of the defeated III Corps. In Arab eyes this could constitute a propaganda gain for the Iraqi regime; as he subsequently told me, General Khalid considered the Americans should, and could, have held out for a member of Saddam

Hussein's Revolutionary Command Council to participate in this act of submission.

We shared this concern that the American military should not monopolise the agenda. Together with the Saudis and Kuwaitis, we had a particular interest in ensuring that provision was made at Safwan for the repatriation of civilian detainees in Iraqi hands as well as our prisoners of war. The Kuwaitis put the number of their civilians rounded up and taken off to prison in Iraq in the course of the occupation at several thousand, and the Saudis claimed several of their citizens were being similarly held. In the event the International Committee of the Red Cross subsequently supervised the repatriation of over 6,600 Kuwaitis, though a number still remained unaccounted for thereafter.

The Iraqi round-ups were confirmed to me later by a member of the Kuwaiti Al Sabah family, who described how he and scores of others, some of whom had been active in the resistance, were carted off by truck to imprisonment in Baghdad shortly before the air war began. Their harsh treatment in captivity had apparently improved once the effect of coalition air raids began to suggest to their Iraqi gaolers that defeat was on the cards, in contrast to military prisoners, many of whom were viciously handled up to the finish.

For our own part we had instructions from the FCO to make sure that the cases of British citizens held in Iraq were included in the details of detainees which were to be handed over to the Iraqi representatives at Safwan. The individuals in question were Douglas Brand, who had been caught and convicted of trying to escape from detention in Iraq during the hostage episode, and Ian Richter, a businessman working in Iraq who had been held in prison in Baghdad for some five years. His arrest on charges which we regarded as trumped up had been the subject of sharp protest by the British government during my previous stint in London, and repeated attempts over the years to secure his release, both by direct approach to the Iraqi leadership and through the intercession of intermediaries such as King Hussein. But these had got nowhere with an Iraqi government resentful of Britain's criticism of its human rights record and policy of denying military supplies during the war with Iran.

Now that a concerted approach was to be made by the victorious coalition to secure the release of all detainees, we had no doubt that Ian Richter deserved to be among them. A third Briton, Peter Bluff, who had gone missing with a CBS news team near the Kuwaiti border in January and was known to be held in Baghdad, was promptly released by the Iraqis at the end of hostilities.

Peter de la Billière got back to Riyadh from Safwan during the afternoon and gave me a run-down on how the meeting had gone. It had evidently been a theatrical affair, with Norman Schwarzkopf dominating the discussion, supported by Prince Khalid bin Sultan seated beside him. The other commanders had been ranged behind and had taken no active part. Peter de la Billière had managed to have the names of our detainees included in the lists which had been handed across. The case for immediate release had been firmly pressed on behalf of Kuwaitis, Saudis and other nationalities by Prince Khalid. The Iraqi representatives had responded evasively.

As for the general course of the meeting, I had the impression from Peter de la Billière's account, and from the pictures we had seen on television that morning, that the American command had indeed gone more for effect than for substance. It came as a surprise to learn that no written record had been taken; instead, a tape recording had been made for each side. Fortunately Colin Ferbrache, Peter's personal staff officer, had made his own notes. We agreed he should write these up forthwith while his recollection was still fresh. The Iraqis had been generally acquiescent over the conditions presented to them by Norman Schwarzkopf to govern the military stand-off. But the discussions did not sound to have been conclusive.

This was soon to turn out to have been the case, when within days the Iraqi forces abused a concession they had obtained from General Schwarzkopf over the use of helicopters for communications purposes, by arming these aircraft and using them with deadly effect against the civil uprisings in Basra and other southern cities. As a chagrined Norman Schwarzkopf was subsequently to complain, he had been 'suckered'. On emerging from the conference tent the two joint commanders were beset by the media. Relations between them were not helped by the intrusive CNN microphone catching an abrupt aside of 'don't answer that one' from Norman Schwarzkopf to his Saudi comrade in arms, facing an awkward question from a journalist. The reproof came across distinctly as we watched in Riyadh.

The relationship between the two men, who technically shared command of the international coalition, had predictably had its ups and downs. To some extent it was bound to be uneasy, given the disparity between the two commanders in terms of military experience and forces under their command. This predicament was further aggravated by differences in temperament.

Norman Schwarzkopf had gained a reputation for a short temper and a tendency to ride roughshod over contradiction, to the point where his own staff and commanders were wary of him. At the same time he was a thoroughly professional operator, with a flair for tactics and a determination not to be rushed into action before he was sure of gaining the day.

Very much a soldier's general, his concern for their well-being and to minimise casualties in battle endeared him to the servicemen and women. Having experienced at first hand the military humiliation of Vietnam, he was determined to restore through victory the self-respect of the US Army, an objective he achieved abundantly. Throughout the crisis the conduct of his troops was exemplary.

It was not surprising, therefore, that Prince Khalid should occasionally react with an Arab's sensitivity to this awkward tandem. He had his own quality of decisiveness, which he brought into play effectively at a number of stages in commanding the widely-assorted Arab and Moslem wing of the coalition force. At the same time he was by nature a conciliator, using his genial manner to feel his way towards solutions. Moreover, he carried responsibility for the intensely complex logistic arrangements for making facilities available within the Kingdom to around half a million American troops and their equipment, as well as to other coalition contingents. He and his staff had achieved this feat in impressive fashion. Prince Khalid was also in the lead over operations for the defence of the Kingdom itself, as we had seen in his command of the successful operation to repel the Iraqi incursion at Al Khafji, as well as answering to the King and to his father, Prince Sultan, for the overall handling of military issues. All this added up to a major field of responsibility.

Yet to their credit both commanders kept their sentiments towards each other within bounds. Norman Schwarzkopf duly showed consideration for the lesser experience of his younger counterpart, and for Saudi sensitivity over their status as an equal in the alliance. His own familiarity with the ways of the region, deriving from his upbringing across the Gulf in Iran, where his father had been involved with the Shah's gendarmerie, may have made a fortuitous contribution here. Similarly Norman Schwarzkopf's relationships with Peter de la Billière and the other national commanders were marked by restraint and goodwill, though he was known to be less genial with his subordinates in the American chain of command.

For his part Prince Khalid did everything to ensure the command arrangements operated smoothly, and deferred with good spirit to American overall direction of the offensive into Kuwait and Iraq. The cooperation may have owed something to the particular sense of trust and friendship which developed between Prince Khalid and Peter de la Billière. The two men met often in Prince Khalid's headquarters suite in the Defence Ministry, giving a private chance to compare notes and offer advice as the military scene developed. Prince Khalid had after all begun his officer training with the British Army at Sandhurst, and was at ease with its ways.

The Safwan meeting thus concluded on a somewhat unsatisfactory note, leaving us in Riyadh with the impression of business unfinished and of tricks missed in the haste of the American military to get the Iraqis to the table. The absence of a signed document looked to be a significant omission, affording scope for subsequent dispute over the conditions set by the coalition. The meeting did, however, achieve prompt Iraqi action over the release of prisoners of war, including 12 British RAF and Special Forces personnel, as well as 17 Americans, nine Saudis, a Kuwaiti pilot and the crew of an Italian Tornado. But there were still over 60,000 Iraqi prisoners of war in coalition hands. The bodies of dead military personnel were also returned, with eight British among them.

But the issue of detainees was unresolved, and required a series of further meetings in Riyadh and Geneva during the ensuing weeks under the aegis of the International Committee of the Red Cross, in which the Iraqis first sought unsuccessfully to deny they were holding Kuwaiti civilians and then proceeded to understate the numbers. Derek Plumbly and Peter Gooderham participated with BFME headquarters in the sessions of tough talking held in Riyadh during March, in which our detainees figured on the agenda.

The British government had set a good example to the Iraqis by its scrupulously correct treatment of the troops which our forces had taken prisoner in battle, as well as by the release within a week of the ceasefire of the small number of Iraqi citizens whom it had been considered prudent to intern in Britain at the outset of hostilities. We succeeded in getting Douglas Brand out of Iraq in the middle of the month, but eventually had to separate the Richter case from this process, as Iraqi insistence that it had no connection with the war was threatening to hold up progress over other major ceasefire issues.

Ian Richter's release was eventually obtained by the FCO later in the year following intercession with the Iraqi leadership by Prince Sadruddin Khan, the UN High Commissioner for Refugees, and in return for our agreement to unblock a sizeable portion of Iraq's assets for the purchase of medical and other humanitarian supplies through the British Red Cross. This last action had the approval of the committee set up in New York by the UN Security Council to oversee the application of sanctions. It nevertheless caused Prince Saud to raise his eyebrows at me, and question whether the concession was not inconsistent with our shared wish to see Saddam Hussein's control over his people weakened through the maintenance of sanctions.

The exchange of prisoners of war began on 5 March, with Red Cross chartered aircraft flying the first instalment of Iraqi prisoners to Baghdad

and bringing the first coalition prisoners back to Riyadh. An early problem arose with the repatriation of Iraqis, as a large number refused to go
home for fear of what the regime might do to them by way of retribution.
This was an eventuality which had not been foreseen by the authors of the
1949 Geneva Conventions on the conduct of war. There was no question
of forcing them. In an inspired move, King Fahd found a way round the
problem by declaring those who refused repatriation to be refugees in
Saudi Arabia, thus changing their status at a stroke.

The coalition prisoners arrived in Riyadh in cheerful form, but had
clearly had an unpleasant and degrading time in captivity. Some had suffered physical abuse in flagrant breach of Iraq's obligations under the
Geneva Conventions. It was only with the ceasefire that the Iraqis hon-
oured the requirement to allow access to prisoners of war by the ICRC.
For some the shock of sudden release after incarceration in hostile captivity was considerable. One of the RAF aircrew forced to bale out over
Iraq was handed over by his Iraqi guards at a Baghdad hotel to a pretty
young woman in Red Cross uniform, who was to escort him to the airport. 'Who will be protecting us?' he wanted to know. 'I shall,' she
replied. 'Then who will protect you?' he asked dubiously. 'This is my protection,' she replied, pointing to her Red Cross badge, and led him out
to freedom.

These complex moves over arrangements for a definitive ceasefire,
both on the ground and at the UN in New York, were coinciding with
important political developments on other fronts. Within Iraq reports
began to reach us, even before the Safwan meeting, of unrest among the
largely Shi'a population of Basra and the other southern cities adjacent
to the territory now occupied by American forces as a demilitarised
zone. Hopes began to run high that this might be the beginning of the
end for Iraq's regime, particularly when a few days later there were signs
of similar insurrection among the Kurdish population of northern Iraq.

In Kuwait Crown Prince Saad finally returned home, accompanied by
his ministers, on 5 March and set about the work of re-establishing Al
Sabah authority over a society whose political conventions had been
shaken up by the experience of occupation and resistance. Scores were
already being settled and it was important to see a stop put to summary
reprisals, particularly against members of the large Palestinian community, some of whose members were being accused of collaborating with
the Iraqis.

Intercession on this front was a major feature of Michael Weston's
contacts with the Kuwaitis during the first weeks of recovery. Such pressure on the part of ourselves and the Americans for the restoration of
the due process of law did have some success in restraining excesses,

despite initial vindictiveness and the understandably hostile mood towards anyone suspected of collaboration with an occupation which had caused Kuwaitis much brutal suffering. Those who had played an active part in Kuwait's active resistance movement, many of whom came from the Shi'a community and so tended to be traditionally less attached to the ruling family, were not easily persuaded to lay down their newly-acquired arms and allow the re-establishment of Al Sabah authority. Resentment was apparent on the part of those who had stayed against their countrymen who had sought refuge abroad.

There was the occasional windfall to be had from occupation. We heard of one Kuwaiti who returned to his house, which had been commandeered by an Iraqi officer. The car had been gathering dust in the garage. It was sent in for a service, when the door panels were discovered to be stuffed with gold bars – loot which the occupier had left behind in the rush to escape.

Meanwhile the Amir remained out of sight in Saudi Arabia. A heady mood of wider political representation was in the air, however, and would have to be taken into account by the Al Sabah. The comment in an American newspaper that Kuwait had been made safe for feudalism was a touch uncharitable, though change was not about to come overnight.

In Saudi Arabia the swift victory produced a mood of quiet relief and satisfaction, both at the outcome and in the expectation that life would soon return to its customary state of prosperous insulation. Relations with ourselves and the other Western partners were marked by a friendliness at both government and public level which was probably unprecedented in the Kingdom's 60 years of existence. A few days after the ceasefire we took our first break for some weeks to drive with friends, although still accompanied by our military police team, on an expedition to a lake-bed deep in the dunes below the Tuwaiq escarpment. The still beauty of our surroundings was a tonic, while all along the main highway out of the city we found ourselves exchanging waves and victory signs with Saudi families in their cars. We hardly encountered a checkpoint; the Kingdom clearly wished to put the crisis behind it as quickly as possible.

It was widely assumed that the uprisings within Iraq would soon provoke the overthrow of Saddam Hussein and permit a resumption of Saudi Arabia's traditionally positive relationship with Iraq. The whole Kuwait crisis constituted an embarrassing blot on the record of Arab unity. Crown Prince Abdullah, who among Al Saud ministers probably best understood Iraq, and whose condemnation of Saddam Hussein's actions was vehement, expressed the opinion to me that the ignominy of defeat would bring about the tyrant's removal at the hands of his own army. General Khalid bin Sultan dropped a broad hint in similar terms during a press briefing in Kuwait soon after liberation.

Prince Bandar bin Sultan, the influential Saudi ambassador in Washington, who had played a key part in keeping the Kingdom and the Bush administration in step as the crisis evolved through its most crucial stages, called on John Major in Downing Street just after the ceasefire and expressed the expectation that Iraq's army would rise within a comparatively short period against its discredited leader. He was relieved we had all refused to go along with the ill-conceived Soviet plan for a diplomatic solution halfway through the war, when Saddam Hussein would have been free to salvage his army as well as his reputation.

But this mood of confidence was to prove shortlived. As the days drew into weeks and Saddam Hussein consolidated his hold over his cowed country, so hopes of his fall diminished, to be replaced by a realisation that a long and difficult game of pressure and vigilance still lay ahead. The onset of the fasting month of Ramadan in mid-March, with its dampening effect on public vitality, took some of the spring out of people's steps. It also provided a platform for a more serious backlash at the popular level, fostered by resentful proponents of religious conservatism, now back from their wartime rustication and determined to eradicate all traces of contagion from the infidel forces which had been made so welcome by Saudi Arabia during the crisis.

All these features on the political landscape called for close attention by our embassy, at a time when our numbers were stretched by the need for people to take the extra leave awarded to them for their tireless performance during the crisis. We arranged to take it in turns to have a break over the spring period. It had been an enormous advantage for the continuity of our work together during the long months of crisis that most of us were in the full flush of our spells in the Kingdom and well acquainted with its ways. Almost no one was due for early departure. All had shown real dedication and great good humour, even when the going got rough. This indomitable spirit had been fully shared by our community at large, and once we were all thrown in together even the British press dropped its alarmist tone.

But we were all starting to feel the cumulative effect of fatigue as a result of continuing under such pressure for weeks on end. Concentration was faltering and fuses were becoming a bit short. In addition the remorseless social round, Saudi as well as expatriate, looked like reasserting itself with the ending of hostilities and the threat of Scud attack. Yet there could be no letting up. A new flood of visitors was on its way to us: ministers, commanders, parliamentarians, businessmen, environmentalists – the lot. The only ones to head in the reverse direction were the journalists, in search of new crises.

Some visitors came to congratulate our forces in Kuwait, Saudi Arabia and elsewhere in the theatre on a job well done, and to see at first hand how things looked for the next stages. We had good cause to show pride in the performance of all three services in the campaign, as well as in the care they had taken during the months of waiting to show respect to Saudi society. The headquarters attributed much of this harmony to the ban on alcohol, and certainly there was hardly an instance of ill-behaviour. Instead the task in hand and the stern conditions of the desert imposed their own discipline and close comradeship. Withdrawal was now at the top of the agenda for the politicians and the military, plus provision for the region's future security.

The first to visit us was Tom King, a welcome and familiar figure by now to ourselves and the Saudis. His relationship with Peter de la Billière had not always gone smoothly during the fighting. There had on occasion been a feeling within the BFME headquarters that he was getting too involved with the detail of the campaign, as well as cutting across their intensive relationship with the media in theatre. In our own contacts, whether through the FCO or direct, Tom King had been invariably positive and ready to help with issues that arose in our relations with Prince Sultan and the Saudi military establishment. He had also done his bit to head off unreasonable pressures from the Treasury and other quarters, which might have inhibited the ability of British forces to carry out their task, though there were minor issues over things such as allowances where he had not got his way.

Tom King arrived in Riyadh on the evening after the Safwan talks. We had a very friendly meeting that night with Prince Sultan, marked by mutual satisfaction at the success of the campaign and the way in which our military co-operation had worked over the preceding months. Saudi public opinion, too, had rallied well in the face of hostilities against a fellow Arab state. Both ministers saw a need to keep up the pressure to dislodge Saddam Hussein. At the same time a dilemma was apparent between action to punish Iraq further and the risk that this might have the effect of weakening Baghdad's central authority, with the latest uprisings opening the way to partition and perhaps affording Iran the opportunity to assert her influence.

When Prince Sultan spoke of plans for closer Gulf defence co-operation, Tom King encouraged this and welcomed the idea of Egyptian and Syrian help with future security, plans for which were due to be finalised at a meeting between the Syrians, Egyptians and the six GCC states in Damascus that week. For our part we firmly supported stronger regional defence arrangements. We would soon be withdrawing our forces, but had it in mind to retain the Royal Navy's Armilla patrol in the Gulf. We could also consider occasional joint exercises with local forces with whom we had close connections. Tom King pointed to how our co-operation with the RSAF had been proved in war, and suggested we might now widen this co-operation, building on our experience of combat together. For his part Prince Sultan welcomed a continuing role for the Royal Navy, but urged that our land forces be concentrated in Kuwait as soon as possible. The underlying Saudi sensitivity over the presence of foreign forces on its territory was already reasserting itself.

Tom King's visit gave an opportunity for discussion, together with David Craig, the Chief of Defence Staff, who was also out on a prompt post-war visit, of the mechanics of withdrawal and relocation of our forces. There was a background of considerable apprehensiveness to this exercise, as the ending of hostilities was coinciding with the preparation of far-reaching proposals in Whitehall for post-Cold War reductions in the strength of Britain's armed forces under the 'Options for Change' exercise, for which Tom King was responsible. Some military personnel could be returning to the prospect of redundancy. It was evident that politicians at home were already impatient to pull out of the Gulf. Yet, as we made clear to the Defence Secretary, we still had only a provisional and precarious ceasefire.

It was decided that withdrawal could begin within days, starting with the return of the territorial military hospital based at Riyadh airport. Mercifully the predicted high level of casualties had not materialised out of the lightning offensive, and in any case the NHS needed its staff back. Meanwhile, the headquarters would set in hand plans for its own early run-down and the concentration of our rear party at Jubail to undertake the lengthy process of backloading all the land equipment.

No sooner had Tom King departed than the Prime Minister arrived, having decided to fit in a quick detour to Saudi Arabia and Kuwait on the return leg of a visit to the USSR. He came into Dhahran at the grim hour of 4.30am in torrential rain. We took him to the sumptuously-appointed royal guest palace for a brief turnaround to change and have a briefing in preparation for his call on King Fahd in Riyadh later that evening. Despite lack of sleep, John Major was in lively form and looking forward to visiting British troops in Kuwait. While we were talking in his suite he asked my advice on what to wear for a day to be divided between soldiers in the battlefield and a call on Crown Prince Saad, reinstalled in his office in Kuwait City. We opted for informality in the shape of a jersey and slacks. It came as a shock to see the conversation on this point of detail lampooned almost word for word in *Private Eye* magazine a couple of weeks later. Some journalist in the party accompanying the Prime Minister had come to know his subject pretty well.

Having seen the Prime Minister, accompanied by his private secretary, Charles Powell, off in a RAF Hercules to Kuwait with Peter de la Billière, I went on to a briefing session in Al Khobar with a pioneer group of British businessmen who had volunteered to form the vanguard of our operation to secure a share of work in Kuwait's reconstruction. Late in the afternoon John Major returned from Kuwait and was given a boisterous greeting by the RAF Tornado crews and BAe technicians working with the RSAF at Dhahran airbase. We also drove out to see the vast bomb and ammunition storage park which our forces had set up in a corner of the huge airfield. The Prime Minister reacted with exhilaration to his welcome. The aircrews made it plain to him, as the soldiers had done in Kuwait earlier in the day, that they were looking for an early return home. The Prime Minister's ready commitment on this point was to give us problems in the weeks ahead.

The day in Kuwait had not, however, been plain sailing. Rain and sandstorms, as well as dense smoke from the oil fires, had forced diversion to another airstrip in order to reach the troops in the desert. A second aircraft carrying the press party could not follow, with the result that the journalists missed the Prime Minister's encounter to congratulate those he had seen on their way into battle only eight weeks earlier. They did catch up with the party for the Kuwait City stage, but raised a fuss which quickly came bouncing back to us in Dhahran, not that there was anything we could do about the predicament. But the mishap unsettled the Prime Minister and his party.

By the time we all reached Riyadh from Dhahran that evening for a meeting with King Fahd, the Prime Minister was becoming anxious to avoid delay in taking off for the overnight flight back to London, where he had a Cabinet meeting the next morning. Those of us familiar with the King's predilection for nocturnal meetings were keeping our fingers crossed. This encounter, within days of the successful end to hostilities, represented a consummation of our months of close alliance to counter Iraq's aggression, and would set the scene for an even stronger association in the future. There was much at stake for both countries, and from Britain's point of view not least the response which King Fahd had promised to the Prime Minister's request for a contribution towards the costs of our military deployment to help see off Saddam Hussein's threat.

John Major was met at Riyadh's military airport by the governor of Riyadh, Prince Salman, and the Minister of Petroleum and Mines, Hisham Nazer, who had been appointed to escort him. The meeting with King Fahd, which took place after slight delay in the King's villa in the grounds of the Al Yamamah palace, was every bit as friendly and positive as we could have hoped. It was an occasion for mutual congratulations over the way the coalition had arrived with so little loss of life at its objective of seeing Iraq out of Kuwait. King Fahd spoke warmly of the contribution made by British troops and also by our community who had stayed on to support the Kingdom, while the Prime Minister paid a genuine tribute to the King's tenacity of purpose to see Iraq's invasion reversed, and his achievement in mobilising and holding together the unprecedented international coalition.

There was a hope in our minds that the unrest now spreading through Iraq would bring a change of regime and spell the end of Saddam Hussein. At the same time there was concern that the public encouragement now being given by the Iranian government to the Shi'a uprising in the south, and the reported presence among the insurgents of a force composed of Iraqi Shi'a refugees in Iran and known as the Badr Brigade, would have a counterproductive effect on opinion elsewhere in Iraq and serve to reinforce Saddam Hussein's authority.

John Major agreed to put this concern to the Iranians, and when Douglas Hurd had a chance in New York a few days later to see the Iranian Foreign Minister, Velayati, the matter was raised. Velayati assured him that the support was confined to medicines and food, and that Iran gave her backing to all elements in the spectrum of opposition groups now trying to sink their differences to create a government-in-waiting for Iraq. A meeting of these factions was taking place in Beirut that week, though it did little more than reveal the extent of the divisions between them.

The Prime Minister was told Saudi Arabia would be contributing $1 billion towards Britain's military costs. This was a generous offer, coming on top of the local costs of fuel, rations and accommodation which the Saudis were bearing. Moreover, it was made despite a sense of chagrin that British clearing banks had declined to participate in the loan which the Saudi government was finding itself obliged, against all tradition, to raise on the international market to help cover the heavy burden of war expenditure. We had reason to be grateful for this substantial contribution, and John Major made his appreciation clear. King Fahd was as good as his word; when we followed up promptly with the Saudi Monetary Agency it was to be told that the sum was already being transferred to a startled Bank of England.

We also took the opportunity of the warm mood of the meeting to request clemency to permit a British citizen, Neville Norton, who had been detained in Saudi Arabia over a business debt for some ten years and had appealed to the courts for compensation, to leave the country at last.

Responding to the plea made to him by the troops he had seen in the field, the Prime Minister followed up his return to London with a statement to the House of Commons that our forces would start to withdraw. This well-intended undertaking set a cat among the pigeons at our end. While for reasons of domestic politics the Saudis wanted to see Western and other foreign military contingents out of the Kingdom as soon as possible, they fully shared the concern of the Kuwait government over the need to ensure protection against any lingering gesture of defiance by Saddam Hussein's still substantial forces now operating in strength in southern Iraq in a ruthless action to put down the uprising there. Some form of effective military screen needed to be kept in place in Kuwait for this purpose, at least until the ceasefire had been formalised in the UN Security Council and accepted by Iraq.

Moreover, it was becoming clear that the conditions which deserved to be included in a definitive ceasefire resolution were multiplying fast to cover such issues as disarmament, compensation, repatriation, recognition and the continuation of sanctions. Initial expectations on the part of the Americans and ourselves that a final ceasefire resolution could be put together quickly, and that the temporary occupation of a demilitarised area of southern Iraq by American troops could soon be ended, were met by Saudi and Kuwaiti pressure to take things more steadily to ensure the resolution was comprehensive. These concerns were discussed in detail by the Saudis with the American Secretary of State, when he came to Riyadh on 10 March to lay plans for the next stages and saw the King and Prince Saud.

The move into slower gear over a ceasefire resolution reinforced the case against our precipitate withdrawal. Apart from considerations of security, it was plain that by pulling out ahead of our partners we were jeopardising the enormous fund of goodwill which our participation in the action to liberate Kuwait had secured for us in the area, and the dividend in terms of future co-operation and business which we could expect this to generate in the period ahead.

The Prime Minister's announcement unsettled the Saudis. It resulted in requests from Prince Saud and his deputy minister, Abdul Rahman al Mansouri, from Crown Prince Abdullah and finally, when I took Peter de la Billière on a farewell call on 24 March, from Prince Sultan, that we join the Americans and French in keeping some fighting troops in Kuwait until the ceasefire looked set. I put the arguments against a premature pull-out in successive telegrams to Whitehall during March, to the point where I was beginning to make myself unpopular. The arguments were repeated to Paddy Hine and senior army commanders like Michael Wilkes and David Ramsbotham when they came out from High Wycombe.

BFME headquarters in Riyadh were now planning on pulling out all fighting troops within as little as six weeks, while Peter de la Billière himself was getting ready to leave, together with Bill Wratten, the RAF commander. On 14 March I had a chance to raise these concerns with the chief of the general staff, General Sir John Chapple. I had another go when the House of Commons Defence Committee, led by Michael Mates, visited Riyadh three days later, stressing the damage which would be done if we chose to throw away the credit we had gained.

All were sympathetic, but it was clear that the Prime Minister's undertaking had created a strong political current in London to bring the troops home. Some Royal Engineers would stay on to help clear up ordnance and mines in Kuwait, but we would leave no fighting units. Trooping charter contracts had already been arranged. The ground units also had a time limit on their service, so an extension would involve a rotation with a new battalion. I suspected a Treasury hand in this exercise, which was beginning to look unstoppable. Somehow we had got our priorities wrong. The government seemed to have boxed itself in over early withdrawal.

It was a great relief to hear from the FCO on 25 March that there were signs of a change of heart. Two days later it was confirmed that ministers had decided to retain a battle group in Kuwait, together with an RAF presence for a while longer. The news came just in time to forearm me for a visit I was making up to Kuwait with Peter Sincock, the defence attaché, to see Michael Weston and take him some supplies. We had also arranged to take advantage of the landing and take-off capabilities of the Army Islander to drop in on 4 Brigade in their positions in northern Kuwait, from which they were already being withdrawn to their bases in Britain and Germany. As we left Riyadh, Peter Sincock warned me that the brigade commander, Chris Hammerbeck, wanted me to speak to those elements of his troops whose misfortune it had been to be held back at short notice from withdrawal, in order to compose the battle group which was to stay behind until replacements could arrive from Britain.

As we flew north in clear weather there was a fine view from the co-pilot's seat of the breaches which the coalition forces had made across the border through the Iraqi front-line defences four weeks earlier. Inert hulks of burnt-out Iraqi tanks and guns sat in scraped-out hollows below us, at intervals along the line. Their crews had suffered a savage pounding from the weeks of barrage and air bombardment in such exposed positions. A wide black smudge in the sky to the north-east indicated the smoke from the burning oilfields.

We came down on a makeshift sand runway near an RAF Hercules, being boarded by a line of soldiers on the first stage of their homeward journey, and were met by Chris Hammerbeck. He drove us immediately to where his battle group had been assembled about two kilometres away, explaining that he hoped I could put it across to the men why they were having to stay behind. There was resentment, as they had been confidently led to expect early withdrawal. Some of them had even had to be disembarked from transport aircraft they had just boarded. Clearly I was not to expect an easy encounter, particularly as I was seen as being behind the decision that they should remain.

Those who had drawn this short straw comprised a company of the 3rd Royal Regiment of Fusiliers, a squadron of the 14/20th Hussars, and a Royal Artillery battery. They gathered with their officers in a semicircle in the sand. Chris Hammerbeck introduced me, saying I had been involved in the decision to keep a battle group in Kuwait and could explain the background to them. There was a disconsolate tone to their mood – understandable enough, I felt, in the light of their having been given to believe they were on their way home.

I was helped by a discussion ten days earlier with the Fusiliers' chaplain, Adrian Pollard, our former colleague in Algiers, who had hitched a flight down to take a break with us in Riyadh shortly after the ceasefire. In addition to his welcome sacramental ministration, Adrian had joined us in a post-war feast out at Prince Abdullah bin Faisal's desert camp. He also came to a hospitable dinner given for Peter de la Billière by Sheikh Abdul Aziz al Towaijri, the much-respected *wakil* to the National Guard, at which General Prince Mitab, the Sandhurst-trained son of the Crown Prince, was present. Very much a 'hands on' chaplain, Adrian Pollard had given tireless spiritual support to his battalion during the fighting – with the help, as he told us, of St Mark's gospel. When I raised with him my concern over the effect of dashed expectations on those we were asking should stay behind, he responded that if it was properly explained to the men they would take it in their stride. The Army had now put me on the spot.

I told those gathered around how it would be a grave mistake if, after all they and their fellows had achieved so magnificently in helping to drive the Iraqis out of Kuwait, Britain was to leave the field before the job was complete. As yet there was no final ceasefire arrangement in place, though our representatives in New York were going hard to put this together. Meanwhile Saddam Hussein retained considerable military strength. Given his vindictive and unpredictable nature, some further act of aggression could not be ruled out. Kuwait needed to have a defensive screen for a while longer, and it was right that Britain should take her part alongside her Western and Arab allies in forming this. If the task were prolonged I expected replacement troops would come out to relieve them. But it would be wrong to throw away all the trust and goodwill we had gained with the Kuwaitis and our partners by leaving them to carry on at this stage, and after those present had achieved so much and above all sacrificed so much. For it was the 3rd Fusiliers who had lost nine men in the tragic air strike by supporting US aircraft during the heat of battle. I finished by saying that we therefore had to leave some teeth in Kuwait. That important role fell to them.

There was a silence as the men pondered what I had said. Then a diminutive fusilier, sitting in the sand all encumbered with his battle kit, climbed to his feet. 'Sir,' he said in a broad Geordie voice, 'you tell us we've got to leave some teeth behind. Well,' putting his hand to his mouth and drawing out a set of false teeth which he threw down on the sand, 'there's me teeth and I'll stay with them.' The spell was broken and everyone rocked with laughter. I could have embraced that fusilier.

We all had a friendly brew of tea before Peter Sincock and I went back to the Islander and flew on to Kuwait City. Our arrival was a grim experience. We came along the line of the highway running north out of the city towards the Iraqi border over the Mutla Ridge, the route which had been dubbed the 'Highway of Death' in the Western press when thousands of Iraqi troops, laden with booty and seeking to flee Kuwait three weeks earlier, had been caught and decimated by coalition air and armoured attack. The highway now looked a graveyard of blackened vehicles, mostly civilian but with the occasional tank lying lopsided with armour pierced.

Two kilometres or so from the airport we flew into a choking cloud of black smoke from the oilwell fires, which blazed to within a few hundred metres of the end of the runway. The smoke only cleared as we came into land. The airport itself was a scene of pillage and devastation. We taxied to near where the tailplane of the British Airways jumbo, which had been caught on the ground at the moment of the Iraqi invasion in the early hours of 2 August the previous summer, stood like a gaunt memorial, severed from its fuselage in an enthusiastic attack on the airfield by US Marines Harriers.

Kuwait City itself presented a dilapidated sight, although apart from a few government buildings the damage did not look as extensive as we had expected. It was a strange feeling to come back to the handsome old embassy building, built in the heyday of British Indian rule, where I had spent those hot summer months 30 years earlier during the previous British action to defend Kuwait against an Iraqi threat. Now it looked rather sad, with its entrance shot up in the assault by the Special Forces sent to reoccupy it and with Royal Engineers busy putting the place back into commission.

Michael Weston and his small staff were in good heart. We sat out on the cool veranda and took advantage of the fare Grania had provided for our lunch, interrupted by occasional loud explosions from over the compound wall as French engineers got on with clearing the shore of mines, a huge task which was to keep our own ordnance disposal experts busy across the country for weeks to come. Some days earlier, when the Energy Secretary, John Wakeham, had been staying in the embassy, the French happened to detonate a particularly large store of mines just as he was having his morning shave. The blast showered him with window glass, producing the rueful reflection when he stopped through Riyadh on his return journey that, having been fortunate enough to survive an IRA bomb in Brighton, the French were now trying to get him in Kuwait.

From what Michael Weston told us, it was taking time for Crown Prince Saad to re-establish Al Sabah authority. The Amir had not yet returned from Saudi Arabia. Together with the American ambassador, Michael Weston was regularly seeing Sheikh Saad and his ministers to discourage reprisals, especially against Palestinian residents, of which some evidence had begun to appear, and urge due trial for those suspected of collaboration. But animosity remained close to the surface. Reports of vicious Iraqi interrogation of Kuwaitis with resort to torture were now being confirmed. Much equipment and property had been looted. A few British had managed to survive in hiding during the occupation. The Kuwaitis were clearly keen that we should keep a military presence for a while yet. They were proving less enthusiastic at the prospect of Egyptian and Syrian troops staying on.

The embassy was also setting about ensuring that British firms secured a good share of the work of refurbishing Kuwait's infrastructure, in the face of strong American efforts to monopolise this activity through the US Corps of Engineers. An experienced Arabist, Lawrie Walker, had been appointed to head trade promotion and a senior British business delegation, including financiers as well as the construction sector, had lost no time in visiting the country – producing the incongruous sight of a clutch of dark-suited businessmen with their briefcases disembarking into a smoke-filled Kuwait from an operational RAF Hercules.

In another enterprising venture, which Peter de la Billière had a hand in setting up, a group of British contractors was taking over a compound in Kuwait, formerly used by the British Army training mission, to serve as a base for the provision of artisan skills. The idea was put into effect at short notice by Alan Cockshaw of AMEC, who galvanised the hardware sector of the Riyadh souk one day by purchasing tools by the gross to be flown immediately to Kuwait on the RAF shuttle.

Already we were taking a hand in several areas of Kuwait's recuperation. A Saudi veterinary team from the gazelle breeding station north of Riyadh, which came to help Kuwait's zoo soon after the end of hostilities, included a specialist from the London Zoological Society. They found a grim scene, with animals having been slaughtered by the Iraqi troops for food. An elephant was found alive as a result of rations brought to it by loyal keepers, but suffering from gunshot wounds, while one of the few animals to have been spared was a shaggy Highland cow. Perhaps the invaders had not known what sort of beast it was. The support given to Kuwait's zoo by the London society was recognised by the Amir through a donation a year later, which helped avert London Zoo's closure.

We had to get back to Riyadh by dark, so took off for home with the plane laden with a selection of Kalashnikov rifles and other trophies which the two members of my accompanying protection team had assembled from what was still lying around in Kuwait. For the first half-hour our Air Corps pilot took us on a never-to-be-forgotten ride through the thick of the oil fires to the south of the city. As we banked about and passed through spirals of smoke which turned daylight into night, flames spewed from the ground close below us amid a desolate landscape of charred desert and lakes of crude oil. The penumbra of smoke stretched across the whole horizon. How, one wondered, would it ever be possible to extinguish such an inferno and bring the huge oilfield back under control? Yet remarkably all 600 fires were put out by the end of the year, thanks to the expertise and sheer courage of teams of firefighters brought to Kuwait from North America, Britain and Hungary, among whom the most prominent was the legendary Red Adair company of Houston.

We flew on, crossing a military airfield in southern Kuwait where a gaping hole in the roof of a hardened concrete hangar testified to the accuracy of the coalition's precision bombing. Near the frontier we came at last into clean air. Below us there was emptiness where only shortly before half a million men and their equipment had awaited the signal to advance. Their tracks criss-crossed the sands. Some attributed the unusually dense sandstorms we were experiencing that spring to the pulverising of the desert's fragile crust.

Meanwhile our headquarters in Riyadh was running down rapidly. Ian MacFadyen, the chief of staff, was to take over command from Peter de la Billière. A Welsh artist, Andrew Vicari, who knew the Kingdom well, was engaged by Prince Khalid to record the war and its personalities. We flew him up with the Army Air Corps to experience the oil fires.

There were many loose ends to tie up. Among these was the surprisingly sensitive question of military awards. I firmly supported the proposal from the FCO that the honour of knighthood should be awarded in equal degree to both General Schwarzkopf and his counterpart, Prince Khalid bin Sultan. Both were admitted to the Order of the Bath, an anachronistic title which was to cause some puzzlement when translated into Arabic.

Grania and I gave a farewell dinner for Peter de la Billière, Bill Wratten and Rupert Smith on the eve of their departure. It was a very special occasion, attended by Norman Schwarzkopf and Chuck Horner, themselves about to leave the theatre, as well as by the French commander. Over 50 guests crowded into our dining room, still with its ceiling bare from the dilapidations of the nearby Scud a month before. Jeremy Phipps, the Director of Special Forces, was out from London, and Norman Schwarzkopf made a point of expressing his appreciation for the brave work these units had done behind Iraqi lines. Coming from a commander who had been initially sceptical of the Special Forces role, this was a real tribute.

Our exchanges of speeches and farewells were not without emotion. We all felt real regret at Peter de la Billière's going. It had been a terrific collaboration, and the way he had made a point of working so closely with us in the embassy had meant a great deal to the effectiveness of our relations with the Saudis, and in our occasional dissonances with Whitehall too. He had established ideal working relations with our Saudi hosts, and the Americans as the dominant military partner, and had used his experience and influence to real effect in both quarters. His troops held him in the highest regard. In all ways it had been a remarkable performance. As he left Peter remarked that it seemed wrong for him to be going while we all stayed on. Somehow, I reflected, such crises were for diplomats part and parcel of the job.

All this activity was taking place against an unsettled and ominous background in Iraq. Within days of the ceasefire and the occupation of an area between Basra and the Kuwaiti frontier by American forces, a major uprising against Saddam Hussein and his Ba'athist regime occurred on the part of the mainly Shi'a populations of Iraq's southern cities. Reports which came to us in Riyadh from military reconnaissance, and messages passed via Iraqi exiles with whom we kept in contact, said the insurgents were initially joined by units of the Iraqi army, forced to retreat in the face of the coalition onslaught and resentful of the failure of their leadership. Members of the Sunni, as well as Shi'a, communities were participating.

Information was sketchy, but within days it became evident that irregular military units composed of Iraqi Shi'a who had taken refuge in Iran during her war with Iraq had joined the uprising, which was also receiving vocal support from the Iranian government. There were rumours that Iranian revolutionary guards were involved in the fighting. These last reports were not confirmed, but were enough to arouse second thoughts on the part of the Saudis as to where this keenly-awaited uprising against Iraq's regime might now be leading. As King Fahd had made clear to the Prime Minister, the prospect of a Shi'a breakaway enclave in southern Iraq, under the influence of revolutionary Iran, presented a serious dilemma for the regional policy of Saudi Arabia and her GCC partners.

The ferocity of the uprising, accentuated by the violent retribution which those who had come in from Iran were said to be exacting against members of the regional administration and other non-Shi'a elements, had the effect of alienating some of those who had initially given support to it. The Sunni community in particular, fearful of the fanaticism being shown by many of their Shi'a compatriots, began to see it as a threat to their dominant status within the social fabric. As an Iraqi friend described the predicament to me, the Sunnis of Baghdad and other Iraqis of moderate outlook saw the prospect of a vengeful civil war as even worse than a continuation of Saddam Hussein's rule of terror.

Seeing the tide begin to turn, Saddam Hussein moved swiftly to capitalise on these fears by using 24 army divisions, including the Republican Guard which he had kept in reserve outside the Kuwait theatre, to overcome the insurgency in savage fashion. Far from turning his swords into ploughshares, he was instead turning them on his own people. Shrines in the Shi'a holy cities of Kerbala and Najaf were desecrated, and an implacable revenge was wreaked upon the Shi'a population. It has been estimated that over four times as many civilians perished in southern Iraq at the hands of the regime in the three weeks it took to put down the uprising as died in all the intense coalition air activity of the preceding six weeks.

Appeals began to reach Riyadh for military help, stimulated in part by the earlier remarks of President Bush and other coalition leaders inviting the Iraqi people to put an end to their regime. But no response came. As early as 5 March when the Iraqi army was launching its counteroffensive in Basra, a White House spokesman made it clear that the USA did not intend to become involved in Iraq's internal affairs. Indeed it had never been the intention of the Western partners in the coalition, and certainly not of the Saudis and other Arab participants, to become engaged directly in the snare of Iraq's politics, or support upheaval which might see her territorial unity put at risk. As Prince Saud had consistently put it to the Americans and ourselves, Iraq must at all events remain intact for the sake of maintaining the region's precarious security balance.

Towards the end of March, when Saddam Hussein was facing uprisings both in the south and from the Kurdish population in the northern mountains of Iraq, President Bush repeated his hope that the turmoil would lead to the Iraqi leader's downfall. But at the same time the White House made it clear there would be no American military intervention; such a move would not be welcome in the region, nor did the American people have the appetite for it. Even Iraq's brazen exploitation of a loophole in the ceasefire arrangements negotiated at Safwan, by using helicopters to mount air attacks on the insurgents, was met with no more than a reproof which was ignored. Saddam Hussein thus found himself with virtually a free hand to suppress the uprising, and did so in merciless fashion, causing thousands of civilians to flee from Basra and other cities to seek refuge in Iran, in the remote marshes of southern Iraq, and in makeshift camps on the Kuwait frontier within the area still controlled by American troops.

We watched the ruthless extinguishing of the Basra revolt, and saw the Iraqi leadership preparing to administer similar punishment to the Kurds in the north, with a sense of helpless regret. There was no question in our minds of the correctness of the decision not to follow through to Baghdad in the hope of installing an alternative authority of a more benign complexion. As Mrs Thatcher had aptly put it at the outset of the crisis, we should avoid getting our arm caught in the mangle, though paradoxically she was now among those urging more positive action to remove Iraq's leader. But to witness Saddam Hussein reasserting his repressive control by turning insurgency to his advantage in this opportunist and ruthless fashion came as a bitter pill.

It was clear from our regular talks with the Saudis that they fully shared the sense of chagrin, and were having to resign themselves to the prospect of Saddam Hussein's survival, with the concomitant need for continued economic restraints and military vigilance so long as he could present a threat. A tedious diplomatic road stretched ahead. Eventual assassination at the hands of his own military apparatus now looked the more likely eventuality, but who could predict when that might occur, and in any case would a successor dictatorship be any less malevolent?

Yet Saddam Hussein came close to being toppled in the first days of the Basra revolt. There were some who speculated with hindsight that, had American forces been permitted another 24 hours in which to complete their occupation of the pocket to the south of Basra, Saddam Hussein would not have been able to retaliate so effectively. Saudi thinking, however, was not entirely consistent; while determined to see Iraq preserved as a unitary state, there were yet questions as to why their Western allies had encouraged an uprising and then left the insurgents to their fate. I could see that in the back of some minds lurked latent suspicions of Western motives. Might it even be our private intention to see Saddam Hussein survive, as a pretext for continued Western intervention? Old myths continued to die hard.

It was the revolt among the Kurds which finally produced intervention by the Western community. The Shi'a insurgency in the south had lacked coherent publicity through the international media. Journalists who had tried to slip into the area during early March had been turned back. This was not the case with the Kurds, whose plight in the face of the Iraqi army's retribution from the end of March onward, when nearly two million refugees struggled to escape into eastern Turkey and Iran, was recorded in its grim misery on television around the world. Moreover the Kurdish people, who had so long suffered from Saddam Hussein's repression, had well-established lobbies in Western political circles.

Their predicament aroused its most acute reaction in Britain, and led to a personal initiative by John Major to mobilise European and American support for direct intervention. His ideas broke new ground, by introducing the concept of humanitarian action under Western military protection and underpinned by a UN Security Council resolution to safeguard a community within a sovereign state from the actions of its own government. This was a bold departure from previous UN practice, and was only possible to achieve within the context of Iraq's earlier delinquency.

There was initial American opposition, but within the EC the response was more positive. By the second week in April, the British initiative had produced a plan for 'safe havens' within northern Iraq, to which the refugees in the mountains of south-eastern Turkey were being encouraged to return under the protection of British, French, Dutch, Italian and American troops. These were based in Turkey, albeit with somewhat grudging Turkish acquiescence.

The operation was backed by the carefully-worded Resolution 688, which the British representative in New York, David Hannay, succeeded in piloting through the Council on 8 April. It called for an end to repression and required Iraq to allow humanitarian access to her population. The resolution, accepted with predictable bad grace by Iraq, was followed up by an agreement between the UN and the Iraqis to permit the stationing of a UN police force in the country to oversee the observance of the resolution. This new type of force was to find its activities constantly harassed and obstructed by the Iraqis, particularly over relief work in the south.

In the Kurdish area the safe haven policy achieved its main purpose, as well as setting a precedent for subsequent international pressure on the Iraqi regime. It evoked a mixed reaction, however, on the part of the Saudi government, who saw in the plan a possible precursor to a separate Kurdish entity. Indeed, this thought was probably present in Kurdish minds too, as attempts by the centrist elements within the fragmented Iraqi opposition movement to forge a democratic front, which would be credible to opinion within Iraq, were making little progress owing to internal differences and the inclination of both the Kurdish and the clerical Shi'a wings to follow their own factional agendas. An opposition Iraqi National Congress was in the process of being formed, with encouragement from London and Washington. But Iraq's neighbours in the region, notably Iran and Syria but also Saudi Arabia, were showing predictable favour to the groups among the exiles whom they saw as best suiting their interests. It was a discordant endeavour.

This turmoil within Iraq contributed to a delay in the formulation within the UN Security Council of a resolution to set definitive terms for the coalition's ceasefire. As thought was given to Iraq's renewed militancy, so the variety of eventualities for which it was considered desirable to provide in the ceasefire resolution grew in number, a cause of particular impatience to the British government with its target of early withdrawal of forces. The major issues of concern included the destruction of Iraq's sinister capability in weapons of mass destruction, her recognition of Kuwait's sovereignty and frontier, and her renunciation of terrorism. A UN observer force would need to be posted along the border before coalition forces on both sides of it could complete their withdrawal.

The Kuwaitis and Saudis additionally laid stress on the return of the several thousand Arab detainees still in Iraqi hands, provision for Iraq to pay compensation, and measures to ensure that the basic needs of the Iraqi people in food and medical supplies were provided for. The French with their large outstanding debts and contractual obligations in Iraq pressed for Iraqi assurances in this complex area. It was not until 4 April that this marathon exercise was concluded with the adoption by the Council of Resolution 687, running to 34 executive paragraphs and known to those who had laboured over it as the 'Christmas tree' for having had so much hung upon it. Economic sanctions were meanwhile to remain in force. The interdiction on Iraqi oil and other exports was not to be lifted until Iraq had complied with the stringent conditions for the inspection and destruction of her mass destruction weapons.

Iraq accepted the resolution two days later, though describing it as unjust. A formal ceasefire came into effect on 11 April. Iraqi compliance with the weapons inspection provisions continued to be obstructive and devious, and was to lead to recurring confrontation with the UN Security Council and leading members of the coalition in the months to come. But the American withdrawal from Iraqi territory could at last go ahead.

This produced a crisis over the 40,000 or so refugees from southern Iraq now gathered on the Kuwait frontier under an international protection shared between the UNHCR and the International Red Cross. Overwhelmed by the problems of putting their own house back in order, and anxious not to set a precedent for the absorption of their own large stateless community, known as the 'bidoon', the Kuwaiti government refused flatly to take in these victims of Saddam Hussein's internal repression.

We therefore turned our attention to the Saudis, who, despite considerable reluctance to be saddled with a large refugee community composed of Shi'a Moslems and perhaps including elements which the Iraqi regime could use for subversive purposes, responded to appeals from ourselves, the Americans and the international organisations, and took them in. A camp at Rafha in the north of the Kingdom near the Kuwaiti border was made available to accommodate the refugees, together with Iraqi war prisoners who had refused repatriation. After an initial spell under the control of the Saudi security forces, when some problems arose over order, the direction was put under the authority of General Prince Khalid and his military command, who set about rebuilding the camp to a high standard at the expense of the Saudi government to make their enforced exile more tolerable for its inmates.

It was with real relief that Grania and I took a break at the end of March from all these post-war pressures. Before going we bade a grateful farewell to our close protection team, who were returning to England. Steve Brumpton and his men had become real friends to all in the embassy. Their unobtrusive guard against a terrorist attempt had been a great comfort. Perhaps as a result of their vigilance, the only live action they had seen was when one of the team, on guard at the residence one evening while we were out, had taken too literally a remark I had made about wanting to see the end of a tom-cat which used to vie with the Scuds to disturb our sleep. Spying it in the garden, he despatched it with a shotgun. This brought a Saudi policeman on to the scene to investigate the sound of shooting at the British embassy in the midst of a war. His disquiet was not easily assuaged. I had forgotten that to the military a wish is as good as a command.

We flew to Venice for a week of tranquillity. It was unreal to find ourselves by the Grand Canal, with all the frenzy and eventfulness of the war behind us. It made for a wonderful convalescence. With our strength restored, we went on to London in time for our sons' 21st birthday. The

FCO had organised a conference to review the lessons to be drawn from the experience of the past few months for British policy in the Middle East, and for the handling of future crises. There was no doubt in our minds that we had to redouble our efforts and assistance to enable our friends in the Gulf to develop their ability to see off potential future threats. Meanwhile the containment of Iraq, at least so long as Saddam Hussein could throw his weight about, would have to remain a priority.

It was also good to connect with all those in the FCO with whom we had been working so intensively by telegram and telephone over the preceding weeks, and find them released from the confines of the emergency centre in the depths of the old India Office. It had been a great collaboration across a vast range of political, military and consular issues. Their guidance and forbearance right round the clock, as they worked long shifts in Whitehall, starting well before the winter dawn in order to tie in with our Middle Eastern time zone, had been an enormous support to all of us in the Middle East missions. But we had little time to rest on diplomatic laurels. These had yet to be won and the peace secured.

CHAPTER 17

Profit and Loss

By mid-April we were back in Riyadh. There was a certain change of mood within the Kingdom. Determination to see the back of Saddam Hussein seemed as firm as ever, and feelers which he was understood to have put out to the Saudi government in March had been firmly rebuffed. Yet people were already trying to put the nightmare of the Kuwait crisis behind them, as a shameful aberration in Arab relations of which they were reluctant to be reminded.

There were signs, too, at the popular level of an Islamic backlash in reaction to the presence of Western troops over so many months. This mood, incited by more conservative preachers and reflected among elements of the religious police and other zealots whose prejudices had been muzzled during the hostilities, was leading to renewed harrassment of the foreign community now that the servicemen were less in evidence. More significantly it was being translated into the beginnings of a political campaign directed at the Saudi regime, with calls for a stricter application of Islamic standards to government policy. This campaign also reflected in some degree the spirit of more open debate which was emerging out of the shock of the crisis.

A contrary strand of opinion was at the same time being articulated by liberal elements in Saudi society. Their petition, which had been circulated the preceding autumn and called for a range of reforms aimed at wider participation over matters of policy, was served up afresh in early April. As one young Saudi woman put it to us, the war meant that 'we lost our innocence'. Yet improved status for women was a significant omission from even the liberals' platform. The shock tactics adopted by the women who had defiantly driven down a Riyadh thoroughfare during November in the height of the crisis had misfired, and set back their cause with Saudi opinion.

King Fahd responded with encouragement to the modernist camp through references in his traditional speech marking the end of Ramadan to changes in inter-Arab relationships, to the need for greater self-reliance in defence, and, most significantly, to his plans for administrative reform including the establishment of a consultative council.

343

The ultra-conservative elements took this cautious expression of royal support for more representative rule as a threat to the religious author-ity they sought to install, and countered by opposing such innovation unless it was combined with an Islamic imprint. Faced with these turbu-lent currents, the King, ever-careful to avoid tearing the fabric of national consensus, showed no hurry to introduce change. But the coun-try was at least acquiring a taste for political debate.

On the regional scene the enthusiasm for building on the partnership with Egypt and Syria to form a new combination for Gulf defence, which had emerged as a key feature of Saudi diplomacy in the course of the cri-sis, was already starting to abate with the recovery of Kuwait. Second thoughts were manifesting themselves over the political desirability of offering two such powerful Arab states, with their republican traditions, a formal role in the defence of the Gulf's traditional monarchies. Even the Kuwaitis, still within Iraqi gunshot range, shared these hesitations and had irritated their Egyptian and Syrian allies through their vacilla-tion over whether their troops should be asked to stay on alongside Western contingents as part of a defensive screen.

In consequence the important declaration providing for closer co-operation, including the security field, which the six GCC states led by Saudi Arabia had signed with Egypt and Syria in Damascus on 6 March in the immediate aftermath of hostilities, was already requiring to have its defence clauses diluted in an awkward sequel. It also appeared that suspicion of Iran continued to overshadow the Saudi outlook, despite the settlement after tough negotiations of the disagreements over the quota of pilgrims for Iran's resumed participation in the 1991 *haj*, and the re-establishment of diplomatic relations. This act of outward recon-ciliation had the seal set on it with a visit to Tehran by Prince Saud during June, shortly before the start of the pilgrimage month.

But there lurked suspicions of an overzealous Iranian hand behind the way in which the uprising in southern Iraq had misfired. The Iranians had also begun to jockey with pressures to discourage ideas among their Gulf neighbours for a wider Arab defence arrangement, and for renewed security agreements with Western countries. At the same time they put a price on closer regional collaboration between themselves and the GCC by resurrecting claims to financial compensation for damage during their war with Iraq. In the light of these manoeuvres, Saudi scepticism over Iran's intentions seemed quite understandable.

We had a timely opportunity to bring all this regional activity into bet-ter focus with a visit to Jedda by Douglas Hurd at the beginning of May to see the King and Prince Saud. Our talks with the latter covered the whole gamut of regional issues, to useful purpose. An issue of major significance for both sides was the relaunching of the Arab–Israel peace process. With solid backing from the Saudis, as from ourselves, James Baker was in the process of restarting negotiations, taking advantage of the way in which the outcome of the Kuwait crisis had enhanced the authority of the more moderate and conciliatory elements within the Arab world and among the Palestinians themselves, while discrediting the PLO leadership and other radical voices.

At the same time he was employing a blend of persuasion and raw pressure on the hard-line Likud government, led by Itzhak Shamir, to put across the case for Israel entering into simultaneous dialogue with Palestinians from within the occupied territories and with adjacent Arab states. Iraq's missile attacks had demonstrated that Israel could no longer rely on the occupation of buffer territory for her defence. Moreover, the three years of the *intifada*, the uprising on the part of Palestinians in the occupied territories which Israel had all but failed to repress, had brought about a shift within Israeli opinion over the merits of continued occupation. The decline in the influence of the USSR had also removed an important prop for the Arab radicals, thus invalidating one of Israel's main objections to the holding of an international conference.

There were signs that in these new circumstances the Bush administration was losing patience with the entrenched position which Israel's right-wing government sought to sustain, and was even prepared to lean on Israel by linking financial guarantees for US loans, needed to help with the settlement of Jews now flooding into Israel out of Russia, to progress over peace negotiations. Shamir's resistance was proving stiff, but it was beginning to look as if at the end of the day he would have little option but to move in the direction the Americans sought to draw him.

On the Arab side, too, new realities were apparent. In its weakened state the PLO leadership was having to yield to the idea of negotiations being headed by an alternative team from within the occupied territories, whose background made for a more constructive approach towards the Israelis. Yasir Arafat's wholehearted endorsement of Iraq, on the back of the emotional wave of frustrated identification with Iraq's leader which had afflicted Palestinians throughout the region, had been compounded in Saudi eyes by his action in going to Baghdad at the height of the fighting to receive from Saddam Hussein the hastily-instituted Order of the Mother of all Battles.

The suspension of the Saudi subsidy of some $6 million a month to the PLO in consequence of its support for Saddam Hussein was emerging as an important element in cutting the organisation down to size and obliging it to modify its hard-line stance. Its financial predicament was further aggravated by the evaporation of the subvention, not far short of the Saudi amount, which it had been receiving from Iraq.

A PLO contact whom I saw in May left no doubt that Yasir Arafat was in no position to challenge the moves being made by leading Palestinians within the occupied territories to make the running in fresh talks. At the same time he discounted prospects for a change of leadership within the PLO itself, a development to which the Saudis had been giving discreet encouragement, as a way of preserving the framework of Palestinian politics while changing the cast and heading off a challenge from the Islamic right through the emerging Hamas organisation. A major problem here was that most of those who might have been credible candidates to replace Yasir Arafat were no longer around, some having met violent deaths.

The Saudis were quick to perceive this significant shift in the balance of Palestinian leadership as a result of the Kuwait affair, as well as the intensified need to find a settlement to a problem which lay like a cancer at the heart of Middle Eastern politics and had fed the seductive rhetoric of the Iraqi tyrant. They were ready to help mobilise moderate Arab governments, and get things moving while the climate for negotiations was favourable.

The arguments for direct talks over Palestine between Israel and adjacent Arab states were discussed with James Baker when he came to Riyadh in early March with a fresh American initiative over Palestine in mind. He followed up with two further visits to the area in an effort to prevail on Israel and her neighbours to embark on an imaginative formula for talks on a bilateral basis, with regional discussions in parallel.

These rounds would be held under the umbrella of an international forum and led jointly by the Americans and the USSR, but there would on this occasion be no attempt to dictate agendas. It was clear Jordan would have a particularly important role in giving political cover to whoever was to attend from the occupied territories on behalf of the Palestinians. From the Saudi side strong encouragement was being given in Washington by Prince Bandar bin Sultan, the Kingdom's influential ambassador. There were nevertheless Saudi hesitations over becoming a party to the bilateral talks themselves. They did not after all share a border with Israel, and preferred to bring their influence to bear from the position of observers. Their offer to take a seat jointly with their partners in the GCC at the international conference was, however, a considerable help in getting things moving.

Thus it was that when Douglas Hurd came to Jedda in early May, the prospects for turning the experience of the Kuwait crisis to advantage over a Palestine settlement occupied a central place in his talks with Prince Saud, and subsequently with King Fahd. The Foreign Secretary was concerned to see whether there was yet scope for an easing in the severe strains which the crisis had produced in the Kingdom's relations with Jordan. This was regarded as desirable in view of the part which King Hussein would have to play in securing Israeli agreement to Palestinian participation in any conference. Jordan's key role in the Arab–Israeli context was acknowledged. But it was evident that for the present there could be no prospect of reconciliation so long as Jordan's position over support for Saddam Hussein remained unclear. The same went for Yemen, whose foreign minister had asked to see Douglas Hurd in Cairo, his next stop, in a bid to restore respectability.

As for the American initiative over talks, there seemed a risk of this becoming bogged down over the composition of the international conference and the role to be played by the UN, about which the Israelis harboured strong misgivings. We pressed the Saudis on the idea of an easing of the Arab boycott on Israel in return for a freezing of Israel's programme of new settlements in the occupied lands, but it was plain they did not see this as a fair exchange. To try and get round the problem of UN status, Douglas Hurd agreed to take up with the Americans the idea of substituting a sponsorship by the five permanent members of the Security Council, a theme which with subsequent modification to permit joint attendance by the members of the EC was carried forward into the conference held in Madrid that autumn.

The discussions in Jedda ranged well beyond Palestine. It was now clear that pressures on Saddam Hussein's regime in Iraq would have to be maintained to hold in check a resumption of his threat to stability. It was essential that the exercise launched by the UN to seek out and destroy Iraq's capability in weapons of mass destruction should be carried through, despite the obstructions and efforts at concealment which the inspection teams were already facing. There was no doubt that Iraq had more of such weaponry hidden away than she had so far admitted, or for that matter than we had all estimated when we had gone for confrontation over the seizure of Kuwait.

Meanwhile sanctions would have to be kept in place, including the naval inspection blockade of the Jordanian port of Aqaba and in the northern Gulf. The Saudis hoped that we would keep some troops in Kuwait for a while yet, until the new UN observer force, to be known as UNIKOM, to patrol the Kuwait–Iraq border was in place. This would be made up of personnel from a variety of states including the Soviets, thus at last giving the latter some element of that direct involvement in Gulf security which they had sought so long.

Douglas Hurd described the success of the safe haven operation to shield the Kurds in northern Iraq, and applauded the shelter which the Saudis were giving to refugees from the abortive Basra uprising. On the matter of future security it was very much part of our policy to encourage the Saudis and their GCC partners to develop ideas for closer integration of their defence effort, though this would still need underpinning from outside for some while. The Saudis made it plain they had no objection to other smaller Gulf states seeking security co-operation with the West, though there was no question of their taking this road themselves. We had gathered that recent American soundings over stockpiling equipment in the Kingdom had run into problems over control.

After a swim in a sea made rough by a bout of sandstorms, which made it difficult to appreciate the brilliant colours of the fish and coral along Jedda's reef, we set off up the coast to the King's island retreat where he was taking a break from the strains of the past few months. As we drove across the causeway, the low-built house seemed dwarfed by the elegant bulk of the royal yacht moored behind it.

The King was in forthcoming and buoyant mood. In addition to Prince Saud the meeting was attended by the King's brother, Prince Salman, governor of Riyadh. The reason for his presence became apparent when Douglas Hurd reverted to the subject of Neville Norton's detention, which had been broached by the Prime Minister after the ceasefire. Prince Salman subsequently took a most helpful hand in expediting the complex legal cases involved, with the result that Neville Norton was finally able to quit the Kingdom a few months later with all outstanding court actions resolved and with compensation. Clive Woodland made a point of seeing him right on to the aircraft. After the long saga of his case, the release constituted a small yet significant Saudi gesture in the wake of our collaboration over Kuwait.

There was no doubt that the King remained on his guard so long as Saddam Hussein stayed in control of Iraq. The Iraqi leader had aimed to make himself the new Caliph of Baghdad, a preposterous notion, and had shown he could not be trusted. The King spoke of his plans for wider public consultation through the establishment of a consultative council, or *majlis al shura*. This was encouraging to hear, and we did not doubt that the developments of the past months had played a part in the relaunching of this important constitutional proposal.

For the next few weeks the stream of visitors meant that we had hardly time to turn around between despatching one personality and getting our briefs prepared for the next. With the end of Ramadan the tempo of regular work also began to build up. We encouraged early visits by British exporters to explore the new opportunities in a market flush with funds from the contracting and supply work the war had generated, and where our national stock was running very high. Having seen Douglas Hurd and his party off to Cairo I flew up to Yanbu, the new industrial city on the Red Sea coast, to join a group of senior figures from major British firms, whom our MoD and their advisers, Schroder Asseily, had lost no time in bringing out to the Kingdom to look for opportunities to invest with local industry under the Al Yamamah offset programme. The port was full of French troops of the Daguet division in the final stages of their withdrawal; the French forces had used Yanbu's ample dock facilities as their port of supply, just as we had moved through Jubail on the Gulf.

The British community was by now back in strength. Families had lost no time in reuniting in the Kingdom as soon as hostilities ceased. Their numbers were growing fast, and with the arrival of new expatriates already looked like surpassing the total of some 30,000 at the time of Iraq's invasion. The British schools were all back in business. No one seemed greatly put out by the stricter observance of Islamic dress codes, which the religious police in their post-war fervour had started to enforce. Indeed, it had its humorous side. In a reaction to the hot-weather dress worn by some Western troops the custodians of virtue put up notices in English in certain supermarkets stipulating that men should not wear 'knickers' – a slip of the lexicon.

We arranged to hold the annual Queen's Birthday Party reception in Riyadh at the end of April. Ian MacFadyen agreed to let us have a musical interlude by the fifes and drums of the Royal Anglian Regiment, which had recently arrived in Kuwait to take over from the Fusiliers battle group. When the musicians, in their desert camouflage, surged on to the balcony overlooking the residence garden, some of our several hundred guests made a startled exit. Later in the evening two pipers from the King's Own Scottish Borderers and the Royal Irish Rangers played from the roof. It only emerged at the last minute that Scottish and Irish bagpipes have difficulty in playing together as, perhaps intentionally, there is a semitone or so difference in their pitch. So the pipers played alternately against a moonlit sky. The effect was magical.

We also maintained our support for colleagues who had gone back into Kuwait, where conditions were far from easy. Two supply runs were arranged from the Riyadh embassy during April. On one of these Chris Wilton took a convoy of vehicles up the coast highway, the Kuwaiti stage of which was by now in a very poor state, having been pounded by months of military traffic. The oilfire smoke was so thick that headlights had to be used in full daylight. The vehicles included a fuel bowser, driven by Derek Smith, who had exchanged his communication and clerical role for a spell of trucking. Phil Hagger recorded the journey on film for posterity.

The Secretary of State for the Environment, Michael Heseltine, was the next minister to visit Saudi Arabia. Following Iraq's wanton act in January in releasing oil into the waters of the Gulf, he had led with a British government donation of £1 million towards an international operation to clean up the consequences. We flew north from Dhahran on a clear morning in mid-May in a cargo helicopter of the Saudi Frontier Force. Its rear ramp hung open, giving us a fine view of the booms surrounding the key water inlets to the refineries, water desalination plants and power stations which the Iraqis had unsuccessfully sought to damage through intake of crude oil. It had been a close-run thing, but the floating slick of oil had mercifully become trapped in the angle of the Abu Ali peninsula, not far to the north of the Jubail installations. Only a small amount had floated on south to threaten the towns and fisheries of the eastern cities and the island of Bahrain.

Northwards, however, the coastline of creeks and sandshoals was black with oil deposit as far as the eye could see, stretching to where a pall of smoke indicated the burning wells in Kuwait. The breeding grounds for the Gulf's fishing industry would take a long time to recover. The bird-washing centre which Prince Abdullah bin Faisal had set up with our help during the hostilities had done much to save birdlife. But the habitats below us looked ravaged. The Saudi authorities had, however, made a start with the cleaning-up operation. There were men standing in the mangrove swamps, hosing down the twisted trunks of the bushes; it must have been dispiriting work. On some sandbanks the blackened sand had been scraped away to open patches for the rare seaturtles to nest. We had a splendid view of one of these ungainly creatures swimming in blue water just below us. Elsewhere Aramco was at work with pumps and skimmer boats, drawing oil off the surface of the water into large reservoirs dug on the shoreline. It was not a vain endeavour; some ten million barrels of crude were eventually recovered and taken off to be refined.

I left Michael Heseltine in Jubail with Prince Abdulla bin Faisal and returned to Riyadh for a dinner which Prince Saud was giving for the Soviet Foreign Minister, Bessmertnykh. This was the first visit to the Kingdom by a Soviet figure of such standing. It symptomised the remarkable scenery change which was taking place in international affairs, in which the crisis over Kuwait was playing no insignificant part. The newly-appointed Soviet ambassador, Gennadi Tarasov, had recently arrived from Moscow to take up his post, and was beginning to find his bearings amid Saudi Arabia's guarded society. We had struck up a good rapport and, with the Cold War ended, were frequently to find ourselves pulling on the same end of the rope in the months ahead – a novel experience.

When he reached Riyadh the next day Michael Heseltine called on Prince Sultan, whose responsibilities combined defence with the environment. This was a happy conjuncture as he and Michael Heseltine were old friends, having set up the Al Yamamah programme together seven years earlier. Prince Sultan made no secret of his satisfaction with our co-operation.

We next had a visit by the House of Commons Foreign Affairs Committee, as part of a tour to assess the results of the Gulf conflict. Under their chairman, David Howell, they had meetings with Prince Saud and the Finance Minister, Mohammed Aba al Khail, which gave them a feel for the way tensions were by no means over, and for the financial burdens the Kingdom now faced as it met the costs of the political and military alliance it had so staunchly sustained. The visitors also had a chance to sample some of the more dissentient views now emerging among Saudi opinion.

No sooner were they on their way than Tom King returned. I went across in the Islander to connect with him in Jubail, where we gathered for a meeting in a hotel. Michael Weston drove down from Kuwait with the Defence Secretary. On our agenda once again was the vexed matter of withdrawal. The rear party of infantry in Jubail, composed of the King's Own Scottish Borderers, was returning home, and it was planned to move the Royal Anglians down from Kuwait to carry on with guard duty for the remaining couple of months until the backloading of British equipment was complete. I had, however, again had approaches from the Saudis asking us to keep our final withdrawal from Kuwait more or less in step with other Western contingents. Michael Weston was under similar pressure in Kuwait. Tom King saw the force of our arguments, but he was also having to keep a Whitehall eye on costs. Finally he agreed that a party of the Royal Anglians should stay on in Kuwait, together with the engineers at work on the dangerous business of ordnance disposal.

We spent the next morning seeing the KOSB troops engaged in sorting and salvaging unexpended ammunition from the land battle. It was tedious work in the heat of the desert, but they were in good spirits. Here, I reflected, was a real life case of 40 maids with 40 mops, though they were only taking half the time allowed by the walrus and carpenter for the task. In the port battered armoured vehicles were being loaded on to roll-on ships for the long run back to Europe, while all around lay acres of vehicles, mostly American, awaiting shipment, together with a proud selection of Iraqi armour to be taken home as trophies. It gave us no satisfaction to discover a French-made Exocet missile of recent date among the Iraqi prizes which the British forces were bringing home.

On getting to Riyadh Tom King had a good talk with Prince Sultan, who was relieved to learn of the decision to keep a token presence in Kuwait a while longer. We told him that Peter de la Billière would, in his new role as a special adviser to the Defence Secretary, be keeping his links with the armed forces of the region and advising on future co-operation between us, a subject on which Tom King had some proposals to put forward. There were already indications of differences of approach within the GCC over measures for closer defence integration, for which the Omanis were preparing a blueprint. The Saudi military were also co-operating with the Americans in a post-war study, intended to illustrate the strength of forces the Kingdom would need to resist a threat from either of her powerful neighbours to the north and east. The upshot would be far beyond their capacity to handle alone.

Tom King also took the opportunity to see the deputy commander of the National Guard, Prince Badr, and paid a farewell call on General Prince Khalid. With the latter he raised the old question of our residual military costs in the Kingdom, which the Saudis had undertaken to reimburse under the terms of the understanding we had reached in January on host nation support. The casual approach towards account-ing procedures, which our MoD had adopted during the early months of the crisis, had returned to plague us. With some justification the Saudi military authorities responsible for settling outstanding claims by coalition partners made it clear they were not prepared to reimburse bills which were not properly backed-up by account documents. Belated MoD efforts to untangle this area had only achieved limited success, with the result that we had claims outstanding estimated at tens of millions of pounds, on top of the local costs which the Saudis had already paid on our behalf and King Fahd's munificent contribution of $1 billion to the Prime Minister. In the event a salutary lesson was learnt.

Tom King's night in Riyadh coincided with the dinner we were giving to bid farewell to Ian MacFadyen and the BFME headquarters, which was closing down. Command of the few remaining British elements in the Kingdom was being transferred to Jubail to complete the final stages of evacuation. Among the items they bequeathed us was enough sacra-mental beverage to last us into the next century.

There was further debate over medals. The Saudis had struck a cam-paign medal to commemorate Kuwait's liberation, and proposed to award this to all coalition troops. But under the long-standing British rule whereby foreign honours and awards cannot be accepted without the sovereign's special permission, we should strictly speaking have had to decline the Saudi campaign medal on behalf of all British servicemen in theatre, an action bound to cause deep affront to our ally. The practice was said to date back to the reign of Queen Elizabeth I, who was purported to have decreed that 'my dogs shall not wear other people's collars'. The Canadian ambassador, Allan Lever, told me that Canada, as a realm, was in the same bind.

Anxious to avoid the situation where we refused this Saudi courtesy, I pressed on the MoD a course whereby the medal would be accepted and distributed to those entitled to it, with the proviso that it should not be worn unless on service in the Kingdom, for example in one of our military advisory missions. Fortunately this formula was approved and honour was saved. But Whitehall's parsimonious financiers got their own back by insisting that the costs of distribution be met by the recipients. There was disappointment among some of our diplomatic and military staff in Riyadh and elsewhere in the Gulf to find themselves ineligible for the British Gulf War campaign medal, despite having worked so closely alongside the British forces during the crisis. After review by the FCO it was decided that this self-denying ordinance on the part of the diplomatic service should remain in place; to alter things now would, it was argued, raise too many awkward precedents involving previous military actions dating back to the Second World War.

Meanwhile the frigates of the Armilla patrol continued to operate along Gulf sea lanes to keep an eye out for cargoes which might be in breach of the blockade on Iraq. The flotilla of minesweepers was also still busy in the northern Gulf. An offer by the German government to contribute minehunting vessels as soon as hostilities ceased was seen by the Saudi government as coming too late. But a minehunting force from Japan was on its way, the first occasion in which Japanese forces had engaged in active service since the Second World War. Their appearance in the Gulf after the long voyage from Japan produced a twist of historical irony in the shape of a telegram which I received one morning through civilian channels from the commander of the flotilla. In most courteous English he announced its arrival and asked to place the Japanese naval operation under Royal Navy supervision. I made sure that Trevor Waddington sent this telegram back to the Admiralty for the archives.

So far as Saudi military activity was concerned, the final stage was the holding at the beginning of June of a grand parade of their armed forces and civil defence units to commemorate the victory. This event was probably without precedent in the 60 years of the Kingdom's history as a nation. Indeed, given the absence of military pomp in Saudi custom, in contrast to the practice in most Arab states, they possibly hoped it would be the last too.

The parade took place well away from the public gaze on the new King Fahd airport some kilometres outside Dammam. This huge project was still incomplete when Iraq's invasion took place. The airfield had been quickly converted into a major airbase for the USAF, which had now departed. Diplomats and attachés, representing no less than 37 countries which had contributed, even in small measure, to the defence of Saudi Arabia or the liberation of Kuwait, gathered under an awning amid tarmac and sand.

With King Fahd and senior members of his family and government, as well as the Kingdom's military establishment, we watched a well-rehearsed parade of armour, artillery, infantry and marines, plus the fire and civil defence services. I felt my Irish colleague deserved to have been invited in recognition of his compatriots who had fought in some numbers with British regiments, and the Nepalese too on behalf of the Ghurkas. Combat and transport aircraft of the RSAF, including elements of their Tornado and Hawk squadrons, flew low overhead in close formation.

It was a brave show, and everyone enjoyed themselves. For the Saudis it was a celebration to close a chapter. King Fahd invested Prince Khalid with the sash of the King Abdul Aziz Order, and we all took the opportunity to pay our respects to the monarch and his commander who had together seen things through so steadfastly to their satisfactory conclusion. As the afternoon drew to its close the wind blew a dark, oil-laden cloud down from the north, a sombre reminder of the destruction which the operation had brought in its wake.

It was on this high note that General Prince Khalid bin Sultan ended his military service. His departure came as something of a surprise. The work which he and his military staff, headed by Brigadier Abdul Aziz Al al Sheikh, had carried out to co-ordinate Saudi logistic support for all the disparate elements of the coalition, both in his own Moslem forces and on the Western side, had been a substantial achievement. He had succeeded, too, in keeping his end up in the company of commanders of far greater experience in the business of war. Perhaps there was no longer space within Saudi Arabia's small peacetime military hierarchy for someone of his pre-eminence. Hubris may also have played a part in his decision; there had been comment on his outspoken views on a more integrated Gulf defence. T-shirts were being marketed by enterprising merchants with his image displayed in tank commander's garb. Such projection went against the grain of Saudi tradition. Prince Khalid retired on promotion to general's rank, and with firm friendships and respect established during the long months of crisis.

Meanwhile the repercussions of the two abortive uprisings, so savagely repressed by the Ba'athist regime, continued to echo through to us from Iraq. In June, when British units recently returned from the Gulf were parading to a popular ovation and a well-deserved 'welcome home' reception by the City of London, our Iraqi exile contacts were telling us of harsh new operations by the Iraqi army against Shi'a refugees in the marsh country south of Basra. Troops were also said to be marshalling to harass the Kurds, grouped under UN protection in the north. At the same time the teams investigating Iraq's nuclear programme became the object of frequent, and sometimes violent, harrassment. We began to wonder if Saddam Hussein was seeking to provoke a fresh showdown.

The withdrawal of the last British forces from Kuwait and Jubail was nevertheless completed in late July. Operation GRANBY had been an effective and professional show, and had achieved its military aims with mercifully few casualties. There was little reason to suspect that a year later RAF Tornadoes would again be patrolling the Iraqi skies out of Dhahran.

CHAPTER 18

The Fourth Estate

'The essential thing in war is news, news, news, an insatiable
demand for news.'

Frank Gillard, BBC Second World War correspondent,
speaking on BBC television in May 1995

The part played by press and television throughout the Kuwait crisis
merits a chapter to itself. Their role was a highly influential one in terms
of public sentiment and of government responses too – and nowhere
more so than in the USA and Britain. Pressure by the media for access in
overwhelming numbers to the theatre of action developed into something of a running sore with their Saudi hosts. It also took up a great deal
of embassy time and attention right through the crisis. There were certain aspects to the media's participation in the crisis, both political and
technological, which were without precedent. These gave the experience
a unique quality, while holding lessons for the future pattern of war
reporting and its control.

One of the most significant of these new features was the breakthrough
in technology which enabled events to be reported instantly by satellite,
not only by voice but in pictures too, to a home base thousands of kilometres away with the aid of a compact mobile transmitter. This real-time
access to the public audience had the effect of reducing the scope for the
imposition of a regime for the comprehensive scrutiny of journalists'
material, for example during the period of military activity when security
of information became of paramount importance. Instead, such discipline could only be instituted on a partial basis while also depending on
voluntary adherence by the media to agreed 'ground rules'. Those who
had the advantage of direct transmission facilities could, if they chose,
ignore the filter. Yet to have tried to prohibit the use of direct satellite
transmission would have been a vain move, and bound to antagonise
correspondents whose co-operation was being sought on a basis of trust.

This feature coincided with the appearance of another new phenomenon in international broadcasting – the arrival of the world's first
round-the-clock satellite television news service in the shape of CNN,

operating out of Atlanta in the USA and available by dish receiver throughout the Middle East and around much of the globe via a linkage with a Russian satellite. The Kuwait crisis made CNN's reputation, transforming the station from a pilot news project of limited appeal into a compelling global information service. The instant visual coverage it suddenly made available of a crisis which had a mesmerised world in its grip endowed CNN almost overnight in the summer of 1990 with unprecedented power to influence the perception of events by the public and governments. Its application of this influence was at times to prove erratic and naive. This was compounded by the irritating practice of flitting from item to item, on the assumption that the attention span of its audience was about on a par with that of a spaniel. Yet the homespun superficiality of its commentaries was more than offset by the vivid and colourful imagery of its pictorial record.

In Saudi Arabia the station became virtually an addiction, with its images constituting a ubiquitous and distracting backdrop in the offices of officials with whom we did our business. For the public, too, it formed a major source of information of the course of events, once, with the launching of hostilities, the English-language channel of Saudi television was given over almost entirely to its coverage. We had entered the age of the 'CNN curve'; henceforward history would have to pause until the network arrived.

One of the reasons behind CNN's appeal to a wide audience within the region was the presence it contrived to retain in Baghdad throughout the duration of the Kuwait crisis. But the network paid a price in integrity for the privilege of keeping this commercially valuable foot in the enemy camp. Other Western television services also broadcast by satellite out of the Iraqi capital from the early stages of the crisis right up to the first days of the air war in January.

Indeed, during this period it was part of Iraq's ever-agile information policy to encourage such a foreign presence, including journalists from those countries which were taking a lead in opposing her occupation of Kuwait. The aim was to secure a propaganda gain from their presence. It was a bold tactic, and one not seen in recent situations of military confrontation. Western journalists had for example been uncommon in Hanoi during the war in Vietnam, and there had been none on hand to speak for the Argentinian occupiers during the Falklands conflict. In the event a few were deceived into playing the Iraqi tune, though as a more rigorous censorship closed in upon the reports which these correspondents were permitted to despatch, many of them indulged to their credit in elaborate deception tactics to avoid becoming mere mouthpieces.

With the unleashing of the coalition's bombing campaign however, the presence of Western journalists in Baghdad, with their capacity to transmit live reports of damage caused by the remarkable precision of the Tomahawk cruise missiles, became a two-edged sword for the Iraqi authorities. We were astonished by an eye-witness description of the science fiction precision of the Tomahawks, with their computer memories tracing the configuration of Baghdad's streets in search of preset objectives, given by John Simpson of the BBC as he watched a missile fly past his window in the Al Rashid hotel and turn the next street corner. There was also well-founded scepticism at the scale of Iraqi claims of civilian damage and loss of life as a result of coalition bombing, and more than a suspicion of elaborate theatricals being laid on for the benefit of the closely-shepherded Western correspondents. Several of these, like Robert Fox of *The Daily Telegraph* and Richard Beeston of *The Times* as well as John Simpson, saw through the Iraqi game. Despite assiduous screening by the Iraqi censorship, their reports sometimes contained nuggets of information which were of value to the coalition. In consequence Western correspondents were bundled out of Iraq for a spell.

CNN was allowed to stay, however, and retain the privilege of its satellite transmission equipment. Indeed, there were occasions when we began to wonder whether it was not becoming an Iraqi mouthpiece. On 28 January its correspondent in Baghdad, Peter Arnett, whose apparent readiness to swallow Iraq's propaganda had been a source of irritation to other Western journalists in the city, was granted the favour of a live television interview with Saddam Hussein himself, in which the Iraqi leader gave vent to a renewed outburst of malevolence, claiming Iraqi victory and threatening the shedding of blood. The ready provision of such a platform by an influential representative of the Western media during the thick of hostilities amounted in the eyes of all of us in Riyadh to behaviour that was not merely opportunist but shameful.

CNN went on to compound this complicity with uncritical repetition of other material fed to it by the Iraqi hosts. In one such report, showing bomb damage inflicted on a factory in the vicinity of Baghdad which had been identified as involved in the manufacture of ingredients for Iraq's chemical weapons programme, the Iraqi cover story that it had been solely engaged in the manufacture of babies' milk was repeated without a trace of scepticism. Such gratuitous air-time for Iraq's propaganda machine seemed bound to have its impact among some portion of the large audience which the novelty of CNN had succeeded in capturing in the Arab world and beyond.

It was thus a prime objective for the international coalition to counter Iraq's pervasive information offensive by ensuring that the world's media obtained the fullest possible access consistent with operational security to the policies and activities being put in place to reverse her aggression. The focal point for such dissemination had to be Saudi Arabia, in her dual role as a key co-ordinator of the international coalition and launch point for any eventual military offensive to enforce Iraq's withdrawal from Kuwait. The MoD, and Tom King himself, were inclined to fret at this arrangement. They may have hankered to keep the media initiative at the London end, as had been the case with the Falklands campaign nine years previously, rather than seeing Peter de la Billière and his team in the eye of the camera. But there was no real choice, as the world's press were camped in Riyadh where the action lay. The French tried for a while to co-ordinate their press briefing from Paris, but had eventually to yield.

To be effective, however, the arrangement required the wholehearted co-operation of the Saudi authorities. Their response was in the early stages inhibited by an endemic aversion to contact with the international media. This mistrust of outside public comment had become deeply rooted in the attitudes of the senior generation of the Al Saud. It derived from a determination to shield the Kingdom, with its conservative systems of government, law and custom, from the inquisitive eyes of the outside world, where certain contemporary standards and attitudes were perceived as erosive of Saudi traditions of stability and strict religious orthodoxy.

These suspicions had if anything been reinforced by frequent instances of disparaging and sensationalist reporting of events in the life of the Kingdom which had caught international attention. The inquisitive, and sometimes prurient, tone of such journalism gave offence, not just to the regime but to important sections of Saudi popular opinion too.

A celebrated case had been the showing on British television in 1980 of a film which recorded in lurid and secondhand fashion an episode three years previously in which a young princess of the Al Saud and her Saudi paramour had been executed for adultery, in accordance with Saudi Arabia's strict application of Islamic *shari'a* law. The screening of this film aroused deep indignation within the Kingdom. Relations with Britain passed through a tense few months, during which time the British ambassador, James Craig, was required by King Khalid bin Abdul Aziz to leave the country for a spell. The film was not only regarded as an insult to the country's traditions, however at variance these might be with Western practice, but also as a deceitful attempt on the part of the Western media to breach the carefully-guarded screen of privacy with which Saudi society sought to surround itself.

This episode, and others in similar if less prominent vein, had over the years earned for the British press a particularly malign image in Saudi perceptions. Constant efforts on the part of the FCO and the embassy to counter this prejudice had met with only limited success. Thus it was that when Kuwait was invaded in August 1990 and British forces were promptly deployed to the Kingdom in response to the Saudi request for assistance in meeting the threat of armed attack, representatives of the British media who naturally sought to cover this startling turn of affairs found themselves unable to secure the necessary visas to enter Saudi Arabia. Moreover, it soon became apparent that American journalists were not suffering under the same handicap. CNN, for example, was on hand to record the arrival of US warplanes and Marines units on the east coast within days of the crisis erupting.

The outcry from the British press was not long in reaching us. The MoD were for their part anxious to have the troop deployment fully portrayed for the purpose of engaging public support. For the FCO and ourselves the absence of a press presence was a factor contributing to the wave of sensational and misleading reporting in Britain on the threat to the Kingdom and, more particularly, to the large British community resident there, echoes of which had begun to cause needless distress to some of our citizens as alarm was relayed back to them from worried relatives. Anxiety at home was intensified by the unhelpful impact of an alarmist programme on BBC television about the dangers of chemical and biological weapons. Thus began a saga over the participation of the British press and media which was to form the only significant issue of controversy between the Saudi authorities and ourselves in all the eight months of our close and productive co-operation in the crisis over Kuwait.

An influential source for this negative approach towards access for the British media was the Minister of Information, Ali Sha'ir. A former general in the army and a member of a family with close ties to the Al Saud, he was ever-conscious of what he saw as his responsibility to hold at bay inquisitive or derogatory attention on the part of the world's press. The Kingdom's own national press presented no such problem as, albeit without a formal mechanism of censorship, they were accustomed to take a careful cue from his Ministry in what they wrote, and the television network was a department of the Ministry with no appetite for controversy.

The Minister therefore contemplated with disquiet the prospect of the crisis affording the opportunity for foreign journalists to have the run of the country in large numbers, poking their noses into corners for topics suitable for criticism or ridicule. Unfortunately for the British press this restrictive view appeared to be shared by the Saudi ambassador

to the UK, Sheikh Nasser al Manqour, a charming man with long experience of government business, but who had had his own brushes over
media interest in Saudi Arabia and her singular ways. The ambassador
was accordingly disinclined to facilitate the entry of British journalists
without clear instructions from Riyadh.

For our part we had regularly taken the line with those who managed
the Kingdom's relations with the foreign press that the way to counter
what they regarded as obsessive prying into private aspects of Saudi life
and traditions was to open doors and become more accessible. If the
fruit no longer appeared to be forbidden, the novelty would soon wear
off, to be replaced by more serious and constructive comment. At the
same time it was the wrong tactic to stand aside from debate and expect
others to correct tendentious reporting from abroad. The Kingdom had
instead to argue the toss for itself, as it was well equipped to do. There
were several within the Saudi establishment, both ministers and officials, who shared this thinking. But the arguments ran contrary to the
instincts of the senior generation, some of whom were extremely sensitive on the issue and regarded a more liberal approach as an invitation
to yet further malicious reporting.

By late August things had reached the point where the American
press, led by CNN, was present in the Kingdom in strength, with many
French and Arab journalists. It was apparent that the Saudi ambassador
in Washington, Prince Bandar bin Sultan, and his colleague in Paris,
Jamil al Hejailan, had chosen to adopt an open-handed approach over
the granting of visas. The British media were conspicuous by their
absence, with the exception of a few agile Middle East hands who had
managed to secure entry through nearby Saudi diplomatic missions.

Faced with the refusal of the Saudi embassy in London to issue press
visas, the MoD went to the lengths of flying out a plane-load of British
journalists by RAF Hercules to Dhahran, where with the full co-operation
of the RSAF base commander, Prince Turki bin Nasser, they saw the
Tornado squadron undertaking patrols and had briefings from Air Vice
Marshal Sandy Wilson and myself. So long as they stayed on the airbase
no entry formalities were involved. It was a relief to us when, under the
vigilant eye of their RAF minder, they trooped back on to the Hercules
at the end of the day for the slow haul back to Brize Norton. But the
situation had become unacceptable. Somehow we had to find a way of
getting the block on visas for the British press corps lifted.

We found help from the director of the foreign press department of
the Information Ministry, Shihab Jamjoom, a member of a leading Jedda
merchant family with local press interests who held the rank of assistant
minister. Over the months ahead he played a tireless part in facilitating

access by British journalists and media technicians, finding his way around obstacles and even turning the occasional blind eye when they took predictable, yet provocative, liberties with the rules.

Shihab Jamjoom carried a heavy responsibility throughout the crisis for overseeing the background arrangements for the veritable army of foreign press representatives which descended on the Kingdom. During the fighting phase their number exceeded 1,000. He set up extensive briefing centres in the International Hotel beside Dhahran airport, and subsequently at the imposing Hyatt Regency Hotel in Riyadh where coalition commanders and spokesmen delivered their daily operational briefings throughout the hostilities. At the same time he opened doors to visiting journalists on an unprecedented scale, overcoming in the process instinctive reluctance among many of his counterparts within the Saudi establishment.

Visas, however, were a matter for the Minister himself. We decided to tackle the problem by stages. As a first step we gave support to an application for a visa made by the well-respected Middle East correspondent of the BBC World Service, Barnaby Mason. Relations between the BBC and the Minister of Information were in particularly good shape following a visit to the Kingdom the previous spring by Marmaduke Hussey, the chairman of the BBC's board of governors, as the guest of Ali Sha'ir. Shihab Jamjoom had laid on a most hospitable programme for the visit, including a turn on one of the flight simulators at Saudia's modern pilot training centre in Jedda, when 'Duke' Hussey and I managed to crash-land a Boeing 747 at Geneva.

Given the international standing of the BBC World Service and the large audience which its Arabic service enjoyed within the Kingdom, from the Royal Diwan down to the man in the street and in the tent too, it made no sense to deny access to its correspondent. Moreover, Barnaby Mason was based in Egypt, who had shown herself to be an important ally to Saudi Arabia in the crisis. The Saudi embassy in Cairo might prove more relaxed than London over the issue of a visa.

The approach worked and Barnaby Mason gained entry in late August. But there was still no movement at the London end. To complicate things a new cause for complaint now arose against British media reporting, involving the BBC Arabic service. From their habitual listening to the BBC news bulletins, the Saudis had formed the impression of a bias towards Iraq's version of events in the presentation of the crisis by the Arabic service. Prince Saud raised this worry during a discussion on press visas. He suggested it might be a consequence of the presence of a number of Palestinians among the editors and newsreaders on the London staff of the Arabic service. Iraq's seizure of Kuwait and Saddam

Hussein's facile attempt to link this with Israel's occupation of Palestinian territory was having the intended effect of arousing support among many Palestinians. Similar allegations of bias began to reach us from other quarters, to the point where they were evidently contributing to the problem of British press access.

The BBC World Service at Bush House rightly took the charge seriously, and set in hand a scrutiny to check for any tendency towards bias. They claimed to find none. We recognised that to some extent the Saudis would inevitably find it hard to accept that the BBC, with all its influence among Arab audiences, needed to pursue its aim of objectivity by allowing a voice to those showing sympathy with the Iraqi aggressor. We nevertheless undertook our own embassy survey, from which it did seem to us that there were instances when the editorial balance between reports appeared to give Iraq's standpoint a prominence it did not deserve. Part of the problem, however, stemmed from the traditional Saudi reluctance to respond in public debate.

Nevertheless the BBC's response helped to moderate Saudi concern. By early September a limited number of visas was being issued by the embassy in London to both press and television. This was the phoney war period of initial military build-up, when there was little novel to report. The journalists who came out were for the most part defence specialists, whose interest was therefore directed towards the troops and their training rather than more general issues affecting Saudi Arabia. They were given a remarkably free rein within the Kingdom.

For their part the Saudi government had sensibly elected to avoid action which might afford a focus for controversy or prying interest. Capital punishment in the shape of public executions was quietly suspended lest it attract lurid comment. To help satisfy the appetite for news we made early arrangements for BFME headquarters to set up a forces information bureau alongside the Americans and Saudis in the Dhahran press centre, and carried out our own regular briefing in Riyadh of British and other journalists on the diplomatic background. Meanwhile there was a splendid response from a number of British tabloids to a request from the headquarters public affairs staff for backing for the weekly newspaper, *The Sandy Times*, which was being launched locally for the benefit of British troops in the theatre.

But this was a tedious period of waiting for the world's press, now assembling in the Kingdom and caught between pressure from editors' deadlines and little action to file. Their frustration tended to show. When a newsworthy event did occur, they took on the appearance of a voracious pack of raptors, as when the three British engineers who had boldly made it to Saudi Arabia in a small boat from detention in Iraq ran the gauntlet of their clamorous interrogation in Dhahran during October.

Among more serious commentators it was frequently the Americans who produced the most perceptive material. Two who took particular pains to understand the Kingdom and cultivate influential Saudi contacts were Dean Fisher of *Time* magazine and Judith Miller of the *New York Times*. On the British side the *Economist, The Guardian* and *The Daily Telegraph* were among those with good performers in the field, who handled information with responsibility and an eye to our common purpose in the crisis. We helped them out where we could, and they found a number of Saudis who were accustomed to the ways of the Western press and ready to provide them with the unwonted flavour of the Kingdom at war. There was also keen competition for news stories among the three television news services, BBC, ITN and the relative newcomer, Sky.

There was, however, a handful of representatives of influential British newspapers for whom preconception seemed to us on occasion to count for more than actuality. Robert Fisk of *The Independent* had the justified reputation of being one of the most knowledgeable and respected commentators on Middle Eastern affairs. A specialist on Palestine, he had also had a spell in the Gulf prior to the Kuwait crisis and knew the area's problems well. Through the Saudi embassy in Bahrain he was one of the first to secure an entry visa.

During all the stages of the crisis he put his credentials and experience of the Kingdom to good journalistic effect, preferring to plough his own furrow while enjoying access to an extent which gained him the envy of others – a kind of Scarlet Pimpernel act. At one point, irked by military controls of journalists' movements, he went so far as to argue publicly that if correspondents were trusted to make their own way to the front, observing operational confidentiality and having responsibility for their own security, all restrictions could be abolished. It was not only in his movements, however, that he kept apart from the main pack. In his writing too there often emerged a tendency to challenge the actions of the coalition to the point where it sometimes seemed to verge on personal prejudice.

From an early stage Robert Fisk's reporting showed a negative attitude towards the military, questioning morale and the effectiveness of combat capability. One early piece, written following contacts with American servicemen, queried their will to face combat, a suggestion which was amply confuted by their performance when it came to hostilities. The British Army came in for similar disparagement, with querulous comment on the Challenger tanks with which Patrick Cordingley's 7th Armoured Brigade was equipped, and subsequent comparisons with the mud of Flanders when the desert going turned wet and heavy in the New Year. February found him casting doubt on the Saudi will to see the air offensive sustained as it ran into a second month.

Whatever the sources for such reports, their derogatory pitch was out of all proportion. For their part our service colleagues discounted such carping as the latest round in a history of antipathy towards the military on Robert Fisk's part. Having given vent to irritation on more than one occasion, a rumour came back to me from the press corps that I had interceded with the Saudis to get him removed. This was absurd, though the Saudis shared our indignation. All the embassy's effort was being devoted to securing greater rather than less access for members of the British press, whatever their prejudices.

Another journalist to cause us concern was the Middle East corre-spondent of *The Times*, Christopher Walker. During January and February when the main thrust of international media attention was rightly focused on the preparation and conduct of the coalition offen-sive, he went out of his way to produce a series of reports in tabloid vein, an aim of which seemed to be an attempt to drive wedges between the Saudis and their Western comrades and create mischief for our working relationship. There was speculation about pork in the British rations, an unfounded allegation that the Saudis had prevented British troops from holding a service on the eve of battle, and a report attributing deroga-tory remarks about Saudi Arabia to British servicemen.

He also questioned Saudi popular resolve over the launching of the land war, with the claim that each day of Iraq's resistance to the coalition was seen as a victory for Saddam Hussein. This was far from the reality, though it made an opportunist story. Another report later in February on growing unease among Saudis over the prolonged duration of the bombing campaign was closer to the mark. But it all had a meretricious quality, which we felt was denying the readership an appreciation of the major issues at stake, and unworthy of *The Times*' august masthead. It did, however, lead to a comic sequel, when Peter de la Billière, to whom I had grumbled about one Christopher Walker writing on the taboo subject of worship, took to task a startled British Army chaplain who, as ill-luck would have it, was also called Christopher Walker and happened to have written a letter to *The Times*... another instance of 'Murphy' at work.

Occasionally we would receive visits from senior figures in the British press whose factious reputation was deemed by the MoD to entitle them to special attention. One such was Andrew Neil, editor of *The Sunday Times*, who came round to the house for a talk one evening in October before being spirited off down to Oman by the military, for the privilege of joining an RAF Nimrod surveillance patrol over the sea approaches to the Gulf which operated out of the base at Masirah. It was an inspired idea, which kept Andrew Neil airborne and out of contact for several hours of his short visit.

On taking over command of British forces from Sandy Wilson, Peter de la Billière made a point of giving the British press contingent an early briefing in Dhahran and at my house in Riyadh on the growing likelihood that things would have to come to a fight. He stressed that any conflict would be a short one. We could cope with Iraq's possible use of illegal chemical weapons, but further reinforcements might be needed.

Towards the end of October, however, a situation arose which threatened once again to restrict the access to Saudi Arabia which we had managed to secure for the British media. This was a period when the limited-term visas granted to the first wave of British journalists were starting to expire. With welcome help from the governor of the Eastern Province, Prince Mohammed bin Fahd, who had been consistently forthcoming with briefings and hospitality for the foreign press, and with some adroit juggling with accreditations on the part of Shihab Jamjoom, temporary extensions were secured to cover the arrival of 7th Armoured Brigade. But the curtain then fell, and no less than 20 of the 42 British media personnel by now present in the Kingdom were asked to leave. They happened to include the entire ITN contingent.

I made our dismay at this retrograde move plain to the Information Minister and to his helpful deputy, Dr. Fuad al Farsi, and pressed for the visas to be extended, deploying the argument that Britain's military involvement in the crisis needed to be reported in full detail so that public opinion at home should be well-informed and supportive. Moreover, the record of reporting by British correspondents had hitherto been a responsible one, and had afforded the Saudis no cause for concern. To reduce their numbers in mid-stream was bound to have a negative impact at home.

The Information Ministry appeared unmoved. Their response was that they were now facing irresistible pressures from all round the globe to admit press teams, to the point where numbers looked like getting out of hand. The British contingent was disproportionately large and had to be reduced to make place for others. This international clamour for media accreditation was indeed presenting real difficulties for the Saudis, accustomed as they were to strict monitoring of press access to the country.

But, as I told them in reply, there could be no comparison between the position of the UK as a major troop contributor and that of other countries which were mere spectators. The suggestion was also conveyed that their action might even involve a discriminatory element; we were aware that the press contingents from our two main Western partners, the USA and France, were not meeting similar restriction, as a result of the open-handed approach over media access adopted by the Saudi embassies in Washington and Paris. Indeed, it was said that one flight out of the French capital brought well over 100 correspondents to cover the crisis.

Finding these exchanges were making little progress, we sought to broaden our lobbying by bringing in the Foreign Ministry and individuals like Prince Abdullah bin Faisal in Jubail, who were familiar with our press. Finally I took our problem to the King through his personal staff, with an expression of serious disquiet over the likely repercussions of imposing a penalty of this scale on British press numbers. This produced a helpful assurance that the British media strength could stay at its present level, though there had to be some new faces.

A limited number of new visas were issued by the London embassy, but problems soon surfaced again. Still influenced by a measure of mistrust, the Information Ministry asked for the British government to take a part in the selection of journalists to be issued with visas. This we firmly declined to do. Ironically, matters were in danger of reaching the point where Iraq was more open with visas for British journalists than Saudi Arabia.

Meanwhile the Saudis had themselves taken some bold steps into uncharted territory in the management of their domestic media. Faced with an insidious radio campaign from Iraq designed to erode public support for Kuwait and exploit religious sensitivity over the presence of non-Moslem forces so near to Islam's holy places, the initial Saudi response was ponderous and unconvincing, relying on standard invocations of patriotic rhetoric with little attempt to go on the offensive and challenge Iraq on her own ground. We began to give some technical help to the Saudis in establishing their own counter-propaganda exercise into Iraq and Kuwait, which might evade Iraq's dense radio-jamming defences.

But something also needed to be done to capture the attention of opinion within Saudi Arabia herself. In the course of October the Information Ministry made it clear to the Saudi press that it should make greater use of its own initiative in writing on the crisis. This was followed by an unprecedented act of encouraging the publication of daily newspapers in tabloid form, in which it was hoped that the increasing number of reports of Iraqi atrocities coming out of Kuwait would be highlighted. There was no shortage of such black material. Once they overcame their initial disbelief at such permissiveness, the Saudi press houses responded enthusiastically with vivid journalism that did not lack for hyperbole and had immediate appeal for a jaded readership. Television projection of the crisis was perked up with the retransmission of CNN coverage, though this turned out to be a mixed blessing.

In mid-December, with the UN Security Council deadline for Iraq's withdrawal only a month away and no sign of any intention on Saddam Hussein's part to comply with it, I took up the visa impasse once again with Prince Saud. In his ever-helpful way he suggested a resourceful solution through a formula which could combine a minimal official endorsement on our part of journalists' credentials to meet the reservations of the Information Ministry, with open selection and an ample ceiling. We worked up this idea together, and I tried it on Archie Hamilton, the Minister of State for Defence, when he came out to visit the troops shortly before Christmas. He thought it would run in Whitehall.

By this time, however, we had hit another snag. BBC television's *Panorama*, a weekly current affairs programme with a justified reputation for provocative and controversial comment, had applied to send a team to Saudi Arabia in December to film the country on the eve of war. Naturally the programme's producer, David Lomax, was keen to cover as many strands of opinion within the Kingdom as possible, ranging from interviews with senior Al Saud figures in government to urban and pastoral society, and taking in the conservative Islamic elements which had been voicing concern over the allegedly unwholesome influence upon Saudi society of the presence of foreign forces.

To their credit, particularly as the application followed on the heels of the ladies' driving episode which had led to much controversy in the foreign press, the Information Ministry, after some urging from ourselves and Saudi contacts favouring a more open approach to the foreign media, gave their blessing.

David Lomax and his production team obtained access to a wide cross-section of Saudi opinion around the country. They went with Faisal Bashir, a former planning minister, to join the bedouin camp of his ageing father, a senior sheikh of the Anaiza tribe; they discussed Saudi Arabia's traditions of government in detail with Prince Khalid Al Faisal, the able and enlightened governor of the Asir province on the frontier with Yemen; they mingled somewhat uneasily after prayers with the people of the puritanical region of Qassim; and they took opinions, freely given, from all around, including the stimulating views of Khalid Maeena, editor-in-chief of the Jedda-based *Arab News* and one of the Kingdom's most articulate journalists. Prince Abdullah bin Faisal, who had appeared previously in *Panorama* programmes, gave the team considerable time, as did Shihab Jamjoom in the co-ordination of the visit. Indeed, Saudi co-operation was excellent.

The programme was due to be screened in Britain on 5 January. As the date neared, however, reports began to get back to the Saudis, no doubt from their embassy, that, notwithstanding the particular circumstances of the crisis, *Panorama* intended to resurrect criticism of certain of the more sensitive features of Saudi society. These rumours had the effect of inducing anxiety at a high level in the Kingdom, to a point which began to affect once again the provision of additional visas for the British press.

We had by this time devised an overall control plan for the British media contingent in the event of hostilities, and I had agreed this with Prince Saud. The brigadier responsible for public relations in the MoD came out from London during December to set up with the BFME headquarters, and in liaison with the American military, a scheme involving the formation of five official pools, composed of around 80 British journalists and television and radio personnel, with accreditation as war correspondents. Four of these would accompany Army units into Kuwait, while the fifth would be afloat with the Royal Navy.

To expedite transmission these groups would share a satellite facility close to the area of combat. Under the pooling arrangements their product would be available to all. A BBC bid for a separate dedicated link was not accepted. Rudimentary screening of material would be applied in the field to ensure no breach of security or prejudice to coalition policy in the conflict, and the journalists concerned would be expected to observe ground rules of military confidentiality.

These proposals for pooling arrangements with prompt clearance in the field were designed to get away from the rigid and slow system of news management which had been applied during the Falklands operation nine years previously, and which had been much resented by the media in Britain. The Americans were proposing to adopt pooling arrangements for their press on similarly open-handed lines. For them this represented a departure from their earlier, more restrictive, practice in Vietnam. In the event the British pools proved to have an advantage in rapid despatch of material. American screening arrangements were said to be more cumbersome, and material had to reach Dhahran or Riyadh before it could be transmitted. But the American pool system appeared to have operated with greater flexibility of movement.

These plans were fine so far as they went. But it was clear that the numbers we had been planning for were quite inadequate; access would be needed for about twice that number, owing mainly to the large numbers of technical staff required by the television channels. We therefore had to devise two categories for the press contingent, with about half of them accredited to the pools with their element of protection and supervision, and the rest operating outside this circle and registered as freelance. There was resentment and some sharp frustration on the part of some who found themselves excluded from the official pools, though others seemed to prefer going it alone and taking their own chances in the reporting of combat.

The size of this second category, swollen by scores of press representatives from around the world who enjoyed no access to pool arrangements, meant that there needed to be a system for full and constant briefing on the military situation by all the combatants, including the Saudis, in both Riyadh and Dhahran. Given the voracious press appetite for news and their ready access to satellite communications, it made no sense to be parsimonious with information. This would create frustration and encourage speculative and capricious reporting of the kind we sought to discourage. Disclosure had, of course, to be tailored to operational security and political considerations, and take account of such factors as coalition solidarity and morale. Within these general bounds it was decided that the various headquarters should aim for maximum briefing, to hold press attention and keep them well plied with detail. This was, after all, what news editors were demanding to fill their bulletins.

We accordingly put to the Saudis a total ceiling of 170 for British journalists and technicians, all to be selected by their own enterprises but to have their professional credentials vouched for to the Saudi embassy by the MoD. I took Prince Saud a letter from Douglas Hurd, explaining these arrangements and reinforcing the request that the embassy in London be authorised to grant the necessary visas. As the Foreign Secretary put it, we were all praying for peace yet had to prepare for war.

By now, however, the incubus of the imminent *Panorama* programme was hanging over the whole exercise, and had rekindled the Information Minister's misgivings which we had been at such pains to allay. Ali Sha'ir raised his unease with me on the eve of the programme being shown. In London there had been considerable discussion during the previous days between the Saudi embassy and the FCO, and also with the BBC, over the tone the programme would adopt. As we explained to the Saudis, the BBC understandably insisted on its right to editorial independence. At the same time they were not insensitive to the consideration that this was not the moment for introducing controversy into a very significant relationship of alliance. As producer, David Lomax had been given free rein in the Kingdom. It was for him to strike a just balance in putting the programme together.

It was with some trepidation on 7 January that we tuned into the satellite dish, newly installed in the embassy to receive BBC television. I expected that Prince Saud and other senior Saudi figures, for whom we had installed similar reception facilities to serve as an alternative to their diet of CNN, were doing likewise. Shihab Jamjoom had gone to London, and had decided on the bold course of inviting leading editors and journalists to join him in viewing the programme over a dinner arranged in a hotel by the Ministry's contact with the British press, Dermot Graham. There was a large turnout. To our relief the programme came across as informative and balanced. It covered a cross-section of opinion and did not duck areas of Saudi custom which were seen from outside as anachronistic. But the Saudi establishment was given good opportunity to defend such attitudes, and there was no attempt to work up controversy or sensation.

Meanwhile, with only days to go now, the restriction on journalists was turning into a crisis in our relationship. I renewed my urgent representations to the Information and Foreign Ministries as well as to King Fahd's personal office, drawing on a leading article in critical terms which appeared in *The Times* on 9 January. The pressure from London, including from Downing Street, was becoming intense. Prince Saud took the problem up personally with the King and obtained agreement to the immediate issue of visas on the lines we were proposing. In the nick of time everything snapped into gear, with visas forthcoming and the descent of a large addition to the British press contingent. Significantly perhaps, the Saudi ambassador absented himself from his post in London at this stage and did not return until after hostilities had ended. His deputy, Ibrahim al Mosly, did everything he could to be helpful, with support from the Foreign Ministry in Riyadh. It had been a close-run thing.

So far as the international press corps were concerned, the opening of the air offensive brought an end to the weeks of tedious waiting. Scud raids on Riyadh and Dhahran gave them plenty of excitement and made for dramatic television pictures as Patriot missiles went aloft to intercept. It became a difficult choice for pressmen whether to go below to the shelters when the air-raid warning went, or chance it on the hotel roof.

The briefing arrangements set in hand by the coalition forces, using the well-equipped press centres in Riyadh and Dhahran, were operating at full pitch. It was soon found more efficient to run the American, Saudi and British operational briefings together each evening. The British session was supervised by Group Captain Niall Irving, an RAF officer experienced in public relations. It transpired after the war that among the fans of his calm and understated handling of this demanding role on television was Barbara Bush, the American First Lady. The main spot was sometimes taken by Peter de la Billière, who liked to have a free hand with the press and was irked by what he considered to be fussy interference on the part of Tom King and the chief of defence staff in London.

Nick Abbott attended the Riyadh daily briefings while I held periodic sessions in the embassy on the diplomatic background. Our doors were always open to British journalists. For their part the Saudi military absorbed the techniques fast and ran a well-attuned daily briefing performance through their spokesman, Brigadier Al Rubayan. General Prince Khalid sometimes took the stand himself. Norman Schwarzkopf made no secret of his relish of the limelight and gave some rousing performances as he knocked the combat performance of the Iraqis around the ground.

As the land offensive approached those who found themselves outside the pool arrangements chafed increasingly at their inability to get to the front. They had been particularly frustrated to find their efforts blocked to get into Al Khafji during the fighting to retake it from the Iraqis. An ITN team had succeeded in eluding the controls on movement and reached the deserted town in late January, where they recorded some of the air attacks across the frontier and were also the first to notice the release of crude oil and its effect on wildlife. For this unauthorised and hazardous foray through military lines they had had their passes confiscated by the Saudis, and were at risk of expulsion. It took considerable intercession on our part to get them let off with a warning. A CBS television team doing their own reconnoitring had the misfortune to stray over the Kuwaiti border and spent the rest of the war in captivity in Iraq.

By the middle of February many of these 'unilaterals', as they were known, had collected in the northern garrison town of Hafr al Batin as a jumping-off point for their expeditions. A group of reporters, including Richard Dowden of *The Independent*, who set off across the border under their own auspices found themselves receiving the surrender of an Iraqi army unit.

As for those who participated in the five official pools, they were scrupulous in observing silence over the key deception manoeuvre, involving the transfer of the main coalition force inland, away from the Gulf coast where the Iraqis were expecting the main attack to come. They produced some memorable footage. The BBC's Kate Adie joined the Royal Artillery gunners as they sweated to fire off their spectacular barrage of shells and missiles at Iraqi positions in Kuwait. Martin Bell had us a bit worried at one point with sympathetic footage of a REME unit's communion service before battle. But once the attack went in, the coalition forces advanced at such a cracking pace that the pools hardly had time to record events before they had to press on if they were to keep up.

Aboard ship there were scenes of Navy helicopters in action against Iraqi patrol boats and shots of Iraqi prisoners of war. In these reports care was taken to observe Geneva Convention rules prohibiting identification, in sharp contrast to Iraqi action in callously parading British and other captured aircrew on Baghdad television to make forced statements. With the Arab forces there was quite a contingent of Saudi journalists in the unaccustomed role of war correspondents. Khalid Maeena had made sure he was up with the Kuwaiti advance, and reported each day on their jubilant return to their country despite the desolation of oil fires and the wreckage of war.

One of those who chose to plough a lone furrow was Sandy Gall of ITN. Guessing that members of the British media pools might be subject to time delays in issuing their accounts of the fighting, he hit on the idea of attaching himself to one of the Arab formations in the land advance. These units would, he rightly surmised, have a place of honour when it came to entry into Kuwait City. Buoyed up with this ingenious plan he came across to the embassy to tell me about it, with ideas of upstaging the authorised war correspondents. He seemed a touch crestfallen to hear my welcome for his plan and good wishes in his efforts to get aboard the Kuwaiti or Saudi armoured advance. In fact it suited our purposes well to have him flash around the world the participation of Kuwaiti and other Arab forces in the vanguard of the capital's recapture.

At this point our discussion was cut short by a Scud warning, so we adjourned to the nearest gas-proof 'safe haven', which happened to be in our highly-secure communications centre. I asked the obliging Sandy to avert his eyes. It turned out to be a false alarm; the target was the military base of Hafr al Batin, far to the north. In the event Sandy Gall had his ups and downs in getting alongside the Arab forces, but he got his 'scoop' and just made it in time to Kuwait City.

Meanwhile the BBC had redeemed its reputation in Saudi eyes as a result of the more objective standard it was now considered to be achieving in its news bulletins, particularly in comparison with CNN. Peter Arnett's ill-judged interview with Saddam Hussein at the end of January had gone down very badly, and the network's relaying of the display of injured coalition aircrew on Iraqi television had got under Norman Schwarzkopf's skin. After the war he went so far as to describe it as 'aiding and abetting' the enemy, though in practice this uncivilised tactic probably rebounded against Iraq with international opinion.

Panorama also rendered a service with a hard-hitting programme in February on the barbarity of Saddam Hussein's rule. This included videotape of the chilling episode at the outset of his presidency in 1979, when he had convened a meeting of Ba'ath party members at which, between puffing on a cigar and feigning tears, the new leader read out a list of those accused of treason and had their colleagues take them out of the hall to execution. It was a gruesome exercise in ruthless tyranny and mass hysteria, of which we had little doubt the Iraqi President was still capable.

With the liberation of Kuwait the army of journalists lost no time in decamping northwards or heading for home. Suddenly the press centres were deserted. Some courageous individuals tried to infiltrate across the armistice lines into Basra to report on the uprising in the south and the savage action to repress it which was already being undertaken by the Republican Guard. None succeeded. An ITN reporter and cameraman who tried to bluff their way past the Iraqi guards were promptly arrested for their pains and held captive in Basra for over a week. We came under pressure from the FCO to see if we could help get them released, but there was nothing we or the military could do.

Once again Robert Fisk caused us worry by harping on about his expectation of brutal reprisals on the part of the Kuwaiti population against Palestinian residents who had stayed behind, and would be suspected of having collaborated with the Iraqis. We all shared concern on this point, as there was evidence in the first few days after liberation of such scores being settled in arbitrary fashion. From the Cassandra-like tone of Robert Fisk's reporting on the issue during the latter part of February, however, there seemed a risk of his contributing to a self-fulfilling prophecy. In the event, despite understandable rancour on the part of many Kuwaitis, matters did not get out of hand.

Our stream of post-war visitors to Riyadh may have missed the excitement of wartime press 'hype'. For the embassy, however, and above all for the Saudis, it came as a relief. They had treated their demanding media visitors with hospitality and an unwonted confidence. Odd tail-ends of press comment in Britain returned to tease us. When the House of Commons Defence Committee paid a visit to Riyadh shortly after the war, their first request on coming to the house was to see the guest book. The object of their interest turned out to be John Major's signature marking the occasion of his visit shortly before the coalition offensive. In his precise fashion the Prime Minister had added the Downing Street postcode in writing his address. This meticulous entry had evidently been spotted by the sharp eye of a journalist at one of my briefings and had subsequently had fun poked at it in the *Spectator* magazine. Had the Defence Committee members looked further down the page, they would have seen that the next name was that of Hani al Hassan of the PLO, a conjunction which could have given rise to more serious speculation.

CHAPTER 19

Aftermath

In an article published in *The Times* six months after the liberation of Kuwait, Douglas Hurd drew up a balance sheet of what the international operation to liberate Kuwait had achieved. On the positive side the international front which had come together under the aegis of the UN Security Council had secured its main objective – Kuwait's freedom – in strict accordance with the limitations on military action which it had set itself in the UN resolutions. Saddam Hussein's repeated gamble that, if he played for time, the solidarity of the coalition would erode and undermine the effectiveness of sanctions had run up against a resolve, not least on the part of its Arab members, for which he had not bargained. On the wider international front the operation had, moreover, created new opportunities to improve security and promote the settlement of disputes through an enhanced role for the UN, as well as in a regional context in the Gulf and over Palestine.

Yet the article also contained a warning of 'much unfinished business'. The problem of Iraqi aggressiveness under Saddam Hussein's regime was by no means over. Iraq's response during the first months of the UN operation to identify and dismantle her capability in nuclear and other weapons of mass destruction, one of the key elements in the Security Council's ceasefire Resolution 687, had added up to a brazen succession of efforts to conceal stocks and facilities and deceive the inspection teams. Until it was clear that there was no longer a threat from this quarter, the option of force would have to be retained.

Meanwhile the regime was indulging in savage and unacceptable internal repression. Within weeks of the Kuwait ceasefire this had produced an international military intervention in the north to establish a measure of protection for the Kurdish community, and there was now renewed concern over the continuing persecution of the Shi'a population in the south. In words intended perhaps as exhortation, the Foreign Secretary repeated the theme of six months earlier, that no tears would be shed 'if Saddam were toppled'. He reinforced this comment with the caution that 'it is difficult to see how Iraq can meet the conditions laid down by the UN while he remains in power'.

Iraq's behaviour during the five years since she was so conclusively driven out of Kuwait has fully borne out the need for continuing economic and diplomatic pressures, backed up by military vigilance. Throughout this time Saddam Hussein has resorted to a policy of survival at all costs within the bearpit of Iraqi politics. So far he has achieved this by combining the resumption of a rule of terror with repeated gestures of defiance in the face of UN efforts to apply the penalties for aggression. This show of intransigence owes much to that same mixture of impetuosity and self-conceit which contributed to his ill-fated decision to get himself out of a jam by seizing Kuwait and her assets. But it has also no doubt been part of his calculation that defiance in the face of superior odds would continue to appeal to national sentiment among those Iraqis, particularly within the armed forces, who still regarded him as the preferable alternative to internal chaos and a bitter civil war. He may have aimed, too, to touch a wider audience by once again playing on ever-sensitive Arab antipathy towards Western interference.

The fact that the international community has shown itself ready to ensure Iraq complies with the conditions laid upon her, if necessary through force, has rendered such fractious recalcitrance futile. Indeed, the record has shown a succession of Iraqi attempts to obstruct and dissemble being followed by grudging climb-down, to the point where, five years on, the painstaking exercise of destroying her nuclear, chemical and missile programmes and establishing a regime for future monitoring looks nearly complete, though some doubts remain over concealment of missiles and a biological weapons capability.

On the political side Iraq has confirmed her acceptance of Kuwait's sovereignty, and of the frontier as demarcated under UN auspices. Gold bullion looted from Kuwait's central bank at the time of the invasion has been returned, as has a good part of the military equipment and aircraft which the Iraqis took for their own use. Bit by bit Iraqi denials that they were still holding Kuwaiti citizens have been eroded through persistent pressure on the part of Kuwait and the International Red Cross. Successive releases have brought Kuwaiti estimates of missing persons down from over 6,000 following liberation to a core of some 600 by late 1995. The issue of compensation to the victims of invasion and occupation has, however, remained unresolved.

This combination of pressure and containment, under the authority of the UN Security Council and led by the countries which took part in driving Iraq out of Kuwait, has been sustained with a rare unity of purpose. In the initial flush of victory it was claimed as a model for future combined action on the part of the UN in the post-Cold War era to regulate threats to international security, a premature show of confidence which was within a year to lose its way in the political and moral crossfire of Somalia's anarchy and the break-up of Yugoslavia. In the case of Iraq it has been marked by spells of unspectacular tedium punctuated by bouts of confrontation. But it has nevertheless met with success in cutting Saddam Hussein's regime down to size. A pattern soon established itself whereby bursts of Iraqi defiance and threats of physical resistance would be countered by firm international response and a readiness to meet force with force. After noisy exchanges, and occasionally a military brush, the Iraqi leader would back off.

It is difficult to see what Saddam Hussein could secure by such intransigence except for greater disillusionment at home and a reinforcement of international resolve to see him brought to heel. Iraq has found herself virtually isolated within the Arab community, where her abrupt loss of esteem as a result of defeat has not been reversed. Dogged investigation work by the UN Special Commission (UNSCOM) set up under a Swede, Rolf Ekeus, to sort out Iraq's weapons of mass destruction in an operation using Bahrain as the stepping-off point has been conducted in the face of obstruction and harassment, sometimes endangering the safety of the inspectors. The operation has greatly reduced Iraq's scope to mount recidivist threats against her neighbours' security.

The importance of this task has been borne out by the alarming information, which inspections have gradually brought to light, of the extent of Iraq's capability in chemical and biological weapons and missile stocks at the start of the crisis, as well as of the progress she had made in the development of a crude nuclear capacity. Indeed, had Saddam Hussein restrained himself a year or two longer, military confrontation to recover Kuwait could have held far graver implications.

Nor has there been any premature loosening of the screws over the enforcement of sanctions. Saddam Hussein may well have been counting upon pressures to see them eased, notably from France and Russia as former close commercial partners of Iraq who have felt particular pain from prolonged loss of trade and non-payment of large outstanding debts for military equipment. Indeed, some support has materialised in these quarters. Yet the front sustained by the governments, Arab and Western, which took the lead in challenging Iraq's aggression has remained remarkably cohesive and solid in the face of over four years of Iraqi manoeuvres and prevarication.

But in compelling Iraqi compliance with the penalties imposed on her by the UN, the international community has faced an awkward dilemma. Despite the repeated profession that there is no wish to prolong the sufferings of the Iraqi people, the imposition of sanctions and other penalties has inevitably had that very effect. Through denial of revenue to the Iraqi state from oil exports, sanctions have surely made their contribution to the Iraqi leadership's grudging compliance with UN resolutions. But they have proved a two-edged weapon.

With characteristic defiance Saddam Hussein chose to spurn a proposal made by the Security Council in mid-August 1991 whereby, in a move to alleviate the growing hardship of the Iraqi people in the face of sanctions, Iraq would be permitted to sell 1.6 million barrels of oil over a six-month period. The proceeds would be disbursed by the UN, with 30 per cent going towards reparations, and a smaller portion to cover the costs of UNSCOM and other UN activity, including the work of the Border Commission. The major balance would be used to purchase essential food and medicine for distribution within Iraq under UN supervision. This characteristically intransigent response was repeated by the Iraqi leader when in early 1995 he rejected a further Security Council resolution permitting the sale of a larger quantity of oil in return for humanitarian goods over the distribution of which Iraq would retain control.

In rejecting the scheme as an infringement of Iraq's sovereignty, Saddam Hussein chose in effect to hold his people to ransom by causing them to bear the full brunt of sanctions in their daily lives, while naturally casting the blame for their misery on the international community. This specious propaganda exercise met with some success within Iraq and elsewhere, in conveying the image of a vengeful campaign of retaliation led by the West, as conditions of life became ever more harsh for Iraqis. It did not need much to resurrect talk of an American-led conspiracy to sustain a climate of insecurity in the Gulf region through keeping Iraq on the boil.

As months and then years passed without Saddam Hussein's overthrow or assassination, fanciful rumours even went so far as to suggest an intention to keep the Iraqi leader in power, as a pretext for interference. Some Western journalists invited back to Baghdad showed susceptibility to these spurious claims on the part of the Iraqi regime. Meanwhile, limited international efforts to alleviate the worst effects of popular deprivation within Iraq, through schemes run by relief organisations with funds from Western and other governments, met with frequent obstruction.

At the same time Saddam Hussein compounded the misery of his cowed people by renewed brutality and violation of basic human rights. Through successive purges among the military and within the Ba'ath party leadership, he satisfied himself that he was keeping the threat of overthrow at bay. Yet these actions had the constant effect of narrowing the basis for his supreme authority as he came to depend on the bonds of family and tribe for loyalty. Repression was not confined to action against the Kurdish and Shi'a communities. The need to re-establish a basis for support among the country's Sunni population saw no easing in the activity of the regime's secret intelligence apparatus. Increasingly harsh penalties were imposed to discourage black market activity as economic conditions deteriorated.

The UNHCR appointed a former Dutch Foreign Minister, Max van der Stoel, to monitor and report on human rights conditions in Iraq. In a series of reports beginning in early 1992 he recorded a horrifying indictment of state violence against individuals, describing Iraq's human rights abuses as the worst in any country since the Second World War. Three years on, in March 1995, Max van der Stoel reported a policy of intentional starvation of the rural Shi'a population through the deliberate drainage of the southern marshes which provided their home and livelihood. At the same time punishments involving amputation had been introduced for a range of minor crimes, while the growing problem of desertion from the army was being met with the barbarous penalty of severance of an ear and the branding of a tattoo on the forehead.

In Saudi Arabia the government's wish to see the back of Saddam Hussein, or at least to have his power attenuated to the point where he could no longer pose a threat, remained unshakeable. Yet there was also disquiet over the painful predicament of the Iraqi people. It was frequently put to us that the perception of sanctions as victimisation had the effect of rallying support for the leadership rather than detaching it. But no alternative means were to hand to achieve Iraq's compliance with the comprehensive conditions laid down in the Security Council's ceasefire resolution. We could continue to insist that our quarrel was not with the Iraqi people, but so long as their leadership maintained its intransigence it was difficult to carry conviction.

It had been the expectation of the Saudis that, with the withdrawal of foreign forces and the despatch of UN observers to patrol the frontier between Iraq and Kuwait, they could turn their backs on a threat from Iraq and concentrate on the pressing tasks of building up a more secure defence for the future, as well as of tackling the domestic political currents unleashed by the crisis and salvaging their economy from its burdensome costs. But events were to make it impossible for the Kingdom to expunge the bad memory of the crisis and insulate itself from the symptoms of Iraq's continued intransigence.

The Western-led activity initiated out of Turkey in April 1991 to restrain Saddam Hussein's savage retribution following the Kurdish insurgency in the north had little impact on Saudi policy, beyond a paradoxical concern lest the establishment by Western forces of guarded

safe havens for the Kurdish population and the interdiction of Iraqi airforce activity north of the 36th parallel should encourage the partition
of Iraq as a state.

Western moves to encourage diverse Iraqi political elements, in their
scattered exile running from Iran across the Arab world to groups in
London and Washington, to form themselves into an opposition front
which might offer an alternative to the Ba'ath regime in Baghdad also
met with a hesitant response in Riyadh. There was a justified scepticism
over whether these factions could manage to overcome their communal
differences and evident antagonisms to the point where their front
would be credible to the Iraqi people. At the same time there was a suspicion that exile groups would mobilise sponsorship on the part of states
with which they had the closest affinity, to secure a predominant position
within a future government.

The aims of the Kurds and of the Tehran-backed Shi'a religious
opposition presented particular cause for Saudi concern. The Saudis
were themselves tending to show favour to Sunni Arab elements,
though contacts were established more widely across the opposition
spectrum, including with the Shi'a Imam Ibrahim al Bakr, who visited
Saudi Arabia from Iran in 1992 and met King Fahd. Nevertheless the
formation with Western encouragement of an Iraqi National Congress
in exile at a meeting of Iraqi opposition elements in Vienna in June
1992, with the Shi'a religious faction joining it four months later,
aroused little Saudi enthusiasm.

Meanwhile Iraq's obstruction of UN inspection of her military arsenal
came to an early head in the summer of 1991. The inspectors had discovered the existence of facilities for a nuclear weapons enrichment
programme. This had been concealed from them by the Iraqis, who
had resorted to preventing the UNSCOM teams forcibly from visiting
suspected nuclear facilities. This led to an ultimatum from the five permanent members of the Security Council in July that Iraq must disclose
her nuclear programme or face possible military action. Although some
disclosure resulted, the Security Council passed a resolution on 15 May
condemning Iraq's lack of co-operation over the elimination of her
weapons of mass destruction and demanding disclosure of foreign suppliers and unimpeded access for UN inspectors.

The warning of military retaliation in the event of Iraq's non-compliance
meant that urgent plans were set in hand by the Americans and ourselves
to provide for enforcement through air action. This would once again
require the basing of aircraft on the western side of the Gulf. Kuwait was
out of the question, as such facilities as she could offer lay too close to
the Iraqi frontier to be secure.

When Chas Freeman and I received our instructions in early August 1991 to broach this proposal, we had our misgivings whether the Saudi government would give a positive response. American and British forces had just completed withdrawal from the Kingdom, with only a small residual American logistic element and some non-combat aircraft still at Dhahran. A Royal Signals unit had hung in there until an indignant American commander stumbled across it and gave our defence attaché, Mike Holroyd-Smith, who had recently arrived to replace Peter Sincock, a firm steer to have the unit recalled. It was asking a great deal of the Saudis, with foreign troops gone and the public and religious controversy over their presence at last beginning to subside, to take back a Western force, however restricted its role or necessary its purpose. Fortunately Saddam Hussein took the message and his obstruction of inspections eased.

When Prince Saud visited London in September for talks with the Prime Minister and Douglas Hurd, it was plain that Saudi resolve to see an end to Saddam Hussein's ability to renew his threat to the security of the region and upset the balance of Middle East politics was as firm as ever. In particular, Iraq's arsenal of dangerous weapons had to be exposed and destroyed. All this would call for the closest co-operation between us, both directly and within the UN. We agreed that the breakup of the USSR, which had now begun, would pose new challenges for the area.

There was no doubt that as a result of our close collaboration during the crisis our relations looked in strong shape for the future. Already some significant business in the next stages of the Kingdom's economic development was coming the way of British firms. It was gratifying on our side to have been able to show our particular appreciation to two Saudi personalities, Prince Abdullah bin Faisal and Sheikh Abdullah Kanoo, through the award by the Queen of the Order of the British Empire in recognition of the help which they and their organisations had rendered to us during the crisis. Yet already the next issue to put strain on the Kingdom's reinforced post-war relations with her Western partners was casting its shadow ahead. Prince Saud's departure from London was interrupted by a sudden suspension of flights over Yugoslavia, as her peoples took their turn to enter upon an intercommunal conflict which was to set Moslem against Christian and revive a mood of anti-Western sentiment within the Islamic world.

These strains, however, lay in the future. Prince Saud's presence in London coincided with a private visit to the Kingdom by Mrs Thatcher to take leave of her good friend King Fahd. The visit had required preparation at awkwardly short notice between the Saudis and our embassy. It took place in Jedda, after a refuelling stop in Dhahran, and in my absence was handled by Derek Plumbly and Charles Hollis. Mrs Thatcher had a very warm reception from the King, and went with Grania for a call on the senior Al Saud ladies. Her sudden ousting in mid-crisis from the British political scene was, for a Saudi leadership accustomed to a pre-eminent role for personalities in governance, still difficult to comprehend. She now appeared to find the price of the peace with Iraq too high. Had she still been in office, this implacability could, we felt, have produced acute differences with the Saudis, and the American administration too, in the wake of Saddam Hussein's defeat by the coalition she had done so much to forge.

The September of 1991 brought a fresh round of tension over the activities of the weapons inspectors, following Iraq's refusal to allow them to use their own helicopters, supplied by the German government. This was accompanied by a denial that Iraq was holding Kuwaiti prisoners, and a series of violations of the Kuwaiti frontier involving exchanges of fire. There was also renewed obstruction of UN efforts to get relief supplies through to the Kurdish and Shi'a communities. Confronted over the helicopters, the Iraqis shifted their ground by agreeing to their use provided Iraqi representatives were on board to monitor things. This was still unacceptable, and led to a renewed American threat to use armed aircraft as escorts. Suggestions of RAF deployment resurfaced.

A week later the Iraqis responded to the discovery by UN inspectors of documents which contained revelations about Iraq's nuclear pro-gramme at a facility in Baghdad by forcibly detaining the inspectors in the building's car park and insisting they surrendered the documents. Two days later the Iraqis conceded the inspectors could take the docu-ments, provided these were catalogued, and confirmed that helicopter flights would not be restricted. Plans which the Americans had put in hand to send carrier-borne military aircraft to the Gulf were accord-ingly suspended. When inspection of the facility resumed it was found that the interval had been used by the Iraqis to strip the place and arrange for further documents to be concealed.

The UNSCOM inspectors reported to the Security Council in early October that they had uncovered an extensive military nuclear pro-gramme involving enrichment technology, weaponisation and missile delivery. Iraq had been persistently underdeclaring her weapons assets to the UN. New Scud launching facilities had also come to light. Iraq's nuclear weapons programme was understood to be based on a research facility at Al Atheer, south of Baghdad. The Security Council responded to these grave revelations and to Iraq's continuing attempts at obstruc-tion by passing another resolution on 11 October, authorising more aggressive UN inspection and the dismantling of any industrial facility which could be used for weapons production. The Iraqi government reacted with renewed refusal to co-operate.

More sinister yet was the claim shortly afterwards by the UN inspection team to have found plans for an atomic weapon which could have been produced within as little as a year. November brought discovery of a stock of Scud missiles and artillery shells, armed with chemical warheads which could have been used during the Kuwait conflict, though their effectiveness was uncertain.

Meanwhile the post-war initiative to restart negotiations on a settlement of the Arab–Israel dispute bore its first fruit in an international conference in Madrid, under joint American and Soviet chairmanship and with the UN Secretary General present as an observer. The British and French governments attended as part of a joint European group. The Saudi ambassador in Washington, Prince Bandar bin Sultan, who had taken a prominent part since the Kuwait crisis in supporting the new peace initiative, represented the Kingdom within a delegation led by the Secretary General of the GCC. The event marked a considerable personal achievement for James Baker, who had gone to the lengths of effectively strong-arming Israel's right-wing Prime Minister, Itzhak Shamir, into taking part, though he made his reluctance plain. It was an historic moment, which owed more than a little to a mood of realism engendered by the lessons of Iraq's military threats and the fall-out from her subsequent defeat.

Other Arab conferences followed, in which the Saudis gave a lead in calls by summits of the Organisation of the Islamic Conference in Dakar and the GCC, pointedly gathered in Kuwait under the presidency of Amir Jabir of Kuwait, for sanctions to be maintained and for Iraq to comply with UN Security Council resolutions. In the Dakar discussions, where Crown Prince Abdullah represented the Kingdom, both Jordan and Yemen continued to equivocate over sanctions, while Sudan was still contrary enough to oppose the resolution.

The New Year brought further harassment of a group of chemical and biological inspectors in Baghdad, followed by refusal in the February of 1992 to allow the dismantling of ballistic missile facilities. When the Iraqis then sought to trade compliance for an easing of sanctions, the UN Security Council insisted anew that Iraq agreed to destruction under pain of serious consequences. There was fresh talk of American military action. Indications of a less negative Iraqi line, conveyed to the Security Council in March by a delegation led by the Iraqi Deputy Prime Minister, Tariq Aziz, were however met with scepticism and the despatch into the Gulf of an American aircraft carrier.

Iraq responded with greater co-operativeness over her chemical and missile programmes, but continued to play for time on the nuclear side. She was therefore ordered by UNSCOM to destroy the core of the Al Atheer facility. The next months saw the Iraqis carrying forward their game of cat and mouse with the UN by alternating their tactics of intransigence between threats of retaliation against Western aircraft patrolling the northern 'no-fly zone', restrictions on UN relief activity, and rejection of the UN Boundary Commission's recently-completed demarcation of the Kuwait frontier, which had restored to Kuwait portions of land annexed by Iraq since the settlement of 1963.

In July 1992 Iraq again raised the stakes by refusing UNSCOM access to the Agriculture Ministry building in Baghdad, where information on the weapons programme was believed to be stored. This provoked a fresh confrontation with the Americans, who moved troops into the Gulf area for joint exercises and installed Patriot anti-missile defences in Bahrain and Kuwait against possible Iraqi retaliation. In Saudi Arabia the Patriot systems which had been dismantled following the ceasefire were reassembled in the proximity of the Dhahran and Riyadh airbases. It began to look once again as though Saddam Hussein would have to be faced down, if necessary with the threat of retaliation.

Pressure to secure the compliance of the Iraqi regime with the conditions laid down by the UN Security Council as part of the ceasefire had the full support of the Saudi government, concerned as ever to ensure that, so long as he retained his hold on power, Saddam Hussein should not be in a position to renew his menace to his neighbours. For the Saudis the prime objective was now to see his war machine dismantled as quickly as possible, and to resist his attempts to play for time.

Hopes of the tyrant's overthrow from within had by now begun to fade, and it was coming to be accepted that he might remain a feature on the landscape for some while yet. This conclusion tended to increase the sense of unease at the suffering which long-term imposition of sanctions would mean for his people, a brotherly sympathy which was nevertheless tempered by awareness that an early return of Iraqi crude to the market would force an already weak oil price even lower. So far Saddam Hussein had stubbornly refused to accept the conditions for limited oil exports, offered by the UN Security Council to ease Iraq's predicament.

When Prince Saud visited London again for talks in early July, it was agreed that Saddam Hussein must be obliged to comply with all UN resolutions, backed up if necessary by force, and that the Kingdom would continue to play her part. Matters came to a head with a visit to Jedda by the American Secretary of State in late July to discuss with King Fahd a possible ultimatum to Saddam Hussein over the blocking of inspections. It was agreed to allow a few more days; meanwhile we held our breath. To everyone's relief the Iraqi bluff was once again called, and the inspection team was allowed to enter the Agriculture Ministry with the face-saving proviso, agreed with the head of UNSCOM, that it should include no Americans.

This repeated intransigence on the part of the Iraqi regime was accompanied during the early summer of 1992 by an increase in acts of terrorism against UN guards overseeing security in the protected Kurdish region, and with Iraq's refusal in June and again in August to renew the agreement with the UN providing for a humanitarian relief presence to operate in the north and south of the country. One of these attacks, in which four people were killed, was directed against a car convoy in which Mme Françoise Mitterrand, the wife of the French President, was travelling on a visit to Kurdish refugees.

At the same time Saddam Hussein raised the stakes in this new round of confrontation with the UN Security Council and the Western powers engaged in leading the squeeze on him, by stepping up his repression of the Shi'a insurgents who had taken refuge in the southern marshes. This took the form of air attacks on village settlements and military engineering work to drain and clear by fire the close cover which the kilometres of marsh habitat afforded its inhabitants. A major military air-base at Talil near Basra, destroyed during the Gulf offensive, was brought back into use and the regional air defence network was revived. Military units also forcibly prevented the celebration by Iraq's Shi'a community of their annual religious ceremony of Ashura in their holy cities of Najaf and Karbala in southern Iraq.

Publicity over these actions, and those directed against the Kurdish community in the north, was quickly brought to the media's attention by Iraqi opposition groups abroad, and led to a fresh wave of hostile sentiment in the USA and Europe. The Bush administration went back on the political offensive in mid-August with a plan, for which it secured British and French support, to establish a second no-fly zone for Iraqi aircraft in the south of the country below the 32nd parallel, the area in which air attacks against the Shi'a population were taking place. Together with the air interdiction zone already in place in the north, this step meant that as much as a third of Iraq's airspace had been put under international control. John Major gave a warning that Iraqi aircraft would be attacked if they flew within the proscribed area.

The no-fly zone to help protect the Shi'a community in southern Iraq came into effect on 26 August. Like its counterpart in the north, it was not backed by specific UN Security Council authority. Involving as it did the novel and sensitive concept of international intervention in the internal affairs of a member state, a bid for such categoric authorisation could have met with resistance. The three countries engaged in enforcement accordingly presented their action as being in support of the Council's ground-breaking Resolution 688, passed in April 1991 in response to the savage suppression of the Kurdish and Shi'a uprisings following Saddam Hussein's defeat in Kuwait. In it the Security Council called on Iraq to cease repression of her population and permit humanitarian access. In effect this had established a new principle of a *droit d'ingérence* on the part of the UN. By her actions in the south, Iraq was clearly in breach of this requirement.

Significantly no criticism of Western action arose from within the UN Security Council. Indeed, it kept up its own pressure on the Iraqi government with a resolution in late August 1992 endorsing the decisions of the Kuwait Boundary Commission and calling on Iraq and Kuwait to cooperate over its work. This was followed up by action in response to Iraqi refusal to implement Resolutions 706 and 712, authorising limited oil sales to generate funds for compensation, with a resolution providing for the seizure of frozen Iraqi assets and their transfer into a special account for this purpose. The step had British acquiescence, though we faced certain legal problems over its domestic implementation.

Yet, as in the inspection crisis of the previous summer, once the prospect of enforcement became a reality reservations emerged on the part of the Saudi leadership over the provision of basing facilities for a renewed Western air force presence, even on the reduced scale required to establish and control an air exclusion zone in the south of Iraq. As before there was the reaction among Saudi public opinion to be considered. This was now set against a sensitive internal climate in which the more extreme religious elements saw themselves threatened by King Fahd's announcement five months earlier of significant constitutional changes providing for wider public participation in the business of government at national and local level.

These important proposals for change, arising in part from the effect of the Kuwait crisis upon Saudi Arabia's society, did not conform with the kind of prescription for tighter religious supervision of affairs which several hundred citizens representing the more extreme religious strand of opinion had recently, and with some audacity, presented to the government, having published its text abroad. A bout of manoeuvring on the part of the Saudi government had led to the petition being met with a disclaimer, albeit in somewhat equivocal terms, from Sheikh Abdul Aziz bin Baz and the Kingdom's supreme religious council.

Religious antipathy towards the presence of non-Moslem foreigners was also being aggravated by publicity given to the grave predicament of the Moslem community in Bosnia. In a rare incident for Saudi Arabia, two British teachers had been attacked in Al Khobar. There was a suspicion their assailants might have been religious zealots. Moreover, within the Kingdom's conservative Sunni circles the Shi'a sect enjoyed little respect. Measures for its protection in Iraq could thus prove controversial. Even within the Saudi government there remained unease over any move which might encourage autonomy among Iraq's Shi'a population, on account of its sectarian affinity with Iran.

In my absence on summer leave, discussions on possible enforcement of the southern no-fly zone were undertaken in August 1992 on Britain's behalf by Stuart Laing, who had replaced Derek Plumbly as deputy head of our mission at the beginning of the summer. After all we had been through together over the previous three years, it had been sad to see Derek and Nadia Plumbly go. They were posted to the UN in New York, where it was at least a consolation to know that Derek would be joining David Hannay to carry on the endeavour from a seat on the Security Council. Indeed, several others among the embassy's team had moved on since the war, including the irrepressible Charles Hollis, who had stayed long enough to produce a hilarious end-of-year pantomime on the theme of Aladdin. There was a real sense of parting, as we had all seen such special times together.

By the end of the month a joint air force headquarters with excellent command facilities had been set up under the deputy commander of the US Central Air Force, General Record. Air patrols out of the Gulf region, including RAF Tornadoes, began promptly on 28 August, only two days after the declaration of the southern air exclusion zone by the three Western governments. The Iraqis immediately ceased their flying activity against the southern villages, and military force on the ground also appeared to abate.

Following a visit to London in early September by Prince Fahd bin Abdullah, the deputy to Prince Sultan who also had responsibility for our new-found co-operation over environment issues, I returned to Riyadh to find the embassy back in military step. It was handy to have the use of an HS125 again. Ironically I had in London seen Peter de la Billière, whose book about the campaign to liberate Kuwait was on the point of publication. Now here we were on the brink of a second round with Iraq's incorrigible leader. Back in Riyadh the RAF, under Air Commodore Bruce Latton, were occupying a villa adjacent to the RSAF headquarters and shared with the French. It was a tidy set-up, perhaps due in part to the precaution which the MoD had taken on this occasion of appointing an official from the outset to oversee expenditure. Operation GRANBY had evidently left a mark.

We had a visit a week later from Malcolm Rifkind, who had replaced Tom King as Secretary of State during the summer. In Jedda he had his first meeting with Prince Sultan, in which there was discussion on the strengthening of the Kingdom's military capability. This included further supply of equipment under the Al Yamamah programme, which had proved itself to such good effect during the Kuwait crisis. It was clear to us, however, that the Americans were making a strong post-war bid to meet Saudi Arabia's new defence needs, including the supply of combat aircraft hitherto blocked by Congress.

Malcolm Rifkind had a royal flush of calls which included the King, Crown Prince Abdullah and the Interior Minister, Prince Naif. Apart from the continuing problem of Iraq and Saddam Hussein, on which Saudi resolve looked as firm as ever, we found growing concern about the regional ambitions of Iran, who was starting to flex her muscles afresh in the direction of the GCC states through physical reimposition of her control over the disputed Abu Musa island in the Gulf, where sovereignty had in practice been shared with the UAE. Meanwhile the southern no-fly zone over Iraq appeared to be going through a quiet phase, and the northern exclusion zone too.

So they were to remain for most of that autumn, while the UNSCOM weapons inspections went ahead without further interruption. In October Iraq finally renewed the agreement to allow the stationing of UN guards and the provision of humanitarian relief. Economic conditions within Iraq were clearly deteriorating as a consequence of her leader's persistent refusal to accept the UN Security Council's conditions for the raising of sanctions. In response the Iraqi leadership was resorting to harsh penalties, including execution, to deter black market activity among the merchant community. Switches among his ministers were taken to indicate a growing sense of insecurity on the part of Saddam Hussein, and a narrowing of his power base. Yet through a characteristic combination of ruthlessness and playing off factions, he continued to defy predictions of his downfall.

This conciliatory interlude in relations with the UN was again to be shortlived. In December Saddam Hussein chose to mount a fresh confrontation, on a more serious scale than he had attempted previously. Inspection flights by UN helicopters in the vicinity of Baghdad were once again prohibited, and the lists of foreign suppliers of equipment for weapons programmes, which the Security Council had demanded to be handed over to UNSCOM, were not forthcoming. These restrictions were followed at the beginning of January 1993 by a prohibition on the use of UN aircraft by inspection teams flying into Iraq from Bahrain, with a requirement that instead they charter Iraqi aircraft. The confrontation over inspections culminated on 10 January in the barring of a flight bringing a large inspection team back to Baghdad.

In parallel with this burst of defiance on the weapons front, the Iraqis chose to play with fire over the northern and southern no-fly zones. Following the shooting down by a patrolling USAF fighter aircraft on 27 December of an Iraqi warplane which had made a provocative intrusion south of the 32nd parallel, the Iraqis moved anti-aircraft missiles back into the southern area in some strength and began to illuminate patrolling coalition aircraft in hostile fashion with the acquisition radars of these weapons. Further air violations followed. After an ultimatum on 6 January giving Iraq 48 hours to withdraw the missile batteries, the Iraqis attempted to conceal the weapons by moving them around within the zone while maintaining the threat to air patrols. A similar missile threat was introduced into the northern exclusion zone. In a further demonstration of insolence a party of armed Iraqis crossed the demilitarised zone along the newly-demarcated Kuwait border and seized Silkworm missiles and other weapons under the noses of the UN observer group.

This sharp escalation of provocation and harassment came as a surprise. Discussing the motives behind it with our Saudi counterparts, we were inclined to attribute it, as with earlier episodes, to the combination of irascibility and impulsiveness so prominent in the Iraqi leader's temperament coupled with a renewed concern for the sake of his image to strike a posture for home consumption, even when its purpose was forlorn. But on this occasion it was also possible to perceive a deeper political objective, deriving from Saddam Hussein's persistent misreading of the international scene in consequence of his own isolation.

The American presidential elections in November 1992 had produced a Democrat victory, with the new President Bill Clinton due to take over the White House in the middle of January. The ousting of the Bush administration, which had continued to play such a key part in the international exercise to exact penalties from Iraq following her defeat, had been a matter for elation in Baghdad, just as the success of John Major in holding on to power by a narrow margin in the British general election that spring had been a setback. Indeed, Iraq's propaganda had gone so far as to jump the gun at the time with a premature announcement of a Conservative defeat.

Certain comments made by leading Democrat figures during the American election campaign appeared to have been construed by the Iraqi regime as showing sympathy for Iraq's predicament under rigorous

UN tutelage, and could have engendered a hope that, once President Clinton took over, Iraq would have an easier ride. Accordingly it seemed possible that Saddam Hussein, ever one for the bold option, was seeking to raise the temperature of confrontation with the USA, on the calculation that he could subsequently lower the stakes and make terms with the new administration.

These deeper considerations also formed a part of Saudi analysis at this stage. They had their own apprehensions about how firm the Clinton administration would turn out to be over keeping up the pressure on Iraq. It was clear to us from our close consultation with the Saudis during this critical period that they were determined Saddam Hussein should not get away with this latest defiance. This preoccupation was made clear to us during calls by Michael Heseltine on Prince Sultan and Prince Saud, and when King Fahd saw the Minister of State for Defence, Jonathan Aitken, during the second week of January. We put it to the Saudis that in our estimate such suspicions were misplaced. Whatever hesitations some circles within the Democrat party might have expressed in the run up to the Gulf War, there seemed no reason to doubt their party's attachment to the basic principles of human rights, which the Iraqi leader was continuing to flout through the oppression of his own peoples.

A difficulty here was that the post of American ambassador in Riyadh had been vacant since the previous summer, when Chas Freeman had returned to Washington to the regret of his many friends and contacts in the Kingdom. His contribution to the task of keeping American and Saudi policy in close step throughout the vagaries of the Kuwait crisis had been outstanding, and we all felt his absence. The background to his departure was not fully apparent; perhaps he had spelt out the implications for the Saudi relationship of some aspects of American activity post-war rather too clearly for the taste of the Washington policy machine.

His departure was compounded by the failure of the Bush administration to secure Congressional approval for a successor before leaving office at the turn of the year. Indeed it was not until mid-1994 that a new American ambassador to the Kingdom was finally appointed, a curious lacuna given the significance of the Kingdom for American foreign policy. A measure of Saudi frustration became detectable, particularly against a background of political pressure out of Washington for the Kingdom to buy American in its ambitious programme of military and civil development.

As January 1993 advanced with indications that on this occasion Saddam Hussein might not prove so predictable, but was prepared to take confrontation to the brink and perhaps beyond, we felt obliged with full backing from the FCO to set in hand precautions against possible Iraqi retaliation with whatever weaponry he might still have up his sleeve. Our community had by now built up to a number surpassing the total of some 30,000 at which it had stood when Iraq marched into Kuwait. As a result of the earlier crisis we now held a much more comprehensive record.

The wardens were once again put on alert; they were well accustomed to the drill. Clive Woodland and our consular staff reactivated the emergency telephone system for anxious calls from the community. It all had an uneasy feeling of *déjà vu*, particularly as, with his keen nose for news, Sandy Gall, now freelancing for *The Mail on Sunday*, had materialised in Riyadh to cover the second anniversary of the launching of the offensive to liberate Kuwait. Once again he was to be right on the spot.

The commander of the RAF contingent, Group Captain Vaughan Morris, had discussed with me his concern that, as a result of the hostile action of the Iraqi missile radars, air patrolling had been briefly suspended over the southern zone. As he rightly saw it, it was essential that the policeman should get back on the beat and face down the threat. His good relationship with the American joint commander, General Record, helped to get patrols restored. But Iraq's use of targeting radars continued, and in the last days of its life the Bush administration decided, with British and Saudi agreement, that there had to be a retaliation.

Following two statements during the preceding week from the UN Security Council that Iraq's actions put her in breach of the ceasefire resolution, an American-led force of over 100 aircraft, including RAF Tornadoes, attacked Iraqi anti-aircraft missile sites and operational control facilities south of the 32nd parallel on the night of 13 January. The Americans also announced the despatch of a battalion of troops to Kuwait for exercises. Once again the night air over the Gulf was full of the roar of jet engines. But the Saudis, and our own community too, were by now old hands and paid little heed. We had few calls on the consular hot-line.

The raid, which had been postponed for 24 hours by poor weather, led to a ceasing of radar activity in the south, though certain operational control centres remained untouched. Iraq's response, however, was to activate radars in the northern exclusion zone, leading to an American air strike on a radar station and the shooting down of an Iraqi warplane which had intruded into that area. In a simultaneous attempt to bargain over the use of UN aircraft by inspection teams, the Iraqis proposed that these flights could resume provided they made a detour to avoid the southern exclusion zone. This device was rejected by UNSCOM.

On 17 January, virtually its final day in office, the Bush administration sought to break the stalemate over the continuation of weapons inspections by launching a barrage of 45 cruise missiles from US Navy vessels, aimed at a manufacturing facility on the northern edge of Baghdad which had been identified as having played a part in Iraq's uranium enrichment programme. Endorsement of the attack had been obtained from the British and French governments, albeit with some hesitation.

In Riyadh we had only brief warning of the drama through our military channels. The first BBC news reports, from Michael MacMillan who happened to be in the Al Rashid hotel when the Tomahawks came over Baghdad, suggested that things might have gone wrong. It was reported that one missile had impacted off course in front of the hotel, causing loss of life. This seemed to us to be the last word in irony, as the Al Rashid had been one of the places which the coalition had scrupulously forborne to target during the 1991 air war, despite the certainty that it was covering a military command centre. Moreover, it transpired that on the occasion of the present attack a conference of Iraq's supporters from around the Islamic world was being held there. Indeed, it did not seem beyond the bounds of possibility that the Iraqis themselves might have staged an explosion at the hotel for propaganda purposes.

The great majority of the missiles navigated successfully to their targets, however. The Al Rashid hotel had been hit by a dead portion of a Tomahawk, probably brought down by anti-aircraft defences. Had it exploded the repercussions on Arab opinion would have been considerably more serious. Even as it was the resumption of missile and aircraft raids, with some loss of Iraqi lives, was starting to provoke resistance from a Saudi public opinion instinctively concerned to put the political strains of the military confrontation with Iraq behind it. There was also talk of Western double standards, with comparisons being made between readiness to strike at Iraq while declining similar military action to halt Serbian attacks on the Moslem community in Bosnia. We stressed the point to London that retaliation should not be prolonged, lest it put our relationship with the Saudis under strain.

There was, however, one more shot in the locker. Vaughan Morris came round to the embassy on 18 January with the news that a second aircraft raid against Iraqi missile control sites in the southern zone was scheduled to take place soon after dawn. The RAF's allotted target was a key air defence operations bunker just outside the town of Al Najaf on the 32nd parallel. American bombers would attack similar targets.

The mention of Al Najaf startled me, as it was the location of the tomb of Ali bin Abu Talib, son-in-law of the Prophet Mohammed, whose line had, ever since his assassination in 661, been regarded by members of the Shi'a sect as the rightful heirs to the Moslem caliphate. Al Najaf was thus for the Shi'a one of the holiest centres of Islam. The town had been a focus for the abortive Shi'a uprising against Saddam Hussein in the days following his defeat in Kuwait, when the tomb of Ali, unscathed during the coalition's air strikes into Iraq, had suffered damage in the Iraqi army's savage campaign of retribution against the insurgents. With its significance for the Shi'a community, not only in Iraq but throughout the Moslem world and particularly in Iran, Al Najaf was a sensitive vicinity for an air attack.

I put these concerns to Vaughan Morris, who confirmed that the political significance of Al Najaf had not formed part of the target briefing given by the joint headquarters in Riyadh. Command of operations here had been taken over by General Nelson, who had succeeded Chuck Horner as Commander AFCENT following the Gulf War. It looked as though the American headquarters staff were unaware of the implications. On this occasion they lacked a political advisory staff. Vaughan Morris had already told his own command back at High Wycombe of the RAF target and the Tornado crews were being given their instructions.

We spread out an air map on my desk. There were tombs marked in the vicinity of the town, some four kilometres away from the target bunker. The interval looked sufficient, but I pressed home the requirement for accuracy at all costs. If there were any difficulty over target identification or visibility, it would be best to abort the mission. We must give the Iraqis no opportunity to stir the pot with an allegation of a coalition attack on this centre of Shi'a worship. Vaughan Morris accepted these points readily. He undertook to allocate his best aircrews to the operation and put General Nelson in the picture. He was sure things would go right. I believed him, but took the precaution of crossing my fingers.

Vaughan Morris was back in my office early the next morning with a smile on his face. The Tornadoes had taken out the bunker with no error. For extra accuracy the four aircraft had been set to work in pairs, with one operating the laser guidance system while its partner released the 'smart' bomb. The morning was dusty and the first pair had some difficulty on their approach in identifying the well-camouflaged operations bunker. They sensibly overflew, whereupon the second pair made their run, scoring a direct hit. The crews had followed instructions to the letter and the news was a considerable relief. When I saw General Nelson the following day he referred with satisfaction to the success of the attack on the bunker, as confirmed by the Tornadoes' gun cameras. He had not appreciated the full sensitivity of Al Najaf, but had had every confidence in the ability of the RAF to get it right.

The series of raids at last produced a smart turnabout in the Iraqi position. This was just as well, as it would have become politically difficult to have prolonged them. The Iraqi leadership used the pretext of the inauguration of the new American President on 20 January 1993 to declare a unilateral 'ceasefire'. Saddam Hussein backed this with the face-saving suggestion that President Clinton might use the respite to re-examine American policy towards Iraq. Whatever he may have gambled on gaining, he had nothing to show for his six weeks of pertinacity. The antics had also set back any prospect of an early lifting of the prohibition on oil exports. In this latest climb-down Iraq agreed to the resumption of UNSCOM flights and ended her harassment of air patrols. Inspections resumed on all weapons fronts, though the head of UNSCOM warned in March that Iraq was suspected of still concealing some chemical weapons and Scud missiles.

This change of heart was a matter for satisfaction when John Major broke his return journey to London from India in late January for a quick stopover in Riyadh to see the King. Once again the meeting with King Fahd and Prince Sultan took place late at night, following a welcoming banquet attended by members of our business community, royal princes and Saudi ministers. John Major was demonstrating impressive stamina; his working day had begun at dawn in Bombay, then a lunch meeting with Sultan Qaboos in the Oman desert before flying up to Riyadh in the evening. It was past two in the morning when we left the King and the Prime Minister flew on to London. On top of this he had found the time in between official events to issue a libel writ against a British journal. Quite a day in the life of a British Prime Minister.

Yet he stayed on top form, and our late-night meeting confirmed an important decision to inaugurate a new stage of security co-operation through the acquisition by Saudi Arabia of more Tornado aircraft under the Al Yamamah programme. This represented a major dividend from our collaboration throughout the Kuwait crisis. It also sent an opportune signal to Iraq's leadership, and others in the region who might seek to threaten the Kingdom, that the relationship with the UK on the security front remained solid.

When I went across the causeway to Bahrain a few days later and called with Hugh Tunnell on the Amir, Sheikh Issa Al Khalifa, who had given such staunch support to our air force and navy during the Kuwait crisis, he made plain his satisfaction at this sign of our co-operation. It was not long, however, before Saddam Hussein, frustrated perhaps by the absence of any softening in the American position under the new Clinton administration, began to play up yet again.

The next check occurred in April when the Kuwaitis arrested a group, including two Iraqis, found to have smuggled a car bomb into Kuwait for use against former President Bush during a visit he was about to make to the country. This led to calls in Congress for further retaliation against Iraq, in response to the plan to assassinate George Bush. Iraq put herself offside yet again with a refusal in May to accept the final UN demarcation of the frontier with Kuwait, which was confirmed by a Security Council resolution that month.

In June 1993 there was a further attempt to employ Fabian tactics on the inspection front with a refusal to allow the installation of monitoring equipment by UNSCOM or permit the destruction of some chemical production plant. This led to a sharp warning by President Clinton, followed by the launching in late June of a salvo of cruise missiles against the Iraqi Intelligence Service building in Baghdad. The attack was presented by the US administration as retaliation for the attempt against ex-President Bush, in exercise of the right of self-defence. The headquarters of the organisation held responsible for the alleged car bomb plot in Kuwait was thus an appropriate target. On this occasion, however, the missiles caused some adjacent civilian damage. This second missile attack met with considerable criticism within the Arab world, including Kuwait, where those accused of the outrage were still awaiting trial, while expressions of support among the Americans' Western partners were somewhat muted.

By this time Grania and I had left Riyadh, having come to the end of what had been a most eventful and worthwhile tour in Saudi Arabia. David Gore-Booth arrived from London in April to take over as ambassador, a post which, with his previous spell of service in the country ten years earlier and his position at the centre of FCO activity throughout the Kuwait crisis, he was particularly well qualified to fill. We left at the end of the month of Ramadan, with many a backward look and after heartfelt farewells around the Kingdom where we had been privileged to share with our Saudi friends in a remarkable experience.

Before leaving we had managed to fit in a fascinating expedition to the remote Nabatean ruins of Medain Saleh in the north-east of the Kingdom, followed by a trek down the old roadbed of the Hejaz railway to Medina, with derelict locomotives still lying beside the track where they had been sabotaged in joint Arab and British action against the Turks 75 years before. Patrick Fairweather joined us on this trip, having come out to see the results of all that he and his colleagues had from the

FCO end put into Britain's co-operation with the Kingdom during the hectic months of crisis.

In the three years which have followed, the Iraqi leader has continued to alternate between compliance and defiance, while progressively finding himself obliged, as a result of the solid front sustained by the international community, to accept the conditions imposed on his regime for its act of brigandage. The rest of 1993 saw Iraq at last giving way over her weapons development. Information about the advanced stage of her nuclear, chemical and missile programmes was released to the inspectors, and by November she had agreed to UNSCOM conditions for the installation of longer-term monitoring facilities.

In August the destruction finally took place of the massive supergun, for which the barrel, of 350 millimetre bore, had been the subject of sensational litigation in Britain against its manufacturers and of widespread incredulity in Saudi Arabia and elsewhere in the Arab world. There the giant weapon was for all to see, no myth but reality, resting on a mountainside test-bed.

Iraqi diplomacy now switched to the objective of securing an early lifting of oil export sanctions and exploiting divisions within the UN Security Council on this issue. Yet time and again when the question came up for review in the Council, she handed ammunition to those, notably the USA and Britain, who were seeking full prior compliance with all UN ceasefire conditions, by indulging in some new act of internal persecution or fresh prevarication over weapons monitoring. Iraq's endorsement of the frontier with Kuwait was still outstanding, and the matter of detainees had yet to be concluded. South of Basra the process of draining the marshes to destroy the traditional habitat of the Shi'a tribes of the area was pushed forward, drawing protest from a number of international quarters, including the Prince of Wales.

The situation dragged on thus during 1994, until Saddam Hussein chose to provoke a new and major crisis in October, which had the effect of setting back prospects of an easing in sanctions by several months at the least. Seeing perhaps that once again his plea for a lifting of oil sanctions was going to fail, he abruptly recalled Tariq Aziz from lobbying activity in New York and ordered the movement of a large military force to the vicinity of the Kuwait border. This capricious act of defiance appeared once again to stem from a combination of impetuous resentment and a total misreading of its effect on those countries, including members of the UN Security Council, who were arguing that Iraq had now earned some easing of the economic penalties which were making life so difficult for her people. Saddam Hussein may also have felt a need to rally support among his own military through a gesture of aggressiveness, particularly if this brought the perverse satisfaction of causing the Americans and other Western states to respond with a renewed military mobilisation on Arab soil.

In Iraq's reduced military condition it had to be an exercise in bluff. But, given the Iraqi leader's unpredictable reputation, this could not be taken for granted. The manoeuvres certainly gave the Kuwaitis a shock, and they lost no time in putting their own defensive screen into the field. The American reaction, backed by Britain and France, was to send ground troops to Kuwait and a substantial USAF detachment back to Saudi Arabia. They were joined in Kuwait by a Royal Marines battalion, and British and French warplanes returned to the region. A joint headquarters was temporarily established in Riyadh, in which the British commander was Tim Sulivan, who had participated in the CENTCOM planning team for the liberation of Kuwait four years earlier.

But, as Saddam Hussein may have calculated, Saudi Arabia's reaction to this high-profile Western reinforcement proved ambivalent. The regime had in the course of the previous year managed to put a cap on the post-war backlash of resentment on the part of the zealots among religious opinion over the Western military presence. At the start of the year King Fahd had finally judged the moment right to take the plunge and appoint a national consultative council, from which the more extreme shades of Islamic opinion were notably absent. While it was recognised that the Kingdom and its GCC partners could still not afford to take chances with Iraq's intemperate ruler, and that American and Western support remained a tacit ingredient in Gulf defence, there was yet a reluctance to have the earlier controversy over foreign troops reignited, particularly when the threat looked so contrived. Moreover, the Americans presented a bill to the GCC states of $1 billion when President Clinton came to Kuwait and Saudi Arabia later in the year. The Kuwaiti government undertook to pick up half.

I happened to return to Riyadh for a business conference just as the Western reinforcement was taking place, and found a widespread scepticism over the considerable scale of the American response to what was this time seen as Iraqi bluster. Saudi contacts, who had welcomed the arrival of Western troops in 1990, were inclined to dismiss the operation as a gambit to work up domestic support for the Democrat party in the forthcoming mid-term Congressional elections.

But this reaction can have afforded only scant comfort in Baghdad. Within a week Iraq withdrew her forces from the border, on the back of a Russian undertaking to try to secure the lifting of sanctions next time round. Meanwhile the constraints stayed in place and the trial period for the UNSCOM weapons monitoring programme was extended. Iraq followed up with a further concession to the UN by agreeing in November to recognise the frontier and Kuwait's sovereignty.

In the spring of 1995 the UN Security Council, led by France and Russia, responded to these belated steps forward with proposals for easing the earlier conditions governing a limited export of crude oil. Once again the offer was spurned by Iraq, as her leader continued to hold his suffering people to ransom. Nor were the Saudis and Kuwaitis too anxious to see pressure taken off Saddam Hussein. Despite the fact that a welcome rise in world demand for oil meant that Iraqi exports could resume with less chance of a sharp price decline, the continued survival in power of Iraq's leader remained for them a danger signal and allowed for no lowering of their guard. Moreover, UNSCOM had grounds to suspect that Iraq had still not come entirely clean over aspects of her biological and chemical weapons programmes. These queries were sufficient to rule out a lifting of restrictions under the terms of the ceasefire resolution of April 1991. Once again contumacy on the part of Saddam Hussein had done his opponents' work for them.

The Iraqi leader's power base suffered further significant erosion in August with the sudden defection to Amman of two of his sons-in-law and closest military associates, with their wives. One of the pair, General Hussein Kamel Hassan, had occupied a key position in charge of Iraq's weapons programme. His flight to Jordan, where King Hussein, in a belated and welcome move to dissociate himself from Iraq's regime, promptly accorded him asylum, presented Saddam Hussein with the awkward prospect that the reality of Iraq's capability in weapons of mass destruction would finally be divulged.

Initially there was speculation that Hussein Kamel Hassan's breach with his leader and relative might at last portend the nemesis of the Iraqi regime. But this proved a false dawn; given his own complicity he was hardly an attractive alternative candidate for leadership. His escape appeared to spring more from considerations of self-preservation in the face of savage disunity within the regime, originating with Saddam Hussein's malevolent son Udai, than out of protest at the misery of the Iraqi people.

The defection prompted a fresh round of military mobilisation in the vicinity of Kuwait, a move evidently intended for internal consumption. More significantly, however, the Iraqi leadership hastened to offer a further round of disclosures to the head of the UN inspection operation, in a vain and misconceived attempt to limit the damage of what Hussein Kamel Hassan might reveal, and so gain credit with the international community. These included the crucial admission that Iraq had despite denials possessed both artillery and Scud missile warheads at the time of the invasion of Kuwait, ready to be charged with the devastating biological agents, anthrax and botulinum. It was claimed that these stocks had been destroyed after the conflict.

Only now was it finally clear how right the decision had been that our military and civilian communities should take precautions against chemical and germ warfare during the Kuwait crisis. The firm warnings to Baghdad given by the American, and also the British, governments in the prelude to hostilities had been well-founded. Far from helping to achieve an early lifting of sanctions however, these latest revelations caused their further extension that autumn, to give time for investigation of Saddam Hussein's concealment of a horrific biological arsenal, described by Rolf Ekeus in an interview with *Newsweek* magazine as 'an ideal strategic weapon'. Iraq's regime did not yet qualify for a clean bill of health.

For Saudi Arabia the consequence of a decade of Gulf hostilities was to be yet higher preoccupation over her security, and on two fronts simultaneously. While evidence of rearmament on the part of revolutionary Iran was perceived as the major longer-term threat, Saddam Hussein's regime continued to present an aberration in Arab relations with a capacity for aggression which could not be discounted.

Progress towards the goal of closer integration of defence capability among the six GCC states was meanwhile proving fitful, in part due to fears of Saudi domination. For her part Qatar chose to work up territorial quarrels with both the Kingdom and Bahrain, to the point where her contingent did not turn out alongside its partners when the joint GCC brigade was mobilised in support of Kuwait in the flurry of October 1994. A year later GCC solidarity in the face of Iraq came under further strain when the President of the UAE, Sheikh Zaid of Abu Dhabi, made a sudden call for sanctions to be lifted in a spirit of reconciliation with Iraq. His northern neighbours, however, showed no inclination to call it a day so long as UN conditions remained unfulfilled by the Iraqi regime.

Meanwhile the confrontation with Iraq had generated an unprecedented degree of public awareness within Saudi Arabia's own society, and a new confidence in nationhood. It had called forth an impressive record of political resolve on the part of the leadership. As a people the Saudis remained broadly content with their system, and none too convinced of certain aspects of Western life. But the crisis had opened the way to important steps towards broader debate and participation in the country's political system. Things would never be quite the same again as, with ready encouragement from its friends, the world's largest private venture started to go public.

Bibliography

Al Gosaibi, Ghazi A., *The Gulf Crisis: An Attempt to Understand*, London, Kegan Paul International, 1993.

Allen, Charles, *Thunder and Lightning: The RAF in the Gulf*, London, HMSO, 1991.

Armstrong, H. C., *Lord of Arabia: Ibn Saud*, London, Penguin, 1938.

Atkinson, Rick, *Crusade: The Untold Story of the Persian Gulf War*, New York, Houghton Mifflin, 1993.

de la Billière, General Sir Peter, *Storm Command: A Personal Account of the Gulf War*, London, HarperCollins, 1992.

Blunt, Lady Anne, *A Pilgrimage to Nejd*, London, Century Publishing, 1985 (John Murray 1881).

Brittain, Victoria, (editor), *The Gulf Between Us: The Gulf War and Beyond*, London, Virago, 1991.

Cordesman, Anthony H., *After The Storm: The Changing Military Balance in the Middle East*, London, Mansell, 1993.

Cordesman, Anthony H., *Iran and Iraq: The Threat from the Northern Gulf*, Oxford, Westview Press/RUSI, 1994.

Coyne, James P., *Airpower in the Gulf*, Arlington, Virginia, Aerospace Education Foundation, 1992.

Elliott, Capt. T. D., RN, (Ed.), *A Gulf Record; Royal Navy Task Force 321.1*, Dubai, 1991.

Frankel, Glenn, *Beyond The Promised Land: Jews and Arabs on a Hard Road to a New Israel*, New York, Simon & Schuster, 1994.

Fromkin, David, *A Peace to End All Peace: Creating the Modern Middle East, 1914–1922*, London, Penguin, 1989.

Gall, Sandy, *News From The Front: A Television Reporter's Life*, London, Heinemann, 1994.

Godden, John, (editor), *Shield and Storm: Personal Recollections of the Air War in the Gulf*, London, Brassey's, 1994.

Government of Saudi Arabia, Ministry of Information, *The Echoes of the Saudi Position During the Events of the Arab Gulf, 1990–1991*, Riyadh, Saudi Press Agency, 1991.

Hollis, Rosemary (Ed), *The Soviets, Their Successors and the Middle East*, London, St Martin's Press/RUSI, 1993.

Hourani, Albert, *A History of the Arab Peoples*, London, Faber & Faber, 1991.

Hughes, Lieutenant-Colonel B. P., *Battle for Khafji: 29 January – 1 February*, Tavistock, Army Quarterly & Defence Journal, 1993.

International Committee of the Red Cross, *Respect for International Humanitarian Law: ICRC Review of Five Years of Activity (1987–1991)*, Geneva, 1991.

Kaplan, Robert D., *The Arabists: the Romance of an American Elite*, New York, The Free Press, 1993.

Khaled bin Sultan, HRH General, *Desert Warrior: A Personal View of the Gulf War by the Joint Forces Commander*, London, HarperCollins, 1995

Lacey, Robert, *The Kingdom*, London, Hutchinson, 1981.

Makiya, Kanan, (Samir al Khalil), *Republic of Fear*, London, Hutchinson Radius, 1989.

Makiya, Kanan, (Samir al Khalil), *Cruelty & Silence: War, Tyranny, Uprising and the Arab World*, London, Penguin, 1994.

Mansfield, Peter, *The Arabs*, London, Allen Lane, 1976.

McKinnon, Michael, & Vine, Peter, *Tides of War: Eco-disaster in the Gulf*, London, Immel, 1991.

McNab, Andy, *Bravo Two Zero: The True Story of an SAS Patrol behind Enemy Lines in Iraq*, London, Bantam Press, 1993.

Miller, Judith, & Mylroie, Laurie, *Saddam Hussein and the Crisis in the Gulf*, New York, Random House, 1990.

Monroe, Elizabeth, *Britain's Moment in the Middle East 1914–1956*, London, Chatto & Windus, 1963.

Palmer, Michael A., *Guardians of the Gulf: A History of America's Expanding Role in the Persian Gulf, 1833–1992*, New York, The Free Press, 1992.

Powell, General Colin, *Soldier's Way: An Autobiography*, London, Hutchinson, 1995.

Schwarzkopf, General H. Norman, & Petre, Peter, *It Doesn't Take A Hero*, London, Bantam Press, 1992.

Simpson, John, *From The House of War*, London, Arrow Books, 1991.

Taheri, Amir, *Holy Terror: Inside the World of Islamic Terrorism*, London, Century Hutchinson, 1987.

Thatcher, Margaret, *The Downing Street Years*, London, HarperCollins, 1993.

Thomson, Alex, *Smoke Screen – the Media, the Censors, the Gulf*, Tunbridge Wells, Laburnum & Spellmount, 1992.

Viorst, Milton, *How We Went to War in the Gulf, Extract from Sandcastles: the Arabs in Search of the Modern World*, published in Middle East Policy, Vol II, Washington DC, 1993.

Winstone, H. V. F., *Gertrude Bell*, London, Jonathan Cape, 1978.

Works of Fiction

Forsyth, Frederick, *The Fist of God*, London, Bantam Press, 1994.

Mason, David, *Shadow over Babylon*, London, Bloomsbury, 1993.

Index